Baedeker's
CARIBBEAN
Including BERMUDA

⌐. Oistins Bay, on the S coast of
Barbados

232 color photographs
68 maps and plans
1 large map

Text:
Prof. Dr Helmut Blume, Tübingen
  (Political Structure, Topography, Climate, Vegeta-
  tion, Fauna, Population, History, Music, Literature,
  Naive Painting, Economy)
Prof. Dr Hans-Dieter Haas, Munich
Prof. Dr Wolfgang Hassenpflug, Kiel
Helmut Linde, Reutlingen
Dr Udo Moll, Eberdingen-Hochdorf
Dr Rolf Nonnenmann, Pforzheim
Dr George and Inge Scherm, Munich
Hartmut Stelter, Stuttgart
  (The Caribbean from A to Z)

Consultant:
Roger Fortuné, Sainte-Anne (Guadeloupe)

Editorial work:
Baedeker Stuttgart

English Language: Alec Court

© Baedeker Stuttgart
Original German edition

© The Automobile Association
United Kingdom and Ireland 57419

© Jarrold and Sons Ltd
English language edition worldwide

© Prentice Hall, Inc.
English language edition North America

Licenced user:
Mairs Geographischer Verlag GmbH & Co.,
Ostfildern-Kemnat bei Stuttgart

Reproductions:
Gölz Repro-Service, GmbH,
Ludwigsburg

The name *Baedeker* is a registered trademark

Cartography:
Ingenieurbüro für Kartographie
Huber & Oberländer, Munich (maps in text)
Georg Schiffner, Lahr (large map)

Design and layout:
HF Ottmann,
Atelier für Buchgestaltung und Grafik-Design, Leon-
berg

Conception and general direction:
Dr Peter Baumgarten, Baedeker Stuttgart

English translation:
James Hogarth

Source of illustrations: at end of book

Printed in Great Britain by Jarrold & Sons Ltd,
Norwich ★★

0-13-056143-6 US and Canada
0 86145 408 1 UK ISBN

How to Use this Guide

The various groups of islands, individual islands and
towns and areas of tourist interest are described in
alphabetical order. The names of other places referred
to under these general headings can be found in the
Index.

Following the tradition established by Karl Baedeker
in 1844, sights of particular interest and hotels and
restaurants of particular quality are distinguished by
either one or two asterisks.

In the lists of hotels and other accommodation r.=
rooms, b.=beds, SP=swimming pool and T=tennis.

The symbol ⓘ at the beginning of an entry or on a
town plan indicates the local tourist office or other
organization from which further information can be
obtained. The post-horn symbol on a town plan
indicates a post office.

Only a selection of hotels and restaurants can be
given: no reflection is implied, therefore, on establishments not included.

This guidebook forms part of a completely new series of the world-famous Baedeker Guides.

Each volume is the result of long and careful preparation and, true to the traditions of Baedeker, is designed in every respect to meet the needs and expectations of the modern traveler.

The name of Baedeker has long been identified in the field of guidebooks with reliable, comprehensive and up-to-date information, prepared by expert writers who work from detailed, first-hand knowledge of the country concerned. Following a tradition that goes back over 150 years to the date when Karl Baedeker published the first of his handbooks for travelers, these guides have been planned to give the tourist all the essential information about the country and its inhabitants: where to go, how to get there and what to see. Baedeker's account of a country was always based on his personal observation and experience during his travels in that country. This tradition of writing a guidebook in the field rather than at an office desk has been maintained by Baedeker ever since.

Lavishly illustrated with superb color photographs and numerous specially drawn maps and street plans of the major towns, the new Baedeker Guides concentrate on making available to the modern traveler all the information he needs in a format that is both attractive and easy to follow. For every place that appears in the gazetteer, the principal features of architectural, artistic and historic interest are described, as are its main areas of scenic beauty.. Selected hotels and restaurants are also included. Features of exceptional merit are indicated by either one or two asterisks.

A special section at the end of each book contains practical information, details of leisure activities and useful addresses. The separate road map will prove an invaluable aid to planning your route and your travel within the country.

Introduction to the Caribbean

The Caribbean from A to Z

Practical Information

Introduction to the Caribbean
including Bermuda

Holiday paradise in the Bahamas

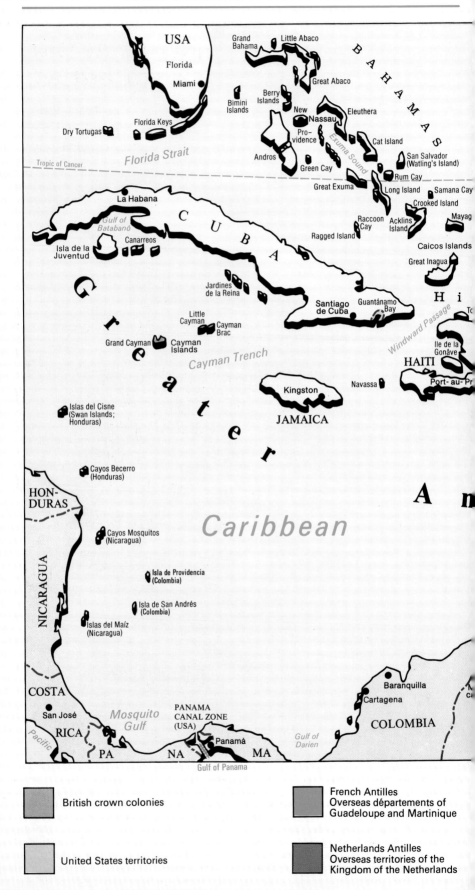

Bermuda – Stonehole Bay

Islands of the West Indies

Bahamas
Greater Antilles
Lesser Antilles

Tropic of Cancer

In addition to the Caribbean islands shown on the map this Guide also covers the popular holiday islands of the **Bermuda** group (formerly known as *Somers Islands*). This archipelago of some 150 small islands, lying not in the Caribbean but far out in the North Atlantic, was discovered in 1503 by the Spanish navigator Juan Bermúdez and occupied by British settlers at the beginning of the 17th c. Since 1684 it has been a British crown colony (administrative center Hamilton).

The constant interplay of land and sea, the tropical landscapes and the mingling of many races combine to make the Caribbean a holiday region of endless variety and attraction, although the rapid development of tourism in recent years has brought great changes in the cultural patterns established during the centuries of colonial rule, particularly on the smaller islands and in the coastal areas of the Greater Antilles.

Exotic rhythms, luxuriant vegetation, palm-fringed beaches of fine sand, warm crystal-clear seas and long coral reefs – visitors find here everything they dream of in a tropical island paradise.

The Caribbean island world, however, is very far from homogeneous. The islands have had very different histories and vary widely as a result not only of the differing political allegiances of the past but also, even more significantly, of the differences in cultural, economic and social conditions to which these have given rise.

It is the object of this Guide, which covers all the main Caribbean islands as well as the Bermuda group far out in the Atlantic, to give prospective visitors some idea of the range and variety of attractions to be found in this region and to help them in deciding where to go and what to see.

Political Structure

The Caribbean islands are, politically, the most highly fragmented area in the world. Within this region there are a dozen sovereign states and as many more separate units in the smaller islands with varying degrees of self-government.

In the 16th c. all the Caribbean islands belonged, at least nominally, to Spain. Later France and Britain became rival colonial powers; and other states – the Netherlands, Denmark, Sweden, Brandenburg, Courland – had possessions in the Antilles at one time or another. The last to appear on the scene were the United States. The present political fragmentation of the islands results from the centuries-long contest between the European powers for possession of what was then one of the richest colonial territories in the world. It is a reflection of this long-continued conflict that the tiny island of Saint-Martin/Sint Maarten is divided into two parts (one French and one Dutch) like the large island of Hispaniola (Haiti and Dominican Republic). All over the Caribbean, islands which were once – and in some cases still are – under British, French and Dutch rule, are juxtaposed and intermingled.

Only a few groups of islands have still retained their colonial status, including the British crown colonies of the British Virgin Islands, the Caymans, Montserrat and the Turks and Caicos Islands.

The French possessions of Guadeloupe and Martinique are now overseas départements within the French Republic. Internal self-government is enjoyed by the British associated island of Anguilla, the Netherlands Antilles and the US territory of Puerto Rico. Antigua, St Kitts and Nevis, the Bahamas, Barbados, Dominica, Grenada, Jamaica, St Lucia, St Vincent/Grenadines and Trinidad and Tobago are former British colonies which have attained independence since

the 1960s. In many of the new mini-states, with their grave economic and social problems, the political power structure is still highly unstable.

In the spring of 1980 mass emigrations from Cuba and Haiti on political and economic grounds highlighted the considerable tensions still prevailing on these and other Caribbean islands – tensions transcending the political status of the particular island. Apart from external influences connected with the geo-strategical interests of the great powers and with economic considerations, other factors which are now increasingly giving rise to conflicts are the sharp cultural and social contrasts, the almost insoluble economic problems (partly due to unfavorable natural conditions) and the tremendous population pressure. The standard of living on the different islands varies widely according to the natural and economic circumstances. The United States and the former European colonial powers contribute large sums by way of assistance to their former dependent territories. Some of the more recently established island states are seeking a solution to their social conflicts in a policy of economic growth, while others are trying to follow the Cuban or other socialist models.

Strong feelings of political independence hinder the development of wider forms of political association in the Caribbean. Earlier attempts in this direction have been unsuccessful, such as the West Indies Federation of former British colonies which was established in 1958 but fell apart in 1962. Little has so far been achieved by the Caribbean Common Market (Caricom or CCM), which in 1973 succeeded the Caribbean Free Trade Area (Carifta) founded in 1968. It may be that a further stimulus towards political unification will come from the associations of many of the states, either direct or indirect, with the European Community.

Islands	Political status (WIAS=West Indies Associated State)	Area in sq. miles (sq. km)	Population	Capital or administrative center
Anguilla	Self-governing state associated with Britain (WIAS)	34 (88)	7,000	The Valley
Antigua and Barbuda	Independent state within British Commonwealth	171 (442)	75,000	St John's (Antigua)
Bahamas	Independent state within British Commonwealth	5,380 (13,939)	240,000	Nassau (New Providence)
Barbados	Independent state within British Commonwealth	166 (431)	280,000	Bridgetown
Cayman Islands	British crown colony	100 (260)	17,000	George Town (Grand Cayman)
Cuba	Socialist republic	44,218 (114,524)	9,710,000	La Habana (Havana)
Dominica	Independent republic within British Commonwealth	290 (751)	82,000	Roseau
Grenada Southern Grenadines	Independent state within British Commonwealth	133 (345)	107,000	St George's (Grenada)
Guadeloupe St Martin (N part), St-Barthélemy	French overseas département	687 (1,780)	335,000	Basse-Terre (Guadeloupe)
HISPANIOLA **Dominican Republic**	Presidential republic	18,699 (48,442)	5,690,000	Santo Domingo
Haiti	Presidential republic	10,714 (27,750)	5,300,000	Port-au-Prince
Jamaica	Independent state within British Commonwealth	4,244 (10,991)	2,225,000	Kingston
Margarita	In Venezuelan state of Neuva Esparta	444 (1,150)	90,000	La Asunción
Martinique	French overseas département	416 (1,080)	330,000	Fort-de-France
Montserrat	British crown colony	39 (102)	13,000	Plymouth
Netherlands Antilles Curaçao, Aruba, Bonaire; Sint Maarten (S part), Sint Eustatius, Saba	Self-governing territories of Kingdom of Netherlands	383 (993)	256,000	Willemstad (Curaçao)
Puerto Rico	Self-governing state associated with USA	3,435 (8,897)	3,240,000	San Juan
St Kitts and Nevis Sombrero	Self-governing state within British Commonwealth (WIAS)	101 (262)	60,000	Basseterre (St Kitts)
St Lucia	Self-governing state associated with Britain (WIAS)	238 (616)	150,000	Castries
St Vincent and Grenadines Northern Grenadines	Self-governing state associated with Britain (WIAS)	150 (389)	125,000	Kingston (St Vincent)
Trinidad and Tobago	Presidential republic within British Commonwealth	1,980 (5,128)	1,240,000	Port of Spain (Trinidad)
Turks and Caicos Islands	British crown colony	166 (430)	7,500	Cockburn Town (Grand Turk)
VIRGIN ISLANDS **British Virgin Islands**	British crown colony	59 (153)	12,000	Road Town (Tortola)
U.S. Virgin Islands	US territory	132 (342)	102,000	Charlotte Amalie (St Thomas)
Bermuda	British crown colony with internal autonomy	20 (53)	55,000	Hamilton

Boston Bay, Jamaica

Topography

The **CARIBBEAN ISLANDS** extend in a wide arc almost 2500 miles long from Florida to the northeastern coast of Venezuela. They vary widely in size, with a total land area 90,350 sq. miles (234,000 sq. km) less than that of the United Kingdom, roughly half of it consisting of uplands and half of plains.

Some 95% of the land area of the Caribbean islands is in the **Antilles** (named after the legendary island of Antilia which, before the discovery of America, was believed to lie between Europe and Asia), the chain of islands which begins some 125 miles E of the Yucatán peninsula in Mexico with Cuba, by far the largest of the Caribbean islands, lying only some 110 miles off the southern tip of Florida. Together with *Jamaica* to the S and *Hispaniola* and *Puerto Rico* to the E, Cuba forms the **Greater Antilles**, which account for almost 90% of the land area of the Caribbean islands. To the E, curving southward, are the **Lesser Antilles**, a string of smaller islands and islets which extends from the Virgin Islands in the N to Trinidad in the S. The northern part of the chain is known as the *Leeward Islands*, the southern part as the *Windward Islands*. Finally a chain of islands runs parallel to the South American coast from the Venezuelan island of Margarita in the E to the Dutch island of Aruba in the W.

NE of Cuba and NW of Hispaniola are the **Bahamas** and the *Turks and Caicos Islands*, a scatter of islands and cays (small flat islets and banks: pronounced "keys") running SE from the coast of Florida. – To the S of Cuba are the most isolated islands in the Caribbean, the *Caymans*, lying widely separated from one another on a submarine ridge.

With the exception of the Bahamas the Caribbean islands lie between latitude 10° N and the Tropic of Cancer (23°27′ N), and are thus all tropical islands. Climatic conditions vary considerably between the islands, however, as a result of their differing topography.

The name of Haiti, the republic which now occupies the western part of the large island of Hispaniola, means "land of mountains" in the language of the original Indian inhabitants; and indeed Hispaniola is a very mountainous island, traversed by several parallel ranges, with the Cordillera Central rising to a height of 10,417 ft/ 3175 m in the Pico Duarte. These mountains are the continuation of the North American cordilleras, which bear eastward in Central America and run into the Greater Antilles, reaching a height of 6470 ft/1972 m in the Pico Turquino (Sierra Maestra) in southern Cuba. The mountains of Jamaica (Blue Mountain Peak, 7402 ft/2256 m) and Puerto Rico (El Yunque, 3494 ft/1065 m) are also part of the cordillera system. In geological terms this is a relatively young region of faulted and folded mountains, a fragile section of the earth's crust much broken up by tectonic action. Some parts of the area – the mountain ranges – were thrust upwards in recent geological times, while others subsided, like the Enriquillo rift valley between the Central and Southern Cordilleras on Hispaniola. Tectonic movements are still continuing, giving rise every now and then to earthquakes. Since the Caribbean islands are surrounded by sea of considerable depth, with great trenches plunging down to 29,500 ft/ 9000 m, the overall relief pattern is on an impressive scale, with height differences of 33,000–39,000 ft/10,000–12,000 m. Although the **cordilleras** of the Antilles are as high as the Alps at some points, the

Gonaïves plain, Haiti

relief is not of Alpine type, since the Caribbean mountains were not exposed to glacial action during the ice ages: it is characteristic, rather, of mountains of medium height, though the valleys are usually deeper and more steeply scarped than in regions of this type in Europe – a consequence of vigorous erosion by the rivers, fed by the high tropical rainfall.

An offshoot of the American cordillera system also runs down the Lesser Antilles; and the South American cordilleras, turning E in Venezuela, continue along the chain of islands from Aruba to Trinidad, rising to some height only on Margarita (Pico San Juan, 3019 ft/920 m) and in the Northern Range on Trinidad (Cerro del Aripo, 3087 ft/941 m).

A very different pattern is found in the volcanic Leeward and Windward Islands. The only islands on which there is still volcanic activity are Martinique, Guadeloupe and St Vincent. The great eruption of *Mont Pelé* on Martinique in 1902 destroyed all life in the town of Saint-Pierre in the space of a few minutes; *Soufrière* on St Vincent last erupted in 1979; and the 4813 ft/1467 m high volcano of the same name on Guadeloupe erupted in 1956 and 1976, making it necessary to evacuate the whole population of the surrounding area for safety's sake. The danger arose not so much from flows of lava as from the expulsion of great masses of detritus. In the eruption of Mont Pelé (4584 ft/1397 m) in 1902 a glowing cloud travelled down the slopes of the mountain. The aftermath of earlier volcanic activity can be seen in the solfataras and fumaroles on St Lucia. The relief pattern of the volcanic regions varies considerably. Some of the younger volcanoes form handsome cones, such as Quill (1949 ft/594 m) on the Dutch island

of Sint Eustatius, but for the most part they are mere volcanic ruins. Particularly striking are the volcanic plugs like the Pitons which forms such distinctive landmarks on St Lucia.

Areas of **plain** occur here and there between the upland regions, particularly along the coasts and in the lower reaches of river valleys. They feature prominently only on Cuba, the largest island in the Antilles. For the most part they consist of low tracts of limestone country of rather featureless character. The Bahamas, consisting of limestones and calcareous sandstones, are also flat, as are the islands in the outer arc of the Lesser Antilles, from Anguilla in the N by way of Antigua to Barbados in the S, to the E of the volcanic islands. All these low-lying limestone plateaux have been much affected by karstic action (underground drainage, with many cavities, etc., caused by dissolution of rock), with large expanses of "swallowhole karst" characterized by dolines and dry valleys. A type of karst peculiar to humid tropical regions, with characteristic conical or "haystack" formations, is found locally on Cuba, Hispaniola, Jamaica, Puerto Rico and Guadeloupe.

In addition to the islands shown on this map (Bahamas, Greater Antilles, Lesser Antilles) this Guide also covers **Bermuda**, an archipelago lying far out in the North Atlantic (latitude 32°18′ N, longitude 64°46′ W) which, with its pleasant subtropical climate and the abundance of fish in its waters, attracts large numbers of visitors.

Geologically the Bermuda archipelago is made up of limestones, sandstones and – thanks to the warmth brought by the Gulf Stream – corals, resting on a submarine

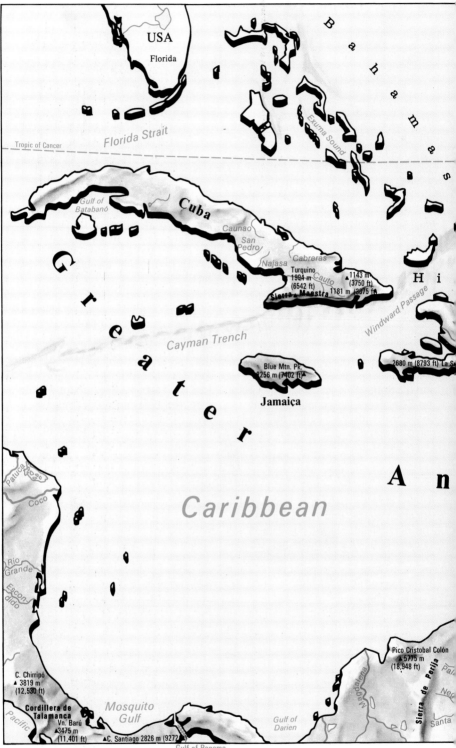

base of volcanic rock. The islands, with their beautiful park-like interiors, are edged by bizarrely shaped cliffs and beautiful beaches. There are numbers of caves and caverns, the result of vigorous karstic action.

The Caribbean islands, washed by seas which are warm throughout the year, form a barrier between the **CARIBBEAN SEA** and the Atlantic Ocean. The average temperature at the water-surface is about 82 °F/28 °C in the warmest month, 77 °F/

A beach in Bermuda

Terrestrial and Submarine Relief

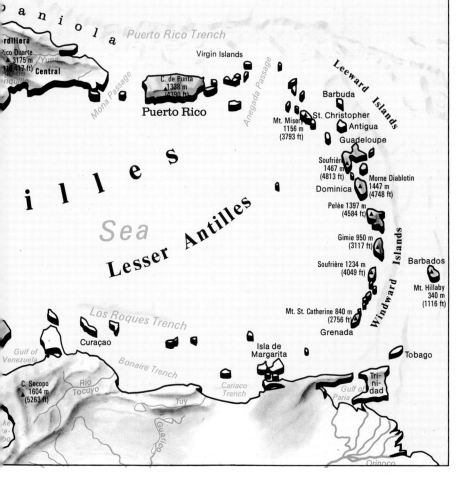

Tropic of Cancer

Atlantic

Puerto Rico Trench

Virgin Islands

rdlllera
?ico Duarte
▲ 3175 m
(10,417 ft) Central
rique

Mona Passage

C. de Punta
▲1338 m
(4390 ft)

Puerto Rico

Anegada Passage

Leeward Islands

Barbuda

Mt. Miser
1156 m
(3793 ft)

St. Christopher
Antigua
Guadeloupe

Soufrièr
1467 m
(4813 ft)
Dominica

Morne Diablotin
1447 m
(4748 ft)

Pelée 1397 m
(4584 ft)

illes

Sea

Lesser Antilles

Gimie 950 m
(3117 ft)

Soufrière 1234 m
(4049 ft)

Windward Islands

Barbados

Mt. Hillaby
340 m
(1116 ft)

Mt. St. Catherine 840 m
(2756 ft)

Grenada

Los Roques Trench

Curaçao

Gulf of
Venezuela

Bonaire Trench

C. Secopo
▲ 1604 m
(5263 ft)

Rio
Tocuyo

Tuy

Cariaco
Trench

Isla de
Margarita

Tobago

Tri-
ni-
dad

Gulf of
Paria

Guarico

Orinoco

25 °C in the coldest. In the subtropical Bahamas the temperature falls during the winter months to 75–73 °F/24–23 °C.

The trade winds, blowing throughout the year, drive great masses of water from the Atlantic through the passages between the Lesser Antilles into the Caribbean, in what is known as the **North Equatorial Current**. During the dry winter months, when the trade winds blow particularly strongly and steadily, the current, now

Sunset, Fort-de-France (Martinique)

known as the **Caribbean Current**, reaches speeds of 1.2–1.6 knots, increasing in speed as it flows into the Gulf of Mexico through the Yucatán Channel between Cuba and the Yucatán peninsula. The current which flows back into the Atlantic through the Florida Strait between Cuba and Florida also increases in speed, reaching as much as 3.7 knots. During the age of sail shipping took full advantage of these currents: the Spanish galleons sailed into the Caribbean through the various passages in the chain of the Lesser Antilles but always returned through the Florida Strait. In coastal waters, of course, there are often local currents for which sailing enthusiasts must watch out; but one feature which makes life easier both for them and for divers and bathers is the lack of tides in the Caribbean (with a movement of only 8–16 in./0.2–0.4 m).

Much of the sea around the Caribbean islands is on the continental shelf. This is true particularly of the Bahamas, which lie on the Great Bahama Bank, only 65 ft/ 20 m below the surface. Around Cuba and Trinidad there are also great expanses of **shallow sea**, the result of a rise in sea level which has taken place only since the last cold period (i.e. within the last 10,000 years). – The rest of the Caribbean is a region of **deep sea**. It is broken up into a number of basins between 13,000 ft/ 4000 m and 16,500 ft/5000 m deep and

traversed by a number of trenches of still greater depth. The *Cayman Trench*, which extends from the Gulf of Honduras along the S coast of Cuba to the Windward Passage between Cuba and Hispaniola, is up to 23,800 ft/7250 m deep, and the *Puerto Rico Trench*, on the outer side of the Antilles, reaches 28,000 ft/8540 m, with a maximum of 30,250 ft/9219 m in the *Milwaukee Depth*. These trenches, in which the thinness of the earth's crust produces gravity anomalies, are frequently the epicenters of seaquakes; and, as already noted, the neighboring islands are tectonically fragile.

The upthrust of the islands is demonstrated on many stretches of coast by a step-like succession of fossil *abrasion terraces* in the coralline limestone, often with cavities gouged out in the past by the surf. The best examples are to be seen on Cape Maisi, at the E end of Cuba, and in northwestern Hispaniola. Elsewhere the coast has been submerged by the sea: thus the *bolsas* ("pouches") on the coast of Cuba and the similarly shaped inlets known as *bocas* on the Dutch islands in the southern Antilles are the result of marine transgressions. These inlets make magnificent natural harbors, such as that of Havana and the Schottegat in Curaçao. They are sheltered from the open sea since they have only a narrow entrance, usually a river valley drowned by the rise in sea level.

A palm-fringed beach, Jacmel (Haiti)

The Caribbean islands have the finest **coral reefs** within the Atlantic province. Thanks to the influence of the Gulf Stream, these formations, built up by the tiny marine creatures called Anthozoa, reach northward to Bermuda. The coasts of the islands are fringed by *barrier reefs*, divided into clearly marked zones – the outer reef, the main ridge, the reef platform and the inner reef which bounds the sheltered lagoon. Some miles out from the islands are the so-called *bank reefs*, ranging in depth from 33 ft/10 m to just below the surface. They show less differentiation of structure than the barrier reefs and are not, like them, associated with nearby land masses. – The coral reefs are a biotope in which great numbers of marine creatures achieve a characteristic pattern of symbiosis (combined existence).

Almost all the Caribbean islands have stretches of **sandy beach** of varying length. Here, instead of the erosional activity found on the rocky coasts, a process of marine sedimentation has been at work, building up the land rather than eating it away. In many places the calcareous sand has been overlaid by "beach rock" formed by the precipitation of chalk. On these gently sloping beaches the water, exposed throughout the day to the strong heat of the sun, becomes very warm. These beaches are the magnet which attracts so many visitors to the Caribbean resorts; but away from the main tourist concentrations these magnificent beaches are still largely unspoiled.

Climate

Apart from Bermuda and the northern Bahamas all the islands described in this Guide lie in the **tropics**: the Tropic of Cancer cuts across the middle of the Bahamian archipelago. In consequence temperatures remain high throughout the year, with an annual average of around 77 °F/25 °C or rather more, even in the Bahamas.

As is normal in tropics, the seasons are not distinguished by differences of temperature: the temperature range over the year is small, usually with a difference of less than $5\frac{1}{2}$ °F/3 °C in the southern Antilles, increasing towards the N (11 °F/6 °C in the Bahamas). The range over the day is greater than the range over the year: again a characteristic of tropical climates. There are no violent extremes of temperature: thus at Pointe-à-Pitre (Guadeloupe), with an annual average temperature of 77.7 °F/25.4 °C, the absolute maximum recorded is 91 °F/33 °C and the absolute minimum 55 °F/13 °C.

Since temperature falls with height, different temperature zones can be distinguished in the upland regions. Up to about 2950 ft/900 m is a warm zone or *tierra caliente*, with an average annual temperature of 70 °F/21 °C; above this, up to about 6550 ft/2000 m, is a temperature zone or *tierra templada* in which the average falls to 61 °F/16 °C; and above this again, at altitudes reached only in a few mountain ranges in the Greater Antilles, is a cold zone or *tierra fría*. On the mountainous islands it is possible to drive, frequently on excellent roads, from the heat of the lowlands to the coolness of the higher regions, where a fire will be welcome, and not merely in the evening.

Although the Caribbean islands have no significant seasonal differences in temperature the seasons are distinguished by variations in rainfall. The *summer rainy season* lasts from May/June to October/November, the *winter dry season* – the preferred tourist season – from December to April. These seasonal differences reflect changes in the position of the sun. During the summer the equatorial trough of low pressure moves towards the Pole, leading to heavy falls (up to 8 in./200 mm in 24 hours) of

Sainte-Anne (Guadeloupe) after a hurricane

"zenithal rain". During the summer the subtropical belt of high pressure moves S, leading as a rule not only to higher air pressures and the settled dry weather which accompanies them but also to an increase in the strength of the trade winds, to which all the Caribbean islands are exposed.

The **trade winds** so called because of their great importance to transoceanic traffic in the age of sail – result from the movement of air from the subtropical areas of high pressure towards the equatorial trough of low pressure. In the northern hemisphere this movement is from NE to SW. The subtropical high pressure areas where the winds originate lie on the E sides of the oceans; and accordingly the originally dry and stable air masses take in great quantities of moisture during their long passage over the ocean and become unstable up to heights of 4900–5900 ft/1500–1800 m. Then when these unstable air masses, charged with moisture, come up against a range of uplands they deposit their moisture in the form of rain on the nearer (windward) side, while the far (leeward) side in the wind shadow remains dry.

The rainfall on the more mountainous islands thus varies considerably between the windward and leeward sides of the mountains, and there may be sharp differences over quite a short distance, with a humid climate on the windward side and a dry climate on the lee side. On the flatter islands these differences do not occur. On the hilly islands the rainfall rises steeply up to the upper limit of the unstable air masses, reaching 350 in./9000 mm or more, and then decreases at higher levels, where the air masses are stable.

The intensity of tropical rainfall is of a different order altogether from the rainfall in non-tropical regions, frequently taking the form of a cloudburst or a persistent drizzle, after which – even during the main rainy season – the sun soon reappears. If the rain lasts a long time or is exceptionally heavy (as at Fort-de-France on Martinique on September 13, 1958, when 3 in./77 mm fell in an hour and $8\frac{1}{4}$ in./220 mm in five hours) there may be severe flooding and washing away of the soil. – The prevailing trade winds are occasionally interrupted during the winter by intrusions of cold air from the central plains of North America, which give rise in the Greater and Lesser Antilles to the formation of stratiform clouds and steady rain lasting several days.

During the summer and autumn the weather pattern set by the trade winds may also be interrupted by **hurricanes**. In an average year there may be seven hurricanes with a diameter of 375–500 miles/600–800 km. In the "eye" of the hurricane, which may have a diameter of some $12\frac{1}{2}$ miles/20 km, the pressure falls below 950 millibars, and the sharp pressure gradients give rise to wind speeds of over 125 m.p.h./200 km.p.h. (Hurricane Allen, 1980, attained some 175 m.p.h./280 km p.h.). While the winds swirl around the eye of the hurricane in a clockwise direction, moving upward and thus discharging rain, in the eye itself the air moves downward and there are few clouds and no wind.

These tropical cyclones, mainly originating over the sea to the E of the Lesser Antilles and travelling W over the Caribbean Sea and the islands, cause great damage to settlements and crops as a result of the extraordinarily high winds and also whip up tidal waves which devastate the coastal regions, while the heavy rains which accompany them usually cause catastrophic floods and landslides. Thus in November 1909 a hurricane produced a rainfall of 135 in./3428 mm in a week (29 in./728 mm in one day alone) in the Blue Mountains of Jamaica. – Thanks to its situation near the Equator and to the increase in Coriolis force (deflection due to the earth's rotation) towards the Equator, Trinidad is free from hurricanes.

Since the hurricanes on the fringes of the tropics bear NE on a parabolic course many of them ravage the southern coastal regions of the United States, and the US government has set up an efficient observation and early warning system, using air reconnaissance and radiolocation, which covers the whole Caribbean area.

Like earthquakes and volcanic eruptions, hurricanes are negative factors in the structural and climatic pattern of the Caribbean. Other unfavorable elements are the danger of drought in the areas of low rainfall, flooding due to unusually high tides and severe erosion of the soil.

For visitors coming from the temperate zone the climate of the Caribbean islands is very agreeable. This is particularly so during the dry winter months, but even during the summer rainy season the high humidity of the air and the resulting mugginess are rendered tolerable, at least in coastal areas, by the fairly constant wind movement. On the mountainous islands, too, there is a regular alternation between land and sea winds on the leeward side: almost at the same time every morning the land wind blowing towards the sea gives place to a sea wind blowing on to the land. On the S coast of Jamaica, where the change in wind direction is clearly signalled by the smoke from a cement factory chimney to the E of Kingston, the sea breeze, regarded by the local people as particularly healthy, is known as the "Doctor Wind". The trade winds blow strongly, but are unpleasant only over the dry islands of the southern Antilles, where the trunks of the trees are driven into a horizontal position by the unremitting force of the wind.

One great attraction of the Caribbean for visitors from more northern climes is the amount of **sunshine** in the islands, with the exception only of the mountainous regions. Thus Fort-de-France on Martinique, with an annual rainfall of 72 in./1840 mm, has an average of 2787 hours of sunshine in the year. Moreover, there is little variation in the amount of sunshine over the year, as there is in the temperate zone. Although the summer months have heavy rain, it falls in such violent downpours and is over so soon that the average number of hours of sunshine is much the same as in winter: thus at Fort-de-France the average daily hours of sunshine in August, the rainiest month, is 8.3, compared with 7.3 in December.

The difference in the amount of sunshine between the Caribbean and more northerly regions, however, reflects not only the different climatic conditions but also the difference in the length of the day resulting from the lower latitude. Visitors from Europe or North America have to adjust to the idea that in the tropics the day is shorter in summer and longer in winter than at home. In the Caribbean the sun rises all year round at about 6 a.m. and sets about 6 p.m., and the period of half light in the morning and twilight at night is much shorter than in more northern latitudes.

As a result of the high air temperatures prevailing throughout the year *sea temperatures*, except for short periods in Bermuda and the northern Bahamas, are consistently above 68 °F/20 °C and in July rise to 81–82 °F/27–28 °C. In consequence corals, which

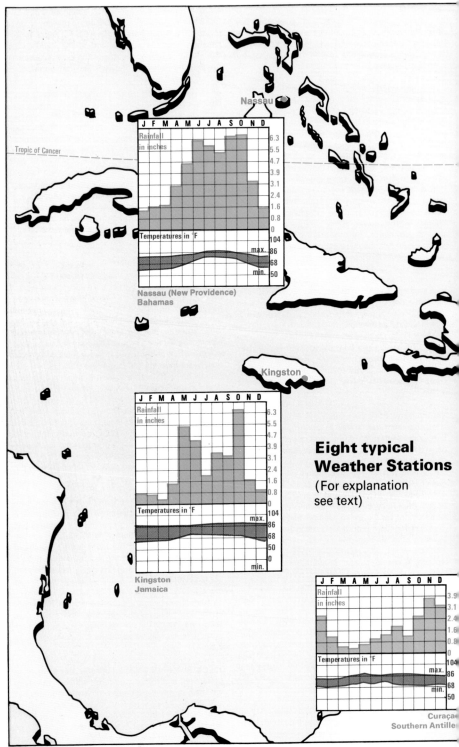

Nassau

Tropic of Cancer

J F M A M J J A S O N D

Rainfall
in inches

6.3
5.5
4.7
3.9
3.1
2.4
1.6
0.8
0

Temperatures in °F

104
max. 86
68
min. 50

Nassau (New Providence)
Bahamas

Kingston

J F M A M J J A S O N D

Rainfall
in inches

6.3
5.5
4.7
3.9
3.1
2.4
1.6
0.8
0

Temperatures in °F

104
max. 86
68
50
0
min.

Kingston
Jamaica

Eight typical Weather Stations

(For explanation
see text)

J F M A M J J A S O N D

Rainfall
in inches

3.9
3.1
2.4
1.6
0.8
0

Temperatures in °F

104
max. 86
68
min. 50

Curaçao
Southern Antilles

Prepared by Prof. Dr Wolfgang Hassenpflug

prefer warm water, are found widely throughout the Caribbean: indeed it is the corals that have created many of the islands.

The climatic characteristics of selected islands are shown in the climatic diagrams above which give the monthly average temperature and rainfall. The blue columns show the rainfall in inches, in accordance with the scale in the right-hand margin. The orange band shows the temperature in °F, the upper edge giving the average maximum day temperature, the lower edge the average minimum night temperature, in accordance with the orange scale in the margin.

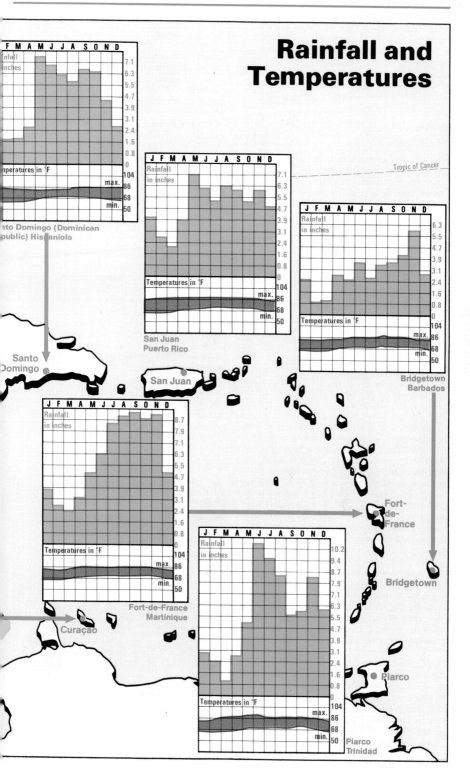

Rainfall and Temperatures

Tropic of Cancer

Santo Domingo (Dominican Republic) Hispaniola

Santo Domingo

San Juan
Puerto Rico

San Juan

Bridgetown
Barbados

Fort-de-France

Bridgetown

Fort-de-France
Martinique

Curaçao

Piarco

Piarco
Trinidad

Bahamas
Nassau weather station (New Providence)

The climate of the Bahamas offers ideal holiday weather all year round; it ranges from tropical to subtropical according to the situation of the particular island between latitude 20° and 27° N. The capital, Nassau (on New Providence), is in the same latitude as the southernmost tip of Florida. – The clear, warm water, without which the corals could not grow, is also one of the major tourist assets of the Bahamas.

From May to August the wind blows mainly from the SE, during the rest of the year from the NE. The Gulf

Stream which flows through the archipelago brings additional warmth in winter. – The number of days on which rain falls is 9 in November and December, 6 in January–April, 11 in March and 14–17 in other months. Between the showers there are long periods of sunshine – 264 hours in May (the highest figure), 210 in October (the lowest).

Jamaica
Kingston weather station

Kingston, on the south coast of Jamaica, has an annual rainfall of 32 in./811 mm. In the Blue Mountains at the east end of the island, rising to over 6560 ft/2000 m, the average annual rainfall is over 157 in./4000 mm; at Mooretown (alt. 655 ft/200 m), on the eastern slopes of the hills, the high figure of 220 in./5600 mm has been recorded. The southern and western coastal area, facing away from the trade winds, is much drier, with an annual rainfall of less than 40 in./1000 mm. The decrease in rainfall from E to W is also reflected in the number of days with rain – over 200 in the Blue Mountains, 157 at Kingston, only 70–80 farther to the SW – and in the increased incidence of plants such as thorny scrub, cactuses and other succulents which can grow in very dry conditions. The rain falls mainly during the afternoon in the form of thunder-showers; less than 20% falls during the night.

Hispaniola
(Haiti and Dominican Republic)
Santo Domingo weather station

Hispaniola, a relatively large island with a varied pattern of relief, shows considerable local deviations from the figures recorded at the Santo Domingo weather station. As on the other islands, temperature falls and rainfall rises with increasing altitude. The NE of the island, exposed to the trade winds, has a high rainfall; the lowlands in the wind shadow of the mountains, on the other hand, are markedly arid. – Temperatures fall with increasing altitude, until on the highest summits the minimum is only just over 32 °F/ 0 °C and the maximum day temperature only a little over 50 °F/10 °C.

The wettest areas (some of them with annual rainfalls of over 80 in./2000 mm), are, in addition to the central highlands, near Samaná, in the uplands between Gonaïves and Cap-Haïtien and in the bay of Les Cayes. Southwestern Hispaniola is also brought heavy rain by the S winds, which blow much more rarely than the prevailing northerly winds.

There are arid regions (with a rainfall of under 12 in./ 300 mm a year) in the coastal area around Gonaïves, in the lowlands W of Santiago, in the rift valley E of Port-au-Prince, with its salt lakes lying below sea level, and in the Azua plain. – Temperature fluctuations over the day increase in arid regions and in areas remote from the coast, where maximum temperatures occasionally rise above 104 °F/40 °C.

In the western three-quarters of the island the rainy periods in April–June and August–November, when the sun is at its highest, are clearly marked off from one another by a brief dry season in July. In the eastern part of the island the aridity of July is less marked. The rainiest months are May and June, when rain falls on average on 11–12 days in the month, mostly in the form of violent showers in the afternoon. At Port-au-Prince the rain falls mostly at night, with only a third of the total amount falling during the day.

Puerto Rico
San Juan weather station

Unlike Kingston (Jamaica), the San Juan weather station lies on the N side of the island and, with a similar temperature pattern, has a markedly higher rainfall (60 in./1534 mm a year). On the northern and eastern slopes of the central massif the rainfall figures are still higher. Only a narrow strip of land along the S coast is dry: Ponce, for example, has an annual rainfall of only 35 in./900 mm, with rain on 95 days in the year (compared with 163 days at San Juan). February and March are the driest months everywhere, with rain falling on an average of 10 days in each month (against 12–16 days during the rainy season). – The number of hours of sunshine ranges between 210 hours in November and 266 in August.

Martinique
Fort-de-France weather station

Fort-de-France, on the W coast of Martinique, has a hot and predominantly humid climate. From December to March maximum temperatures remain below 86 °F/30 °C, with relatively little rainfall; from April to June both temperatures and rainfall rise; and from July to November it is hot and wet.

At an altitude of 1640 ft/500 m temperatures are 3½–5½ °F/2–3 °C lower than on the coast and rainfall some 40 in./1000 mm higher. The driest areas are the S end of the island and the strip of coast between Fort-de-France and St-Pierre. The number of days with rain is at its lowest in February (17 days), but rises during the rainy season to between 22 and 27. – The number of hours of sunshine ranges between 211 and 256 per month. – The wind blows throughout the year from the E and NE at forces between 5 and 7.

Barbados
Bridgetown weather station

The climate of Barbados is claimed to be the healthiest in the West Indies. Bridgetown weather station lies on

Platinum Coast, Barbados

Coastal scenery, northern Trinidad

the SW coast, in the lee of hills rising to 1000 ft/300 m. The NE trade winds blow over the whole island, but are less strong in the summer months as a result of its southerly situation. The annual rainfall at Bridgetown is 50 in./1276 mm, rising to over 80 in./2000 mm in the central hills and 100 in./2500 mm on the E coast. During the months of February–April there are 7 days of rain a month, in May 9, in the other months 14–18. The rainfall is concentrated in violent showers, with long periods of clear weather in between. – Lying so far S, the island is little troubled by hurricanes.

Trinidad
Piarco weather station

Trinidad is the most southerly of the West Indian islands. Piarco is the meteorological station of the island's central airfield. In autumn, during the rainy season, the NE trade winds blow less strongly. From January to June temperatures rise by $3\frac{1}{2}$–$5\frac{1}{2}$ °F/2–3 °C and then fall slightly at the beginning of the rainy season (highest rainfall in June–July). Piarco itself has an annual rainfall of 70 in./1750 mm; in the hills to the NE the figure rises to 150 in./3800 mm, while on the dry W coast it falls to 59–47 in./1500–1200 mm. – Trinidad is not troubled by hurricanes.

Southern Antilles
Curaçao weather station

The islands lying off the coast of Venezuela have a very dry climate. The average annual rainfall is between 20 in./500 mm and 24 in./600 mm, and this, combined with high temperatures throughout the year (annual average 81–82 °F/27–28 °C), a high rate of evaporation and the water-permeable limestone subsoil found in many areas, permits only a scanty vegetation cover of thorny scrub and cactuses. The islands are now supplied with water by desalinization plants processing sea water.

Bermuda, lying in latitude 32°18′ N, is, thanks to the warming influence of the *Gulf Stream*, the most northerly outpost of tropical climatic conditions and the world's most northerly coral reef. The climate is maritime to subtropical. The warmest month is July, with a mean temperature of 73 °F/23 °C, February the coldest with 59 °F/15 °C. – Seasonal variations are small, though rather greater than on the Caribbean islands. – Annual rainfall rises to about 100 in./2500 mm; April is the rainiest month, October the driest. – Throughout the year the air has a high humidity content; in summer it is muggy, and from July to September there are frequent thunderstorms.

Vegetation

Climatically the Caribbean region belongs to the tropics, and its vegetation is tropical, or more precisely neo-tropical (i.e. belonging to the New World tropical zone). The **neo-tropical flora** includes many species belonging to the large pan-tropical (i.e. found throughout the tropical zone) families of the **palms** (*Chamaedorea*, the mountain palm; *Mauritia*, the fan palm; *Euterpe*, the Assai palm; *Jubaea*, the wine palm; *Sabal*, the palmetto), *Araceae* (arum family), *Zingiberaceae* (ginger family), *Lauraceae* (laurel family), *Myrtaceae* (myrtle family), *Melastomataceae*, *Euphorbiaceae* (spurge family, to which the highly poisonous manchineel tree belongs), *Piperaceae* (pepper family), *Moraceae* (mulberry family), *Asclepiaceae*, *Hymenophyllaceae* (filmy ferns), *Cycadaceae* (palm ferns) and *Gesneriaceae*, as well as the specifically neo-tropical families (mostly with numerous species) of the *Cactaceae* (cactuses), *Cannaceae* (cannas), *Tropaeolaceae* (nasturtium family), *Loasaceae* and *Malpighiaceae* and the neo-tropical genera of *Agava*, *Yucca* and *Polemonium* (Jacob's ladder).

Within the neo-tropical vegetation zone, characterized by steady high temperatures (annual average around 77 °F/25 °C; minimum 55 °F/13 °C), vegetation patterns are differentiated by varying degrees of humidity. A factor of decisive impor-

Bougainvillea (Trinidad)

tance in determining levels of rainfall is the fact that beyond the Tropic of Cancer the trade winds, reversing the direction of wind movement in both hemispheres, blow from NE to SW or from SE to NW. In consequence the humidity zones – and with them the vegetation patterns – of the Caribbean range from humid neo-tropical in the E and NE to arid neo-tropical in the SW and W. An area is classified as humid when rainfall exceeds evaporation and as arid when the rate of evaporation is greater than the rainfall. Where there are no marked weather barriers the transition between humid and arid zones is gradual. In areas with considerable variations in relief, on the other hand, the change can be quite abrupt; in particular there is a sharp contrast between vegetation patterns on the windward and the lee sides of hills. Altitude also affects the type of vegetation cover, and it is notable that changes in vegetation type take place at lower levels on the windward side than on the lee side of hills.

Although vegetation patterns are largely determined by climatic conditions, variations may result from differences in the nature of the soil or from human intervention. The separation of the Caribbean islands from the mainland has also pro-

Coconut palms (Guadeloupe)

moted the development of endemism (the occurrence of particular species within a localized area); this is found particularly in the Leeward and Windward Islands.

The lower-lying areas, particularly in the Greater Antilles, and the windward slopes of the hills – which form the *tierra caliente* or hot zone, reaching up to 3300 ft/1000 m – are the region of **evergreen tropical rain forest**, the world's most luxuriant growth of vegetation, with a rich variety of species, stratified according to height. The growing period continues throughout the year, and even trees of the same species shed their leaves at different times, so that the forest always appears green. Similarly the period of blossoming and ripening is spread over the whole year, with no single period offering an overpowering show of blossom. Stem-flowering plants are numerous.

The trees reach upwards towards the light, ranging in height up to 130 ft/40 m, with

Philodendron (Guadeloupe)

Heliconia (Trinidad)

trunks of no great thickness (up to 40 in./ 1 m in diameter). The spreading crowns allow little light to penetrate to the ground, only some 3% of the available daylight reaching the interior of the forest. The shrubby undergrowth shows a lesser variety of species, consisting largely of saplings of the forest trees. Since growth is continuous there are no clearly marked growth rings, and the trees thus yield excellent timber with little grain, much of it notable for its hardness and pliability; particularly esteemed is Cuban mahogany (*Swietenia mahagoni*). The roots do not strike deep, since most of the meagre nourishment available is in the uppermost layers of soil. The branches and crowns of the trees are knitted together into an

impenetrable jungle by a dense growth of epiphytes (plants parasitic on trees, such as *Philodendron*). Particularly common are bromeliads, orchids, ferns, lichens and mosses. The lack of light means that there is little or no low-growing vegetation. – A good example of tropical rain forest, with many tree ferns and palms, can be seen in the Sierra de Luquillo nature reserve on Puerto Rico, made easily accessible by roads and waymarked footpaths.

In the *tierra templada* or temperate zone (3300–6500 ft/1000–2000 m) and the *tierra fría* or cold zone (6500–13,000 ft/ 2000–4000 m) the tropical rain forest thins out into the **evergreen mountain rain forest** and **montane cloud forest**. Here too growth is continuous through-out the year, but there are fewer species and growth is slower than in the sub-montane rain forest. The trees are farther apart and their trunks are thicker. With increasing altitude the creeping plants so common in the *tierra caliente* disappear, but epiphytic plants of many different species are present in great abundance, particularly notable being the bromeliad called Spanish moss (*Tillandsia usneoides*).

In areas with periodic dry seasons the evergreen tropical rain forest gives place to **green humid and dry forests**. Here the trees shed their leaves during the dry season and enter into a state of quie-scence corresponding to the winter period of quiescence in the temperate zone.

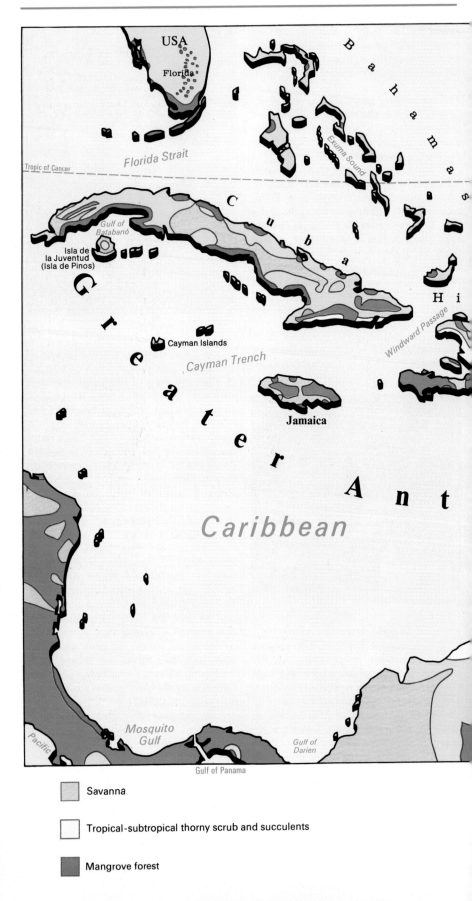

Savanna

Tropical-subtropical thorny scrub and succulents

Mangrove forest

Heliconia collinsiana in Jamaica

Vegetation Zones in the Caribbean

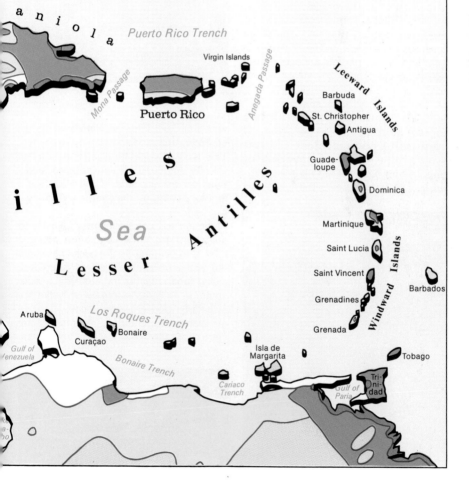

Tropic of Cancer

Atlantic

Hispaniola

Puerto Rico Trench

Virgin Islands

Mona Passage

Anegada Passage

Puerto Rico

Leeward Islands

Barbuda

St. Christopher

Antigua

Guade-
loupe

Dominica

illes

Sea

Antilles

Martinique

Saint Lucia

Windward Islands

Lesser

Saint Vincent

Barbados

Grenadines

Aruba

Los Roques Trench

Bonaire

Grenada

Curaçao

*Gulf of
Venezuela*

Bonaire Trench

Isla de
Margarita

Tobago

*Cariaco
Trench*

*Gulf of
Paria*

Tri-
ni-
dad

Evergreen tropical rain forest
Evergreen mountain rain forest, montane cloud forest

Green humid and dry forest

Xerophytic vegetation on Curaçao

Particularly striking representatives of this vegetation pattern are the kapok tree (*Ceiba pentandra*) with its characteristic spreading crown, the handsome royal palm (*Roystonea regia*) widely distributed in the Greater Antilles, and the curious bottle palm (*Colpothrinax wrightii*) of Cuba. Epiphytes are rare, and lianas are entirely absent. There are numerous trees belonging to the order of Leguminosae, in particular various species of acacia. There are also areas of thorny scrub.

Bay grapes (Grand Cayman)

The driest regions in the Antilles have a **tropical-subtropical vegetation of thorny scrub and succulents**, a sparse covering of thorny shrubs, agaves, spiny opuntias and cactuses, the latter contributing a striking note to the landscape with their extraordinary variety of forms, globular, columnar and many-branched. This type of vegetation is found on the Greater Antilles only in sheltered situations on the lee side of hills but is the regular pattern on the southern Antilles.

Particular soil conditions may give rise to deviations from the vegetation patterns related to climate. Such special cases are the areas of almost treeless grassland, called *sabana* by the Indians, which were common on Cuba before the arrival of the Spaniards and the periodically flooded grasslands on Trinidad, resembling the *llanos* of the Orinoco in Venezuela.

Mangroves on Trinidad

Cacao (Grenada)

Mention must also be made here of the **coniferous forests** (*Pinus caribaea*), common in the Caribbean only in the *tierra caliente* and *tierra templada*, which are also found on the neighboring North American and Central American mainland. The Cuban Isla de Pinos (Isla de la Juventud) takes its name from this type of forest.

Another vegetation pattern determined by particular soil conditions is the **mangrove forest** found on flat and sheltered coasts, sometimes covering considerable areas (3.6% of the total area of Guadeloupe, 2.5% of the area of Martinique; also on Cuba, Trinidad and other islands). In consequence of its highly specialized habitat the mangrove has only four main species (*Rhizophora mangle*, the red mangrove; *Avicennia nitida*, the black or honey mangrove; *Laguncularia racemosa*, the white mangrove; *Conocarpus erecta*, the button mangrove). These salt-loving plants with thick evergreen leaves grow in separate belts in an amphibious scrub forest, with the stilt-rooted red mangrove giving place farther inland to the black mangrove with its upward-branching roots (pneumatophores). – Common on beaches are thickets of the evergreen broad-leaved *bay grape* or sea grape (*Coccoloba uvifera*).

Centuries of cultivation, first by the in-digenous Indian inhabitants and later by white settlers, largely destroyed or altered the original vegetation pattern, now preserved only in patches. In some areas the changes have been so radical that it is almost impossible to decide whether they are the result of soil conditions or of human action. It seems clear, however, that the large tracts of savanna country were produced by the clearance of the original tropical forest.

Where the land has been cultivated by man in an organized fashion the indigenous plants have been supplemented or superseded by new introductions. The most notable example of this is **sugar-cane** (*Saccharum officinarum*), a plant which probably came from South-East Asia and has been cultivated in the Antilles since the 16th c. Refined to

Pineapple (Guadeloupe)

produce cane sugar or distilled to produce rum (particularly on Jamaica, Martinique and Guadeloupe), sugar-cane is one of the chief economic resources of the Caribbean. Other important crops are *tobacco* (*Nicotiana tabacum* var. *havannensis*) on Cuba (Havana cigars) and Hispaniola, *caçao* (*Theobroma caçao*) on Jamaica, Trinidad, Tobago, Hispaniola and Guadeloupe, and *sisal* on Cuba and Hispaniola – all native to the New World. The Europeans brought *coffee* (Trinidad, Tobago, Guadeloupe, Hispaniola, Jamaica), *bananas* (Jamaica, Guadeloupe, Trinidad, Tobago, Bahamas, Hispaniola), *citrus fruits* (Cuba, Jamaica, Trinidad, Tobago, Bahamas), *coconuts* (Trinidad, Tobago, Jamaica)

Sugar-cane (Jamaica)

Hibiscus (Trinidad)

Breadfruit tree (Grand Cayman)

and *rice* (Cuba, Hispaniola); but *cotton* (Cuba, Hispaniola) was already known to the Indians. From Asia came *ginger* (*Zingiber officinale*) and *nutmeg* (*Myristica fragrans*), which are grown on Jamaica and Grenada, together with the indigenous *pepper* plant (*Pimenta officinalis*). The *pineapple* (*Ananas sativus*), a native of tropical South America, was brought to Europe from Guadeloupe by Columbus in 1492; it is now an important crop in the Bahamas (and five pineapples feature in the coat of arms of Jamaica).

Typical Caribbean fruits include the *avocado* (*Persea gratissima*), much esteemed by the Indians under the name of ahuacatl; the luscious *mango* (*Mangifera indica*); the *pawpaw* (*Carica papaya*), known in Cuba as *fruta bomba*; and the *ackee* (*Blighia sapida*), introduced from Africa in the 18th c. to provide food for black slaves, and which, cooked, is still popular in Jamaica as an accompaniment to salt fish. Another plant brought in as a cheap source of food for slaves was the *breadfruit* (*Artocarpus altilis*), a native of the Pacific islands. Weighing up to $4\frac{1}{2}$ lb/2 kg and rich in carbohydrates and vitamins,

the breadfruit is either eaten boiled or roasted or ground to produce flour. A leaf of the breadfruit tree appears on the flag of St Vincent and the Grenadines.

A variant pattern of vegetation is found in many parks and gardens, offering a profusion of glorious color all year round to which native, pan-tropical, palaeo-tropical (from the tropics of the Old World) and subtropical plants all make their contribution. Numerous fantastically formed species of *orchids* add a strikingly exotic note. *Bougainvillea, oleander, hibiscus, parkinsonia* and *heliconia* (which also grows wild on the Lesser Antilles) are ubiquitous, as are the profusely flowering *coral tree* (*Erythrina poeppigiana*), the *rubber tree*, the *yucca* and the *thorn-apple* (*Datura arborea*). – The brilliantly blue flower of the *lignum vitae* tree (*Guaiacum officinale*) is Jamaica's national flower. Almost every part of the tree serves some medicinal purpose, and it also yields a very hard and heavy timber.

Animal Life

As with most other archipelagoes, the Caribbean islands show a relatively limited range of species, particularly in the case of the mammals. The oceanic situation either brought the evolutionary process to a stop or directed it into specific channels, leading to the emergence of endemic species. Although animal life may vary considerably from island to island, all the islands have much closer relationships with each other than with the mainland. Accordingly the animal life of the Caribbean islands is grouped by zoogeographers into a West Indian region.

The only exception to this generalization is Trinidad, which was cut off from the South American mainland only some 8000 years ago and has the same wealth of animal species as Central America. Here are still to be found *anteaters* (*Myrmecophagidae*), *tiger cats* (*Felis pardalis*), *pine martens* (*Mustela barbara*), *racoons* (*Procyon lotor*) and *howling monkeys* (*Alouatta seniculus*, the red howling monkey; *Alouatta villosa*, the black howling monkey).

The *Haitian solenodon* (*Solenodon paradoxus*), an insect-eater weighing up to 2¼ lb/1 kg, survives only in the mountain forests of Hispaniola, but the *Cuban solenodon* (*Atopogale cubana*) appears now to be extinct. – *Bats* in great variety are found on all the Caribbean islands but particularly on Trinidad, where they are the subject of organized research.

More numerous than the mammals on the Caribbean islands are the **reptiles** and **amphibians**. The *cayman*, which gives the Cayman Islands their name and features above the coat of arms of Jamaica, is still found on Cuba in two endemic species. There are many species of *teju* (*Teiidae*), the New World counterpart of the Old World lizard, and the *iguana* is not uncommon, occurring on Hispaniola in an endemic species, *Cyclura cornuta*, the horned iguana, which can reach a length of 40 in./1 m. The *least gecko* (*Sphaerodactylus*) is a genus confined to the Caribbean area. – Less numerous than the lizards are the *snakes*, the only poisonous species of which are the *lance-head snakes* (*Bothrops caribaeus* and *B. lanceolatus*) found on

Martinique and St Lucia. Here again Trinidad forms an exception, with a wide range of snakes, including a number of poisonous species and the majestic *boa constrictor*. – Amphibians found in the Caribbean include several endemic species of whistling frogs belonging to the genus *Eleutherodactylus*.

In contrast to the terrestrial life, the **birds** of the Caribbean are notable for their color and variety, with many endemic species; and in addition hosts of migratory birds winter on the islands. Particularly characteristic of the neo-tropics (New World) are the numerous *parrots* (*Psittaciformes*) and *hummingbirds* (*Trochilidae*). The Greater Antilles have four species of *todies* (*Todidae*), living mainly on insects, which they catch in flight, and nesting in burrows in the earth.

Flamingoes on Mayaguana (Bahamas)

There are numerous water birds, in particular *brown pelicans* (*Pelecanus occidentalis*) and *flamingoes* (*Phoenicopterus*), the great flocks of which on Bonaire have earned it the name of Flamingo Island. The extensive mangrove forests of Trinidad are the home of the *scarlet ibis* (*Eudocimus ruber*). – With little in the way of inland waters, the Caribbean islands have little fresh-water life.

The **marine life** of the Caribbean is abundant and varied, making the coastal waters of the islands a happy hunting ground for the diving enthusiast. The sea bottom is covered with forests of fantastically shaped **corals**, particularly common being the *stony corals* (*Madrepora*), comprising the *stag coral* and *elkhorn coral* genera; *Neptune's brain* (*Diploria*); and the *horny corals* (*Gorgonaria*), represented by *Venus's fan* and the *gorgonia bush*. The tiny marine creatures (coelenterata) which inhabit the tropical seas in such vast numbers and build up

Scarlet ibises (Trinidad)

their limestone colonies to form coral have not only given the sea floor its colorful pattern but have also created numbers of atolls in the Caribbean Sea.

With their intricately ramified structures the banks of coral provide shelter and

Finger coral (Cayman Islands)

protection for great numbers of **fish**, most of them brilliantly coloured and many of them bizarrely formed. Typical denizens of this tropical submarine world are the colorful *parrotfishes* (*Sparisoma abildgaardi, Scarus vetula, Sparisoma viride*, etc.), the *queen triggerfish* (*Balistes veluta*), the *hogfish* (*Lachnolaimus maximum*), several species of *boxfish* (*Ostracionidae*), encased in their bony plates, the *butterflyfish* and *angelfish* (*Chaetodontidae*), the *surgeonfish* (*Acanthurus*), the curious *porcupinefish* (*Diodon hystrix*) and various species of *flying fish*

Jellyfish (Cayman Islands)

(*Exocoetidae*). – Predatory fish include the *barracuda* (*Sphyraena barracuda*), the *blue shark* (*Prionace glauca*), the *shovelnose shark* (*Notidanus griseus*), the *nurse shark* (*Ginglymostoma cirratum*) and the *smooth hammerhead shark* (*Sphyrna zigaena*). Large numbers of *marlins* (*Makaira*) and swordfish (*Xiphias gladius*), locally known as *balau*, are caught by fishermen.

Common **marine mammmals** are the *dolphin* and the *porpoise*. The *manatee* (*Trichechus manatus*) can occasionally be seen in flat coastal areas and brackish water, where it grazes on seaweed.

Queen triggerfish (Cayman Islands)

The **turtles** of the Caribbean have been decimated by human action – in particular the *green turtle* (*Chelonia mydas*) and the *hawksbill turtle* (*Eretmochelys imbricata*), which yields the much sought-after tortoiseshell. Turtles are now systematically bred on Grand Cayman and elsewhere. – *Prawns*, *crayfish* and other crustaceans grow to considerable size in the warm waters of the Caribbean. – *Crinoids*, *sea urchins* and *starfishes* are ubiquitous. – The *abalone* (*Haliotis*) is a much prized delicacy. Banks of *oysters* and *mussels* are cultivated in many places; the Venezuelan island of Margarita was once renowned for its cultivated oyster beds.

Population

Two direct effects of the past histories of the Caribbean islands are, in the first place, the mingling of races on each of the islands and, secondly, the specific characteristics which result from their former allegiance to the various colonial powers – Spanish, French, British or Dutch.

A feature common to all the islands is that there are hardly any remnants of the indigenous Indian population. In up-country areas in Cuba and the Dominican Republic, it is true, white people are sometimes encountered with facial characteristics pointing to some Indian blood. The Arawak Indian population of the Greater Antilles was wiped out relatively quickly, but the **Caribs** held out longer on the Lesser Antilles. On St Vincent and particularly on Dominica there are still small numbers of "black Caribs", with a mingling of Carib and negro blood. Most of this mixed population, however, was deported by the British authorities to the Mosquito Coast and the Bay Islands in 1796. Finally the Dutch island of Aruba and the Venezuelan island of Margarita off the South American coast have populations consisting predominantly of *mestizos*, people of mixed white and Indian blood.

Otherwise the population of the Caribbean islands consists of the descendants of incomers. During the colonial period *Europeans* of various nationalities and languages settled on the islands, coming either directly from Europe or from the North American colonies. Then hundreds of thousands of *negroes* were forcibly transported from Africa by the colonial powers. After the abolition of slavery the British and French brought in indentured laborers from *India* to work on the sugar plantations. Smaller groups of immigrants also came from *China* and *Lebanon*.

There are no reliable statistics on the racial composition of the population of the Caribbean islands. Part of the difficulty is that of the many mulattoes descended from unions between whites and blacks those with light-colored skins are frequently counted as white and those with dark skins as black. A cautious estimate might reckon 40% of the population to be *white* and 40% *black*, with 18% of *mulattoes*. The remaining 2% consists predominantly of (Asian) Indians.

With the exception of a few very small islands the population shows no racial homogeneity: each island displays its own characteristic **ethnic pluralism**. The former French and British possessions show a marked predominance of blacks, with a high proportion of mulattoes on the French islands. In both cases, however, more than 90% of the population are colored. In the former Spanish islands, in contrast, the white element in the population predominates (80% in Puerto Rico,

Girls in traditional costume, Martinique

73% in Cuba). The predominance of mulattoes (60%) in the population of the Dominican Republic, formerly a Spanish territory, is an exception resulting from the two occupations of the country by Haiti. These considerable differences in racial composition reflect differing economic developments during the colonial period. The early plantation economy, based on slave labor, in the British and French colonies produced the present predominance of blacks on these islands. Asian Indians are found only in the former French and British possessions; in Trinidad they make up 40% of the population. The smaller proportion of blacks in the former Spanish possessions results from the fact that the early plantation system did not develop in these areas. By the time large sugar plantations of modern type were established on these islands slavery had been abolished, and the necessary labor force was provided by incomers from Spain and the Canary Islands.

The **languages** spoken on the various Caribbean islands are also a reflection of their history and their former colonial allegiance. Some small and remote islands still preserve old dialects inherited from the original settlers: thus on the French island of Saint-Barthélemy a 17th c. Norman dialect is still spoken. In general the country people of the former British and French possessions speak an *English* or *French* interspersed with many Africanisms. The people of the Dutch islands in the southern Antilles speak *Papiamento*, a language which evolved in the 18th c. out of a mingling of Spanish, Portuguese, Dutch, English, Indian and African elements. – The official languages of the various Caribbean states are those of the former colonial powers – though in Puerto Rico, with its Spanish-speaking population, the close association with the United States has led to English becoming a second official language. In the Lesser Antilles it can happen, as a result of a change of colonial master in the past, that the official language and the language of everyday life are not the same: thus a French patois is spoken on the islands of Grenada and St Lucia, which are members of the British Commonwealth, while English is spoken in the French part of the island of St-Martin.

The total population of the Caribbean islands is almost 30 million, giving an average **population density** of 313 to the sq. mile (125 to the sq. km). This average, however, conceals wide variations. The most thinly populated islands are Turks and Caicos (36 to the sq. mile/14 to the sq. km) and the Bahamas (52 to the sq. mile/20 to the sq. km), the most densely populated Barbados (1505 to the sq. mile/581 to the sq. km). High population densities are also found on other islands in the Lesser Antilles and in Haiti (454 to the sq. mile/181 to the sq. km), Jamaica (482 to the sq. mile/186 to the sq. km) and above all Puerto Rico (966 to the sq. mile/373 to the sq. km); all these areas are over-populated. These are hilly islands on which there is no further scope for extending the area under cultivation and (with the exception of Puerto Rico) industry has been inadequately developed. Birth rates remain high and there is now little scope for emigration; as a result the high rates of population increase, over-population and unemployment or under-employment are problems of desperate importance on these islands. The situation is very different in Cuba and the Dominican Republic, since there is still land which can be brought under cultivation and the density of population is in any case considerably lower (Cuba 228 to the sq. mile//88 to the sq. km, Dominican Republic 274 to the sq. mile/115 to the sq. km). In neither country, therefore, is there any population pressure.

The Spanish colonies, with their numerous foundations of towns, had traditionally a high proportion of urban population. The high figures shown by present-day Cuba (69%) and Puerto Rico (58%), however, also reflect the modern development of industry in these countries. A moderately high degree of urbanization is also shown by Trinidad (55%), the Dominican Republic (54%) and Jamaica (45%), but on most of the other islands the proportion of urban population is still extraordinarily low: in Haiti, for example, it is only about 24%. – These figures clearly indicate that in spite of political decolonialization most of the Caribbean islands are still predominantly agricultural.

Patterns of **rural settlement** still show features inherited from the differing economic development of the various islands. The main distinction is between the areas in which the plantation system was established and those which were worked in small peasant holdings; villages predominate in the former; in the latter small individual farmhouses.

The *plantations* of the colonial period were large establishments which included both agricultural and industrial installations and living accommodation. Central features were the sugar-cane press and the boiling house, near which were the farm buildings, the slaves' quarters and the house of the slave-master; the owner's mansion was some distance away. Here and there visitors will encounter the remains of plantation buildings of the colonial period; in particular many fine plantation houses have been preserved. The present-day plantations usually have specially built settlements for workers situated near the sugar factories, laid out on a regular plan and usually including a school and modest service facilities. On the state farms (*granjas estatales*) of Cuba these little settlements of traditional-style houses give place to larger housing estates of almost urban character.

In the peasant farming areas there are some *villages*, usually of irregular layout, but the normal pattern is the *individual holding*, sometimes (e.g. in Haiti) very widely dispersed. In consequence the little peasant farmhouses lie away from the few roads, accessible only by footpath or bridle track.

In the former Spanish colonies the traditional *bohío* is still everywhere to be seen: a plank-built cottage roofed with palm leaves or straw of a type inherited from the indigenous Indian population. – House types are more varied in the former British and French colonies. The walls may be built of planks or of wattle and daub. There are often wide overhanging roofs, allowing work to continue during rain. The fireplace is in the open outside the house, forming a focus around which the daily life of the household revolves. – On islands where development is more recent the traditional types of house have increasingly given place to concrete structures with corrugated iron roofs.

The **towns** of the Caribbean islands, all foundations of the colonial period, still preserve the grid plan characteristic of all colonial towns whatever their political allegiance; departures from the principle are found only where the topography makes this unavoidable. In the old town center is a square (often originally called the Plaza de Armas or Place d'Armes) surrounded by public buildings (government offices, the church). Many towns still have well-preserved buildings in colonial style, in each case reflecting the architectural fashions of the mother country. Thus the old Spanish colonial towns have houses with a patio of Andalusian type and handsome wrought-iron balconies. The Cathedral of Santa María la Menor in Santo Domingo, capital of the Dominican Republic, the oldest church in the New World (1523–41), combines Romanesque, Gothic and Plateresque elements, but other churches in the former Spanish colonies are younger, dating from the Baroque period. Spanish colonial architecture can be seen in the older parts of Santo Domingo, Havana (Cuba), San Juan (Puerto Rico) and other towns; perhaps the finest examples are to be found in the town of Trinidad (Cuba).

Icecream seller, Haiti

Characteristic of the old British colonial towns are their white-painted wooden houses built on stone foundations and their Georgian or Victorian public buildings. Basseterre, capital of St Kitts, still preserves the atmosphere of a small British colonial town. – The center of Pointe-à-Pitre (Guadeloupe) preserves the type of a French colonial town with its closely packed houses of two or three storys; Willemstad, on the Dutch island of Curaçao, has all the atmosphere of an 18th c. Dutch town, with its narrow houses and crow-stepped gables; and Danish traditions are reflected in the substantial merchants' houses of Christiansted on St Croix, now one of the

United States Virgin Islands. – The Caribbean towns have been little affected by high-rise developments of North American type. Exceptions are the Cuban capital of Havana and San Juan on Puerto Rico, with its modern business district of Hato Rey and the numerous tower-block hotels of Condado.

Apart from their administrative functions the towns of the Caribbean islands also have an important role as centers of external trade. Almost all of them are port towns; and the principal port on an island is usually also its capital. Each of these towns is the administrative, cultural and economic heart of the whole island and accordingly by far the largest settlement on each island, sometimes containing more than a quarter of the total population. Thus in 1970 the Metropolitan Area of San Juan already had almost a third of the total population of Puerto Rico, and since then the city has continued to grow. The population of the Havana metropolitan area had reached almost 2 million by 1981 and was likewise continuing to grow – to such an extent that the Cuban government banned any further movement of population into the capital. The same drift from the country to the towns, though not on the same scale as in the case of these two cities, is taking place all over the Caribbean islands. Neither the industrial nor the services sector of the economy is achieving the growth necessary to provide jobs and homes for those who flock to the towns, and in consequence there has been a massive development of shanty towns and slums which become hotbeds of crime and social unrest.

There are only 19 towns of over 100,000 inhabitants on the Caribbean islands, 14 of them in the former Spanish colonies (including 9 on Cuba alone). On the British islands only Kingston, Spanish Town and Montego Bay (Jamaica) and Port of Spain (Trinidad) have more than 100,000 inhabitants, in the former French colonies only the Haitian capital of Port-au-Prince and Fort-de-France on Martinique.

A further inheritance from the colonial period is a **social structure** which in present conditions appears highly precarious. The old plantation colonies had a small and well-to-do *upper class* and a large *lower class* of poor peasants and

A slum quarter in Port-au-Prince (Haiti)

land workers who made up the mass of the population, with an almost total absence of any intermediate groups. This rigid division into social classes largely coincided with a racial differentiation; and the result was to produce extreme social contrasts and to make any kind of integration between the classes impossible. This was the situation on all the Caribbean islands, though with variations from place to place and differences between the territories of the three main colonial powers. On Cuba this traditional social structure was abolished after Castro's revolution and replaced by a new social order on socialist principles. There have also been changes, varying in degree, on other islands. Apart from Cuba no island has carried through a radical land reform; but wherever modern economic development has begun – in particular where industrialization has made headway and the services sector and the educational system have been developed – a *middle class* has come into being. There is still, however, much poverty in the country areas and also in the towns as a result of the drift from the land into urban areas, and there are still stark social contrasts.

Among the black population in the lower social groups marriage, either civil or in church, is the exception rather than the rule. In Haiti in particular, both in the country areas and in the towns, free unions are normal; and in consequence most of the children are illegitimate. This is a reflection both of African traditions and of economic pressures.

Almost all the Caribbean islands now have well-developed state **educational systems**. These are of relatively recent growth, however, and there is still some illiteracy among adults, varying in degree from island to island. This is true particularly of Haiti, where in 1971 there were still 1.9 million adult illiterates, in spite of a literacy campaign launched in 1958. In Cuba, which had 23% of illiterates in the adult population in 1953, illiteracy has been wiped out as a result of the development of the educational system since the revolution.

On most of the islands the educational system comprises secondary and vocational schools as well as primary schools. There are universities only on the larger islands. The Dominican Republic prides itself on having, in the University of Santo Domingo (founded 1538), the oldest higher educational establishment in Latin America. Haiti has a university in Port-au-Prince, and Cuba has four. The largest university in the Caribbean is Puerto Rico University, in Rio Piedras; and there are also universities on Guadeloupe and Curaçao. There various institutions produce the trained manpower required for the educational system and the health services and also for administration, commerce and industry. Agriculture has long had a training and research center of international reputation in the former Imperial College of Tropical Agriculture in St Augustine (Trinidad), now combined with the former University College of the West Indies in Mona (Jamaica) to form the University of the West Indies, which also has a campus on Barbados.

Freedom of **religion** prevails on all the Caribbean islands. In the former Spanish and French colonies most of the *Christians* belong to the Roman Catholic Church, while on the British islands various Protestant denominations predominate. In Jamaica, for example, the Anglican, Baptist and Methodist churches and the Church of God have the largest numbers of adherents, but there are also a variety of local denominations such as the United Church of Jamaica. On

Hindu priest, Trinidad

Trinidad the descendants of the indentured laborers brought in from India remain true to the faith of their forefathers: 25% of the population are *Hindus* and 6% are *Moslems*. In addition 36% are Roman Catholics, 18% Anglicans and 4% Presbyterians. Visitors to Port of Spain, the capital of Trinidad, will therefore encounter Hindu temples and mosques as well as Christian churches.

Among the black population of the Caribbean islands their African religious heritage is still very much alive. A mingling of Christian elements with pagan African rites is found, for example, in the *Santería* of Cuba, the *Xango* cult of Trinidad and most notably in the *Voodoo* cult of Haiti (see under Haiti).

History

The indigenous population of most of the Caribbean islands consisted of **Indians** belonging to a number of different peoples. In pre-Columbian times the *Arawaks* or Aruaks, a farming people, were widely distributed on the islands. The Caribbean is named after the **Caribs**, a warlike peole who came from South America. The Caribs were largely exterminated in the early colonial period by European settlers coming from the American mainland, but a few hundred of their descendants still live on the island of Dominica.

The history of the Caribbean is usually taken as beginning with the epoch-making discoveries of **Columbus** (1451–1506), who, looking for a western sea route to India, made four voyages across the Atlantic between 1492 and 1504.

1492–93   On his *first voyage* Columbus lands on the small Bahamian island of Guanahani (San Salvador, Watling's Island) on October 12, 1492, and goes on to discover the West Indian islands of Juana (Cuba) and Española (Hispaniola; known to the Indians as Haiti).

1493–96   Columbus's *second voyage* takes him to Dominica and Guadeloupe in the Lesser Antilles and to Puerto Rico and Jamaica.

1498–1500   On his *third voyage* Columbus discovers the island of Trinidad and reaches the northern coast of South America.

1499–1500   The Florentine *Amerigo Vespucci* reaches the coast of Guiana and brings back the first account of the Amazon.
The newly discovered continent is named **America**, after Vespucci's Christian name, by the German cartographer Martin Waldseemüller in 1507.

1502–04   On his *fourth voyage* Columbus reaches the mainland of Central America (Honduras, Nicaragua, Panama).

1503   *Juan Bermúdez*, a Spaniard, discovers Bermuda.

1513   *Juan Ponce de León* (1460–1521), earlier one of Columbus's companions, discovers Florida, which he takes for an island.

1536   The Portuguese navigator *Pedro a Campo* lands on Barbados.

Columbus believes that the islands he has discovered lie off the E coast of Asia, and accordingly the Spaniards name them the *Indias*: hence the name WEST INDIES and the term Indians applied to the natives of the islands.

Spanish conquest and the freebooters (early 16th to mid 17th c.). – Columbus's discoveries lead to the conquest and subjugation by Spain of large territories in Central and South America. The Spaniards' main motive is the quest for gold and silver. The Spanish colonization involves the foundation of a series of towns – Santo Domingo (1496) on Hispaniola, San Juan (1508) on Puerto Rico, Santiago (1514) and Havana (1515) on Cuba.

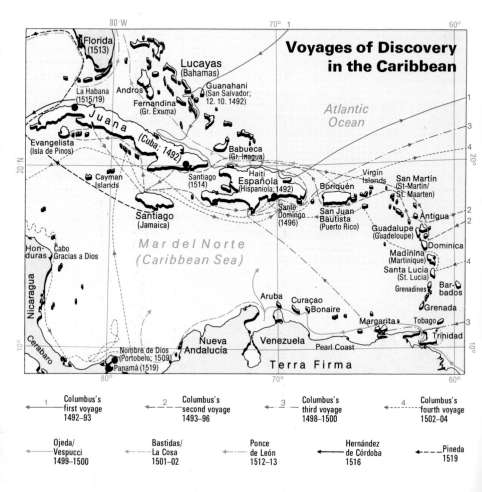

Voyages of Discovery in the Caribbean

1 ← Columbus's first voyage 1492–93	2 ← Columbus's second voyage 1493–96	3 ← Columbus's third voyage 1498–1500	4 ← Columbus's fourth voyage 1502–04
Ojeda/ Vespucci 1499–1500	Bastidas/ La Cosa 1501–02	Ponce de León 1512–13	Hernández de Córdoba 1516 Pineda 1519

The Spanish conquest leads to the destruction of the native Indian population, which is decimated by war, forced labor in the gold-mines and disease. The laws for the protection of the Indians, promulgated in 1542 on the urging of the Dominican friar *Bartolomé de las Casas* (1476–1566), come too late for the native population of the Antilles. During this period the Indians on the Spanish-held islands are almost completely exterminated.

Since the Spaniards find only small quantities of the precious metals they are looking for on the Caribbean islands, while they are present in abundance on the Central and South American mainland, Spanish political and economic interests are concentrated on the mainland. From the middle of the 16th c. the islands are of only secondary importance in the Spanish colonial empire, their main function being to maintain the security of the sea routes used by the galleons carrying the treasures of the New World to Spain. There is little settlement on the islands, but massive forts are built to protect the fine natural harbors on the westward and eastward routes dictated by the prevailing winds and currents.

From 1536   Pirates and freebooters of other European nations seek to capture the Spanish galleons sailing from America to Europe with their valuable cargoes. French corsairs, British privateers and buccaneers and Dutch filibusters not only attack Spanish ships but also plunder Spanish ports in the Caribbean, including Santiago de Cuba (1554), Havana (1555) and Santo Domingo (1586).

1595   A British fleet commanded by Sir John Hawkins and Sir Francis Drake defeats the Spaniards off San Juan (Puerto Rico).

1628   The Spanish silver fleet is captured by the Dutch filibuster Piet Heyn at Matanzas (Cuba).

Competition between the European colonial powers (middle to end of 17th c.). – Western Europeans of different nationalities settle on the Caribbean islands, mainly in the Lesser Antilles but also in the Greater Antilles. Most of the islands change hands several times.

1634   The Dutch take Curaçao.

1635   The French occupy Martinique.

1655   Jamaica, previously Spanish, becomes a British colony; British rule is recognized by Spain in the treaty of Madrid (1670).

1665   French freebooters establish themselves in the western part of the island of Hispaniola (now Haiti). Under the treaty of Rijswijk (1697), signed by France, Britain, the Netherlands and the Empire, French possession of the territory, now known as Saint-Domingue, is ratified.

1671   The Danes land on St Thomas (Virgin Islands).

Rivalry between France and Britain; establishment of the first states (17th–19th c.). – The period until the treaties of Paris of 1814 and 1815 is a time of fierce conflict between the two colonial powers, France and Britain. The islands of the Lesser Antilles are prized by the western European nations as "sugar islands", the possession of which is bitterly contested.
The labor force required for working the plantations is provided by importing black slaves from Africa. A triangular trade develops between Europe (which supplies consumption goods), Africa (which supplies slaves) and the Caribbean islands (which supply sugar).

1763   The peace treaty which ends the Seven Years War brings considerable territorial changes in favor of Britain. The British navy is superior to the French fleet since it possesses bases in the Caribbean equipped with shipbuilding yards. (English Harbour on Antigua still gives some impression of the size of a naval base of this period.)

1782   In the Battle of the Saints, a major naval engagement between British and French fleets in the little island group of the Iles des Saintes (off the S coast of Guadeloupe), Admiral Rodney inflicts a crushing defeat on the French.

1801   After a rising by blacks and mulattoes against the French *François-Dominique Toussaint Louverture* conquers the Spanish (eastern) part of the island of Hispaniola and proclaims the independence of SAINT-DOMINGUE.

1802   The eastern part of Hispaniola is recovered by Spain.

1804   HAITI, the western part of Hispaniola, declares its independence from France under the leadership of "Emperor" *Jean-Jacques Dessalines*, a former slave.

1806–20   Haiti is divided into a negro-state and a mulatto republic.

1814–15   The treaties of Paris at the end of the Napoleonic wars establish the respective possessions of the colonial powers in the Caribbean. Spain retains Cuba, Puerto Rico and eastern Hispaniola. In the Lesser Antilles the French remain in possession of Martinique and Guadeloupe and their associated islands. Curaçao passes finally into Dutch hands. Britain holds Jamaica and most of the Lesser Antilles other than Martinique and Guadeloupe, with the exception of a few small islands which belong to the Dutch and the Danes.

1820–22   The two Haitian states are reunited (1820). The eastern part of Hispaniola declares its independence from Spain (1821) but is soon afterwards occupied by Haiti (1822).

1834   The British Parliament passes the Emancipation Act, which abolishes slavery in the British Empire.

1844   The eastern part of Hispaniola breaks free from Haiti and declares the DOMINICAN REPUBLIC. Spanish resistance, however, delays the final attainment of independence until 1865.

1848   The French declare the abolition of slavery on their islands.

1863   Slavery is abolished on the Dutch islands.

1898   Under the treaty of Paris, which ends the war between the United States and Spain, Cuba – the most important Spanish colony in the Caribbean – is ceded to the United States and thereafter is ruled by an American military governor. Puerto Rico also becomes a United States territory.

Decolonialization (20th c.). – The Caribbean islands are gradually decolonized. Some overseas possessions of the colonial powers are granted internal self-government, including the United States territory of Puerto Rico, the Netherlands Antilles and some British islands; Martinique and Guadeloupe become overseas départements of France; while some colonies achieve full independence. – After becoming independent many states become involved in political and social difficulties; economic reforms, in particular land reform, are frustrated.

1901   CUBA becomes an independent republic.

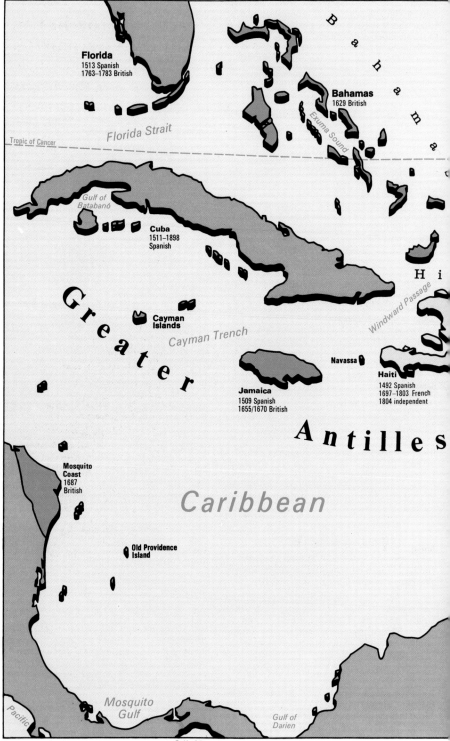

In the 15th and 16th c. practically all the Caribbean islands nominally belonged to the Spanish colonial empire. Later Britain, France and the Netherlands also became colonial powers in the Caribbean; Denmark, Sweden, Courland and Brandenburg had possessions there for varying periods of time; and finally in the 19th c. the United States appeared on the scene (Cuba, Hispaniola, Puerto Rico, the Virgin Islands and some small islands off the Central American coast).

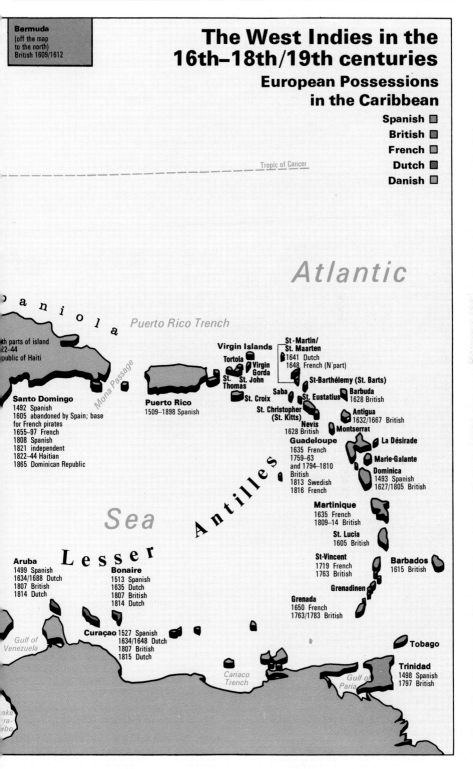

Bermuda
(off the map
to the north)
British 1609/1612

The West Indies in the 16th–18th/19th centuries
European Possessions in the Caribbean

Spanish ▢
British ▣
French ▢
Dutch ▣
Danish ▢

Atlantic

Tropic of Cancer

Puerto Rico Trench

Virgin Islands
Tortola
Virgin Gorda
St. St. John
Thomas
St. Croix

St-Martin/ St. Maarten
1641 Dutch
1648 French (N'part)

St-Barthélemy (St. Barts)

Saba
St. Eustatius

Barbuda
1628 British

Antigua
1632/1667 British

Puerto Rico
1509–1898 Spanish

St. Christopher (St. Kitts)
Nevis
1628 British
Montserrat

Guadeloupe
1635 French
1759–63
and 1794–1810 British
1813 Swedish
1816 French

La Désirade

Marie-Galante

Dominica
1493 Spanish
1627/1805 British

Martinique
1635 French
1809–14 British

St. Lucia
1605 British

St-Vincent
1719 French
1763 British

Grenadinen

Barbados
1615 British

Grenada
1650 French
1763/1783 British

n i o l a

th parts of island
22–44
ublic of Haiti

Santo Domingo
1492 Spanish
1605 abandoned by Spain; base for French pirates
1655–97 French
1808 Spanish
1821 independent
1822–44 Haitian
1865 Dominican Republic

Mona Passage

Sea   *Lesser*   *Antilles*

Aruba
1499 Spanish
1634/1688 Dutch
1807 British
1814 Dutch

Bonaire
1513 Spanish
1635 Dutch
1807 British
1814 Dutch

Curaçao 1527 Spanish
1634/1648 Dutch
1807 British
1815 Dutch

Gulf of Venezuela

Cariaco Trench

Gulf of Paria

Tobago

Trinidad
1498 Spanish
1797 British

ake
ra-
ibo

St Thomas
1666/1672 Danish
(1686 to Brandenburg)

Saba
1640/1648 Dutch

St Croix
1625 Dutch
1645 British
1650 French
1733 Danish

St Eustatius (Statia)
1626 Dutch
1665 British
1674 Dutch

Tortola
1627 Dutch
1672 British
(1695 to Brandenburg)

St Kitts
1623 British
1625 French
1713 British

St-Barthélemy (St Barts)
1648 French
1784 Swedish
1877 French

Montserrat
1632 British
1664 French
1668 British

Tobago
1625 British
1642/1654 to Courland
1655 Dutch
1763/1783 French
1793/1814 British

1902 United States troops leave Cuba.

1903 Under a treaty with Cuba the United States is granted the naval base of Guantánamo. In subsequent years American troops are several times sent to Cuba to protect foreign-owned mines and plantations.

1914 The opening of the Panama Canal brings the Caribbean islands increased international importance.

1915–34 Haiti is occupied by United States troops. In the struggle for power between the blacks and the mulatto elite the Americans support the mulattoes.

1916–24 The United States occupies the Dominican Republic in order to protect American economic interests. It trains modern military forces, under the leadership of Rafael Leónidas Trujillo y Molina.

1917 The people of Puerto Rico receive United States citizenship and a limited degree of self-government. – The United States purchases the Danish Virgin Islands to the E of Puerto Rico.

1930 *Rafael Leónidas Trujillo y Molina* seizes power in the Dominican Republic and, with one brief interruption, rules as a dictator until 1952 (murdered 1961).

1934 Commercial treaty between the United States and Cuba.

1940–44 *Fulgencio E. Batista y Zaldivar*, President of Cuba, with dictatorial powers.

1952 Mutual assistance pact between the United States and Cuba. Batista becomes President again by a putsch. The proposed economic reforms in Cuba are not carried through. From 1953 Fidel Castro wages guerrilla warfare against the Batista regime.

PUERTO RICO becomes the Estado Libre y Asociado de Puerto Rico (Commonwealth of Puerto Rico), with internal self-government.

In the Dominican Republic Rafael Leónidas Trujillo is succeeded by his brother *Hector Bienvenido Trujillo*, who rules until 1960.

1957–71 Haiti, one of the poorest and most densely populated countries in Latin America, is ruled by President *François Duvalier*, who consolidates his dictatorial regime by brutal repression, with the help of a much dreaded secret police. Attempts by Haitian exiles to overthrow him are unsuccessful. – After his death (1971) his son *Jean-Claude Duvalier* becomes President. Under his rule the internal situation is stabilized.

1958 Establishment of the WEST INDIES FEDERATION, consisting of the former British colonies of Jamaica, Barbados, the Leeward Islands, the Windward Islands, Trinidad and Tobago.

1959 After Batista's enforced resignation *Fidel Castro* (b. 1927) becomes Prime Minister of Cuba. A socialist land reform program is carried through and foreign (particularly United States) properties are expropriated. The Soviet Union grants credits for a program of industrialization.

1960 The United States cuts sugar imports from Cuba by 95%. The Soviet Union warns the US against military intervention in Cuba.

1961 The United States breaks off diplomatic relations with Cuba. An attempted landing in the Bay of Pigs by Cuban exiles, with US support, is frustrated. Cuba becomes a socialist republic.

1962 An attempt by the Soviet Union to establish medium-range rocket bases in Cuba sparks off the

Cuban crisis. On October 22 President John F. Kennedy calls on the Soviet government to remove the rockets already delivered and to dismantle the launching ramps, raising the spectre of a nuclear conflict between the two super-powers. On October 28 the Soviet Union accedes to the US demand.

JAMAICA becomes an independent state within the British Commonwealth.

TRINIDAD and TOBAGO becomes a presidential republic within the British Commonwealth. Thanks to its large reserves of oil it prospers.

In both Jamaica and Trinidad the Black Power movement campaigns against other population groups (e.g. Indians) and against foreign economic infiltration.

Juan Bosch Gavino becomes President of the Dominican Republic.

The West Indies Federation is dissolved.

1936 President Juan Bosch Gavino of the Dominican Republic, accused of ''Communist infiltration'', is overthrown by a military coup.

1965 A rising in the Dominican Republic by supporters of ex-President Bosch leads to civil war and to military intervention by the United States in support of the right-wing military junta.

1966 The domestic political crisis in the Dominican Republic is settled.

BARBADOS becomes an independent state within the British Commonwealth.

1967 The islands of Antigua (with Barbuda and Redonda), Anguilla, St Kitts and Nevis (with Sombrero), St Lucia, St Vincent and Dominica enter into a new form of association with Britain as WEST INDIES ASSOCIATED STATES, with internal self-government but with the United Kingdom remaining responsible for external affairs and defence. Each state is entitled to end the association by decision of its legislative council and a popular referendum.

In a plebiscite in Puerto Rico on the political status of the island a majority of the electorate vote for continuing the association with the United States.

1968 Establishment of the Caribbean Free Trade Area (Carifta), aimed at the phased elimination of tariffs and quotas. The founding members are Antigua, Barbados, Guyana and Trinidad and Tobago, who are later joined by Dominica, Grenada, St Kitts and Nevis, Anguilla, St Lucia, St Vincent, Belize (formerly British Honduras), Jamaica and Montserrat.

1969 Foundation of the Caribbean Development Bank (CDB), with its headquarters in Barbados. The principal members are Barbados, Guyana, Jamaica and Trinidad and Tobago, together with the United States, Canada and Venezuela.

1972 Cuba joins the Eastern bloc's Council for Mutual Economic Assistance (Comecon).

1973 The Caribbean Free Trade Area becomes the Caribbean Common Market (Caricom, CCM). The original members are Barbados, Guyana, Jamaica and Trinidad and Tobago; they are later joined by Belize, Dominica, Grenada, Montserrat, St Lucia, Antigua, St Kitts and Nevis and Anguilla.

The BAHAMAS become an independent state within the British Commonwealth.

1974 GRENADA becomes an independent state within the British Commonwealth.

Relationships between the United States and Cuba show signs of improvement. Cubans who want to leave the island are granted permission to settle in the United States, and the American trade embargo is relaxed.

1975 Under the Lomé Convention many developing countries in Africa, the Caribbean and the Pacific (the "ACP" countries) become associated with the European Community. Under this agreement the Community countries undertake not to levy, under any commercial treaty, countervailing duties on any industrial products or on a wide range of agricultural products from the ACP countries. ACP states within the Caribbean are the Bahamas, Barbados, Dominica, Grenada, Jamaica, St Lucia, St Vincent and the Grenadines and Trinidad and Tobago. In addition British, French and Dutch possessions in the Caribbean are associated with the European Community as overseas territories of the mother country

1978 DOMINICA becomes an independent republic within the British Commonwealth.

1979 ST LUCIA and ST VINCENT and the GRENADINES become independent states within the British Commonwealth.

1980 The difficult economic situation in Cuba and political considerations lead to a major Cabinet reshuffle in Cuba; Castro himself gains a stronger hold on the ministries of the interior, defence and culture. – Treaty of friendship and cooperation between Cuba and the German Democratic Republic (June 1).

In an election in Jamaica, which is suffering from an economic crisis the pro-American Labor Party defeats the People's National Party, which has leanings towards Cuba (end of October); *Edward Seaga* becomes Prime Minister in place of Michael Manley.

1981 ANTIGUA and BARBUDA gain independence as a constitutional state in the British Commonwealth.

1983 ST KITTS and NEVIS gain independence as a constitutional state in the British Commonwealth. After serious political disturbances in Grenada the USA invades the island and supports the anti-communist forces by forming a government.

1984 The United States administration supports the setting up of a Caribbean pact.

1986 Mounting unrest leads to the establishment of a military regime in HAITI and to the flight of "Baby Doc", his wife, his retinue and a great deal of money "acquired" during his oppressive dictatorship.

Music

Just as there is a strong infusion of African elements in the folk traditions of the Caribbean islands which find expression particularly in the Carnival, so African influences are evident in the music of the islands, which has attained such a world-wide reputation in recent years. African music and African dances have their roots in three areas in West Africa from which slaves were brought to the Caribbean islands. In the former French possessions the main influences come from the coastal regions of Upper Guinea, particularly from Benin (Dahomey) – influences which are also clearly evident in the Voodoo cult of Haiti. In the British islands the influences come from the Ashanti culture of Ghana (the old Gold Coast), in the former Spanish colonies from the Yoruba culture of Nigeria.

European and African elements fused together in the music and the **dances** of the Caribbean islands at an early stage. An example of this is the *tango* which developed out of the habanera in Cuba in the 19th c., with its Andalusian melodies and the accompanying African rhythms, and was later developed into a ballroom dance in Argentina. Notable among the Afro-Caribbean dances from the Spanish islands which later conquered the world are the *rumba* and *guaracha*, the *mambo* and the *cha-cha-cha*. From Trinidad came the *calypso* with its compelling rhythms. Characteristic of the calypso is its combination of singing and dancing – a living African tradition. The words of the songs are partly traditional, but often too they are specially written – like the music – and performed in a calypso contest, as at Carnival time, with a text which comments humorously and critically on personalities and events of the day. Also of Trinidadian origin is the *limbo* dance, which like the *bamboo*, stems from ancient African rituals.

With the rapid growth of tourism, folk music and dancing are becoming increasingly commercialized, but it is still possible to find authentic exponents of the old traditions, particularly in Haiti, where visitors may occasionally be for-

Limbo dancer, Barbados

tunate enough to come upon a *coumbite*, a gathering at which the work in the fields is performed communally, accompanied by singing to the beat of a drum. – Afro-Caribbean elements are found both in jazz and in international light music, such as *reggae*, which originated in Jamaica and has since conquered the world.

The music of the Caribbean islands uses a variety of **instruments**. The maruga and maracá are of native Indian origin; rhythmic instruments like drums, marimbas, banjos and palitos come from Africa; while Europe has contributed flutes and other wind instruments, guitars and more recently the accordian and saxophone. In contrast the *steelbands*, whose music originated in Trinidad and has spread since the 1940s to the whole Caribbean, use a very limited range of instruments – basically old oil drums of varying size which are beaten into shape to produce different ranges of notes.

More detailed accounts of the music of Cuba, Jamaica and Trinidad can be found in the entries for these islands in the "A to Z" section of this Guide.

Literature

Unlike Afro-Caribbean music and dancing, the literature of the Caribbean islands has only a brief history; and it is also less widely known, although the Antilles now produce more authors, in relation to their size, than any other region in the world. Numbers of novels by Caribbean authors have been translated into other languages, including works by *Alejo Carpentier* of Cuba, *Jacques Roumain* of Haiti, *Vic Read* of Jamaica, *George Lamming* of Barbados and *V. S. Naipaul* – this last particularly well known to English readers.

The early literature of the Antilles – written, like the literature of the present day, in Spanish, English or French – merely copied European models, with no originality of its own. It was only in the 20th c., with the emergence of *indigénisme* in Haiti and *negrismo* in Cuba, that Caribbean literature developed any distinctive individuality. In Haiti this development began during the period of American occupation, when, under the influence of the ethnologist Jean Price-Mars, novelists such as the *Marcelin* brothers with their novel "Le Canapé Vert" and *Edris Saint-Amand* ("Le Flamboyant") depicted the life of the Haitian peasants, still rooted in African traditions. Perhaps the most important work of this period is the novel by *Jacques Roumain*, "Gouverneurs de la Rosée", which has been translated into many languages. – In contrast to this Haitian prose literature, the *negrismo* of Cuba found expression solely in lyric poetry; typical are the verses of *Nicolás Guillén* and *Marcelino Arozarena*, which are recited to the accompaniment of a drum.

From these two schools, *indigénisme* and *negrismo*, developed the literature of **négritude**. In both prose and verse this literature discards European and American values, takes as its themes the values of African tradition and uses African forms of expression. The ideas of négritude have contributed to the emergence of a new national consciousness both in black Africa and in the Caribbean. The founders of the movement were *Léopold Sédar Senghor* (President of the African republic of Senegal 1960–80), *Aimé Césaire* of Martinique and *Léon-Gontran Damas* of Cayenne (French Guiana), who all lived in Paris in the early 1930s. A typical example of the poetry of négritude is the poem by Jacques Roumain, "Guinée".

Guinea

Far is the way to Guinea.
Only death will take you there.
Here are the branches, the trees, the forest;
listen to the rustling of the wind
in its hair of eternal night.
Far is the way to Guinea.
Your fathers wait for you, patiently
by the road; they palaver,
they wait for you.
Here, where the streams chatter and clatter
like chains made of bone.
Far is the way to Guinea;
no splendid reception awaits you
in the black land of the black men.
Under a smoky sky,
pierced by the cries of the birds,
the eyelids of the branches open
round the eye of the pond
to the stagnant brightness.
There, on the edge of the water,
a peaceful village waits for you
and the house of your fathers
and the hard stone of your ancestors
on which to rest your head.

Naive Painting

The painting of the Caribbean islands is even more recent than their literature. Here too the impulses came from Haiti and were rooted in *indigénisme*. Under the influence of the Centre d'Art which was established in Port-au-Prince in 1944 there developed a school of naive popular painters, the principal representative of

Art show, Port-au-Prince (Haiti)

which was *Hector Hyppolite* (d. 1948), a former voodoo priest who decorated the objects used in the ceremonies of the cult and also painted the walls and doors of houses. This naive painting, which depicts in vivid color a wide range of subjects from everyday life, landscapes, plants and flowers and much else besides, is now practiced on almost all the Caribbean islands. The better known artists display their work in galleries, the less well known in the street. Examples of Caribbean painting can now increasingly be seen in the United States and in Western Europe, particularly in France and Britain.

Economy

Although the Caribbean islands produce something like a quarter of the world's total output of sugar, although sugar production is still the basis of the economy of some islands and although sugar is still the islands' principal export they can no longer be called, as they were in colonial times, the "sugar islands" – in the first place because they now grow a much wider range of agricultural produce, and secondly because their economy as a whole has been diversified by the development of industry and tourism.

A primitive sugar-mill in Haiti

The **agriculture** of the Caribbean islands still shows the dualism which developed during the colonial period, the juxtaposition of large plantations and small peasant holdings. The plantations occupy level, easily worked and easily accessible areas of relatively good soil, while the peasant farmers work the poorer land. The black peasant farmers in the former French and British possessions in particular, occupying small and irregularly shaped holdings, practice mixed farming in what often seems a quite haphazard way, growing maize and beans, tubers such as sweet potatoes, manioc (tapioca), taro or yams, bananas, pawpaws and other fruits. In contrast the plantations are laid out in large regular fields and are run on a systematic and uniform basis.

Sugar-cane, traditionally an export-oriented crop, is grown exclusively on large capital-intensive estates. This type of production has been expanded in Cuba, where since the revolution it has been carried out by state farms (*granjas estatales*) on the Soviet model, but on other islands (e.g. on Jamaica and Puerto Rico) it has considerably declined. In the Lesser Antilles the traditional sugar production is of real economic consequence only on Barbados, St Kitts and

Guadeloupe; on some of the other islands (e.g. the US Virgin Islands, Antigua, St Lucia, St Vincent) it has completely disappeared. In some areas new export crops have taken the place of sugar. This is the case particularly on the wetter islands in the Lesser Antilles, which over the last 20 years or so have switched to banana growing; and on these islands

Banana harvest, Dominica

Cuba – Sierra de los Órganos, with portrait of Che Guevara

bananas, grown on small peasant holdings, have become the most important export. Other important agricultural products are *nutmegs* (Grenada), *caçao* (Trinidad), *coffee* (Haiti), *pineapples* (Puerto Rico) and *tobacco* (Cuba), together with citrus fruits, spices and *coconuts*, the kernels of which are dried to form copra.

The islands have inherited from the colonial period an unhealthy agrarian social structure. A beginning has been made with land reform in Jamaica and Puerto Rico; but even the *socialist land reform* in Cuba has failed to get rid of the contrast between the large estates, now transformed into state farms, and the small peasant holdings. Some progress has, however, been achieved: there are no longer any tenant farmers, and the small peasant holdings, averaging some 37 acres, are well above the average size of such holdings elsewhere in the Antilles. The traditional structures have thus been significantly changed in Cuba, even though the original plan for breaking up the large estates has not been achieved; for economic as well as social considerations have been taken into account in the execution of the Cuban land reform. It is beyond doubt that land reform is urgently necessary on the other Caribbean islands. Poverty is widespread in rural areas, leading to a considerable *flight from the land* which the island governments have been unable to check. And yet in spite of the over-population and under-employment in rural areas many of the large estates are short of manpower, partly because agricultural wages are very low, partly because of the country people's dislike of paid labor.

The development of **industry** is seen as a means of getting rid of unemployment and under-employment on the over-populated Caribbean islands; but conditions for industrialization are not favorable, since the islands have few industrial raw materials and are short of skilled workers and above all of capital. A further difficulty is the limited capacity of the domestic market. Nevertheless some islands have made notable progress in developing industry, in particular those which possess raw materials, including Cuba (*metal ores*), Trinidad (*oil*) and Jamaica (*bauxite*): thus industry accounts for 58% of the gross domestic product in Cuba, 50% in Trinidad and Tobago and 39% in Jamaica. Particularly striking is the case of Puerto Rico, where industry contributes 37% of the gross domestic product in spite of the island's almost total lack of industrial raw materials. Over-populated Puerto Rico, once the "poorhouse of the Antilles", has become a model for other underdeveloped countries; and the Puerto Rican example in promoting the development of industry has been followed by other Caribbean islands, notably by Jamaica and Trinidad but also by Barbados and the Dominican Republic.

Textile factory, Kingston (Jamaica)

The industrialization program in **Puerto Rico** would not have achieved such rapid success without the special advantages flowing from the island's association with the United States. As a result of a lower tax burden (Puerto Rico being exempt from US federal taxes) and a lower wage level than in the United States the costs of production are correspondingly lower; and many firms, European as well as American, have taken advantage of this and established factories in Puerto Rico for supplying the American market. The Economic Development Administration set up in 1950 promoted the establishment of industry by offering a wide range of inducements and facilities – market research, assistance in installation and financing, training of staff, provision of sites and ready-made factory buildings (often on industrial estates), exemption from income tax for up to 30 years, etc.

Three stages can be distinguished in the industrial development of Puerto Rico. During the first phase, in the 1940s, factories were established – at first state-run, later privately owned – using local raw materials like limestone, clay and sand and producing for the domestic market. The factories established during the second phase, in the 1950s, were mostly concerned with producing for the large US market, using raw materials and intermediate products imported from the United States to make finished and semi-finished products. Most of these factories were in the textile and clothing industry, which employed 34% of all industrial workers in 1968. The third phase, beginning in the 1960s, was mainly devoted to the capital goods sector of industry – oil refineries and petrochemical works, together with engineering plants, factories producing fertilizers, pharmaceuticals, etc. While the first phase was directed towards the production of import substitutes, the subsequent phases have been export-oriented. – The measures taken in Jamaica and Trinidad to promote the development of industry have likewise led to the establishment of foreign-owned and export-oriented factories which do not use locally available raw materials and do not produce for the domestic market.

Comparison with the successful Puerto Rican industrialization program highlights a number of negative features which have accompanied or followed attempts to develop industry on other Caribbean islands. All efforts to establish industry in rural areas have failed. Such industrial development as has taken place is concentrated in the towns, and in particular in and around the capital of the island. This has accelerated the flight from the land and the growth of the towns and has considerably aggravated the regional *imbalance between town and country*. Unemployment and under-employment have remained high as a result of the continuing drift of population to the towns, the high rate of population increase and the loss of jobs resulting from rationalization. In consequence of the export orientation of the foreign-owned factories, which import all their raw materials, there is little integration or cooperation between factories and a heavy dependence on imports.

Although the political decolonization of the Caribbean islands has largely been achieved the same cannot be said of their economies. Most of the smaller islands still live by exporting particular agricultural products and, as in colonial times, are dependent on the import of foodstuffs and consumption goods. Those states which have achieved some degree of industrial development have changed the nature of their dependence, but the dependence still remains. This is true both of socialist Cuba, in which industrial development stagnated for a decade and a half after Castro's revolution, and of the other

independent states. Thus the rich deposits of bauxite in Jamaica, which occupies the leading place among the bauxite-producing countries of the world with an annual output of 11.5 million tons, are worked by American and Canadian firms, and the processing of the bauxite to produce aluminum takes place not on the island but on the North American mainland, to which the bauxite is exported. The oil industry of Trinidad, with its rich offshore oilfields, operates in the same way. – The final elimination of all structures inherited from the colonial period is perhaps the most important task now confronting the Caribbean islands. So far, however, it has not been possible to find a way to break out of the vicious circle of poverty and do away with the dependences which have come down from the past.

Given the economic difficulties with which the Caribbean islands have to contend, **tourism** has become a factor of major importance in their economy, and each of the islands has been eager to participate in the great tourist boom of the last 20 years or so. Between 1959 and 1979 the number of visitors to the Caribbean islands rose from some 1.3 million to over 6.5 million; but the number of visitors and the rate of growth of the tourist trade differ considerably from island to island. Before the Castro revolution Cuba was a favorite holiday area, attracting some 300,000 visitors in 1958, and its closure to United States vacationers in 1961 led to a sharp increase in the number of visitors to other Caribbean islands, particularly the Bahamas, Puerto Rico, the United States Virgin Islands and Jamaica. In 1979 the leading tourist island, by a considerable margin, was Puerto Rico, with 2.1 million visitors, followed by the Bahamas with 1.4 million and the US Virgin Islands with 900,000. Earlier the tourist trade was wholly concentrated in the winter months, but this is no longer the case, and the airlines, travel operators and hotels have been successful in their efforts to attract visitors to the islands throughout the year. Nevertheless winter, climatically the most favored season, is still the most popular time for a Caribbean vacation, even though during the winter (December to April) hotel rates are considerbly higher than during the rest of the year.

On some islands, notably the Bahamas,

Sunset on the S coast of Grenada

tourism is now the main element in the economy; on others it is steadily increasing in importance, as in Puerto Rico, where it is now the third largest source of revenue, after industry and agriculture. But even a flourishing tourist trade can be unhealthy if it leads, as it sometimes does, to the neglect of other elements in the economy. Tourism is, after all, no more crisis-proof than any other form of monoculture.

The Caribbean islands have traditionally ranked with Hawaii as the tropical holiday paradise of the Americans and Canadians, but in recent years they have attracted steadily increasing numbers of visitors from Europe, and many travel operators now offer tempting vacations in the Caribbean. These may involve either air travel or a cruise, or a combination of both.

The number of cruises run by North American and European shipping lines, generally during the winter, has increased enormously in recent years.

Most visitors to the Caribbean travel by air, and practically all the islands are now brought within easy reach by an extensive network of air services as well as the many charter flights which are now available. There are large international airports, with direct flights from Europe and both North and South America, on Puerto Rico, Jamaica, Guadeloupe and Trinidad; and San Juan Airport on Puerto Rico in particular has become a major center of international air traffic. The various islands are linked by regional airlines flying regular services, so that "island hopping", which allows the individual traveler wide scope for following his preferences, has become very much a matter of course.

Caribbean
including Bermuda
A to Z

Empress Josephine monument, Fort-de-France, Martinique

Abaco Islands

Bahama Islands
Commonwealth of the Bahamas

Islands: Great Abaco, Little Abaco, Elbow Cay, Great Guana Cay, Walker's Cay, Treasure Cay, Green Turtle Cay, Gorda Cay, Man o' War Cay, Pelican Cays.
Area: 650 sq. miles/1680 sq. km
Population: 7000.
Administrative center: Nassau (on New Providence).
Vehicles travel on the left.

ⓘ **Abaco Chamber of Commerce,**
P.O. Box 428,
Marsh Harbour,
Abaco, Bahamas.
Hope Town Agencies,
Hope Town,
Abaco, Bahamas.
See also Practical Information.

HOTELS. – MARSH HARBOUR: *Ambassador Inn* (no rest.), 6 r.; *Conch Inn* (no rest.), 14 r., SP; *Lofty Fig Villas* (no rest.), 6 r., SP; etc. – HOPE TOWN/ELBOW CAY: *Abaco Inn*, White Sound, 10 r., SP; *Beach Houses* (no rest.), White Sound, 12 r.; *Elbow Cay Club*, Hope Town, 12 r.; *Hope Town Harbour Lodge*, Hope Town, 21 r., SP; etc. – GREAT GUANA CAY: *Guana Harbour Club*, 19 r.; *Pinder's Cottages*, 6 r.; etc. – WALKER'S CAY: *Walker's Cay Hotel and Marina*, 44 r., SP, T. – TREASURE CAY: *Treasure Cay Beach Hotel and Villas*, 193 r., SP, T, golf. – GREEN TURTLE CAY: *Green Turtle Club*, 33 r., SP, T; *Bluff House* (no rest.), 15 r.; *Linton's Beach Cottages* (no rest.), 4 r.; *New Plymouth Inn*, 8 r., SP; *Sea Star Beach Cottages* (no rest.), 12 r., SP; etc. – Several GUEST-HOUSES and HOLIDAY APARTMENTS.

RESTAURANTS. – GREEN TURTLE CAY: *Blue Bar and Restaurant*, *Plymouth Rock*, *Seaview Restaurant and Bar.*

EVENTS. – *Abaco Fishing Tournament* (April). – *Walker's Cay Billfish Championship* (April–May). – *Abaco Regatta* (July). – *Abaco Week* (November).

RECREATION and SPORT. – Sailing, deep-sea fishing, wind-surfing, scuba diving, snorkeling, swimming and sunbathing; golf, tennis, riding, shooting.

AIR SERVICES. – Regular services from Marsh Harbour and Treasure Cay to Nassau (New Providence) and Miami.

SHIPPING. – Mail boat services to Nassau from most ports on Great Abaco and all the inhabited smaller islands.

The most southerly of the *Abaco Islands lies some 55 miles N of Nassau. The main island in the group is the boomerang-shaped Great Abaco, with a fringe of cliffs and narrow islets off its E coast and another dense cluster of islands half way down the W coast. From its narrow northern tip, reaching towards Walker's Cay, the most

northerly of the Bahamas, it curves round southeastward and then southwestward to enclose a shallow inland sea.

The Abaco Islands were settled in the mid 17th c. by immigrants from Britain and in the late 18th c. by American Loyalists, and these origins are still reflected in the style of building and the way of life. – The traditional activities of boatbuilding and fishing have now almost died out, and their place has been taken in recent years by a considerable development of the tourist trade. Recently, too, Great Abaco in particular has gained increased revenue from the growing of vegetables for export, the felling of timber for pulpwood and the cultivation of sugar-cane.

SIGHTS. – The principal settlement is the lively little town of **Marsh Harbour** (pop. 4000), the third largest town in the Bahamas, situated at the point on Great Abaco where the island changes direction from SE to SW, with an airfield and a large yacht harbor. On the outskirts of the town stands the turquoise-colored *Cottman's Castle*, home of the well-known Bahamian doctor and writer Evans Cottman. – To the S of Marsh Harbour stretches the *Pelican Cays National Park* (2000 acres), a nature park containing numbers of islets and reefs with an extraordinarily abundant and varied range of underwater life.

Some 15 miles/25 km S of Marsh Harbour is *Eight Mile Bay*, bounded on the NE by the picturesque settlement of *Cherokee Sound* and on the SW by the *Crossing Rocks*, the narrowest part of the island. Eight Mile Bay is famous for its magnificent beach.

At the SW end of the island, surrounded by coconut palms, the pretty little settlement of *Sandy Point*, has a small airstrip. Lying out to the NW is *Gorda Cay*, a little island much favored by fishermen and scuba divers. – SE of Sandy Point is the village of **Cross Harbour**, in the bay of the same name. A lighthouse stands on the southernmost tip of the island, known as the *Hole in the Wall*, and to the SW of this are a number of caves and grottoes some 100 ft/30 m below the surface which are a favorite haunt of scuba divers. – N of Marsh Harbour is **Man o' War Cay**, an old boatbuilding center. Near here lies the wreck of *USS*

Hope Town, Elbow Cay (Abaco Islands)

"Adirondack", a Federal warship sunk during the American Civil War. – Farther N is the long straggling **Great Guana Cay**, noted for its beautiful *beaches and scuba diving grounds.

To the E of Marsh Harbour, on another long narrow island, **Elbow Cay**, we find the picturesque little port of ***Hope Town**, with its much photographed *Lighthouse* (118 ft/36 m), candy-striped in red and white.

From Marsh Harbour a road to the N passes through the *Wild Boar Country*, an extensive area where sportsmen hunt wild boar and in 25 miles/40 km it reaches the luxurious resort settlement of ***Treasure Cay**, with a marina, a beach, a golf-course and an airstrip. – Offshore to the N is **Green Turtle Cay**, a resort island only a few miles long with hilly and varied scenery, once noted for the number of turtles caught off its shores. **New Plymouth** has the air of a typical little New England town; Albert Lowe's Museum contains interesting historical relics and *ship models.

Some 40 miles/65 km N of Marsh Harbour is **Cooper's Town**, an attractive little place which is the starting-point for a trip to **Little Abaco**, a tongue of land running W from the northern tip of Great Abaco, with its two sleepy little settlements of *Fox*

Town and *Crown Haven*. – Little Abaco is fringed by reefs and islets, among them *Spanish Cay* and the *Pensacola Cays* off the N coast, which are popular with deep-sea fishermen. ***Walker's Cay**, the most northerly of the Bahamas, is an exclusive deep-sea fishing center, with a luxurious resort complex. – Offshore to the S lie the *Grand Cays*, which are serviced from Walker's Cay.

See also **Bahamas**.

Acklins

Bahama Islands
Commonwealth of the Bahamas

Islands: Acklins, Castle Island, Mira Por Vos, Fish Cay, Wood Cay, Plana Cays, Samana.
Area: 150 sq. miles/388 sq. km
Population: 1500.
Administrative center: Nassau (on New Providence).
Vehicles travel on the left.

ⓘ **Ministry of Tourism,**
Nassau Court, P.O. Box N 3220,
Nassau,
New Providence, Bahamas;
tel. (809) 322 7505.
See also Practical Information.

HOTEL. – *Williamson's Hilltop View*, Pine Field, 4 r.

RECREATION and SPORT. – Sailing, deep-sea fishing, scuba diving, snorkeling, swimming and sunbathing; shooting; walking.

SHIPPING. – Regular mail boat services via Crooked Island and Long Cay to Nassau and Mayaguana. Ferry services between Crooked Island and Acklins.

*Acklins, one of the least known of the Bahama Islands, lies between latitude 22°20′ and 22°50′ N and between longitude 73°50′ and 74°20′ W, forming the S and SE part of an atoll-like chain which encloses the shallow Bight of Acklins, once noted for the many sponges found there.

This hilly and rocky island, to which the Spanish navigators paid little attention, was settled at the end of the 18th c. by American Loyalists, who at first tried to grow cotton here. When this failed they turned to the more lucrative trade of extracting salt from the sea – possible only at certain points on the island – and later, on a smaller scale, to diving for sponges in the **Bight of Acklins**. The inhabitants now earn their living by fishing and a little farming.

In recent years efforts have been made to develop tourism on this beautiful island with its bizarre rock formations, extensive beaches and varied plant and animal life. As a first step in this direction a new road has been built from *Lovely Bay* (ferry from Crooked Island) in the N to *Salina Point* in the S, running past a number of attractive villages and bays with beaches.

Off the southern tip of Acklins is little **Castle Island**, with a conspicuous lighthouse (1867). – Some 12 miles SW are the **Mira Por Vos** islets. – To the N of Northeast Point are the **Samana Cays**.

See also ****Bahamas**.

American Virgin Islands

See United States Virgin Islands

Andros

Bahama Islands
Commonwealth of the Bahamas

Islands: Andros Islands, Joulter's Cays, Big Wood Cay, Yellow Cay, Mangrove Cay, Curley Cut Cays.
Area: 2300 sq. miles/5955 sq. km.
Population: 8000.
Administrative center: Nassau (on New Providence).
Vehicles travel on the left.
ⓘ**Ministry of Tourism,**
Nassau Court,
P.O. Box N 3220,
Nassau,
New Providence, Bahamas;
tel. (809) 322 7505.
See also Practical Information.

HOTELS. – NORTH ANDROS: **Andros Beach Hotel and Villas*, Nicholl's Town, 65 r., SP, T; **San Andros Inn and Tennis Club*, San Andros, 22 r., SP, T; etc. – ANDROS TOWN AND VICINITY: *Chickcharnie Hotel*, Fresh Creek, 8 r.; *Small Hope Bay Lodge*, Fresh Creek, 20 r.; *Charlie's Haven*, Behring Point, 5 r. – MANGROVE CAY: *Bannister House*, 6 r.; *Diana's Guest-House*, 4 r.; *Moxey's Guesthouse*, 6 r.; etc. – SOUTH ANDROS: **Las Palmas Hotel*, Congo Town, 25 r., SP, T.

EVENTS. *August Monday Regatta.*

RECREATION and SPORT. – Sailing, deep-sea fishing, scuba diving, snorkeling, swimming and sunbathing; riding.

AIR SERVICES. – Regular services from San Andros, Andros Town, Mangrove Cay and South Andros to Nassau. Occasional charter flights to neighboring islands.

SHIPPING. – Mail boat services from Mastic Point, Fresh Creek and Mangrove Cay to Nassau.

Some 30 miles/48 km W of New Providence lies *Andros, the largest of the Bahamas – a flat island broken up by numerous inlets and inland lakes, both well stocked with fish. The hilly E coast has a number of good beaches, but the W coast is exceptionally flat and muddy. The landscape of the island is made up of extensive forests (pines, palms, mahogany), scrub and mangrove swamps, the haunt of huge colonies of seabirds. – Off the E coast stretches one of the longest barrier reefs in the world, the E side of which plunges down to a depth of 4900 ft/1500 m in the Tongue of the Ocean. Notable features are the Blue Holes, deep caverns under the sea.

This still undeveloped island is a land of legend, the home of the "chickcharnies" (red-eyed pixies with three fingers and three toes) and the Lusca (a dragon-like sea monster). In the 18th c. it provided a refuge for Seminole Indians driven out of Florida by the Spaniards; the first British settlers came in the 19th c. Since 1963 there has been an accelerated development of agriculture and forestry and a large-scale promotion of tourism.

SIGHTS. – One of the oldest settlements is *Coakley Town*, on Fresh Creek. Also in this creek, farther S, is the resort settlement of **Andros Town**, founded by the Swedish industrialist Dr Axel Wenner-Gren. Near the airstrip is *Twin Lake Farm*, which has pioneered the growing of fruit, vegetables and spices. – 4 miles/6 km S of Andros Town is the test center of the Atlantic Undersea Testing and Evaluation Company (AUTEC, 1966), and near this is a development project initiated by a businessman named Reynolds with interests in the aluminum industry. – 12½ miles/20 km farther S the village of *Behring Point* has a small harbor.

N of Coakley Town the charming little village of *Love Hill* stands on the hill of that name. – A few miles farther on is the village of *Staniard Creek*, with a beautiful beach. Here too is the Androsia Factory, which produces artistic batik work. *Small Hope Bay*, with a resort village, is much favored by scuba divers.

At San Andros in the N of the island – formerly an area which provided good shooting – a development project (vegetable-growing, etc.) was initiated only a few years ago by the North Andros Development Company (NADCO); it has an airstrip and a hotel.

On the E coast is the settlement of **Mastic Point**, with a small harbor which served the local population. Neville Chamberlain, British Prime Minister at the beginning of the Second World War, once owned sisal plantations in this area. – 6 miles/10 km farther N is *Nicholls Town (pop. 1000), a little settlement of gaily painted houses inhabited by farmers and fishermen. – To the NE, in the rugged cliffs of *Morgan's Bluff*, is a cave which is said to have been used as a base by the notorious pirate Henry Morgan. Off the N coast are **Joulter's Cays**, much frequented by wildfowlers. To the W of Nicholl's Town in the San Andros development area are extensive pinewoods and many pretty little lakes and ponds. **Red Bay Village**,

on the W coast, is of special interest for the traditional way of life and customs still preserved here.

The central part of the island, much indented by inlets of the sea, offers good shooting, fishing and sailing. Particularly notable are the *North, Middle* and *South Bights* and the islands *Big Wood Cay, Yellow Cay* and *Mangrove Cay*. On Mangrove Cay the settlement of **Moxey Town** has accommodation for visitors.

On *Drigg's Hill*, in the S of the island, is the new holiday settlement of **Congo Town**, with its own airstrip. – On the road running S through the development are first the little hamlet known as the *Bluffs* and then *Long Bay Cays*, where the pirate Edward Teach, alias Blackbeard, is said to be buried. From *Mars Bay*, at the end of the road, there are possible excursions to *Cistern Point* and to *Curley Cut Cays* and *Water Cays*, off the S coast of Andros.

See also ****Bahamas**.

Anegada

Lesser Antilles
British Virgin Islands
British Crown Colony

Area: 13 sq. miles/34 sq. km
Population: 300.
Administrative center: Road Town (on Tortola).
Vehicles travel on the left.

(i) **British Virgin Islands Tourist Board**,
P.O. Box 134,
Road Town,
Tortola, B.V.I.;
tel. (809) 49 43134.
See also Practical Information.

HOTEL. – *Anegada Reefs Hotel*, 12 r., with beach.

RECREATION and SPORT. – Sailing, deep-sea fishing, scuba diving, snorkeling, swimming and sunbathing; walking.

AIR SERVICES. – Air-taxis to Virgin Gorda, Tortola and St Thomas, linking up with international air services via San Juan (Puerto Rico).

SHIPPING. – Cargo boats and charters to neighboring islands.

*Anegada, the most northeasterly of the British Virgin Islands, lies in latitude 18°44' N and longitude 64°20' W. This island of coral limestone and calcareous sandstone, once an atoll, is a popular base for sea fishermen.

SIGHTS. – The principal settlement, **Anegada**, and the small airstrip lie on the S coast, with roads leading from there to all parts of the island (the highest point on which rises barely 33 ft/10 m above the sea).

In the W of the island is *Flamingo Pond*, once a nesting-place for these birds, which are now rare. The only accommodation for visitors is on a narrow strip of land between Flamingo Pond and the S coast. At the W end of the island are unspoiled beaches.

The best swimming is to be had in a series of coves on the N coast – from W to E *Bone Bay*, *Jack Bay*, *Loblolly Bay*, *Deep Bay* and *Table Bay*, with Cooper Rock.

At the E end of the island is the interesting *Sinking Pond*, a long stretch of swamp which merges imperceptibly into the *Salt Pond*, formerly used to produce salt.

The island is surrounded by magnificent *coral reefs* which are a favorite haunt of scuba divers and snorkelers. There are also numbers of wrecks, although the exact number is not known. – The relatively clean sea in this area, the precipitous chasm of the Puerto Rico Trench to the N and the Anegada Passage to the E of the island provide ideal conditions for sea fishing. Several record catches have been made here.

See also *British Virgin Islands.*

Anguilla
Lesser Antilles
Leeward Islands
British Associated State

Area: 34 sq. miles/88 sq. km.
Population: 7500
Administrative center: The Valley.
Vehicles travel on the left.
(i) **Anguilla Department of Tourism,**
The Valley,
Anguilla, W.I.;
tel. 451, 759.
See also Practical Information.

HOTELS. – Camora, South Hill, 10 r.; *Cul-de-Sac*, Blowing Point, 8 r., SP; *Lloyd's*, The Valley, 12 r.; *Rendezvous Bay*, 20 r.; etc. – Some GUEST-HOUSES and HOLIDAY APARTMENTS.

RESTAURANTS. – *Harbour View, South Hill.*

PUBLIC HOLIDAYS and EVENTS. – *New Year's Day.* – *Freedom Day* (February 10). – *Good Friday.* – *Easter Monday*, with a great regatta. – *May 31*, anniversary of the separation from St Kitts and Nevis. – *Whit Monday.* – *Queen's Birthday* (second Saturday in June). – *August Monday* (first Monday in August), commemorating the liberation of the slaves. – *August Yacht Race.* – *Christmas Day.* – *Boxing Day* (December 26).

RECREATION and SPORT. – Swimming and sunbathing; boat trips, deep-sea fishing; scuba diving, snorkeling; tennis.

AIR SERVICES. – Daily (except Sundays) to and from St-Martin/St Maarten (Juliana Airport) and Marigot; also to Antigua, St Thomas and Tortola.

SHIPPING. – Ferry services to and from St-Martin/St Maarten (Marigot).

The long flat limestone island of Anguilla, in latitude 18°12′ N and longitude 63°5′ W, rises above the sea from the Anguilla Bank, lying only 180 ft/55 m below the surface.

The narrower W end of the island, with beautiful beaches and lagoons, has little rainfall and only a scanty covering of forest. The wider eastern part is a region of karstic hills and depressions.

HISTORY. – After being discovered by Spaniards at the end of the 15th c. the island was given the name *Anguila*, from the Spanish for "eel". The first real settlers, however, came from England in the 17th c., followed in 1698 by Irish Catholics. At the end of the 18th c. the island was held briefly by the French. From 1871 to 1956 it was administered as one of the Leeward Islands, and from 1958 to 1962 belonged to the West Indies Federation. In 1967 Anguilla was to be combined with St Kitts and Nevis as an associated state within the Commonwealth, but the population of the island refused to accept this and declared the independence of Anguilla, whereupon British troops were sent to the island to maintain order. In 1971 the new administrative unit of *Anguilla* was established under British protection, and in 1976 it was granted domestic self-government.

POPULATION and ECONOMY. – The population consists mainly of blacks and mulattoes, the descendants of African slaves, with smaller numbers of whites of European descent. They belong to nine different religious denominations, mainly Protestant. – In view of the unfavorable natural conditions, particularly for agriculture, many of the island's inhabitants have been obliged until quite recent times to seek work in other countries, and their remittances to their families on the island have been a major contribution to the economy.

Thanks to the island's location in some of the best fishing grounds in the Caribbean there has been a considerable development of the fishing industry; in particular large quantities of crayfish are exported to the tourist centers of the neighboring islands. Another export-oriented industry is the production of sea salt, which is sent to Trinidad for use in the petrochemicals industry. The development of **tourism** is being pursued with great caution in order to avoid the unfortunate consequences experienced elsewhere.

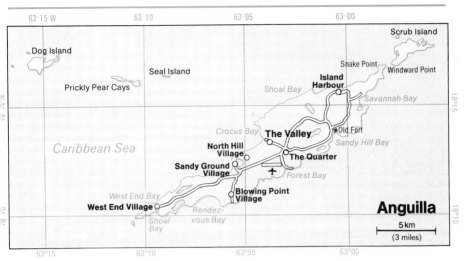

TOUR OF THE ISLAND. – The chief town on the island is the settlement known as **The Valley**, near Crocus Bay (good fishing), where the French landed in the 18th c. In Wallblake House is an exhibition illustrating the history of the island. The small airstrip is to the S of the settlement.

4 miles/6 km NE of the Valley is *Shoal Bay*, with a beautiful underwater garden. 2 miles/3 km farther E is the sheltered fishing village of *Island Harbour*, to the E of which rises Navigation Hill (150 ft/ 46 m), commanding extensive views. This is a good base from which to explore the northeastern tip of the island, with Goat Cave, and the two scrub-covered islands appropriately named Scrub Island and Little Scrub Island, which have much fissured coral rocks. – From Island Harbour the road runs S past Savannah Bay to *Sandy Hill*, in the bay of that name, with the ruined Old Fort. 4 miles/6 km W, beyond the *Long Salt Pond*, at *Forest Bay*, are reefs – a happy hunting ground for scuba divers.

4 miles/6 km W of the Valley is the busy little settlement of **Sandy Ground Village**, situated on a narrow strip of land between Road Bay and the *Road Salt Pond* (used for the production of salt) at the foot of the steep-sided *North Hill* (203 ft/62 m).

Farther down the S coast is **Blowing Point Harbour**, from where a ferry crosses to St-Martin/St Maarten. To the W of this is the beautiful crescent-shaped *Rendezvous Bay*, popular with sunbathers and shell-collectors. Farther W are *Cove Bay*, fringed by coconut palms, and

beyond this *Maunday's Bay, Shoal Bay* and *Sherrick's Bay*, all bounded on the landward side by lagoons, some of which are used for the production of salt.

On the N coast of the western part of the island, at **Long Bay Village** and **West End Village**, are imposing cliffs.

Attractive trips for those who seek unspoiled natural beauty are to *Anguillita Island*, off the W end of Anguilla, and to **Sandy Island** and **Prickly Pear Cays**, to the NW. – Some 10 miles/16 km NW of Anguilla lies the privately owned **Dog Island** which the United States Navy recently attempted to secure for use as a training ground. – Some 35 miles/56 km NW is the flat limestone island of **Sombrero** (belonging to St Kitts and Nevis), an isolated islet with a lighthouse at the entrance to the busy shipping route through the Anegada Passage.

Antigua

Lesser Antilles
Leeward Islands
Antigua and Barbuda

Area of state: 170 sq. miles/442 sq. km (Antigua 108 sq. miles/280 sq. km, Barbuda 62 sq. miles/ 160 sq. km, Redonda $\frac{1}{2}$ sq. mile/1.5 sq. km).
Capital: St John's.
Population: 78,000.
Religion: Protestant (over 70%); Roman Catholic minority.
Language: English.
Currency: East Caribbean dollar (EC$) of 100 cents.
Weights and measures: British/American system.
Time: Atlantic Time (4 hours behind GMT).
Vehicles travel on the left.
Travel documents: passport, immigration card, onward or return ticket.

(i) **Antigua Tourist Board,**
P.O. Box 363,
St John's,
Antigua, W.I.;
tel. 20029 and 20480.
See also Practical Information.

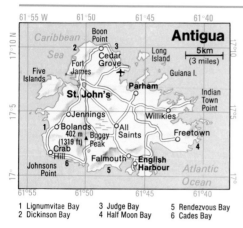

1 Lignumvitae Bay   3 Judge Bay   5 Rendezvous Bay
2 Dickinson Bay   4 Half Moon Bay   6 Cades Bay

HOTELS. – *Anchorage, Dickenson Bay, 99 r., SP, T; *Galley Bay Surf Club, Galley Bay, 28 r., T, beach; *Half Moon Bay Hotel, Half Moon Bay, 100 r., SP, T, golf; *Hawksbill Beach Hotel, Hawksbill Beach, 50 r., T, beaches; *Hyatt Halcyon Cove, Dickenson Bay, 104 r., SP, T; Admiral's Inn, English Harbour, 14 r.; Antigua Beach Hotel, Hodges Bay, 42 r., SP, T, golf; Antigua Horizons, Long Bay, 36 r., T; Atlantic Beach Hotel, Crosbies, 24 r., SP; Barrymore Hotel, St John's, 23 r., SP, T; Blue Waters Beach Hotel, Soldiers Bay, 49 r., SP, T; Callaloo Beach Hotel, Morris Bay, 16 r.; Castle Harbour Club and Casino, St John's, 50 r., SP, casino; Catamaran Hotel, Falmouth Harbour, 12 r.; Curtain Bluff Hotel, on SW coast, 50 r.; English Harbour Inn, T, beach; Holiday Inn, Marmora Bay, 100 r., SP, T; Jolly Beach Hotel, Lignumvitae Bay, 77 r., T; Long Bay Hotel, on NE coast, 20 r.; White Sands Hotel, Hodges Bay, 40 r., SP; etc.

Several GUEST-HOUSES and many HOLIDAY APARTMENTS.

RESTAURANTS in most hotels; also Admiral's Inn, Nelson's Dockyard; Brother B's, Darcy's, Golden Peanut and Maurice's, St John's.

NIGHT CLUBS. – Castle Harbour Club and Third World Club, both just outside St John's.

Casino in Castle Harbour Club.

SHOPPING. – There are many stores in St John's catering for passengers on the cruise ships and other visitors. Local specialities are pottery and cotton goods.

PUBLIC HOLIDAYS and EVENTS. – *New Year's Day, with dancing in the streets and a masquerade. – Tennis Week (January). – St Valentine's Day (February 14), with a beauty contest. – Good Friday. – Easter. – *Sailing Week (April–May), with a big program of events; the last day is Dockyard Day, with historical contests and displays. – Labour Day (May 1). – Whitsun. – Red Cross Week (June). – Queen's Birthday (June), with a parade. – *Midsummer Carnival (July–August), lasting ten days, with the election of a Carnival Queen, calypso contests, processions and other celebrations. – Police Week (September), with a program of events. – Caribbean Trade Fair (September), an agricultural and industrial show. – State Day (November 1), commemorating the foundation of the state, with official receptions, parades and sporting events. – Christmas Day. – Boxing Day (December 26).

RECREATION and SPORT. – Sailing, wind-surfing, water-skiing, deep-sea fishing, scuba diving, snorkeling, swimming and sunbathing; golf, riding, tennis, walking.

AIR SERVICES. – Direct connections with Miami and New York (USA), Toronto and Montreal (Canada), London (UK), San Juan (Puerto Rico), St Croix and St Thomas (US Virgin Islands), Tortola (British Virgin Islands), St Maarten (N.A.), St Kitts, Nevis and Montserrat (B.W.I.), Guadeloupe and Martinique (F.W.I.), Dominica, St Lucia and Barbados.

SHIPPING. – Some Caribbean cruise ships call in at St John's, normally coming from Miami (USA), San Juan (Puerto Rico), Barbados and Curaçao (N.I.), and sometimes from other islands. – Occasional cargo boats to neighboring islands.

With its many * beaches of incomparable beauty, * Antigua (pronounced Anteega) is one of the most popular islands in the Lesser Antilles, situated in latitude 17°05′ N and longitude 61°45′ W. It is the main element in the West Indies State of Antigua and Barbuda (independent since November 1, 1981), with a population of almost 80,000.

The almost impregnable naval base of English Harbour, from which Nelson operated when commander of the dockyard, was the main stronghold of British colonial rule in the Caribbean.

The island, fringed by coral reefs, consists mainly of limestones built up in hills around a central plain. Only in the SW are there traces of very ancient volcanic action, and in this area is the island's highest point (1358 ft/414 m). The coastline is much indented by inlets, coves and natural harbors, almost all with magnificent sandy beaches, which offer facilities for every kind of water sport and provide beautiful settings for luxurious hotels.

The original vegetation of this semi-arid island – with average temperatures ranging over the year between 72.5 °F/22.5 °C and 86 °F/30 °C – has been much reduced over the past 300 years by the establishment and expansion of sugar-cane plantations; but these plantations in turn have been almost wiped out by the frequent droughts and little ability to compete commercially. The central plain and the hills around it were formerly covered with sugar-cane, but large areas of the island are now overgrown with secondary forest or used only for grazing. Attempts are now being made to render this basically fertile island more attractive to agriculture by the construction of reservoirs to store the available water.

HISTORY. – The island was discovered by Columbus in 1493 and named after the Church of Santa Maria la Antigua in Seville. Attempts were made to settle the island by the Spaniards and the French (landing by Belain d'Esnambuc, 1629), but it was finally occupied in 1632 by English settlers from St Kitts. With the exception of a brief period of French occupation in 1666 (ended by the treaty of Breda in 1667) Antigua remained a British possession until 1967.

During the 17th and 18th c. the island was strongly fortified, and English Harbour became one of the best known British naval bases. In 1784 Horatio Nelson took over command of the Leeward Islands Squadron, in which the future King William IV served as captain of HMS "Pegasus". In 1843 the island was ravaged by a severe earthquake. From 1871 to 1956 Antigua – which became a major US base during the Second World War – was part of the British colony of the Leeward Islands, and from 1958 to 1962 it belonged to the West Indies Federation. From 1967 Antigua, together with the neighboring island of Barbuda and the uninhabited islet of Redonda, formed a West Indies Associated State within the British Commonwealth, enjoying internal self-government. Full independence was achieved in 1981.

GOVERNMENT and ADMINISTRATION. – The Queen, as head of state, is represented by a Governor. Parliament consists of a Senate of ten appointed members and a House of Representatives of 17 elected members. The Prime Minister and his Cabinet are responsible to Parliament. – The island is divided for local government purposes into six parishes.

POPULATION and ECONOMY. – The population consists predominantly of the descendants of black slaves brought in from Africa: only some 2% are whites, mostly of European origin. The majority of the population belongs to various Protestant denominations, the Anglican Church being the largest. The percentage of illiteracy, at almost 20%, is high compared with neighboring islands. Roughly a third of the population live in the capital, St John's – a feature characteristic of other Caribbean islands.

Favored by the deep-water harbor of St John's, the infrastructures built up by American forces during the Second World War and fiscal legislation designed to encourage investment, **tourism** has developed into a major pillar of the economy. The number of visitors rose from 46,000 in 1964 to some 157,000 in 1982 (90,000 coming by air and 67,000 on cruise ships). In 1980 roughly half the gross domestic product was accounted for by the tourist trade. Efforts are under way to achieve a considerable increase in bed capacity, about 1500 at that time. At present work is in progress to open up Deep Bay.

Compared with this sector of the economy the island's once-flourishing 300-year-old sugar-cane industry is in a lamentable state. Much of the extensive area once occupied by sugar-cane plantations is now waste land or grazing for livestock. A succession of catastrophic droughts halved the production of sugar and led in 1966 to the closing of the only sugar refinery. Cotton-growing has managed to survive, particularly in the drier eastern part of the island. It has given rise to a modest textile industry and makes a contribution to Antigua's export trade. On the volcanic soils in the SW of the island fruit and vegetables are grown, primarily for domestic consumption. Much of the annual catch of fish (some 7000 tons) is exported. – Attempts to establish industry on Antigua have been unsuccessful and have had little effect on the high unemployment rate, reliably estimated at around 40%. Much was hoped for from a modern oil refinery established at St John's, but this was inoperative between 1980 and 1982.

*St John's (sea level; pop. 25,000), capital and economic center of Antigua-Barbuda, lies in the NW of the island at the head of a beautiful sheltered inlet, deep enough to take quite large cruising liners. Previously a quiet little colonial town, it

Antigua – a beach on the N coast

has been given a fresh lease on life by the growth of the tourist trade.

SIGHTS. – By the harbor is the *Public Market* (a colorful scene particularly on Fridays and Saturdays), and adjoining this are the *Industrial School for the Blind*, where charming craft articles can be bought, and the *Post Office*, which sells the much prized Antigua *stamps. In Market Street stands the old **Court House** (1748–50), seat of the island's Parliament, which was damaged by earthquakes in 1843 and 1974. In the Parliament Chamber are portraits of King George III and Queen Caroline, attributed to Sir Joshua Reynolds.

Opposite the Court House is the police headquarters, once an Arsenal. – In Church Lane we find the imposing **St John's Cathedral* (1847), successor to a church of 1745 which was destroyed in the 1843 earthquake. The original church was dedicated in 1683.

The INTERIOR is completely faced with pitchpine. The iron railings at the entrance date from 1789. The figures of John the Baptist and John the Evangelist are believed to have come from a French ship during the Napoleonic wars.

At the corner of East Street and High Street a handsome *Cenotaph* commemorates the dead of both world wars. – The *George Westerby Memorial* was erected in 1888 in honor of the bishop of that name. **Government House**, originally a timber-built 17th c. mansion, was from 1801 the residence of Lord Lavington, owner of the Carlisle estate. It has a fine dining room in typical Georgian style.

SURROUNDINGS of St John's. – On the little **Rat Island** by the harbor is the *Antigua Rum Distillery* (1932), which can be seen by appointment.

To the W of the town lies the little settlement of **Green Bay**, founded by Moravian Brethren in the 19th c. for freed slaves. – 2½ miles/4 km farther W, above **Deep Bay**, stands *Fort Barrington* (1780).

On the N side of the town is the *West Indies Oil Refinery*, a modern plant established to give a stimulus to the economy but which had to be temporarily closed down in 1980.

On the eastern outskirts of the town are the **Botanical Gardens*, small but very attractive, which give an excellent picture of the island's native vegetation.

St John's to Dickenson Bay (4 miles/6.5 km). – The road NW from St John's along the N side of the harbor inlet comes in 2 miles/3.5 km to **Fort James* (1704–39), commandingly situated on St John's Point. The road then continues N through an area of reclaimed swamp to the beautiful **Dickenson Bay*, with a carefully tended beach and luxurious hotels. From *Hyatt Halcyon Cove* a funicular goes up to a restaurant from which there are extensive views.

St John's to the N coast (round trip 11 miles/ 18 km). – The road runs NE from St John's, passing a number of factories.

4 miles/6 km: **Coolidge Airport**, which handles a considerable local traffic.

The road then continues N to a number of excellent beaches, now equipped to cater for vacationers.

3 miles/5 km: **Cedar Grove*, a charming litle bay on the N coast.

The return is by way of *Mount Pleasant* (443 ft/ 135 m) to – 4½ miles/7 km: **St John's**.

St John's to Indian Town (12½ miles/20 km or 15 miles/24 km). – Leave St John's on a road which leads E to –

3½ miles/5.5 km: the sugar-refinery (now closed) of *Antigua Syndicates Ltd.*

2 miles/3.5 km: side road to the little settlement of **Parham**, 1¼ miles/2 km N.

In Parham stands the handsome *St Peter's Church* (by Thomas Weekes, 1840), an Italian-style building on an attractive octagonal plan, originally with rich stucco decoration. Outside the village are two well-maintained houses of the colonial period, *Parham Hill* and *Mercer's Creek*, which can be seen by appointment.

¾ mile/1 km: two side roads leading to the Atlantic coast. The more northerly of the two passes through the attractive villages of *Pares* and *Willikies* to **Indian Town*, a protected area of natural beauty and archaeological interest.

6 miles/10 km: **Devil's Bridge*, a natural bridge formed by the action of the heavy surf at the mouth of *Indian Creek*, is a popular tourist attraction. Near here are several "blowing holes", also carved out by the waves, through which the spray surges noisily up.

In the area near *Indian Creek*, between the more northerly road to Indian Town and the southerly road, which ends in 9 miles/14 km at the very beautiful **Half Moon Bay*, much archaeological evidence of pre-Columbian cultures has been discovered in recent years. Many finds have also been made at *Mill Reef*, near Half Moon Bay. The Antigua Archaeological Society runs excursions, by arrangement, to the Indian sites.

St John's to English Harbour (round trip 32 miles/ 51 km). – The road runs SE, past the *Castle Harbour Club and Casino*.

5½ miles/9 km: **All Saints**, an attractive village in an area where the traditional craft of pottery is still practiced.

2 miles/3 km: **Liberta**, one of the first settlements founded by freed slaves. The 19th c. parish church of St Barnabas is a "chapel of ease". – To the E of the village, on *Monk's Hill*, is **Fort George** (17th c.), primarily intended as a place of refuge for women and children.

1½ miles/2.5 km: **Falmouth**, situated in a charming bay and surrounded by former sugar-cane plantations, with several abandoned sugar mills. St George's Church (18th–19th c., restored) was a military church in Nelson's time.

2 miles/3.5 km: *English Harbour, in an inlet on the SE coast, one of the safest natural harbors in the world, deep enough to take seagoing ships but barely visible from the sea. It is now an exclusive but very busy yacht harbor. Throughout the 18th and 19th c., from 1707 to 1899, it was the main British naval base in the West Indies.

A naval base was built between 1725 and 1746 on a narrow promontory in the bay and was later given the name of *Nelson's Dockyard. During the Seven Years War this base played a major part in establishing British naval superiority over the French. Later it was used by Rodney and Hood, in addition to Nelson, as an operational base.

The military installations were restored some years ago. The *Admiral's Inn* is now a hotel and restaurant, and the *Admiral's House* contains a museum which gives a picture of Antigua in its heyday. The *Officer's Quarters* and the *Copper and Lumber Store* have also been restored.

On a low hill above the dockyard stands *Clarence House, built for Prince William, Duke of Clarence (later William IV), who was appointed to command HMS "Pegasus" in 1787. The house, finely appointed (valuable furniture, old maps and plans), is now the Governor's country residence, but can be seen by arrangement. Princess Margaret and Lord Snowdon spent part of their honeymoon here.

On the W side of the harbor entrance is **Fort Berkeley**, which with the *Horseshoe Battery*, facing it, and Fort Charlotte to the N protected the naval base.

Above the harbor to the N are *Shirley Heights, fortified in 1787 by General Shirley, then Governor of the Leeward Islands, from which there are magnificent views. The *Blockhouse* is well preserved. Nearby in a military cemetery stands an obelisk in honor of the 54th Regiment.

On *Dow's Hill*, within the NASA tracking station constructed in connection with the "Apollo" program, interesting material of the Arawak and Carib cultures has been found.

From English Harbour return to Liberta and just beyond the settlement (4½ miles/7 km) turn off into **Fig Tree Drive** (in Antigua fig is the name for a banana), which traverses the volcanic region in the SW of the island with its luxuriant growth of vegetation.

¾ mile/1 km: *Sweet's*, a pleasant little village, from which the *Body Ponds*, a short distance NE, can be visited. – The road continues SW, passing the little village of *John Hughes*.

2 miles/3 km: *Wallings Reservoir*, one of the reservoirs constructed to provide water for irrigation.

2 miles/3 km: *Old Road*, a settlement on *Carlisle Bay, with a mgnificent beach.

1½ miles/2.5 km: *Cades Bay*, where the growing of the sweet black pineapple of Antigua has been revived.

1¼ miles/2 km: *Urlins*, a little village on the slopes of a southern outlier of *Boggy Peak* (1358 ft/414 m), the island's highest peak.

The road continues past *Johnson's Point*, the SW tip of the island, to –

1¼ miles/2 km: *Crab Hill*. Then N to –

1¼ miles/2 km: *Lignumvitae Bay*, with a beautiful beach on the edge of a salt-water swamp.

The road then returns, via *Bolans* and *Jennings*, to –

6 miles/10 km: **St John's**.

The origin and purpose of the *megaliths on **Greencastle Hill** have not been established. It has been suggested that they are an unusual geological phenomenon, or alternatively that they are an Indian cult site.

Some 30 miles/48 km W of Antigua is the uninhabited islet of **Redonda** (area ½ sq. mile/1.5 sq. km), part of the arc of volcanic formations in the Antilles.

Barbuda: see separate entry.

Aruba
Southern Antilles
Netherlands Antilles

Area: 74 sq. miles/193 sq. km.
Population: 67,000.
Administrative center: Willemstad (on Curaçao).
Vehicles travel on the right.
(i) **Aruba Toeristenbureau,**
A. Schuttestraat 2,
Orangjestad,
Aruba, N.I.;
tel. 23777.
See also Practical Information.

HOTELS. – ORANJESTAD: *Talk of the Town Resort Hotel*, 64 r., SP. – DRUIF BAAI BEACH: *Aruba Beach Club*, 131 r., SP, T; *Dividivi Beach Hotel*, 148 r., SP, T; *Tamarijn Beach Hotel*, 150 r., SP, T. – MANCHEBO BEACH: *Manchebo Beach Resort Hotel*, 72 r., SP, T. – PALM BEACH: *Americana Aruba Hotel and Casino*, 200 r., SP, T, beach, casino; *Aruba Caribbean Hotel and Casino*, 200 r., SP, T, beach, casino; *Aruba Concorde*, 543 r., SP, T, beach, casino; *Aruba Holiday Inn*, 390 r., SP, T, beach, casino; *Aruba Sheraton Hotel*, 200 r., SP, T, beach, casino; *Basti Ruti Beach Hotel*, 15 r. – Several PENSIONS and HOLIDAY APARTMENTS.

RESTAURANTS. – In most hotels; also ORANJESTAD: *Ball Floating Restaurant*, Lloyd Smith Boulevard (Indonesian); *Papiamento*, Wilhelminastraat; *Dragon Phoenix*, Havenstraat; *Trocadero*, Nassaustraat; PALM BEACH: *De Olde Molen*; SAVANETA: *Brisas del Mar*.

NIGHT CLUBS and CASINOS in the leading hotels on Palm Beach.

SHOPPING. – The main shopping street is Nassau-straat in Oranjestad, where optical goods, electronic apparatus, jewelry, perfume and alcoholic drinks can be bought at very advantageous prices.

PUBLIC HOLIDAYS and EVENTS. – *New Year's Day.* – *Carnival (mid January to Ash Wednesday), with colorful and cheerful parades. The main events are the Tumba Contest for musicians, the election of the Carnival Queen, the Grand Parade and the Jump-Up (check exact date with Toeristenbureau). – *Good Friday.* – *Easter.* – *Queen's Birthday* (April 30). – *Labour Day* (May 1). – *Ascension.* – *Pentecost.* – *Kingdom Day* (December 15), the national day. – *Christmas* (December 24–26). – *New Year's Eve* (December 31).

RECREATION and SPORT. – Sailing, wind-surfing, deep-sea fishing, parasailing, water-skiing, water-scootering, scuba diving, snorkeling, swimming and sunbathing; cycling, walking, ball games, dune sliding.

AIR SERVICES. – Direct connections with Curaçao, Bonaire and St Maarten (N.I.), Port of Spain (Trinidad), San Juan (Puerto Rico), Caracas and Maracaibo (Venezuela), Georgetown (Guyana), Paramaribo (Surinam), Barranquilla and Medellín (Colombia), and Miami and New York.

SHIPPING. – Some of the regular Caribbean cruise ships call in at Oranjestad, usually from Miami (USA) or San Juan (Puerto Rico) and occasionally from other islands. – Regular ferry services to Curaçao and Bonaire and to Punto Fijo (Venezuela).

*Aruba, the most westerly of the Dutch "ABC" islands (Aruba, Bonaire, Curaçao), lies in latitude 12°13′ N and longitude 70° W at the entrance to the Gulf of Venezuela which, with the region of Lake Maracaibo, has rich reserves of oil. This situation explains the presence on Aruba of a huge oil refinery. – The island's long beaches of white sand, combined with its excellent hotel resources and facilities for all kinds of water sports, have made Aruba a very popular vacationers' island.

Like the two neighboring islands of Curaçao and Bonaire, Aruba belongs geologically to the Venezuelan coastal cordillera. The basement rocks form a

gently rolling upland region in the center of the island, with hills of Cretaceous sedimentary rocks rising out of the older formations. In the Quaternary era the island lay considerably lower than it does today, so that the coral reefs which are now such a striking feature were built up around the old mountain core, to be preserved in their present form as the result of a later upthrust. The younger reefs along the S coast serve a valuable protective function, particularly for the movement of shipping. The climate and biosphere of the island are notable for their aridity: the average annual rainfall at Oranjestad is 17 in./440mm. Aruba lies outside the Caribbean hurricane belt.

HISTORY. – Aruba, then occupied by Arawak Indians, was discovered in 1499 by the Spanish navigator Alonso de Ojeda. The Spaniards took little interest in the island and forcibly transferred many of the Indian inhabitants to work on Hispaniola. In 1643 Peter Stuyvesant – later Governor of New Amsterdam (New York) – was appointed Governor of Aruba and the other islands in the Netherlands Antilles. During the 19th c. the island was held briefly by Britain. Gold was discovered on Aruba in 1824, but gold-working ceased in 1913. In 1860 the aloe, a native of the arid regions of Africa, was introduced into Aruba, and during the first half of the 20th c. some 70% of total world production of aloes (used for medicinal purposes) came from here. The *dividivi* tree which grows wild on Aruba and is still a characteristic feature of the landscape, leaning in the direction of the trade winds, was formerly of considerable economic importance, since its yellow fruits have a high tannin content and were in much demand for export until a synthetic substitute was produced. The rearing of cochineal insects, which feed on opuntias, for the production of a dye is another activity which has succumbed to the advance of science. – The Aruba oil refinery came into operation in 1929, when it was the largest refinery in the world. The present huge plant, belonging to Exxon (Esso), is the island's largest source of employment. With more than 300 large tanks (total capacity some 30 million barrels), it can process something like 525,000 barrels of crude oil a day.

Since the Second World War Aruba has developed into an important resort island, with 2150 rooms for visitors, most of them in luxury hotels, which are occupied to a very high proportion of capacity. More than 160,000 visitors come to the island every year. In 1980 120,000 from North America alone spent their vacation on Aruba. In spite of this prospering tourist trade and a flourishing oil industry, however, the unemployment rate is about 20%. In an attempt to alleviate this problem some 800 new jobs in industry have been created within the last few years. – In a referendum held in 1977 some 57% of those entitled to vote favored breaking away from the Netherlands. The island is to be given a special political status in 1986. In 1986 Aruba is to have special status and in 1996 it will be granted complete independence.

*Oranjestad (sea level; pop. *c.* 20,000), capital of the island, lies in Paardenbaai. The old part of the town is in Dutch colonial style with a mingling of Spanish features such as balconies, patios and gardens enclosed by high iron railings.

SIGHTS. – The principal landmark of the town is the *Willem III Toren (1867; museum), an old lighthouse and part of the fortifications of Fort Zoutman (1797), which formerly defended the town against attack. A colorful feature of the town is the *Schooner Market, a floating market enlivened by the presence of Venezuelan fish, fruit and vegetable sellers in their small boats. In Lloyd G. Smith Boulevard, named after a former manager of the Lago refinery, are a number of office buildings and the *Wilhelmina Park, laid out in 1955 on the occasion of a visit by Queen Juliana and Prince Bernhard. The carefully tended gardens are a riot of tropical flowers (hibiscus, bougainvillea, orchids, frangipani, etc.). There is also an imposing marble statue of Queen Wilhelmina by Arnoldo Lualdi.

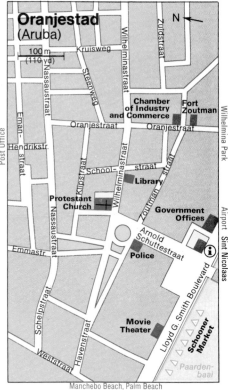

Nassaustraat, the town's principal shopping street, is a thoroughfare bustling with activity in which high quality goods can be bought duty-free.

Oranjestad to Sint Nicolaas (round trip 24 miles/ 39 km). – Leave Oranjestad on Nassaustraat, going E. Then, after passing the *Cultureel Centrum* (Cultural Center: folk art, etc.; exhibitions) to –

2 miles/3 km: **Princess Beatrix Luchthaven**, the airport which handles a busy tourist trade. Then past modern industrial plants to –

3 miles/5 km: **Spaans Lagoen** (Spanish Lagoon). The road now winds its way up to the abandoned gold-mine of *Balashi*, near *Frenchman's Pass*, with the remains of old smelting works – relics of a brief gold rush in the first half of the 19th c.

4 miles/6 km: **Savaneta**, a village on the S coast which was once a place of some consequence thanks to the nearby salt-pans and, under the name of Commandeursbaai, was capital of the island until 1797. Beautiful beach.

2 miles/3 km: **Sint Nicolaas** (*San Nicolás*), the second largest settlement on the island, with the *oil refinery of the Lago Oil and Transport Company, established by Standard Oil of New Jersey in 1929, when it was the world's largest oil refinery. The American staff of the refinery live in a bungalow village. To the NE are extensive sports and recreational facilities, including the Aruba Golf Club. – At the eastern tip of the island stands the *Seroa Colorado* lighthouse.

From Sint Nicolaas the road continues N through country bearing the mark of the trade winds which blow almost all the time, leading to a number of caves of the type common on the island, some of them with rock paintings and engravings of the Indian period. Particularly notable are the *Seroe Pretoe Cave* ¾ mile/ 1 km N of Sint Nicolaas, which is also a sanctuary of the Virgin and a place of pilgrimage, the *Huliba Cave*, the *Guadirikiri Cave* and the very interesting *Fontein Cave* on the way to Boca Prins on the N coast.

5 miles/8 km: *Boca Prins, one of the great tourist attractions of the island. Here the extensive fields of dunes are constantly being reshaped by the trade winds. The dunes offer scope, to an extent rarely found elsewhere, for the popular local sport of "dune sliding".

¾ mile/1 km: a narrow side road goes off to *Dos Playa*, a magnificent beach NW of Boca Prins.

2 miles/3 km: *Miramar Pass*, with one of the finest views of the island. Near here are the remains of abandoned gold-mines. To the S is *Mt Yamanota* (617 ft/188 m), the highest point on Aruba.

3 miles/5 km: **Santa Cruz**, one of the island's larger settlements. To the W is the much photographed silhouette of the *Hooiberg* (499 ft/152 m). A flight of several hundred steps leads up to the summit, from which the Venezuelan coast can be seen in clear weather.

Beyond Santa Cruz, under the S side of the Hooiberg in the **Canashito** area, are caves which were once inhabited by Arawak Indians and Caribs, some of them containing rock engravings.

3 miles/5 km: **Oranjestad**.

Oranjestad to Boca Mahos (round trip 12 miles/ 19 km). – Leave Oranjestad on Emmastraat, going N. 1¼ miles/2 km from the town is a historic old cemetery.

2 miles/3 km: *Paradera*, from which we take a road running E to the *Casibari* area, littered with huge rocks hollowed out by weathering.

Aruba – a bird's-eye view of Oranjestad

This type of weathering can be observed at a number of points on Aruba. The enormous blocks of volcanic rock are fashioned into bizarre shapes by chemical and physical weathering processes and by the action of the trade winds.

1 mile/1.5 km: road junction, where we take a road going NE.

2 miles/3 km: **Ayo**, another area noted for its weathered rocks. From here a narrow road runs down to the N coast.

2 miles/3 km: ***Boca Mahos**, a wild and romantic bay shaped by the fierce surf. – ¾ mile/1 km E is *De Gold Molen* (15th–16th c.), a ruined inn once frequented by gold prospectors and also, it is said, by pirates. At *Andicouri*, ¾ mile/1 km farther E near the *Noordkaap* (North Cape), is an imposing *natural arch formed by the action of the waves.

Above Boca Mahos, on the way back to Oranjestad, is –

1¼ miles/2 km: *Bushiribana*, an abandoned gold-mine. Nearby is the *Crystalberg*. – Then via Paradera to –

3½ miles/5.5 km: **Oranjestad**.

Oranjestad to Druif (round trip 14 miles/23 km). – Leave Oranjestad on the Lloyd G. Smith Boulevard, going W.

2 miles/ 3 km: **Manchebo**, with the *Old Eagle Pier*. This is the beginning of the almost continuous beach of fine sand which extends along the W coast, with luxury hotels strung along it like pearls. – Passing *Eagle Beach*, we come to –

2 miles/3 km: ***Palm Beach**, the finest stretch of beach, with celebrated hotels. Beyond the Aruba Caribbean Hotel is an unusual attraction – De Olde Molen, a 19th c. windmill brought here from Holland.

The road continues NW past *Bastiroeti Beach* and *Hadikoerabi Beach* to –

2½ miles/4 km: **Malmok**, a little settlement with another beautiful beach. Offshore is the wreck of a German cargo ship, the "Antilia", which ran aground here at the beginning of the Second World War.

1¼ miles/2 km: *California*. Here, at the NW tip of the island, are extensive sand-dunes, forming a landscape of strange and striking aspect. Then E from the California lighthouse to –

1¼ miles/2 km: **Druif**, on the N coast, with two large petrochemical plants built in the 1960s.

From here we return SE on a country road.

2½ miles/4 km: **Noord**, a small village, with the Santa Anna Kerk, which has a fine carved wooden altar by a 17th c. Dutch master. – From here a side road (2 miles/3 km) branches off to the charming little *Alto Vista* chapel on the N coast, from which there are extensive views.

Then, passing a historic old cemetery, back to –

3 miles/5 km: **Oranjestad**.

See also ***Bonaire** and **Curaçao**.

Bahamas

Bahama Islands
Commonwealth of the Bahamas

Nationality letters: BS.
Area: 5380 sq. miles/13,935 sq. km.
Capital: Nassau (on New Providence).
Population: 235,000.
Religions: Protestant (over 70%), Roman Catholic (20%). Jewish minority.
Language: English.
Currency: Bahama dollar (B$) of 100 cents.
Weights and measures: British/American system.
Time: Eastern Standard Time (5 hours behind GMT).
Vehicles travel on the left.
Travel documents: passport, immigration card, onward or return ticket.

(i) **Ministry of Tourism,**
Nassau Court,
P.O. Box N 3220,
Nassau, Bahamas;
tel. (809) 322 7505.
See also Practical Information.

The **Bahamas (from Spanish "baja mar" shallow sea) enjoy a marvelous climate and are for many the very quintessence of a vacation paradise. Magnificent lonely beaches fringed by palms, fascinating underwater hunting grounds for skin divers, gay with rare corals, waters teeming with fish, facilities for every kind of water sport: to these natural advantages are added a host of man-made amenities – luxury hotels, exclusive holiday complexes, splendid secluded private villas, casinos, marinas, golf-courses, tennis courts and every conceivable form of recreation and leisure pursuit. The islands have long had the reputation of a retreat for the wealthy, and it is only since the end of the Second World War that there has been an increased influx of tourists, mainly from the United States and Canada. The tourists have been catered for by massive new developments, involving in particular the islands of New Providence, with the Bahamian capital of Nassau, and Grand Bahama, with the new town of Freeport-Lucaya. In the last few years, too, the so-called "Out Islands" have begun to attract the attention of powerful financial interests, encouraged by fiscal legislation which is generous to capital. This former British colony became an independent state within the Commonwealth in 1973.

The Bahamas consist of some 700 islands of varying size and some 2400 uninhabited islets and rocks lying between latitude 20°50' and 27°25' N and between longitude 72°37' and 80°32' W. The archipelago extends from about 50 miles off the coast of Florida for a distance of almost 750 miles in a southeasterly direction. The islands, predominantly flat, reaching their highest point of only 207 ft/ 63 m on Cat Island, have a total land area of 5380 sq. miles/13,935 sq. km. By far the largest island is Andros, with an area of 2299 sq. miles/5955 sq. km; the smallest of the inhabited islands is Spanish Wells ($\frac{1}{2}$ sq. mile/1.3 sq. km). New Providence, with the capital city of Nassau, is one of the smaller islands, with an area of 80 sq. miles/207 sq. km.

A typical limestone cave in the Bahamas

The Bahama Islands rise out of the Bahama Banks, which lie barely 65 ft/ 20 m under the sea, their sides falling steeply away to great depths. They are built up from more than 13,000 ft/4000 m of oolitic limestones and calcareous sandstones and coral reefs. Old beach-lines, cliffs and marine transgressions bear witness to variations in sea level and tectonic movements. Beaches of fine light-colored sand are frequently enclosed by bizarre rock formations, and harbors and anchorages lie within the shelter of jagged cliffs. In contrast to most of the other islands, the long narrow islets bordering the Atlantic tend to be hilly. The flatter parts on the islands are areas of sea bed which have been raised above water level, while the individual ranges of hills are old dunes which are now consolidated, the sharper contours representing the older dunes and the gentler land forms being younger dunes, often not yet consolidated. Particularly large accumulations of sand produce the type of terrain known as "white lands"; if vegetation is able to establish itself these areas become darker in color and yield agricultural land of very moderate quality ("provision land"). Good agricultural soils are found only in particularly sheltered situations. Since surface watercourses are lacking as a result of karstic action (which also produces impressive caves) many areas have to bring in their drinking water at considerable expense. On some of the islands shallow depressions are filled by lakes or covered by salt-flats and swamps.

CLIMATE. – The Bahamas lie on the edge of the subtropical anticyclone belt. The trade winds which blow almost continuously give them an agreeable climate, rather cooler and wetter on the more northerly islands, warmer and drier on the more southerly ones. The average day temperature in winter is about 70 °F/ 21 °C, in summer about 81 °F/27 °C; highs above 90 °F/32 °C and lows below 55 °F/13 °C are rare. The annual rainfall ranges according to situation between 39 in./1000 mm and 59 in./1500 mm, with most of the rain falling in heavy showers from June to October. The predominant direction of the wind is NE from October to April, SE from June to August; in May and September the winds blow generally from the E. The Bahamas are exposed to devastating tropical hurricanes between mid July and November. Thanks to an average of over 7 hours sunshine a day and to a water temperature which remains above 73 °F/23 °C all year round the islands attract beachgoers throughout the year, with the main season in the dry and pleasantly warm winter months.

HISTORY. – When Columbus landed on the Bahamian island of San Salvador on October 12, 1492, believing that he had reached the E coast of India by the western route, the archipelago was occupied by Lucayans (Lukku-Cairi), descendants of a tribe of Arawak Indians from South America who had been driven northward by the Caribs in the 8th–9th c. Few traces are now left of the culture of these Indians. Since the islands were of no great economic value to the Spaniards they established only small and temporary settlements, and deported the native population, estimated at some 20,000, to provide a cheap labor force on the large East Indian islands of Hispaniola and Cuba with their valuable deposits of gold and silver. In 1513 Ponce de León discovered the peninsula of Florida during a quest for the Fountain of Youth, known only to the Indians, and believed to be on one of the northern Bahamas.

When merchant shipping traffic began to develop between the West Indian islands and Europe, particularly Spain, pirates and beachcombers established themselves on the Bahamas, which with their fringes of coral reefs were well suited for their purposes. – The islands were first treated as a British possession in 1629, when they were granted by Charles I to Sir Robert Heath. In 1647–48 the "Eleutheran Adventurers", led by William Sayle, a former governor of Bermuda, landed on the island of Eleuthera and founded the first republic in the New World. Sayle was also responsible for the colonization in 1666 of New Providence, now the most important of the islands in economic terms, with the capital, Nassau.

Queen's Birthday parade in Nassau

Under a charter of 1670 six "Lords Proprietors" were granted possession of the islands, which were ruled for the next 50 years by a succession of weak and undistinguished governors, leading to economic decline and lawlessness. In 1703 a Spanish and French fleet captured New Providence, and at this time pirates, including Hornigold, Major Stede Bonnett and Edward Teach ("Blackbeard"), as well as Mary Read and Ann Bonny, became renowned throughout the Spanish Main. In 1718, however, Woodes Rogers was appointed first royal Governor and set about restoring law and order. Fort Nassau was recommissioned and a local militia established. In 1728 an Assembly of 24 members was constituted and passed the islands' first laws. Rogers died in 1732, and thereafter the islanders returned to their smuggling and plundering of shipping. During the 18th and 19th c. the "wreckers" pursued a profitable trade, luring ships on to the rocks with lights. It is significant that the first lighthouse was not erected until 1816 at the entrance to Nassau harbor.

In 1776 New Providence became involved in the conflict between Britain and its rebellious American colonies. In 1782 it was occupied by Spanish forces, but was recovered in the following year by Col. Andrew Deveaux, later a member of the Bahamian Parliament. Many North American Loyalists, attracted by the prospect of acquiring land, settled in the islands, bringing their slaves with them, and within a short time the number of whites doubled and of blacks tripled. Soon, however, the exhaustion of the soil and insect pests made the newly established cotton plantations uneconomic, and many planters left the islands. In the 1830s the slaves were freed – many of them because their former owners were no longer able to feed and maintain them. The Emancipation Act was passed on August 1, 1838, a date still celebrated in a gay and colorful festival.

With the outbreak of the American Civil War in 1861 and the blockade of the Southern ports Nassau became the haunt of blockade-runners and refugees from the southern states. After the end of the war the colony relapsed into economic depression. Towards the end of the 19th c. the export of sponges became a considerable source of revenue for many islanders, but this soon declined as a result of pollution of the habitat of the sponges. Thereafter the planting of pineapples and sisal was expanded, but these too enjoyed only a brief period of prosperity.

The introduction of Prohibition in the United States in 1919 brought a revival of the smuggling trade. Nassau was the main center of this activity, but West End on Grand Bahama and the Bimini Islands were also much involved in the illicit trade. The first casino was opened in Nassau in 1920, and nine years later an air service between Miami and Nassau was established. During this period the Bahamas were discovered by American millionaires as a resort area and a place for investment. The Canadian financier Harry Oakes, who began to invest in the Bahamas in 1934, was seen as a benefactor of the islands at a time when unemployment was rife. – During the Second World War the islands played an important part as naval bases and training grounds for Allied troops. From 1940 to 1945 the Duke of Windsor (ex-King Edward VIII) was Governor of the Bahamas. In 1942 social problems led to the outbreak of serious riots on New Providence and to the murder, in circumstances never explained, of Sir Harry Oakes.

After the end of the Second World War the tourist trade developed at a tremendous rate. In 1950 45,000 visitors came to the Bahamas: 29 years later the figure had risen to 1.7 million, an increase promoted by the exclusion of American tourists from Cuba. Among major projects undertaken in recent years have been the establishment of an exclusive resort on Paradise Island, off New Providence, and the development of Grand Bahama, with the foundation by the American financier Wallace Groves of the industrial town and free port of Freeport and the resort settlement of Lucaya. The development of the Out Islands is now also under way.

In 1963 the Bahamas were given a new constitution on the British model; in 1964 they were granted self-government in internal affairs; and on July 10, 1973 the Commonwealth of the Bahamas became an independent state within the British Commonwealth.

GOVERNMENT and ADMINISTRATION. – The head of state is the Queen, who is represented by a Governor-General. The government is headed by the Prime Minister. The legislature consists of a Senate of 15 members appointed by the Governor-General and a House of Representatives of 38 members elected for a five-year term. – The various islands are governed direct from Nassau: there is only an embryonic pattern of local government.

The Commonwealth of the Bahamas is a member of the United Nations, and also has links with the Organization of American States (OAS).

ECONOMY. – The Bahamas are predestined by nature as vacation islands, and tourism is the predominant factor in the economy, accounting for more than 60% of the gross national product and providing two-thirds of the islands' employment. There are at present more than 12,000 rooms available for visitors, over 5000 in Nassau and on Paradise Island and almost 4000 on Grand Bahama. In 1982 about 70% of the total number of visitors (nearly 2 million; in 1959 264,000) came from the United States, 12% from Canada and 9% from Europe, mainly Britain and Germany. The tourist trade of the Bahamas is affected by political and economic changes both in other competing vacation areas and in the countries from which the visitors come, making it necessary for the Bahamians to watch the market carefully and be ready to meet changing requirements. Thus the islands benefited enormously from the disappearance of Cuba as a resort for Americans, while in more recent years economic difficulties in the United States led to a decline of 14% in the number of visitors between 1972 and 1979. As a result, the government is now turning away from its earlier concentration on developing tourist projects on the less known islands, and seeking instead to promote other branches of the economy by special incentives and to involve the remoter islands in the general economic development of the Bahamas.

Favorable fiscal and economic legislation has enabled the Bahamas to become an important financial center, with the headquarters of many trusts and holding companies, which have become an increasingly important source of employment. In 1977 these activities already accounted for 6% of the gross domestic product. Nassau is now the world's largest eurodollar market after London. At the end of 1979 there were 285 banks registered here. Since there are practically no income, property, capital gains or inheritance taxes the state's main sources of revenue are customs duties, fees for company registrations and indirect taxes and duties.

Particular attention is now being given to the promotion of agriculture, which in the past has lagged behind, mainly for lack of fertile soil but also as a result of water shortage and poor communications. Since 1978 both national and international agencies have been seeking, with increasing success, to develop new crops (pineapples, citrus fruits, onions, cucumbers, tomatoes, etc.) and to build up a livestock industry (dairy cattle, poultry) which will help to meet domestic demands. There are now more than 62,000 acres in agricultural use. On some particularly suitable islands modern farms and processing plants have been established and have now begun to produce for export. – A significant contribution is also made to the economy by the forests of Grand Bahama, Abaco and Andros. The pines which are found in large numbers provide building timber and pulpwood for the American papermaking industry, while tropical hardwoods such as mahogany and ebony are used in boatbuilding and furniture manufacture. Recently the government has been particularly concerned to ensure that deforested areas are replanted. – The waters of the Bahamas are well stocked with fish, which not only supply sport but meet part of the domestic demand. Considerable quantities of shellfish and crustaceans are exported to the United States.

Local craft products in the Straw Market, Nassau

Shell jewelry from the Bahamas

special position as a port for the shipment of sea salt. Numerous mail and freight services link Nassau with all the inhabited islands. A network of well-equipped yacht harbors cater for the needs of sailors and deep-sea fishermen.

The road system on the islands of New Providence, Grand Bahama and Eleuthera, the most extensively developed of the Bahamas, is excellent. More than half the vehicles registered in the Bahamas are on New Providence, with its 375 miles/600 km of roads. The other islands are being gradually opened up by the construction of new roads.

POPULATION. – with a population of 235,000 in 1980, the Bahamas had a population density of 44 people to the sq. mile (17 to the sq km), compared with 31 to the sq. mile (12 to the sq. km) in 1970. In 1920 the population was only 53,000. This tremendous increase is primarily due to a large influx of population from outside, reaching critical proportions in recent years with the arrival of thousands of refugees from Haiti, which restrictive measures taken by the government have been unable to stem. The problems of finding enough jobs for this increasing population is aggravated by the fact that almost half the inhabitants of the Bahamas are under 25. The unemployment rate is estimated at 30%, with unemployment among young people reaching disquieting proportions. More than 60% of the working population are employed in the services sector, predominantly in the tourist trade but with a significant proportion in finance. Other important sources of employment are trades and crafts, the construction industries, agriculture and fishing.

The **industry** of the Bahamas is mainly concentrated around the new port of Freeport on Grand Bahama, which was developed during the 1950s. With the largest oil bunkering installations in the western hemisphere, an oil refinery, a cement plant and numerous other capital-intensive industries, Freeport developed within a few years into the second largest town in the Bahamas. In addition to products intended mainly for export and therefore subject to favorable rates of duty (alcoholic drinks, canned foods, pharmaceuticals, electronic apparatus, etc.) many firms also produce traditional art and craft goods designed to appeal to visitors, much of their output being sold in the "straw markets" of Nassau and Freeport. – There are large plants for the provision of drinking water and electric power. There are believed to be deposits of oil and natural gas in the Bahamas, but it is uncertain how far they can be worked to meet the islands' needs. Other minerals of some economic importance are aragonite (in the Biminis), limestone and sea salt (on Great Inagua and Long Island). These raw materials are exported to the United States and Trinidad.

The distribution of population reflects the degree of economic development of the islands. Almost 60% of the total population live on New Providence, mostly in the capital, Nassau. A long way after this comes Grand Bahama, with the rising port and industrial town of Freeport, followed by Eleuthera and Andros.

Over 80% of the population are blacks and mulattoes, mostly the descendants of slaves. Whites, of British and American origin, are in a majority only on a few of the smaller islands. Of the more than 20 churches and other religious denominations, mainly Christian, on the islands the Anglican and Roman Catholic churches have the largest numbers of adherents, followed by Baptists and Methodists.

The educational system of the Bahamas is based on the British model, and gives particular attention to vocational education. The Commonwealth of the Bahamas contributes to the financing of the University of the West Indies.

Air services play an important part in Bahamian **transport**. Good connections with major cities in the United States and Canada, in Central and South America and in recent years increasingly in Europe mean that most visitors and businesspeople now come to the Bahamas by air. Much internal traffic is also handled by air services. In addition to the two international airports of Nassau and Freeport there are some 60 other airfields, airstrips and flying-boat harbors serving all the islands involved in the tourist trade.

Sea transport, however, is still of importance. The main ports are Nassau and Freeport, which handle a considerable proportion of the islands' external trade and are also major ports of call for the Caribbean cruise ships. Matthew Town on Great Inagua occupies a

Junkanoo parade, Nassau

See also *Abaco Islands, *Acklins, *Andros, Berry Islands, *Bimini Islands, *Cat Island, *Crooked Island (and *Long Cay*), *Eleuthera, *Exumas, *Grand Bahama, *Inagua, *Long Island, *Mayaguana, *Nassau, **New Providence, *Ragged Island Range, *Rum Cay and *San Salvador.

Bahía de Samaná

See Samaná

Barbados

Lesser Antilles
Windward Islands
Independent state within the British Commonwealth

Nationality letters: BDS.
Area: 166 sq. miles/431 sq. km.
Capital: Bridgetown.
Population: 280,000.
Local administration: 7 parishes.
Religion: Anglican (over 70%), Methodists and Moravian Brethren (25%), Roman Catholic minority.
Languages: English; some French; Bajan.
Currency: Barbados dollar (BDS$) of 100 cents.
Weights and measures: Metric is replacing the British/American system.
Time: Atlantic Time (4 hours behind GMT).
Vehicles travel on the left.
Travel documents: passport, immigration card, onward or return ticket.

(i) **Barbados Board of Tourism,**
Harbour Road,
P.O. Box 242,
Bridgetown,
Barbados;
tel. 72623–4, 64656.
See also Practical Information.

HOTELS. – Only a small selection out of the enormous range of hotels can be given:

ST MICHAEL: *Hilton, 188 r., SP, T, beach; *Holiday Inn, 138 r., SP, T; *Paradise Beach, 152 r., SP, T; Island Inn, 22 r.; etc. – HASTINGS: Asta, 60 r.; Caribee, 53 r.; Ocean View, 40 r.; Regency Cove, 66 r.; etc. – ST LAWRENCE: Bagshot House, 16 r.; Southern Palms, 93 r.; etc. – CHRIST CHURCH: *Rockley Resort, 246 r., SP, T; Accra Beach Hotel, 32 r.; Arawak Inn, 22 r., SP; etc. – ST PHILIP: *Marriott's Beach Resort (formerly *Sam Lord's Castle, home of an 18th c. buccaneer), 270 r., SP, T, golf, beach; Crane Beach, 20 r., SP; etc.

ST JAMES: *Sandy Lane, 115 r., SP, T, golf, beach; *Sunset Crest Resort, 840 r., SP, T, beach; Barbados Beach Village, 82 r., SP; Buccaneer Bay, 38 r.; Coconut Creek, 34 r., SP, beach; Colony Club, 75 r., SP; Coral Reef Club, 77 r., SP; Discovery Bay Inn, 75 r., SP; Miramar, 90 r., SP, T; Sandpiper Inn, 24 r., SP; Tamarind Cove, 50 r.; etc. – ST PETER: Cobbler's Cove, 38 r., SP; Eastry House, 35 r., SP; etc.

Many GUEST-HOUSES and HOLIDAY APARTMENTS. – FOR YOUNG PEOPLE: South Hostel, Yoga Centre, Worthing; YMCA, Bridgetown.

RESTAURANTS in hotels; also in BRIDGETOWN: Flying Fish. – ST MICHAEL: Alexandra's, Bishop Court Hill. – ST THOMAS: Bagatelle Great House; Nick's Smoochery. – ST GEORGE: *La Bonne Auberge (French). – CHRIST CHURCH: *Pisces; Dinner Bell.

The "**Barbados bombshell**" is a refreshing cocktail made from rum, Pernod, freshly pressed lime juice and grenadine syrup.

SHOPPING. – Broad Street in Bridgetown offers a wide range of luxury goods, particularly watches and jewelry, with many duty-free shops. There are numerous skilled tailors who make clothes to measure at very reasonable prices. Local handicrafts of excellent quality can be bought in the Government Handicraft Centre in Pelican Village (between the town center and the harbor). Caribatik Island Fabrics, at the Crane Beach Hotel in St Philip, sell quality batik work.

PUBLIC HOLIDAYS and EVENTS. – New Year's Day. – Stately Homes of Barbados visits (January–March). – Barbados Turf Club Horse Race Meetings March, May, August, November). – Barbados Game Fishing Contests (March–April). – Good Friday. – Easter Monday. – May Day (May 1), Labour Day. – Whit Monday. – *Crop Over Festival (June–July), celebrating the end of the sugar-cane harvest, with carnival parades. – Cricket matches (June–January). – Kadomet Day (first Monday in June). – Caricom Day (August 1), commemorating the signature of the Caricom agreement. – United Nations Day (first Monday in October). – Festival of Creative Arts

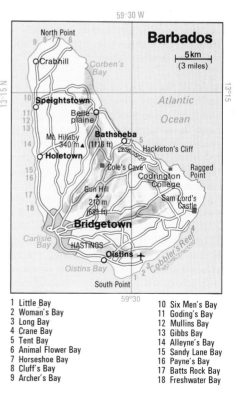

Barbados

| 5 km |
(3 miles)

1 Little Bay
2 Woman's Bay
3 Long Bay
4 Crane Bay
5 Tent Bay
6 Animal Flower Bay
7 Horseshoe Bay
8 Cluff's Bay
9 Archer's Bay

10 Six Men's Bay
11 Goding's Bay
12 Mullins Bay
13 Gibbs Bay
14 Alleyne's Bay
15 Sandy Lane Bay
16 Payne's Bay
17 Batts Rock Bay
18 Freshwater Bay

(November). – *Independence Day* (November 30). – *Christmas Day*. – *Boxing Day* (December 26).

RECREATION and SPORT. – Sailing, deep-sea fishing, wind-surfing, water-skiing, parasailing, scuba diving, snorkeling, swimming and sunbathing; golf, riding, polo, tennis, cricket.

AIR SERVICES. – Regular direct connections with Atlanta, Boston, Chicago, Miami, New York and Washington (USA), Montreal and Toronto (Canada), San Juan (Puerto Rico), Antigua, Guadeloupe, Dominica, Martinique, St Lucia, St Vincent, Port of Spain (Trinidad), Kingston (Jamaica), Grand Cayman, La Habana (Cuba), Caracas (Venezuela), London (UK), Luxembourg and Copenhagen (Denmark). There are occasional charter flights to some of the neighboring islands, Quebec (Canada) and Frankfurt am Main (Germany).

SHIPPING. – A few shipping lines sail between Barbados and the USA, Canada, the United Kingdom and Western Europe, South America, New Zealand and Australia. There are regular calls by mixed cargo and passenger vessels and Caribbean cruise ships and occasional cargo and passenger boats to neighboring islands.

*Barbados, with a climate which has long made it a popular holiday resort, lies in latitude 13°4′ N and longitude 59°37′ W – the most easterly of the West Indies, lying some 100 miles from the southern string of islands. With 1500 inhabitants to the sq. mile (600 to the sq. km) it is one of the most densely populated places in the world. This "Island in the Sun", with its long palm-fringed beaches and its huge sugar-cane plantations, is also known as "Little England" – bearing as it does the imprint of 300 years of British rule.

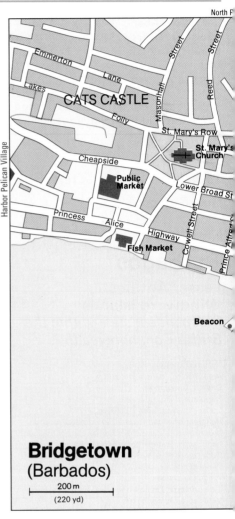

Bridgetown
(Barbados)

|—— 200 m ——|
(220 yd)

Most of the island of Barbados is occupied by a gently rolling plateau of coralline limestone up to 295 ft/90 m thick, which rises in terraces towards the NE and reaches its highest point in Mount Hillaby (1116 ft/340 m). The landscape is patterned by extensive plantations of sugarcane and dolines and dry valleys with a luxuriant growth of tropical vegetation. In the NE the plateau ends at Hackleton's Cliff, which plunges sharply down to the Scotland District, a region consisting mainly of Tertiary sediments and deeply slashed by a number of rivers, with a rugged coastline carved into bizarre rock formations by the Atlantic breakers. On the W and SW coast, facing on to the Caribbean, there are beautiful sandy beaches, many of them developed to cater for tourists, with an excellent range of facilities. In the sheltered Carlisle Bay in the SW of the island is the capital,

Bridgetown, with a new deep-water harbor. Here, in the town and its suburbs, is the island's main concentration of population. A dense network of roads radiating from Bridgetown promoted the development of Barbados from an early stage.

HISTORY. – Barbados was probably inhabited in pre-Columbian times by Arawak Indians. There are also

Bridgetown Harbour

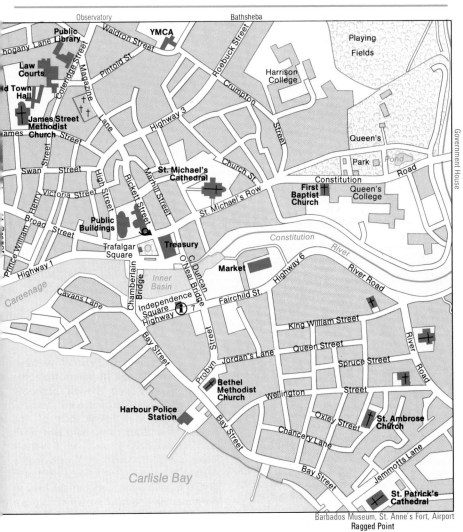

Observatory · Bathsheba

Barbados Museum, St. Anne's Fort, Airport
Ragged Point

traces of settlement by the Caribs who moved into Barbados from the S and drove out the Arawaks. The name *Isla de los Barbados* ("Island of the Bearded" – believed to be a reference to the bearded fig-trees which grow on the island) appears for the first time in 1511. Other documents of the early 16th c. refer to the island as Bernados, San Bernados or Barbudosa. The Portuguese navigator Pedro a Campos landed here in 1536 on his way to Brazil. The first Englishmen appeared on the W coast of the island about 1625, and in 1627 an expedition financed by Sir William Courteen established Jamestown, the first English settlement, near present-day Holetown. This was followed in 1628 by the foundation of a rival settlement at Bridgetown. The tobacco, cotton and sugar-cane which the settlers brought from Guiana yielded good harvests, and by the middle of the 17th c. the basic structures of the island's economy, still in effect today, had been established. The monoculture of sugar-cane was extended with the help of thousands of black slaves brought in from West Africa and promoted by the large English landowners. In 1639 the island was given its first Parliament. Some years later Jews from Pernambuco settled on Barbados. In spite of severe devastation by hurricanes in 1675 and 1780 and a series of epidemics, the island developed into a flourishing colony and a major center of maritime trade which attracted many immigrants from

Britain, particularly during the 18th and 19th c. In 1834 slavery was abolished.

After years of preparation Barbados achieved independence on November 30, 1966, and in the following year it became a member of the United Nations. – Its constitution and government are based on the British model. The head of state is the Queen, who is represented by a Governor-General, who in turn appoints the Prime Minister and the members of the Cabinet (on the nomination of the Prime Minister). The Barbadian Parliament has two chambers, the Senate and the House of Assembly.

POPULATION and ECONOMY. – Some 95% of the population are colored – descendants of black slaves, American Indians, Europeans, Jews and Asian Indians. The white minority is mainly of British origin. More than 70 religious denominations are represented on the island, the largest by far being the Anglican Church, with substantial numbers of Methodists, Moravian Brethren, Roman Catholics and Jews. The educational system of Barbados is well developed and ranks as one of the best in the Caribbean. – Traditionally the economy has been based on the monoculture of sugar-cane, and this is still an important economic activity, some 60% of the available agricultural land being used for this purpose,

The Careenage, Bridgetown (Barbados)

usually on large estates. The main exports are sugar, molasses, syrup and rum, which are produced by a number of fairly large concerns. Vegetables and fruit are grown, chiefly for domestic consumption, on a large number of smallholdings. Thanks to the abundance of fish in the waters of Barbados the fisheries are highly productive. Crustaceans and shellfish are exported. There are nine industrial estates, with factories producing foodstuffs, textiles, household requisites, chemicals and refinery products. Prospecting for oil has been in progress for some time in the coastal waters, and the deposits of natural gas in the Tertiary rocks in the NE of the island and smaller discoveries of oil in the southern part have recently begun to make a contribution to local power requirements.

Tourism has played a part in the economy of the island since at least the 19th c., and it was considerably developed from 1932 onwards by the Barbados Publicity Committee. Within recent years the huge increase in the number of visitors has made the tourist trade a major element in the economy. While in 1965 the number of visitors was only 61,600, by 1980 it had risen to more than 370,000 (excluding passengers on cruise liners). At the beginning of 1980 there were fully 12,500 beds available for visitors. This has completely altered the employment structure of Barbados; and there are now some 10,000 jobs directly, and another 20,000 indirectly, dependent on tourism. About 160,000 passengers on cruises visit the island every year, and they are important for the trade in souvenirs.

*Bridgetown** (sea level; pop. 95,000, including outer districts), the busy capital of the island, was founded in 1628 by the Earl of Carlisle. It is the only town in the SW of the island, with its rather featureless suburbs now reaching far inland.

SIGHTS. – The old part of the town lies on both sides of the *Careenage**, the picturesque old harbor, crowded with boats, at the mouth of *Constitution River*. The settlement took its name from the *Chamberlain Bridge*, which probably occupies the position of an earlier Indian-built bridge. On the N side of the Careenage is *Trafalgar Square*, laid out in 1874 (previously known as Egleton's Green), with Sir Richard Westmacott's *Nelson Monument*, which was erected in 1815 (i.e. before the more famous Nelson Monument in London). Also in the square is the *Dolphin Fountain* (1865), with a basin of local coral limestone, commemorating the construction of the municipal water supply system. Behind it stands the *Financial Building*, a modern office tower (good view from roof).

On the N side of the square, in an area destroyed by fire in 1860, are the neo-Gothic *Public Buildings** (W wing 1872, E wing 1874).

In the E wing are the **Houses of Parliament**. The *House of Assembly* has stained-glass windows with portraits of British monarchs. The fine *Speaker's Chair* was presented by the Indian government when Barbados became independent.

From Trafalgar Square *Broad Street*, an elegant shopping street, runs W through the town center, which has a number of attractive colonial buildings. It crosses Prince William Henry Street, named after the future William IV, who spent some time on Barbados in 1786. To the N is Victoria Street, a narrow street with many attractive little shops, and beyond this Swan Street (fine balconies).

Sunset on the S coast of Barbados

Farther N, in James Street, stands *James Street Methodist Church* (19th c.), and beyond this the *Old Town Hall* (now the police headquarters), the 18th c. *Law Courts* and the *Public Library* (1905). Farther N still, in Clapham Street, is the *Harry Bailey Observatory*, a very popular Planetarium.

A little way E, in Magazine Lane (named after a powder magazine which once stood here), we find the well-known *Montefiore Library*. Farther S is the *Synagogue* (17th and 19th c.), which was damaged by a hurricane in 1831 and how houses legal records.

At the W end of Broad Street, set in gardens, is the venerable *St Mary's Church* (18th c.). A short distance away to the SW lies the large *Public Market*, and farther S, on the seafront, the colorful *Fish Market* – both the scene of lively activity.

To the W along Princess Alice Highway, on land recently reclaimed from the sea, *Pelican Village, with its characteristic pyramidal roofs, is a popular shopping center for local arts and crafts and souvenirs. Farther NW at the deep-water **Bridgetown Harbour**, there is a large industrial estate (large sugar warehouse, molasses terminal, etc.). Nearby is *Kensington Oval* (1882), the town's main cricket ground.

From Trafalgar Square *St Michael's Row* leads E to *St Michael's Cathedral* (17th and 18th c.), which was destroyed by a hurricane in 1780 and later rebuilt. Notable features of the interior are the font and a number of monuments. – Farther E in *Queen's Park* are a number of schools, extensive sports grounds and the *First Baptist Church* (19th c.). The headquarters of the British forces in the West Indies were once here.

On the far side of the river, on the eastern edge of the select residential district of BELLEVILLE, stands *Government House, set in beautiful gardens. Built in the 17th c., this has been the residence of the Governor – and now the Governor-General – since 1702.

From the *Inner Basin* of the Careenage *Bay Street* runs S past the Harbour Police Station to the Roman Catholic *St Patrick's Cathedral* (19th c.), which was devastated by fire in 1897 and subsequently rebuilt. Farther S are the *Bay Street Esplanade* and a number of government buildings. At the corner of Bay Street and Chelsea Road stands *Washington House*, where George Washington is said to have stayed with his brother in 1751 – allegedly his only visit to a foreign country. In this area too is the handsome *Bay Mansion* (18th c.), with fine furniture and furnishings, including tapestries and Chinese porcelain. – To the SW, on *Needham's Point* (beautiful beaches), are extensive vacation and recreational facilities, with some of the best hotels and sailing clubs on the island. At the SW tip of the promontory are the ruins of *Fort Charles* (17th–18th c.). – Farther E is *St Anne's Fort (1702)*, part of a system of fortifications begun in 1694. Well-preserved features are the *Signal Tower* (1703) and the *Guard House* (with bell-tower), which was damaged by a hurricane in 1831. In front of the fort extends the *Garrison Savannah* (parade ground), where the famous Barbados Turf Club race meeting is held. In the Military Detention Barracks (1853) to the NE the *Barbados Museum houses extensive collections on the natural history, culture and history of the island. Particularly interesting are an exhibition illustrating the history of sugar-growing and a library containing old maps and documents on the West Indies.

Bridgetown to Ragged Point (round trip 31 miles/ 50 km). – Leave Bridgetown on Highway 7, which runs SE through the suburbs of HASTINGS, MARINE GARDENS and ROCKLEY, with magnificent hotels and beautiful beaches.

3 miles/5 km: **Oistins**, a small fishing village charmingly situated in the bay of the same name. It has an old inn, Ye Mermaid's Inn, in which the charter of Barbados was signed in 1652, requiring the royalist islanders to render strict obedience to Cromwell and the Commonwealth Parliament. – To the SE of the village, near *South Point* (the southernmost tip of Barbados), are three beaches – *Little Bay, Woman's Bay* and *Long Bay.* – Commandingly situated on a hill to the E of the village stands Christ Church parish church. In the churchyard is the legendary *Chase Vault*, noted in the 19th c. for the great "coffin mystery" (the unexplained movement of coffins within the sealed vault).

2½ miles/4 km E is *Grantley Adams International Airport*, much enlarged in 1979, and nearby an industrial estate. – From here the road continues NE, running parallel to the beautiful SE coast with its bizarre rock formations – *Pennyhole Rock, Salt Cave Point, Green Point, New Fall Cliff* – to *Crane Bay, which ranks as the most beautiful beach on the island. This was once an anchorage for cargo vessels, and there are remains of the crane used for loading and discharging them. – Farther NE is *Sam Lord's Castle, a Georgian mansion built in the early 19th c. on the foundations of an old plantation house by Samuel Hall Lord, reputed to have been a wrecker who lured ships on to the rocks and plundered them. Now a luxury hotel, the house has magnificent stucco decoration and fine period furniture. Remains of an Arawak settlement were found nearby. – In this area there are several beautiful bays and impressive rock formations. The SE tip of the island is rugged and much indented, with dangerous reefs lying just off the coast. From *Ragged Point* (lighthouse) there are rewarding walks to the many beauty-spots in the area.

4 miles/6 km W of Ragged Point on Highway 4B, on *Pollard's Plantation* (established 1628), can be seen a well-preserved sugar mill dating from about 1750. – Farther W is *Drax Hall (c. 1650), one of the finest colonial mansions on the island. A short distance S stands another fine old house, *Bentley Mansion*. – From here the road continues W to Bridgetown.

Bridgetown to Bathsheba (round trip 34 miles/ 55 km). – Leave Bridgetown on Highway 4, going E, and in 3 miles/5 km turn left into Highway 3B. Running NE, this comes in 2 miles/3 km to *St George's Church* (17th and 18th c.), which was devastated by

A bay on the Atlantic Ocean near Bathsheda (Barbados)

a hurricane in 1780; it has a fine *altarpiece by Benjamin West. – The road continues uphill to *Gun Hill*, once an important British military camp and signal station, with an imposing British *lion 10 ft/3 m high and 16 ft/5 m long hewn from a limestone outcrop in the time of Col. H. J. Wilkinson (1868). – 2 miles/3 km NE, at *St Jude's Vicarage*, is a fine 17th c. sugar mill. Near here the commandingly situated *Villa Nova* (1834), an elegant mansion set in beautiful gardens, once belonged to Sir Anthony Eden.

Farther S, Highway 4, reaches *Ashford Bird Park*. 3 miles/5 km E, near Conset Bay, is the famous *Codrington College, one of the earliest institutions of higher education in the western hemisphere, later a theological college. It was founded by Christopher Codrington (1662–1716), a native of Barbados who became Governor of the Leeward Islands. It has a fine avenue and park with tall king palms.

2½ miles/4 km NW, in a situation commanding extensive views, stands *St John's Church*, built in 1836 to replace an earlier church destroyed by a hurricane in 1831. In the churchyard is the grave of Ferdinando Palaeologus, said to be a descendant of a Byzantine emperor, who had fled from Constantinople to escape the Turks. – The road continues past the sheer *Hackleton's Cliff and descends to beautiful *Tent Bay*, on the rugged E coast. Above the bay are the magnificent *Andromeda Gardens*, with pools, cascades and a riot of tropical vegetation (orchids). – Farther N, framed in high cliffs, lies the fishing village and holiday resort of **Bathsheba**, with the best beaches on the E coast. Flying fish can often be seen here.

3 miles/5 km NW, above the panoramic East Coast Road, rise the peaks of *Chalky Mount*, noted for the ochre-colored clay which the local people fashion into artistic pottery. Farther N is the charming village of **Belleplaine**. From here the route continues S on Highway 2 past *Mount Hillaby* (1116 ft/340 m), the highest point on the island. 4½ miles/7 km farther on *Vault Road*, commemorates mysterious happenings said to have taken place in the burial vault of the Williams family. The family owned *Welchman's Hall Gully*, a short distance farther S – a rocky valley shaped by karstic action which was converted into a tropical garden in the 19th c. and later reverted to nature. It is now a nature reserve and one of the island's principal tourist attractions, noted in particular for its many caves. In one of the caves can be seen one of the largest stalagmites in the world (diameter 4 ft/121 cm). A little way S is Cole's Cave, another large cave traversed by a stream which flows into the sea in Freshwater Bay, N of Bridgetown. The cave, up to 16 ft/5 m high, divides into two some 100 yd/90 m from the entrance. A great many blind cave-dwelling crayfish live in large pools in the cave. – Nearby is the less well-known *Harrison's Cave*, which also belongs to the much ramified underground river system in this area. To the NE stands *Canefield House*, once an elegant plantation mansion. – From here Highway 2 returns to Bridgetown.

Bridgetown to North Point (round trip 37 miles/ 60 km). – Leave Bridgetown on Highway 1, which runs N along the W coast, known as the *Platinum Coast* on account of its magnificent palm-fringed beaches. This has long been a fashionable vacationers' retreat with splendid villas and luxury hotels. First comes Freshwater Bay, with the famous *Paradise Beach*, where the underground stream from Cole's Cave flows into the sea. Beyond this is *Bats

Rock Bay, off which lies the wreck of the Greek freighter "Stavronika", destroyed by fire in 1976 and, after long-drawn-out negotiations, scuttled in 1978. – Farther N, on *Holder's Hill*, above beautiful *Payne's Bay*, is a large polo ground. *Sandy Lane Bay* has one of the finest beaches on the island.

Beyond this we come to **Holetown**, named after its small natural harbor, where the first British settlers landed in 1625. Plantation Fort, or Fort St James (18th c.), is now the police station. St James's Church, built in 1872 to replace an earlier wooden church, has a fine 17th c. font. An obelisk erected in 1905 commemorates an earlier English landing supposed (erroneously) to have taken place in 1605. To the E of the village is *Porters, a fine 17th c. mansion set in beautiful grounds which belonged for 200 years to the influential Alleyne family and was several times enlarged. – In the surrounding area are other old mansions and sumptuous villas, many of them with equally magnificent gardens.

The road continues N past *Alleyne's Bay* and *Gibbs Bay* to *Mullins Bay*, above which is the old plantation mansion of *Mullins Mill* (1831). The three oldest rooms in the house, furnished with valuable antiques, give some impression of life in Barbados in earlier days.

Farther N, beyond *Goding's Bay*, is **Speightstown**, the second largest place on the island and once an important sugar port. Its links with the English port of Bristol earned it the name of "Little Bristol". In the Manse (17th c.), believed to be the oldest building in the town, services were held after the church was destroyed by a hurricane in 1831. There are only scanty remains of Denmark Fort (18th c.).

EXCURSION from Speightstown. – First N to *Six Men's Bay*, once an important whaling station, well fortified, as the many cannon still show. – Then on Highway 1B to the picturesque **North Point**, with attractive vacation houses. Beautiful beaches – *Horseshoe Bay*, *Cluff's Bay* and *Archer's Bay* to the W, *Animal Flower Bay* to the E. There are impressive underwater caverns which can be reached only by scuba divers and also marvelous sea caves, the most popular of which is the *Animal Flower Cave*, accessible only on foot; it is named after the sea anemones which live in pools on the rocks and in the cave. Round trip 7½ miles/12 km.

From Six Men's Bay Highway 1C leads to *River Bay*, a quiet and very beautiful beach on the NE coast . Round trip 4½ miles/12 km.

From Speightstown Highway 1 runs E, coming in 3 miles/5 km to *Farley Hill*, a finely situated mansion offering extensive views.

The house was built in 1861 on the occasion of a visit to Barbados by Prince Alfred, Duke of Edinburgh, and has been visited on several occasions by members of the royal family. It was used as the setting of the film "Island in the Sun". After being damaged by fire in 1965 it was taken over by the government.

Farley Hill lies in the *Farley Hill National Park*, in the northern part of the very beautiful *Scotland District*. To the E, approached by a fine avenue of casuarina and mahogany-trees, is *Cherry Tree Hill* (850 ft/259 m), once covered with cherry-trees, from which there is a superb *view of Scotland District. Many capuchin monkeys, originally brought in from the Old World, still live on the hill.

Nearby is *Nicholas Abbey (c. 1750), one of the oldest mansions on the island, with four corner chimneys which seem a little out of place in this setting. – A few miles farther N is Pico Teneriffe, with far-ranging views of the rugged Atlantic coast.

To the S of Cherry Tree Hill stands the *Morgan Lewis Mill (17th–18th c.), the only well-preserved survivor of the numerous Dutch-style windmills built in the early days of the sugar-cane plantations by Dutch Jews from Brazil.

The road continues S, passing St Andrew's Church (18th c.). Half way between the Morgan Lewis Mill and Holetown are *Turner's Hall Woods, 45 acres of natural forest which give some idea of the island's original vegetation cover. Here too there are many monkeys. The Boiling Spring is a source of natural gas. – Then via Holetown back to Bridgetown.

Barbuda
Lesser Antilles
Windward Islands
Antigua and Barbuda

Area/ 62 sq. miles/160 sq. km.
Population: 1300.
Administrative center: St John's (on Antigua).
Vehicles travel on the left.
(i) **Antigua Department of Tourism**
   P.O. Box 363,
   St John's,
   Antigua, B.W.I.;
   tel. 20029 and 20480.
   See also Practical Information.

HOTEL. – Cocoa Point Lodge, 14 r.

RECREATION and SPORT. – Swimming and sunbathing, deep-sea fishing, scuba diving, snorkeling; shooting.

AIR SERVICES. – Irregular connections with Antigua (Coolidge International Airport) and St Kitts.

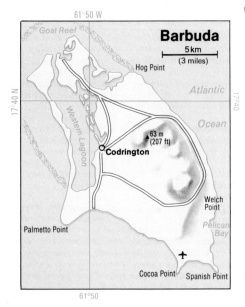

SHIPPING. – Irregular boat connections with Antigua and St Kitts.

The low and arid coral island of Barbuda, some 25 miles N of Antigua, is a paradise for scuba divers, with some 50 or 60 wrecks lying off its coasts, and has some excellent beaches. The inhabitants live mainly by fishing, farming and salt-working.

The chief town on the island is **Codrington** (pop. 1000), on the SE side of the Western Lagoon, which provides excellent facilities for water sports. – At the southern tip of the island is Cocoa Point Lodge, with a small airstrip. To the E is a beautiful promontory, Spanish Point. – The interior of the island and the range of hills which rise to 207 ft/63 m in the E are well stocked with game and attract many sportsmen.

See also *Antigua (and Redonda).

Bequia
See under Grenadines

Bermuda
British Crown Colony

Area/ 20½ sq. miles/53 sq. km.
Population: 54,000.
Administrative center: Hamilton.
Vehicles travel on the left.
(i) **Bermuda Department of Tourism,**
   Old Town Hall,
   Hamilton 5–23,
   Bermuda;
   tel. (809) 292 0023.
   Visitors' Service Bureau,
   King's Square,
   St George's,
   Bermuda;
   tel. 7 1642.
   Visitors' Service Bureau,
   Ferry Terminal,
   Hamilton,
   Bermuda;
   tel. 5 1480.
   Visitors' Service Bureau,
   Civil Air Terminal,
   Kindley Airport,
   Bermuda;
   tel. 3 0736.
   See also Practical Information.

HOTELS. – ST GEORGE'S: *Holiday Inn, 900 b., SP, T, beach, golf; etc. – HAMILTON PARISH: *Castle Harbour Hotel, Beach and Golf Club, 800 b., SP, T, beach, golf; *Grotto Bay Beach Hotel and Tennis Club, 494 b., SP,

Yacht harbor, Hamilton, Bermuda

T, beach; etc. – FLATTS VILLAGE: *Coral Island Hotel*, 201 b., SP; *Palmetto Bay Hotel and Cottages*, 116 b., SP, beach; etc. – PEMBROKE PARISH: **Bermudiana Hotel*, 751 b., SP, T, beach; **Hamilton Princess Hotel*, 1000 b., SP, beach, golf; *Rosedon*, 103 b., SP; *Sherwood's Hotel*, 223 b., SP, T; *Waterloo House*, 75 b., SP, T, beach; etc. – PAGET PARISH: **Elbow Beach Hotel*, 883 b., SP, T, beach; **Inverurie*, 420 b., SP, T, beach; *Glencoe*, 65 b., *Harmony Hall Hotel*, 212 b., SP, beach; *Newstead*, 120 b., SP; *White Sands Hotel and Cottages*, 100 b., SP, beach; etc. – WARWICK PARISH: **Belmont Hotel and Golf Club*, 414 b., SP, T, beach, golf; **Mermaid Beach Club*, 237 b., SP, beach; etc. – SOUTHAMPTON PARISH: **Sonesta Beach Hotel*, 937 b., SP, T, beach; **Southampton Princess Hotel*, 1500 b., SP, T, golf, beach; *Pompano Beach Club*, 158 b., SP, beach; *Reefs Beach Club*, 142 b., SP, T, beach; etc. – Many GUEST-HOUSES and HOLIDAY APARTMENTS. – CAMPING: limited facilities.

RESTAURANTS. – ST GEORGE'S: *Carriage House*, Somers Wharf; *White Horse Tavern*, King's Square. – HAMILTON PARISH: *Plantation Club*, at Leamington Caves; *Tom Moore's Tavern*, in Walsingham Bay. – PEMBROKE PARISH: *Ding Ho*, Pitt's Bay Road (Chinese and Polynesian). – HAMILTON: **Lobster Pot*, Bermudiana Road (fish); **Penthouse Club*, Front Street (French); **Waterfront*, on harbour (fish); *Fisherman's Reef*, Burnaby Street; *Gay Venture*, floating restaurant at Albuoy's Point (British and Scandinavian); *Harbour Front Club*, Front Street; *Hog Penny*, Burnaby Street (British and German); *Horse and Buggy*, Queen Street; *Rum-Runners*, Front Street. – PAGET PARISH: *Four Ways Inn*, Middle Road. – SOUTHAMPTON PARISH: *Henry VIII*, South Road; *Beach House*, Horseshoe Bay; and many others.

NIGHT CLUBS. – DEVONSHIRE PARISH: *Clayhouse Inn*, North Shore. – HAMILTON: *Forty Thieves*, Front Street.

DANCING. – PEMBROKE PARISH: *Robin Hood*, Richmond Road. – HAMILTON: *2001 Discothèque*, Bermudiana Road.

SHOPPING. – The central area of Hamilton is rated one of the best shopping centers in the western hemisphere. Front Street, Queen Street and Reid Street are lined with stores selling textiles (Shetland woollens, cashmeres), perfume, crystal, porcelain, cameras and watches of the highest quality, rare antiques and much else to tempt the visitor.

> **Bermuda swizzle**, the Bermudian national drink, is a refreshing cocktail of various kinds of rum and fruit juices, served ice-cold.

PUBLIC HOLIDAYS and EVENTS. – *New Year's Day*, with performances by gombey dancers. – **Bermuda Festival* (January–February), a festival of music, dance and drama, with artists of international reputation. – *Bermuda Bridge Tournament* (February), an international event. – *Annual Invitation Amateur Golf Championship for Men* (March), on Port Royal course, Southampton. – *Bermuda Homes and Garden Tours* (Wednesday afternoons, March–May). – *College Weeks* (March), with a full program of events for visiting college students. – *Good Friday*, with traditional kite-flying. – *Easter Sunday*, with many open-air events. – *Agricultural Exhibition* (last week in April), in Paget Botanical Gardens. – *Beating of Retreat* by the Bermuda Regiment in Front Street, Hamilton (April–October, last Wednesday in month). – *Peppercorn Ceremony* (Last week in April), parade by Bermuda Regiment in King's Square, St George's. – *International Race Week* (April–May), international sailing regatta. – *Commonwealth Day* (last week in May), with dinghy races in St George's Harbour and a marathon race from Hamilton to Somerset. – *Sandys Flower Show* (May), in Springfield, Somerset. – *All-Breed Club of Bermuda Dog Show* (May), in Paget Botanical Gardens. – *Queen's Birthday* (second week in June), with military parade in Front Street, Hamilton. – *Bermuda Open Golf Championship* (June), on Port Royal course. – ***Newport-Bermuda Ocean Yacht Race* (June in even-numbered years), one of the world's great yacht races, from Newport (Rhode Island, USA) to Hamilton. – *Blue Water Cruising Race* (June in odd-numbered years), yacht race from Marion (Mass., USA) to Bermuda. – *Biennial Multi-Hull Race* (end of June in odd-numbered years), yacht race from Newport (R.I.) to Bermuda. – *Annual Bermuda International Light Tackle Tournament* (July), deep-sea fishing competition. – *Cup Match Cricket Festival and Somers Day* (end of July/beginning of August), a major and very colorful occasion, with cricket championship and folk displays, including gombey dancing. – *Tennis Tournaments* (August), in Pembroke Tennis Stadium. – *Belmont Open Golf Tournament* (September), organized by Belmont Hotel, Warwick. – *Bermuda Open Tennis Tournament* (September), in Pembroke Tennis Stadium. – *Convening of Parliament* (October), ceremonial opening of the parliamentary session. – *Remembrance Day* (second week in November), with military parade and laying of wreaths on Cenotaph. – *Castle Harbour Pro-Am and Beefeater Pro-Am Tournament* (November), golf tournament on Port Royal course. – *Bermuda Invitational Four-Ball Championship for Men* (November), on Port Royal course. – *Bermuda Kennel Club Championship Dog Show* (November), in Paget Botanical Gardens. – *Conservation Sunday* (November), special service in Bermuda Cathedral, splendidly decorated for the occasion. – *Bermuda at Home* (December–March), a program of special events during the winter season. – *Goodwill Golf Tournament* (beginning of December), the year's biggest golfing event. – *Christmas Pantomime* (December), in Hamilton City Hall Theatre. – *Christmas Concert* (December), in Hamilton. – *Carol Singing* (December), at the flagstaff in Front Street, Hamilton. – *Christmas Eve*, with candle procession in Bermuda Cathedral and midnight mass in St Theresa's Church. – *Christmas Day*. – *Boxing Day* (December 26), with colorful parades of gombey dancers.

Gombey, related to the Caribbean *goombay*, is an Afro-Bermudian dance whose origins go back to the days of slavery. It is danced by colored dancers wearing brightly hued masks and costumes, usually to celebrate some festival or other special occasion.

RECREATION and SPORT. – *Golf; *sailing, motor-boating, deep-sea fishing, water-skiing, wind-surfing, scuba diving, snorkeling, swimming and sunbathing; tennis, cycling, walking.

AIR SERVICES. – Direct connections with London (UK), Baltimore, Boston, Chicago, Detroit, Philadelphia, New York, Washington (USA), Halifax, Montreal, Toronto (Canada), Nassau (Bahamas), Antigua, Barbados and Port of Spain (Trinidad).

SHIPPING. – Cruise ships weekly April–November from and to Nassau (Bahamas) and New York, occasionally from Baltimore, Boston, Charleston, Miami, Norfolk and Philadelphia (USA) and Southampton (UK).

Bermuda – the "still-vexed Bermoothes" of Shakespeare's "Tempest" – is an isolated archipelago of more than 150 islands and islets of varying size, with a total land area of some 20 sq. miles/52 sq. km, lying in the western Atlantic in latitude 32°18′ N and longitude 64°46′ W. The islands are the highest parts of a mass of limestone capping a substructure of volcanic rock, with a fringe of old consolidated sand-dunes and banks of coral. They are the most northerly coral islands in the world, thanks to a climate favored by the Gulf Stream. Formerly notorious as the "Isles of the Devil" on account of the reefs which wrecked so many ships (over 120 wrecks recorded) and provided a rich booty for beachcombers, they are now a fashionable and exclusive resort area – thanks not only to their healthy climate but also to a fiscal system which makes them an attractive tax haven.

The "**Bermuda Triangle**" is the triangular area of sea bounded by Bermuda, Puerto Rico and a point in the Gulf of Mexico in which many ships and aircraft have been lost – as a result, some people maintain, of unknown and mysterious forces.

Lying 600 miles/965 km from Cape Hatteras on the North American mainland, the group of islands extends over a distance of some 22 miles/35 km from NE to SW, with an average width of $1\frac{1}{4}$ miles/2 km. The intricately patterned coastlines of the islands – a maze of inlets enclosed by tiny islets, arms of sea, peninsulas, sandbanks, coral reefs, outlying rocks and rose-pink beaches bounded by striking rock formations – are evidence, like the varying levels of the sea bottom and the old beach lines, of a complex geological development. As a result of karstic action

Marley Beach, Bermuda

Passenger liners in Hamilton harbor

the islands have no surface watercourses of any size, but by the same token they have magnificent caves and underground caverns, often containing pools of salt water.

CLIMATE. – Bermuda owes its maritime subtropical climate to the influence of the *Gulf Stream*. The average annual temperature is 70.2 °F/21.2 °C, the average summer maximum 89.8 °F/32.1 °C. the average winter minimum 46.9 °F/8.3 °C. The average humidity of the air is about 77%. The rainfall is distributed evenly over the year, with an annual average of 59 in./1500 mm; the upper and lower limits are on average, about 91 in./2300 mm and 39 in./1000 mm. Two seasons can be distinguished, a summer lasting from April to November and a winter lasting from December to March. The prevailing winds are southwesterly, occasionally interrupted during the winter by strong N and northeasterly winds. Very rarely the islands are affected by offshoots of the dreaded hurricanes which travel NE from the Caribbean area.

varied, including two which are peculiar to Bermuda, chameleon-like lizards and whistling frogs. The steeply shelving sea bottom, varied submarine relief and exceptionally clean sea water provide very favorable habitats for a wide range of sea creatures

HISTORY. – The reference to Bermuda in Peter Martyr's "Legatio Babylonica" (1511) shows that the islands were known at the beginning of the 16th c. Hernando de Oviedo, who sailed close to Bermuda in 1515 ascribed the discovery of the islands to his fellow-countryman Juan Bermúdez, who probably passed this way in 1503. The islands were granted to Hernando Camelo by Philip II of Spain in 1527. They were described in 1593 by an Englishman named Henry May who was driven ashore here, and ten years later by the Spanish captain Diego Ramírez. In 1609 the "Sea Venture", flagship of the second expedition sent to America by the Virginia Company of London under the command of Admiral Sir George Somers,

Temperatures in Bermuda

Day Temperatures[1] (Monthly Averages)

January	68 °F (20.0 °C)
February	67 °F (19.4 °C)
March	68 °F (20.0 °C)
April	71 °F (21.7 °C)
May	75 °F (23.9 °C)
June	80 °F (26.7 °C)
July	85 °F (29.4 °C)
August	86 °F (30.0 °C)
September	84 °F (28.9 °C)
October	79 °F (26.1 °C)
November	74 °F (23.3 °C)
December	70 °F (21.1 °C)

[1]Night temperatures are roughly 10 °F (5.5 °C) lower

Bermuda Cathedral, Hamilton

PLANT and ANIMAL LIFE. – The reddish-brown soils of Bermuda, composed of shell and coral sand, support a varied subtropical vegetation, the best known native species being the *Bermuda cedar (unfortunately much reduced in numbers by disease and over-felling), the Bermuda iris, the dwarf palm and the maidenhair fern. The very common *Easter lily, the national plant of Bermuda, was brought in from Japan by a clergyman. – Animal species are also

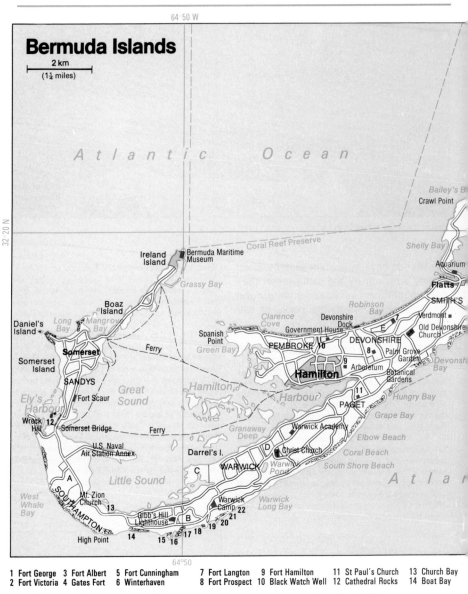

Bermuda Islands

2 km
(1¼ miles)

1 Fort George	3 Fort Albert	5 Fort Cunningham	7 Fort Langton	9 Fort Hamilton	11 St Paul's Church	13 Church Bay
2 Fort Victoria	4 Gates Fort	6 Winterhaven	8 Fort Prospect	10 Black Watch Well	12 Cathedral Rocks	14 Boat Bay

A Port Royal Golf Course	C Riddell's Bay Golf Course	E Queens Park Golf Course
B Princess Golf Course	D Belmont Golf Course	F Mid Ocean Golf Course

was wrecked off St George's Island during a violent storm – providing the theme of Shakespeare's "Tempest". The survivors built two new ships, the "Deliverance" and the "Patience", and sailed on to Virginia a year later. Sir George Somers, however, returned a few weeks later to Bermuda, where he died shortly afterwards. The Virginia Company took possession of the islands, and in 1612 a further 60 English settlers were sent out, together with the first Governor. Soon afterwards the islands' capital of St George's was founded, and only four years later the first slaves were brought in – mainly Africans, and later also Indians from North America, Scottish prisoners and Irishmen. The first meeting of the island parliament was held in 1620.

Thereafter the economy of the islands flourished, primarily through shipbuilding and maritime trade. The Turks Islands in the West Indies were colonized from Bermuda. In 1775 gunpowder was stolen from a camp in St George's for the use of the American rebels,

in return for which the Bermudians received food and a letter of thanks from George Washington. In the meantime the islands had become a base for privateers and pirates – a consequence of the flourishing trade in piracy which was carried on in the West Indies with British government sanction. The war between Britain and the United States in 1812–15 also benefited the Bermudians, and the burning of Washington in 1814 was initiated from Bermuda.

In 1815 Hamilton replaced St George's as capital of the islands. Slavery was abolished in 1834. The Hamilton Hotel, of which the foundation stone had been laid in 1852, was opened in 1863, marking the first step in the development of Bermuda's rapidly growing tourist trade. The first "tourists" to come in any numbers, however, were blockade-runners, spies and secessionists during the American Civil War. In the second half of the 19th c. an export-oriented agriculture was developed with the help of peasant settlers brought in from the Azores. In 1872 a steamer

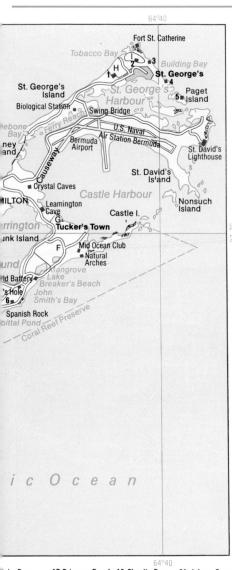

64°40

Fort St. Catherine
Tobacco Bay
H
3 Building Bay
St. George's
4
St. George's
Island
St. George's
Harbour
5 Paget
Island
Biological Station
Swing Bridge
ebone
Bay
Ferry Reach
U.S. Naval
Air Station Bermuda
ney
and
Bermuda
Airport
St. David's
Lighthouse
Causeway
Crystal Caves
St. David's
Island
ILTON
Leamington
Cave
Castle Harbour
Nonsuch
Island
32°20
rrington
Tucker's Town
Castle I.
unk Island
F
G
und
Mid Ocean Club
Natural
Arches
Mangrove
Lake
ld Battery
Breaker's Beach
's Hole
John
6
Smith's Bay
Spanish Rock
oittal Pond
Coral Reef Preserve

i c   O c e a n

64°40

| inky Bay | 17 Princess Beach | 19 Chaplin Bay | 21 Jobson Cove |
| ast Whale Bay | 18 Horseshoe Bay | 20 Stonehole Bay | 22 Frank's Bay |

astle Harbour Golf Course ose Hill Golf Course I Holiday Inn Golf Course

service began to operate between Bermuda and New York. During the Boer War (1900–02) some of the smaller islands were used for the internment of prisoners from South Africa. The first yacht race from Newport, Rhode Island, to Bermuda was held in 1906.

After the First World War there was a considerable expansion of hotel accommodation on the islands, and during the Prohibition years of the 1920s there was a large increase in the number of visitors from the United States. In 1930 Bermuda's agriculture was thrown into a grave crisis by US restrictions on imports, and the whole economy of the islands had to be reoriented. In 1931 the first trains ran on the Bermuda Railway – a short-lived enterprise, for it was sold to British Guiana in 1947. The first flying boat of Imperial Airways (now British Airways) arrived in 1937.

During the Second World War the United States built a military base in Bermuda, and a number of important military conferences were held here after the war. The first political party was founded in 1963, and five years later a new constitution gave Bermuda control of its domestic affairs. In 1972 the Bermuda dollar was given parity with the US dollar. The way is now being prepared for complete independence.

ADMINISTRATION. – The government of Bermuda, the oldest British colony responsible for its own affairs, is based on the British model with the Governor as representative of the Crown. The Cabinet, of 12 members, is headed by the Premier, who comes from the largest party in the House of Assembly (the lower house of Parliament), which has 40 members elected by popular vote. The 11 members of the Legislative Council (the upper house) are appointed by the Governor (5), the Prime Minister (4) and the leader of the Opposition (2). Bills brought in by the House of Assembly are reviewed by the Legislative Council and submitted by them to the Governor, who promulgates the legislation. The islands are divided for administrative purposes into nine parishes of roughly the same size – St George's, Hamilton, Smith's, Devonshire, Pembroke, Paget, Warwick, Southampton and Sandys.

POPULATION. – The islands have a population of some 54,000, giving a density of about 2634 to the sq. mile (1019 to the sq km). Some 40% of the population are whites, predominantly of European descent; the majority are colored, most of them the descendants of African slaves. Illiteracy and unemployment are practically unknown on the islands. Some 40 different churches and religious communities are active in Bermuda, the African Methodist, Anglican and Roman Catholic churches having the largest numbers of adherents. – The two principal settlements are the towns of Hamilton and St George's, but their density of population is little greater than that of the surrounding areas.

ECONOMY. – The economy of Bermuda was formerly based on its cedar forests, which yielded timber for shipbuilding. It developed a flourishing maritime trade, particularly during periods of political crisis, and until 1930 also exported vegetables to the United States. Bermuda has never had any heavy industry, and still has little light industry. In consequence most goods must be imported, giving rise to a relatively high cost of living. The main source of revenue has long been tourism, which was promoted at an early stage by the building of hotels and the introduction of good shipping and later air services. In 1980 some 610,000 visitors came to Bermuda, mostly from the United States and Canada, with a small proportion from Western Europe, and are conservatively estimated to have spent about 210 million Bermuda dollars. As a result of special fiscal and economic legislation, which have given the islands the name of a tax paradise, many international companies are registered in Bermuda, representing its second largest source of employment. Significant contributions are also made to the economy by the British and American bases in the islands. In terms of living standards and income levels Bermuda takes a high place among the countries of the world.

ARCHITECTURE. –The pastel-colored houses with their whitewashed stepped roofs – some of them one or two centuries old – fit harmoniously into the landscape. Their builders had the advantage of the easily worked calcareous sandstone which underlies the sandy soil and becomes extremely hard when exposed to the air. Thus it is possible to saw thin stone slabs, which are then laid in stepped formation on the

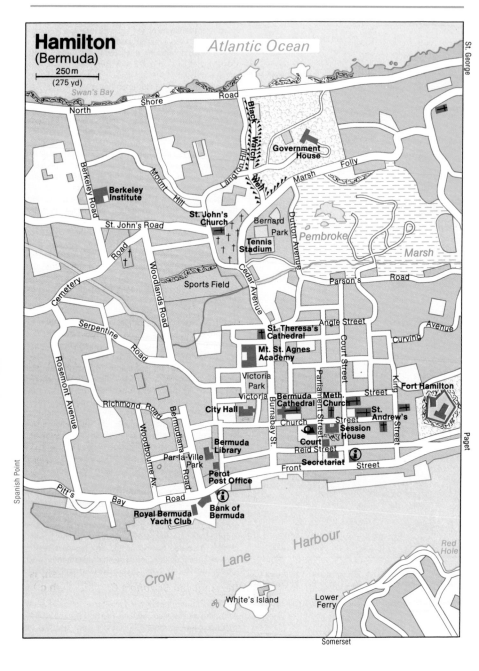

cedarwood rafters so as to collect rainwater and direct it into special tanks. Above the windows are projections also designed to collect water. The tall chimneys running up the outside of the walls carry the smoke well above the houses. Many houses still have the old "butteries" – rooms designed for coolness, with slit windows and raised floors, now used as living rooms. The local type of garden gate known as a "moon gate" was an idea brought back by sea-captains on the China run.

*Hamilton (sea level; pop. 3000), founded in 1793 and laid out on the pattern of a British colonial town, was chosen as the new capital of the islands in 1815 on account of its central situation,

and soon became a center of the tourist trade.

SIGHTS. – Flanking the busy **harbor** is *Front Street, with numerous luxury shops, many of them in buildings dating from Hamilton's earliest days. At the W end of the street stands the modern seven-story building of the *Bank of Bermuda*, and beyond it the famous *Royal Bermuda Yacht Club* (1844), the rendezvous of international celebrities. A little way N, in Par-la-Ville Park, the former residence of W. B. Perot (1818–62), the colony's first postmaster, now houses the well-stocked *Bermuda Library* (with a collection of newspapers since 1887) and the *Bermuda Historical Society Museum* (material on the history of the islands, coins, silver, cedarwood furniture, ship models, etc.).

In Queen Street is the restored *Perot Post Office* (1842), in which Perot produced the early Bermuda stamps, now much sought after. In Church Street, to the NE, stands the fine **City Hall** (1960), with a theater, art gallery and conference hall. A weathervane on top of the tower takes the form of the "Sea Venture". In front of the building is an attractive garden, with fountains. Higher up, to the E, stands *Bermuda Cathedral, built between 1886 and 1911 on the site of the earlier Holy Trinity Church which was burned down in 1884. The present neo-Gothic building incorporates material from Scotland, Normandy, Nova Scotia and Indiana. It has three notable stained-glass windows, the Lefroy Window on the N side of the nave and the War Memorial Window and Reid Window in the S porch. – A little way E is the 19th c. *Methodist Church.*

Session House, Hamilton

Opposite the Methodist Church, on the highest point in the town, is the **Session House**, with a façade in Italian Renaissance style and the *Jubilee Clock Tower*, built in honour of Queen Victoria's Jubilee. This is the seat of the *House of Assembly* (the lower house of Parliament) and the *Supreme Court*. Lower down the former *Post Office* (1869), is also occupied by the Supreme Court. Facing it, to

Cabinet Building, Hamilton

the SE, is the **Cabinet Building** (Secretariat, 1838), meeting-place of the *Legislative Council* (the upper house of Parliament). In the Council Chamber is the fine cedarwood Throne (1642) on which the Governor sits. In front of the Cabinet Building stands the *Cenotaph* (1920), a smaller version of the Cenotaph in Whitehall, London. Lower down, in Front Street (to the SE), is the *Old Town Hall* (1794), one of the oldest buildings in the town, now occupied by the Department of Tourism.

On the E side of the town rises the imposing *Fort Hamilton, a massive Victorian stronghold with a maze of underground passages. – Below City Hall, to the N, lies *Victoria Park*, with fine old trees. On the N side of the park stands the venerable *Mount St Agnes Academy* (1889), and above this, in Cedar Avenue, *St Theresa's Cathedral (R.C.), a handsome building in Spanish style erected in 1931. Some 500 yd/457 m N, outside the town in Pembroke parish, is the Anglican *St John's Church* (19th c.), adjoining the large *Tennis Stadium*. On *Mount Langton*, to the NE, stands *Government House, a Victorian mansion in a magnificent subtropical park; it is the Governor's residence and a guesthouse for distinguished visitors. Below this, to the W is the *Black Watch Well*, a deep shaft dug by the well-known Scottish regiment during a severe drought in 1849.

SURROUNDINGS of Hamilton. – **To Spanish Point**: Take *Pitt's Bay Road, which runs W through the exclusive hotel district, including the *Bermudiana Hotel* (1924) and the *Hamilton Princess Hotel* (1885). 2 miles/3 km farther NW, on Clarence Hill, is *Admiralty House* (19th c.), famous for its many underground passages and cellars. On the coast below lies the sheltered *Clarence Cove*, the subject of many tales and legends. ¾ mile/1 km farther W we come to *Spanish Point*, where, on the evidence of numerous finds made here, the Spanish captain Diego

Replica of the "Deliverance", St George's

*replica of the "Deliverance", which was built in 1610 to take the shipwrecked crew of the "Sea Venture" on to America. In *King's Square*, the town's picturesque main square (flagstaff, cannon, pillory, stocks), stands the *Town Hall* (1782). To the W is *Somers Wharf*, beautifully restored, with shops and restaurants. The *Carriage Museum*, in Water Street houses well-preserved examples of the horse-drawn carriages formerly used on the islands. Diagonally across from this is *Tucker House* (1711), an exceptionally fine example of Bermudian architecture which was the residence (1775–1800) of the Colonial Secretary, Henry Tucker.

The *Drawing Room* of Tucker House contains elegant 18th c. furniture of mahogany and Bermuda cedarwood. In the *Dining Room* is a large Cuban mahogany table. The cupboard and four-poster bed in the *Large Bedroom* date from about 1760. In the *Nursery* are a very fine secretaire (*c.* 1750) and a cradle, both of cedarwood. The *Silver Room* displays the Tucker family silver, with their coat of arms. The old *Kitchen* to the rear once provided a place of refuge for Joseph Hayne Rainey (1832–87), the first black member of the US House of Representatives (elected 1870). The basement was once occupied by the family slaves.

Ramírez is believed to have landed in 1603. Outside the harbor are the remains of what was in the 19th c. the largest floating dock in the world.

St George's (sea level; pop. 2000), the oldest continuously inhabited British settlement outside Britain, occupies a picturesque and sheltered site on the most northerly of the Bermuda islands, surrounded by a number of forts. The historic core of the town is well preserved. The development of St George's, which was the chief place in the islands from 1612 onwards, was brought to a halt when the capital was transferred to Hamilton in 1815, and began to recover its position only with the development of the tourist trade.

SIGHTS. – On the little *Ordnance Island*, where the cruise ships put in, is a faithful

Higher up, to the NW, is Duke of York Street, with the venerable *Ebenezer Methodist Church* (1841), overlooked by the pastel-colored building which was formerly *St George's Hotel* (Rose Hill Golf Club). Farther W is the *Opera* (19th c.), and below this, to the S, *Penno's Wharf*, which is also used by cruise ships.

St Peter's Church, St George's

Somers Wharf, St George's

Fort St Catherine, St George's Island

To the N of King's Square is the charming *St Peter's Church (1713), successor to the earliest Anglican church in the western hemisphere. It is a typically Bermudian building of calcareous sandstone and cedarwood.

In the INTERIOR are a beautiful cedarwood altar (1624) and a 15th c. font with a handsome silver basin presented by Governor Browne (1782). The magnificent communion silver was presented by King William III. – The western part of the interesting churchyard adjoining the church was formerly reserved for slaves.

The former Globe Hotel (1698), opposite the church, a center of Confederate activity during the American Civil War, houses the *Confederate Museum*, with many relics of that period. Higher up to the NW, in Queen Street, is *Stuart Hall* (1706), a handsome colonial building which now contains the Municipal Library. Farther N the Queen-Anne-style *Old Rectory* (1703) was once the home of a reformed pirate who rose to become naval judge. Above this, on Turkey Hill, stands the *A. M. E. Church* (19th c.), SE of which, in Governor's Alley, is the little *Salvation Army Hall* (19th c.), and farther S the *Church Roslyn Ruins*, an unfinished 19th c. church. – Duke of Kent Street leads S to the narrow Featherbed Alley, in which, housed in a building of 1725, can be found the *St George's Historical Society Museum*, with a very interesting collection of material on the history of the islands. In the adjoining *Print Shop* is a 17th c. printing press, still in working order. To the SE, in Duke of York Street,

lies the quiet little *Somers Garden*, with an obelisk commemorating Sir George Somers. Opposite this, to the S, is *State House* (1619), the oldest government building of its kind in the western hemisphere. A little way W is the *Bridge House Gallery* (exhibitions of work by local artists).

SURROUNDINGS of St George's. – On the N side of the town is *Gunpowder Cavern*, an 18th c. munition store with a maze of underground passages. It was from here that gunpowder was stolen in 1775 and shipped to the American rebels from Tobacco Bay, to the N. On the hill above are the remains of *Fort Victoria* and *Fort Albert* (19th c.), now in the grounds of the Holiday Inn. On the coast below lies *Gates Bay*, with a beautiful beach. On the northernmost tip of the island stands the well-preserved 18th c. *Fort St Catherine*, the largest fort in Bermuda, which contains interesting displays illustrating the history of the islands (diorama, wax museum) and reproductions of the British crown jewels. On the eastern

State House, St George's

tip of St George's Island *Alexandra's Battery* (18th c.) commands *Buildings Bay*, in which the survivors of the wrecked "Sea Venture" built the "Patience" and the "Deliverance" which were to take them on their way to Virginia. Farther E is the little *Gates Fort* (reconstructed), one of the oldest defensive works on the islands.

To the W of the town, on a hill with extensive views, is *Fort George* (18th–19th c.), now a weather and signal station, beyond which is a golf-course. – To the SW is the little settlement of **Wellington**, situated on a small peninsula in the picturesque fjord-like *Mullet Bay*, whose development of which into a busy yacht harbor began as long ago as 1865. – Farther W, in Ferry Reach, near the *Swing Bridge* (1864), is the **Bermuda Biological Station**, an internationally known center of marine biological research which was established here in 1931, on the basis of an agreement originally reached in 1903 between the Bermuda Natural History Society, Harvard University and New York University.

The Swing Bridge leads on to *St David's Island*, most of which is occupied by **Bermuda Airport** and the *US Naval Air Station*, established during the Second World War. On the highest point in the eastern part of the island is *St David's Lighthouse* (1879), from which extensive views may be enjoyed. To the N, on the eastern slopes of *Skinner's Hill*, is the beautiful **Great Head National Park**, with *St David's Battery* (19th c.) and the rugged *Great Head*. To the N, above Red Hole Bay, are remains of the *Old Fort* (18th c.).

Hamilton to St George's (round trip 22 miles/ 3 km). – Leave Hamilton, going E, and continue along Foot of Crow Lane to Berry Hill, with the *King Edward VII Memorial Hospital* and the **Botanical Gardens** (1898). Here can be seen some of the native plants which have now become rare, in particular Bermuda cedars, dwarf palms (palmettos) and junipers. There are also many species brought in by settlers, including Surinam cherries, bottle gourds, rubber trees, paw-paws, hibiscus, oleander and bougainvillea. There is a special garden for the blind. In the middle of the

gardens is *Camden House*, an 18th c. mansion which now houses a museum of horticulture, with outbuildings in which arrowroot used to be prepared. – To the S lies *Hungry Bay*, a small and sheltered natural yacht harbor. To the N is a beautiful *Arboretum*, with rare trees, dominated by the 19th c. *Fort Prospect*, which was occupied by British garrison forces until 1958.

¾ mile/1 km NE of the Botanical Gardens stands *Christ Church* (mid 19th c.), in Early English style. Nearby *Old Devonshire Church* (1716) was built of the local limestone and cedarwood in the technique of the old shipwrights. The present building is the successor to an earlier church which was the scene in 1673 of a dramatic confrontation between Quakers and Puritans. ¾ mile/1 km farther S, in South Road, is the large *Palm Grove*, with beautiful gardens and an aviary of tropical birds. A short distance SE, above Devonshire Bay (fine beach), we find the *Old Fort*, a small 17th c. defensive work. 1¼ miles/2 km NE, on *Collector's Hill*, *Verdmont House*, an elegantly appointed 18th c. mansion is now a mansion. ¾ mile/1 km farther E we come to the pretty *St Mark's Church* (19th c.). To the E, lower down, lies *Spittal Pond*, a well-known bird sanctuary. *Spanish Rock* on the coast has an inscription which is thought to have been carved by a 16th c. Spanish navigator. Nearby is *Jeffrey's Hole*, a curious rock formation. – Continuing W along South Road, past *Albuoy's Point*, we come in another ¾ mile/ 1 km to the 17th c. *Winterhaven Farm Cottage* (restored).

A short distance N, at the SE corner of HARRINGTON SOUND, is the *Devil's Hole*, originally a sea cave the roof of which has fallen in; it is now used for rearing fish and turtles. – ¾ mile/1 km NE, on Mangrove Lake, the *North Nature Reserve* has interesting plant and animal life. Nearby, on the Atlantic coast, is the *Old Battery*, one of the oldest structures in Tucker's Town. To the NE extends the magnificent *Mid-Ocean Golf Course*, laid out by Charles McDonald, the father of American golf, which belongs to the exclusive **Mid-Ocean Golf Club**, founded during the boom years of the 1920s. Leading international statesmen have played on this course during high-level conferences in Bermuda. On the beach are the *Natural Arches*, spectacular rock formations.

To the N, on the tongue of land, fringed by beautiful beaches and picturesque coves, which bounds the S side of CASTLE HARBOUR, lies **Tucker's Town**, originally a settlement founded by Governor Daniel Tucker in the 17th c. which failed to prosper. With its magnificent villas, yacht harbors and beaches, it is now one of the world's most exclusive residential areas. – Offshore, to the E, are *Castle Island*, named after its ruined 17th c. fort, and *Nonsuch Island*, now a bird sanctuary. – To the NW stands the *Castle Harbour Hotel*, with beautiful gardens, a golf-course and other sports facilities. The *Shark's Hole*, an impressive sea cave at the E corner of Harrington Sound, can be entered only by water. ¾ mile/1 km N is *Leamington Cave*, with rocks ranging in hue from yellow to orange and a massive stalagmite rising out of a small lagoon. In *Walsingham Bay*, a short distance farther N, **Tom Moore's Tavern**, was once the haunt of the 19th c. Irish poet; in front of it is the calabash-tree which he celebrated in a poem. – ¾ mile/1 km W, on the N side of Harrington Sound, stands the picturesquely situated *Holy Trinity Church* (1623). Above it is an 18th c. mansion, *Mount Wyndham*, once the residence of a British admiral, where the 1812 attack on Washington in which the White House was burned down was planned. A little way farther N are the *Perfume Factory* and the *Bermuda Pottery*,

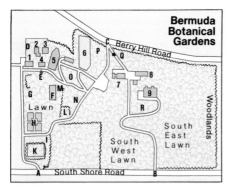

Bermuda Botanical Gardens

A South West Gate
B South Gate
C North Gate
D Rock Garden
E Economic Plants
F Garden for the Sightless
G Ficus Collection
H Formal Garden
I Juniper Collection
K Orchard

L Rose Garden
M Palm Garden
N Eastern Lawn;
   Shrub Collection
O Montrose Orchard
P Oleander Hill
Q Flower Trials;
   Conifer Collection
R Ceremonial Lawn

1 Main Office
2 Horticultural Hall (toilets)
3 Exhibition Building
4 Orchid House
5 Exotic Plant House

6 Exhibition Ring
7 Restaurant
8 Fern House; Aviary
9 Camden House

Stalactites and stalagmites, Crystal Cave

a smugglers' haven and now a popular base for scuba divers operating in the extensive *Coral Reef Preserve, offshore to the NW. 2 miles/3 km SW, on the Ocean View Golf Course above Robinson Bay, is the hexagonal Fort Langton (19th c.). ¾ mile/1 km W is Devonshire Dock, a picturesque old fishing harbor. From here the route continues by way of the Black Watch Well to **Hamilton**.

Hamilton to Somerset (round trip 29 miles/ 46 km). – Leave Hamilton, going E, passing through the select residential district of PAGET and coming in ¾ mile/1 km to the imposing *Waterville House, headquarters of the National Trust, a splendidly appointed 18th c. mansion on the S side of Foot of Crow Lane. On Trimingham Hill are many villas, some of them extremely luxurious, set in beautiful gardens.

Government Aquarium, Bermuda

where traditional local crafts are still practiced. To the E is the *Crystal Cave, with light-colored stalactites and stalagmites and a salt-water lagoon. Farther E again we find the Blue Grotto Dolphin Show, charmingly situated on the shores of Castle Harbour. To the N the Causeway (1871) leads to the airport on St David's Island and by way of the Swing Bridge to **St George's**.

The return to Hamilton is by way of the *North Shore Road, along Bailey's Bay and Shelly Bay (small sandy beach). At the SW corner of Harrington Sound stands the *Government Aquarium, one of the best of its kind in the world, with a fine collection of subtropical and tropical marine creatures ranging from the tiny seahorse to the Galapagos turtle. Associated with the Aquarium are a well-stocked *Natural History Museum, with collections illustrating the development of the Bermuda islands, and a Zoological Garden (magnificent aviary of tropical birds). – Beyond the narrow entrance to Harrington Sound is **Flatts**, once

Farther W, above the beautiful Red Hole Bay, is the late Georgian Villa Clermont, were tennis was played for the first time in the New World in 1873. To the S lies the *Paget Marsh, a nature reserve with a dense growth of vegetation. On the S side is St Paul's Church (18th and 19th c), the parish church. – Harbour Road

Southampton Princess Hotel, Bermuda

continues W to *Salt Kettle Bay*, once a center of the salt trade in *Granaway Deep*, along the W side of which are a number of islets, which provide an opportunity of "getting away from it all". Farther S, on Middle Road, we come to *Warwick Academy*, the oldest school in Bermuda, founded in 1660. Farther SW, on the edge of *Belmont Golf Course*, is *Christ Church* (1719), believed to be the oldest Presbyterian church in the British colonies. *Thorburn Hall* (1890) nearby was named after the Rev. Walter Thorburn who was minister here from 1852 to 1886. Just under ¾ mile/1 km W, beside *Warwick Pond*, stands the attractive *St Mary's Church* (1832), with a tower modeled on an Italian campanile. To the N, on Granaway Deep, the well-preserved 17th c. mansion of *Spithead was once owned by the 18th c. privateer Hezekiah Frith, whose ships captured and plundered many French and Spanish galleons, and later the property of the American playwright Eugene O'Neill. To the NW lies *Darrel's Island*, with the former airfield. – Farther W extends *Riddell's Bay Golf Course*, in Riddell's Bay, once an anchorage used by trading vessels. Beyond this, in Jew's Bay, is the old *Waterlot Inn* (17th c.); and on a hill to the S the *Southampton Princess Hotel*, the largest hotel on the island (1500 beds), situated in beautiful grounds (golf course). To the W rises *Gibb's Hill* (246 ft/75 m), one of the highest points in Bermuda, with the looming *Gibb's Hill Lighthouse* (118 ft/36 m), the first lighthouse in Bermuda (1846).

The road continues W to Frank's Bay and then NW to Evans Bay, after which it passes *Port Royal Golf Course* and comes to *White Hill*, in Sandys parish. To the E is the *US Naval Air Station Annex*, constructed on what were formerly Tucker's Island and Morgan's Island.

Wreck Hill (141 ft/43 m) to the NW was once a fortified post on which, it is said, beacons were lit to guide ships caught in a storm, which then ran aground on the reefs and were plundered by the local people. Off the W coast, where the reefs stretch far out to sea, there are 39 wrecks. To the N is the picturesque *Wreck Bay*, with a beautiful sandy beach.

Somerset Bridge, Bermuda

Middle Road leads N to *Somerset Bridge (17th c.), said to be the smallest bascule bridge (a drawbridge balanced by a counterpoise) in the world, which links Somerset Island with the main island. To the NW, in **Ely's Harbour** (named after William Eli, who settled here in 1621), are the strikingly shaped *Cathedral Rocks*. – N of the bridge is *Fort Scaur* (19th c.), now

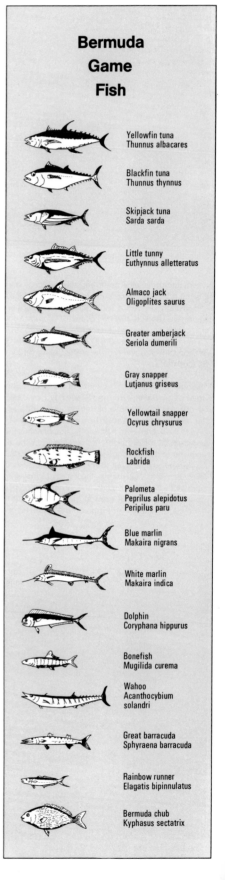

Bermuda Game Fish

Yellowfin tuna
Thunnus albacares

Blackfin tuna
Thunnus thynnus

Skipjack tuna
Sarda sarda

Little tunny
Euthynnus alletteratus

Almaco jack
Oligoplites saurus

Greater amberjack
Seriola dumerili

Gray snapper
Lutjanus griseus

Yellowtail snapper
Ocyrus chrysurus

Rockfish
Labrida

Palometa
Peprilus alepidotus
Peripilus paru

Blue marlin
Makaira nigrans

White marlin
Makaira indica

Dolphin
Coryphana hippurus

Bonefish
Mugilida curema

Wahoo
Acanthocybium
solandri

Great barracuda
Sphyraena barracuda

Rainbow runner
Elagatis bipinnulatus

Bermuda chub
Kyphasus sectatrix

part of a public park. On the coast below this, to the SE, is *Boiling Hole Grotto*, into which the sea surges noisily. – Farther N, above a pretty little bay on the W coast, stands *St James's Church* (1789), successor to an earlier church which was destroyed in a hurricane. Farther NW at *Daniel's Head* are a number of small coves and a Canadian military station. To the W lies *Long Bay*, most of which is a nature reserve (beautiful beach).

Mangrove Bay to the E is sheltered on all sides and has a number of beautiful beaches. *Mangrove Bay Wharf* is the starting-point of many deep-sea fishing expeditions. A little way S in the *Gilbert and Springfield Nature Reserve*, a former plantation which is now an open-air museum, are interesting and well-preserved 17th c. buildings, including the handsomely appointed plantation house.

The road continues N over *Watford Bridge* (1903) to Watford Island and Boaz Island, then over *Grey's Bridge* to Ireland Island, the northern part of which is occupied by the extensive installations of the former *Royal Naval Dockyard*. One of the largest of British naval dockyards, this was begun in 1809 and was constructed by several thousand slaves and forced laborers, many of whom died of yellow fever. The most interesting part is the *Floating Dock*, the largest in the world when it was built at the beginning of this century. An old Victorian fort houses the *Bermuda Maritime Musem*, with a fine collection illustrating the seafaring traditions of Bermuda, including ship models, old prints and the world-famous **Tucker Treasure*, a collection of relics and valuables from ships wrecked off Bermuda.

Part of the dockyard is now a free port which makes a significant contribution to Bermuda's economy. – At the S end of Ireland Island is the *Royal Naval Cemetery*.

The first part of the return route to Hamilton is on the same road. Soon after Frank's Bay *South Road (the coast road) branches off and runs S to the *Old Fort* (18th c.). To the E, above *Church Bay* with its beach of fine sand, is *St Anne's Church* (18th c.). The road then continues E, past the beautifully situated *Sonesta Beach Hotel*, to a series of charming little coves, with beaches of fine sand enclosed by fantastically shaped rock formations, in the area of the Rifle Range. The finest of these are *East Whale Bay*, *Horseshoe Bay*, *Chaplin Bay* and *Stonehole Bay*. Above the coast is *Warwick Camp*, built in 1870 as part of Bermuda's

Warwick Beach, Bermuda

defensive system, and which is now the headquarters of the small Bermuda Regiment. To the SE lies *Warwick Long Bay*, with a long and beautiful beach. Passing numerous hotels and recreation facilities, the road turns NE to *Saphir Bay*, with a famous beach, and on to *Coral Beach* and *Elbow Beach*, two magnificent and very popular beaches. Farther NE is *Grape Bay*, after which the road runs N to **Hamilton**.

Berry Islands
Bahama Islands
Commonwealth of the Bahamas

Area: 12 sq. miles/31 sq. km.
Population: 600.
Administrative center: Nassau (on New Providence).
Vehicles travel on the left.

(i) **Ministry of Tourism,**
P.O. Box N 3220,
Nassau,
Bahamas;
tel. (809) 322 7505.
See also Practical Information.

HOTELS. – CHUB CAY: *Chub Cay Club*, 55 r., Sp, T. GREAT HARBOUR CAY: *Great Harbour Club*, 133 r., SP, T, golf.

EVENTS. – *Chub Cay Blue Marlin Tournament* (July), a deep-sea fishing competition.

RECREATION and SPORT. – Sailing, deep-sea fishing, scuba diving, snorkeling, swimming and sunbathing; golf, tennis.

AIR SERVICES. – Regular services from Chub Cay and Great Harbour Cay to Nassau (New Providence).

SHIPPING. – Mail boat services from Chub Cay and Great Harbour Cay to Nassau.

The Berry Islands, 30 miles/48 km N of New Providence, are a string of some 30 islets. They have beautiful beaches and waters, well stocked with fish and have a reputation as holiday retreats for millionaires. Only a few of the islands have any permanent population.

At the S end of the chain of islands is *Chub Cay, a good base for fishermen and scuba divers. Off its SE coast are marvelous submarine gardens. A famous local feature is *Mamma Rhoda Rock*, a spiky coral reef 16 ft/5 m high.

On **Little Whale Cay** is a sumptuous villa with an aviary (peacocks, flamingoes) belonging to the American financier Wallace Groves, founder of Freeport.

The reefs round the Whale Cays are excellent hunting grounds for scuba divers, as is *Hoffman's Cay*, $12\frac{1}{2}$ miles/ 20 km farther N.

On* **Great Harbour Cay**, at the N end of the chain of islands, is a very exclusive resort settlement with its own airstrip. – Just to the S of this lies *Anderson Cay*, with a handsome lighthouse. – To the N of Great Harbour Cay, between *Little Stirrup Cay* and *Great Stirrup Cay* (lighthouse), is the wreck of an unidentified ship.

See also * * **Bahamas.**

Bimini Islands

Bahama Islands
Commonwealth of the Bahamas

Islands: North Bimini, South Bimini.
Area: 11 sq. miles/28 sq. km.
Population: 1500.
Administrative center: Nassau (on New Providence).
Vehicles travel on the left.

(i) **Ministry of Tourism,**
Nassau Court,
P.O. Box N 3220,
Nassau,
Bahamas;
tel. (809) 322 7505.
See also Practical Information.

HOTELS. – NORTH BIMINI: *Anchors Aweigh Hotel*, 12 r.; *Bimini Big Game Fishing Club*, 55 r., SP; *Bimini Blue Waters*, 12 r., SP; *Bimini Inn*, 25 r., SP, T; *Brown's Hotel*, 28 r.; *Compleat Angler Hotel*, 15 r.; etc.

EVENTS. – *Bimini Big Game Blue Marlin Tournament* (June). – *Cat Cay Billfish Tournament* (August), a fishing competition for local people.

RECREATION and SPORT. – Deep-sea fishing, sailing, scuba diving, swimming.

AIR SERVICES. – Irregular services to Nassau (Bahamas) and Miami and Fort Lauderdale.

SHIPPING. – Mail boat services from Alice Town to Cat Cay and Nassau (Bahamas) and Miami.

The * **Biminis are a string of islands some 40 miles/65 km long lying 50 miles/80 km from the coast of Florida which are an internationally renowned center of big game fishing. Ponce de León sailed past the islands in 1513 during his quest for the fabled "fountain of perpetual youth" which was supposed to be on the Biminis and discovered Florida instead. Later the islands became the haunt of rum-runners and wreckers, who sought to entice ships on to the rocks and plunder them. Ernest Hemingway found the inspiration of his novel "The Old Man and the Sea" while staying here.**

At the S end of the island of **North Bimini**, which has a whole series of yacht harbors, is **Alice Town**, the busy little settlement which is the chief place in the group. This is the starting-point of the world-famous annual game fishing competitions.

In the *Compleat Angler Hotel* is an interesting *Hemingway exhibition. Close by is the former home of the world-famous author. The *Anchors Aweigh Hotel* has a "Fisherman's Hall of Fame" with information about record catches

Big game fishing off the Bimini Islands

and famous visitors. The **Lerner Maritime Laboratory** is a marine biological research station run by the *American Museum of Natural History*, with an *Aquarium containing brilliantly colored fish and a display collection.

In the N of the island, round **Bailey Town**, are very fine *beaches. Farther N, on Paradise Point, is a splendid mansion belonging to the American inventor George Bert Lyon. – Off the coast of North Bimini, in 30 ft/9 m of water, are blocks of dressed stone, the origin of which has not been explained.

The island of **South Bimini** is largely agricultural. Near the airport is the legendary *Fountain of Youth.* – Off the S coast of the island are large numbers of small islets and reefs, ending in the imposing *South Riding Rock*.

Off the shores of the Bimini Islands are many wrecks, including some which have not been precisely located. Among them are the US warship "Seminole" and a number of Spanish galleons.

See also * *Bahamas.

Bonaire

Lesser Antilles
Netherlands Antilles

Area: 112 sq. miles/290 sq. km.
Population: 10,000.
Administrative center: Willemstad (on Curaçao).
Vehicles travel on the right.
(i) **Bonaire Toeristenbureau,**
Breedestraat 1,
Kralendijk,
Bonaire, N.A.;
tel. 8322 and 8649.
See also Practical Information.

HOTELS. – *Hotel Bonaire and Casino*, Kralendijk, 134 r., SP, T, beach, casino; *Flamingo Beach Hotel*, Kralendijk, 100 r., SP, beach; *Habitat Bonaire*, Kralendijk.; etc. – HOLIDAY APARTMENTS, 9 villas; *Rochaline*, 25 r.; and GUEST-HOUSES.

RESTAURANTS in hotels listed; also in KRALENDIJK: *Beefeater*, Breedestraat; *China Garden*, Breedestraat; *Den Laman*; *Mona Lisa*; *Zeezicht*, at harbor; etc.

NIGHT CLUB and CASINO in Bonaire Hotel.

DISCOTHEQUE. – *E Wowo.*

PUBLIC HOLIDAYS and EVENTS. – *New Year's Day.* – *Canival* (February), with processions. – *Good Friday.* – *Easter.* – *Queen's Birthday* (April 30). – *Labour Day* (May 1). – *Ascension.* – *Pentecost.* – *Día de San Juan* (June 24), St John's Day, with many folk events. – *Día de San Pedro* (June 29), St Peter's Day. – *Annual International Sailing Regatta* (October). – *Kingdom Day* (December 15), National Day. –

Christmas (December 24–26). – *New Year's Eve* (December 31).

RECREATION and SPORT. – Scuba diving, snorkeling, deep-sea fishing, sailing, wind-surfing, water-skiing, swimming and sunbathing; tennis, bird-watching walks.

AIR SERVICES. – Direct connections with Curaçao and Aruba.

SHIPPING. – Occasional boats to Curaçao and the Venezuelan mainland. Some cruise ships call in.

Bonaire, well known to scuba divers (more than 50 diving grounds) and bird-watchers, lies off the N coast of the South American land mass in latitude 12°5′ N and longitude 68°17′ W, 28 miles/45 km E of Curaçao. Hilly in the N and predominantly flat in the S, it is an arid island which in some places takes on the aspect of a semi-desert.

Like the neighboring islands of Curaçao and Aruba, Bonaire is a detached fragment of the Venezuelan coastal cordillera. It formerly lay much lower, leading to the formation of the remarkable coral reefs around the island. It has a notably dry climate, with an annual rainfall of barely 10 in./250 mm at Kralendijk. Hence the characteristic vegetation pattern, with numerous cactuses and other drought-loving plants; hence also the salt-pans which until quite recently fostered a lucrative trade. Typical of Bonaire are the many caves and grottos and the little windswept Divi-Divi trees.

HISTORY. – The island, then inhabited by Arawak Indians, was discovered by Amerigo Vespucci in 1499. The Spaniards developed some limited stock-farming activity and began to recover sea salt in artificial salt-pans. In the 17th c. the Dutch arrived and made Bonaire an important market for the slave trade. At the beginning of the 19th c. the island was occupied for a time by British forces, but was recovered by Holland in 1815. During the Second World War German prisoners of war were interned here. During the 1950s and 1960s, thanks largely to its abundant bird life and its fascinating offshore banks of coral, Bonaire began to come into its own as a resort, and some 18,000 people now visit the island every year. – A few years ago an oil refinery was established on Bonaire, substantially improving the island's economic situation. Another quite recent development is the *Trans World Radio* transmitter, one of the most powerful in the world.

Kralendijk ("Coral Dyke"; sea level; pop. 1500), the island's capital, lies in an attractive setting on the W coast, sheltered from the trade winds. It is a little town of pastel-colored houses in Dutch colonial style. A charming promenade runs along the harbor with its many fishing boats. In the town's main street, the Breedestraat, are a number of shops selling luxury articles at very reasonable prices. There is an interesting old fort, still with a cannon. The Fish Market is the scene of bustling activity in the mornings. Near the Post Office is the well-stocked Fundashon Arte i Industria Bonairiano (Handicraft Center). The Instituto de Folklore Bonairiano has a museum devoted to the life and traditions of the island. Bonaire Marine Park includes coral reefs around Bonaire. The Radio Nederland Museum (Wereldomroep) is also worth seeing.

Kralendijk to Rincón (round trip 23 miles/37 km). – Leave Kralendijk on a road which runs NW along the quiet W coast, sheltered by the uninhabited offshore island of Klein Bonaire. The road passes many imposing banks of coral, now left high and dry. Footpaths lead down to the coast.

9 miles/15 km: *Goto Meer*, a charming coastal lagoon which is now a flamingo sanctuary. To the N is *Mount Brandaris* (784 ft/239 m), the highest point on the island. – 2½ miles/4 km W of the Goto Meer is *Nukove*, one of Bonaire's finest snorkeling areas.

The northern part of the island is occupied by *Washington National Park (17,514 acres/ 7088 ha), in which more than 130 species of birds can be seen. Along the coast are attractive beaches and hidden caves. A circular road (22 miles/36 km) runs through the park.

2½ miles/4 km: * **Rincón**, the oldest settlement on the island, with picturesque little pastel-colored houses.

2 miles/3 km: **Onima**, above the wild and romantic bay of the same name on the NE coast. Near the village are caves with expressive rock engravings by Indians of the pre-colonial period.

From here a scenic road cuts through the interior of the island to –

9 miles/15 km: **Kralendijk**.

Kralendijk to the Pekelmeer (round trip 19 miles/ 31 km). – From Kralendijk the road runs S along the SW coast.

5 miles/8 km: **Cabaje**, a small village with some restored 18th c. slave huts and an obelisk of salt which formerly served as a seamark.

To the S is the lagoon of **Pekelmeer**, with salt beds worked by the Antilles International Salt Company, flanked by long rows of shimmering white salt pyramids. In the dunes along the narrow spit of land between the lagoon and the sea live thousands of flamingoes (bird sanctuary).

6 miles/10 km: Willemstoren lighthouse, on the SE coast (good views). – To the N the superb beach of Sorabon is unfortunately disfigured by the shell of an abandoned hotel.

4 miles/6 km: **Lac Baai**, a beautiful beach fringed by mangroves: from glass-bottomed boats the fascinating underwater world can be observed.

4½ miles/7 km: **Kralendijk**.

See also * **Aruba** and * * **Curaçao**

British Virgin Islands

Lesser Antilles
Leeward Islands
British Crown Colony

Area: 59 sq. miles/153 sq. km.
Population: 12,000.
Administrative center: Road Town (on Tortola).
Currency: US dollar.
Vehicles travel on the left.

ⓘ **British Virgin Islands Tourist Board,**
P.O. Box 134,
Road Town,
Tortola, B.V.I.;
tel. (809) 49 43134.
See also Practical Information.

PUBLIC HOLIDAYS and EVENTS. – *New Year's Day.* – *Good Friday.* – *Easter;* on Virgin Gorda * **Easter Festival**, reaching its climax in the *Festival Queen Parade* in the Valley. – * *B.V.I. Spring Regatta* (March–April), on Tortola. – *Commonwealth Day* (May). – *Whitsun.* – *Queen's Birthday* (June), with parades. – *Territory Day* (July 1), with sports contests. – *August Monday (first week in August), commemorating the liberation of the slaves, with cheerful and relaxed celebrations; on Tortola the Tortola Festival. – *St Ursula's Day* (October 21). – *Prince of Wales's Birthday* (November 14). – *Christmas Day.* – *Boxing Day* (December 26).

RECREATION and SPORT. – Sailing, deep-sea fishing, scuba diving, snorkeling, wind-surfing, swimming and sunbathing; tennis, walking.

AIR SERVICES. – From Beef Island, Tortola, to San Juan (Puerto Rico), St Thomas and St Croix (US Virgin Islands) and Antigua; occasional flights to Miami and other cities on the E coast of the United States. – From Virgin Gorda to San Juan (Puerto Rico) and St Thomas (US Virgin Islands).

Frequent services between the islands of Tortola, Virgin Gorda and Anegada.

SHIPPING. – Ferry services from Spanish Town (Virgin Gorda) and Road Town and West End (Tortola) to St Thomas (U.S. Virgin Islands). – Cargo boats and charters between the various islands.

The * British Virgin Islands lie between latitude 18°18' and 18° 46' N and between longitude 64°15' and 64°52' W. Together with the United States Virgin Islands they form a link between the Greater Antilles to the W and the Lesser Antilles curving down to the SE. – The British part of the Virgin Islands group consists of more than 50 islands and islets, only 16 of which are inhabited. The principal islands are Tortola (with the capital, Road Town), Beef Island (recently linked with Tortola by a bridge), Virgin Gorda, Anegada and Jost van Dyke.

With the exception of Anegada the islands consist of Cretaceous sediments and metamorphic and volcanic rocks. They lie on a continental shelf some 215 ft/65 m below the sea which is bounded on the N by the Puerto Rico Trench and on the E by the Anegada Passage. A variety of geological forces have given the islands a hilly topography, with the highest point (1782 ft/543 m) on Tortola. The climate, influenced by the trade winds, is extremely agreeable. Day temperatures range between 77 °F/25 °C and 86 °F/ 30 °C, and night temperatures rarely fall below 68 °F/20 °C. – The uncontrolled plantation development and over-grazing of the past have left only a few remnants of the original forest cover, now replaced by a secondary growth of scrub. There are considerable variations in the amount of rainfall, reflected by the occurrence of drought-loving vegetation in certain areas.

HISTORY. – The islands were discovered by Columbus in 1493, and remained in Spanish hands until the arrival in 1595 of Sir Francis Drake, sailing through the channel S of Tortola which now bears his name. After conflicts with the Spanish and the Dutch Britain annexed Tortola in 1672. Thereafter Tortola and some of the neighboring islands became the haunts of

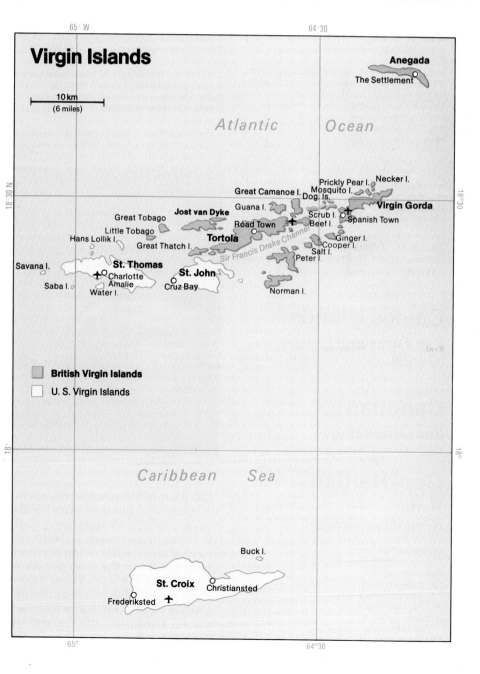

pirates, providing the inspiration for Robert Louis Stevenson's "Treasure Island". Later increased numbers of British planters settled on the islands, and the 18th c. saw the establishment of a Quaker colony which sought to set up a separate island government under the British crown. From 1871 to 1956 the British Virgin Islands were administered as part of the Leeward Islands group. Since 1971 they have been a crown colony with a limited degree of internal self-government. – The head of state is the Queen, who is represented by a Governor. The Governor, the Prime Minister, two other ministers and two ex-officio members form the Executive Council. The legislature consists of a Speaker, two ex-officio members, one nominated member and seven elected representatives.

POPULATION and ECONOMY. – Something like a third of the population of the British Virgin Islands live in Road Town on Tortola. The overwhelming majority of the inhabitants are the descendants of African slaves; a minority are of European or North American origin. The majority of the population belong to various Protestant denominations.

Some 60% of the land area is devoted to agriculture – roughly 2500 acres producing fruit and vegetables, 5000 acres of other arable land, the rest pastureland. The sugar-cane plantations are in a bad way, as is shown by the spread of secondary scrub and waste land. **Tourism** has developed in recent years into the major element in the economy, producing an estimated four-fifths of the islands' revenue. In 1972 there were 350 beds available for visitors: by 1979 the number had tripled. It now appears – having regard particularly to the effect on the environment – that saturation point has almost been reached, and accordingly the further development of tourism is proceeding with great caution.

See also *Anegada, Tortola, Virgin Gorda and *United States Virgin Islands.

Caicos Islands
See Turks and Caicos Islands

Canouan
See Grenadines

Cap-Haïtien
Haiti
République d'Haïti

Département du Nord.
Altitude: sea level.
Population: 68,000
(i) Office National du Tourisme,
Avenue Marie-Jeanne,
Port-au-Prince,
Haïti;
tel. 2 1720.
See also Practical Information.

HOTELS. – *Mont Joli*, 43 r., SP; *Cormier Beach*, 20 r., SP; *Hostellerie du Roi Christophe*, 18 r.; *Hotel Beck*, 25 r., SP; *Imperial Hotel*, 28 r., SP, T; *Brise de Mer*, 10 r.; etc. – Several PENSIONS.

SHOPPING. – A wide range of typical local products can be bought here, particularly on the "cruise ship days" when the cruise liners call in and countless little shops and stalls open up for the benefit of the passengers. High quality handicrafts can be found in the *Mahogany Factory* and the *Guy Benjamin Shop* (both woodcarving), *Carlos*, the *Coockoo's Nest* and the *Cobaha Shop* (which is run by the Baptist Mission). – The main art galleries are the *Flamingo Gallery*, *L'Ile Galerie d'Art*, *Marassa Art Gallery*, *Galerie Max Gerbier* and *Obin Studio*.

RECREATION and SPORT. – Swimming and sun-bathing, scuba diving, snorkeling, boat trips; walking.

AIR SERVICES. – Direct connections with Port-au-Prince (Haiti) and Fort Lauderdale and Miami.

SHIPPING. – Regular calls by cruise ships coming from or going to Miami (USA), San Juan (Puerto Rico) and various Caribbean ports, according to season. – Boat trips to Labadie.

ROAD TRANSPORT. – Buses, rented cars and taxis to Milot, the Citadelle La Ferrière and Port-au-Prince.

Houses in Cap-Haïtien

*Cap-Haïtien, situated on the northern (Atlantic) coast of Haiti, is the country's second largest town, capital of the Département du Nord and the economic center of the northern plain. Known to the local people as "Le Cap", it is Haiti's finest town, which has not only many particular features of interest but which has largely preserved its distinctive character.**

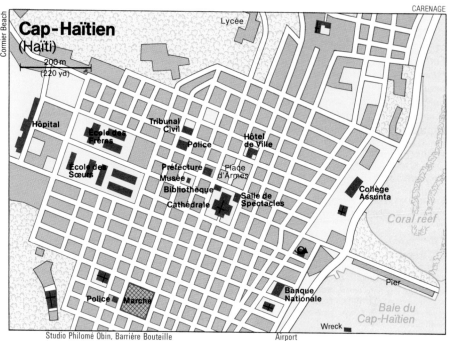

Cap-Haïtien (Haïti)

Milot (Palais Sans-Souci; Citadelle La Ferrière)

The town has little industry – a sugar factory, the Usine Citadelle Caldos, a rum distillery and a few factories processing agricultural produce. The government's development plans, however, provide for an expansion of the town's economic role within the context of their decentralization measures, and new factories are to be established on an industrial estate which is at the planning stage. The town's small airport and the harbor, which is the only one in the country apart from Port-au-Prince harbor at which cruise ships and commercial shipping lines regularly call, are also to be developed. – In the northern plain, which extends from Cap-Haïtien to Fort-Liberté, the principal crops are sugar-cane and sisal. In the hills around the town there are many large mango groves, and on the higher slopes there are extensive plantations of coffee.

HISTORY. – The town was founded in 1670 by French pirates from the Ile de la Tortue to the NW. During the French colonial period, under the name of Cap-Français, it became one of the finest and wealthiest towns in the New World, the "Paris of the Antilles", and for many years was capital of the French colony of Saint-Domingue. The troubled years of the wars of independence, however, left their mark on the town: it was burned down in November 1791, sacked in June 1793 and again devastated by fire in January 1802. Thereafter it enjoyed a brief period of splendor when Pauline Bonaparte, Napoleon's sister and wife of the commander of the French expeditionary force, General Leclerc, held court here; but these days of glory came to an end with the defeat of the French forces.

When the fortunes of war during the struggle between the French and the rebellious blacks and mulattoes turned in favor of the Haitians the French could no longer hold Cap-Français. The town, defended by General Rochambeau and his remaining troops, was attacked by the Haitian commander Jean-Jacques Dessalines on November 10, 1803 and captured, after fierce fighting, on November 29. During the reign of Henry I the town – renamed Cap-Haïtien and, for a time, Cap-Henry – became the capital of the North Haitian kingdom, though the royal residence was outside the town at Milot. After the fall of the monarchy Cap-Haïtien was unable to compete with Port-au-Prince, which increased steadily in importance. – A very violent earthquake which devastated northern Haiti in 1842 destroyed much of the town, including many houses of the French colonial period.

SIGHTS. – The picturesque streets and lanes with their pastel-colored houses bear witness to the town's colonial past, as do the extensive fortifications. The *Cathedral, originally dating from the 18th and 19th c., was destroyed by the 1842 earthquake and rebuilt in the original style exactly a hundred years later. The *Pier* is a scene of great activity, with frequent calls by cruise ships. On the W side of the town is the *Hospital*, originally built by the French. To the S is the *Studio of Philomée Obin*, the leading contemporary Haitian painter and founder of the Cap-Haïtien Art School. A little way farther S stands the *Barrière Bouteille*, an old town gate with three openings. – On the N side of the town is the *Séminaire*, an important educational institution.

To the N, in the outlying district of CARENAGE, are three relics of the period of French colonial rule – *Fort Magny* and *Fort St-Joseph* (both 18th c.), and the *Palais Pauline Bonaparte*, once the residence of Napoleon's sister and her husband General Leclerc. – Farther N are *Rival Beach* (swimming) and the ruins of another 18th c. French fort, *Fort Picoulet*.

SURROUNDINGS. – 4 miles/6 km N, on the Atlantic coast, is *Cormier Beach*, a beautiful beach (hotel). *Coco Beach*, to the west is equally fine.

6 miles/9 km W of the town is the *Baie de Labadie*, a beach in a magnificent tropical setting, with a picturesque little settlement which can be reached only by boat. Nearby are remains of fortifications.

Cap-Haïtien to the Citadelle La Ferrière. 12 miles/19 km S of Cap-Haïtien is **Milot**, which King Henry-Christophe set out to develop into a sumptuous royal residence. Above the town to the S are the ruins of the *Palais Sans-Souci*, the former royal palace, which was destroyed in the 1842 earthquake.

Ruins of Sans-Souci Palace, Milot

Both the name and the architecture of the palace were based on Frederick the Great's palace at Potsdam; and the strict court ceremonial introduced by Henry-Christophe likewise followed the pattern of contemporary European courts. The structure and appointments of the palace showed a lavishness quite out of keeping with the circumstances of the time and the financial resources of Haiti. The rooms were walled and floored with precious woods, hung with French tapestries and illuminated by crystal chandeliers, and Italian marble was imported to enhance the effect. A mountain stream was diverted so that its water could circulate under the floors in a system of pipes to moderate the tropical heat. – A broad flight of steps flanked by two sentry-boxes leads up into the palace. The domed *chapel*, well preserved, contains a contemporary marble altar. The bronze lions which formerly guarded the entrances to the palace are now in the Ministry of Justice in Port-au-Prince. The flight of steps at the main entrance, originally dominated by a fountain, leads on to a magnificent double *staircase* giving access to the royal apartments. Visitors pass through spacious reception rooms, drawing-rooms, banqueting halls and ballrooms, now stripped of their sumptuous appointments, roofless and exposed to the ravages of the tropical rain and sun. To the rear are the extensive ruins of the domestic offices and the quarters of the royal retinue.

Above Sans-Souci, on the hill to the S known as the *Bonnet de l'Evêque* (Bishop's Cap", over 3300 ft/ 1000 m high; road for part of the way, then on foot or muleback), stands the **Citadelle La Ferrière,** begun in 1804 by Dessalines and completed in 1817, during the reign of Henry-Christophe.

Henry I, also known as *Henry-Christophe*, ranks with "Emperor" Faustin I of Haiti and "Papa Doc" as one of the most colorful and controversial figures in Haitian history. Henry-Christophe was born a slave (1767) in the British colony of St Kitts, and later worked for many years as a waiter in Cap-Français. Then, during the long struggle for independence, his extraordinary military skill and valor made him one of the principal generals and leaders of the rebels. When Haiti was divided into two states after the murder of Jean-Jacques Dessalines in 1806 Henry became President of the northern state. The President of the southern state was Alexandre Pétion, who gave support to Simón Bolívar in his fight for independence. In February 1807 Henry was appointed President for life, and in June 1811 he had himself proclaimed king. Since every kingdom must have its nobility Henry created numbers of new Haitian nobles with such unlikely titles as Duc de Marmelade and Comte de Limonade; and following medieval precedent all nobles were given grants of land. During his reign Henry built himself no fewer than nine palaces and residences, most of them now in ruins or difficult to get to for lack of roads. Apart from his main palace of Sans-Souci the best known is the Palais des 365 Portes at Petite Rivière de l'Artibonite. In addition to his *folie de grandeur* and lust for power Henry seems to have suffered from severe mental disorder, in particular from persecution mania. According to contemporary accounts he saw himself as God's deputy on earth. He is said to have answered the thunder of a tropical storm with a salvo from his cannon, in order to demonstrate that his power was as great as that of the forces of nature. His rule encountered increasing resistance from the population; then, while hearing mass at Limonade, he suffered a stroke and became partly paralyzed. Popular unrest continued. Finally when reviewing his troops two months later he collapsed and had to be carried back to Sans-Souci; and when news was brought to him that the palace guard had joined the rebels he saw no way out other than suicide, and on October 20, 1820 shot himself with a silver bullet (or, according to some accounts, a golden one).

This colossal stronghold in the immediate vicinity of the royal residence was intended on the one hand to demonstrate the power and security of the royal house and on the other to provide an impregnable refuge for the king and his court in the event – still expected – of a French invasion.

The **Citadel**, with 365 cannon ranged in three galleries, could accommodate 15,000 men in case of need and was stocked with sufficient provisions to withstand a year's siege. Large cisterns on the roof stored rainwater for the use of the garrison. The number of iron cannonballs still stored in the fortress is estimated at 45,000. In the early 19th c. Haitian military preparations were always directed against the threat of an invasion by one of the countries where slavery was still rife. It is said that on one occasion

Citadelle La Ferrière, Milot

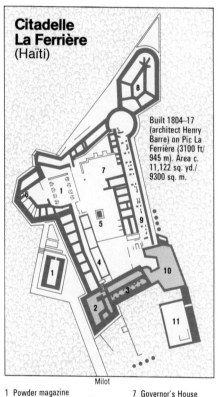

Citadelle La Ferrière (Haïti)

8

Built 1804–17 (architect Henry Barre) on Pic La Ferrière (3100 ft/ 945 m). Area c. 11,122 sq. yd./ 9300 sq. m.

Milot

1 Powder magazine
2 Batterie du Prince Royal
3 Batterie de la Reine
4 Kitchen
5 Tomb of Henry-Christophe
6 Batterie Marie-Louise
7 Governor's House
8 Batterie Coidavid
9 Batterie Royale
10 Batterie des Princesses
11 Hospital

Henry-Christophe, in order to convince a British diplomat of the fearlessness and discipline of his troops, ordered a detachment of soldiers to march off the upper gallery of the Citadel and into the abyss below: whereupon, it is reported, the troops blindly obeyed the order without a moment's hesitation. But the Citadel – still largely preserved in its original state – never had to face enemy attack. Some 200,000 men are said to have worked on its construction, at least 20,000 of them losing their lives in the process.

The Citadel, which vaguely resembles the form of a ship, occupies an area of some 10,750 sq. yd/9000 sq. m. At the N end is a massive projecting bastion, and there are two flanking bastions facing the crest of the hill. From the bastions and the upper gun gallery there is a magnificent *view (in the morning only,

since heat haze begins to build up from about 10 o'clock) extending over the hills to the N and the plain around Cap-Haïtien.

The *walls* are up to 140 ft/43 m high in places and up to 13 ft/4 m thick. The Citadel is entered through a massive iron-bound door. The great gloomy *casemates* and the barrack-rooms occupied by the garrison have been stripped of their contents, though several hundred cannon, some of them still on their carriages of fine hardwood, remain in the damp gun galleries. Most of the cannon were captured from Spanish, British and French forces during the fight for independence. Henry-Christophe himself is buried in the *inner ward* of the fortress. His pyramid-shaped tomb has a bronze tablet with the inscription "Here lies King Henry-Christophe, born October 6, 1767, died October 20, 1820, whose motto was 'I shall be reborn from my ashes'."

19 miles/30 km S of Cap-Haïtien, at **Dondon** in the northern hills, are interesting caves with remains of pre-Columbian occupation.

*EXCURSION from Cap-Haïtien to **Port-au-Prince** (170 miles/275 km; 5 hours by car, 10 hours by bus). – The road leads S over the *Plaine du Nord* and through the *Chaîne de Belance*, continues over the *Plaine des Gonaïves* and down the *Artibonite valley* and finally runs along the coast to Port-au-Prince. The scenery offers striking contrasts between hills and plain, karstic uplands and lush tropical vegetation, sandy beaches and mangrove swamps.

See also **Haiti** and **Hispaniola**.

Carriacou
See Grenadines

Cat Island
Bahama Islands
Commonwealth of the Bahamas

Area: 150 sq. miles/388 sq. km.
Population: 4000.
Administrative center: Nassau (on New Providence).
Vehicles travel on the left.
(i) **Ministry of Tourism,**
Nassau Court,
P.O. Box N 3220,
Nassau,
Bahamas;
tel. (809) 322 7505.
See also Practical Information.

HOTELS. – THE BIGHT: *Cutlass Bay Yacht Club*, 10 r., SP, T; etc. – PORT HOWE: *Greenwood Inn*, 16 r., SP. – HAWK'S NEST: *Hawk's Nest Club*, 10 r.

EVENTS. – *Cat Island Regatta* (first Monday in August), at Arthur's Town. – *Junkanoo* (Boxing Day and New Year), a colorful costume parade.

RECREATION and SPORT. – Sailing, deep-sea fishing, scuba diving, snorkeling, swimming and sunbathing; walking.

AIR SERVICES. – Regular connections with the island of San Salvador and Nassau (New Providence).

SHIPPING. – Mail boat connections with the islands of San Salvador and Rum Cay, George Town (Great Exuma) and Nassau (New Providence).

*Cat Island, one of the most beautiful and most fertile islands in the Bahamas, lies 100 miles/160 km SE of New Providence. Evidence of earlier Indian cultures can be seen at many places on the island, which was occupied only briefly by the Spaniards. At the end of the 18th c. American Loyalists settled here and established cotton plantations, which later gave place to arable land and fields of vegetables. In the past 20 years the island has become an increasingly popular resort.

The chief place on the island, *The Bight, is a picturesque village of thatched cottages. The fine Roman Catholic church (1948), built by Father Jerome, has good frescoes. Of Armbrister House, a colonial-period mansion, only the façade survives. – To the N rises ***Mount Alvernia** (207 ft/63 m), the highest point in the Bahamas, on the summit of which is the *Hermitage*, a building in Southern European style erected by Father Jerome, an Anglican priest who became a convert to Roman Catholicism.

From The Bight a road leads S to the old settlement of **Moss Town** and (9 miles/15 km) the charming little coastal town of ***Port Howe**, with the remains of the Deveaux Mansion, an 18th c. plantation house. – 3 miles/5 km beyond this is *Columbus Point*, the southernmost tip of the island, with a cave which was inhabited in pre-Columbian times.

To the W of Port Howe, past the small airfield, lies *Cutlass Bay*, a fisherman's paradise. Farther W is **Hawk's Nest**, a rising tourist center (deep-sea fishing).

From The Bight a road runs towards the N of the island, which becomes steadily narrower, passing through pleasant farming villages. In 19 miles/30 km it reaches **Pigeon Cay**, a peninsula with a magnificent *beach and coastal lagoons, to the N of which is *Bennett's Harbour*. 5 miles/8 km beyond this is **Arthur's Town**, the largest place in the northern part of the island and a good base from which to explore its many beauties. The actor Sidney Poitier spent his childhood here.

Some 12 miles W of Arthur's Town, half way between Cat Island and Eleuthera, is the island of ***Little San Salvador**, a port of call for the "Norway" (formerly "France"), the world's largest cruise ship.

See also ****Bahamas** and ***San Salvador** (*Watling's Island*).

Les Cayes
Haiti
République d'Haïti

Département du Sud.
Altitude: sea level.
Population: 36,000.
ⓘ **Office National du Tourisme,**
Avenue Marie-Jeanne,
Port-au-Prince,
Haïti;
tel. 2 1720.
See also Practical Information.

HOTELS. – *Concorde*, 21 r., SP; *Ideal*, 8 r.; etc.

AIR SERVICES. – Regular service to Port-au-Prince, daily except Sundays.

Les Cayes Cathedral, Haiti

*Les Cayes, Haiti's fourth largest town and capital of the Département du Sud, was founded by the French in 1719. Simón Bolívar took refuge here in 1815 and was supplied with arms by President Pétion.

A pleasant town of wide streets and gardens, Les Cayes is of some economic importance as a port for the shipment of coffee and has one of the country's three large sugar factories. The town received an economic boost by the reconstruction and resurfacing of the Route Nationale 200 to Port-au-Prince. Plans have been made for an industrial area for the stimulation of manufacturing industry. The port installations are also to be modernised.

SIGHTS. – Around the harbor, now badly silted up (the sacks of coffee must be transferred to seagoing ships by lighter),

The Saut Mathurine, near Les Cayes

are the remains of fortifications of the colonial period. Other features of interest are the **Cathedral** (19th c.) and a number of attractive old houses in typical French colonial style.

SURROUNDINGS – 19 miles/30 km N of the town is the *Saut Mathurine, an impressive waterfall surrounded by luxuriant tropical vegetation (difficult access).

22 miles/35 km NW, on the Citadelle des Platons (2460 ft/750 m), is the tomb of the composer Nicolas Geffrard. Farther N the Pic de Macaya (7701 ft/ 2347 m), highest point in the **Massif de la Hotte**, can be seen at the W end of the southern Haitian peninsula.

16 miles/26 km SW (inquire about state of road), at **Port Salut**, is the developing tourist resort of Macaya Beach, with a superb beach.

From Les Cayes there is an attractive boat trip to the *Ile à Vache (7 miles SE), which for a long time, particularly in the 17th c., was a buccaneers' lair. Henry Morgan set out from here with a considerable fleet to raid Panama.

Inland from Les Cayes is the *Plaine des Cayes, one of Haiti's most fertile plains. Here, in addition to numbers of small farms, there are large plantations of sugar-cane and vetiver, a plant which yields a fragrant oil used in the manufacture of perfumes. Scattered over the plain are the imposing remains of plantation buildings of the colonial period. Many of the ruined buildings still contain the remnants of machinery which bear witness to the high technical standards of the processes of sugar production. These industrial buildings, together with the remains of irrigation channels and the plantation owners' mansions, still impressive even in ruin, demonstrate the prosperity of the old colonial plantations – a prosperity which benefited only a small white minority. Near the ruined plantation houses can often be seen the primitive sugar-cane presses used by smallholders. In these presses, worked by a pair of oxen, the cane was crushed between wooden rollers and the juice conveyed to the vats in which it was boiled to produce the brown sugar, and the brown rum which was the popular local drink.

See also **Haiti and **Hispaniola.

Cayman Islands
British Crown Colony

Islands: Grand Cayman, Little Cayman, Cayman Brac.
Area: 100 sq. miles/259 sq. km.
Population: 17,000.
Administrative center: George Town (on Grand Cayman).
Currency: Cayman Dollar (CI $).
Vehicles travel on the left.
ⓘ **Cayman Islands Department of Tourism,**
P.O. Box 67,
George Town,
Grand Cayman, B.W.I.;
tel. 9 4844.
See also Practical Information.

HOTELS ON GRAND CAYMAN. SEVEN MILE BEACH: Royal Palms, 102 r., SP; Grand Caymanian Holiday Inn, 183 r., SP, T; Beach Club Colony, 38 r., SP, T; Caribbean Club, 36 r., SP; Galleon Beach Hotel, 35 r., SP, T. – NORTH COAST: Spanish Bay Reef Resort, 18 r. – SOUTH OF GEORGE TOWN: Casa Bertmar, 16 r., SP; Seaview Hotel, 19 r., SP; Sunset House, 37 r. – EAST COAST: Tortuga Club, 14 r., T. – RUM POINT: 10 r.; Cayman Kai, 52 r., SP; and many others. – Many HOLIDAY APARTMENTS.

Resort complex, Grand Cayman

RESTAURANTS in most hotels; also *Almond Tree*, *Cayman Arms* and *Lobster Pot*, all in George Town; *Grand Old House*, outside the town, to the S.

HOTEL ON LITTLE CAYMAN. – *Kingston Bight Lodge*, 8 r. – HOLIDAY APARTMENTS.

HOTELS ON CAYMAN BRAC. – *Brac Reef Hotel*, 30 r., SP; *Buccaneer's Inn*, 34 r. – HOLIDAY APARTMENTS.

RECREATION and SPORT. – Scuba diving, snorkeling, boat trips, deep-sea fishing, wind-surfing, water-skiing, swimming and sunbathing; tennis.

AIR SERVICES. – Regular services between George Town and Miami and Houston (USA), Kingston (Jamaica) and San José (Costa Rica). Flights to little Cayman and Cayman Brac according to demand.

SHIPPING. – Some cruise ships call at George Town. Services to Little Cayman and Cayman Brac according to demand.

PUBLIC HOLIDAYS and EVENTS. – *New Year's Day*. – *Ash Wednesday*, with agricultural show and beauty contest. – *Good Friday*. – *Easter Monday*. – *Grand Court Opening Ceremony* (May), ceremonial opening of law courts. – *Discovery Day* (third Monday in May), commemorating Columbus's discovery of the islands, with a regatta. – *Flower Show* (June). – *Queen's Birthday* (second week in June), with parade. – *Constitution Day* (first Monday in July), with regatta. – *Pirates Week* (end of October–beginning of November), with a "pirate landing", sporting contests and costume balls. – *Bank Holiday* (November), with a regatta. – *Remembrance Day* (November), with various ceremonies. – *Christmas Eve*, with carol singing, fireworks and dancing. – *Christmas Day*. – *Boxing Day* (December 26). – *New Year's Eve*.

The three *Cayman Islands lie between latitude 19°15' and 19°45' N and between longitude 79°44' and 81°27' W on a submarine ridge in the Caribbean which runs W from the Sierra Maestra on Cuba to Belize (formerly British Honduras) in Central America, separating the Yucatán Basin to the N from the Cayman Trench, the deepest part of the Caribbean (25,200 ft/7680 m).

Grand Cayman, Little Cayman and Cayman Brac form a British crown colony with internal self-government, which thanks to generous tax and investment laws enjoys considerable prosperity (tax haven).

HISTORY. – The Cayman Islands were discovered by Columbus on his last voyage in 1503 and were at first known as the Tortugas, after the large numbers of turtles found here. The name Caymanas (from the Indian name of a species of lizard) first appeared in 1530. The first Englishman to visit the islands was Sir Francis Drake, who came here from Santo Domingo in 1586. Four years later Captain William King landed on Grand Cayman and began the slaughter of the turtles. The first settlers are believed to have been deserters from Cromwell's army, then engaged in wresting Jamaica from the Spaniards, in the second half of the 17th c. After the treaty of Madrid in 1670, and particularly after the treaty of Utrecht in 1713, the islands fell into the hands of pirates, chief among them Sir Henry Morgan, Thomas Anstis, Edward Low, George Lowther and Neil Walker. The inspiration for Robert Louis Stevenson's "Treasure Island" came from Edward Teach, better known as "Blackbeard", who was active about 1717. Settlers again began to come to the island in 1734, most of them fishermen of Scottish origin. In 1788 ten merchant ships sailing in convoy from Jamaica were wrecked off the E coast of Grand Cayman and their crews were saved only by the heroic efforts of the islanders – in return for which, it is said, George III promised them exemption from taxation.

At the beginning of the 19th c. the islands had a population of about 1000 (more than half of them slaves), living primarily by fishing and farming. The

Iron Shore, on the SW coast of Grand Cayman

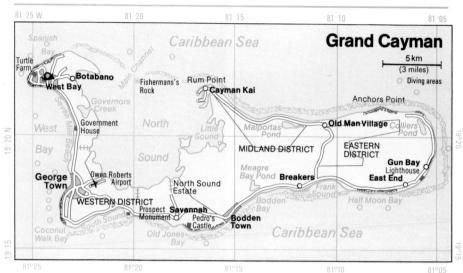

Grand Cayman

5 km
(3 miles)

○ Diving areas

Spanish Bay

Turtle Farm

Botabano
West Bay

Caribbean Sea

Fishermans's Rock

Rum Point
Cayman Kai

Anchors Point

Governors Creek

Government House

North

Little Sound

Malportas Pond

Old Man Village

Colliers Pond

West Bay

Sound

MIDLAND DISTRICT

EASTERN DISTRICT

Meagre Bay Pond

Breakers

Gun Bay
Lighthouse
East End

George Town

Owen Roberts Airport

North Sound Estate

Bodden Bay

Frank Sound

Half Moon Bay

WESTERN DISTRICT

Prospect
Savannah
Monument
Pedro's Castle

Bodden Town

Coconut Walk Bay

South Sound

Old Jones Bay

Caribbean Sea

islands' Legislative Assembly was established in 1832. A few years later slavery was abolished. In 1898 the Governor of Jamaica, whose writ also ran in the Cayman Islands (which had been formally constituted as such in 1863), appointed commissioners who set up various important public institutions in the islands. After the end of the Second World War tourism began to develop in the Caymans. In 1959 the islands were given a constitution granting them internal self-government; in 1962 they were separated, politically and administratively, from Jamaica; and in 1972 the newly created crown colony received its present constitution. – The government of the islands is in the hands of the Governor, representing the Queen, and a seven-member Executive Council. The Governor also presides over the Legislative Assembly, which has 15 members.

POPULATION and ECONOMY. – The present population of the Caymans is about 17,000 (26% blacks, 54% mulattoes, 19% whites, 1% others), more than 15,000 of them living on Grand Cayman and about a third of these in the capital, George Town. They belong to a variety of religious denominations, with the United Church of Jamaica and Grand Cayman (Presbyterian), the Anglican Church, the Baptists, the Pilgrim Holiness Church, the Church of God, the Roman Catholic Church, the Seventh Day Adventists and the Methodists claiming the largest numbers of adherents. – In the past the poor state of the islands' economy led to considerable losses of population through emigration, but since the end of the 19th c., and particularly since the last war, the population has shown a rising trend. At the beginning of this century shipping and fishing were still the main sources of revenue; but since the end of the Second World War, and more particularly since 1962, there has been a considerable development of **tourism**, promoted not only by an increased number of calls by cruise ships but also by very liberal tax laws and inducements to attract investment. The islands are considered to be one of the finest tax havens in the world. Whereas there were barely 2000 visitors to the islands in 1962 the number had risen to over 180,000 by 1981. Apart from the tourist trade the main sources of employment are the offices of more than 300 banks and finance companies, mainly foreign, and the public service, followed by the construction industries, aquaculture (the "farming" of turtles, crayfish and tropical freshwater fish) and fishing.

Grand Cayman

*Grand Cayman (area 76 sq. miles/ 197 sq. km; pop. 15,500) is the largest and most westerly island in the group. The center of the island consists of Tertiary limestones, the highest point being only 60 ft/18 m above sea level. The flat coastal areas, almost completely surrounded by a fringe of reefs, are made up of coral limestones, coral sands and marls. The North Sound, a marine transgression, divides the island into a western half, mostly covered by dry forest, and an eastern half with expanses of mangrove and freshwater swamps

The oldest settlements are on the S coast, sheltered by its fringing reef, and in the southern part of the W coast. The excellent beaches on the W and S coasts have long been a magnet for visitors; and in recent years the North Sound has been developed as a fine natural harbor protected by its barrier reef.

PLANT and ANIMAL LIFE. – Like the other Caribbean islands, the Caymans have a varied pattern of vegetation, much influenced by the hand of man. Grand Cayman is notable for its southern pines and its profusion of lilies and orchids. – Turtles and iguanas, which were numerous on the island at the time of its discovery by the Spaniards, are now practically extinct in the wild state; and in recent years the cream-colored land crabs and the hare-like agoutis have also become rare. More than 100 species of birds, however, can be observed on the island throughout the year.

TOUR OF THE ISLAND. – *George Town (pop. 5000), capital of the colony, lies in *Hog Sty Bay*, a little bay near the S end of the W coast which has been developed into a harbor.

Bank, George Town

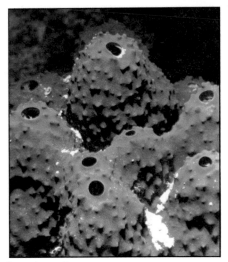

Lavender coral

On the seafront are a number of old buildings, some of them now occupied by duty-free shops. **Elmslie Memorial Church** is an attractive 19th c. church (restored). Nearby are the scanty remains of *Fort George* (17th–18th c.), built to provide protection against attack by Spaniards or pirates. Inland from the harbor are numbers of modern office buildings occupied by lawyers and the representatives of more than 200 foreign banks and trusts. Between Panton Avenue and Edward Street is the *Law Court*, in contemporary style; and facing this, to the N, are two other modern buildings, the *Legislative Assembly Building* and the *Town Hall*, with a monument to King George V in front of them. Outside the town, to the SE, are the palatial *Government Administration Building* (1975) and other new government offices.

1¼ miles/2 km E, beyond *Half Way Pond*, is the *Owen Roberts Airport*, with the interesting *Tropical Gardens* at its SE end. To the N are the ruins of the former turtle farm.

N of George Town lies *Seven Mile Beach*, one of the finest in the Caribbean, with many hotels, apartment buildings and villas, including *Government House*, the Governor's residence. – On *North Sound*, a much indented stretch of coast with a fringe of mangroves which offers excellent facilities for water sports, are recently established marinas and holiday houses. At its NW end is the little fishing village of **Botabano**, starting-point for boat trips to the northern barrier reef.

At the N end of Seven Mile Beach is **West Bay**, the second largest settlement on the island, in the bay of that name. Beyond this, on the NW coast, an area of hard coral limestones, is the *Turtle Farm, the only establishment of its kind in the world, where some 65,000 turtles are reared in large tanks and marketed when they reach a given age.

Originally the turtles were hatched from eggs collected in Surinam, Costa Rica and Ascension Island, but in 1973 the farm scored a notable success when the first turtle eggs were laid in captivity. Thereafter it no longer had to rely on the import of eggs, which had attracted criticism from the World Wildlife Fund. In 1978 exports from the farm (turtle meat, leather, tortoiseshell, cosmetics, etc.) had a value of almost £1,000,000, making it by far the largest productive establishment in the colony.

To the E of the Turtle Farm, in the rugged area known as Hell, stands the famous *Hell Post Office*, with its own postmark, "Hell, Grand Cayman". Here too is the *Inferno Club*, an old established hostelry.

At the SW tip of the island is *Coconut Walk Bay*, with a lighthouse and a beautiful beach. To the E extends *South Sound*, sheltered by its barrier reef, with a wreck

The coastal waters of Grand Cayman are an *UNDERWATER PARADISE. Thanks to the good quality of the water and the varied submarine relief the marine life to be found here shows an unusually wide range of species. Particularly notable are the **black corals – much used in the creation of exquisite jewelry and ornaments – which are commonly found here though rare elsewhere. Scuba-diving enthusiasts will encounter finger corals, antler corals, fire corals and many other less common corals, orange-colored tube sponges, azure-blue cup sponges, dark-colored stovepipe sponges and trumpet sponges, sea anemones, sea ferns and the marvelously beautiful flamingo tongues, together with a wide range of fishes, from the little trumpetfish, the butterflyfish, the angelfish and the tarpon to the manta, the moray eel, the barracuda and the shark.

Divers can also explore the numerous wrecks of ships which have gone to the bottom as a result of navigational errors, storms or the activities of pirates and wreckers.

Wreck of the "Balboa"

Hell Post Office, Grand Cayman

Bodden Town, which in the past frequently suffered in pirate raids. In Gun Square is a cannon which formerly commanded the channel through the reef. On the landward side of the town an old defensive wall almost 4 miles/6 km long follows a U-shaped line. – 3 miles/5 km farther E, beyond *Meagre Bay Pond*, in the little village of **Breakers**, is the famous Lighthouse Club. Beyond can be seen the wide expanse of *Frank Sound*, with beautiful beaches. Then comes the delightful *Half Moon Bay*, and between this and the village of **East End** extends a range of impressive cliffs, with "blowing holes" through which the sea surges noisily up. Farther NE, beyond *Gorling Bluff Lighthouse* and the *Radio Cayman* transmitter, is **Gun Bay**, with a picturesque church, belfry and churchyard. Offshore lies the reef which was the scene of the "Wreck of Ten Sails" in 1788, when a convoy of ten vessels was lost. – 2½ miles/4 km beyond this, at the NE corner of the island, is the *Tortuga Club*, a well-known hostelry.

at the western entrance. It has a fine sandy beach. – Farther E, on Prospect Point, rises a monument built by William Bodden (1776–1823) commemorating *Fort Prospect*, once the headquarters of the island's government. On the E side of the point is the little *Prospect Beach*, with another wreck on its sheltering reef. Near the road are a number of interesting old graves. To the N of the main road lies the recently established settlement of *Prospect Park*, immediately N of which, on North Sound, is the developing water sports and resort center of *Omega Gardens*.

To the E of Prospect Beach is *Spotts Bay*, with the rugged *High Bluff* and *Bats' Cave Beach*, named after a cave which is still inhabited by bats. To the N are the *Matilda Ponds*, the nesting-place of rare birds. – Farther E is the little township of **Savannah*, and to the SE of this, above Old Jones Bay, the historic **Pedro's Castle*, the oldest building in the Cayman Islands, said to have been erected about 1635 by a Spanish settler and strongly fortified by the British in 1780. – N of Savannah is the *North Sound Estate*, a resort for sailing enthusiasts.

3 miles/5 km E of Savannah, in Bodden Bay with its protective barrier reef, lies the little settlement of

A typical old grave, Grand Cayman

Turtles on the Turtle Farm, Grand Cayman

Young rubber tree

From Frank Sound a road runs N through striking tropical scenery, coming in 4½ miles/7 km to **Old Man Village**, in Old Man Bay. From there the coast road continues W past *Malportas Pond, Grape Tree Point* (beautiful churchyard) and *Bowse Bluff* to (6 miles/ 10 km) Rum Point, at the NE corner of North Sound, with an idyllic beach. Here is the far-famed *Rum Point Club*, and nearby the complex of *Cayman Kai*, with a marina.

Little Cayman

The island of Little Cayman, much of which is covered by mangrove swamps, has an area of 10½ sq. miles/ 27 sq. km (length 9 miles/15 km, greatest width 2 miles/3 km). It was settled by Europeans in the 17th c., but was later abandoned after repeated pirate raids, and it was not until 1833 that fresh settlers came to the island from Grand Cayman. Now with a population of barely three dozen people, Little Cayman is an ideal base for deep-sea fishing and scuba diving.

The chief settlement is **South Town**, in the SW of the island. Along the S coast, protected by an almost continuous line of reefs, are a series of unspoiled beaches. – At the rocky western end of the island stands a lighthouse. Farther W is *Spot Bay*, where it is planned to establish a large oil terminal. Close by is *Bloody Bay*, a favorite area with scuba divers, who can prospect here for old wrecks. Along the N coast runs a coral reef, with a number of openings. At the end of the road along the

N coast is **Callabash Spot**, the site of an old settlement.

Cayman Brac

The island of Cayman Brac (area 14 sq. miles/36 sq. km) consists of a tabular formation of Tertiary limestones, much affected by karstic action, which falls away to the SW and is bounded on the E by rugged cliffs dropping steeply down to the sea. Most of the island is covered by dry forest. The narrow coastal strip is formed of Pleistocene coral limestones, and coral reefs fringe the western and central parts of the S coast and the eastern part of the N coast. The 1600 inhabitants live almost exclusively on the sheltered N coast. The island is a favorite haunt of scuba divers.

The village of **West End**, now a small resort with the island's airstrip, was established in the 17th c. by Scottish settlers who gave the island its name (from Gaelic *brac*, "bluff"). Near the famous Buccaneer's Inn are the impressive "*blowing holes*", carved out of the coral limestone by wave action. Near West End are a number of beautiful beaches, particularly on *Isaac's Point*, in the extreme W of the island, and at Brac Reef Hotel in reef-fringed *Dick Sessinger's Bay*.

At the NE end of the road along the S coast are a number of the stalactitic caves which can be found all over the island, some of them difficult to reach. In some of the caves there are still a few * iguanas, lizard-like creatures some 3 ft/1 m long which are now almost extinct and in need of protection.

The road along the N coast passes *Frenchman's Fort*, site of a historic old settlement, to rugged *Stake Bay*, where there are a few government buildings and a radio transmitter. From here a footpath runs through beautiful scenery to the little settlements of *Tibbet's Turn* and *Creek* and the island's largest village, **Spot Bay**, at the end of the road. It is possible to continue on foot to *North East Point* (165 ft/50 m; lighthouse), a steep-sided promontory commanding extensive views, with fierce breakers beating around its base.

Half way along the island a road (opened 1978) crosses the central plateau, an area with some expanses of good agricultural soil which is to be developed in the next few years.

Crooked Island

Bahama Islands
Commonwealth of the Bahamas

Islands: Crooked Island, Long Cay.
Area: 92 sq. miles/238 sq. km.
Population: 1000.
Administrative center: Nassau (on New Providence).
Vehicles travel on the left.

ⓘ **Ministry of Tourism,**
Nassau Court,
P.O. Box N 3220,
Nassau,
Bahamas;
tel. (809) 322 7505.
See also Practical Information.

HOTELS. – *Pittstown Point Landings*, Pittstown, 12 r.; *Sunny Lea Guest House*, Colonel Hill, 4 r.; *T & S Guest House*, Cabbage Hill, 9 r.

RECREATION and SPORT. – Sailing, deep-sea fishing, scuba diving, snorkeling, swimming and sunbathing; shooting.

AIR SERVICES. – Connections with Nassau (New Providence) and some neighboring islands.

SHIPPING. – Mail boat services to Nassau, Acklins and Mayaguana.

*Crooked Island and Long Cay form the NW part of a system of atolls, extending between latitude 22°10′ and 22°50′ N and between longitude 73°50′ and 74°20′ W, which encloses the Bight of Acklins, once notable for its abundance of sponges. The islands lie on the SE side of the Crooked Island Passage, an important shipping route to Central and South America.

The Spaniards paid little attention to Crooked Island and Long Cay, which served on occasion as convenient bases for buccaneers and wreckers. – From 1783 American Loyalists began to settle on the islands, and by the beginning of the 19th c. there were some 40 cotton plantations employing a total of a thousand slaves. After the decline of cotton growing the population turned to the extraction of salt from the sea.

It was only in the sixties of this century that the two islands acquired a satisfactory system of roads and services, and in recent years their natural advantages – beautiful beaches, good fishing and diving grounds, an abundance of bird life on the cliffs and reefs around the islands, magnificent karstic caves – have lead to the beginnings of development for tourism, particularly on the NE tip of Crooked Island, on *Colonel Hill* and in **Albert Town**, the chief settlement on the island of Long Cay. – On the NW coast, at **French Wells**, are the remains of fortifications of the colonial period, including an old cannon. On the northern cliffs stands *Bird Rock Lighthouse* (112 ft/ 34 m). Nearby is the *Marine Farm*, an old British fortification.

See also ****Bahamas**.

Culebra

Puerto Rico
Estado Libro y Asociado de Puerto Rico
Commonwealth of Puerto Rico

Area: 11 sq. miles/28 sq. km.
Population: 700.
Vehicles travel on the right.

ⓘ **Puerto Rico Tourism Company,**
Edificio Banco de Ponce,
Muñoz Rivera Avenue,
San Juan/Hato Rey, P.R. 00708,
Puerto Rico;
tel. (809) 754 9292.
See also Practical Information.

HOTELS. – *Punta Aloe*, 27 r.; *Seafarer's Inn*, 19 r.; etc.

RESTAURANT. – *Flamboyan*.

RECREATION and SPORT. – Sailing, deep-sea fishing, scuba diving, snorkeling, swimming and sunbathing.

AIR SERVICES. – Regular services to San Juan (Puerto Rico). Charter flights to neighboring islands.

SHIPPING. – Regular services to Vieques and Fajardo (Puerto Rico).

*Culebra, lying 20 miles E of Puerto Rico, belongs in terms of geological structure to the Virgin Islands. It is an island of great scenic beauty, with hills rising to something over 330 ft/100 m, but is not yet overrun by visitors.

The chief place on the island is **Dewy**, beautifully situated in the *Ensenada Honda*. – On the N coast is the *Playa Flamenco, a magnificent beach

EXCURSIONS. – Three little coral islands which attract many sailing enthusiasts are the *Cayo de Luis Peña* (to W), the *Cayo Norte* (to E) and *Culebrita*.

Curaçao
Southern Antilles
Netherlands Antilles

Area: 171 sq. miles/444 sq. km.
Population: 162,000.
Administrative center: Willemstad.
Vehicles travel on the right.

(i) **Curaçao Tourist Information,**
Plaza Piar,
Willemstad,
Curaçao, N.A.;
tel. 61 33 97 and 61 19 67.
See also Practical Information.

HOTELS. – *Arthur Frommer Hotel*, Piscadera Beach, 100 r., SP, T, beach; *Curaçao Hilton*, Piscadera Bay, 200 r., SP, T, beach, casino; *Curaçao CP Plaza*, St Anna's Bay, 260 r., SP, casino; *Holiday Beach Hotel*, Willemstad, 200 r., SP, T, beach, casino; *Princess Beach Hotel*, Willemstad, 140 r., SP, T, beach, casino; *Airport Hotel Bianca*, 20 r., SP; *Avila Beach Hotel*, Willemstad, 44 r.; *Coral Cliff Hotel*, Martha Bay, 40 r., T; *Country Inn*, 70 r., SP, T; *Madeira*, 60 r., SP; *Park Hotel*, 80 r.; *San Marco*, Willemstad, 60 r.; etc. – Many PENSIONS and HOLIDAY APARTMENTS.

RESTAURANTS in most hotels; also in WILLEMSTAD: *Café Restaurant Fort Nassau*, Schottegat; *Fort Waakzaamheid*, Otrabanda; *Golden Star*, Socratesstraat; *La Bistroëlle*, off the Promenade (French); *La Hacienda*, at Princess Isles Hotel; etc.

NIGHT CLUBS and CASINOS in the leading hotels.

SHOPPING. – **Punda**, the oldest part of Willemstad, is one of the best shopping areas in the Caribbean, thanks largely to the island's status as a free port. The principal shopping streets are *Breedestraat, Madurostraat* and *Heerenstraat*. Madurostraat and Heerenstraat are pedestrian precincts, as is the *Gomezplein*. There are countless shops offering luxury articles from many different countries. Particularly good value are jewelry, porcelain, optical and electronic appliances and textiles.

PUBLIC HOLIDAYS and EVENTS. – *New Year's Day*. – *Carnival* (February–March), with colorful and carefree processions. – *Good Friday. – Easter. – Queen's Birthday* (April 30). – *Labour Day* (May 1). – *Ascension. – Pentecost. – Kingdom Day* (December 15), National Day. – *Christmas* (December 24–26). – *New Year's Eve* (December 31).

Some national minorities celebrate their own festivals – the Chinese New Year, the Indian National Day, the US Independence Day.

RECREATION and SPORT. – Sailing, wind-surfing, deep-sea fishing, water-skiing, water-scootering, scuba diving, snorkeling, swimming and sunbathing; golf, riding, tennis, walking.

AIR SERVICES. – Direct connections with Aruba, Bonaire and St Maarten (Netherlands Antilles), St Kitts (B.W.I.), Port of Spain (Trinidad), San Juan (Puerto Rico), Santo Domingo (Dominican Republic), Port-au-Prince (Haiti), Kingston (Jamaica), Caracas (Venezuela), Georgetown (Guyana), Paramaribo (Surinam), Barranquilla and Medellín (Colombia), Panama City (Panama), Miami and New York (USA) and Amsterdam (Netherlands).

SHIPPING. – Willemstad is a port of call for many Caribbean cruise ships, mostly from Miami, New York (USA) and San Juan (Puerto Rico), less frequently from other islands. – Regular ferry serices to Aruba, Bonaire and Coro (Venezuela).

** Curaçao, the largest of the Netherlands Antilles, is famous for the liqueur which bears its name but it has much else to offer. Well situated from the point of view of communications, it became a major center of maritime trade in early colonial times. Present-day Curaçao has some of the largest oil-refining installations in the western hemisphere, and its capital, Willemstad, is a cosmopolitan shopping center familiar to the passengers of countless cruise liners. In addition the island has splendidly equipped hotels and idyllic beaches which have made it a popular tourist area, attracting increasing numbers of visitors especially from Western Europe.

Lying off the N coast of the South American continent, the island belongs in geological structure to the Coro highlands in Venezuela. The interior consists of gently rolling uplands, out of which rise hills formed of Cretaceous sediments such as St Christoffelberg (1230 ft/375 m).

During the Quaterny era the island lay at a lower level than it does today, so that large coral reefs were built up around the old mountain core. As a result of a subsequent upthrust these have been preserved, showing the ring-shaped formation characteristic of a former atoll. At points where the sea broke through the enclosing ring there were formed the so-called *binnenwater*, in which sheltered harbors could be established, such as Willemstad's harbor in the Schottegat.

CLIMATE. – Like the other islands in the Netherlands Antilles, Curaçao has a climate of extreme aridity. The average annual rainfall at Willemstad is only about 20 in./500 mm, mostly in the form of brief but violent showers, particularly during the months of October and November. The temperature is tropically high, with an annual mean of some 81 °F/27 °C and a very limited range of variation. The aridity of the island is increased by the large expanses of permeable limestones. The trade winds which blow throughout the year make the climate very tolerable for visitors from North America and Northern Europe. Curaçao lies outside the hurricane belt.

PLANT LIFE. – In this arid climate the dominant species are cactuses, agaves and thorny scrub. On the hillsides there are areas of dry forest. The varied

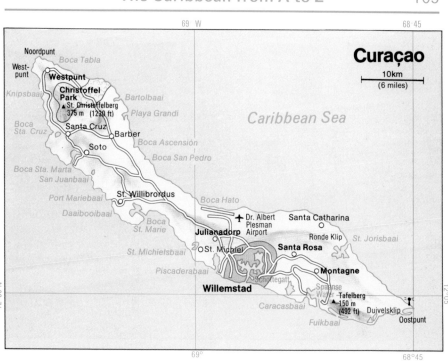

vegetation cover of which some remains can be found here and there on St Christoffelsberg has fallen victim elsewhere on the island to the lowering of the ground-water level. Large areas were formerly covered by wild pineapples and a variety of epiphytic plants (plants growing on another species).

HISTORY. – When it was discovered by the Spanish navigator Alonso de Ojeda in 1499 the island was still occupied by Arawak Indians, who were soon dis-placed by Spanish settlers. In 1634 the Dutch took the Spanish town of Santa Ana and renamed it Willem-stad, and in 1642 Peter Stuyvesant, later governor of New Amsterdam (New York), became governor of the island. Later Curaçao developed into a market for contraband goods, and it also played an important part in the slave trade. From this period dates the high proportion of blacks and mulattoes in the population. Between 1666 and the early years of the 19th c. Britain and France tried in turn to gain control of the island.

The population was increased by a considerable influx of Portuguese Jews, who numbered some 2000 by 1750. After the Paris treaties of 1815 Curaçao was finally recognized as a Dutch possession. The island's economy was mainly based on trade, and although plantations were established on Curaçao the climatic conditions were unfavorable and they made only a modest contribution to the economy. Willemstad continued to thrive as a busy transit port, and its importance increased after the opening of the Panama Canal. – The administration and the running of the port remained in the hands of a small upper stratum of Dutch officials and settlers; the Portuguese Jews were involved in trade; and the great mass of the population, consisting mostly of black and mulattoes, were employed as port workers, agricultural workers and straw-plaiters – a craft which still provided occupation for some 15% of the population at the end of the Second World War. Dilapidated old mansions in Dutch Baroque style still recall the old sugar-cane plantations, which depended on artificial irrigation and a large labor force, but were prevented from

making any great headway by the fall in the ground-water level. Until the end of the Second World War, however, many of these old irrigated *hofjes* survived, providing fruit and vegetables for domestic consump-tion.

Curaçao became internationally known for the orange liqueur named after it. The aromatic skins of the bitter oranges from which it is made began to be exported to Holland for processing in 1752.

After the First World War Royal Dutch Shell built a huge oil refinery on Curaçao, which at first processed crude oil from the nearby Lake Maracaibo area.

In 1942 the colonial status of the island was modified with the object of preparing it for a stage-by-stage move to independence. Curaçao now has 12 repre-sentatives in the Staten, the parliament of the Netherlands Antilles. In 1969 a strike by refinery workers led to disturbances which almost took on the proportions of civil war and led to a leftward move in island politics. It is the intention of the Netherlands government to prepare the Netherlands Antilles for independence under the leadership of Curaçao; but

Huts of traditional type, Curaçao

Street scene, Willemstad (Curaçao)

these plans have encountered considerable resistance on the other islands, which fear the enhancement of Curaçao's economic and political hegemony.

POPULATION. – Curaçao is a cosmopolitan island with a population of many different nationalities (about 50 all told). About a fifth of the present population were born outside the Netherlands Antilles. The island is notable, therefore, for its racial and religious tolerance, and the varied origins of the population are reflected in the variety of their religions – Roman Catholics, Protestants, Jews, Moslems and many other denominations – and the endless range of festivals and celebrations in the island's calendar. Most of the inhabitants are descended from Spanish, Dutch, Portuguese, French and British settlers, black slaves and immigrants from Asia and South America, large numbers of whom were attracted to Curaçao as indentured laborers by the boom in the oil industry. The main concentration of population is in and around Willemstad, where more than two-thirds of the inhabitants live.

ECONOMY. – The pattern of the island's economy reflects its convenient situation from the point of view of communications and its shortage of water. The extraction of salt from the salt-pans in its lagoons is of little economic importance. More important is the working of phosphates (100,000 tons annually) on the Tafelberg, which for thousands of years was the nesting-place of countless seabirds. The central element in the economy of Curaçao, however, is the oil refinery originally established by Royal Dutch Shell in 1915 and still one of the largest in the world. After an extraordinary boom in employment it became necessary to reduce the labor force from 7000 to 3000 between 1952 and 1980 as a result of increased automation, and attempts are now being made to create new jobs by the establishment of light industries and the expansion of oil storage capacity. Efforts are also under way to relieve the shortage of drinking water by setting up desalinization plants to process sea water. So far, however, it has been possible to create only about 5000 new jobs.

Particular attention is being given to the development of **tourism**, which it is hoped will give a boost to the local food industries and to trade and craft production. More than 30,000 tourist and business visitors come to Curaçao each year, together with well over 270,000 passengers on cruise ships, making tourism the second largest element in the island's economy. Curaçao has recently become known as a tax haven.

***Willemstad** (sea level; pop. *c.* 52,000), capital of the Netherlands Antilles, is a town of very Dutch aspect. In PUNDA, the picturesque quarter which is the oldest part of the town, visitors find themselves transported into a little 17th c. Dutch town, with narrow streets and handsome tall gabled buildings.

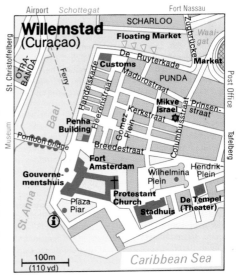

SIGHTS. – *Handelskade*, at the entrance to **St Anna Baai**, the narrow channel giving access to the natural harbor of **Schottegat**, N of the town, is lined with fine yellow and red brick houses. From here the famous *Koningin Emma Brug*, a pontoon bridge, leads over St Anna Baai into the western district of Otrabanda.

The bridge, constructed in 1939 in place of a 50-year-old predecessor, is opened at least 20 times a day to let ships through into the Schottegat.

At the E end of the bridge stands the 18th c. *Fort Amsterdam, in and around which are many public institutions and banks. On the W side is an attractive arcade.

At the W entrance to the fort is *Gouvernementehuis*, seat of the island's government. On the E side is a notable church, the *Fort Kerk* (1763; Protestant).

Immediately S of the fort is Plaza Piar, named after one of Bolívar's generals. Dominating the square the *Curaçao Plaza Hotel* occupies the site of another old fort, the Waterfort.

To the E of Fort Amsterdam is Curaçao's principal square, the **Wilhelmina Plein**, on the S side of which are the *Stadhuis*, the *Raadzaal* (Town Hall) and *Statenzaal*, which houses the parliament of the Netherlands Antilles. To the E of the square lies the *Wilhelmina Park*, at the SE corner of which is the *Tempel Emanuel*, now a theater.

Running E from the Queen Emma Bridge to the Hendrikplein is the *Breedestraat, the principal thoroughfare of the old town. Together with the side streets branching off it to the N (*Handelskade*, *Heerenstraat*, *Gómez Plein* and *Columbusstraat*) and the *Kerstraat* and *Madurostraat* it forms one of the most popular shopping areas in the Caribbean, with numerous luxury shops selling jewelry, porcelain, watches, cameras, spirits, etc., at very advantageous prices.

At the corner of Columbusstraat and Kerkstraat stands the *Joodse Synagoge Mikve Israel (1732), the oldest synagogue in the New World and one of the finest surviving examples of Dutch colonial architecture.

INTERIOR. – In the center of the synagogue, around the altar, is strewn white sand, symbolizing the children of Israel's journey through the desert to the Promised Land. From the mahogany ceiling hang four superb candelabra, each with 24 candles – reproductions of candelabra in the Portuguese Synagogue in Amsterdam.

In the Rabbi's house adjoining the synagogue are a rich **Jewish Museum** and a 300-year-old *mikvah*, formerly used for ritual ablutions.

Farther N, alongside the *De Ruyterkade* (quay), we come to the picturesque *Floating Market – a row of small sailing ships with their characteristic brown sails, in the shade of which dealers from the South American mainland offer a varied selection of fruit, vegetables and fish.

Floating Market, Willemstad

To the E, beyond a drawbridge, are the Waaigat (a small harbor basin) and the Market.

To the N of the Waaigat, in the old Jewish quarter, SCHARLOO, the architecture shows strong European influence. In this area are the *Cultureel Centrum* (Cultural Center) and to the E, the *Bolivarplein*, with a statue of Bolívar and the *Casa Bolívar* (1812), now a museum.

N of Scharloo, in St Annaboulevard, is *Roosevelt House*, presented by the Netherlands to the United States in gratitude for their help during the Second World War. It is now occupied by the US Consulate-General. – To the W St Anna Baai is spanned by the *Koningin Juliana Brug*, a modern high-level bridge (1974) which affords extensive views. Farther N, at the point where St Anna Baai runs into the Schottegat, stands the 19th c. *Fort Nassau*, from which shipping traffic in St Anna Baai is controlled.

To the W of the Queen Emma Bridge lies the OTRABANDA district. Its principal square is the **Brionplein**, with a statue commemorating the town's most famous son.

Pedro Luis Brion, leader of the island's militia at the beginning of the 19th c., distinguished himself in the defense of the town against British attacks. In 1814 he became an admiral in Bolívar's service and fought for the independence of Venezuela and Colombia. He is buried in the Pantheon in Caracas.

To the S of the Brionplein is the *Riffort* (1768), which, with the Waterfort, defended the entrance to the harbor. – To the W of the square stands a venerable old church, the *St Anna Kerk*. Some 550 yd/500 m farther W an old Dutch plantation house (1853) houses the *Curaçao Museum*, with an interesting collection of material on the history of the island (art, furniture). To the S is *Coney Island Amusement Park* (open only at weekends and on public holidays). Nearby is one of the earliest sea-water desalinization plants in the world.

SURROUNDINGS of Willemstad

Around the Schottegat. – At the SE corner of the Schottegat, Willemstad's natural harbor, is the *Autonomy Monument* (by J. Fresco). This depicts six young birds leaving the maternal nest, symbolizing the six Dutch islands in the Caribbean which were granted self-government in internal affairs on December 15, 1954. Close by is the *Centro Pro-Arte*, a theater which is used for a great variety of cultural events. A little way N is found the *Amstel Brewery*, a branch of the famous Amsterdam firm of brewers (conducted visits).

On the N side of the Schottegat is the *Raffinaderij Shell Curaçao*, one of the largest oil refineries in the world, with a capacity of 500,000 barrels a day and a labor force of 3000.

The *Beth Haim Cemetery* at the NW corner of the Schottegat is the oldest Jewish cemetery in the New World (17th c.) and one of the largest, with more than 2500 graves.

EXCURSIONS from Willemstad

Willemstad to the Tafelberg (round trip 9 miles/15 km). – Leave Willemstad on the Caracasbaaiweg, going E.

2 miles/3.5 km: **Landhuis Chobolobo**, a Dutch colonial mansion, now occupied by the *Curaçao Liqueur Distilleri* (conducted tours), in which the world-famous liqueur is manufactured, using the skins of bitter oranges. – Nearby are a fine Botanic Garden, a Zoo and a children's traffic training ground presented by the Shell Corporation.

1¼ miles/2 km: side road (2½ miles/4 km) to the *Spaanse Water*, a beautiful sheltered natural harbor now equipped as a yacht marina, with many sailing and other clubs for water sports enthusiasts. Close by is the Caracasbaai, where the large cruise ships put in.

On the E side of this bay stands *Fort Beekenburg*, with a well-preserved tower. To the W of the bay is the privately run *Jan Thiel holiday home*, open to visitors (charge).

4 miles/6.5 km: *Landhuis Santa Barbara*, a charming old plantation house on the E side of the Spaanse Water. Farther S is a fine beach, above which rises the –

*Tafelberg** (490 ft/150 m), for thousands of years the haunt of seabirds.

The guano deposited here was dissolved by rainwater and combined with the underlying coral limestone to produce stone with a high phosphoric acid content. Some 100,000 tons of phosphate a year are extracted here by opencast working.

2 miles/3 km: **Nieuwpoort**, a little settlement in *Fuikbaai*, below the S side of the Tafelberg. From here there is a charming walk by way of the wild *Duivelsklip* (Devil's Cliff) to Punt Kanon, the easternmost tip of the island, from which there are extensive views.

Willemstad to Sint Jorisbaai (round trip 8½ miles/14 km). – Leave Willemstad on the Schottegatweg Oost and Sta Rosaweg, going NE.

5 miles/8 km: **Santa Rosa**, a suburb of Willemstad, with an interesting parish church.

4 miles/6 km: *Sint Jorisbaai*, a sheltered inlet, with varied scenery, which is linked by a narrow channel with the exposed NE coast. The surrounding country has long been under cultivation, as is shown by a series of plantations – *Santa Catarina* and *Coraal Tabak* to the N, *Groot Sint Joris* to the W, *Choloma* and *Klein Sint Joris* to the S – with their fine old colonial-style buildings.

*Willemstad to Westpunt** (round trip 52 miles/83 km). – Leave Willemstad on Pater Eeuwensweg going W. On the western outskirts of the town is the beautiful *Piscaderabaai*, with several luxury hotels. – The road now turns N.

4½ miles/7 km: **Julianadorp**, a suburb of Willemstad, where is situated the University of the Netherlands Antilles.

2½ miles/4 km SW of Julianadorp is the pretty little fishing village of **Sint Michiel**, with the remains of fortifications. S of the village, in the *Blauwbaai*, is a beach well equipped for swimming.

5 miles/8 km NW of Julianadorp, past the *Salina St Michiel*, we find the *Bullenbaai* oil terminal.

2½ miles/4 km N of Julianadorp we come to the **Dr Albert Plesman Airport**, one of the best airports in the Caribbean. Nearby is the *Hato Cave*, with old Indian rock engravings. – The road continues NW.

2½ miles/4 km: *Landhuis Papaya*, an attractive pastel-colored plantation house.

¾ mile/1 km: *Landhuis Ceru Grandi*, another fine old colonial house. Situated on the **Grote Berg**, it has magnificent views of the Hato plain and the N coast. – A short distance farther on are a small chapel and an art gallery.

2 miles/3 km: **Daniel** (road junction).

3 miles/5 km W lies the little village of **Sint Willibrordus**, a good base for walks in the beautiful *Rif*, between the Salina St Marie and the sea. – To the W and NW of the village are beautiful and unfrequented beaches, including the *Daaibooibaai*, the *Portomaribaai*, the *Playa Hunku*, the *Valentijnsbaai*, the *Play' i Shon*, the *Playa Chikitu*, the *Playa Boto* and the *Playa Largu*, which is bounded on the N by *Punt Halve Dag*. – On the E side of the village the well-preserved *Landhuis Jankok* (17th–18th c.) now houses a museum on the history of the island. A notable feature is the bell which summoned the slaves back from their work on the salt-pans. The cellar under the house once served as a salt store and a prison for slaves. To the E is the *Boca San Pedro*, a romantic stretch of coastal scenery.

The road continues NW, running parallel to the coast.

3 miles/5 km: side road to **Fontein**. The main road continues N.

2½ miles/4 km: *Landhuis Ascension*, an excellently restored 17th c. plantation house above a small bay, now a training center for marines.

¾ mile/1 km: *Landhuis Doktorstuin*, the residence of the district medical officer.

1¼ miles/2 km: **Barber**, a small village with a notable church, the Sint Jozefskerk. – The road continues into the hilly northern part of the island through dry savanna country, where cactuses, agaves and thorny scrub, as well as many of the characteristic dividivi trees are found. The *Sint Antonieberg* (564 ft/172 m) is passed, then *Sint Hironymus* (755 ft/230 m).

5 miles/8 km: *Landhuis Savonet*, a charming 18th c. plantation house. Entrance to the *St Christoffelberg National Park, centered on the island's highest hill, the St Christoffelberg (1230 ft/375 m).

The ****National Park** (area 3500 acres) gives a good impression of the original vegetation pattern of Curaçao. Nature-lovers come here to see the dividivi trees, rare species of palms, wild pineapples, various epiphytic plants and orchids as well as species of reptiles and birds which have now become rare. – There are attractive roads and footpaths running through the National Park, and from the summit of St Christoffelberg there are breath-taking panoramic **views. In the lower hill to the E are four interesting *caves* with unusual rock formations and rock engravings which bear witness to occupation by Indians.

1¼ miles/2 km: *Boca Tabla*, with a cave carved out by the fierce breakers which is famed for its acoustic effects.

Along the rugged N coast there are other stretches of scenery which are scarcely less spectacular, including the *Boca Wandomi*, the *Boca Costalein*, the *Boca Platé*, the *Boca Mansalina*, the *Boca Djegu* and the *Dos Boca* – all accessible only on foot.

2½ miles/4 km: **Westpunt**, a picturesque fishing village with a fine beach of dark-colored sand. From here there is a pleasant walk to the *Noordpunt*, the northernmost tip of the island.

The road now turns S along the W coast, passing the beach of *Playa Abao*, the *Landhuis Knip* and two bays which offer good swimming, *Knipsbaai* and *Playa Jeremi*.

4 miles/6 km: **Lagún**, a small village with an attractive beach. – The road continues SE, passing another fine old plantation house, *Landhuis Santa Cruz*.

4½ miles/7 km: **Soto**, imposingly perched above *Sta Martabaai*. In early colonial days the Caiquetios were driven back into this area. Later salt was worked in the bay. The area is now being developed for tourism.

Then back via *Pannekoek* to –

18 miles/29 km: **Willemstad**.

La Désirade

Lesser Antilles
Windward Islands
French Antilles
Overseas Département of Guadeloupe

Area: 8½ sq. miles/22 sq. km.
Population: 2000.
Administrative center: Basse-Terre (on Guadeloupe).
Vehicles travel on the right.

ⓘ **Office Départemental du Tourisme,**
Place de la Victoire,
BP 1099,
F-97110 **Pointe-à-Pitre**,
Guadeloupe, A.F.;
tel. 820930.
See also Practical Information.

HOTEL. – *La Guitoune*.

RECREATION and SPORT. – Sailing, deep-sea fishing, scuba diving, snorkeling, swimming and sunbathing; walking.

EVENTS. – *Fête Communale* (Assumption), in Grande-Anse.

AIR SERVICES. – Daily scheduled service from Grande-Anse to Guadeloupe (Le Raizet).

SHIPPING. – Launches to Saint-François (Guadeloupe).

***La Désirade, lying 5 miles/8 km off the eastern tip of Guadeloupe, is an island of tabular limestone much affected by karstic action; it rises to a height of 900 ft/275 m and falls away to the NW. 7 miles/11 km long and 1¼ miles/2 km across, it is, thanks to the nature of its soil, notable for its aridity. For more than 200 years it was a leper colony, a compulsory place of residence for persons suffering from the disease.**

The chief place on the island is ***Grande-Anse**, which has a magnificent beach sheltered by a barrier reef. From here the island's only road runs N along the coast, under the steep face of the limestone plateau, and passes through the hamlet of **Souffleur** and past *Baie-Mahault*, to end at the old leper colony formerly run by the Sœurs de la Charité (closed 1954).

WALKS. – From the W side of Grande-Anse a footpath (1 hour) leads to the *Pointe du Nord*, from which there are fine views of the steep and rugged N coast, with the very impressive *Porte d'Enfer ("Gate of Hell") in the foreground.

From the E side of Grande-Anse there is a footpath (1½ hours) to the *Grande Montagne* (896 ft/273 m), which commands extensive views.

From Souffleur a steep path (1 hour) leads up the *Morne Souffleur* (679 ft/207 m), which also affords fine views.

From Baie-Mahault it is a ½ hour's walk NE to the Station Météorologique (lighthouse), above the *Pointe Double*; superb *views.

See also ****Guadeloupe**, ***Marie-Galante** and ***Iles des Saintes**.

Dog Island
See Anguilla

Dominica
Lesser Antilles
Windward Islands
Commonwealth of Dominica

Nationality letters: WD.
Area: 290 sq. miles/751 sq. km.
Capital: Roseau.
Population: 74,000.
Local administration: 2 town councils and 25 village councils.
Religion: Protestant (over 60%); Roman Catholic.
Language: English; Creole French (patois).
Currency: Eastern Caribbean dollar (EC$) of 100 cents.
Weights and measures: British/American system.
Time: Atlantic Time (4 hours behind GMT).
Vehicles travel on the left.
Travel documents: passport, visa, onward or return ticket.

(i) **Dominica Tourist Board,**
    Cork Street,
    P.O. Box 73,
    Roseau,
    Dominica, W.I.
    See also Practical Information.

HOTELS. – ROSEAU AND SURROUNDINGS: *Anchorage Hotel*, 36 r., SP; *Asta Hotel*, 16 r., *Fort Young*, 25 r., SP; *Island House*, 18 r., SP; *Reigate Hall Hotel*, 8 r., SP, T; *Sisserou Hotel*, 20 r.; etc. – ON TRANSINSULAR ROAD: *Rivière la Croix Hotel*, 10 r. – NORTH OF ST JOSEPH: *Castaways*, 30 r. – PORTSMOUTH: *Douglas Guest House*, 7 r.; *Portsmouth Beach*, 50 r.

RESTAURANTS in most of these hotels; also IN ROSEAU: *La Robe Créole*.

PUBLIC HOLIDAYS and EVENTS. – *New Year's Day*. – *Samedi Gras* (Saturday before Ash Wednesday), with lively dancing displays. – *Carnival* (Monday and Tuesday before Ash Wednesday), street carnival, with processions and dancing. – *Good Friday*. – *Easter Monday*. – *Labour Day* (May 1), with events organized by trade unions. – *Pentecost*. – *Caribbean Day* (July), commemorating the signature of the Caricom agreement. – *Emancipation Day* (August 1), commemorating the emancipation of the slaves. – *National Day* (November 3–4), with folk displays and carnival events. – *Christmas Day*. – *Boxing Day* (December 26), with dancing.

RECREATION and SPORT. – Safaris and excursions into the interior of the island; scuba diving, fishing; swimming and sunbathing.

The road system of this relatively undeveloped island has not yet been brought up to modern standards, and there is little in the way of public transport. For excursions into the interior it is advisable to rent a car, preferably a cross-country vehicle with a knowledgeable local driver. – There are cleared and waymarked paths only to certain particular beauty-spots. For safaris and excursions into the remoter parts of the island – which will often be extremely strenuous – appropriate clothing should be worn, and it is essential to have a local guide.

AIR SERVICES. – Daily connections with Guadeloupe (Aéroport Le Raizet/Pointe-à-Pitre), Antigua (Coolidge International Airport), Martinique (Aéroport du Lamentin/Fort-de-France), St Lucia (Castries) and Barbados (Grantley Adams International Airport).

SHIPPING. – Occasional calls by cruise ships and banana boats with passenger cabins plying between Roseau and Western Europe. – Irregular sailings to neighboring islands by cargo boats with accommodation for passengers.

*Dominica, the hilliest island in the inner arc of the volcanic Antilles, lies roughly half way between the two French overseas territories of Guadeloupe and Martinique, between latitude 15°12′ and 15°40′ N and between longitude 61°15′ and 61°30′ W. It is an island of magnificent mountain scenery, difficult of access with its three principal massifs, rising to a height of 4748 ft/ 1447 m in the centrally situated Morne Diablotin, and more than 350 rivers and streams. Here are still to be found rare plants and animals which have long since disappeared from the neighboring islands.

Many fumaroles (volcanic crevices, from which hot vapour issues), hot springs and sulphur springs, the most famous of which is the Boiling Lake, bear witness to the volcanic activity which has not yet died down. The greater part of this rainy island is covered with dense evergreen rain forest. Sparse tropical mountain forest (cloud forest) is found in the summit zones of the highest mountains, green dry forest in the sheltered coastal areas on the Caribbean side of the island, the most favored regions of human settlement. On the windward side, facing the Atlantic, the hills fall steeply down to the sea, though there is room for the island's airport in the northern part of this coastal area. Only near the mouths of rivers and in sheltered bays are there beaches of dark-colored sand and small natural harbors.

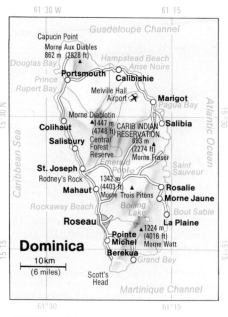

HISTORY. – Columbus discovered the island, then inhabited by warlike Caribs, on Sunday November 3, 1493 during his second voyage and accordingly named it *Dominica* (Sunday Island). In 1627 Charles I presented the island to the Earl of Carlisle, but subsequent English attempts to establish settlements were frustrated by the Caribs – estimated to number about 2000 at the beginning of the 18th c. – as were later enterprises by the French. In the treaty of Aix-la-Chapelle (1748) Britain and France agreed that the island should remain in the hands of the original inhabitants; but, tempted by the fertility of the soil, the French in particular disregarded this agreement and established a number of settlements and plantations. During the second half of the 18th c. there was bitter fighting between French and British forces for control of the island, to which the native Caribs now gave the name of *Waitukubuli* ("land of many battles"). Finally in 1805, in return for a payment of £12,000, France ceded Dominica to Britain, after first burning down the capital, Roseau. From 1871 to 1940 the island was administered as part of the British Leeward Islands, and from 1940 to 1956 as part of the British Windward Islands. It then became a crown colony; from 1958 to 1962 it belonged to the West Indies Federation, and in 1967 it was granted the status of a state associated with Britain but enjoying internal self-government. On November 3, 1978 it attained independence as the Commonwealth of Dominica, and on December 18 became the 151st member of the United Nations. –

The Dominican parliament consists of a 21-member House of Assembly, presided over by the Speaker, and a 9-member Senate, from which three ministers are elected. – In the late summer of 1979 Hurricanes David and Frederick caused widespread devastation on the island. In 1981 a plot against the ruler, Eugenia Charles, was uncovered. In 1983 Dominica took part in the invasion of Grenada by US and Caribbean forces.

POPULATION and ECONOMY. – Blacks and mulattoes form the great majority of the population, some 40% of whom belong to the Roman Catholic Church and 60% to various Protestant denominations. In a reserve on the E coast there live some 400 people of predominantly Indian descent, though only a few are pure-blooded Caribs. – Although only a fifth of the island's area is under cultivation agriculture is the most important element in the economy. In the 19th c. Dominica's principal export was coffee, but after the trees were affected by disease coffee-growing gave way to the cultivation of limes, and the use of limes in dyeing and as a means of preventing scurvy in the Royal Navy enabled Dominica to become the world's largest producer of lime concentrates. Then in the 1930s a further outbreak of plant disease led to the gradual displacement of the lime by the banana, which is now the island's chief export. Consequent upon the terrible damage by hurricanes in recent years, banana production is now in a critical situation. Other products are coconut oil, cocoa, tobacco and laurel oil. Citrus fruits are exported to the neighboring islands and Western Europe. The old method of clearing land for agriculture by burning is still practiced in some areas. Fishing and craft industry (boatbuilding, arts and crafts) are traditional activities which are likely to retain their importance, in view particularly of the expected expansion of the tourist trade (28,000 visitors in 1979). The average income of the inhabitants, however, is barely £50/$80 a month, and accordingly many Dominicans seek to better themselves by the direct sale of local products (fruit, vegetables, hand-made articles) or by seeking employment elsewhere, particularly on the neighboring islands of Guadeloupe and Martinique with their better developed economy and flourishing tourist trade.

The island's capital, *Roseau (pop, 20,000), a typical little town of the colonial period which was rebuilt on a planned layout after a fire in 1805, lies at the mouth of the Roseau River on the SW coast.

SIGHTS. – The harbor front (small vessels only: larger ships anchor offshore) is lined by warehouses and other commercial

Street in Roseau (Dominica)

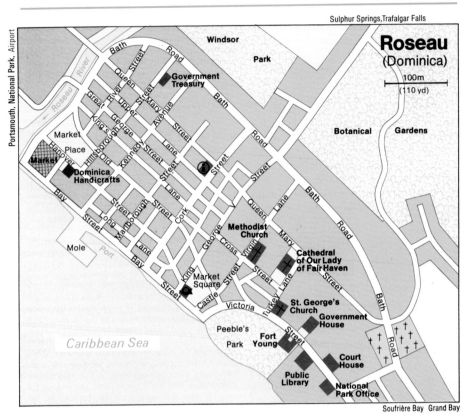

Sulphur Springs, Trafalgar Falls

Roseau
(Dominica)

Portsmouth, National Park, Airport

Windsor Park

Government Treasury

Botanical   Gardens

100m
(110 yd)

Market Place

Market

Dominica Handicrafts

Mole

Port

Methodist Church

Cathedral of Our Lady of Fair Haven

Market Square

St. George's Church

Government House

Caribbean Sea

Peeble's Park

Fort Young

Public Library

Court House

National Park Office

Soufrière Bay   Grand Bay

buildings, with colorful markets at the N and S ends. In Victoria Street, in the southern part of the town, *Fort Young* (now a hotel) was originally built in the 18th c. and later enlarged several times. In this area are several public buildings in Georgian style – the *Public Library* and, on the opposite side of the street, *Government House* and the venerable *Court House*. Nearby stands *St George's Church*, a handsome 19th c. building (Anglican). To the N is the island's principal Roman Catholic church, the *Cathedral of Our Lady of Fair Haven* (19th c.). In the town center, a district of modest wooden houses with a few buildings of stone and concrete, are several handicraft centers selling attractive local products (basketwork, naturally dyed fabrics, verti-verti mats, wood-carving, souvenirs made from coconut shells and bamboo). – Above the town to the W, on the slopes of Morne Bruce (once occupied by a fort), are the magnificent *Botanical Gardens* (110 acres), laid out at the end of the 19th c., with rare plants both native and imported.

E of Roseau lies the ****Morne Trois Pitons National Park** (25 sq. miles/ 64 sq. km), established in 1975. This is one of the finest nature parks in Central America, with magnificent scenery of volcanic origin and a varied range of plant and animal life.

Within the National Park, at **Pont Cassé** (on the road from Roseau to Melville Hall Airport), a side road branches off and runs through superb primeval forest to the *Emerald Pool, a small basin surrounded by

Primeval forest near the Emerald Pool (Dominica)

rocks, with a waterfall. – S of Pont Cassé is the *Morne Trois Pitons (4403 ft/1342 m), a three-peaked hill which climbers will find difficult.

From Roseau a road follows the valley of the *Roseau River*, with side roads leading to the striking *Sulphur Springs, bubbling and emitting sulphurous fumes, and the *Trafalgar Falls, one of the finest waterfalls on the island. The road continues up the valley past the wild *Ti Trou Gorge* to the *Morne Macaque* (3501 ft/1067 m) and the picturesque *Freshwater Lake, a deep lake filling the crater of an extinct volcano. To the N, through a forest of giant ferns, is *Boeri Lake*, also in a beautiful setting. – To the S of Freshwater Lake, in the *Valley of Desolation*, is the **Boiling Lake (diameter almost 330 ft/100 m), discovered in 1922. This is part of a solfatara field in which a violent explosion of steam took place in 1880. One of the largest solfatara lakes in the world, it "boils" at regular intervals. Much of the vegetation around the lake has been killed by the sulphurous fumes.

From Roseau a difficult road runs 10 miles/16 km SE to *Grand Bay*, a wide bay on the S coast with a beautiful beach and a fine view of Martinique. Farther E is *Pointe Saint-Jean*, on the Atlantic coast. To the S of Roseau the village of *Pointe Michel* was established by Martiniquais fleeing from the catastrophic explosion of Mont Pelé. Farther S is *Soufrière Bay*, with a good sandy beach and plenty of scope for scuba divers. Above the bay are the Soufrière Sulphur Springs. To the S, on Scott's Head, stands the Old Semaphore Station, with a fine view of Martinique.

Transinsular Road (Melville Hall Airport to Roseau, 40 miles/65 km). – The road runs S from the airport via Marigot (population 5000), the largest settlement on the Atlantic coast, to the beautiful *Pagua Bay*, with a beach of dark-colored sand.

From Pagua Bay a road leads S to the * *Carib Indian Reservation, beyond the village of *Salibia*. Established in 1903, the reservation has an area of some 3750 acres. Of the 1000 or so inhabitants some 400 are of predominantly Indian stock, but very few indeed are pure-blooded Caribs. Some of them still live in the traditional type of hut constructed of branches and leaves, but most of the old huts have been replaced by the common Caribbean type of Creole wooden hut standing on low piles. The most notable Carib products, apart from artistic woodcarving and basketwork, are the dugouts made from the trunks of rubber trees which are still widely used as fishing boats all over the island. These canoes are still made on the beach at the little fishing village of *Castle Bruce*, to the S of the reservation.

The main road continues SW from Pagua Bay, through plantations of limes and bananas and past mighty rubber trees, to the interesting *Central Forest Reserve, with the *Wet Area Agriculture Station*, and Pont Cassé, a central junction point from which roads descend through the fertile valley of the *Layou River* (plantations of bananas, citrus fruits, cacao and tobacco) to the W coast and, in the opposite direction, to the Atlantic coast.

The road to the E passes the Emerald Pool and reaches the Atlantic coast at Rosalie, a small village surrounded by banana plantations, with a small beach. Near the village an impressive waterfall plunges down into the sea. To the N lies the beautiful bay of *Petite Soufrière, where another waterfall tumbles into the sea, and beyond this is the little bay of *Saint Sauveur*. – To the S, beyond *Bout Sable* with its beach of dark-colored sand, are the little village of La Plaine and the *Pointe Mulâtre* from which the road leads up to Delices.

From Pont Cassé the road to the W coast descends through a deeply indented

In the Carib Indian Reservation, Dominica

valley, past the *Rivière La Croix* plantation, to the coast and then turns S to Roseau.

Roseau to Portsmouth by the coast road (50 miles/80 km). – The road runs N, with fine views, past little *Woodbridge Bay* and the beautiful *Rockaway Beach*, and continues through plantations of limes to *Massacre* and **Mahaut**, which has a number of small factories (coconut products, canning, sugar).

Farther N are the rugged *Rodney's Rock* and the strikingly impressive mouth of the *Layou River*; then on by way of St Joseph and the *Castaways* resort complex, with a beach of dark-colored sand; and through the little villages of *Salisbury*, *Colihaut* and *Dublanc* to the *Pointe Ronde*. From here it is possible to climb the *Morne Diablotin* (4748 ft/1447 m), the island's highest summit, to the SE. In the almost impenetrable forests which cover its slopes there are still a few of the rare sisserou parrots.

The route continues along *Prince Rupert Bay, where on April 12, 1782 a naval battle was fought between the French and the more powerful English forces, the latter being victorious. There are still many

the island, lies on an excellent natural harbor, but its development has been hampered by the swampy nature of the surrounding country. On a promontory to the NW are the ruins of *Fort Shirley (18th and 19th c.), with a few old cannon. – The road continues N through teak plantations to *Douglas Bay* and little Toucari Bay (beaches with some areas of light-colored sand), at the foot of the *Morne aux Diables* (2828 ft/862 m). From *Capucin Point*, at the northern tip of the island, there is a good view of the Iles des Saintes.

Melville Hall Airport to Portsmouth (25 miles/40 km). – From the airport the road runs N above *Londonderry Bay*, with a beach of dark-colored sand, to beautiful Woodford Hill Bay, the *Anse Noire* and *Hodges Beach* (with light-colored sand), from which scuba divers can explore the magnificent banks of *coral (brain corals, sea ferns; rare tropical fish). From here too there is a good view of the island of Marie-Galante in the Guadeloupe archipelago. – The road continues W, passing close to *Baptiste Beach* and *Hampstead Beach*, palm-fringed beaches of light-colored sand. Beyond this a side road goes off to **Vieille Case**, on the NW coast. The main road continues through banana plantations to **Portsmouth**.

The north coast of Dominica

cannon on the sea bed. A trip along the *Indian River*, which flows into the sea here, is an enjoyable experience for the dense tropical rain forest is the home of many rare birds and orchids.

The attractive little town of **Portsmouth** (pop. 4500), the second largest place on

Dominican Republic

Hispaniola

República Dominicana

Nationality letters: DOM.
Area: 18,816 sq. miles/48,734 sq. km.
Capital: Santo Domingo.
Population: 5,622,000.
Local administration: 27 provinces.
Religion: Roman Catholic; Protestant minority.
Language: Spanish.
Currency: Dominican peso (RD$) of 100 centavos.
Weights and measures: metric.
Time: Eastern Standard Time (EST), 5 hours behind GMT.
Vehicles travel on the right.
Travel documents: US and Canadian citizens, proof of citizenship and tourist card; for others, passport.

ⓘ **Dirección Nacional de Turismo e Información,**
César Nicolás Pensón/Rosa Duarte,
P.O. Box 497,
Santo Domingo,
República Dominicana;
tel. (809) 688 5537.
See also Practical Information.

The **Dominican Republic (República Dominicana), the second largest West Indian state (after Cuba), occupies the eastern part of the island of Hispaniola in the Greater Antilles. It has an area of 18,816 sq. miles/48,734 sq. km. Bordered on the W by the republic of Haiti, which occupies more than a third of the island, it is bounded on the N by the Atlantic Ocean and on the S by the Caribbean Sea, which stretches between the West Indian islands and the coasts of South and Central America. Its neighbor to the E is the island of Puerto Rico, from which it is separated by the 70-mile-wide Mona Passage. It lies some 685 miles/1102 km SE of the southern tip of Florida and 375 miles/603 km N of Punta Gallinas, the most northerly point in South America.

Hispaniola is the most mountainous of the West Indian islands, and the highest peaks in the Caribbean archipelago lie within the territory of the Dominican Republic. The backbone of the country is the **Cordillera Central**, with *Pico Duarte* (10,417 ft/ 3175 m) and *Loma la Rucilla* (9938 ft/ 3029 m). This range of mountains which traverses the country from NW to SE belongs, together with three other parallel ranges, to the eastern belt of the American cordillera system. All four ranges have been subjected in geologically recent times to upward thrusts, and the earthquakes which occur with some frequency, sometimes causing considerable damage, are clear evidence that in this region the earth's crust has not yet settled down.

A second characteristic feature of the geological structure of Hispaniola is represented by the three large rift valleys which lie between the island's four mountain ranges. The most striking of these long narrow depressions is the Enriquillo valley, the deepest part of which, the Lago de Enriquillo in the SW of the Dominican Republic, is 144 ft/44 m below sea level. The difference in altitude between this lake and the summit of Pico Duarte (10,562 ft/3219 m), however, is very far from reflecting the full extent of the upward and downward movement of the earth's crust in this area, as is shown by the conformation of the sea bottom: only 30 miles/48 km N of Hispaniola is the Puerto Rico Trench, which plunges down to 30,248 ft/9219 m in the Milwaukee Depth.

CLIMATE. – The Dominican Republic lies in the outer tropical climatic zone, with relatively little variation in temperature between summer and winter. In July, the warmest month in the year, average temperatures at sea level are about 82 °F/28 °C, falling in January to 73 °F/23 °C. Seasonal climatic differences are reflected more clearly in the rainfall: a dry winter (December–March) is followed by two rainy periods (April–June and August–November), corresponding to the zenithal position of the sun. A determinant factor is the NE trade wind, blowing throughout the

year, which gives rise to downward air movements, usually hindering the formation of rain-bringing clouds. The strong summer sunshine, however, leads to the formation of strong convectional currents in the lower levels of the atmosphere, and the rising air masses frequently break through the otherwise stable movement of the trade winds, leading to increased cloud formation and a tendency to showers.

Unusually large climatic variations are produced by the varied pattern of relief, affecting both the temperature and, even more markedly, the rainfall. Three distinct temperature zones determined by altitude can be distinguished: up to about 2950 ft/ 900 m is the *tierra caliente* (warm zone), with a mean annual temperature of over 70 °F/21 °C, and above this is the *tierra templada* (temperate zone), with temperatures ranging between 70 °F/21 °C and 61 °F/ 16 °C, followed above 6560 ft/2000 m by the *tierra fría* (cold zone), with temperatures below 61 °F/16 °C. The distribution of rainfall is determined in every area by altitude, for the rain-bringing trade winds, blowing constantly from the NE, come up against the mountain ranges running at right angles to their direction of movement, so that the rainfall is considerably heavier on the weather side than on the lee side of the mountains. The rainiest areas are, therefore, in the NE of the country (up to 75 in./1900 mm) and in the high Cordillera Central, while in some southern areas the rainfall may be as low as 12 in./300 mm or even less. The driest part of the country is the Enriquillo valley with its slightly brackish lakes.

This range of variation, from high humidity to total aridity, aggravated by the great differences in altitude – an extreme range found scarcely anywhere else in the world within such a relatively small area – is reflected in the distribution of the natural vegetation. This ranges from the evergreen tropical rain forests, varying in type with altitude, and the mangrove swamps of the northern coastal area by way of the humid forest of the intermediate areas to the thorny scrub and succulents of the Enriquillo valley; and there are similarly marked variations in the crops grown in different parts of the country from N to S.

HISTORY. – The island of Hispaniola was discovered by Columbus on December 6, 1492 on his first voyage to the New World. The inhabitants were Arawak Indians, of advanced cultural level, who lived mainly by agriculture (manioc and maize) and on the coast also by fishing. European settlement started a year after the discovery of the island, and the natives were then decimated by enslavement and disease. Within a short period they had been wiped out altogether, and from 1509 black slaves began to be brought in to work the gold- and silver-mines for the Spaniards. During this period Santo Domingo became capital of all the Spanish colonies in America and a base for further voyages of discovery. After the island's mines had been worked out, however, the main center of Spanish activities moved to South America, and from 1530 onwards the once-flourishing colony started to decline. Soon afterwards the French began to extend their sphere of influence to America, and in 1697 Spain was compelled under the treaty of Rijswijk to cede the western part of Hispaniola to France. The eastern part of the island – the territory of the present-day Dominican Republic – remained in Spanish hands, under the name of the Audiencia Española de Santo Domingo; but barely a hundred years later (1795) France gained possession of the whole island with the help of the black fighter for independence Toussaint L'ouverture. In 1802 the Spanish Creoles, with British support, broke away from Haiti and returned to Spanish rule. In 1821, however, the Dominican people rose against Spain, and Haiti took advantage of the situation to annex the eastern part of the island. Finally in 1844 the Dominican Republic was established; but in view of the continuing threat from its French-speaking neighbor country the new republic voluntarily put itself under the protection of Spain in 1861. Only four years later, however, this further colonial interlude was ended by a revolution. The following hundred years were marked by perpetually recurring domestic difficulties. From 1916 to 1924 the country was annexed by the United States, anxious to protect its economic interests; then in 1930, with US support, the army commander, Rafael Leónidas Trujillo y Molina, seized power. He was succeeded in 1952 by his brother H. B. Trujillo y Molina, but retained his dictatorial powers until his murder in 1961. By plundering and exploiting the country, the Trujillos made themselves one of the wealthiest families in the world. The new President was Juan Bosch, who was displaced by a military junta only two years later, in 1963. A further attempted putsch in 1965 led to civil war, which was ended by the intervention of a US force of 30,000 men. In 1966 Joaquín Balaguer became President, followed in 1978 by Silvestre Antonio Gúzman Fernández. The victor in the 1982 election was Salvator Jorge Blanco.

GOVERNMENT and ADMINISTRATION. – The President, who is elected for a four-year term, is head of state, head of the government and commander of the army and police. He is, to say the least, in a very strong position. The Dominican parliament (Congress) consists of two chambers, the Senate (27 members) and the House of Representatives (91 members), which together form the National Assembly. The country is divided into 26 provinces and the district of Santo Domingo. The administration of each province is headed by a governor appointed by the President.

POPULATION and ECONOMY. – The marked racial differences in the population of the Antilles derive from the differing economic structure of the former British (Jamaica, Barbados, Windward and Leeward Islands) and French colonies (Saint-Domingue/Haiti, Martinique and Guadeloupe) on the one hand and the Spanish colonies (Cuba, Puerto Rico, Santo Domingo) on the other. While the British and French colonies were, until the end of the 19th c., prosperous and densely populated sugar islands with a flourishing plantation economy based on cheap slave labour, the thinly populated Spanish colonies depended on extensive cattle-rearing and subsistence farming on

small peasant holdings. In these territories a plantation economy based on the concentration of land ownership in a small number of large estates (latifundia) came into being only in the post-colonial period, at the beginning of the 20th c. As a result of these different patterns of development the former British and French territories still have fairly high population densities and a high proportion of blacks, while the old Spanish colonies are much less densely populated, with a predominance of whites.

The population of the Dominican Republic shows a very different pattern from either of these. Neither the black nor the white inhabitants (who are predominantly of Spanish origin) enjoy numerical superiority, accounting respectively for 12% and 28% of the total population. The majority (60%) are mulattoes. The explanation for this difference lies in the two periods of rule by Haiti, which was a French colony from 1697 until the 19th c. and had a correspondingly numerous black population, many thousands of whom moved into the less densely populated eastern part of the island of Hispaniola. This movement still continues on an illegal basis, since the level of economic development of the Dominican Republic is considerably higher than that of Haiti and offers the blacks who slip over the frontier the hope of improving their fortunes.

A slum area in Santo Domingo

The annual rate of population increase in the Dominican Republic is 2.9% – the highest in the West Indies, excluding the Bahamas (4.2%). In spite of this the density of population is still relatively low – an average of 272 to the sq. mile (105 to the sq. km) for the whole country. This national average, however, covers wide variations. Some 47% of the population live in towns, at higher densities, reaching 1450 to the sq. mile (560 to the sq. km) in the capital, Santo Domingo de Guzmán; in the Valle del Cibao, the most northerly of the island's three longitudinal valleys, it is still 492 to the sq. mile (190 to the sq. km); but outside these two concentrations it falls to well below 259 to the sq. mile (100 to the sq. km).

The Dominican Republic is predominantly an agricultural country, and agricultural produce accounts for some 79% of its exports. The principal crop is sugar (40–50% of exports by value), followed by coffee, bananas, cocoa and tobacco. More than half the country's area is under cultivation, and some 40% of this is in large holdings of 250 acres and over – though these represent no more than 0.7% of the total number of holdings. Most of the large estates are in the sugarcane-growing area in the southern coastal region, followed by the cacao-growing area in the Río Yaqui valley (Valle del Cibao) and the coffee-growing area on the slopes of the Sierra de Baoruco in the SW of the country. The NW is devoted primarily to the growing of bananas, mostly for the US-owned United Fruit

National Palace, Santo Domingo

Company. The smaller holdings are not much involved in growing cash crops for export but produce mainly for domestic consumption – rice, maize and beans, together with onions, sweet potatoes, tapioca and tropical tubers. There is also a certain amount of stock farming inherited from the colonial period.

Apart from agriculture the only other economic activity of any real importance is the working and export of *bauxite* (annual output about 100,000 tons). It is also planned in future to work copper, nickel and chromium ore on a substantial scale, and further deposits of gold and silver have also been discovered. Industry, however, still plays a very subordinate part: apart from a few sugar processing plants there are a few textile and clothing factories of very minor importance.

An important contribution is now being made by **tourism** (over 700,000 visitors in 1983), which is only now being recognized as a valuable labor-intensive sector of the economy. In addition to the capital, Santo Domingo – the oldest colonial town in the New World – increasing numbers of visitors are now being attracted to the fashionable seaside resort of La Romana in the SE of the country, the coastal area around Samaná in the NE and the N coast round Puerto Plata. The government promotes investment in tourism by offering tax inducements and is also carrying out a number of large-scale projects on its own account, including the development of the Playa Grande/Playa Dorada area.

The people of the Dominican Republic regard **amber** (*ámbar*) as their national stone. This fossil resin dating from the Tertiary era – ranging in color from light yellow to blackish brown and usually translucent – is found in the mountains in the central and northeastern parts of the country and is worked by local craftsmen and artists into beautiful and intricately carved jewelry and ornaments which are sought after by visitors as souvenirs.

The range of amber articles to be seen in jewelers' shops is wide – from bracelets, earrings and brooches to chessmen, pipe mouthpieces and vessels of various kinds. Also very popular are cut pieces of amber in which an insect is imprisoned.

The largest piece of amber so far found weighed 21 lb/9.5 kg and was about the size of the upper part of a child's body.

See also ****Bahía de Samaná**, ***Higüey**, ***La Romana, Puerto Plata, Santiago de los Caballeros** and ****Santo Domingo.**

Eleuthera

Bahama Islands
Commonwealth of the Bahamas

Islands: Eleuthera, Cupid's Cay, Windemere Island, St George's Cay, Harbour Island.
Area: 200 sq. miles/518 sq. km.
Population: 9000.
Administrative center: Nassau (on New Providence).
Vehicles travel on the left.

(i) **Ministry of Tourism,**
Nassau Court,
P.O. Box N 3220,
Nassau,
Bahamas;
tel. (809) 322 7505.
See also Practical Information.

HOTELS. – SPANISH WELLS: *Roberts·Beach Resort,* 16 r., T; *Roberts Harbour Club,* 14 r., T; *Sawyers Marina,* 12 r., SP; etc. – HARBOUR ISLAND: **Romora Bay Club,* 25 r., T; **Valentine's Yacht Club,* 26 r., SP, T; *Coral Sands Hotel,* 30 r., T; *Dunmore Beach Hotel,* 30 r., T; *Ocean View Club,* 10 r.; *Pink Sands Lodge,* 53 r., T; *Runaway Hill Club,* 7 r., SP; *Sunset Inn,* 6 r.; etc. – NORTH ELEUTHERA: *Current Yacht and Diving Club,* Current, 19 r.; *La Renaissance,* Ridley Head, 10 r., SP; *Whale Point Hotel,* Whale Point, 40 r.; etc. – GREGORY TOWN: *Cambridge Villas,* 16 r.; *Caridon Cottages,* 6 r.; etc. – HATCHET BAY: *Rainbow Inn,* 27 r., T; *Cigatoo Inn,* 20 r., SP, T; etc. – GOVERNOR'S HARBOUR: **Club Méditerranée French Leaves,* 300 r., SP, T; **Potlach Club,* 18 r., SP, T; *Buccaneer's Club,* 8 r., SP, T; etc. – WINDEMERE ISLAND: *Windemere Island Club,* 79 r., SP. – TARPUM BAY: *Cartwright's Ocean View Cottages,* 5 r.; *Culmer House,* 6 r.; *Hilton's Heaven Hotel,* 10 r.; etc. – ROCK SOUND (and surrounding area): **Cape Eleuthera Resort and Yacht Club,* 128 r., SP, T, golf; **Cotton Bay Club,* 76 r., SP, T, golf; *Nu-View Hotel,* 8 r.; *Winding Bay Beach Cottages,* 36 r., SP, T; etc.

RECREATION and SPORT. – Sailing, deep-sea fishing, parasailing, water-skiing, scuba diving, snorkeling, wind-surfing, swimming and sunbathing; tennis, golf, walking.

AIR SERVICES. – Regular flights from North Eleuthera, Governor's Harbour and Rock Sound to Nassau, Freeport, Fort Lauderdale (USA) and Miami.

SHIPPING. – Mail boat services from Spanish Wells, Harbour Island, The Bluff, Hatchet Bay, Governor's Harbour, Rock Sound, Davis Harbour, Wemyss Bight and Bannerman Town to Nassau.

Some 40 miles/65 km E of New Providence lies the long, straggling, sickle-shaped island of *Eleuthera (about 112 miles/180 km long, but only a few miles/km wide), the most highly developed of all the Bahamian Out Islands. There is a long tradition of agriculture on the island, and tourism – with Eleuthera's rose-pink beaches as a powerful attraction – is also well established.

In 1649 a few dozen pioneers from England and Bermuda, the Eleutherian

A beach on Eleuthera

Adventurers (from Greek *eleutheria*, "freedom"), were shipwrecked off the island and founded the first republic in the New World here. Something of the atmosphere of the early colony is still preserved in the pretty little settlements with their pastel-colored houses.

The largest place on the island, **Rock Sound**, lying on an imposing natural harbor, is now a rapidly developing resort. Around the town are large cattle farms. – Exclusive new resorts have been established on the S of Rock Sound in *Cotton Bay* and to the SW on *Cape Eleuthera*, where Bruce Devlin and Bob van Hagge have laid out one of the finest championship golf-courses in the world. – At the S end of the island are *Davis Harbour* (yacht harbor) and *Wemyss Bight*, an idyllic little fishing harbor. At *Millers* are the well-preserved remains of an old plantation house.

The attractive little settlement of **Bannerman Town** lies near East End Point, with a lighthouse and a beautiful beach. – N of Rock Sound is the picturesque fishing village of **Tarpum Bay**, with a new resort center.

In an idyllic bay half way down the island is *Governor's Harbour*, a popular resort, with an interesting straw market and art gallery. – A causeway leads to *Cupid's Cay*, where the first settlers are believed to have landed in 1649. – 9 miles/15 km SE is the pleasant little fishing village of **Savannah Sound**. Offshore, to the E, lies *Windemere Island*, with a new resort hotel.

To the N of Governor's Harbour is the airfield, and a mile or two beyond this the quiet little fishing village of James Cistern. The road continues via *Alice Town* to **Hatchet Bay**, the main poultry-farming

and dairying center in the Bahamas. Nearby are karstic *caves* with magnificent stalactites and stalagmites.

The road continues N through an area of pastureland to **Gregory Town**, well known for its food and drinks industries (including pineapple punch). The *Cove* is a small harbor, formerly a buccaneers' lair. In the surrounding area are large pineapple plantations. – To the N of Gregory Town is the *Glass Window*, a fragment of a natural arch which once spanned the island here at its narrowest point. There is a striking contrast between the deep blue water of the Atlantic to the E and the turquoise-colored water of the shallow *Middle Ground* to the W.

The Glass Window, Eleuthera

Current, at the northwestern tip of the island, is the largest settlement in the northern part of Eleuthera. Offshore is a labyrinth of coral reefs in which many blockade-runners came to grief during the American Civil War. Experienced scuba divers can explore the numerous wrecks in this area. Here too is the *Boiling Hole*, a cavity in an offshore sandbank which "boils" at the turn of the tide. – SE of Current, near the airfield, are the little villages of *Lower Bogue* and *Upper Bogue*. – NE of Current is the *Bluff*, a small harbor. – At the N end of the island is the *Preacher's Cave*, in which the Eleutherian Adventurers took refuge after their shipwreck.

On the little island of **St George's Cay**, off the N coast of Eleuthera, lies the picturesque little town of *Spanish Wells* (pop. 800). It was here that pirates and others found fresh water. Built on a steep-sided hill above an excellent natural harbor, it was burned down by American troops in 1812. Good diving grounds and fine beaches in the surrounding area.

Off the E coast of northern Eleuthera is
*Harbour Island (area $1\frac{1}{2}$ sq. miles/4 sq.
km; pop. 1500), now a popular resort,
with picturesque gardens and rose-pink
beaches. The island was occupied by
English settlers in 1694, and the inhabitants ("Brilanders") still speak an
old-world form of English. The chief place
on the island, formerly the home of
boatbuilders and wreckers, is *Dunmore
Town, a little colonial township named
after the Earl of Dunmore, Governor of the
Bahamas 1786–97, who used to spend
the summer here. The fine *Methodist
Church* (1835) is one of the largest
churches in the Bahamas.

See also **Bahamas.

Exumas

Bahama Islands
*Commonwealth of the
Bahamas*

Scuba diver in the Exumas

Islands: Great Exuma, Little Exuma, Exuma Cays.
Area: 112 sq. miles/290 sq. km.
Administrative center: Nassau (on New Providence).
Vehicles travel on the left.
ⓘ Ministry of Tourism,
   Nassau Court,
   P.O. Box N 3220,
   Nassau,
   Bahamas;
   tel. (809) 322 7505.
   See also Practical Information.

HOTELS. – GREAT EXUMA: *Out Island Inn, George
Town, 88 r., SP, T; Hotel Peace and Plenty, George
Town, 32 r., SP; John Marshall's Guest-House,
George Town, 13 r.; Regatta Point, George Town, 6 r.;
Bahama Sound Beach Club, Bahama Sound, 13 r.;
etc. – STANIEL CAY: Happy People Marina, 11 r.; Sand
Dollar Beach Hotel, 24 r., SP; Staniel Cay Yacht Club,
6 r., SP. – NORMAN'S CAY: Norman's Cay Club, 16 r., T.

EVENTS. – *Out Island Regatta (April), George Town.
– Bahama Bonefish Bonanza (September), deep-sea
fishing competition, starting from George Town.

RECREATION and SPORT. – Sailing, deep-sea
fishing, wind-surfing, scuba diving, snorkeling, swimming and sunbathing; tennis, walking.

AIR SERVICES. – Scheduled services from George
Town to Stella Maris, Long Island, Crooked Island and
Nassau (Bahamas) and Miami.

SHIPPING. – Mail boat services from George Town,
Staniel Cay, Black Point, Farmer's Cay and Barraterre
to Nassau.

The *Exumas are a long string of
islets and cays, beginning some

40 miles/65 km SE of New Providence and extending for more than
125 miles/201 km in a southeasterly
direction. The largest island, near
the end of the chain, is Great Exuma,
with the chief place, George Town.
The Exumas offer some of the finest
sailing waters in the western hemisphere, with the additional attractions of their unspoiled natural
beauty and idyllic beaches.

*Great Exuma, the largest island in the
chain, is also the hilliest. Many American
Loyalists sought refuge here and introduced cotton growing, and in consequence the island is well developed for
agriculture. The chief place, *George
Town (pop. 800), a rising tourist resort
and the site of the famous Out Island
Regatta, lies on *Elizabeth Harbour, one
of the finest harbors in the Bahamas and
once the haunt of buccaneers. It is a little
township of pastel-colored houses, some
of them dating from the colonial period,
and has a busy straw market. The Peace
and Plenty Hotel occupies the site of the
former slave market. An obelisk is a
prominent landmark. – In recent years
many hotels and vacation or retirement

homes for well-to-do Americans have been built in the surrounding area.

Off George Town, to the E, is a little islet known as **Stocking Island**, noted for its *Mysterious Cave*, accessible only to divers, and its beautiful beaches. – A short distance S of George Town is the old-world little farming township of *Rolle Town*, with pretty pastel-colored houses of the 18th and 19th c. Here visitors can see a number of *Loyalist tombs*, including one with a fine marble monument. – At the S end of the island, rather off the beaten track, lies the hamlet of **Harts Ville**, with some handsome 18th c. stone houses. – On **Man-o'-War Cay** are the ruins of an old fort. In *Pretty Molly Bay*, the subject of a local legend, and on the nearby **Pigeon Cay** are good beaches.

On a hill 4½ miles/7 km NW of George Town is the old township of **Hermitage**, with large stone tombs known as the "brick tombs". – A little way N *Gilbert Grant*, a particularly picturesque example of a Bahamian island village, has thatched houses dating from the colonial period. – 10½ miles/17 km farther NW is the quiet little settlement of **Steventon**, once the center of a cotton-growing area. This was the residence of Lord Rolle, who presented his large estates to his slaves when they were liberated in 1835, resulting in many families, as well as a number of townships, to adopt his name. – In the surrounding area are many old 18th c. plantation houses, some of them in ruins, which were built by American Loyalists from the southern states who established cotton plantations in the Exumas. Here also are two large nature reserves, *Anderson National Park* and the *Bahamas National Park*. – 5 miles/8 km beyond this, at the N end of the island, is the old-world little settlement of **Rolleville**, with pastel-colored 18th c. houses – now the center of a busy farming area.

Little Exuma is reached by way of a bascule bridge known as the "Ferry". Just beyond the bridge we find the attractive hamlet of *Forbes Hill*. **Williams Town**, the chief place on this island and once the haunt of buccaneers, lies at the S end. In the surrounding area are many relics of the cotton era. On the *Hermitage Estate*, an old cotton plantation, is a well-preserved 18th c. *plantation house (open to visitors). – Beside the *Great Salt Pond* stands

an obelisk, a landmark visible far and wide.

The *Exuma Cays are a narrow string of islets running NW from Great Exuma. **Lee Stocking Island** 6 miles/10 km farther NW has a marine biological research station. – 35 miles/56 km beyond this is *Staniel Cay, one of the most popular and best equipped yacht anchorages in the Bahamas, with beautiful beaches. Nearby can be seen the famous *Thunderball Grotto*, in which some of the scenes in the James Bond film "Thunderball" were shot. – Farther NW is **Sampson Cay**, also popular with sailing enthusiasts. – To the NW extends the **Exuma Land and Sea National Park**, a nature reserve established in 1959, well over 150 sq. miles/400 sq. km in area, containing countless islets and cays with almost virgin beaches, magnificent coral reefs and submarine gardens, in many places lying only 3–10 ft/1–3 m below the surface. A few iguanas still live in caves and grottoes here, and there are several dozen species of tropical birds now rarely to be seen elsewhere. – To the N of the National Park is *Norman's Cay, now an exclusive yachting center. – 6 miles/10 km farther N, on **Highbourn Cay**, lies the wreck of a buccaneers' ship which ran on to the reef in 1560.

See also **Bahamas**.

French Antilles

See **La Désirade, Guadeloupe, Marie-Galante, Martinique, Saint-Barthélemy, Saint-Martin** and **Iles des Saintes.**

Gonaïves

Haiti
République d'Haïti

Département de l'Artibonite.
Altitude: sea level.
Population: 34,000.
ⓘ **Office National du Tourisme,**
Avenue Marie-Jeanne,
Port-au-Prince,
Haïti;
tel. 2 1720.
See also Practical Information.

*Gonaïves, capital of the département of l'Artibonite, is a quiet little town charmingly situated in the sheltered Baie des Gonaïves. It has a cotton mill which plays an important part in the economy of the surrounding area.

HISTORY. – The independence of Haiti was proclaimed in Gonaïves on January 1, 1804 by Jean-Jacques Dessalines, leader of the revolutionary forces and later first emperor of Haiti (Jacques I). The town was once a major port for the shipment of cotton and coffee and has the typical checkerboard layout of the colonial period.

SIGHTS. – In the middle of the town is the colorful *Market (Marché). The Cathédrale à Mémoire and a number of other monuments were erected to commemorate the 150th anniversary of the proclamation of independence. – While the center of the town has brightly painted colonial-style houses the outer districts consist largely of mud huts of rural type.

Street in Gonaïves

Inland from the town extends the *Plaine des Gonaïves, an agricultural area which is faced with great difficulties owing to the shortage of water. The aridity of the climate is reflected in the drought-loving natural vegetation. With development assistance from the German Federal Republic deep wells have been bored in the Cul-de-Sac and Gonaïves plains in order to provide water for irrigation and thus increase the agricultural output. The German project in the Gonaïves plain will benefit some 3000 families with small peasant holdings whose incomes have hitherto tended to fall short of the minimum required for subsistence. In addition to the production of food crops it is hoped to promote the growing of cotton, for which the climate is well adapted. A sizeable cotton-mill which will process the cotton produced has already

been built on the outskirts of Gonaïves, and it is planned to establish a plant for extracting cottonseed oil.

See also **Haiti and **Hispaniola.

Ile de la Gonâve
Haiti
République d'Haïti

Département de l'Ouest.
Area: 255 sq. miles/660 sq. km.
Population: 60,000.
Administrative center: Port-au-Prince (on Hispaniola).
Vehicles travel on the right.

ⓘ Office National du Tourisme,
Avenue Marie-Jeanne,
Port-au-Prince,
Haïti;
tel. 2 1720
See also Practical Information.

SHIPPING. – Occasionally small boats to Port-au-Prince and St-Marc.

The *Ile de la Gonâve, Haiti's largest subsidiary island, lies in the Golfe de la Gonâve. Consisting mainly of limestones, it has been much affected by karstic action. Its coasts are difficult of access, being fringed by a broad belt of mangrove swamps, shallows and coral reefs.

In the 17th c. the island served as a pirates' lair; in the 18th c. it was a place of refuge for runaway slaves. – The aridity of the climate offers little scope for agriculture, and the people gain a very modest subsistence from fishing. Although the island has a number of beautiful and completely unspoiled beaches there are no facilities for visitors. – The largest settlements on the island are Anse à Galets, with a small airstrip, on the NE coast, Grand Boucan, and Pointe à Raquette on the W coast. There are a number of mule-tracks and footpaths leading into the interior of the island, the highest points of which are the Montagne Daudeville (1214 ft/370 m) in the W and the Montagne la Pierre (2562 ft/781 m) and Montagne Chien (2526 ft/770 m) in the SE.

Grand Bahama

Bahama Islands
Commonwealth of the Bahamas

Area: 530 sq. miles/1372 sq. km.
Population: 35,000.
Administrative center: Nassau (on New Providence).
Vehicles travel on the left.

(i) **Ministry of Tourism,**
International Bazaar,
Freeport,
Bahamas;
tel. 352 8044.
See also Practical Information.

HOTELS. – FREEPORT:LUCAYA: *Arawak Hotel Golf and Tennis Club*, 120 r., SP, T, golf; *Atlantic Beach Hotel*, 175 r., SP, T; *Bahamas Princess Hotel*, 800 r., SP, T, golf; *Holiday Inn*, 490 r., SP, T, golf; *Princess Tower*, 400 r., SP, T, golf; *Silver Sands*, 164 r., SP, T; *Xanadu Beach Hotel*, 177 r., SP, T; *Coral Beach Hotel*, 50 r., SP; *Lucayan Bay Hotel*, 168 r., SP, T; *Shalimar Hotel*, 150 r., SP, T; *Victoria Inn and Scuba Club*, 40 r., SP, T; *Castaways Resort*, 137 r., SP; *Freeport Inn*, 148 r., SP; *Lucayan Harbour Inn*, 143 r.; *Islander Hotel*, 100 r., SP.   WEST END: *Grand Bahama Hotel and Country Club*, 577 r., SP, T, golf.

RESTAURANTS in hotels; also in FREEPORT/LUCAYA: *El Morocco*, in Casino; *Captain's Charthouse*, E. Sunrise/Beachway Drive; *Stoned Crab*, Taino Beach; *Café Michel* (French), *Japanese Steakhouse* and *China Temple*, all in International Bazaar; *Island Lobster House* (Polynesian), *Marcella's* (Italian), *Sir Winston Churchill Pub* and *Pub on the Mall*, all on the Mall.

NIGHT SPOTS in some hotels; also in FREEPORT: *Kasbah* in Casino; *Orbit*, Pioneer's Way.

International casino: *El Casino*, Ranfurly Circus.

SHOPPING. – Freeport is the most popular shopping center in the Bahamas after Nassau. The best place for shoppers is the large *International Bazaar, which offers goods from all over the world at very advantageous prices. Close by is the *Straw Market*, where visitors will be tempted by local handicrafts, in particular attractive straw articles. – There are also many shops offering a variety of interesting wares at reasonable prices in *Churchill Square*, in the middle of town.

International Bazaar, Freeport (Grand Bahama)

EVENTS. – New Year's Day Junkanoo Parade, a colorful parade in costume. – Labour Day Parade (first Friday in June). – Bahamas 500 (June), a motorboat race, followed by a masked ball. – Independence Celebrations (July). – *Goombay Holiday (July), colorful goombay parades by the Jumpin dancers, folk displays, music by Royal Bahamas Police Force Band. – Emancipation Day (first Monday in August), commemorating the liberation of the slaves. Discovery Day (October 12), mussel cracking contest in McLean's Town. – Boxing Day Junkanoo Parade (December 26).

RECREATION and SPORT. – Golf (six courses): sailing (six marinas), motor-boating, deep-sea fishing; para-sailing, wind-surfing, water-skiing, scuba diving,

El Casino, Freeport

snorkeling; swimming and sunbathing; tennis, ball games.

AIR SERVICES. – Scheduled services from Freeport to Nassau and to Atlanta, Fort Lauderdale and Miami. – Occasional charter flights to various destinations.

SHIPPING. – Regular cruise ships to Nassau, Miami (USA) and San Juan (Puerto Rico); occasionally cruise ships to other Caribbean destinations. Regular mail boat services to Nassau.

The rapidly developing island of *Grand Bahama, with its fringe of islets, lies only some 60 miles/97 km from the coast of Florida, from which it is separated by the Florida Strait. Some 120 miles/193 km NW lies Nassau (New Providence), across the Northwest Providence Channel. The planned tourist and industrial development of the island began only after the Second World War, making Grand Bahama second only to New Providence in economic importance within the Bahamas.

Extending from E to W for a distance of some 75 miles/120 km and up to 15 miles/25 km across, Grand Bahama attracted the early English settlers with its rich resources of wood in the form of the scrub and pine forests which still pattern the landscape. The island has excellent beaches as well as large areas of mangrove swamp. It is flat, with its highest point only 69 ft/21 m above sea level.

*Freeport/Lucaya (sea level; pop., with suburbs, c. 30,000), a rapidly growing town which is now the second largest in the Bahamas, lies on the S coast of Grand Bahama. Founded as recently as 1955 by an American businessman named Wallace Groves, it is the largest industrial area in the Bahamas and a very popular resort.

In Ranfurly Circus, the town's main hub of tourist activity, is *El Casino, one of the largest gaming casinos in the western hemisphere. A Moorish-style building erected in the 1960s, it is equipped with every amenity. The adjoining *International Bazaar, a shoppers' paradise, offers a tempting array of goods from all over the world, with restaurants serving an equally international range of dishes. Beyond this is the *Straw Market*, where local handicrafts including plaited straw articles can be bought. – Opposite the Casino stands the star-shaped *Bahama

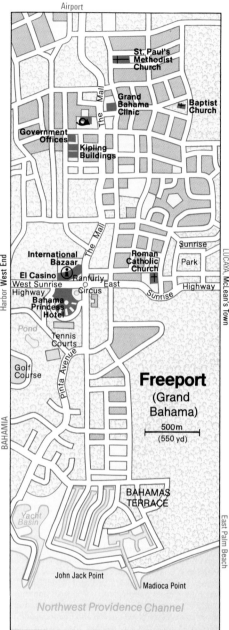

Freeport
(Grand Bahama)

500 m
(550 yd)

Princess Hotel (1250 beds), one of the largest resort hotels in the Caribbean.

From Ranfurly Circus the busy *Mall* runs N to the business quarter of FREEPORT with its modern office towers. To the W of the Mall the most notable buildings are *Kipling Buildings*, the *Radio Tower* and the *Post Office*. On the E side of the town stands the fine *Baptist Church* and at the N end the imposing *St Paul's Methodist Church* with its associated school. – To the N, near the coast, is **Freeport International Airport** (1965).

From Ranfurly Circus East Sunrise Highway runs E, past the fine *Roman Catholic Church*, to the resort district of LUCAYA, with its magnificent villas and leisure facilities. Here are to be seen the *Gardens of the Groves*, a luxuriant tropical park which commemorates the founder of the town. In the gardens the *Freeport/Lucaya Development Museum* houses interesting displays illustrating the history of the town. On **Bell Channel Bay**, a much ramified inlet and yachting harbor lined by luxury hotels, is the famous *Underwater Explorers Club*, with a Museum of Underwater Exploration. Close by is the landing-stage used by the largest glass-bottomed boat in the world.

To the N of the town extends the *Rand Memorial Nature Centre* (100 acres), a magnificently colorful botanic garden with specimens of Caribbean plants which are now extremely rare. There is also a charming aviary of tropical birds.

From Ranfurly Circus West Sunrise Highway runs to FREEPORT HARBOUR, in *Hawksbill Creek*, enlarged and deepened in 1955 to form a deep-water harbor. A large industrial zone has grown up around the harbor, with a huge oil storage installation (1958), a refinery belonging to the Bahamas Oil Refining Company (BORCO, 1960), a cement plant of the US Steel Corporation, a tube factory (1975) and various factories producing pharmaceuticals and foodstuffs.

Freeport to West End (27 miles/43 km). – Leave Freeport on the Queen's Highway, going W. Beyond Hawksbill Creek this joins West End Road, which comes in 12½ miles/20 km to **Eight Mile Rock**, a rising little coastal settlement. – The road continues along the coast, with varied scenery, passes through the pretty villages of *Hanna Hill* and *Seagrape* and in another 9 miles/14 km reaches *Hydro Flora Gardens* (hydroponic agriculture, growing plants without soil). – In another 5½ miles/9 km, after passing Bootle Bay, the road comes to –

West End (sea level; pop. 1000), one of the best known bases for the illicit alcohol trade during the Prohibition period, with dilapidated port installations and warehouses to bear witness to its former activity. West End is now a well-known resort, with the *Grand Bahama Hotel and Country Club*, an excellent golf-course, a well-equipped yacht harbor, a convention center (with seating for 1150), a fine beach and an airfield. – At *West End Point* are underwater caves, which are a happy hunting ground for scuba divers, beautiful beaches and a bird sanctuary.

Freeport to McLean's Town (50 miles/80 km). – Leave Freeport on the Queen's Highway, going E. This leads into the developing **Freeport Ridge** area, with two large agricultural estates, Grand Bahama Farms

and Hydroponics Farms. In 6 miles/10 km the road crosses the new *Grand Lucayan Waterway* for sailing and fishing enthusiasts which runs deep inland, with many ramifications. Beyond this is the developing resort area of *Lucaya Estates*.

11 miles/18 km farther on, on the S coast, is the fishing village of *Freetown*, near which is an American military base. – The coast road continues E, passing a number of development projects and lonely coves with good beaches. In 9 miles/15 km it reaches *High Rock* and in another 13 miles/21 km *Pelican Point*, two small fishing villages in delightful settings. 10 miles/16 km farther on is **McLean's Town**, the most easterly settlement on the island, where the road ends. Offshore, to the SE, are numerous small islets much favored by fishermen for the abundance of fish to be found there. Among the best known are *Deep Water Cay* and *Sweeting Cay*, with accommodation for visitors and an airstrip.

DIVING EXPEDITIONS. – From Freeport/Lucaya to the *Treasure Reef*, where treasure worth more than a million dollars was found in 1964. – 5 miles/8 km W of Lucaya is the *Zoo Hole*, a cavern with many varieties of marine animals and plants. – The *Caves* are large caverns in a coral reef.

See also **Bahamas**.

Grenada
Lesser Antilles
Windward Islands
State of Grenada

Nationality letters: WG.
Area: 133 sq. miles/344 sq. km.
Capital: St George's.
Population: 120,000.
Local administration: 6 parishes.
Religion: Roman Catholic and Protestant.
Language: English; French patois.
Currency: Eastern Caribbean dollar (EC$) of 100 cents.
Weights and measures: British/American system.
Time: Atlantic Time (4 hours behind GMT).
Vehicles travel on the left.
Travel documents: passport, immigration card, onward or return ticket.

(i) **Grenada Tourist Board,**
P.O. Box 293,
St George's,
Grenada, W.I.;
tel. 2279.
See also Practical Information.

HOTELS. – ROSS POINT and surrounding area: *Crescent Inn*, 15 r.; *Ross Point Hotel*, 13 r. – GRAND ANSE BAY: *Cinnamon Hill*, 40 r., SP; *Holiday Inn*, 185 r., SP, T, beach; *Blue Horizons*, 32 r., SP; *Silver Sands*, 30 r.; *Spice Island Inn*, 30 r., SP; etc. – LANCE AUX EPINES: *Calabash*, 44 r., SP, T; *Secret Harbour*, 20 r., SP, T; *Horseshoe Bay*, 24 r., SP; *12° North*, 12 r. – Several GUEST-HOUSES and HOLIDAY APARTMENTS. – FOR YOUNG PEOPLE: *Adam's Guest-House*.

RESTAURANTS in most of the hotels listed; also in ST GEORGE'S: *The Nutmeg, Pastry Man, Rudolf's*. – GRAND ANSE BAY: *Casa Mia, Bird's Nest*. – LANCE AUX EPINES: *Red Crab Pub*. – CALIVIGNY ESTATE: *Island View*.

NIGHT CLUBS. – *Evening Palace*, St George's; *Blanco's Beach Club* and *Sugar Mill*, both outside St George's.

SHOPPING. – St George's has several luxury shops catering chiefly for passengers on cruise ships, and which offer a wide range of goods, often at low rates of duty – Objets d'art, fine jewelry, crystal, modern textiles, etc. Local specialties are baskets of spices, perfume and hand-made articles of mahogany, palm leaves and sisal.

PUBLIC HOLIDAYS and EVENTS. – *New Year's Day*. – *Independence Day* (February 7). – *National Day* (March 13) – *Carnival* (Saturday before Ash Wednesday to Ash Wednesday), lasting four days, with selection of the Carnival Queen, dancing and processions in the streets, and steelband, calypso and beauty contests. The climax is reached on *Mardi Gras* (Shrove Tuesday) until the invasion. – *Good Friday*. – *Easter* (from Easter Day to the following Tuesday), with a *Water Festival* (program of events, including sailing and fishing contests). – *Labour Day* (first Monday in May). – *Pentecost*. – *Corpus Christi*, with processions at various places. – *Emancipation Day* (first Monday in August), commemorating the liberation of the slaves. – *Christmas Day*. – *Boxing Day* (December 26).

AIR SERVICES. – Direct connections with Barbados, St Vincent and Carriacou (Grenadines) and Port of Spain (Trinidad). Charter services to all the neighboring islands.

SHIPPING. – St George's is a frequent port of call on Caribbean cruises, particularly during the winter season. – Regional services by freighters to Isle de Ronde, Carriacou, Petit Martinique and the northern Grenadines.

Grenada, world-famed as the "Spice Island", is one of the most beautiful islands in the West Indies, with a varied landscape shaped by volcanic action; its capital, St George's, is magnificently situated on a superb natural harbor. Long disputed between Britain and France in earlier centuries, the island became independent in 1974 together with three of the Grenadines to the N. In 1983 the island was brought into the focus of world publicity after an invasion by US forces.

Mahogany planks

Lying between latitude 12° and 12°15' N and between longitude 61°35' and 61°50' W, Grenada belongs geologically to the inner volcanic arc of the Lesser Antilles. Evidence of volcanic action is provided by two crater lakes, Lake Antoine in the NE of the island and the Grand Etang in the center, and by the extinct volcano Mount St Catherine (2756 ft/840 m), the highest point on the island. Like the other hills on the island, Mount St Catherine is covered with luxuriant tropical rain forest. The hills descend in stages towards the S, broken up by numerous rivers, streams and waterfalls. A series of parallel river valleys, the lowest parts of which are below sea level, give the S coast a varied scenic pattern, with beautiful natural harbors and small sandy bays.

CLIMATE. – The climate of the island is tropical, with periods of varying humidity over the year. On the windward side of the hills to the NE, (exposed to the trade winds) the average annual rainfall is over 200 in./5000 mm, and even on the lee side, to the SW, it is still well over 60 in./1500 mm. The mean annual temperature is about 82 °F/28 °C. From June to October there is a danger of hurricanes.

VEGETATION. – Except in the more inaccessible parts of the island the natural vegetation has been reduced or driven out by the development of a plantation economy. The old cotton plantations, however, have given place in more recent times to trees, and since the devastation wrought by Hurricane Janet in 1955, these in turn have been replaced by mixed-crop farming. The predominant crops are now nutmegs at the higher levels and cacao lower down, interplanted in both cases with bananas.

HISTORY. – Columbus discovered the island, then inhabited by Caribs, on August 15, 1498, though he himself never landed on it. The Spaniards at first named it Concepción, but this was later changed to Granada, no doubt after the Andalusian town; the present form of the name (pronounced Gren-ay-da) shows the influence of the French form, Grenade. The

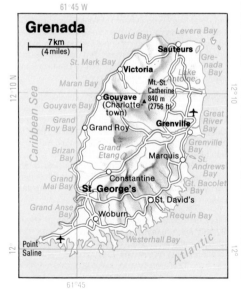

Grenada

7 km
(4 miles)

61°45 W
61°45

David Bay
Levera Bay
Sauteurs
Grenada Bay
St. Mark Bay
Victoria
Lake Antoine
Maran Bay
Mt. St. Catherine
840 m
Gouyave Bay
Gouyave (Charlotte town)
(2756 ft)
Great River Bay
Grand Roy Bay
Grand Roy
Grenville
Brizan Bay
Grand Etang
Grenville Bay
Marquis
St. Andrews Bay
Grand Mal Bay
Constantine
Gt. Bacolet Bay
St. George's
Grand Anse Bay
St. David's
Woburn
Requin Bay
Westerhall Bay
Point Saline
Atlantic

Caribbean Sea

12°10 N
12°10
12
12

first attempt to establish a colony was made by London merchants in 1609 but was frustrated by the hostility of the natives. In 1650, however, a settlement was established by the French, led by Du Parquet and Le Comte, on a site near present-day St George's. In 1664 the island passed into the hands of the Compagnie Française des Indes Occidentales, and in 1674 it became a possession of the French crown. After a brief period of peaceful coexistence the French gained control of the whole island from the native Caribs after a series of battles, and finally the last surviving Caribs threw themselves off a precipice on the N coast into the sea, at the spot known as the Caribs' Leap (French, Morne des Sauteurs).

In 1762 Britain challenged the French control of the island, and the French were able to reassert their position only in 1779. Under the treaty of Versailles in 1783, however, Grenada was ceded to Britain. At the beginning of the colonial period the island's principal crops were tobacco and indigo, but by the middle of the 18th c. the principal products were cotton, coffee and sugar. British settlers extended the area devoted to sugar-cane, consolidated the plantation system and brought in increased numbers of slaves. In 1795 Julien Fedon, a black planter inspired by the ideas of the French Revolution, led a bloody rebellion against British rule, and the resultant tensions did not die down until 1834, after the abolition of slavery. The blacks then settled in the interior of the island or emigrated to Trinidad, which offered better working conditions. In subsequent years shortage of labor led to a marked decline in the growing of sugar-cane, and attempts to bring in large numbers of Indian and Malay indentured laborers were unsuccessful. – In 1877 Grenada became a British crown colony; in 1967 it was declared a British associated state; and finally in 1974 it was granted full independence. In 1979 a

Nutmegs

bloodless coup overthrew the government of the controversial Sir Eric Gairy, who was seeking to establish a dictatorial regime with a secret police popularly known as the "Mongoose Gang" and was increasingly leading the country into isolation.

The pro-Cuban government under Maurice Bishop cultivated economic and political links with Cuba and with the Soviet Union. The construction of an international airport, which was necessary because of the growth of the tourist industry, was begun with the help of the European Economic Community and subsequently extended under Cuban control; this gave rise to suspicion in the USA. Internal strife between Maurice Bishop and Vice-president Bernard Coard culminated on October 19, 1983 in the murder of President Bishop and several of his ministers. This was the decisive moment for an invasion of Grenada by the USA supported by several Caribbean states, an invasion which had been prepared for some time. There were some 250 fatalities. This triggered off worldwide argument as to the legality of the invasion and how far Grenada was to have been made a Soviet strongpoint in the Caribbean.

GOVERNMENT and ADMINISTRATION. – The head of state is the Queen, who is represented by a Governor-General. Parliament consists of two chambers, a Senate of seven appointed members and a House of Representatives of 15 elected members. The Cabinet, headed by the Prime Minister, is responsible to Parliament. For administrative purposes the island is divided into six parishes. The islands in the Grenadines which are dependencies of Grenada form separate administrative units.

POPULATION and ECONOMY. – The overwhelming majority of the population are descendants of the black slaves brought to the island by the French and British. They are mostly Roman Catholics. There is also a minority (5%) of Indians, descended from the indentured laborers brought from India in the 19th c.; most of them are still Hindus. The thousand or so whites are predominantly of Western European origin; many of them belong to various Protestant denominations.

More than 35% of the working population of about 30,000 are employed in agriculture. Most of the island's arable area (about 35,000 acres) is given over to the growing of nutmegs, together with cacao and bananas. These account for some 90% of Grenada's total exports, and Grenada is the world's third largest

A cacao pod

producer of nutmegs and mace. Other products include coconuts, citrus fruits, a variety of spices and arrowroot, the growing of which has recently been reintroduced. Some sugar-cane and cotton are also still grown.

The island's industry is primarily concerned with processing its agricultural produce, the principal products being sugar, rum, soap, vegetable oils, perfume and foodstuffs. Many workshops are also engaged in producing souvenirs for tourists.

Thanks to the island's magnificent scenic attractions **tourism** has developed into a major element in its economy. While in 1963 only some 9000 hotel visitors came to the island, there were in 1979 about 32,000 as well as an additional 140,000 tourists who came by cruise ships. Further impetus to tourism was interrupted by the worsening of internal political wrangling and the change of course by the Bishop government as well as by the US invasion. As a consequence of the opening of the new international airport Point Saline and planned measures of improvement, a noticeable rise in the number of visitors is to be expected. With the help of private investors from the USA, tourism, small industries and agriculture are being expanded.

A special factor in the economy is the Medical School of St George's which is attended by between 500 and 1000 American medical students who have failed to find places at American universities.

***St George's** (0–410 ft/0–125 m; pop. 31,000), capital of Grenada, lies on a beautiful natural harbor. Founded by French settlers at the beginning of the

18th c., the town is a popular port of call with cruise ships and sailing yachts. The pastel-colored houses with their red and green roofs, built on the slopes of the hills around the harbor, give the town a character which is part French and part Georgian. It is divided into two parts by a promontory crowned by an old fort.

SIGHTS. – From the pier Wharf Road skirts the picturesque ***Carenage**, the inner harbor, and leads past the Theatre and other public buildings to the *Government Handicraft Centre* and the ***National Museum**, which contains interesting pre-Columbian material and relics of the colonial period.

Imposingly situated above the harbor is ***Fort George**, built by the French in the early 18th c. as Fort Royal. On the extensive defense works are cannon which are still used to fire salutes. Visitors are shown a maze of underground passages, guard-rooms and dungeons. The fort, the name of which was changed to Fort Rupert after the murder of Rupert Bishop, served as police headquarters for many years. In 1983 it was bombed by American invasion troops.

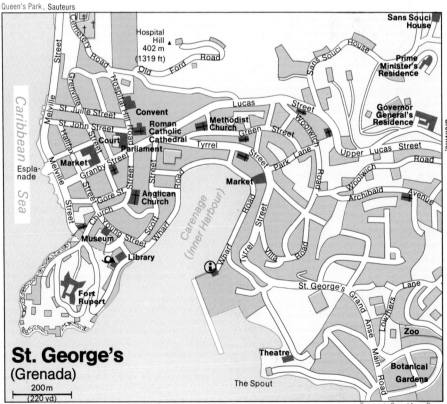

St. George's
(Grenada)
200m
(220 yd)

Queen's Park, Sauteurs

Freeport, Grand Anse Bay

St George's (Grenada)

The *Sendall Tunnel*, cut by the French at the beginning of the 18th c., runs under the promontory on which the fort stands. At its W end is Melville Street, a seafront promenade skirting the busy western half of the town. From the *Esplanade* overlooking the sea, Granby Street runs up to the *Market* (fruit, vegetables, baskets of spices), which is particularly lively and colorful on Saturdays. In the market square the *Yellow Poui Art Gallery* houses an interesting collection of work by Caribbean artists. On the E side of the square (Grenville Street) stands the *Town Hall*, which contains a charming *exhibition of handicrafts and folk art (woodcarving, pictures, articles made from coconut shells, seashells, straw, etc.). Higher up, in Church Street, is the impressive *Roman Catholic Cathedral*, with the venerable *Supreme Court* and the Registry opposite it. In the lower part of Church Street the pastel-colored *Anglican Church* (1690), the old garrison church, has a magnificent marble altar, fine frescoes and beautiful stained glass. To the SW, rising high above the Sendall Tunnel, is the **Kirk**, a Scottish Presbyterian church built in 1830, with a spire which is a conspicuous landmark.

Lucas Street leads up to the *Old Fort* (18th c.) on Wireless Hill, to the building of which both the French and the British contributed. – Farther E, on the slopes of *Mount Royal* above Upper Lucas Street, is *Government House* (18th c.), residence of the Governor-General, in a setting commanding extensive views. Higher up stands the former Prime Minister's Residence, and beyond this *Sans Souci House*, a charming 18th c. mansion.

On the southeastern outskirts of the town are the beautiful *Botanical Gardens, with rare plants and animals of the Caribbean area.

SURROUNDINGS of St George's. – To the N of the town, reached by way of Melville Street and the old *Green Bridge* over St John's River, is *Queen's Park*, with extensive sports facilities.

To the S, around the *Lagoon*, lies the charming little settlement of **Belmont Village**, bounded on the W by *Santa Maria Hill* (161 ft/49 m).

SE of the town, on *Richmond Hill* (722 ft/220 m), are the ruins of *Fort Adolphus* (18th–19th c.).

St George's to the S coast (round trip 15 miles/25 km). – Leave St George's on St George's Grand Anse Main Road, going S.

1½ miles/2.5 km: *Martin's Bay*, bounded on the S by *Ross Point*. Beyond this is *Grand Anse Bay*, which has been developed as a resort area, with facilities for all kinds of water sports. – To the S, beyond *Goat Point*, a narrow rocky promontory, lies *Morne Rouge Bay*, with a beautiful beach.

¾ mile/1 km: *Grand Anse Estate*, a small village with a rum distillery. – From here a narrow road (1¼ miles/2 km) runs S to *Lance aux Epines*, with an excellent beach.

3 miles/5 km SW of Grand Anse Estate on a minor road which passes the picturesque *True Blue Estate*, we come to the impressive *Point Salines, the SW tip of Grenada, near which pre-Columbian remains have been found. Here is situated the new airport and there are several idyllic beaches, including *Grand Bay, Cato Bay* and *Black Bay* on the S side of the promontory and *Canoe Bay* and the *Trou Jab* on the N side. Off the coast lies the wreck of the "Biance C".

From Grand Anse Estate the main road continues through the sugar-cane plantations of *Woodlands Estate* (small sugar refinery) to –

Grand Etang

2½ miles/4 km: **Woburn**, a picturesque little fishing village which provided the setting for the film "Island in the Sun". It overlooks Clarkes Court Bay, in which are two small islands, *Hog Island* (closed military area) and *Calivigny Island*.

1½ miles/2.5 km: *Calivigny Estate*. 2 miles/3 km farther S, on a promontory between Chemin Bay, with *Calivigny Harbour*, to the E and the long inlet of *Port Egmont* (yacht harbor) to the W, are the ruins of *Fort Jeudi* (18th c.).

1¼ miles/2 km: *Westerhall Estate*, in a beautiful setting above the bay of the same name. A road runs along the promontory to *Bacaye Point* (view).

1¼ miles/2 km: *Bacolet Estate*, above Bacolet Bay. From here the road climbs to –

2 miles/3 km: *Perdmontemps* (Piedmontagne), below the S side of *Mount Maitland* (1713 ft/522 m). The road now traverses some outlying districts to –

5 miles/8 km: **St George's**.

St George's to Grenville (round trip 32 miles/51 km). – Leave St George's on River Road, going NE. The road winds its way up the valley of *St John's River*, with fine views, passing through many little villages and hamlets amid beautiful scenery.

4½ miles/7 km: **Constantine**. From here a narrow road climbs N to the *Annandale Falls*, surrounded by luxuriant vegetation, where the water plunges down 50 ft/16 m into a blue-green pool.

The road now climbs E below the NW side of *Mount Sinai* (2307 ft/703 m) into the *Grand Etang Forest Reserve*, an area of unspoiled tropical forest which is the home of many rare birds including the long-billed doctor birds.

3 miles/5 km: *Grand Etang (alt. 1690 ft/515 m; area 2 sq. miles/5.3 sq. km), a spectacular lake in the crater of an extinct volcano. It is not known how deep the lake is. On its N side is *Mount Qua Qua* (2303 ft/702 m).

From the Grand Etang the road winds its way down through forests of tree ferns and plantations of nutmeg, cacao and bananas into the *Great River Valley*, passing pretty little villages with names which hark back to the French colonial period and the time when the slaves were liberated. To the N rises the island's highest summit, *Mount St Catherine* (2756 ft/840 m), an extinct volcano.

7 miles/11 km: **Grenville** (sea level; pop. 6000), the second largest town on the island, situated on the E coast bay of the same name, with a colorful fruit and vegetable market and a lively fish market. Here a visit

can be made to the island's largest factory for the processing of nutmegs. – 2 miles/3 km N is *Pearls Airport*, near which many remains of pre-Columbian settlement have been found.

The return route to St George's leads S along Grenville Bay, coming in 2 miles/3 km to *Grand Marquis*, an old French settlement on the far side of *Battle Hill*, the name of which recalls the colonial conflicts of the past. Offshore is the rocky *Marquis Island*.

At the S end of St Andrew's Bay the road begins to climb, and then pursues a winding course high above the S coast with its numerous bays and secret little coves.

15 miles/25 km: **St George's**.

St George's to Sauteurs (round trip 48 miles/77 km). – Leave St George's by way of Melville Street, going N along the W coast with its cliffs and pretty little bays. Tiny fishing villages such as *Happy Hill* and *Grand Roy* cling to the steep hillside.

5 miles/8 km: *Halifax Harbour*, a beautiful bay with two little rivers flowing into it. – The road continues, with many bends, to –

2½ miles/4 km: *Grand Roy*, an attractive little fishing village in the bay of the same name.

The road skirts the long sweep of *Palmiste Bay*, passes below *Mount Nesbit* (443 ft/135 m) and reaches –

3 miles/5 km: *Gouyave* (sea level; pop. 5000), a picturesque town on the NW coast, with a number of spice plantations in the surrounding area.

3 miles/5 km: *Victoria*, a fishing village with a small nutmeg processing factory.

2½ miles/4 km: *Duquesne Bay*, with a pretty beach. – The road now runs SE up the valley of the *Duquesne River* to *Union Estate*, an intensively cultivated spice-growing area, and then descends the valley of the *Little St Patrick River*.

4½ miles/7 km: *Sauteurs* (sea level; pop. 3000), in a spectacular setting on the N coast. Beyond the Roman Catholic church is the cliff known as the *Caribs' Leap

Sauteurs, seen from the Caribs' Leap

(Morne des Sauteurs) from which the last Caribs are said to have jumped to their death rather than submit to the French.

NW of Sauteurs lies *Sauteurs Bay, 1¼ miles/2 km long, with a superb beach. There is a delightful walk (45 minutes) along the bay to the wild and precipitous *David Point.

2½ miles/4 km: *Levera Bay, a fine beach in a magnificent setting. Offshore, to the E, are three little islets much frequented by sailing enthusiasts, the Sugar Loaf, Green Island and Sandy Island.' – To the S of the bay is the Levera Pond, a crater lake, on the W side of which is Levera Hill (846 ft/258 m). – On Bedford Point, at the northeastern tip of the island, are the ruins of an old fort.

The road now continues S along the shores of beautiful *Grenada Bay.

2½ miles/4 km: River Sallee, an attractive farming village. N of the village are mineral springs with an abundant flow of water. – The road then climbs S, with views of High Cliff and Antoine Bay.

2¼ miles/4 km: *Lake Antoine, an almost circular crater lake. – Then S to –

5½ miles/9 km: Grenville. From here the road crosses the island, past the Grand Etang, to –

14 miles/23 km: St George's.

Grenadines
Lesser Antilles
Windward Islands
State of Grenada and St Vincent/Grenadines

(i) Grenada Tourist Board,
P.O. Box 293,
St George's,
Grenada, W.I.;
tel. 2279.
St Vincent Tourist Board,
Halifax Street,
Kingstown,
St Vincent, W.I.;
tel. 6 1224.
See also Practical Information.

The **Grenadines, a scattered group of eight larger and more than 120 smaller islands between St Vincent in the N and Grenada in the S, are everyone's idea of a tropical island paradise. This island world has long been renowned as one of the world's finest sailing areas and as an exclusive retreat for the wealthy.**

Many of the Grenadines are the summits of underwater volcanoes in the inner arc of the Antilles; others are coral reefs built up on the top of submarine volcanoes. The highest point is 1099 ft/335 m. Many of the islands have a central hill and precipi-

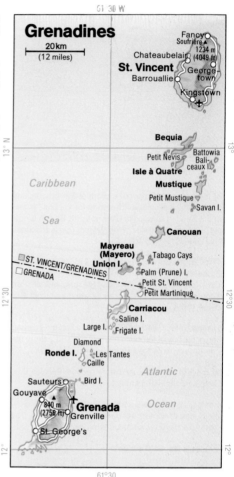

tous coastal cliffs, between which are superb beaches. Almost all of them have a sheltering girdle of coral reefs.

The rainfall averages between 31 in./800 mm and 63 in./1600 mm, with periods of drought between the rainy seasons. The islands are rarely troubled by hurricanes, though great devastation was caused by Hurricane Janet in 1955.

Only some ten of the islands – which were settled by the French in the 17th c. – are inhabited throughout the year. Their population structure is similar to that of the parent islands of Grenada and St Vincent. The principal islands are Bequia, Mustique, Canouan and Carriacou.

The Grenadines became a base for whalers at an early stage. The plantation system was established on the islands in the 17th c., and sugar-cane and cotton flourished. Over-felling of the trees, however, led to severe erosion of the soil. Agriculture is now of minor importance, serving only to meet domestic needs.

Bequia

State: St Vincent/Grenadines.
Area: 7 sq. miles/18 sq. km.
Population: 6000.

(i) **Bequia Tourist Office,**
Port Elizabeth,
Bequia,
St Vincent, W.I.;
tel. 8 3286.
St Vincent Tourist Board,
Halifax Street,
Kingstown,
St Vincent, W.I.;
tel. 6 1224.
See also Practical Information.

HOTELS. – *Sunny Caribbec*, Belmont, 25 r.; *Spring on Bequia*, Spring, 12 r.; *Julies and Isola*, Port Elizabeth, 20 r.; *Frangipani*, Admiralty Bay, 10 r.; *Friendship Bay*, Friendship Bay, 28 r.; etc.

RESTAURANT. – *Whaleboner*, Port Elizabeth.

RECREATION and SPORT. – Sailing, deep-sea fishing, scuba diving, snorkeling, swimming and sunbathing; walking.

SHIPPING. – Frequent ferry services to Kingstown (St Vincent), and several times weekly to Mustique, Union and Carriacou. Excursions to some of the neighboring Grenadines.

The picturesque island of *Bequia, **second largest of the Grenadines, lies 10 miles/16 km S of St Vincent. It is a popular haunt of yacht-owners and from March to June is a whaling base. Apart from tourism and fishing boatbuilding still makes a contribution to the island's economy.**

From the highest point on Bequia there are breath-taking panoramic ** views. The chief place is **Port Elizabeth**, in *Admiralty Bay* (yacht harbor). From the old fort there is a good view of the harbor. *Paget Farm Village* is the whaling base. The resort complex of *Moon Hole*, built into the cliffs on the S coast, is a fine example of contemporary architecture. On the E coast is the beautiful *Friendship Bay*, which has been developed as a resort area (yacht harbor, beach).

BOAT TRIPS. – 1¼ miles/2 km S is the tiny island of *Petit Nevis*, where the whalers cut up their catch.

2½ miles/4 km S is the **Isle à Quatre**, a quiet little resort island.

Mustique

State: St Vincent/Grenadines.
Area: 2½ sq. miles/6 sq. km.
Population: 400.

(i) **St Vincent Tourist Board,**
Halifax Street,
Kingstown,
St Vincent, W.I.;
tel. 6 1224.
See also Practical Information.

HOTEL. – *Cotton House*, 19 r., SP, T, riding, beaches.
– BAR. – *Basil's Bar*.

RECREATION and SPORT. – Sailing, deep-sea fishing, scuba diving, snorkeling, swimming and sunbathing; riding, tennis, walking.

AIR SERVICES. – Regular flights to St Vincent, Canouan, Union, Carriacou and Martinique.

SHIPPING. – Ferry services several times weekly to St Vincent, Bequia, Carriacou and Union. Occasional charters and excursions to neighboring islands in the Grenadines.

*Mustique lies 15 miles/24 km S of St Vincent. Owned since 1959 by the wealthy Scottish landowner Colin Tenant, it is one of the most exclusive retreats in the Caribbean and attracts many well-known personalities.**

Until recently little known to the outside world, Mustique is now increasingly being developed for tourism. Princess Margaret has a vacation home on *Gun Hill*, a beautiful spot at the southern tip of the island.

The two largest settlements are **Lovell's Village** and **Dover's Village**, on the W coast. All around the island are fine beaches and little hidden coves, while off the coasts are magnificent banks of coral and many small islets.

Off the N coast lies the wreck of the French cruise ship "Antilles", which struck a reef here in January 1971 and was burned out, all the passengers and crew being saved by the local people.

BOAT TRIPS. – 1¼ miles/2 km S of Mustique is the coral-fringed island of *Petit Mustique* (highest point 351 ft/107 m), a quiet retreat for yacht-owners. – 4 miles/6 km farther S are the lonely *Savan Islands*.

4½ miles/7 km N of Mustique are *Baliceaux Island* and *Battowia Island*, pleasant places for a relaxing vacation.

Canouan – a bird's-eye view

Canouan

State: St Vincent/Grenadines.
Area: 3 sq. miles/8 sq. km.
Population: 700.
(i) **St Vincent Tourist Board,**
Halifax Street,
Kingstown,
St Vincent, W.I.;
tel. 6 1224.
See also Practical Information.

HOTEL. – *Crystal Sands Beach*, 10 r.

RECREATION and SPORT. – Sailing, deep-sea fishing, scuba diving, snorkeling, swimming and sunbathing; walking.

AIR SERVICES. – Regular flights to St Vincent, Union, Mustique and Carriacou.

SHIPPING. – Ferry services several times weekly to St Vincent, Bequia, Mustique, Union and Carriacou. Occasional charters and excursions to neighboring islands in the Grenadines.

*Canouan, formerly a lonely island at which only the occasional yacht called, is now attracting increasing numbers of visitors to its superb beaches and is being developed to cater for their needs.

Attractive spots on Canouan are *Charlestown Bay, New Bay* and *Rameau Bay* on the W coast, *Hyambook Bay* and *Maho Bay* on the N coast and little *Carenage Bay* on the E coast. On the NE coast are the wild and romantic *Billy Hole* and *Cloey Hole.*

Union Island

State: St Vincent/Grenadines.
Area: 2½ sq. miles/7 sq. km.
Population: 2000.
(i) **St Vincent Tourist Board,**
Halifax Street,
Kingstown,
St Vincent, W.I.;
tel. 6 1224.
See also Practical Information.

HOTEL. – *Sunny Grenadines*, 10 r.; *Anchorage Yacht Club*, 10 r., *Clifton Beach* 10 r.

RECREATION and SPORT. – Sailing, wind-surfing, deep-sea fishing, scuba diving, snorkeling, swimming and sunbathing; walking.

AIR SERVICES. – Regular flights to St Vincent, Canouan, Mustique and Carriacou.

SHIPPING. – Ferry services several times weekly to St Vincent, Bequia, Mustique, Canouan and Carriacou. Occasional charters and excursions to neighboring islands in the Grenadines.

With its hilly terrain *Union Island is one of the most attractive of the Grenadines, an exclusive rendez-vous for sailing enthusiasts from all over the world.

The chief town on the island is **Clifton**, on the SE coast, which has a sheltered harbor for sail boats. Above the little town is *Fort Hill* (400 ft/122 m), the most easterly hill on the island. Off the E coast lies the little *Red Island*.

Half way along the S coast is **Ashton**, another popular sailing harbor. Offshore can be seen the narrow *Frigate Island*. A happy hunting ground for snorkelers, it is part of the *Lagoon Reef* which protects almost the whole of the S coast. To the W of the harbor rises *Mount Taboi* (1000 ft/ 305 m), one of the highest hills in the Grenadines. Below this hill and *Mount Olympus* (637 ft/194 m) to the N is *Chatham Bay, a beautiful and secluded bay on the E coast . Other attractive bays are *Bloody Bay* in the NW of the island and *Richmond Bay* and *Belmont Bay* to the N.

1¼ miles/2 km SE of Clifton Harbour is the idyllic *Palm Island or *Prune Island* (hotel: *Palm Island Beach Club, 40 r., SP, T), which has been developed into a resort by two sailing enthusiasts, the Caldwells. There are excellent facilities for water sports, a small airstrip served by regular flights and a beautiful tropical garden.

4½ miles/7 km SE, near the boundary between St Vincent and Grenada, lies the little island paradise of *Petit St-Vincent (hotel: *Petit St-Vincent, 45 r., SP, T, beach), also privately owned, an exclusive retreat frequented by wealthy sailing enthusiasts.

2 miles/3 km N is the picturesque little tropical island of *Mayreau, an occasional port of call for yacht-owners.

4½ miles/7 km NE are the * *Tobago Cays, a scatter of islets which are sheltered from the Atlantic swell by the *Horseshoe Reef* to the E. With their enchantingly beautiful palm-fringed beaches of white sand and their abundance of marine life these cays are among the most popular anchorages in the Caribbean, with somewhat too many visitors at the height of the season.

Carriacou

State: Grenada.
Area: 13 sq. miles/34 sq. km.
Population: 10,000.
Ⓘ **Carriacou Tourist Board,**
Hillsborough,
Carriacou, Grenada, W.I.
Grenada Tourist Board,
P.O. Box 293,
Pier,
St George's,
Grenada, W.I.;
tel. 2279.
See also Practical Information.

HOTELS. – *Mermaid Inn*, 12 r.; *Silver Beach Cottages*, 8 r.; etc. – Several HOLIDAY APARTMENTS.

EVENTS. – *Carriacou Regatta* (August).

RECREATION and SPORT. – Sailing, deep-sea fishing, scuba diving, snorkeling, swimming and sunbathing; walking.

AIR SERVICES. – Regular flights to Grenada, St Vincent, Union, Canouan and Mustique. Charter flights to neighboring islands.

SHIPPING. – Regular ferry and mail boat services to St George's (Grenada), Isle de Ronde, Petit Martinique, Union, Canouan, Mustique, Bequia and Kingstown (St Vincent). Charters to some of the neighboring islands.

*Carriacou, the largest of the Grenadines and once a great sugar-growing island, is an internationally famed rendezvous for sailors. In its lagoons thrive "free oysters", much favored by connoisseurs.**

The island is traversed from N to S by a central range of hills, rising to almost 1000 ft/300 m in places. Around the coasts are a string of fine beaches and sheltered natural harbors. English and French place-names and the ruins of old plantation houses recall the island's colonial past. The old sugar-cane fields are now used for growing cotton, ground-nuts and limes or have given place to pasture. – The inhabitants are predominantly the descendants of black slaves. On this sequestered island they have preserved many old cultural and spiritual traditions resembling the Xango of Trinidad and the Voodoo cult of Haiti.

The chief town is the port of **Hillsborough** on the W coast, with venerable old stone merchants' houses which bear witness to the island's former economic importance. * **Tyrell Bay** is one of the finest natural harbors in the West Indies, a long inlet which offers yachts excellent shelter in a hurricane. – Nearby lies the picturesque village of *Harvey Vale.*

Off Carriacou are spectacular coral reefs and numbers of small islets. Notable among them are *Saline Island*, *Frigate Island* and *Large Island* off the S coast, all with superb beaches.

BOAT TRIPS. – 3 miles/5 km NE of Carriacou is the small island of **Petit Martinique**, whose 500 inhabitants are mostly descended from French settlers. They are noted for their seafaring skill.

10 miles/16 km S of Carriacou is the **Isle Ronde**, an island rising out of the sea to a height of 490 ft/150 m, edged by precipitous cliffs. On the NW coast is an excellent beach. – Here too are *Diamond Island*, *Les Tantes* and *Caille*, all favorite anchorages for sail boats.

Guadeloupe

Lesser Antilles
Windward Islands
French Antilles
Overseas Département

Area: 583 sq. miles/1510 sq. km.
Population: 335,000.
Administrative center: Basse-Terre.

ⓘ **Office de Tourisme de Guadeloupe,**
5 Square de la Banque,
B.P. 1099,
F-97159 **Pointe-à-Pitre,**
Guadeloupe, A.F.;
tel. 82 09 30.
Bureau d'Informations,
Aéroport du Raizet,
F-97110 **Pointe-à-Pitre,**
Guadeloupe, A.F.;
tel. 82 11 81.
Gare Maritime,
F-97110 **Pointe-à-Pitre,**
Guadeloupe, A.F.;
tel. 82 00 68.
Chambre de Commerce
et d'Industrie,
6 Rue Victor Hugues,
F-97100 **Basse-Terre,**
Guadeloupe, A.F.;
tel. 81 16 56.
See also Practical Information.

HOTELS. – Of the numerous hotels in Guadeloupe
only a small selection can be given here.

POINTE-À-PITRE: *Le Bougainvillée*, 40 r.; *Normandie*,
7 r.; *Schoelcher*, 10 r. – GOSIER: **Auberge de la Vieille
Tour*, 82 r., SP, T, beach; **Frantel*, 200 r., SP, T, beach;
*Holiday Inn, 156 r., SP, T, beach; **Novotel Fleur
d'Epée*, Bas-du-Fort, 180 r., SP, T, beach; **PLM
Arawak*, 150 r., SP, T, beach; **Salako*, 120 r., SP, T,
beach; *PLM Village Soleil*, 105 r.; *Callinago Beach
Hotel*, 41 r., SP, T, beach; *Ecotel*, 40 r., SP, T; *Les
Flamboyants*, 12 r.; *Serge's Guest House*, 22 r.;
Auberge J.J., 7 r.; etc. –STE-ANNE: **Club Méditerranée
Caravelle*, 300 r., SP, T, beach; *Auberge du Grande
Large*, 10 r.;**Le Relais du Moulin*, 40 r.; **Motel de Ste-
Anne*, 8 r. – ST-FRANÇOIS: ** Méridien Guadeloupe*,
270 r., SP, T, golf, beach; **Hamak*, 56 villas, T, golf,
beach; *Trois Mâts*, 36 r., T, golf, beach; *Honoré's
Hotel*, 7 r.; *V.V.F.G.*, 80 r., SP, T, beach. – LE MOULE:
*Caraibe Copatel, 212 r., SP, T, beach; **PLM Les
Alizés*, 110 r., SP, T, beach; *Le Rejeton*, 8 r. – BASSE-
TERRE: *Hotel de Basse-Terre*, 14 r.; *Hotel Relaxe*, 13 r.
–ST-CLAUDE: *Hotel Relais de la Grande Soufrière*, 20 r.
– VIEUX-HABITANTS: *Hotel de Recroy*, 12 r. – DESHAIES:
*Club Méditerranée Fort Royal, 231 r., SP, T, beach. –
Many HOLIDAY APARTMENTS. – Several modest
PENSIONS. – CAMPING. – DESHAIES: *Sable d'or*,
limited scope.

RESTAURANTS in most hotels: also in POINTE-À-
PITRE: *Auberge Henri-IV*, 83 rue Henri-IV; *Chick-
ekebab*, 28 rue Schoelcher (Oriental); *Danieli*, 36 rue
Schoelcher; *Oiseau des Iles* and *Madras*, both at
Aéroport du Raizet; etc. – GOSIER: **Chez Rosette*; **Le
Bistrot*, Petit Havre; *La Réserve chez Jeanne*, Route de
Ste-Anne; *Auberge des Châtaigniers*; *La Chaubette*. –
STE-ANNE: *Le Bistrot*. – ST-FRANÇOIS: *La Ciboulette*;
Madame Jerco; *Ranch*. – BASSE-TERRE: *Gargantua*, 42
rue de la République; *Relais d'Orléans*, near Préfec-

ture; *Tropic*, on Market; etc. – MATOUBA: *Chez Paul*. –
DESHAIES: *Le Karacoli*.

NIGHT CLUBS in the large hotels; also in GOSIER:
Domino; *Le Boukarou*; *La Cocoteraie*; *Marie-Lou*. –
ST-FRANÇOIS: *Le Casino*.

Casino (blackjack, baccarat, roulette) in Hôtel
Méridien Guadeloupe, St-François.

SHOPPING. – The island's main shopping and
commercial center is Pointe-à-Pitre. The best shopping streets are *Rue Frébault*, *Rue Schoelcher* and *Rue
Nozières*. Between the market and the old harbor there
are many street traders from Dominica and Haiti
selling fruit and vegetables and sometimes also
excellent hand-made articles. In the immediate
neighborhood of the Gare Maritime are a number of
shops selling imported goods (e.g. crystal, porcelain
and perfume from France) at very advantageous
(duty-free) prices.

A number of native artists have rediscovered the
calabash and revived the old tradition, going back to
pre-Columbian times, of creating objects of artistic
quality from the bottle gourd.

PUBLIC HOLIDAYS and EVENTS. – *Jour de l'An*,
New Year's Day. – **Carnaval* (first Sunday after
Epiphany to Ash Wednesday), a lively carnival, with
big parades and other events, which reaches its climax
between *Samedi Gras* (Saturday before Ash Wednes-
day) and *Mercredi des Cendres* (Ash Wednesday) and
ends with the burning of the "Vaval". – *Vendredi
Saint*, Good Friday, with a great procession at
Abymes. – *Pâques*, Easter. – *Fête du Travail* (May 1),
Labour Day. – *Ascension*. – *Pentecôte*, Whitsun. –
Fêtes Communales (July–October), colorful parish
festivals, usually in honor of the local patron saint. –
Fête Nationale (July 14), the French National Day. –
Fête du Carmel (July 16), a religious festival in Basse-
Terre. – *Schoelcher* (July 21), Schoelcher Memorial
Day. – **Assumption* (August 15), with great celebra-
tions in many places. – **Fêtes des Cuisinières*
(August–September), the traditional festival of the
cooks (mostly colored) of Guadeloupe, with a mass in
honor of St Lawrence, followed by a colorful
procession. – **Toussaint* (November 1), All Saints
Day; after dark, processions bearing candles to many
churchyards. – *Jour des Morts* (November 2), All
Souls Day; ceremonies in many places remembering
the dead. – *Fête de la Sainte-Famille* (November 4), a
religious festival in honor of the Holy Family, Goyave.
– *Armistice* (November 11). – *Christ-Roi* (last Sunday
in the church year), festival of Christ the King, Les
Mangles. – *Noël*, Christmas.

Cockfights (*Combats de coqs*) are very popular
sporting occasions in Guadeloupe, particularly in
Grande-Terre. Almost every village has a cockpit
in which fights are regularly held between cocks
armed with knife-sharp steel spurs and weighted
to make them heavier. Most of the spectators lay
bets on the result of the contest, which lasts about
a quarter of an hour, and urge on their favorite with
vociferous shouts and gestures. The time and
place of these events, which often draw spectators
from the neighboring islands, are announced in
the newspapers.

RECREATION and SPORT. – Flying; sailing, deep-sea
fishing, wind-surfing, water-skiing, scuba diving,

Tree fern, Guadeloupe

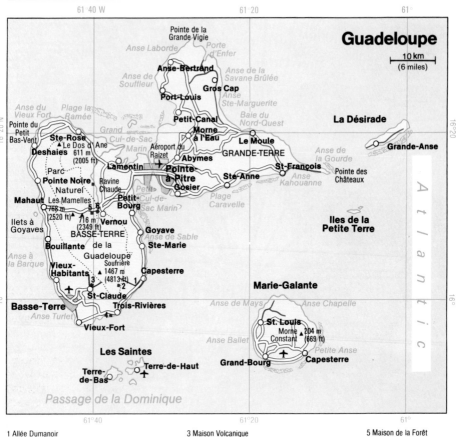

1 Allée Dumanoir   3 Maison Volcanique   5 Maison de la Forêt
2 Chutes du Carbet   4 Roches Gravées   6 Cascade aux Ecrevisses

snorkeling, swimming and sunbathing; riding, golf, tennis, walking.

AIR SERVICES. – Regular flights from the Aéroport International du Raizet to Dominica, Martinique, St Lucia, Barbados, Grenada, St Vincent, Trinidad, Caracas (Venezuela), Cayenne (French Guiana), Antigua, Montserrat, St Kitts, St-Barthélemy, St-Martin, St Thomas, St Croix, Tortola, St Eustatius, Saba, San Juan (Puerto Rico), Port-au-Prince (Haiti), Santo Domingo (Dominican Republic), Miami and New York (USA), Montreal (Canada), Paris (France), Brussels (Belgium), Basle/Mulhouse (Switzerland/France), Geneva (Switzerland) and Frankfurt am Main (Germany). – Frequent local services to Marie-Galante, La Désirade and Iles des Saintes from Pointe-à-Pitre (Le Raizet) and Basse-Terre (Baillif).

SHIPPING. – From the Gare Maritime, Pointe-à-Pitre, cruise ships sometimes sail to Miami (USA), San Juan (Puerto Rico) and other destinations in the Caribbean. – Regular freighter sailings from Pointe-à-Pitre and Basse-Terre to Le Havre and Marseilles (France), Britain and various Caribbean destinations. – Small cargo boat sailings daily to Marie-Galante, La Désirade, St-Barthélemy, St-Martin and Dominica. – Ferry services from Trois-Rivières and Basse-Terre to Iles des Saintes.

The butterfly-shaped island of ****Guadeloupe**, consisting of a hilly western part made up of volcanic rocks (Basse-Terre) and a lower eastern half formed of limestones (Grande-Terre), lies between latitude 15°50′ and 18°5′ N and between longitude 61°3′ and 63°5′ W. Known to the pre-Columbian inhabitants as Karukera, "Land of the Beautiful Waters", it was given the name of Santa María de Guadalupe de Estremadura by Columbus. – Together with the neighboring islands of Les Saintes, Marie-Galante and La Désirade, the island of St-Barthélemy, 125 miles/201 km farther N, and the French part of St Maarten/St-Martin, Guadeloupe now constitutes a French overseas département.

The butterfly form of the main island reflects the different geological history of the two parts of the island. The roughly triangular eastern half, **Grande-Terre**, consists of beds of limestone broken up by tectonic action, the central area having a particularly varied pattern of relief – hills much distorted by karstic action which are known to the natives as "montagnes russes" (switchbacks) and the so-called Fonds, which are residual areas of plain at

Pointe-à-Pitre and the Petit Cul-de-Sac Marin, Guadeloupe

heights of up to 446 ft/136 m, much weathered and eroded. This region falls down towards the Riviéra du Sud, the stretch of coast, sheltered by banks of coral, which extends from Pointe-à-Pitre to the eastern tip of the island, the rugged Pointe des Châteaux. The fine beaches of white sand and sheltered bays with turquoise-colored water are now being developed for tourism on a massive scale. The main resort centers are the town of Gosier and the townships of Ste-Anne and St-François. – To the N and E the central uplands fall down to a coastal plain lying between 130 ft/40 m and 200 ft/60 m, with extensive sugar-cane plantations. The NW coast of Grande-Terre, between the airport of Le Raizet and the fishing village of Port-Louis, is fringed by large areas of mangrove swamp, while the NE and E coasts are bounded by imposing cliffs, interrupted at intervals by the mouths of rivers and excellent beaches.

The smaller island of La Désirade and the Iles de la Petite Terre, to the SE, and Marie-Galante to the S are, like Grande-Terre, built up of limestones. To the NW they fall down to the sea in varying degrees of steepness, depending on the extent of the upthrust they have undergone. Here again the beaches, almost untouched by the hand of man, are sheltered by coral reefs.

The line of division between the two parts of the island is the *Rivière Salée*. This narrow channel flanked by mangrove swamps which links the **Grand Cul-de-Sac Marin**, the large bay to the N which is traversed by numerous banks of coral and contains an abundance of fish, with its southern counterpart, the **Petit Cul-de-Sac Marin**, also with banks of coral. At the sheltered NE end of the Petit Cul-de-Sac is Pointe-à-Pitre, the economic center of Guadeloupe.

The western half of the island, **Basse-Terre**, has something of the shape of an egg when seen from the air. Forming part of the Eastern Caribbean volcanic axis, this half of the island shows a vigorous pattern of relief very different from that of the eastern part. The summits increase in height from N to S, from the Piton de Ste-Rose (1171 ft/357 m) by way of Les Mamelles (2520 ft/768 m) to 4813 ft/ 1467 m in the still active volcano of La Soufrière, and then fall down to the sea again to the S of the Monts Caraïbes (1880 ft/573 m). The Iles des Saintes, to the S of Basse-Terre, also owe their existence to an upthrust resulting from volcanic action.

Topographically Basse-Terre is made up of five different landscape units. The eastern coastal zone is relatively flat and is broken up by many watercourses. This area has extensive banana plantations, as has the steeply scarped region rising to the mountains, with its impressive gorges and tumbling waterfalls. The highest peaks in the central range which are for the most part covered with dense tropical forest, reach up into the zone of sparser mountain forest (cloud forest) with its typical vegetation cover. On the SE and S coasts are long fjord-like inlets, at the head of which there are often beaches of black sand. The W coast is marked by wild gorges and small areas of alluvial soil at the mouths of rivers; and here, in contrast to the E coast, the beaches are not

Heliconia caribaea

sheltered by banks of coral and are repeatedly ravaged by storm tides.

Below the W side of the Soufrière massif is Basse-Terre, the Island's capital, with its main administrative institutions.

CLIMATE. – The Guadeloupe archipelago lies on the western margin of the Atlantic in the zone of the tropical trade winds. As on the other Caribbean islands, altitude has a determining influence on the climate. The trade winds, blowing from the ENE on some 300 days in the year, bring moisture with them; and when the air masses are forced up by the fairly high mountains of Basse-Terre the resultant cooling of the air brings down an abundant rainfall. While the average annual rainfall at the eastern tip of Grande-Terre is about 28 in./700 mm, the figure rises at Pointe-à-Pitre to 39–47 in./1000–1200 mm and in the Soufrière region on Basse-Terre reaches no less than 315–395 in./8000–10,000 mm. Three-quarters of this rainfall occurs between July and December; the two driest months are February and March, the period of Carême (Lent). The mean annual day temperature at sea level is about 77 °F/25 °C, with a range of 9–16 °F/5–9 °C between maximum and minimum. The difference in temperature between the warmest and the coldest month is about 9 °F/5 °C. The Basse-Terre heights, however, contribute to leveling out the temperature. Given its situation, the archipelago is exposed to the danger of inflows of cold air from the North American continent: thus on the Soufrière temperatures approaching 32 °F/0 °C have on occasion been recorded. Other hazards, particularly between July and September, are violent tropical storms and terrifying hurricanes, which can wreak catastrophic damage. Guadeloupe was visited by catastrophes of this kind on September 12, 1928, August 11, 1956 (Hurricane Betsy), September 27, 1966 (Hurricane Ines) and August 29, 1979 (Hurricane David), on each occasion suffering heavy damage.

HISTORY. – It is supposed that Guadeloupe, like some of the neighboring islands, was settled by Arawak Indians from Venezuela some 2000 years ago. The evidence of archaeology suggests that this people had already reached a fairly advanced cultural stage. The warlike Caribs probably arrived on the island only about A.D. 1000 The scanty finds indicate that they had a less evolved culture than their predecessors.

The island was discovered by Columbus on November 4, 1493; but since it possessed no useful minerals the Spaniards soon lost interest in it. Until the end of the 16th c. there were only occasional landings by Europeans, who were discouraged from settling by the hostile attitude of the islanders.

About 1635 Richelieu decided, on the advice of the governor of St-Christophe, Belain d'Esnambuc, to send out an expedition from France to colonize the island. Under the leadership of Liénard de l'Olive and Duplessis d'Ossonville, two Norman nobles, a first party of settlers sailed for Guadeloupe. This consisted of missionaries and volunteers who paid for their passage by contracting with the Compagnie des Iles d'Amérique to give their labor for three years. The settlers encountered great difficulties, partly as a result of differences of opinion between the two leaders and partly because of the hostile attitude of the Indians. In 1644 Charles Houël began to grow sugar-cane on the islands, and this labor-intensive crop led to the introduction of slave labor. In 1664 Guadeloupe became the responsibility of the newly established Compagnie des Indes Occidentales, but only ten years later, after the collapse of the company, it became part of the Domaine Royal (Crown property). The administration of the island had previously (1669) been made subordinate to that of Martinique. During the first half of the 18th c. further crops were introduced – first indigo and then cotton, coffee, cacao and tobacco. The additional labor force required was recruited from freed galley slaves, Protestants, prostitutes and black slaves from Africa. A vivid description of life on the island in the first quarter of the 18th c. is given by the Dominican friar Père Labat in his "Nouveau Voyage aux Iles de l'Amérique" (1722).

In 1759 and again in 1763 the island was occupied by Britain, but under the Peace of Paris it was returned to France. Between 1789 and 1815 it was involved in the troubled period of the French Revolution, and there were a number of battles between royalists and supporters of the new ideas. The royalists called on British help, but Victor Hugues, the *commissaire* appointed by the Committee of Public Safety, defeated the British forces and in 1794 issued a decree abolishing slavery. Under his rule many planters were executed, and the white population went into hiding or sought safety in Louisiana on the North American mainland. Finally Hugues' rigorous measures led to his recall.

Under General Richepance, who was appointed governor of the island by Napoleon, slavery was re-introduced in 1802, and there followed a period of reactionary rule. Between 1810 and 1816 Guadeloupe was several times occupied by British forces. – In 1848 slavery was finally abolished, a prominent part in its abolition being played by Victor Schoelcher, the national hero who is also honored in Martinique. During the second half of the 19th c. the island's economy took on its present form. More than half the usable land was acquired by large companies who employed great numbers of poor settlers as well as more than 40,000 Indian indentured laborers, and numbers of Chinese and black Africans. The varied origins of the population were a major factor in the severe social conflicts which later gave rise to the demand for self-government.

During the Second World War the island at first sided with the Vichy regime, but in 1943 it went over to the Committee of National Liberation. In 1946 it became a French overseas département (*département d'outre-mer*), and is now a French region within the European Community. – For many years a number of leftist groups, some of them militant, have been campaigning for independence from France.

ADMINISTRATION. – The overseas département of Guadeloupe has the same form of administration as any other French département. The chief town, with the Prefecture, is Basse-Terre, and there are sub-prefectures at Pointe-à-Pitre and St-Martin. The département is represented in the French Parliament by three deputies and two senators. There is a Regional Council of 41 members and an Economic and Social Council of 35 members. The Conseil Général of the département has 36 members representing the individual communes and cantons.

POPULATION. – Guadeloupe has a population of some 335,000, predominantly of mixed blood, the descendants of French settlers, African black slaves and Indian indentured laborers. Only a small proportion of the population, most of whom belong to the Roman Catholic Church, is of pure European descent.

Over 52% of the population are under 20 – a reflection of the high surplus of births over deaths which is found here as on other Caribbean islands. The annual rate of population increase is between 1.5% and 2%. In order to reduce the pressure of population the government has supported family planning measures and has also promoted programs of resettlement under which between 2500 and 3000 people annually are moved to thinly populated French overseas territories such as French Guiana or to France itself. About a quarter of the working population is employed in the primary sector, chiefly in agriculture; another quarter work in productive industry; and fully half are engaged in the service trades (commerce, tourism, administration).

The main concentration of population is at Pointe-à-Pitre, with some 110,000 people living in the town and suburbs. The second largest town is the island's capital, Basse-Terre, with a population of some 50,000 including the adjoining communes.

In recent years considerable sums have been spent on improving the island's social and educational facilities, so that Guadeloupe now ranks among the best developed territories in the Caribbean.

ECONOMY. – The **agriculture** of Guadeloupe is based primarily on the growing of sugar-cane and bananas. Of its 150,000 acres of agricultural land 60,000 acres are devoted to sugar-cane, mostly grown on Grande-Terre. The total crop comes to some 965,000 tons, producing 91,000 tons of sugar, 40,000 tons of molasses and 2,000,000 gallons of rum. Most of this output is exported to France and other EEC countries. At present, however, the sugar and rum industries of Guadeloupe are experiencing serious marketing problems, as a result of the worldwide over-production of sugar and the steep increase in costs of production.

Banana plantations occupy some 18,000 acres, chiefly in the southeastern part of Basse-Terre. The total crop is about 150,000 tons; most of it was exported to France and other EEC countries.

An increasingly important branch of agriculture is the growing of vegetables, which at present occupy some 12,500 acres. Exports in 1977 amounted to some 4000 tons, principally egg plants. – In spite of a steady increase in the area under cultivation it is still necessary to import some 13,000 tons of fruit and vegetables every year.

The remaining agricultural land, some 54,000 acres, consists of pasture. Great efforts are being made to reduce the present large imports of milk, beef, pork, poultry and eggs by increasing domestic production.

Almost a third of the island's area is occupied by forest, although the local topography makes it difficult to exploit these resources. Some 5000 tons of timber are felled annually – insufficient to meet domestic needs.

Guadeloupe's 800 fishermen have an annual catch of some 7500 tons of fish and seafood, most of which is exported.

The efforts made in recent years to force the pace of industrialization have had some success. The main concentration of **industry** is in the Pointe-à-Pitre area. The oldest establishments are the sugar refineries and rum distilleries, which have recently been subjected to a painful slimming-down process made necessary by marketing difficulties. Later developments included factories producing soft drinks and canned foods. In the last few years the construction industries have prospered, thanks to the building of a large power station and a cement plant. Further stimulus has been given to the development of industry by the establishment of a 314 acre industrial estate at Pointe Jarry and the provision of new industrial sites at Basse-Terre.

More than 5000 people are employed in wholesale and retail trade, and other major sources of employment are various government agencies, which have sought to limit unemployment among young people by making provision for short-term employment opportunities. – In recent years a considerable boost has been given to the economy by the development of **tourism**. Most visitors come by air, using the excellently equipped airport of Le Raizet, which handles more than a million passengers per year. In a given year, too, more than 70,000 cruise ship passengers land on Guadeloupe, spending a few hours in sightseeing and giving a further boost to the island's trade.

Pointe-à-Pitre

*__Pointe-à-Pitre__ (alt. 0–100 ft/0–30 m; pop. 30,000), Guadeloupe's main economic center, lies at the junction of the two parts of the island. It has a fine natural harbor.

HISTORY. – The town's name is derived from a Dutch fisherman of Jewish origin who was expelled from Brazil by the Portuguese. For many years an unimportant little settlement, it became a place of some

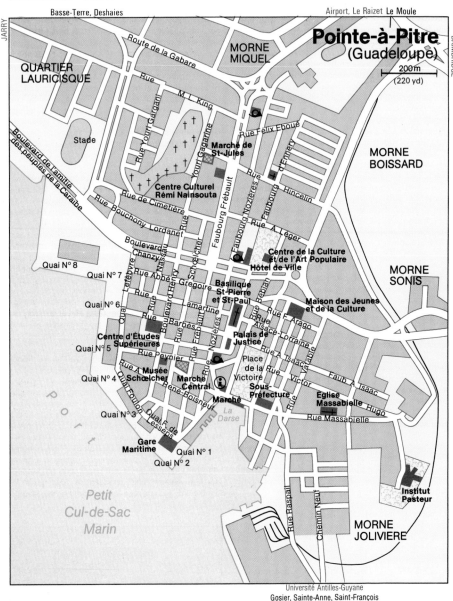

Pointe-à-Pitre (Guadeloupe)

economic consequence when the inhabitants of the inland township of Abymes built a road to the harbor to enable them to market their produce. The final establishment of the town took place in 1759, during the Seven Years War. The harbor was now improved by the British occupants, but under the Peace of Paris (1763) they had to cede the town to the French, who strengthened its fortifications. By the time of the French Revolution Pointe-à-Pitre had grown substantially in size. In 1843 much of the town was destroyed in an earthquake, but it was quickly rebuilt. Despite a cholera epidemic in 1865 it continued to develop, and became an important banking and commercial capital. In 1898 a third of the town was destroyed by fire, and in 1928 it was devastated by a cyclone which claimed several hundred lives. In 1967 Pointe-à-Pitre was the scene of violent disturbances, arising primarily from social problems. Much damage was caused in 1979 by Hurricanes David and Frederick.

The heart of the town is formed by the old harbor or *Darse, the quays of which are now occupied by a colorful street market, and the *Place de la Victoire, the name of which commemorates Victor Hugues' victory over British forces. At the SE corner of the palm-shaded square stands the *Sous-Préfecture*, and on the opposite side the *Office du Tourisme* – both very typical examples of French colonial architecture. A little way NE, linked with the square by a huddle of souvenir and refreshment stalls spreading out from the harbor, is the *Marché Central, the scene of bustling activity, with piles of vegetables, fruit and spices. To the S of the market are many offices, banks and duty-free shops selling imported goods, the *Gare Maritime* (where the cruise ships moor) and other port installations. The oldest of the town's major thoroughfares is *"Rue Frébault*, which runs N from the market. This is the principal shopping street, but the two parallel streets, Rue Nozières and Rue Schoelcher, and the cross streets which link them are scarcely less busy.

Just to the W of the market can be found the *"Musée Schoelcher*, commemorating the great fighter for the abolition of slavery. Nearby, in Rue Sadi-Carnot, is the *Chambre d'Agriculture* (19th c.), another notable example of French colonial architecture.

NE of the market is Place Gourbeyre, with a bust of the French admiral of that name. On the S side of the square stands the modest *Palais de Justice* (Law Court). *The Basilique Saint-Pierre et Saint-Paul* (1847), on the N side, dominates its surroundings. This large church, reinforced by iron girders, which has suffered much damage from the elements in the past, has fine stained glass. Farther N, on the boulevard bounding the old town, are a number of good modern developments in the older northern districts of the town. Particularly notable are the avant-garde *Banque Nationale de Paris*, the new Head Post Office, the very modern *Hôtel de Ville* (Town Hall) and the excellently equipped *"Centre de la Culture et de l'Art Populaire* (1978), which has given fresh stimulus to the previously very modest cultural life of the town.

In the Faubourg Frébault, the main road out of the town to the N, can be found the *Centre Culturel Rémi Nainsouta*, where there are periodic exhibitions and other events. – Farther N is the district of MIQUEL, with the offices of many public institutions and agencies. A short distance SE the old *Grand Hotel*, built in the style of a passenger liner of the early 20th c., now houses the Chamber of Commerce.

To the E, above the old harbor, is the handsome *Eglise Massabielle* (19th c.), now overtopped by the *Tour Massabielle*, a high rise building from which far-ranging views may be enjoyed. – Farther E, on the Morne Jolivière, are the extensive buildings of the *Hôpital Général* and *Institut Pasteur*.

Basse-Terre
(Guadeloupe)
500 m
(550 yd)

At the S end of the town, beyond the *Usine Darboussier* (one of the oldest and largest sugar and rum factories on the island), is the little harbor known as the **Carénage**, above which rear the new buildings of the **Université Antilles-Guyane**.

On the far side of the bay is the **Jarry** industrial estate, a promising attempt to provide new jobs. There is another industrial estate at **Le Raizet** on the northern outskirts of the town, where the modern airport has given a considerable impetus to development.

*****Basse-Terre** (sea level; pop. 17,000), capital of Guadeloupe, the see of a bishop and an important banana-shipping port, lies at the foot of the volcano of *La Soufrière* on the SW coast of the eastern part of the island.

HISTORY. – Basse-Terre is one of the oldest French colonial towns in the Caribbean, founded by Charles Houël around 1640, when Fort St-Charles, on the S side of the town, was also built. In the second half of the 17th c. the town extended from the fort to the Rivière aux Herbes. In 1702, and again during the Seven Years War, the town was attacked by British forces. In the last quarter of the 18th c. Basse-Terre was torn by social unrest and the French Revolution, and in 1794 it was occupied by British forces. In 1802 the town was the scene of conflict betwen General Richepance, commissioned by Napoleon to restore the institution of slavery which had been abolished by the revolutionary government, and Col. Louis Delgrès, a Guadeloupe patriot who commanded the Basse-Terre forces. Finally on May 28, 1802 Delgrès and more than 200 of his men threw themselves to their deaths rather than submit to the Napoleonic forces.

The town has had to be evacuated on several occasions because of threatened eruptions of the volcano of La Soufrière, most recently in 1976, when more than 70,000 inhabitants of Basse-Terre and the surrounding area were rehoused elsewhere for almost five months. On September 28–29, 1979 the town was ravaged by Hurricane David, and a few days later by offshoots of Hurricane Frederick.

Summit zone, La Soufrière (Guadeloupe)

Overlooking the **Harbor**, with its installations for the shipment of bananas, are the *Capitainerie* (Harbor Office) and *Hôtel de Ville* (Town Hall). Behind these buildings are two shopping streets, Rue des Corsaires and Rue du Docteur-Cabre; at the S end of the latter stands the *Cathedral* (19th c.),. with an imposing *façade.

Beyond the *Rivière aux Herbes* in the southern part of the town are many office buildings. Between Rue de la République and the Boulevard du Général-de-Gaulle, which runs alongside the harbor, is the colorful **Marché Central**. To the S, at the corner of Avenue Félix-Eboué, stands the *Palais du Conseil Général*, meeting-place of the département's "parliament", and opposite this is the *Palais de Justice* (Law Court), adjoining which are two sports grounds. Higher up, beyond the beautiful *Jardin Pichon*, we come to the *Place du Champ d'Arbaud**, a charming square surrounded by handsome colonial-period buildings, with a large monument in the center. – 550 yd/500 m farther uphill is the superb *Jardin Botanique**.

To the S, above Rue de Lardenoy, are the extensive buildings of the **Préfecture**, with the *Palais d'Orléans**, built in the 1930s to house receptions and other great occasions. – The much frequented church of *Notre Dame du Mont-Carmel*, a little way downhill, probably occupies the site of the first church founded in the colony. It contains fine grave slabs. Pilgrimage on July 16.

Farther S rises the imposing *Fort St-Charles**, on a projecting spur of hill above the *Rivière du Galion*. This was the point around which the town developed. The massive structure with its extensive outworks is well preserved. General Richepance and Admiral Gourbeyre are buried in the fort. To the S is the new Marina Rivière Sens (120 capacity).

SURROUNDINGS of Basse-Terre. – 3 miles/5 km NE, above the town, is *St-Claude (1870 ft/570 m; pop. 10,000), with a pleasant climate which makes it a favored residential and vacation resort. The town was founded in the 18th c. by French planters who had survived an expedition to Guiana. A large hospital was built here in 1823. There is an interesting *Maison du Volcan, with displays and documentation on volcanic activity, in particular on the development of La Soufrière. – 2 miles/3 km farther N and higher up, in a wild and romantic setting, lies the little village of **Matouba**, once a favorite place of residence for incomers from the East Indies, now noted for its mineral springs with an abundant flow of water. Just before the entrance to the village stands a *monument to Col. Delgrès* (see above under History).

Matouba is the starting-point of the *Trace Victor-Hugues, a strenuous but very rewarding hill path (19 miles/30 km; 10 hours' walk), with magnificent views. The path climbs by way of the *Savane aux Ananas* (3288 ft/1002 m) to *Sans-Toucher* (4442 ft/1354 m), goes over the *Col de la Matéliane* (4259 ft/1298 m) to the *Ajoupa Moynac* and then descends NE to **Montebello**, on the E coast of Basse-Terre. – At the Ajoupa Moynac another fine path, the *Trace Merwart, branches off, running past the *Morne Moustique* (3675 ft/1120 m; extensive views) and the *Montagne Merwart* to **Vernou**.

St-Claude to La Soufrière. – From the Maison du Volcan in St-Claude a narrow road (4 miles/6 km) climbs steeply past the *Aire du Soleil,* a picnic site with panoramic views, and through dense tropical mountain forest to the *Bains-Jaunes* (3117 ft/950 m), a hot chalybeate spring at the foot of the *Morne Goyave,* from which it continues to a large car park on the *Savane à Mulets,* an ancient plateau out of which rears the massive bulk of the still active volcano which is the highest peak in the Lesser Antilles.

****La Soufrière** (4813 ft/1467 m) has the form of a truncated cone more than 1000 ft/300 m in height, with a diameter at the base of some 2950 ft/900 m and at the top of some 1300 ft/400 m. Its rocky and rugged slopes fall steeply down, with only a scanty growth of vegetation – as a result of the sulphurous fumes constantly emitted by the volcano and the very high rainfall (some 400 in./10,000 mm annually). The volcanic dome, consisting of slow-flowing acidic lava which solidified on the spot, is split by a deep cleft running from N to S.

The volcano has erupted several times since the beginning of the colonial period. There appears to have been a catastrophic eruption of magma (molten mineral matter) in 1590, and phreatic eruptions (i.e. spectacular explosions of steam caused when rising magma comes into contact with ground water), sometimes lasting for weeks, took place in 1797–98, 1836–37, 1956 and 1975–77. These eruptions were accompanied by the emission of acid gases, the ejection of ash and stone and flows of viscous lava, and had in each case been preceded by a period of increased seismic activity. – Also in the La Soufrière massif are the *Carmichaël* peaks (4639 ft/1414 m) to the NW, the *Col de l'Echelle* (4584 ft/1397 m) and the old volcanic crater of *La Citerne* (3619 ft/1103 m) to the SE.

Ascent of La Soufrière (1–2 hours; good footwear and rainproof clothing essential; magnificent views on dry days from December to April). – From the car park

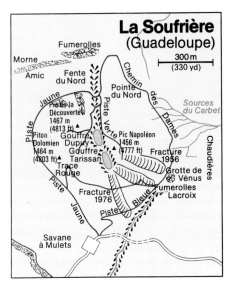

on the Savane à Mulets the *Chemin des Dames* ascends the W flank of the volcanic dome to the *Fente du Nord,* the northern part of the deep cleft, from which the difficult *Piste Verte* continues up to the summit area, passing a number of fumaroles. In the cleft are the *Gouffre Dupuy and the **Gouffre Tarissan,* two volcanic chasms which constantly emit fumes and rumblings. On clear days there are excellent *views from the volcano's two highest peaks, the *Pic de la Découverte* (4813 ft/1467 m) and the *Piton Dolomieu* (4803 ft/1464 m).

Warning. – As a result of weathering and volcanic activity some sections of the marked paths are difficult, and visibility is reduced by swirling clouds of mist. Particular care is required in the summit area with its many crevices, precipitous gullies, fumaroles and mud ponds.

Tour of Grande-Terre from Pointe-à-Pitre (74 miles/119 km). – Leave Pointe-à-Pitre on N 4, going S. Soon after leaving the town the road passes the **Bas-du-Fort** yacht harbor (capacity 600), crowded with sail boats, and then continues E along the **Riviéra du Sud,** coming in 2 miles/3 km to –

La Grande Baie, with a number of luxury hotels, carefully tended beaches and extensive sports facilities. Above the bay is the well-preserved ***Fort Fleur d'Epée** (18th c.), a massive structure on a hill surrounded by a deep moat.

The fort has had an eventful history. It was difficult to defend against attack from the landward side, and was taken by British forces in 1794, being recovered by the French only after a long effort.

2 miles/3 km: ***Gosier,** the island's principal tourist area, with a beautiful beach and many hotels, restaurants and places of entertainment. Offshore is a small wooded islet encircled by a sandy beach, the **Ilot de Gosier,* with a lighthouse.

2½ miles/4 km: *St-Félix,* a small hamlet with a beautiful beach to the S. – The road continues E through the southern outliers of the Grands Fonds.

Lava flow on the Col de l'Echelle

Resort area, Gosier, from the air

6 miles/10 km: *Ste-Anne, a developing resort with a good beach sheltered by a reef. The settlement was founded in the 17th c., prospered as a sugar-exporting port and soon became the chief place in Grande-Terre. It was sacked by British forces in 1759. – To the W of the town, in a secluded setting, we find the luxurious and strikingly designed holiday settlement of *Caravelle*, with a superb *beach of fine sand. – Around the town are many ruined sugar-mills. – From Ste-Anne a minor road (D 105) runs NW through the *Grands Fonds area to Pointe-à-Pitre. This very beautiful region, popularly known as the "Montagnes Russes" ("Switchback"), is a limestone plain which has been broken down into small residual patches, with hills much affected by karstic action and a tangle of deeply slashed valleys, which after heavy rain become an almost impassable series of lakes. – Beyond Ste-Anne N 4 continues E into the low *Plaine de la Simonière*.

8 miles/15 km: *Ste-François, a picturesque fishing village with an 18th c. church and an interesting Hindu cemetery. At the entrance to the village is the *Plage des Raisins Clairs*, with a vacation village. On the E side of the village, where the old salt-pans have been converted into a marina (capacity 275), stands the luxury *Hôtel Méridien Guadeloupe*, with its own airstrip, golfcourse, casino and other leisure facilities, where President Carter, Prime Minister Callaghan, Chancellor Schmidt and President Giscard d'Estaing had a summit meeting on January 5–6, 1979. To the N of the village is the new *Ste-Marthe* sugar factory, which can be visited. 2 miles/3 km farther NE is the pretty *Anse de la Baie*, above which stands the *Chapelle Baie Olive*.

Detour to the Pointe des Châteaux. – From St-François a narrow road runs E along a promontory of arid soil, with drought-loving vegetation. In 4½ miles/7 km an unsurfaced road branches off on the left and continues a few hundred yards N to the *Anse de la Gourde*, a charming little beach. Next to it lies the naturist beach *Plage de Tavare*. – 2½ miles/4 km beyond the junction the *Pointe des Châteaux, the easternmost tip of Guadeloupe, has been hewn into jagged and fantastic shapes by the fierce Atlantic breakers. From the highest point, the *Pointe des Colibris* (141 ft/43 m; cross) there are breath-taking ** views of the S and E coasts of Guadeloupe, the uninhabited **Iles de la Petite Terre**, a favorite sailing area, to the S and the rugged limestone cliffs of La Désirade to the E. The sunrises here are magnificent. Below the Pointe des Colibris is a very beautiful sandy beach.

> **Warning.** – Swimming is prohibited here, since the very strong surf makes it highly dangerous.

NW of the Pointe des Châteaux are old salt-pans, within the shelter of the reef.

From St-François N 5 continues N through large sugar-cane fields.

4 miles/6 km: *Zevallos, a majestic mansion of the colonial period, once the center of one of the largest sugar plantations on the island. From here a country road (1¼ miles/2 km) leads to the *Porte d'Enfer* ("Gate of Hell"), a precipitous cliff on the E coast.

4 miles/6 km: *Le Moule (0–33 ft/0–10 m; pop. 17,000), one of the largest towns on the island and the only port on the Atlantic coast.

Founded at the end of the 17th c., Le Moule was once an important sugar port and for a time capital of Guadeloupe. It was the target of British attacks in 1794 and 1809. In 1928 it suffered heavy damage in a hurricane.

At the S end of the town is *L'Autre Bord*, where the Gardel ravine meets the sea; this is a popular anchorage for sail boats. To the E is a fine beach, with hotels and other facilities. – The town itself has an imposing 19th c. church in neo-classical style. By the

Plage Caravelle, Ste-Anne (Grande-Terre, Guadeloupe)

Pointe des Châteaux (Grande-Terre, Guadeloupe)

harbor are the ruins of an 18th c. fort. – On the NW outskirts of the town, in the *Baie du Nord-Ouest*, is the luxury *Hôtel Caraïbe Copatel*. A little way to the N can be seen the remains of an Arawak Indian settlement.

From Le Moule D 101 runs W to Pointe-à-Pitre via **Château Gaillard**, passing through beautiful open scenery.

The main road continues N from Le Moule, keeping close to the coast, and comes in 2 miles/3 km to a road junction. Continue on N 7.

1¼ miles/2 km: *Palais*. The road (unsurfaced) con-. tinues N, passing through Ste-Marguerite.

5 miles/8 km: road junction at **Gros Cap**. A side road (1¼ miles/2 km) runs E to the *pilgrimage chapel of Ste-Anne* (feast on July 26), high above the *Anse de la Savane Brûlée*.

2½ miles/4 km: *Mahaudière*, an old sugar factory. The road continues W, passing through the village of *Campêche*. – In 1¼ miles/2 km turn N into D 122.

1¼ miles/2 km: *Marie-Thérèse*, with a small pond. Detour N from here to the impressive fjord-like *Porte d'Enfer* ("Gate of Hell"), with fine caves and a beautiful beach. – Continue NW from Marie-Thérèse on D 120.

4½ miles/7 km: **Anse-Bertrand**, the most northerly settlement on Guadeloupe and the final retreat of the Caribs, whose last descendants were still living here in the 19th c. A little way N of the village is the *Anse Laborde*, with an excellent beach.

Detour to the Pointe de la Grande Vigie. – From Anse-Bertrand an unsurfaced road (4 miles/6 km) runs NE past the *Anse Castavia* and through an area of drought-loving vegetation to the *Pointe de la Grande Vigie* (276 ft/84 m), the most northerly point on Guadeloupe, from which there are far-ranging views. There is a beautiful *walk along the cliff-fringed coast past the *Anse Pistolet* (beach of fine sand) to the Porte d'Enfer.

From Anse-Bernard N 6 continues S, passing several ruined sugar-mills.

5 miles/8 km: **Port-Louis** (0–33 ft/0–10 m; pop. 7000), the agricultural center of the N.

This old fishing town has had an eventful history. It was bombarded and severely damaged by the Royal Navy in 1809. Catastrophic damage was caused by the 1928 hurricane.

On the northern outskirts of the town is the *Plage du Souffleur*, one of the best known beaches on the island, particularly beautiful at sunset and when the flame-trees (flamboyants) are in flower. 1¼ miles/2 km farther N is the *Pointe d'Antigues* (wide views). On the E side of the town stands the *Beauport* foodstuffs factory (including meat and dairy products), originally an old-established sugar-mill. – The road continues S.

5½ miles/9 km: **Petit-Canal**, a fishing village on the mangrove-fringed N coast. 2½ miles/4 km farther W lies the village of **Les Mangles**, where the feast of Christ the King is celebrated on the last day of the liturgical year. – The road continues S through large plantations of sugar cane.

4½ miles/7 km: **Morne-à-l'Eau** (6½ ft/2 m; pop. 16,000), a town founded about 1800, situated on the edge of a large mangrove swamp. In 1826 it was linked with the Grand Cul-de-Sac Marin by the construction of the *Canal des Rotours*. An impressive *procession of candle-bearers in the cemetery takes place on All Saints Day.

The beautiful hilly region of karstic scenery S of Morne-à-l'Eau, with the villages of **Jabrun du Sud** and **Jabrun du Nord**, is the home of the Blancs Matignon, a mysterious white-skinned and predominantly fair-haired population group who are believed to be the descendants of aristocratic families who escaped the blood-bath perpetrated by Victor Hugues during the French Revolution. It is said that they are related to the princely house of Monaco.

¾ mile/1 km: D 107 branches off and runs SW through swampy country.

4 miles/6 km: *Vieux-Bourg*, a charming fishing village on the Grand Cul-de-Sac Marin, formerly the chief town in what is now the commune of Morne-à-l'Eau. – Continue S on D 106.

5 miles/8 km: **Abymes**, an administrative center founded at the beginning of the 18th c., which took the lead in the later development of the harbor of Pointe-à-Pitre. – The road passes the modern airport of *Le Raizet* and returns to –

3 miles/5 km: **Pointe-à-Pitre**.

Tour of Basse-Terre from Pointe-à-Pitre (97 miles/156 km). – Leave Pointe-à-Pitre on an expressway which runs W over the **Rivière Salée**. This is the mangrove-fringed waterway at the junction of Grande-Terre and Basse-Terre which links the **Grand Cul-de-Sac Marin** to the N with the **Petit Cul-de-Sac Marin** to the S.

A fascinating experience for visitors is a boat trip into the unique amphibian world of mangrove swamps and coral reefs in the two bays.

2 miles/3 km: side road on left running SW to the *Jarry* industrial estate, which has developed considerably in recent years. – The main road continues W, passing a large barracks.

2 miles/3 km: junction of three main roads at the Baie Mahault. Take N 2, going N.

1¼ miles/2 km: **Baie Mahault**, on the bay of the same name, an old buccaneers' lair named after a species of mangrove, with a boating harbor and a large racecourse. – Continue W on N 2.

4 miles/6 km: **Lamentin**, a rural township with a number of well-preserved colonial buildings, amid large plantations of sugar-cane. To the N is the wide mouth, overgrown with mangroves, of the *Grande Rivière à Goyaves*, the longest and largest river on the island.

4 miles/6 km: S of Lamentin is **Ravine Chaude**, widely known for its hot sulphur springs. – The main road continues NW.

7½ miles/12 km: **Ste-Rose**, an attractive little fishing village which is developing into the principal resort on the Grand Cul-de-Sac Marin.

Above Ste-Rose, 4 miles/6 km SW, is the hamlet of *Sofaia*, a good base for walkers, who can climb the *Belvédère* (1595 ft/486 m; extensive views) or follow the *Trace Sofaia-Baille-Argent*, a trail which runs along the main ridge through magnificent tropical mountain forest.

From Ste-Rose the road continues NW past the beautiful *Plage la Ramée* and the old-established *Distillerie du Comte de Lohéac*.

4½ miles/7 km: **Anse du Vieux-Fort**, a picturesque bay with the charming *Plage de Clugny* (swimming dangerous), where the first French settlers led by Du Plessis d'Ossonville and Liénard de l'Olive landed and built a small fort in 1635. A narrow track (⅔ mile/1 km) leads from here to the *Pointe Allègre*, the most northerly point on Basse-Terre. – Offshore, to the W, is the tiny *Ilet à Kahouanne* (226 ft/69 m), a haunt of yacht-owners and deep-sea fishermen. – The road continues S through the varied scenery of the W coast of Basse-Terre.

2½ miles/4 km: *Club Méditerranée Fort-Royal*, a luxurious complex with a beach on the rugged *Pointe du Petit Bas-Vent*; a good base for fishing and diving expeditions.

The coast road follows a winding course S, passing the *Anse de la Perle* and the *Grande Anse*, two bays with fine beaches.

4½ miles/7 km: **Deshaies**, a small fishing village picturesquely situated in a bay, with the *Pointe du Gros-Morne* (673 ft/205m) rising above it on the N. – The hilly road continues S, with many bends passing the *Anse Baille-Argent*, with a quiet beach, at the end of the footpath from Sofaia.

9 miles/15 km: **Pointe-Noire**, a settlement founded in the 17th c. which takes its name from the dark volcanic rock of the surrounding area. Features of interest are the war memorial and the ruins of an old fort. From the S end of the village a footpath, *Chemin des Contrebandiers* ("Smugglers' Trail"), leads into the range of hills running from N to S.

5 miles/8 km: *Pointe de Malendure* (121 ft/37 m), from which there are magnificent *views of the dark-colored beaches of *Plage de Malendure* and *Plage de Galets* and of the *Ilets à Goyaves* or Ilets de Pigeon, lying just offshore. These islets form part of the ***Parc Naturel Sous-Marin** (Underwater Nature Park), with an abundance of underwater life which can be observed from a glass-bottomed boat.

2½ miles/4 km: **Pigeon**, a little fishing village with a good beach.

2 miles/3 km: **Bouillante**, one of the oldest villages on the island, noted as the site of an active geothermal anomaly, with several steam vents and sulphur and chalybeate thermal springs, some of them lying below sea level.

The hyperthermalism (abnormally high ground temperature) in this area, the result of volcanic activity, has been under investigation since 1968 as a possible source of energy. A number of borings have been carried out and temperatures of up to 500 °F/260 °C have been recorded.

To the E of the village, rising above the extensive *Forêt Espérance*, are the *Pitons de Bouillante* (3570 ft/ 1088 m). – N 2 continues S, passing through a particularly attractive stretch of coastal scenery, with quiet little inlets reaching far into the land.

4½ miles/7 km: *Anse de la Barque*, one of the most beautiful bays on Guadeloupe, shaded by coconut palms. This is the starting-point of the splendid *Trace des Crêtes*, a trail which runs N along the ridge of hills, affording extensive views. At the S end of the bay is the picturesque little settlement of *Marigot*.

3 miles/5 km: **Vieux-Habitants**, a picturesque little township founded in the first half of the 17th c. It has the oldest parish church on Guadeloupe, several times renovated. On the outskirts of the village is a beautiful beach.

1¼ miles/2 km: *Plage de Rocroy*, another excellent beach, with a hotel. – A little way S a footpath (1650 yd/1500 m) goes off to the *Roche Gravée* (pre-Columbian rock engravings).

4 miles/6 km: **Baillif**, one of the oldest settlements of the colonial period, twice sacked by British forces

around 1700. It is now, for all practical purposes, part of Basse-Terre. On the outskirts are the small airfield of Basse-Terre and a small industrial estate.

2½ miles/4 km: **Basse-Terre**. – The route continues on the well-engineered N 1, which runs E, climbing gradually.

4 miles/6 km: **Gourbeyre** (pop. 7000), a little town founded only in the 19th c., which has grown rapidly since then.

From here there is a rewarding climb (2 hours) to the *Etang As de Pique (alt. 2454 ft/748 m, area 5 acres), a lake above the town to the NE which was formed when a lava flow from the *Volcan de la Citerne* dammed its outflow.

1¼ miles/2 km: *Dos d'Ane*, a good base from which to explore the *Monts Caraïbes (2254 ft/687 m), the southernmost outliers of the main volcanic ridge of Basse-Terre. – The new N 1 continues straight ahead, affording fine views, through a forest of tree ferns, interrupted at intervals by banana plantations.

The old N 1 runs downhill, with many bends.

¾ mile/1 km: **Capes Dolé**, with a well-known warm mineral spring.

2 miles/3 km: D 6 branches off.

Detour to Vieux-Fort (5½ miles/9 km). – The narrow and winding coast road (D 6) passes the Grande Anse with its beach of dark-colored sand and then continues W along the slopes of the Monts Caraïbes, with extensive views, to Vieux-Fort, at the southern tip of Basse-Terre, which was ravaged by Hurricane David in 1979. The old fort, strategically situated, was established by Liénard de l'Olive. The main occupations of the inhabitants are fishing and the traditional *embroidery. From the lighthouse there is a fine view of the Iles des Saints to the SE.

¾ mile/1 km: **Trois Rivières** (pop. 9000), the inhabitants of which held out stubbornly against a British attack in 1703. Ferry to the Iles des Saintes.

Near the ferry port is the **Parc Archéologique des Roches Gravées**, one of the island's principal tourist sights, with a huge collection of petroglyphs (rock engravings) which are now thought to have been the work not of the pre-Columbian Caribs but of their predecessors the Arawaks. The exhibition rooms contain numerous displays and commentaries explaining the engravings. This open-air archaeological museum is set in a botanic garden with many species of plants native to Guadeloupe.

The coast road continues N along the SE coast of Basse-Terre, with fine views.

4½ miles/7 km: **Bananier**, a banana-growing center.

1¼ miles/2 km: **St-Sauveur**. D 4 goes off on the left and climbs steeply up (5 miles/8 km) to the Grand Etang and near the *Chutes du Carbet.

Walk to the waterfalls. – The *Carbet, which emerges from the E side of the volcano as a boiling hot spring, plunges impressively down in three separate falls some distance apart. – From the car park it is a half-hour walk down to the *Troisième Chute du Carbet. Although it is only 65 ft/20 m high this is the grandest of the waterfalls because of its size. – It is a

15-minute climb to the *Second Chute du Carbet*, which is 360 ft/110 m high. From here it is a strenuous climb (1½ hours) to the *Première Chute du Carbet*, the highest of the three (375 ft/115 m).

¾ mile/1 km: side road to the *Habitation Bois Debout*, where the French poet Saint-John Perse (real name Marie-René-Auguste-Alexis Léger, 1887–1975; Nobel Prize for literature 1960) spent his holidays as a boy.

¾ mile/1 km: bridge over the Carbet. Here too is the beginning of the *Allée Dumanoir, an avenue of royal palms planted in the 19th c. by the Guadeloupe writer Pinel Dumanoir. On clear days there are fine views from here of the Soufrière massif and the falls on the Carbet.

1¼ miles/2 km: **Capesterre-Belle-Eau** (0–65 ft/ 0–20 m; pop. 18,000), the center of an intensely cultivated plain (bananas, sugar-cane, pineapples). The road on the N side of the town forms a beautiful arch over the flame-trees.

1¼ miles/2 km: *Ilet Pérou*, a narrow tongue of land bounded on the S by the Rivière du Pérou and on the N by the Grande Rivière de la Capesterre. To the W, on the eastern slopes of the *Montagne de la Capesterre* (3721 ft/1134 m), is the *Forêt de Féfé*.

1¼ miles/2 km: *Carangaise*, a small hamlet with a Hindu temple.

¾ mile/1 km: road on left (2½ miles/4 km) running up to **Neuf-Château**, with a research station of the *Institut Français de Recherches Fruitières*.

¾ mile/1 km: **Ste-Marie**, where Columbus landed on November 4, 1493, has a Columbus Memorial by Bacci, 1916. On the Pointe du Carénage is a small beach. Offshore lies a coral reef with great quantities of fish.

The road continues N, passing the *Anse du Sable*, with a beach of fine sand.

4 miles/6 km: **Goyave**, founded in the second half of the 17th c. and for long the smallest commune on the island. The feast of the Holy Family on November 4 attracts large numbers of worshippers. Offshore, to the NE, is the *Ilet Fortune*, a sun-worshippers' paradise with a beautiful beach.

3 miles/5 km: **Montebello**, starting-point of the magnificent *Trace Victor-Hugues*, a 19 mile/30 km long footpath which runs SW over the main range of hills to St-Claude.

1¼ miles/2 km: **Petit Bourg**, a growing township from which there are fine views over the offshore coral reefs to Pointe-à-Pitre and Gosier. From here N 1, now of expressway standard, runs N to –

9 miles/14 km: **Pointe-à-Pitre**.

Route de la Traversée (16 miles/26 km). – This E–W road running through the *Parc Naturel de la Guadeloupe (established 1971) branches off the road to Basse-Terre (N 1) 6 miles/10 km SW of Pointe-à-Pitre, numbered D 23, and traverses the main range of hills to Mahaut on the W coast.

The *Parc Naturel de la Guadeloupe, a combination of nature reserve and open-air museum designed not only to preserve the island's natural heritage but also to provide visitors with an alternative to the standard attractions of "sun, sand and sea". The park, the home of a species of racoon, takes in some 62,000 acres of tropical mountain forest in Basse-Terre, together with such unique natural features as the Soufrière volcano and the Carbet falls. Documentation centres, some of them dealing with particular fields of interest in the manner of an open-air museum, have been established not only in Basse-Terre but also in Grande-Terre.

Saut des Ecrevisses, Guadeloupe

4½ miles/7 km: from the main road D 23 comes to a junction at *Barbotteau*, near the *Grande Rivière à Goyaves*. 1¼ miles/2 km S the village of **Vernou** lies at the end of the scenic footpath known as the *Trace Merwart*. Beyond the village is the *Saut de la Lézarde*, a beautiful tropical waterfall. – 3 miles/5 km W, above D 23 (car park), is another much visited beauty-spot, the *Cascade aux Ecrevisses*. – 2 miles/3 km beyond this, higher up, we reach the *Parc Tropical de Bras-David*, an area of unspoiled tropical mountain forest, with a nature trail. Here too is the *Maison de la Forêt*, with informative documentation on tropical forests and their plant and animal life. – 2½ miles/4 km farther on D 23 reaches a pass (extensive views) between the *Morne Léger* (2090 ft/637 m) to the N and the *Mamelle de Petit-Bourg* (2349 ft/716 m) and *Mamelle de Pigeon* (2520 ft/768 m) to the S. From here there are beautiful paths into the hills. – ¾ mile/1 km beyond the pass a concrete road goes off to the *Morne à Louis* (2438 ft/743 m; television relay station), from which there are breath-taking views of the northern part of Basse-Terre, the two Culs-de-Sac Marins and Grande-Terre. – The road then descends the N side of the *Colas* valley to **Mahaut**, at the N end of the Parc Naturel Sous-Marin, and the junction of D 23 with N 2.

See also *La Désirade, *Iles des Saintes and *Marie-Galante.

Guanahani
See San Salvador

Haiti
Hispaniola
République d'Haïti

Nationality letters: RH.
Area: 10,714 sq. miles/27,750 sq. km.
Capital: Port-au-Prince.
Population: 5,300,000, not including Haitians living abroad.
Local administration: 9 départements.
Religion: Roman Catholic (90%); Protestant (c. 10%); the Voodoo cult is widespread.
Language: French; Creole patois, Créole.
Currency: gourde (G) of 100 centimes. The US dollar is also an officially approved currency: 5 gourdes = $1 (fixed exchange rate since 1921).
Weights and measures: metric.
Time: Eastern Standard Time (EST), 5 hours behind GMT.
Vehicles travel on the right.
Travel documents: passport, fiche d'immigration.
ⓘ **Office National du Tourisme,**
   Avenue Marie-Jeanne,
   Port-au-Prince,
   Haïti;
   tel. 2 1720.
   See also Practical Information.

The Republic of **Haiti – which its inhabitants, with pardonable exaggeration, like to call the "Pearl of the Antilles" – is a land of contrasts, in terms both of scenery and of social conditions. Haiti is considered to be the poorest country in the Western hemisphere. In spite of the

In the sailing-ship harbor, Port-au-Prince

great poverty of the mass of the population, the marked extremes between rich and poor, and a variety of other problems Haiti has one of the lowest crime rates in the world. Its people are cheerful, colorful, optimistic and proud of their past.

The tidal wave of tourism has not yet reached Haiti. Only a few of its beaches have facilities for visitors, and large areas of the country are still difficult to reach. This has enabled Haiti to preserve unspoiled its distinctive character and originality; and visitors to this lively and charming country will find it fascinatingly new and different.

SITUATION and TOPOGRAPHY. – With an area of 10,714 sq. miles/27,750 sq. km the Republic of Haiti is the third largest state in the West Indies, after Cuba and the Dominican Republic. It occupies the western end of the island of Hispaniola in the Greater Antilles, the eastern two-thirds of which form the Dominican Republic, and is separated from its western neighbor, Cuba, by the 55 mile/88 km wide Windward Passage. Although the coastline of Haiti is much indented it has few offshore islands; the largest of these are the Ile de la Gonâve off the W coast, the Ile de la Tortue off the Atlantic coast to the N, and the Ile-à-Vache off the peninsula at the SW end of Haiti, in the Caribbean. Between this peninsula and a smaller peninsula to the N is the Golfe de la Gonâve. – Three ranges of hills separated by areas of plain traverse Haiti from SE to NW and E to W.

Among the principal areas of plain are the Artibonite valley in central Haiti, the northern coastal plain around Cap-Haïtien and Fort-Liberté, the Cul-de-Sac plain in the S, which is bounded on the Dominican frontier by the Etang Saumâtre, and the plain of Les Cayes at the W end of the southwestern peninsula. The dominant feature of the country's topography, however, are the extensive highland regions, which even at the higher altitudes have the character of uplands rather than mountains. In the N are the Massif du Nord and the north-western highlands, which form the basic structure of the northern peninsula. In the central region is the high basin of the Plateau Central, which is continued on the Dominican side by the Valle de San Juan and is separated from the central

A coastal sailing vessel in Gonaïves harbor (Haiti)

Haitian highlands – consisting of the Montagnes Noires, the Chaîne des Matheux and the Montagnes du Trou d'Eau – by the Artibonite valley and the Cul-de-Sac plain. The southwestern peninsula consists of the Massif de la Hotte and the Massif de la Selle, in which is the highest peak in the country, the Pic la Selle (8793 ft/2680 m). Only about a fifth of the country consists of coastal and river plains and other land under 650 ft/ 200 m. The hilly character of so much of Haiti has hampered the provision of an adequate system of communications and held back the economic development of large areas of the country.

The uplands are composed of crystalline schists, Cretaceous sediments, volcanic rocks and sedimentary deposits of the Tertiary era. Limestones in particular are widely distributed, and accordingly there is much evidence of karstic action. There are no active volcanic features on the island.

CLIMATE. – The tropically hot climate, tempered by altitude in the highland areas, is predominantly influenced by the NE trade winds. The amount and distribution of rainfall are largely conditioned by the relief. Rainfall is highest in the parts of the country exposed to the NE wind, much lower on the lee side of the hills. Thus Le Borgne on the Atlantic coast of the northwestern peninsula has an annual rainfall of almost 78 in./2000 mm, while Gonaïves on the Caribbean coast of the peninsula has only 22 in./560 mm.

The plains between the mountain ranges, sheltered as they are from the winds, suffer from extreme aridity. This regular alternation of plains and uplands, with rainfall patterns ranging from aridity to high humidity, gives Haiti every variety of tropical climate. Particularly during the summer months it is exposed to the threat of tropical hurricanes.

Average monthly temperatures, reflecting the island's tropical location, are uniformly high throughout the year, ranging at low altitudes between 72 °F/22 °C and 77 °F/25 °C in the coldest month and between 81 °F/27 °C and 82 °F/28 °C in the warmest month. The daily variation in temperature between day and night, at about 18 °F/10 °C, is much greater than the variation over the year. The atmosphere is muggy throughout the day in summer and around midday in winter. The relative humidity of the air in summer is about 55%. In the highland regions climatic conditions are pleasanter, since temperatures fall by about 0.9 °F/0.5 °C for every 300 ft/100 m of altitude, and in the coastal plains the tropical heat is much moderated by the winds constantly blowing off the sea.

HISTORY. – On December 6, 1492 the first Spaniards set foot on Haiti, in the bay now occupied by the little town of Môle St-Nicolas at the extreme northwestern tip of the country, and a few miles E, probably near the present town of Cap-Haïtien, the "Santa Maria", flagship of Columbus's little fleet, ran aground. The first attempts at settlement were frustrated by the local Indians, but later attempts, supported by Spanish troops, were more successful. As the Spaniards found no worthwhile deposits of gold in western Hispaniola they concentrated their efforts on the territory which is now the Dominican Republic. Later, this power vacuum in the western part of the island was filled by French, English and Dutch freebooters or "filibusters", for whom the long, hilly coast of Haiti offered a whole range of convenient hiding-places. The principal base of these pirates, whose main targets were the Spanish gold and silver fleets, was the island of Tortuga (Ile de la Tortue). Apart from the pirates' lairs the only settlements in the 17th c. were a few scattered villages, particularly on the N coast, where the "habitants" lived by some modest farming activity. In addition there were numbers of "buccaneers" (a term which came to mean the same as pirate) who ranged over the island hunting livestock which had gone wild and supplied the filibusters and the habitants with meat.

A factor which decisively influenced the later history of this area was the predominance of people of French origin in an otherwise very heterogeneous population. This led the French Government, which was already concerned to extend its influence in the Caribbean, to aim at wresting the western part of the island from Spain. In 1640 the island of Tortuga as annexed by France and the activities of the pirates, which had stood in the way of the proper economic development of the area, were gradually brought under control. Towards the end of the 17th c. increased numbers of French settlers came to the western part of Hispaniola.

From the beginning of the 18th c. western Hispaniola, which under the treaty of Rijswijk (1697) had officially become a French colony under the name of Saint-Domingue, enjoyed a period of prosperity which soon made it the richest colony in the New World. Its wealth was derived from its plantations of sugar-cane, coffee, cotton and indigo, owned by a small white upper stratum of the population, mostly of aristocratic origin. In 1790 there were no fewer than 793 sugar-cane plantations, 3117 plantations of coffee, 789 of cotton, 3160 of indigo and 54 of cacao in the colony of Saint-Domingue.

The labor force for the plantations was provided by bringing in increasing numbers of slaves from West Africa – some 23,000 a year in the period from 1780 to 1789 alone. Unions between white planters and slaves produced a rapidly growing population of mixed blood, who were usually given their freedom by the planters and often granted certain economic advantages. These colored people, known as libres or affranchis, together with black slaves who had been given their freedom, soon gained great economic influence in the colony. By the end of the 18th c. they owned about a third of the cultivated land and a quarter of the slaves. On the eve of the French Revolution, in 1789, the population of Saint-Domingue consisted of about 31,000 whites, 28,000 free colored people and 465,000 slaves.

The outbreak of the French Revolution had far-reaching consequences. In 1790 the aspirations of the colored population towards full legal and political equality found expression in a mulatto rising, and a year later the inhuman living conditions of the black population resulted in a great slave rebellion led by a Voodoo priest named Boukman. France dispatched various commissions and a military force but was unable, in the long term, to re-establish order.

The wars in which the young French republic became involved in Europe from 1793 onwards also involved Saint-Domingue and brought further chaos to the colony. The Spaniards contrived to win over the leaders of the slave revolt and occupied large areas of the colony, and there were also landings by British forces. The French commissaires, who now became responsible for running the colony, sought to win the allegiance of the black troops by proclaiming the liberation of all slaves; and with the help of Toussaint L'ouverture, leader of the slaves, first the Spaniards and in 1798 the British were compelled to withdraw from Saint-Domingue, after long and bloody fighting. Officially Saint-Domingue was still under French rule, but in fact power lay in the hands of the black general Toussaint L'ouverture.

France, however, had won freedom of action by the conclusion of the peace treaties of Amiens and Lunéville, and was not prepared to give up its profitable colony without a struggle. The economic importance attached to Saint-Domingue was reflected in the size of the military effort involved in sending an expeditionary corps of 22,000 men in 86 ships in 1801. The object of the expedition, which was led by General Leclerc, was to restore French sovereignty and the economic status quo, including slavery; but in the end the French forces, weakened by bloody fighting and by yellow fever, were compelled to withdraw from Saint-Domingue.

On January 1, 1804 the independence of Haiti was proclaimed in the town of Gonaïves by Jean-Jacques Dessalines, who had become the country's new leader after the capture of Toussaint L'ouverture. After being appointed President for life Dessalines, encouraged by Napoleon's coronation as emperor, had himself crowned as emperor of Haiti under the style of Jacques I. The new emperor was murdered during a campaign against rebels, and Haiti then fell into two parts, with President Pétion ruling in the S and W and a kingdom ruled by Henry I in the N. In the second half of the 19th c. there were actually three separate states on Haitian territory following a rising against President Salnave. These unstable political conditions went hand in hand with a chronic financial shortage. Soon after the achievement of independence high military expenditure occasioned by the fear of renewed military intervention by the French began to swallow up much of the national budget; and the diplomatic recognition of the new state by France in 1825 brought further burdens in the form of compensation to displaced French planters. In the second half of the 19th c. large amounts of German and French capital were invested in Haiti, and with increasing European influence Haiti became the object of European gunboat diplomacy. Thus in the Lüders affair in 1897, when a German national named Emil Lüders was wrongly sentenced to imprisonment, the Haitian government was compelled by the dispatch of two German warships and an ultimatum with a four hour time limit to pay compensation of 20,000 US dollars, send a letter of apology and give a 21-gun salute to the German flag.

A totally chaotic domestic political situation, amounting almost to civil war, and a succession of four Presidents within two years led in 1915 to the intervention of the United States, and American troops remained in the country until 1934. During this period the Haitian infrastructure was much improved. A brief period of internal stability after the end of the American occupation was followed by further unrest, leading in the mid 1950s to a severe government crisis. Between December 1956 and September 1957 there were no fewer than five governments, including one military government. Finally on September 22, 1957 Dr François Duvalier was elected President and the "Révolution Duvaliériste" began. "Papa Doc", himself a black, laid great stress on the African cultural features in Haitian life. During his reign – he was appointed President for life in 1964 – the old mulatto ruling class in the army and the administration were replaced by a new black elite, with the help of the most brutal measures. After Papa Doc's death he was succeeded by his 19-year-old son Jean-Claude Duvalier ("Baby Doc"), also appointed President for life, who succeeded in establishing a degree of political stability. From 1978 Haiti was subjected to a new political philosophy created by the then president. Under "Jean-Claudismus", on the one hand the political revolution of François Duvalier was to be continued, on the other hand however, an economic revolution realized. In recent years mass emigration from Haiti – caused primarily by the sterile state of the economy – has brought Haiti again and again to the notice of the world. Early in 1986 "Baby Doc" was deposed by the military and was forced to flee.

GOVERNMENT and ADMINISTRATION. – The country's parliament, the Chambre des Députés, consists of 58 members elected for a six-year term; but in accordance with the authoritarian pattern of Haitian government only the Parti de l'Unité Nationale, the government party, is represented in parliament. There is nothing in the nature of an effective parliamentary Opposition on the western model. Political parties or groups outside the government are without influence or are banned. Trade unions are not allowed and unrestricted reporting in the media is not possible. Widespread corruption, which was rampant on several levels of the state administration, has been a lasting check on development.

The government of Haiti is centralized, on the French pattern, with the capital enjoying disproportionate importance and the provincial areas relegated to relative political, economic and cultural insignificance. The country is divided into nine départements, which in turn are subdivided into arrondissements and communes. Each département is administered through a provincial capital; it is planned to give these towns, hitherto of little importance, an increased role by intensive measures of decentralization. The capital and seat of government of Haiti is Port-au-Prince.

Haiti is a member of the United Nations and its specialized agencies and of the Organization of American States, as well as of the Latin-American Economic System (Sistema Económico Latino-americano, SELA), founded in 1975. It is also seeking extraordinary membership of the Caribbean Common Market (Caricom).

ECONOMY. – The most important element in the Haitian economy is agriculture, in which some 75% of the working population are employed. The land is worked by peasant farmers, with holdings usually averaging under $3\frac{3}{4}$ acres, originally formed by the redistribution of the old plantations after independence. The land usually belongs to the peasants, though very few of them could produce written evidence of their title. In contrast to most other Latin American countries, Haiti has relatively few rented holdings and few large estates.

In their continual quest for new cultivable land the people of Haiti have cleared all but a few remnants of the natural forests which once covered the hills, and the large-scale export of building timber and fine woods such as logwood and mahogany during the 19th c. caused irreparable ecological harm. The destruction of the forests has been accelerated by the use of wood and charcoal by the poorer classes of the population, who can afford no other form of fuel – a practice which has continued down to the present day. Thus the visitor arriving at Port-au-Prince international airport sees great expanses of bare hills, deforested and ravaged by karstic action and erosion.

The most important agricultural export is coffee, which is grown in the highland areas, again on innumerable smallholdings rather than on plantations. After the harvest the coffee beans, dried and shelled, are taken by the peasant farmers in small quantities to the village markets, where they are bought by the middlemen known as *spéculateurs*.

Piles of shells, Cap de Léogâne (Haiti)

Other important agricultural products are sisal, manioc, bananas, sugar-cane, maize, tobacco and cotton. In the valley of the Artibonite, Haiti's largest river, rice is increasingly being grown in large irrigated paddy-fields.

It is planned to increase agricultural production in the Haitian plains, which have good soil but insufficient rainfall, by the boring of deep wells and the development of irrigation systems.

Although almost three-quarters of the population are engaged in agriculture this is a relatively unproductive sector of the economy. The average annual income of the peasants is less than $150, and agriculture contributes only some 40% of the gross domestic product. Everywhere in Haiti can be found so-called "subsistence enterprises", producing food solely for consumption by the peasant family and not for the market.

In spite of Haiti's 930 km/1500 km coastline the fisheries have been until now without great economic importance, being confined to primitive beach and coastal fishing. Only about half of the domestic requirement of the island can be met.

Minerals do not play any great part in the Haitian economy. Bauxite was worked at Miragoane in the SW of the peninsula by a US company. However, the deposits are now worked out and mining has ceased. Prospecting, more especially in the north of the country, has revealed deposits of copper which could well become productive in the future.

Haitian industry is relatively undeveloped, providing employment only for some 7% of the working population. Most industrial establishments are at Port-au-Prince, which has excellent facilities – an adequate supply of electric power, a container port, and the country's only international airport.

Industry is in a difficult marketing situation; because of the limited purchasing power of the population – Haiti has one of the lowest per capita incomes in the world – it has only a very small domestic market. The main products are the simplest consumption goods and textiles. The processing of agricultural products is also of some importance, the main fields of activity being the production of canned foods and fruit juices and above all the sugar industry. The largest sugar refinery is that of the Haitian American Sugar Company (HASCO) on the northern outskirts of Port-au-Prince, and in the country areas there are many old-fashioned cane-presses and small boiling-houses. An important export is essential oils, distilled in small factories.

The low level of wages in Haiti has encouraged foreign firms to transfer labour-intensive work to Haiti, particularly clothing and electronics. The most important foreign trade partner of the country is the USA.

Haitian trade is much overmanned – a feature reflected in the thousands of small shops and street dealers, shoeshine boys and sellers of lottery tickets in the streets of Port-au-Prince, gaining the smallest of incomes against intense competition. The development of tourist facilities, in particular an increase in the number of hotels and provision for swimming, etc., although limited at present, is expected to give some stimulus to the economy; and **tourism**, which has brought increased numbers of visitors to Haiti since the early seventies, is already one of the country's principal sources of foreign currency.

POPULATION. – With a population of some 5.3 million, Haiti is the most populous state in the West Indies after Cuba, and with roughly 520 inhabitants to the sq. mile (200 to the sq. km) it is the most densely populated country in the Greater Antilles. The most intensively settled areas are the economically important coastal plains, including the Plaine du Nord, the Plaine de Léogâne and the Les Cayes plain. Even in the highland areas, however, densities of over 775 to the sq. mile (300 to the sq. km) are sometimes found. Given the hilly nature of the country and the limited amount of land suitable for agriculture, this high density creates major economic problems.

Country market, Haiti

The over-population of the country led to massive migration. It is estimated that there are not less than 1 million Haitians living abroad. Several hundred thousand Haitians are now living in the Dominican Republic. Over 30,000 are employed every year in that country helping with the harvesting of sugar cane. The pay and conditions of these seasonal workers are exceptionally poor. More recently they have been going – illegally – to the USA, Canada, the Bahamas or to the French overseas départements. In New York alone there are believed to be some 250,000–300,000 Haitians. According to official statistics an average of 20,000–25,000 leave the country every year.

The annual rate of population increase is about 1.5% – a relatively low figure which is exceeded by most other Latin American countries – as a result not only of the high emigration rate but also of high infant and child mortality rates and a low expectation of life (in 1980: 53 years) all attributable to inadequate medical care and malnutrition. The number of adults over 14 who can neither read nor write amounts to some 75% and is the highest in the whole of Latin America.

The people of Haiti are descended from the slaves brought to the island during the colonial period and from the white planters. Some 90% of the population are black. The mulattoes who make up the remainder of the population live mainly in the towns, particularly in the capital; they form the dominant middle class, known in Haiti as the "elite". Whites represent a very small proportion of the population, amounting to no more than a few thousand at most.

Voodoo in Haiti

Just as French is the official language of Haiti, so Roman Catholicism is the official faith of most Haitians. In practice some 85% of the whole population adhere, more or less openly, to the Voodoo cult.

The practices and beliefs of **Voodoo** (*Voudou, Vaudou, Wodu*) are not laid down in writing, and can vary from area to area, indeed from village to village. In addition to deities revered throughout Haiti there are domestic gods, personal protective gods and nature spirits; and any profound personal experience, perhaps a dream, can give rise to the creation of new divinities. The Voodoo cult is thus not static but is in a process of constant change. Its origins go back to the religions which the slaves brought with them from their African homeland. The very name of Voodoo comes from Africa: in the language of the Fon people of Benin (formerly Dahomey) it means "god" or "spirit".

The religious beliefs brought from Africa by the slaves came into contact in the French colony with the teachings of Christianity. In the eyes of the white settlers the employment of slaves was justified, or at any rate excused, by the obligatory baptism and the cursory instruction in the Christian faith given to the slaves, who were thus directed into the path of salvation. The slaves were not prepared, however, to jettison the whole of their own religious heritage, and in this enforced contact with Christianity elements of their natural religions fused with Roman Catholic rituals and beliefs to produce the magical cult of Voodoo.

The Voodoo divinities, known as *loas*, are many and vary in importance. Many of them bear African names, such as *Papa Legba*, god of crossroads, who maintains the link between heaven and earth and must therefore be invoked in all cult actions; *Ogoun*, god of war; *Agoué Taroyo*, god of the seas; *Erzulie Fréda*, a coquettish goddess of love. Other gods have French names, including *Baron Samedi*, lord of the dead, a figure very similar to the Christian Devil, whose name was applied to President "Papa Doc" Duvalier at the height of his reign of terror. – Many loas correspond to Christian saints and are depicted with appropriate symbols. Erzulie Fréda resembles the Virgin Mary, and is represented with a pierced heart. Ogoun corresponds to St James, Agoué Taroyo to St Ulrich, with the respective attributes of armor and a fish.

The principal Voodoo divinities are divided into four groups – the spirits of water, air, fire and earth. There are also a host of domestic and protective gods and nature spirits inhabiting particular trees or stones. The Voodoo gods and goddesses are by no means remote celestial figures: they have distinctly human traits, they behave like Haitian peasants, enjoy good food and drink, fall in love, quarrel with one another; they are ambitious and strive for power and influence, measured by the number of worshippers they attract.

The Voodoo rituals are conducted by priests (*houngans*) and priestesses (*mambos*), who are attended during the ceremonies by numerous assistants. These officiants include drummers, the *laplace* (a kind of master of ceremonies), *hounsicanzos* (believers who have been inducted into the first order of attendants) and men and women who have on several occasions become a *cheval* (i.e. they have been possessed by a god and have become his medium). Central elements in almost all cult ceremonies are an animal sacrifice and the "possession" of one or more of the participants.

The ceremonies take place in a special hut known as the *hounfort*, and are usually held during the night between Saturday and Sunday. Dancing, singing and the beating of sacred drums, apparently representing the pulsing of life, are important elements in the ceremonies, which are accompanied by long invocations and litanies and center on the sacrifice of an animal. According to the importance of the occasion the animal may be a cock, a goat, a pig or an ox. The sacrifices are offered to the gods on magical figures known as *vèvès*. These occult patterns, symbolizing the presence of the god, are traced on the floor of the hut by the priest, using flour, ashes or dust; and, combined with the sacrifice offered by the assembled worshippers, they cause the divinity invoked to manifest himself.

If the loa who is being invoked is satisfied with the sacrifice and accepts it he himself joins the assembly by "taking possession" of one of the worshippers, or frequently of the priest. The chosen vessel, the *cheval*, who thus becomes the intermediary between gods and men, is caught up during the cult dances into a trance-like ecstasy in which his face becomes grotesquely distorted, his body writhes and his hands describe figures and symbols. He is "possessed", and god and man are now inhabiting the same body. During this phase of ecstasy the god can be asked for advice and for an oracle for the future. – Frequently the appearance of the loa who has been invoked will be accompanied by the manifestation of a rival divinity, who will take possession of the body of some other worshipper.

In addition to the *houngan* and *mambo* the Voodoo cult also features another magician, the *bocor* or *gangan*, who practices black magic. The most popular conceptions in this field are the *loup-garou* (werewolf) and the *zombi* (usual English spelling zombie). The loup-garou is a human being who is able to leave his body at night and suck the blood of other men or women (most commonly of children). Some magicians are credited with the ability to make a person appear to die but in fact to remain alive: this is the zombie, who is disinterred by the magician after his burial and given all the faculties of a living human being except his will and the realization of his situation, and thereafter serves as the magician's servant and tool.

Although Voodoo has at times been vigorously combated by the Roman Catholic and other Christian churches it has lost none of its importance for the people of Haiti. It offers the uneducated mass of the population comprehensible explanations of the events and processes they observe in their restricted experience of life. Every Voodoo believer has his personal protective god whom he seeks to propitiate by taking part in cult ceremonies and making him offerings. If some misfortune comes his way he does not seek a rational explanation but attributes it to some failing on his own part in his dealings with the god: the loa must be offended or angry, or perhaps he is involved in conflict with some other powerful god. This fatalism often militates against economic advance. Thus peasants will attribute their poor living conditions to the displeasure of gods or spirits and will seek to improve matters by ceremonies and sacrifices rather than by rationally directed action, for example by adopting better farming methods.

Since Haiti achieved independence Voodoo has found its way back to Africa, carried by blacks who have returned there. In many West African countries believers in Voodoo already form substantial religious minorities: in Togo, for example, over 200,000 people, out of a population of some 2,500,000, are believed to be Voodoo worshippers.

TOWNS and VILLAGES. – Some 70% of the population of Haiti live in the country, mostly in scattered

Peasant huts in the Massif du Nord (Haiti)

settlements, small hamlets or small separate farms consisting of one or two huts. Apart from the capital, Port-au-Prince, which has a population of some 800,000 there are only a few towns. In Port-au-Prince alone live about 60% of all the town-dwellers of the country. As a consequence of migration from the rural districts, principally to Port-au-Prince, the growth rate of the capital greatly exceeds the national average. All in all Haiti is a country in which, both in economic and settlement patterns, the rural element is predominant.

Almost all Haiti's towns go back to French settlements of the 17th and 18th c., and the regular checkerboard plans still betray this French influence. All the towns of any consequence are on the coast, for the French foundations of the 18th c. were intended to serve as entrepots in the trade between the colony and France.

It is only since the later seventies that the government has been concerned to promote a modest degree of economic growth in the small provincial towns in order to counteract the excessive development of the capital, with the problems to which it has given rise.

Basilica de N.S. de la Altagracia, Higüey.

See also *Cap-Haïtien, *Gonaïves, Ile de la Gonâve, *Jacmel, *Jérémie, *Les Cayes, **Port-au-Prince, Port-de-Paix and *Saint-Marc.

Higüey

Dominican Republic
República Dominicana

Province: La Altagracia.
Altitude: 230–605 ft/70–185 m.
Population: 30,000.

(i) **Dirección Nacional de Turismo e Información,**
César Nicolás Pensón/Rosa Duarte,
Apartado 497,
Santo Domingo,
República Dominicana;
tel. (809) 688 5537.
See also Practical Information.

HOTELS. – *Naranjo*, Los Naranjos 99, 40 r.; etc.

EVENTS. – *Peregrinación Nuestra Señora de Altagracia*, pilgrimage on January 21.

AIR SERVICES. – Occasional flights to international airport of Las Américas.

*Higüey, capital of the province of La Altagracia, lies on the boundary between the southeastern foothills of the Cordillera Oriental at the junction of the Río Duey and the Río Yuma.

The town is dominated by the**Basílica de Nuestra Señora de la Altagracia, one of the finest examples of modern religious architecture in Latin America. The elegant arc of the spire soars up from the powerful bulk of the church, which has very striking stained-glass widows. There is a fine carillon, one of the largest of

its kind in America. Every year on January 21 there is a pilgrimage, attended by worshippers from all over the country, to the Virgin of High Grace, patroness of the republic. – The 16th c. predecessor of the present pilgrimage church still survives.

Also of interest is the fortress-like **Palace of Ponce de León**, which has recently been restored.

Higüey to the Bahía de Yuma (round trip 46 miles/ 74 km). – Leave Higüey on a road which runs S along the Río Yuma and cuts across the eastern part of the southern coastal plain, an area of Pleistocene coral limestones. After passing through *La Matilla* and *El Limón* it comes to –

11 miles/18 km: ruins of the Spanish colonial period on the Río Yuma.

4½ miles/7 km: **San Rafael del Yuma**, chief town of the southern part of the province of La Altagracia.

7½ miles/7 km: **Boca de Yuma**, a small fishing village in the *Bahía de Yuma*, which attracts many fishermen. International deep-sea fishing contests are held annually here from July to October.

E and S of Boca de Yuma are large areas of forest.

To the S of Boca de Yuma is the *Parque Nacional del Este*, which has an area of 166 sq. miles/ 430 sq. km. Established in 1975, the park provides a good impression of the plant and animal life of the southern coastal plain.

Included within the National Park is the *Isla Saona (area 45 sq. miles/117 sq. km; pop. 600), a coral island lying off the coast to the S. With its three large lagoons, *Canto de Playa, Los Flamencos* and *Secucho*, it is the haunt of many species of birds. The coral gardens on the island – which can be reached by boat from either Boca de Yuma or La Romana – contain an extraordinary abundance of marine life.

From here return by the same route to –

23 miles/37 km: **Higüey**.

Higüey to the NE coast through the Sierra del Seibo (round trip *c.* 125 miles/200 km). Leave Higüey on a road which runs W along the S side of the Seibo highlands, passing through a region of small peasant farms. After the villages of *Guanito, La Enea, El Bejuca* and *El Pintado* (junction with the road from La Romana, on the S coast) it comes to –

27 miles/43 km: **El Seibo** (pop. 14,000), chief town of the province of the same name. Like Higüey, it lies at the point of transition between the savannas of the southern coastal plain and the humid forests of the *Sierra del Seibo to the N. Beautifully set on a bend in the *Río Soco*, the town has developed into an important commercial center.

15 miles/24 km W of El Seibo is **Hato Mayor** (pop. 14,000), the third important market town in this area of transition between the hills and the plain.

From El Seibo the road continues N over the main ridge of the Sierra del Seibo (2415 ft/736 m), the forest-covered eastern outlier of the Cordillera Central.

9 miles/14 km: **Pedro Sánchez**, a small hill township. The road continues, with fine views, to –

19 miles/30 km: *Miches (sea level; pop. 5000), a small port at the S entrance to the Bahía de Samaná which is an excellent base for sailing enthusiasts, deep-sea fishermen and coral divers.

To the E of Miches is the *Zona Este, the eastern section of the Dominican Atlantic coast, with 35 beaches which, in terms of natural conditions, are among the best in the world.

The road continues E from Miches, passing the *Laguna Redonda* and the *Laguna Limón*, two coastal lagoons which attract many water sports enthusiasts and wildfowlers.

24 miles/38 km: **Nisibón**, a small settlement near the beautiful *Playa del Muerto.*–The road now turns S past the *Boca de Maimón*.

20 miles/32 km: road on left to **El Macao** (10 miles/16 km NE), a fishing village at the mouth of the *Río Anamuya*, on the beautiful *Playa de Macao*.

From El Macao a narrow coast road runs 22 miles/35 km E, passing the *Laguna Bavaro* (wildfowling), to *Cabo Engaño*, the most easterly point on the island of Hispaniola. 5 miles/8 km S is *Punta Cana, a recently developed and exclusive resort complex in a beautiful setting, with its own airstrip.

From here we return S by way of the easternmost foothills of the Sierra del Seibo to –

12½ miles/20 km: **Higüey**.

See also **Dominican Republic** and **Hispaniola**.

Hispaniola
Greater Antilles
Republic of Haiti and
Dominican Republic

Area: 29,531 sq. miles/76,484 sq. km.
Population: 11,112,000.

ⓘ **Office National du Tourisme,**
Avenue Marie-Jeanne,
Port-au-Prince,
Haiti;
tel. 2 1720.
Dirección Nacional de Turismo e Información,
César Nicolás Pensón/Rosa Duarte,
P.O. Box 497,
Santo Domingo,
República Dominicana;
tel. (809) 688 5537.
See also Practical Information.

**Hispaniola (the "Spanish island"), the most populous and, after Cuba, the largest island in the West Indies, was given its name by Columbus, who discovered it on December 6, 1492. It was known to the Indian inhabitants as Haiti or Aiti, the "mountainous land". The vicissitudes of history in the Caribbean have led to the formation of two independent states on the island. The eastern part of Hispaniola is occupied by the Dominican Republic (area 18,816 sq. miles/48,734 sq. km; pop. 5,620,000), whose inhabitants are predominantly Spanish-speaking mulattoes and whites, while the western part, belonging to the Republic of Haiti (area 10,714 sq. miles/27,750 sq. km; pop. 5,500,000), has a population consisting predominantly of the French-speaking descendants of black slaves. In spite of the similar natural conditions the cultural patterns of the two parts of the island are very different.

Hispaniola, geologically part of two branches of the North American cordillera system, extends for some 410 miles/660 km from E to W and at some points is over 155 miles/250 km wide. It is separated from the neighboring island of Cuba to the W by the 55 mile/88 km wide Windward Passage, from Jamaica to the SW by the 120 mile/193 km wide Jamaica Channel and from the island of Puerto Rico to the E by the 70 mile/113 km wide Mona Passage.

The coastline and superficial topography of the island bear witness to the action of powerful tectonic forces – forces which are still operating on Hispaniola. The Pico Duarte (10,417 ft/3175 m), the highest peak in the West Indies, is barely 190 miles/305 km away from the Milwaukee Depth to the NW which plunges down to 30,248 ft/9219 m. At many points on the coast raised beaches can be observed, as can the competition between different river systems in the mountainous interior, which is traversed by an E–W-oriented system of steep mountain ridges, uplands, plains, valleys and depressions.

The alternation of highland and lowland areas on Hispaniola has given rise to all the variant forms of tropical climate, providing a range of conditions for plant and animal life. There are large areas of evergreen rain forest, but also expanses of dry forest and of semi-desert with a vegetation of succulents.

At the time of its discovery by the Spaniards the island was occupied by a number of Indian states, mainly of Tainos (insular Arawaks). In some places they had established a flourishing culture based on agriculture, in which manioc, sweet potatoes, groundnuts, beans, tobacco and cotton played an important part. The farming methods they employed are still practiced, particularly by the peasant farmers of the Dominican Republic.

The principal Indian settlements were enlarged and developed by the Spaniards soon after their arrival; new settlements were founded, and some of them were in the course of time abandoned. Among the factors which led to the abandonment of some settlements were the rapid working-out by the Spaniards of the known mineral resources of the island and the decimation of the Indian population. Nevertheless Hispaniola remained until the 17th c. the center of the Spanish colonial empire in the New World, and as early as 1496 Santo Domingo, a new Spanish foundation on the S coast of the island, became the seat of the Spanish Viceroy and the cultural capital of the West Indies.

The filibusters and buccaneers who were active in the Caribbean in the 17th c. in effect controlled a lawless territory in western Hispaniola which after a long period of conflict passed into French hands. The new French colony of Saint-Domingue, unlike the Spanish-controlled eastern part of the island, enjoyed considerable prosperity; but the continuing rivalry of the European colonial powers together with slave risings and internal political problems brought on a period of unrest and economic decline. This led in eastern Hispaniola to the expulsion of the Spaniards and the foundation of the Dominican Republic and in the western part of the island to the withdrawal of the French and the establishment of the world's first black republic.

See also **Haiti** and **Dominican Republic**.

Inaguas
Bahama Islands
Commonwealth of the Bahamas

Islands: Great Inagua, Little Inagua.
Area: 645 sq. miles/1670 sq. km.
Population: 1500.
Administrative center: Nassau (on New Providence).
Vehicles travel on the left.
   Ministry of Tourism,
   Nassau Court,
   P.O. Box N 3220,
   Nassau,
   Bahamas;
   tel. (809) 322 7505.
   See also Practical Information.

HOTELS. – *Ford's Inagua Inn*, Matthew Town, 5 r.; *Main House*, Matthew Town, 8 r.

RECREATION and SPORT. – Sailing, deep-sea fishing, scuba diving, snorkeling, swimming; shooting, walking.

AIR SERVICES. – Regular connections with Nassau.

SHIPPING. – Mail boats and freighters from Matthew Town via Acklins and Long Island to Nassau and back.

Great Inagua, the largest of the Inagua Islands, lies some 370 miles/ 595 km SE of Nassau between latitude 20°90′ and 21°20′ N and between longitude 73° and 73°40′ W. Together with Little Inagua, some 6 miles/ 10 km N, it lies at the most southerly point in the Bahama Islands, strategically situated at the entrance to the Windward Passage between Cuba and Hispaniola.

The islands, relatively flat, with numerous salt marshes and lagoons, are thinly populated and accordingly offer a safe nesting-place for many rare species of tropical birds. They still have a population of more than 30,000 flamingoes.

HISTORY. – As its name indicates (from Spanish *lleno*, "full", and *agua*, "water"), Inagua was once within the Spanish sphere of influence. In the middle of the 18th c. the French established a temporary settlement on the island, realizing its strategic importance. By about 1800 the economic potential of the salt marshes had been envisioned, and large installations for extracting and exporting salt, mainly to the United States, were established near the capital, Matthew Town. By the end of the 19th c. the island had become an important labor market. Shipping lines hired stevedores here, and here indentured laborers were recruited for developing areas in Central America – for work on the Panama Canal, building railways in Mexico, and felling timber in the mahogany forests. The First World War put a sudden end to the island's prosperity, and many of its inhabitants emigrated. The period of depression lasted until 1936, when there was an influx of Americans, leading to the revival of the salt-working industry and a fresh economic upswing.

SIGHTS. – The capital of the Inaguas, on Great Inagua, is **Matthew Town** (pop. 1400). Its most notable feature is the *Salt House* (18th–19th c.), an old salt warehouse, whose doorways incorporate stones from the ruined town of Port Royal in Jamaica. In the vicinity of the little town are the large salt works of Morton Salt Crystal Ltd, among the largest of their kind in the world, with an annual output of over 700,000 tons.

The central part of Great Inagua is occupied by the ****Bahamas National Trust Park**. This extensive nature reserve centered on Lake Rosa (Windsor Lake) is the nesting-place of more than 30,000 flamingoes, and the largest breeding ground of this species in the western hemisphere.

On *North East Point*, accessible only with difficulty, are the remains of a house said to have been built as a place of refuge about 1800 by Henry Christophe, later ruler of Haiti.

6 miles/10 km N of Great Inagua lies the reef-fringed island of **Little Inagua** (area 27 sq. miles/70 sq. km), almost untouched by the hand of man. Here live wild goats and donkeys, the descendants of stock introduced by the French, together with a number of rare species of heron.

See also ****Bahamas**.

Jacmel

Haiti
République d'Haïti

Département du Sud-Est.
Altitude: 0–100 ft/0–30 m.
Population: 13,000.
ⓘ **Office du Tourisme,**
Avenue Marie-Jeanne,
Port-au-Prince,
Haiti;
tel. 2 1720.
See also Practical Information.

HOTELS. – *Alexandra*, 11 r.; *Craft*, 12 r.; *La Jacmelienne*, 25 r.

RECREATION and SPORT. – Swimming and sun-bathing, snorkeling, scuba diving.

BEACHES. – *Congo Beach* (palm-fringed; black sand). *Cyvadier Cove* (small beach of white sand; snorkeling). *Ti-Mouillage*. – *Raymond-les-Bains*.

*Jacmel, capital of the Haitian département of the Sud-Est, is charmingly situated on a hill commanding the palm-fringed bay of the same name on the Caribbean coast of the island.

As a result of the silting up of its harbor Jacmel has lost its former importance as a port for the shipment of coffee, cotton and sugar. The town has, however, increasingly become a magnet for tourists, primarily because of its beautiful natural surroundings.

HISTORY. – The advantages of the setting were recognized at an early stage by Spain and Britain, which contended for possession of the area. Later Jacmel became an important pirates' lair. Thereafter, under French rule, the port flourished. – Jacmel featured briefly on the world stage during the South American wars of liberation in the 19th c., when Simón Bolívar, liberator of South America from Spanish rule, assembled his troops here for transport to the mainland. The town had previously, in 1806, provided a refuge for the Venezuelan freedom fighter Francisco de Miranda.

SIGHTS. – More than any other Haitian town Jacmel has preserved the character of a French colonial town. It has many buildings of the colonial period with beautiful wrought-iron balconies and old commercial houses with heavy iron gates. The **Iron Market** (*Marché de Fer*), which at the turn of the 19th c. competed with the Iron Market of Port-au-Prince, bears witness to the former commercial importance of the town, as does the twin-towered **Cathedral**. There is also an interesting *Coffee Sorting Plant*.

SURROUNDINGS. – To the E of the town are a number of fine beaches. 6 miles/10 km away is *Cyvadier Cove*, with a small sheltered beach of white sand, a good place for snorkelers. 4½ miles/7 km beyond this is *Raymond-les-Bains*, one of the best beaches in Haiti. – Other good beaches are *Ti-Mouillage* and the palm-fringed *Congo Beach* (dark-colored volcanic sand).

Within reach of Jacmel, though difficult to get to (guide and mount advisable), are the beautiful *Bassins Bleus (Lac des Palmes, Bassin Palmiste, Bassin Clair)*, to the N.

Here a mountain stream plunges in a series of cascades into three successive basins. There are numerous legends associated with these lakes, which are said to be inhabited by water nymphs and a water goddess. Riches and good fortune await the mortal who shall find the water goddess's lost golden comb.

See also **Haiti and Hispaniola.

Jamaica

Greater Antilles

Independent state within the British Commonwealth

Nationality letters: JA.
Area: 4244 sq. miles/10,991 sq. km.
Capital: Kingston.
Population: 2,225,000.
Local administration: 14 parishes.
Religion: Protestant (over 80%); Roman Catholic (8%); Jewish minority.
Language: English.
Currency: Jamaica dollar (J$) of 100 cents.
Weights and measures: British/American system.
Time: Eastern Standard Time (EST).
Vehicles travel on the left.
Travel documents: passport, immigration card.
(i) **Jamaica Tourist Board,**
    New Kingston Office Complex,
    P.O. Box 284,
    Kingston,
    Jamaica;
    tel. 929 8070.
    See also Practical Information.

****Jamaica is one of the most beautiful islands in the Caribbean. With its magnificent beaches of white sand it is a paradise offering facilities for every kind of water sport – swimming, sailing, snorkeling, scuba diving, water-skiing – as well as golf, tennis and riding. Apart from this it has a variety of other attractions – tours of the interior of the island, visits to sugar-cane plantations and rum distilleries, climbing in the Blue Mountains, adventurous river trips on rafts, and strolling through the colorful local markets.**

A trip to Jamaica still has a touch of exclusiveness about it. Here more than anywhere else visitors are still likely to see film personalities or aristocrats on luxury yachts or great industrial magnates sipping their cocktails on the beach. It is true that much of the James Bond atmosphere of the 1960s (when Ian Fleming was a frequent visitor) has now gone, following changes in the political situation and the opening up of the island to the ordinary visitor. But Jamaica still has on its north coast, not only comfortable guest-houses and holiday apartments, but exclusive luxury hotels unmatched anywhere else in the Caribbean. Even the more reasonably priced hotels often have their own private beach and facilities for water sports, golf, tennis and riding; and cocktail bars, limbo bands and of course swimming pools can almost be taken for granted.

SETTING and TOPOGRAPHY. – With its area of 4244 sq. miles/10,991 sq. km Jamaica is the largest island in the Greater Antilles after Cuba and Hispaniola. Lying only 95 miles/153 km S of Cuba, it consists largely of uplands, with the Blue Mountains in the E rising to almost 7550 ft/2300 m. Some two-thirds of its total area is occupied by limestone plateaux up to more than 1640 ft/500 m in height, with expanses of terra rossa which are now worked for their high bauxite content. The third element in the land-

Tree fern in the Blue Mountains (Jamaica)

scape pattern is formed by the coastal plains which extend around the whole island, reduced along the N coast to a narrow strip.

Where the rainfall is sufficient – mainly in the Blue Mountains and the central highlands – there are large areas of tropical rain forest. The drier parts of the island have thorny scrub and dry savannas. The coasts are fringed with mangrove swamps, the river valleys lined by gallery forest. In the coastal plains, however, the natural vegetation has largely been driven out by the activities of man.

These varied landscape forms have influenced the siting and size of human settlements and the agricultural exploitation of the land. Like the other Caribbean islands with a colonial past, Jamaica is part of "plantation America", with the plain lands occupied by large estates and the upland regions cultivated by peasant farmers. This traditional pattern has been modified over the past 20 years or so by new economic activities. Thus on the limestone plateaux there has been a development of bauxite working, with the associated aluminum oxide industry, and in the plains the large areas given up to the monoculture of sugar-cane and coconut palms have lost ground to the processing industries and, along the coasts, to tourism.

As a result of these developments the old plantation economy of the sugar-cane estates has rapidly lost its economic predominance on the island, and the working of bauxite has promoted the rise of a processing industry.

CLIMATE. – As can be expected from its latitude, the climate of Jamaica is tropically warm throughout the year, with little variation in temperature. In winter the average day temperature is about 79 °F/26 °C, in summer about 86 °F/30 °C. The night temperature never falls below 72 °F/22 °C. The temperature of the water on the coast is about 75 °F/24 °C in winter and 81 °F/27 °C in summer. The trade winds in the N and E and the constant alternation between landward and sea winds in the S and W make even the higher temperatures in summer easily tolerable. The rainiest part of the year begins in August, reaching a maximum in October, and there is frequently also a short rainy period in May. The driest season, which is also the one with the lowest temperatures, is from November to April. There are considerable regional variations in rainfall: while in the Blue Mountains in the E of Jamaica the annual rainfall is over 200 in./5000 mm, the S coast, lying in the rain shadow of the hills, has no more than 40 in./1000 mm. The dreaded hurricanes of the Caribbean area rarely affect Jamaica.

HISTORY. – The name of the island is derived from the Indian *Chaymaka*, "well watered". About A.D. 900 it was settled by Arawak Indians. It was discovered by Columbus on May 4, 1494, and the first Spanish settlement was established in 1509 in St Ann's Bay on the N coast. This was followed by other settlements on the S and E coasts. In 1525 the town of Santiago de la Vega, now Spanish Town, which was for a long time the capital of Jamaica, was established on the banks of the Rio Cobre. Thereafter, the Arawak population was gradually exterminated. The Spaniards planted cacao and coffee on the lower slopes of the Blue Mountains, and in 1517 the first African slaves were brought in to work on the plantations.

In 1655, during the Commonwealth, British forces captured the island from the Spaniards, and it was officially ceded to Britain in 1670, when it had a population of 3000. At first it was used as a base by British pirates, but in the 18th c. settlers began to come to Jamaica from Britain and Ireland, and with the help of an increased force of slave labor it became Britain's principal sugar-producing colony. In the late 17th c. there were 60 sugar and cacao mills in Jamaica, producing 18,000 hundredweight of sugar and large quantities of cocoa annually. There were more than 40 indigo plantations, and during this period the growing of tobacco and cotton also began, and 500 hundredweight of Jamaica pepper were exported every year. By the beginning of the 19th c. Jamaica was, in economic terms, the most valuable British colony in the West Indies.

With the abolition of slavery in 1838 and increasing competition from European beet sugar, the Jamaican cane-sugar industry was faced with increasing difficulties. Efforts were made to combat the crisis by establishing banana plantations, and the first shipment of bananas left Jamaica in 1870. The island had become a crown colony in 1866. Its economic and social problems, however, have continued into recent times, and in 1938 there were serious disorders all over the island. Jamaica received its first constitution in 1944, and this was followed in 1959 by self-government and in 1962 by complete political independence. In the late fifties it belonged briefly to the ill-fated West Indies Federation. – The phase of socialism with stronger links with Cuba (Ara Manley; 1972–80) was halted when the Conservative Seaga was elected Prime Minister in 1980.

GOVERNMENT and ADMINISTRATION. – Jamaica is a parliamentary democracy within the British Commonwealth. The head of state is the Queen, who is represented by the Governor-General; the government is headed by the Prime Minister. The Jamaican Parliament has two chambers, a House of Representatives of 60 members elected for a five-year term and a Senate of 21 appointed members. – For administrative purposes the country is divided into 14 parishes.

Jamaica is a member of the United Nations, the Caribbean Common Market (CCM), the Organisation of American States (OAS) and the Latin American Economic System (Sistema Económico Latino-Americano, SELA) and an associate member of the European Community.

ECONOMY. – Of the island's total area of 4244 sq. miles/10,991 sq. km more than half is devoted to agriculture, a fifth of this being unused or waste land. Just under 10% of the total area is covered by natural forest, while a quarter consists of scrub, swamp and other land unsuitable for agricultural use. This situation is chiefly due to the varying quality of the soil, the island's topography and the rainfall pattern. In addition to sugar-cane and bananas, which account

respectively for 22% and 10% of agricultural output by value, citrus fruits, coconuts, coffee, cocoa, peppers and tobacco are produced in economically significant quantities. The dominant features of Jamaican agriculture are, on the one hand, the export-oriented sugar and banana plantations and, on the other, the innumerable uneconomic peasant holdings, all small and some very tiny indeed. Of a total of 185,000 holdings 145,000 are of less than 5 acres (average size $1\frac{1}{2}$ acres), so that these peasant holdings, less intensively cultivated, represent for the most part a purely subsistence economy. Moreover, between 1954 and 1977, a period during which the area of cultivated land fell from 2,000,000 acres to 1,200,000 acres, the number of holdings actually increased as a result of subdivision. These smallholdings are mainly in the central highland areas, where there is much marginal land threatened with erosion; and their problems are aggravated by over-manning, lack of mechanization, archaic methods of work and difficulties of marketing their produce.

Sugar still plays an important part in the economy of Jamaica, even though the area planted with sugarcane has been considerably reduced since the 19th c. and in recent years has been reduced to eight isolated sectors. After a renewed upswing between 1950 and 1960 the area under cultivation declined again and from 1965 the total value of the output also fell. Between 1965 and 1981 the annual output of sugar dropped from 500,000 tons to 202,000 tons. The reason for this fall lies not only in the world market situation, which is unfavorable to Jamaica, but also in the fact that for most Jamaicans sugar growing is a relic of the colonial period, of which they do not like to be reminded. In the past the sugar industry, a labor-intensive branch of the economy, had the effect of keeping the mass of the population tied to the land and thus had a significant influence on the deployment of the working population within the country.

The traditional sugar industry provides employment for 7% of the working population (9% during the harvest). Work on a sugar plantation is still felt by those who have left the land as a kind of slavery, particularly in view of the ever-widening gap between wages in the sugar industry on the one hand and the bauxite and aluminum oxide industries on the other; and there is little prospect of reducing this gap, since wage costs in the sugar industry amount to 50% compared with only 3% in the bauxite and aluminum oxide industries. Employment in the sugar industry, however, is falling sharply, as are its seasonal fluctuations. Since 1965 five out of a total of 20 sugar factories have closed down because it was no longer economic to run them, and four others are kept in operation only with the help of government subsidies. As a result of the failure to develop mechanization to the full extent, productivity in Jamaica is lower than in other sugar-producing countries, in some of which 1 ton of sugar is obtained from only 7 tons of cane. The introduction of harvesting machines has been banned by the government because of the high unemployment rate; but in any case machines of this kind can be used only on large plantations, and Jamaica has some 25,000 peasant farmers growing sugar-cane on holdings averaging only 3 acres. On average they produce less than 100 tons a year, and with the reduction in the number of sugar factories may have to take their crop a long way for processing. – The drift of population away from the land into the towns has considerably reduced the importance of agriculture as a source of employment, though in 1981 it still accounted for òver 37% of the total working population.

Bauxite working, Claremont (Jamaica)

Bauxite mining, introduced only some 30 years ago, has altered the economic pattern inherited from colonial times and the social structure associated with it, and the process of change is still in full swing. The highly labor-intensive traditional sugar industry of Jamaica now faces the challenge of the capital-intensive and labor-extensive bauxite and aluminum oxide industries; and the recently established processing industries as well as the tourist trade have felt the influence of these industries in many ways. The high iron and aluminum oxide content of Jamaica's terra rossa was discovered as long ago as 1860, but no serious consideration was given to exploiting its economic potential until 1942. The first shipment of bauxite was sent to Canada in 1943; ten years later the firm of Reynolds started exporting it from Ocho Rios, and in the following year Kaiser began shipments from Port Kaiser.

Bauxite mining and the aluminium oxide industry soon became the largest and most dynamic field of economic activity in Jamaica, accounting for some 76.7% of the country's income from exports in 1980. Within 20 years Jamaica has become the world's second largest bauxite producer (after Australia) and its largest bauxite exporter, supplying some 40% of the raw material used by the aluminum industry of North America, which accounts for just under two-thirds of world aluminum production. Jamaica has two advantages over other bauxite-producing countries: in the first place the deposits lie near the surface and not far from the coast, and in the second place Jamaica is well situated geographically for supplying the North American market.

Bauxite is at present being worked in Jamaica by six US and Canadian companies, a majority of the shares in which are now held in Jamaica. Hitherto, the processing of the bauxite has mainly been carried out in North America, and at any rate in the early days the economic benefit which Jamaica has drawn from its bauxite has borne little relationship to the large profits of the aluminum industry.

In spite of the dynamic development of bauxite mining it has had relatively little effect on the critical situation in the labor market, providing a total of no more than 20,000 jobs. Earnings in the bauxite and aluminum oxide industries are three or four times as high as in other types of employment – the minimum daily wage in the bauxite industry has been almost exactly the same as the minimum weekly wage of seamstresses in the clothing industry – and this has had its effects in these other fields.

Apart from the small sugar-mills once so numerous in Jamaica (more than 600 at the beginning of the 19th c., 130 about 1900), the ruins of which are still

Near Port Maria, on the Jamaican N coast

to be seen, the first modest beginnings of industrial development can be detected about 1870 – almost exclusively small foodstuffs factories processing local produce and generating their own power supply. Even in later years, however, the great bulk of Jamaican industrial output was accounted for by sugar, which in 1938 still represented just under half Jamaica's total industrial output, the other half being made up almost entirely of rum, beer, maize flour, copra, vegetable oils and tobacco goods. Even the development of the electricity supply system which began in 1923 gave no great stimulus to industrialization. The decisive impulse was given during the Second World War, when severe restrictions on imports made it difficult to meet the needs of the population. Under this external pressure the first import-saving industries were established, the most important being the footwear and condensed milk industries. Finally in 1947 the Textile Encouragement Law marked the beginning of a period of legislation designed to promote the development of industry by encouraging both foreign and Jamaican entrepreneurs to invest in Jamaican industry. By the end of the 1940s Jamaica had the beginnings of clothing, leatherworking, packaging and fruit-processing industries, and by 1975 some 53,300 people were employed in 1244 firms concerned with the production or repair of industrial goods, although only about 500 of these firms employed 10 or more workers. By October 1981 the total number of people employed in productive industry had reached 82,200.

An analysis of the figures reveals the strong concentration of labor-intensive industry in and around Kingston. Most of the jobs in this area are in the clothing industry; second place is taken by the food and tobacco industries, followed in third place by the metalworking and electrical industries, in which there are small firms. In country areas the food and tobacco industries everywhere occupy the leading place. 80% of what are classed as industrial jobs in Jamaica are in very small firms and workshops of very limited capacity. Almost half of those engaged in industrial work are self-employed, and two-thirds of them are women, whose type of work might more properly be classified as belonging to the services rather than the industrial sector.

Under the pressure of a high unemployment level the Jamaican government has made great efforts to attract foreign capital in order to create new jobs, and has sought in particular to promote the development of export industries which by their nature are less capital-intensive. The aim of considerably reducing unemployment however, has not yet been achieved. Even if it is assumed that for each new job directly created by the industrial promotion campaign another is created indirectly, one must bear in mind that an additional 25,000 people come on to the labor market every year.

The concept of industrialization which has prevailed so far has been little concerned with the country's rural economy. A deliberate plan to establish industry in country areas has been in operation only within the last ten years, with the offer of long-term tax concessions to entrepreneurs. The hoped-for improvement of conditions in rural areas, however, has not been achieved: indeed in some cases the new industries have had adverse effects, for example by pushing up the level of agricultural wages.

With this uneven distribution of industry it is to be feared that the drift from the land into the industrial areas will continue. The aim of economic policy must therefore be to develop relationships between indus-trial firms, and above all to establish the links which have so far not been achieved with the rural sector of the economy; for the future Jamaica's industrial development, like that of a number of other Caribbean islands, lies in the building up of efficient and productive agricultural industries.

In this connection arrangements are under way for establishing a considerable number of tobacco farms with an average area of 22 acres to grow quality tobacco for the Jamaican cigar industry. Also planned is development of a sizeable fruit-canning and meat-processing industry. Investment is required not only in industry but also in agriculture, which must be developed into a productive branch of the economy.

In spite of these difficulties and obstacles the government is still holding fast to its concept of industrialization. Creation of 70,000 new industrial jobs is planned by 1990 – 175% more than the number of jobs available in Jamaica in 1970. This is an ambitious target, and chances of achieving it seem all the more questionable in view of the fact that, in addition to the difficulties just referred to, Jamaican industry is having serious problems in finding markets for its products. The capacity of the domestic market is limited, and it has hitherto been artificially extended by import restrictions introduced to support the industrial promotion program. In the export markets competition is severe, and, apart from sugar, exports amount to less than 10% of industrial production. Even in the textile and clothing industry, which is the largest export industry after oil refining, only a quarter of total output is exported. The government sets high hopes on the Caribbean free trade zone covering the former British colonies in the West Indies which was set up in 1968 as CARIFTA (Caribbean Free Trade Area), and became in 1973 CARICOM, the Caribbean Common Market. Since its establishment 90% of all goods pass duty-free between the member countries.

Tourism is of considerable importance to the economy of Jamaica. With between 600,000 and 700,000 visitors a year Jamaica takes fourth place in the Caribbean tourist league after the Bahamas, Puerto Rico and the Virgin Islands. The main tourist area is the N coast, and only one tourist in four visits Kingston. In 1973 more than three-quarters of the visitors came from the United States and 9% from Canada. Since then, however, the situation has changed. After 1976, when the number of "bed nights" fell catastrophically and the accommodation for visitors was occupied only to a third of capacity,

Half Moon Beach, Montego Bay (Jamaica)

the Jamaican tourist authorities turned their attention increasingly to the European market, and the number of visitors from Europe has considerably increased. Like the bauxite industry during Prime Minister Manley's socialist government (1972–1980) the hotel industry was nationalised. Until then the skilled labor required came almost exclusively from abroad, and with few exceptions the day-to-day requirements were also brought in from the United States.

In addition to the country's political tensions, which restricted the movement of visitors, the increasing American involvement in the bauxite industry aggravated popular resentment of American tourists; and at the same time the Black Power movement stepped up its propaganda about "American exploitation" and whipped up hatred of whites. The Seaga government, which has been in power since 1980, appreciated the necessity of discouraging these emotions, so that the number of tourists from North America can again begin to rise.

Bauxite mining and the aluminum oxide industry have militated against the develoment of tourism in some areas. Thus the resort of Ocho Rios on the N coast now has bauxite-shipping installations in close proximity, and an adjoining beach has lost much of its attraction as a result of the reddish bauxite dust deposited along this section of coast and the movements of the large bauxite-carriers.

POPULATION. – With a population of 2,230,000, Jamaica has the high density of 502 inhabitants to the sq. mile (194 to the sq. km), exceeded in the Greater Antilles only by the over-populated Puerto Rico, which has 966 to the sq. mile (373 to the sq. km). The high density is a fairly recent phenomenon, produced by a sharp rise in the birth rate combined with a fall in the death rate. Within a period of 80 years the population of Jamaica tripled (1891: 639,500), and between 1965 and 1975 alone it increased by a quarter. In the last 20 years the age structure of the population has shown a marked preponderance of the younger age groups: according to the 1970 census 51.5% of Jamaicans were under 20.

The population multiplied threefold in spite of the fact that tens of thousands of Jamaicans left the country in the closing years of the 19th c. and the early years of the 20th. Many islanders of African descent found employment in the building of the Panama Canal, and many others emigrated to Central America (in particular to Costa Rica) to work on the new banana plantations and on the construction of railways. Others went to Cuba for the sugar-cane harvest, and many emigrated to the United States. Between 1881 and 1921 some 146,000 Jamaicans left the island, representing an annual loss of more than 7000. A further mass emigration took place after the Second World War, when, between 1953 and 1962, roughly a tenth of all Jamaicans flocked to Britain. From 1965 to 1970 this movement continued at an annual rate of 26,000. Since the imposition of restrictions by Britain the emigration movement is now directed towards the United States and Canada.

This emigration was harmful to the Jamaican economy by virtue of the fact that those who left the island were predominantly of working age. Between 1972 and 1981 about 20,000 Jamaicans on average emigrated annually to North America or Great Britain. On the other hand the Jamaican economy has profited greatly from the money sent back from the United States by contract workers there.

In spite of this high rate of emigration, the Jamaican government has been unable to remedy the alarming situation in the labor market. As a result of the high birth rate of the 1950s and 1960s many young people are now looking for jobs, and in the last few years unemployment has risen steeply in the towns. Unemployment among young women is high throughout the country but particularly in the capital, Kingston, where the drift from the land makes its effects felt very markedly. More than a third of all Jamaican unemployed are in and around Kingston.

Reggae. – This form of musical expression, which originated in Jamaica and has in recent years attracted much interest in the United States and Western Europe, is a mingling of Indian, European and above all African musical ideas. Reggae (a term formerly current in Jamaica with the sense of feast or festival) developed out of mento (from Sanish mentar, "mention"), one of the oldest forms of Jamaican folk music. Characteristic of reggae is the marked accentuation of the second and fourth elements in the bar, which are normally unstressed; the music is usually in $\frac{4}{4}$ time; and it is this constant displacement of the rhythmic emphasis that gives reggae its specific tension. It also incorporates features of the Cuban rumba, the Trinidadian calypso and, of course, the pan-Caribbean limbo.

Direct forerunners of contemporary reggae were ska, a combination of mento and rhythm-and-blues elements which came to the fore in Britain in the fifties and sixties, and rock steady, which developed in the mid sixties under the influence of beat music, with the bass instruments playing a prominent part. – Reggae, like rock, has now an established place in the "progressive" pop music which is popular particularly with young people. Its forms of expression range from singing with a rhythmic accompaniment to loud articulation with the help of powerful amplifiers.

There are close links, particularly in Jamaica, between reggae and the Rastafarian cult. The texts of the songs often reflect religious and political views, denounce social evils or put forward political demands. Popular themes are the struggle against white predominance and the assertion of the dignity of colored people. – The best known interpreters of reggae music are Bob Marley (d. 1981), Peter Tosh Dillinger and Max Romeo, together with the Wailers and Third World groups.

One of the best known reggae songs, an expression of the social and political struggle of the Rastafarians, is Bob Marley's "Get up, stand up":

Preacher man don't tell me
Heaven is under the earth
I know you don't know
What life is really worth
It's not all that glitters is gold
Half the story has never been told
So now you see the lights
Stand up for our rights
We're sick and tired of our kissing game
To die and go to heaven in Jesus name
We know and understand
Almighty God is a living man
You can fool some people sometimes
But you can't fool all the people all the time

Almost four-fifths of the population are black, the next largest group being the mulattoes (17%). The high proportion of blacks is the result of the plantation system, which during the 17th and 18th c. depended on the cheap labor of slaves. During this period Jamaica was also a major center of the West Indian slave trade. After the abolition of slavery in 1833 Indian indentured laborers were brought in to work on the Jamaican sugar-cane plantations, but the number of Indians in present-day Jamaica is small compared with other countries such as Trinidad and Guyana. Trade, particularly retail trade, is in the hands of Chinese immigrants. The Lebanese who came to Jamaica after the First World War also made a niche for themselves in trade, and more recently they have been active as entrepreneurs in the local industries. Chinese and Lebanese together, however, amount to little more than 1% of the population; and the proportion of whites, once the predominant group in the population, has fallen to less than 1%.

The racial mixture of the population is reflected in a wide range of skin colors, from ebony to white. The mother tongue of the Jamaicans is English, but visitors will frequently hear in the markets the local *patois*, an incomprehensible native dialect.

The majority of the population are Protestants, belonging to a whole range of different churches and denominations. Prominent among them are Anglicans and Baptists. In addition to the Roman Catholic minority there are also Hindu, Moslem and Jewish communities. Many Jamaican sects incorporate elements inherited from West African natural religions.

The Rastafarian sect. – Conspicuous among Jamaica's many religious sects are the Rastafarians. They are readily recognizable by their long matted hair, plaited into "tails", and their woollen caps in the symbolic colors of black, red, gold and green. The term Rastafarian is derived from Ras Tafari, the name borne by the former emperor of Ethiopia, Haile Selassie, before his coronation in 1930 – a year which has the same significance for the Rastafarians as the year of Christ's birth for Christians. Since that date Haile Selassie has been their Lord and Master, their Messiah, and for Rastafarians Ethiopia is the Promised Land to which they aspire to return. The teaching of the sect's founder Marcus Garvey, the Jamaica-born prophet who died in Britain in 1940, distances itself from the social system of the white man and from all school learning.

See also *Kingston, **Montego Bay, **Ocho Rios and *Port Antonio.

Jérémie
Haiti
République Haïti

Département de la Grand'Anse.
Altitude: sea level.
Population: 18,000.
(i) **Office National du Tourisme,**
Avenue Marie-Jeanne,
Port-au-Prince,
Haïti;
tel. 2 1720.
See also Practical Information.

AIR SERVICES. – Scheduled flights to Port-au-Prince daily except Wednesday and Sunday.

*Jérémie, capital of the Haitian département of Grand'Anse, is picturesquely situated at the mouth of the River Grande Anse on the NW coast of the southern peninsula.

The town, which is difficult to reach by land, is an important center of the coastal shipping trade, which is carried on almost entirely by wooden sailing vessels. Because of its isolated position on the coast and the unsatisfactory communications, the town has in the past been able to achieve only minor economic development. It is a pretty little town, its houses mostly washed in green or pink. The town's colonial past is recalled by its regular grid plan and the ruins of *Fort Télémaque* to the S.

The town was the birthplace of Etzel Vilaire, one of Haiti's leading writers, and also of Alexandre Davy de la Pailleterie, born in Jérémie in 1762, who disclaimed the name of his French father and took the name Dumas after his mother, a black woman. He became a general in the French army and was knighted by Napoleon for his valor on the field of battle in Austria and Italy. His son and grandson made the name of Dumas world-famous, the son as the author of "The Count of Monte Cristo" and "The Three Musketeers", the grandson as the author of "La Dame aux Camélias".

SURROUNDINGS. – To the W of the town is the *Anse d'Azur, with a very beautiful beach, almost untouched by man.

25 miles/40 km SW of Jérémie and 40 miles/64 km off the Anse d'Hainault, at the western tip of the island of Hispaniola, is the little island of **Navassa** (2 sq. miles/ 5 sq. km), which belongs to the United States (US naval base) but is claimed by Cuba.

See also **Haiti and **Hispaniola.

Jost van Dyke
See Tortola

Kingston
Jamaica

Altitude: 0–820 ft/0–250 m.

Population: *c.* 200,000; Kingston Metropolitan Area *c.* 650,000.
(i) **Jamaica Tourist Board,**
78 Knutsford Boulevard,
Kingston (New Kingston),
Jamaica;
tel. 929 8070.
See also Practical Information.

DIPLOMATIC MISSIONS. – *British High Commission*, P.O. Box 575, Trafalgar Road, Kingston 10, tel. 926 9050. – *Canadian High Commission*, Royal Bank Building, 30–36 Knutsford Boulevard, P.O. Box 1500, Kingston 5, tel. 926 1500. – *United States Embassy*, Jamaica Mutual Life Centre (3rd floor), 2 Oxford Road, Kingston, tel. 929 4850.

HOTELS. – *Inter-Continental*, King Street, Waterfront, 325 r., T, SP; *New Kingston Sheraton*, New Kingston, 225 r., SP, T; *Pegasus*, New Kingston, 340 r., SP, T; *Casa Monte*, on N side of town, 24 r., SP; *Mayfair*, at Devon House, 32 r.; *Terra Nova*, Waterloo Road, 33 r.; etc. – *Morgan's Harbour*, Port Royal, 24 r., SP, beach. – FOR YOUNG PEOPLE: *YMCA*, 21 Hope Road.

RESTAURANTS in most hotels; also *Cathay*, Orange Street; *Continental*, Worthington Avenue; *Greg Shop*, at Devon House; *Dynasty*, Mall Shopping Centre; etc. – OUT OF TOWN: *Blue Mountain Inn*; *Stony Hill*.

NIGHT SPOTS. – The city's night life is rich and varied. The large hotels put on good shows, and there are "Jamaica Nights" in Devon House (Monday, Wednesday, Friday).

EVENTS. – Active centers of cultural life are the *Institute of Jamaica*, *Devon House* and the *Cultural Centre* (information about activities from the Jamaica Tourist Board or the press). Performances by the *National Dance Theatre Company* and the *Little Theatre Movement* (Christmas musical from Christmas until March). Calypsos and reggae in numerous night clubs and other establishments.

THEATERS. – *The Barn*, Norwood Avenue, Kingston 5; *Creative Arts Centre*, University of the West Indies, Mona; *Little Glyndebourne Theatre*, in the Blue mountain to the N of the town; *Little Theatre*, Tom Redcam Drive, Kingston 5; *Ward Theatre*, North Parade, in city center; *Way Out Theatre*, in Pegasus Hotel.

SHOPPING. – A wide range of typical Jamaican craft products can be found in a number of galleries and specialized shops and in the markets. There are also shops selling imported luxury goods with price reductions of between 20% and 50% on presentation of passport and payment in foreign currency (preferably US dollars or travelers' checks).

ART GALLERIES (a selection). – *Bolivar Gallery*, Grove Road, Hell Way Tree; *Institute of Jamaica*, 12 East Street; *National Art Collection* and *National Gallery*, both in Devon House, 26 Hope Road, Kingston 10; *Olympica Hotel Gallery*, 33 University Crescent, Kingston 6; *School of Art*, Cultural Training Centre.

AIR SERVICES. – INTERNATIONAL: scheduled services from Norman Manley Airport to Atlanta, Chicago, Houston, Miami, Philadelphia and New York (USA), Montreal and Toronto (Canada), San Juan (Puerto Rico), Havana (Cuba), Barbados, Nassau (Bahamas), London (UK) and Frankfurt am Main (German Federal Republic). – DOMESTIC: regular services from Kingston to Montego Bay, Ocho Rios and Port Antonio.

SHIPPING. – Many cruise ships from Miami, Port Everglades, New York (USA), San Juan (Puerto Rico) and other West Indian islands call in at Kingston, sometimes staying for several days. – Occasional passenger-carrying freighters to Europe.

RAIL SERVICES. – Daily service of diesel trains from Kingston to Montego Bay (travel time 5 hours).

*Kingston, capital of Jamaica and its cultural and economic center, a university town and the see of a Roman Catholic archbishop, lies in the eastern part of Jamaica's southern coastal plain, on the seventh largest natural harbor in the world. The town was founded in 1693 after the nearby settlement of Port Royal was destroyed in an earthquake.

At the beginning of the 1960s the town occupied the Liguanea plain above the harbor, which is enclosed by the 9 mile/14 km long tongue of land called the Palisadoes. Since then it has spread far beyond its old boundaries and has now reached the steep lower slopes of the Blue Mountains.

Relics of the colonial period in Kingston include the old pirate harbor of Port Royal to the S, most of the fortifications of which fell into the sea in the 1692 earthquake, and a number of fine old mansions set in beautiful parks. The business district on the seafront is in process of improvement and redevelopment and the port installations are being considerably extended.

To the N of the old town, now much in need of rehabilitation, with extensive slum areas, is New Kingston, a new and enlarged business district with many high-rise buildings.

On the outskirts of the city are exclusive residential districts and also a number of shanty towns, mostly occupied by families from country areas who have drifted to the town in quest of employment.

HISTORY. – Kingston was founded in 1693 in the fertile Liguanea plain, then inhabited by Arawak Indians, in place of Port Royal, a considerable port and notorious pirates' lair which was destroyed by an earthquake in 1692 and largely swallowed up by the sea. At first the town developed rapidly, but during the 19th c. it stagnated in consequence of a series of economic crises. In 1870 Kingston became capital of Jamaica in place of Spanish Town, lying a few miles inland to the W; but neither this promotion nor the construction of a railway gave any great boost to the town's development. In 1871 the population was still only 29,000. In 1907 much of the town was destroyed by an earthquake. By 1921 the population had risen to some 63,000, and thereafter it increased rapidly - to over 200,000 in 1943 and 377,000 in 1960. From the mid seventies there were frequent social and political disturbances in Kingston with not inconsiderable loss of life; this lasted until the end of the Manley era.

Warning

Political, economic and social tensions have led to a serious increase in crime in Kingston. Particularly in the neighborhood of slum areas acts of verbal or physical aggression, theft and robbery with violence are everyday occurrences.

Visitors should therefore avoid going out after dark except with a knowledgeable local escort. They should also deposit anything of value (particularly personal documents, money, travelers' checks, keys) in the hotel safe or at any rate carry such things on their person (and not, for example, in a handbag).

The Kingston police are always anxious to help tourists, but they are faced with massive problems in dealing with crime in the city, often the work of organized gangs, on which they periodically crack down. Not infrequently conflicts between rival gangs or between terrorist groups and the police escalate into situations which almost take on the aspect of civil war and claim many casualties.

SLUMS and CRIME. – Kingston has long been one of the most rapidly growing towns in the West Indies. In 1871 it had only 29,000 inhabitants, but the Kingston Metropolitan Area now houses a population of well over 650,000, many of whom are incomers from the country areas, drawn by the hope of better pay and prospects. Often the head of the household comes to town on his own to look for work, leaving his family to follow later. The incomers settle in the slum areas in the city center, now occupied by a poor and shifting population, or stay with acquaintances in the shanty towns on the outskirts of the city. By 1970 more than two-fifths of all Jamaicans lived in Greater Kingston, and if the 1970s rate of increase continues the proportion will have risen to almost half by 1990. Since the present rate of increase in population is far greater than the number of new jobs being created, in spite of the advantages enjoyed by the city, the problem of housing is becoming steadily more actue. Already more than 30% of Kingston's inhabitants are squatters in slum property, and in some of these slum areas the density of population exceeds 93,000 to the sq. mile (36,000 to the sq. km) – and this in single-story houses with quite inadequate sanitary facilities. Extreme overcrowding, steadily increasing unemployment and a growing feeling of hopelessness have produced very high crime rates; and tourists, regarded by the slum-dwellers as well heeled and therefore fair prey, are frequently the victims of crime.

REDEVELOPMENT PLANS. – Conscious of the growing social problems in the Kingston Metropolitan Area, largely due to economic difficulties, the government has initiated a number of programs designed to relieve the situation. Decentralization schemes combined with efforts to develop industry in the medium-sized Jamaican towns have succeeded in halting the drift away from the land in these areas. In addition various slum clearance and redevelopment projects have been carried out since the beginning of the 1970s, involving the extension of the main business district on the seaward side of the old town, the construction of the modern harbor of Newport West and the expansion of the city into the flat and hitherto unused coastal region S of the Rio Cobre.

This Kingston Redevelopment Plan ranks with the slum clearance and redevelopment program in San Juan (Puerto Rico) as the largest and most important urban renewal project in the Caribbean; and it is the first attempt to carry through a comprehensive town development in Kingston since its foundation in 1693.

Sightseeing in Kingston

City Center

The central area of Kingston is at present in process of rehabilitation and redevelopment. Particularly involved in this program is the **Waterfront** area, which is to become part of the central business district, with shopping facilities, office buildings, hotels, apartment houses, multi-level car parks and cultural facilities. In addition a new landing-place for cruise ships is to be provided. The dominant landmark of the area is the *Inter-Continental Hotel*. The Waterfront district is bounded on the N by Harbour Street, one of the city's principal business streets. At its western end is the *Crafts Market*,

In the Crafts Market, Kingston

one of the most important markets of craft products in the Caribbean, selling not only well-made hand-made articles of wood and straw but also rum and records, produced in numerous small local establishments.

The main axis of the central area, King Street, runs N from the Inter-Continental Hotel, with many shops, offices and public institutions. A short distance E of the *Public Buildings* is the *Institute of Jamaica* (12 East Street), founded in 1870, which contains a natural history collection, material on the history of the town, a valuable library of books on the West Indies and an *art gallery, primarily devoted to the work of Jamaican artists.

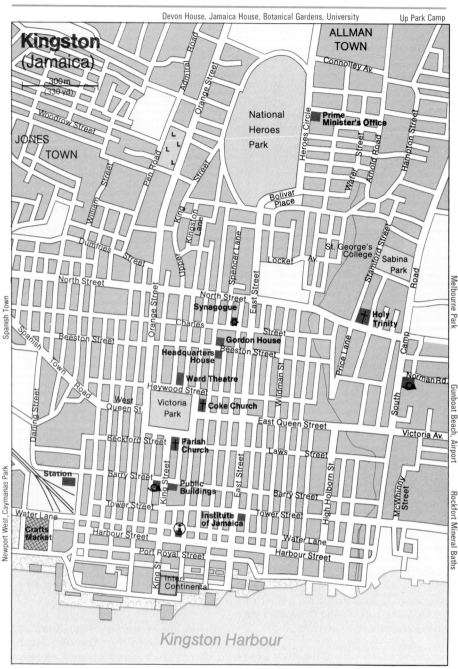

Devon House, Jamaica House, Botanical Gardens, University   Up Park Camp

Kingston (Jamaica)

300m (330 yd)

JONES TOWN

ALLMAN TOWN

Connolley Av.

National Heroes Park

Prime Minister's Office

Woodrow Street

Heroes Circle

Bolivar Place

St. George's College

Sabina Park

North Street

Synagogue

Charles Street

Gordon House

Beeston Street

Headquarters House

Holy Trinity

Ward Theatre

Heywood Street

West Queen St.

Victoria Park

Coke Church

East Queen Street

Beckford Street

Parish Church

Laws Street

Station

Barry Street

Public Buildings

Barry Street

Tower Street

Institute of Jamaica

Tower Street

Water Lane

Harbour Street

Water Lane

Crafts Market

Harbour Street

Port Royal Street

Norman Rd.

Victoria Av.

Inter- Continental

Kingston Harbour

Spanish Town

Melbourne Park

Gunboat Beach, Airport

Rockfort Mineral Baths

Newport West, Caymanas Park

At the N end of King Street is **Victoria Park**, formerly called the Parade, with statues of Norman Manley and Alexander Bustamente, two prominent figures in recent Jamaican history. On the S side of the park stands the *Parish Church*, built in 1910 to replace its predecessor of 1695, destroyed in the 1907 earthquake. The church contains a number of well-preserved 18th c. monuments. On the E side of the park is *Coke Church*, an attractive little Methodist place of wor-

ship. On its N side is the *Ward Theatre* (named after one of Jamaica's leading rum distillers), the largest on the island. To the NE **Gordon House**, named after a mid 19th c. fighter for Jamaican independence, has housed the Jamaican parliament since 1960. Opposite it is *Headquarters House, a notable example of 18th c. British colonial architecture which was the seat of government from 1870 to 1960. A little way N is the *Synagogue*, the only one in

The business district of New Kingston

Jamaica. The little graveyard contains 16th and 17th c. gravestones – relics of the settlement of Jews in Jamaica during the Spanish colonial period.

To the E, in North Street, stands *Holy Trinity Cathedral* (R.C.), a massive domed concrete structure.

To the N of the Cathedral are *St George's College* and the beautiful *Sabina Park*. On the northern edge of the old central area lies *National Heroes Park* (area 75 acres), formerly known as the George VI Memorial Park and originally a racecourse. It contains flowerbeds, playground areas and memorials (including the *Bolívar Memorial*) to great men of the past. On the E side of the park are the Prime Minister's Office and other government offices.

To the W of the park is the slum area of TRENCH TOWN.

New Kingston

To the N of National Heroes Park is the recently developed district of NEW KINGSTON, with the first major concentration of high-rise buildings on the island. This is now an important business and comercial quarter, with banks, large commercial and financial organizations, shopping centers and hotels.

Between National Heroes Park and the center of New Kingston is *Up Park Camp*,

an extensive area occupied by government and other public agencies, several schools and other cultural institutions, including two popular theaters, the *Carib Theatre* and the *Little Theatre*, two important educational establishments, the *Mico Training College* and the *Cultural Training Centre*, and the large **National Stadium**, in which the independence ceremonies were held in August 1962.

The central area of New Kingston is bounded on the E by Old Hope Road, on the W by Half Way Tree Road and on the N by Hope Road. On the outskirts, set in beautiful grounds, are two large hotels, the *Jamaica Pegasus* and the *New Kingston Sheraton*.

At the intersection of Hope Road and Waterloo Road is *Devon House* (19th c.), a mansion of great elegance which is now government property and houses museums, shops and restaurants. The popular *"Jamaican Nights"* are held here three times weekly.

The house was built by George Stiebel, one of the first black millionaires in the West Indies, and is sumptuously appointed, the various rooms being furnished in different styles. Works of art from the national collection are displayed here, and there is also an interesting little museum of African art and history. Note the fine iron *gates at the entrance.

To the NE, in a large and beautifully laid-out park, stands **Jamaica House**, the Prime Minister's residence. Higher up is the Queen-Anne-style *King's House* (1694), residence of the Governor-General

¾ mile/1 km SW of Devon House, at the corner of Hagley Park Road and Eastwood Park Road, we come to *St Andrew's Parish Church*, an attractive church damaged by earthquakes, with fine 17th c. monuments.

Beverly Hills

Above the city center, to the NE, can be found the select residential district of BEVERLY HILLS, extending up the northern slopes of the **Long Mountain**, which rises to 1490 ft/454 m in Wareika Hill. This is an area of handsome and sometimes very elegant villas in striking contrast to the poorer quarters and slum districts lower down.

Mona

On the northeastern outskirts of the city, in the valley of the *Hope River* between *Long Mountain* and *Dallas Mountain*, is the district of MONA, with the renowned *University of the West Indies*. This was founded in 1948 as a college of London University and is now jointly financed by a number of Caribbean states. It is a campus university, on a site previously occupied by a sugar plantation, with remains of the old plantation buildings scattered about in the grounds. Associated with the University is a large hospital. – To the W of the campus is the large *Mona Reservoir*.

To the N of the University are the magnificent *Botanical Gardens*, also on a former plantation, with a small zoo. The beautifully laid-out gardens afford an excellent survey of the plant life of the West Indies. The large collection of orchids is particularly fine.

E of the Botanical Gardens stands the *College of Arts, Science and Technology* to the south of which is the *Olympia Hotel*, with a fine art collection.

The Harbor

Over the last ten years Kingston's harbor has been moved W and considerably enlarged. Marcus Garvey Drive, crossing land reclaimed from the sea, leads to **Newport West**, immediately adjoining which is the government-sponsored *Kingston Industrial Estate*. From here a causeway runs SW, enclosing **Hunts Bay**, where the *Rio Cobre* discharges its load of alluvium. In the flat coastal area S of the river, formerly agricultural land cultivated on an extensive basis, the new suburb of PORTMORE, which will provide 30,000 dwelling units when complete, is now under development. Recreation facilities are provided by the beautiful *Caymanas Park* (horse-racing on Wednesdays, Saturdays and public holidays). In the old fishing settlement of **Port Henderson**, at the far end of *Dawkins Lagoon*, are several old buildings which have been restored by the National Trust, including *Long House* (exhibits on local history) and *Rodney's Look-out*, from which Admiral Rodney used to watch the movement of shipping off the coast.

SURROUNDINGS. – To the S of the town the 9 mile/14 km long strip of land known as the **Palisadoes** follows the S side of Kingston Harbour. The road along the Palisadoes branches off Windward Road, the main road out of Kingston to the E, and reaches the *Rockfort Mineral Baths* and *Fort Nugent* which are situated at the end of the peninsula on the east. Just beyond the fort Palisadoes Road goes off on the right and leads W to beautiful *Gunboat Beach*, with *Palisadoes Park* and the exclusive *Royal Jamaica Yacht Club*, and then on to **Norman Manley International Airport**.

At the end of the Palisadoes is **Port Royal** (which can be reached by boat from Pier 2, Waterfront, Kingston), the prosperous port town, once notorious as a sink of iniquity and a pirates' lair. It was destroyed by the 1692 earthquake and was later partly engulfed by the sea. Efforts were made to rebuild the town, but these were frustrated by devastating fires and storms. One of the few surviving buildings is *Fort Charles* (c. 1660), on the SW tip of the peninsula, which was built by the British colonial authorities to provide protection against Spanish and French attacks. Notable features are the walkway known as Nelson's Quarterdeck and the few cannon which remain out of the original 104. *St Peter's Church* (18th c.), successor to the earlier Christ Church which was swallowed up by the sea, has a finely decorated interior, well restored. It contains a communion vessel said to have been presented by Henry Morgan, who resided here as Governor of the island. The former Naval Hospital is now an archaeological center, from which the excavations and underwater explorations in the Port Royal area are directed. Attached to the center is a small museum with material recovered from the underwater remains (which have also been explored by diving expeditions from Morgan's Harbour Yacht and Beach Club). – Some remains of the fortifications have been excavated on land. From the *National Trust Tower* there is a magnificent *view of Kingston Harbour.

To the S of Port Royal are many little coral islands, the best known of which is *Lime Cay* (boat trips daily from Kingston and Port Royal).

Kingston to Mandeville via Spanish Town
(round trip 160 miles/258 km). – Leave Kingston on
Spanish Town Road (A 1), which runs NW to **Ferry**,
with the historic Ferry Inn.

9 miles/15 km: * White Marl Arawak Museum, on the
site of the largest Arawak settlement so far found on
the island, with interesting pre-Columbian material.
To the N is the famous Caymanas Golf Club.

4½ miles/7 km: * **Spanish Town** (115 ft/35 m; pop.
55,000), formerly the island's capital, founded by the
Spaniards in 1534. The town's population tripled
between 1960 and 1979, largely as a result of the
influx of people from country areas drawn to the
Kingston area by the hope of getting work in industry.

Colbeck Castle, Old Harbour

In the center of Spanish Town – the Spanish colonial
buildings of which have almost entirely given way to
Georgian architecture – is the charming square known
as the * **Park**, around which stand the main public
buildings. On the NW side is the domed * Rodney
Memorial, commemorating Admiral Rodney, who
defeated the French fleet off the Iles des Saintes in
1782. Flanking the Memorial are the National
Archives and the Registry. On the NE side of the
square is the old * House of Assembly (18th c.), now
occupied by municipal offices. On the SE side stands
the 19th c. Court House, now used for concerts, plays,
etc., and on the SW side **King's House** (c. 1760),
formerly the Governor's residence, which now houses
an archaeological museum. Adjoining, in the old
stables, the * Jamaica Folk Museum, which provides
an interesting picture of Jamaican life in earlier days.
In the immediately surrounding area are other
imposing 18th and 19th c. buildings. SE of the Park is
the Queen-Anne-style * **Cathedral of St James**
(Santiago de la Vega, 18th c.), which replaced a
Spanish church of the mid 17th c. destroyed by
Cromwell's Commonwealth troops. The church contains fine monuments and works of art dating from the
Spanish colonial period. – In King Street, the main
traffic artery of Spanish town, is the * Altenheim Art
Studio, with a display of fine arts and crafts, in
particular sculpture showing African inspiration. On
the N side of the town center are the ruins of Trinity
Chapel and, farther NW, the Astor Theatre.

S of Spanish Town the largely unspoiled * Hellshire
Hills, on a peninsula projecting into the Caribbean,
rise to a height of 787 ft/240 m. Off the coast of the
peninsula, much of which is fringed by areas of
swamp, are a string of coral reefs on which many ships
have come to grief, making it a happy hunting ground
for divers in quest of treasure.

The road runs past the little township of **Bushy Park**,
with a well-preserved aqueduct.

12½ miles/20 km: **Old Harbour**, a market village near
Galleon Harbour, an excellent natural harbor much
used in Spanish times. To the N of the village is Little
Ascot Racecourse. – 1¼ miles/2 km NW are the ruins of
Colbeck Castle, said to have been built by Colonel
Colbeck, who came to Jamaica with Cromwell's army
in 1655.

3 miles/5 km: Freetown, from which a road runs S to
the bauxite workings of the Alcoa corporation and the
sugar port of **Salt River**, on Salt River Bay. – 2 miles/
3 km SE of Freetown is Port Esquivel, from which
aluminum oxide is shipped.

9 miles/15 km; **May Pen** (213 ft/65 m.); pop.
32,000), the chief town of Clarendon parish and the

center of an intensively cultivated agricultural region.
To the S and SW extends the largest single sugar-cane
growing area in Jamaica which is irrigated by the Rio
Minho and Milk River.

12½ miles/20 km S of May Pen we come to the little
settlement of **Lionel Town**, a good base from which
to explore the wooded limestone peninsula of
Portland to the S, on the W coast of which are two
beautiful beaches, Carlisle Bay and Jackson Bay. Near
the eastern tip of the peninsula stands a prominent
lighthouse. – To the W of Lionel Town, at **The Alley**,
is the Monymusk Refinery, one of the largest and most
modern sugar factories in the West Indies.

14 miles/23 km SW of May Pen is the spa of * **Milk
River Bath**, with the most highly radioactive hot
spring (91.9 °F/33.3 °C) in the world. To the W of the
little town rises Round Hill (1149 ft/350 m).

The main road continues W from May Pen.

3 miles/5 km: Denbigh Agricultural Show Grounds
(agricultural and industrial show in August).

From here the road at first continues W, and then at
Toll Gate turns N up the valley of the Milk River,
running along the W side of the **Mocho Mounts**, a
limestone plateau, to **Porus**; then, continuing uphill,
via **Hope Village** to –

23 miles/37 km: * **Mandeville** (c. 1970 ft/600 m;
pop. 25,000; Astra Hotel, 25 r.; Mandeville, 68 r.),
main town of Manchester county and the principal
center of the southern limestone plateau. Its agreeable
climate made it a favorite resort during the colonial
period, and it has preserved some attractive old
buildings.

The Horticultural Society holds magnificent flower
shows here in summer. The central feature of the town
is **Crescent Park**, around which are grouped the
principal municipal buildings. On the N side stands
the imposing * **Court House** (19th c.), in Georgian
style, and on the S side the Parish Church (19th c.),
flanked by two other English-style buildings, the
Municipal Library and the Post Office. To the W of the
park are the Odeon Theatre and Tudor Theatre. The
Manchester Golf Club is one of the oldest and most
exclusive on the island.

The prosperity of Mandeville depends in large
measure on the extensive deposits of bauxite in the
neighborhood, which are worked on a large scale by
opencast methods. Many of the staff of the aluminum
firms live in the town.

From Mandeville A 2 runs SW via **Spur Tree** to the imposing rock faces in which the **Figuerero Mountains** (2950 ft/900 m) fall down to the *Black River* plain. Here are the imposing offices of the *Kaiser Bauxite Company*, which owns the aluminum oxide terminal at **Port Kaiser**, 28 miles/45 km SW of Mandeville on *Alligator Pond*, with the pretty little fishing village of the same name. Port Kaiser lies at the end of the firm's railway line, which brings the raw material down from the uplands.

From Alligator Pond a charming coast road (18 miles/ 29 km) skirts the S side of the **May Day Mounts** (highest point *Rose Hill*, 2757 ft/840 m) and past quiet beaches to *Old Woman's Point*. From here it continues via the village of *Gut River* and around Long Bay to Milk River Bath.

The main road continues N from Mandeville, passing the bauxite workings of the Alcan corporation.

13 miles/21 km: **Christina**, the chief place in the eastern part of the *Central Range*. As a range of hills this is not particularly impressive: it is an area of scattered agricultural settlement with a characteristic local farming pattern.

Many descendants of slaves live here, practicing mixed farming on smallholdings. They grow bananas, cacao, coffee, mangoes, pawpaws, yams and other fruits, selling their small surpluses through a network of local middlemen.

The road now runs E into the deeply indented valley of the Rio Minho.

15 miles/24 km: **Frankfield**, the second place of some consequence in this area. – The road continues down the valley, passing under the southern slopes of the *Bull Head* (2782 ft/848 m), to –

11 miles/18 km: **Chapelton**, an agricultural center (citrus fruits). – Then E to –

2 miles/3 km: *Suttons*, with the ruins of a large mansion. – The road now turns NE.

12 miles/19 km: ***Lluidas Vale**, one of the "interior valleys", a large polje (broad sunken area) formed by karstic action and filled with fertile alluvial soil. The rivers which flow through this steep-sided basin rise to the surface at the edge of the basin and then disappear into swallowholes.

8 miles/13 km: **Ewarton**, below *Mount Diablo*, which commands extensive views. The Alcan corporation works deposits of aluminum oxide here. The village lies at the NW corner of the plain of ***St Thomas in the Vale**, on the edge of the plateau, which was brought into cultivation during the colonial period. It is now occupied by large plantations of sugar-cane and citrus fruits.

7 miles/11 km: **Linstead**, a pretty market village, from which the beautiful but winding B 13 climbs to the *Devil's Racecourse*, a notorious stretch of mountain road.

4 miles/6 km: **Bog Walk**, an agricultural center with a large canning factory. – The road now traverses the narrow gorge of the Rio Cobre to Spanish Town and continues to –

24 miles/39 km: **Kingston**.

Kingston to the Blue Mountains (round trip 52 miles/83 km). – Leave Kingston on Old Hope Road, going NE, and continuing on a hill road (difficult; extensive views) to the spectacular ****Blue Mountains**, a range which rises steeply out of the coastal plain and reaches its highest point in the Blue Mountains Peak (7402 ft/2256 m).

The ****Blue Mountains** consist of Cretaceous rocks which have suffered an upthrust at a relatively recent period. The hot springs and the occasional earthquakes show that formation is still in progress. As a result of the high rainfall the mountains are much dissected by valleys. The steep sides of the valleys have been eroded following the poor husbandry of the past, and efforts are now being made to repair the damage by exemplary but expensive measures of reforestation.

6 miles/10 km: *The Cooperage*. The road winds its way up, via *Irish Town* and *Redlight*, to –

12 miles/19 km: **Newcastle**, with an old fort which is still occupied by the Jamaican army. To the NE can be seen *Catherine's Peak* (5059 ft/1542 m; 1½ hours' climb), from which there are breath-taking ****views** of the southern coastal plain and the hills to the E.

The road continues to climb through tropical mountain forest (cloud forest) with its characteristic vegetation pattern to *Hardware Gap* (4009 ft/ 1222 m), and then descends past the **Hollywell Natural Park* (rare orchids and ferns; bird sanctuary; recreation facilities) to –

6 miles/10 km: *Section*. From here the road returns S over the main ridge to –

1¼ miles/2 km: *Silver Hill*, below the SW side of *John Crow Peak* (5752 ft/1753 m). The road now runs down through the wild and romantic **valley of the Yallahs River* by way of *St Peter's* and *Content Gap* (coffee plantations).

Yallahs River, in the Blue Mountains

12½ miles/20 km: **Guava Ridge**, below the N side of *Mount Rosanna* (4000 ft/1219 m).

2½ miles/4 km E of Guava Ridge is **Mavis Bank**, a good climbing base. *Blue Mountains Peak* (7402 ft/ 2256 m; 4 hours' climb), to the NE, is the highest point in the Blue Mountains. – Above Mavis Bank to the N, in the catchment area of the wild *Green River*, are the villages of *Westphalia* and *Cinchonae*, the latter of which is named after the cinchona trees grown there in the 19th c. to provide quinine. To the NE rise *Sir John's Peak* (6332 ft/1930 m) and *High Peak* (6811 ft/2076 m), to the E *Mossman's Peak* (6703 ft/ 2043 m).

From Guava Ridge a narrow and winding road passes through evergreen tropical mountain forest to –

5½ miles/9 km: **Gordon Town**, an attractive little place amid luxuriant aromatic vegetation. The road then continues via The Cooperage to –

8 miles/13 km: **Kingston**.

Kingston to Port Morant (round trip 95 miles/ 153 km). – Leave Kingston on Windward Road, which runs E past the Rockfort Mineral Baths and Fort Nugent.

5 miles/8 km: *Harbour View*, from which the narrow spit of land known as the Palisadoes extends westward.

The road continues E, passing *Brook's Pen* beach near **Seven Mile**, and then crosses the *Cane River*, which tumbles down from the hills in wild *cascades (difficult to reach). It then runs past *Cable Hut* beach, near the settlement of **Palm Beach**, and comes to –

4½ miles/7 km: **Bull Bay**, an attractive little coastal town. Then follows a stretch of varied scenery on the S coast, past the mouth of the *Yallahs River*, to –

11 miles/18 km: **Yallahs**, a rising resort with two beaches *Flemarie* and *Bailey's Beach*. To the east lie the salt pans which are said to have existed in Spanish colonial days. The route continues along the southern slope of *Yallah's Hill* (2396 ft/730 m) to –

7 miles/11 km: **Rozelle Falls**, an idyllic tropical waterfall.

5 miles/8 km: **Morant Bay** (sea level; pop. 6000), on the bay into which the *Morant River* flows, chief settlement in the parish of St Thomas. In 1865 this was the scene of the Morant Bay Rebellion by freed slaves protesting against the deterioration in their living conditions. Although the rising was ruthlessly put down, it led to Jamaica's attaining the status of a British crown colony in 1866. In front of the restored Court House is a statue of Paul Bogle, one of the leaders of the rebellion who was executed together with many others and is now honored as a national hero.

After passing the two beautiful beaches of *Lyssons Providence Pen* and *Prospect Retreat* the road comes to –

7 miles/11 km: **Port Morant**, in the inlet of the same name. The port handles primarily the agricultural produce of the surrounding area.

On the E side of the inlet lies the busy little township of **Bowden**, with large warehouses. To the SE, at *Old Pera* and *New Pera*, are excellent beaches. Farther E extensive rice-fields have been planted in recent years.

From Port Morant the road runs NE to –

6 miles/10 km: *Golden Grove*, from which a visit can be made to *Holland Bay*, with a magnificent beach, and *Morant Point Lighthouse*, on the reef-fringed eastern tip of the island. – The road now runs W along the intensively cultivated valley of the *Plantation Garden River*.

7 miles/11 km: **Bath**, a spa set picturesquely on the SE flanks of the Blue Mountains. Here there is a *Botanic Garden almost 200 years old which is one of the most interesting sights on the island.

The road continues along the S edge of the Blue Mountains through extensive banana plantations, past *Sunny Hill*, *Water Valley*, *White Hall* and *Soho*.

9 miles/15 km: **Seaforth**, the chief town in the *Blue Mountains Valley*. – The road now runs NW up the valley of the *Negro River* to –

10½ miles/17 km: **Cedar Valley**, a farming center with an agreeable climate; it is situated below the S side of *Blue Mountains Peak*. There are large coffee plantations in the sourrounding area.

The road now winds its way down into the valley of the *Yallahs River*, where a program of reforestation and carefully devised patterns of land use has been carried out with the object of preventing further erosion damage.

8 miles/13 km: *Llandewey*, from which the road runs SW by way of *Cambridge Hill* to –

4½ miles/7 km: *Eleven Mile*. Then on A 4 to –

10½ miles/17 km: **Kingston**.

See also **Jamaica.

Long Cay
See Crooked Island

Long Island
Bahama Islands
Commonwealth of the Bahamas

Area: 173 sq. miles/448 sq. km.
Population: 5000.
Administrative center: Nassau (on New Providence).
ⓘ **Ministry of Tourism,**
Nassau Court,
P.O. Box N 3220,
Nassau,
Bahamas;
tel. (809) 322 7505.
See also Practical Information.

HOTELS. – *Stella Maris Inn*, Stella Maris, 42 r., SP, T; *Cape Santa Maria*, Calabash Bay, 10 r.; *Hibiscus Inn*, Stella Maris, 5 r.; *Thompson's Bay Apartments*, Thompson's Bay, 8 r.

EVENTS. – *Long Island Sailing Regatta* (June).

RECREATION and SPORT. – Sailing, deep-sea fishing, scuba diving, snorkeling, swimming and sunbathing; shooting; tennis.

AIR SERVICES. – Regular flights from Cape Santa Maria, Stella Maris, Deadman's Cay and Hard Bargain via George Town (Great Exuma) to Nassau.

SHIPPING. – Regular mail boat services from Stella Maris and Deadman's Cay via George Town (Great Exuma) to Nassau and to Acklins and Inagua.

*Long Island – aptly named, with a total length of some 60 miles/96 km and a breadth which is never greater than a few miles – extends from SSE to NNW between latitude 22°50′ and 23°40′ N. It is an island of very varied landscape pattern, with high cliffs, green hills, gently sloping beaches and expanses of brackish swampland.

This trim and well-cultivated island has long been a center of Bahamian agriculture – particularly stock farming and the traditional form of vegetable growing known as pot-hole farming. Other major sources of revenue are boatbuilding, fishing, the growing tourist trade and the important salt industry, which exports some 500,000 tons of salt annually, much of it extracted from old salt-pans which have been reactivated.

HISTORY. – Archaeological evidence shows that the island had a considerable population of Lucayan Indians in pre-Columbian times. Columbus landed at the N end of Long Island on October 16, 1492. – During the island's eventful history the salt marshes were of major economic importance, and long before the first American Loyalists came here and introduced the growing of cotton, salt was being shipped to Bermuda and New York. After the decline in cotton growing in the 19th c. stock farming and vegetable growing developed into the important elements in the island's economy which they still represent today.

One of the most charming spots in the Bahamas is *Cape Santa Maria, at the northern tip of Long Island, where Columbus landed in 1492. Close by is the magically beautiful *Calabash Bay, with a beach of fine sand over 3 miles/5 km long, now frequented by visitors staying at a nearby hotel. Off the N coast the waters are well stocked with fish, and there are magnificent diving grounds, with rare species of *coral (elkhorn coral, black coral, etc.). – From here the road runs S, past the picturesque little village of Burnt Ground and comes in 6 miles/10 km to the developing resort of Stella Maris, a well-equipped retreat for tourists and well-to-do retired people with its own

airstrip. This is a good base for diving expeditions to the huge underwater caverns and banks of coral off Rum Cay and Conception Island. The road continues S, past Millerton with its cotton gin, to *Simms (7½ miles/12 km), a picturesque Out Islands village with some well-preserved old thatched buildings. Here too are a pastel-colored prison (with the inscription "Her Majesty's Prison") and an old church with an imposing tower. – 4½ miles/7 km farther S lies the quiet little harbor of Wemyss Bight. – Another 4½ miles/7 km S is Salt Pond, starting-point of the *Out Island Regatta, one of the major events in the Bahamian sailing program.

The road continues S, passing unfrequented beaches, attractive little villages and the ruins of Gray's Plantation, to Deadman's Cay (airstrip) and Cartwright's. In the vicinity of these two townships are fine karstic *caves, filled with magnificent stalactitic formations, with rock engravings indicating that they were occupied by man in pre-Columbian times. From New Found Harbour, on the W coast, a dense chain of islets and rocks extends westward to the Ragged Island Range.

From Deadman's Cay the road runs SW, past a number of old cotton plantations, to Clarence Town, the largest place on the island. This is a charming little town of pastel-colored houses built around a small harbor, dominated by St Paul's Church (Anglican) and St Peter's Church (R.C.), both designed by Father Jerome, an Anglican priest who later became a Roman Catholic, in a style influenced by North African architecture. Nearby is the famous Blue Hole, a bell-shaped cavity, not yet fully explored, with a diameter of some 230 ft/70 m. – S of Clarence Town, near the village of Hard Bargain (airstrip), are the extensive salt-pans of the Diamond Crystal Salt Co., which are open to visitors. This is the second largest undertaking of its kind in the Bahamas, with an annual output of some 500,000 tons. – 5 miles/8 km SE of Clarence Town are the ruins of Dunmore Plantation, a relic of the colonial period. Farther S is the charming little village of Roses, and some miles beyond this the beautiful South Point, at the southern tip of the island.

See also **Bahamas.

Isla de Margarita
Lesser Antilles
Leeward Islands
República de Venezuela

Province: Nueva Esparta.
Area: 360 sq. miles/934 sq. km.
Population: 150,000.
Vehicles travel on the right.
ⓘ **Corporacion de Turismo,**
EDO. Nueva Esparta,
Edif. Santiago Mariño,
Av. Santiago Mariño,
Av. Velásquez.
Porlamar,
Venezuela;
tel. 095 24651.
See also Practical Information.

HOTELS. – *Bahía del Morro*; *Bella Vista*; *Caribean*; *Flamingo*; *Margarita Concorde*.

AIR SERVICES. – Regular services to Caracas.

SHIPPING. – Ferries from Punta de Piedras to Cumaná and Puerto La Cruz.

EVENTS. – "El Carite", "La Burriquita", "El Pajaro Guarandol", "Los Chimichimitos", "La Danza del Guacuco", "El Pez Nicolás".

The island of Margarita, lying some 25 miles/40 km off the N coast of Venezuela, is the largest of the islands in the southern Antilles. Together with the neighboring islands of Coche and Cubagua it forms the state of Nueva Esparta.

HISTORY. – The island was discovered by Columbus in 1498, and the Spaniards soon began to fish for pearls on the shell banks around Cubagua. On Cubagua is the site (partly excavated) of the town of Nueva Cádiz, which was destroyed in the 16th c.,

probably by a tidal wave. Tourism has recently begun to make some progress; and the pearl fisheries have recently been revived on the initiative of the government.

Margarita is really two islands linked by the narrow *Istmo Restinga*, some 15 miles/25 km long. On the S side of the isthmus is a much ramified lagoon, the *Albufera de la Restinga*. Almost the whole of the island's population is concentrated in the eastern part, the Isla de Margarita proper, while the western half, known as Macanao, is uninhabited apart from one tiny settlement. The highest point is the *Pico San Juan* (3019 ft/920 m), in the eastern half.

The island's capital, **La Asunción**, founded in 1561, is a little town reminiscent of its colonial past, with low houses, churches and the fort of Santa Rosa.

The tourist and economic center of the island is the little port of **Porlamar** (free port) on the S coast (airstrip; regular boat services from La Guaira), which attracts many visitors (almost exclusively Venezuelan), particularly at weekends.

The only inhabited islands in the southern group are **Coche** (17 sq. miles/43 sq. km) and **Cabagua** (8 sq. miles/22 sq. km). On Cubagua, noted for its pearl fisheries, are the remains of the Spanish settlement of Nueva Cádiz.

Off Margarita are the uninhabited islands of **Tortuga**, to the W, and **Los Testigos**, to the E – arid islands occupied only by herds of goats which have almost completely destroyed the original forest cover by over-grazing.

Nearly all the little islands in the northern group are likewise uninhabited – from E to W, *Los Hermanos*, *La Blanquila*, *Orchila*, **Los Roques** and *Las Aves*. On some of these islands guano, deposited by the countless seabirds nesting there, was worked in the 19th c.

Another island belonging to Venezuela is the **Isla Aves**, which lies many miles away to the NE, W of Dominica.

= Pearl-fishing banks

Marie-Galante

Lesser Antilles
Windward Islands
French Antilles
Overseas Département of
Guadeloupe

Area: 61 sq. miles/158 sq. km.
Population: 16,000.
Administrative center: Basse-Terre
(on Guadeloupe).
Vehicles travel on the right.

(i) **Office du Tourisme de Guadeloupe,**
5 Square de la Banque,
B.P. 1099,
F-97181 **Pointe à Pitre,**
Guadeloupe, A.F.;
tel. 82 09 30.
See also Practical Information.

HOTELS. – *Belvédère*, Grand Bourg, 5 r.; *Soledad*, Grand Bourg, 8 r.; *Le Salut*, St-Louis, 15 r.; etc.

RESTAURANTS. – *Arc-en-Ciel*, St-Louis; *Le Bêkêkê*, Plage de la Feuillère; etc.

RECREATION and SPORT. – Sailing, scuba diving, snorkeling, swimming and sunbathing; walking.

EVENTS. – *Fêtes Communales*, local festivals in Capesterre (July 26), Grand-Bourg (December 8) and St-Louis (August 25).

AIR SERVICES. – Regular flights to Basse-Terre (Aérodrome de Baillif) and Pointe-à-Pitre (Aéroport du Raizet) on Guadeloupe.

SHIPPING. – Regular boat services from Grand-Bourg and St-Louis to Pointe-à-Pitre.

The little sugar island of *Marie-Galante*, **27 miles/44 km S of Pointe-à-Pitre, is, like Grande-Terre on Guadeloupe, a limestone tableland broken up by karstic action. It is divided into two parts by a geological fault which has left its mark on the topography of the island.**

The inhabitants live mainly by sugar growing, with some stock farming and fishing. The sugar-mills in operation in the 19th c., more than 70 in number, have either been demolished or survive only as ruins. The island now has only one large sugar factory and four rum distilleries.

HISTORY. – The island was discovered by Columbus on November 3, 1493 and named after his flagship. It was one of the last refuges of the Caribs, who withdrew to Marie-Galante when they were driven out of Guadeloupe by the French; and when the French landed on the smaller island from 1648 onwards the Indians put up fierce resistance. The island enjoyed a period of prosperity in the 17th c., when indigo, cotton, tobacco, coffee and cacao were grown as well as sugar. In 1691, 1703 and 1754 British forces used Marie-Glante as a base for their attacks on targets in Guadeloupe. During the Napoleonic period, too, the island was several times temporarily occupied by Britain.

TOUR OF THE ISLAND (27 miles/44 km). – From the island's airstrip the road runs E along the S coast to –

2½ miles/4 km: *Petite Anse*, a beautiful beach sheltered by a coral reef.

1¼ miles/2 km: **Capesterre**, in a charming *setting on the *Plage de la Feuillère*, another superb beach within a protective coral reef, with the *Chapelle Ste-Anne*.

2 miles/3 km NE are the *Galeries*, impressive rock formations over 50 ft/16 m high carved out by the surf.

1 mile/1.5 km, above Capesterre: road junction. Take D 201, which runs N, parallel to the reef-fringed E coast.

4½ miles/7.5 km: D 205 branches off, following the **Grande Barre**, the sharply defined fault which divides the higher southern part of the island from the lower northern part, known as **Les Bas**.

2 miles/3 km W is the *Trou à Diable*, a magnificent cave some 550 yd/500 m long with an underground lake (guide essential).

An attractive WALK may be taken along the cliff-fringed *coast, with its rocky promontories and secluded coves, to *Caye Plate* (4¼ miles/7 km N), a steep-sided crag with extensive views, where the local fishermen catch crayfish of exceptional size.

D 205 continues NW into the charming valley of the *Rivière du Vieux-Fort*. 6 miles/9 km: *Anse de Mays*, with a beautiful beach.

1¼ miles/2 km N is the old-world village of **Vieux-Fort**, on another fine beach. Here can be seen some of the *pile dwellings which were common all over the island until the 19th c. 1¼ miles/2 km farther N the *Gueule Grand Gouffre*, a massive natural arch hewn out by the surf on the wild N coast can be seen. 1¼ miles/2 km E is the *Grosse Pointe* (154 ft/47 m), the most northerly point on the island (access difficult).

The road continues W to the *Pointe du Cimetière* and then turns S.

2½ miles/4 km: **St-Louis**, a developing resort with a beautiful mile-long sandy beach. A colorful patronal festival is celebrated here at the end of August.

D 201 runs E to the caves in the southern part of the island known as **Les Hauts** and continues to the Trou à Diable, running parallel to the Grande Barre.

Continue S on N 9.

4 miles/6 km: *Grande Anse* sugar factory, with its own harbor.

1¼ miles/2 km: *Moulin Roussel*, an attractive old sugar-mill.

1¼ miles/2 km: **Grand-Bourg** (sea level; pop. 10,000), the starting-point of French settlement on the island and its principal town. It was badly damaged by fire in 1901.

2½ miles/4 km inland on N 9 is the *Usine Pirogue*, situated on a pond known as the *Mare au Punch*. It takes its name from a riot which is said to have taken place here during the liberation of the slaves, when all the rum and sugar in the factory was poured into the pond.

The road continues along the reef-fringed SW coast.

1 mile/2 km: *Habitation Murat, situated just off the road. Formerly one of the wealthiest estates on the island, this has preserved the ruins of a windmill and a sugar factory. The *Château* is a classical-style colonial mansion (18th c.) which was destroyed by an earthquake in 1843.

1¼ miles/2 km: *Moulin des Basses*, an excellently preserved old sugar-mill.

1¼ miles/2 km: **Aérodrome** (the island's airfield).

See also *La Désirade, **Guadeloupe and *Iles des Saintes.

Martinique
Lesser Antilles
Windward Islands
French Antilles
Overseas Département

Area: 427 sq. miles/1106 sq. km.
Population: 350,000.
Administrative center: Fort-de-France.
Vehicles travel on the right.

ⓘ Office du Tourisme,
   Boulevard Alfassa,
   Bord de Mer,
   B.P. 520,
   F-97206 Fort-de-France,
   Martinique, A.F.;
   tel. 71 79 60.
   Bureau d'Informations,
   Aéroport du Lamentin;
   tel. 74 28 55.
   See also Practical Information.

HOTELS. – Only a selection of the large number of hotels on Martinique can be given here.

FORT-DE-FRANCE: *Impératrice*, Rue de la Libération, 24 r.; *Victoria*, Route de Didier, 20 r., SP; *Le Duparquet*, Avenue des Caraïbes, 20 r.; *Malmaison*, Rue de la Liberté, 19 r.; *Le Gommier*, Rue J.-Cazotte, 18 r.; *Le Balisier*, Rue Victor-Hugo, 18 r.; *Un Coin de Paris*, Rue Lazare-Carnot, 14 r.; *Bristol*, Rue Martin-Luther-King, 10 r.; *Au Rêve Bleu*, Rue Lazare-Carnot, 10 r.; *Anna*, Rue Lazare-Carnot, 6 r. – TROIS-ILETS: *Méridien*, 307 r., SP, T, beach; *Frantel*, 213 r., SP, T, beach; *Bakoua*, 99 r., SP, T, beach; *La Marina*, 170 r., SP, T; *Bambou*, 24 r.; *Eden Beach Paradise*, 22 r.; *Madinina*, 20 r.; *Auberge de l'Anse Mitan*, 20 r.; *Caraïbe Auberge*, 14 r.; *Chez André*, 11 r. – SCHOELCHER: *PLM La Batelière*, 200 r., SP, T, beach. – LE CARBET: *Latitude*, 92 r., SP, beach. – ANSE A L'ÂNE: *Calalou*, 20 r.; *Reflets de la Mer*, 6 r. – STE-ANNE: *Manoir de Beauregard*, 27 r., SP, beach; *Dunette*, 11 r. – SP. – LE DIAMANT: *Novotel du Diamant*, Pointe de la Chéry, 182 r., SP, T; *Diamant-les-Bains*, 15 r. – LE VAUCLIN: *Auberge de l'Atlantique*, 11 r.; *Chez Julot*, 10 r.; *Ranch Macabou*, 10 r.; *Les Alizés*, 6 r. – LE FRANÇOIS: *Bungalows de la Prairie*, 10 r.; *Les Brisants*, 6 r.

– BASSSE-POINTE: *Plantation de Leyritz*, 24 r., SP. – MORNE-ROUGE: *Le Vieux Chalet*, 9 r. – MORNE-VERT: *Chez Coecilia*, 4 r. – CASE-PILOTE: *Auberge du Vare*, 7 r., SP; *Le Vétiver*, 25 bungalows, SP, T. – TARTANE: *Le Madras*, 14 r. – LA TRINITÉ: *St-Aubin*, 15 r.

RESTAURANTS in most hotels; also in FORT-DE-FRANCE: *Le Royal* (French); *La Grand'Voile*, Pointe Simon; *La Pampa*, Boulevard du Général-de-Gaulle; *Typic Bellevue*, Boulevard de la Marne; *La Madrague*, Boulevard Chevalier-Sainte-Marthe; *El Raco*, Rue Lazare-Carnot (Catalan); *Lotus d'Asie*, Boulevard de la Marne (Vietnamese); *Le Bristol*, Rue Martin-Luther-King (Oriental); *Constellation*, Aéroport du Lamentin; etc. – POINTE DU BOUT AND TROIS-ILETS: *Chez Sidonie*; *Le Cantonnais*, Marina Pointe du Bout (Chinese). – ANSE MITAN AND LES ANSES D'ARLET: *La Bonne Auberge*; *Case à Cha-Cha*; *Tamarins Plage*; *California Saloon*. – STE-LUCE AND STE-ANNE: *Aux Délices de la Mer*; *Pol et Virginie*; *Les Filets Bleus*. – ATLANTIC COAST: *Madras*, Tartane; *Le Mont St-Michel*, Le François; *Auberge de l'Atlantique*, Ste-Marie. – NW COAST: *La Baie d'Along*, Schoelcher; *Le Foulard*, Schoelcher; *Le Bouddha*, Fond-Lahaye (Chinese); *Grain d'Or*, Le Carbet; *La Guinguette*, St-Pierre; *La Factorerie*, St-Pierre. – NE: *Chez Madame Labridy*, Morne des Esses; etc.

NIGHT CLUBS in some of the larger hotels (*Bakoua*, *Méridien*, *Frantel*); also in FORT-DE-FRANCE: *Sweety*, Rue du Capitaine-Rose; *Le Privé*, Rue F.-Arago; *Le Manoir*, Route des Religieuses; *Tam Tam*, Route de Rédoute. – LE LAMENTIN: *Club Perfecta*, Cité Petit Manoir. – LA TRINITÉ: *Le Tonneau*.

Casinos (blackjack, roulette, baccarat, craps) in the Méridien and La Batelière Hotels.

SHOPPING. – The main commercial center on the island is Fort-de-France, and its principal shopping streets are *Rue Victor-Hugo*, *Rue Schoelcher* and *Rue Antoine-Siger*. In these streets there are enticing boutiques on the Paris model, jewelers' shops and shops selling local craft products. French *haute couture*, leather goods and perfume can also be bought in Fort-de-France at advantageous prices, as well as the best French wines and spirits, food, kitchen and domestic equipment, tobacco goods, cosmetics and much else besides.

Martinique basketwork

PUBLIC HOLIDAYS and EVENTS. – *Jour de l'An*, New Year's Day. – *Carnaval* (first Sunday after Epiphany to Ash Wednesday), a lively Carnival, with processions and other events. It reaches its climax on *Mardi Gras* (Shrove Tuesday) and *Mercredi des Cendres* (Ash Wednesday), and ends with the burning of the "Vaval". – *Vendredi Saint*, Good Friday. – *Pâques*, Easter. – *Fête du Travail* (May 1), Labour Day. – *Ascension*. – *Pentecôte*, Whitsun. – *Fêtes*

Patronales (July–October), colorful communal festivals, usually in honor of the local patron saint. – *Fête Nationale* (July 14), the French National Day. – *Schoelcher* (July 21), Schoelcher Day. – *Assomption* (August 15), Assumption, with great celebrations in many places. – *Toussaint* (November 1), All Saints, when numbers of small candles are lit in cemeteries after dark. – *Jour des Morts*, All Souls. – *Armistice* (November 11). – *Christ-Roi* (last Sunday in the church year), festival of Christ the King. – *Noël*, Christmas.

Fighting cock, Martinique

Cockfights (*combats de coqs*) are very popular sporting occasions in Martinique, as they are in Guadeloupe. The cocks are armed with knife-sharp metal spurs and weighted to make them heavier, and fight in special cockpits which are found in many towns and villages, e.g. at Le Lamentin, Rivière-Pilote, Ste-Anne, St-Pierre and Morne-Rouge. Most of the spectators lay bets on the result of the contest, which lasts about a quarter of an hour, and urge on their favorite with vociferous shouts and gestures. The defeated cock, usually badly injured, is killed immediately; the victor is cosseted and set to fight again. The time and place of these events, which often draw spectators from the neighboring islands, are announced in the newspapers.

RECREATION and SPORT. – Flying; sailing, deep-sea fishing, wind-surfing, water-skiing, scuba diving, snorkeling, swimming and sunbathing; riding, golf, tennis, walking.

AIR SERVICES. – Regular flights from the Aéroport International du Lamentin to Guadeloupe, St-Martin, Antigua, Dominica, St Lucia, Barbados, Grenada, St Vincent, Union Island, Caracas (Venezuela), Cayenne (French Guyana), Lyons (France), Miami (USA), Montreal (Canada), Mulhouse/Basle (France/Switzerland), New York (USA), Paris (France), Port-au-Prince (Haiti), Port of Spain (Trinidad), Santo Domingo (Dominican Republic) and San Juan (Puerto Rico).

SHIPPING. – Many cruise ships call at Fort-de-France. – Freighters sail regularly between Fort-de-France and ports in France, including the banana boats of the Compagnie Générale Maritime (usually weekly sailings). These boats sail to and from Dieppe, Rouen, Le Havre and Bordeaux, usually taking nine days and carrying 10–12 passengers. Advance booking necessary, since berths on these boats are much in demand. – Small cargo boats sail daily to the neighboring islands, and there are also excursion boats to St-Pierre and other places. – Passenger ferries from Fort-de-France to Pointe du Bout.

The French island of **Martinique in the Lesser Antilles lies some 25 miles/40 km S of the Dominican Republic and 20 miles/32 km N of the British associated island of St Lucia between latitude 14°23' and 14°53' N and longitude 61° W. It is one of the most popular tourist destinations in the Caribbean, particularly with European visitors, since it combines great beauty and variety of scenery and the exotic attractions of the tropics with the advantages of the French way of life and the comfort and amenities of Europe. Martinique, like Guadeloupe, is fully integrated into the French Republic as a département and thus belongs to the European Community.

The island has a total length from N to S of almost 37 miles/60 km, with a width which is never more than 19 miles/30 km and at its narrowest is barely 6 miles/10 km across. It is predominantly hilly, reaching its highest point in Mont Pelé (Montagne Pelée) (4584 ft/1397 m), a still active volcano in the N of the island. The coast is rugged and much indented on the E side but has a gentler pattern on the W. All around the island are magnificent beaches, which in the S and SE have excellent facilities for swimming but in the NE are sometimes dangerous on account of the heavy surf: in some places, indeed, bathing is prohibited. There is accommodation for visitors in hotels and guesthouses of all categories near the finest beaches, including many luxury hotels with prices to match.

The name of Martinique is derived by some authorities from the Indian term Madinina or Madinia, which is said to mean "island of flowers" in the Carib language; but although this explanation is still commonly repeated it is disputed by other writers. An alternative theory is that when Columbus discovered the island in 1493 he took it for the legendary island of Martinino, home of the Amazons – which might also explain why he did not set foot on the island. It is perhaps more probable that Columbus, following the common

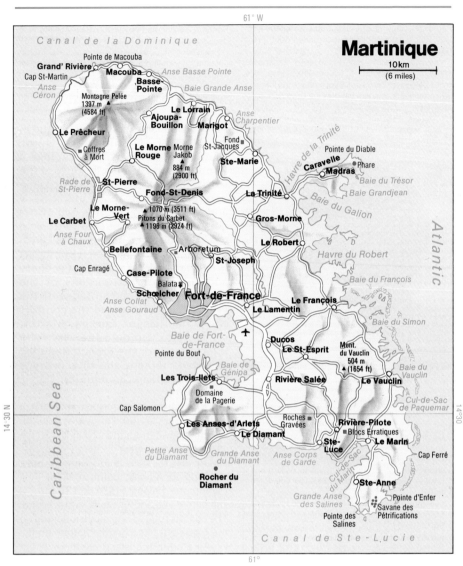

In the **north** of the island evidence of relatively recent volcanic activity is provided by Mont Pelé (4584 ft/1397 m), Martinique's highest peak, and the Pitons du Carbet (3924 ft/1196 m), which rear up behind the capital, Fort-de-France. These two massifs, extending like fingers towards the coast, are dissected by a bewildering network of rivers and streams.

practice of those days, named it after a saint – in this case St Martin.

The romantic name, "Island of Flowers" is entirely appropriate, for the vegetation of Martinique is of unrivalled beauty. It has a profusion of orchids, bougainvilleas, lilies and other tropical flowers, and has also considerable areas of forest; and its many species of trees, both native and imported – mangroves, coconut palms, tree ferns, bananas, tree bamboos, mahogany – contribute to the impression made on many visitors that Martinique is one large garden.

From a distance the island, which consists mostly of volcanic rocks, appears rugged and forbidding; but at closer quarters it can be seen to break down into three large topographical units.

Alluvial deposits cover the **Lamentin plain**, around the Baie de Fort-de-France, which reaches far into the W side of the island, and small areas of plain on the coasts.

The **south** is hilly, though not so high as the N. Characteristic of this region are the hills known as *mornes*, with flat or rounded tops and steeply scarped sides.

With the exception of the Volcan du Vauclin they are all under 1640 ft/500 m. A feature of particular interest is the *Savane des Pétrifications*, with petrified trees; semi-precious stones like jasper are also quite commonly found here. – The southeastern tip of the island is formed of Tertiary limestones, with a profusion of characteristic rock formations. – Through the hills flow many rivers and streams, forming beautiful waterfalls, deep defiles and gorges on their way to the sea and depositing broad fans of alluvial soil at their mouths. – Fumaroles and hot springs bear witness to volcanic forces now quiescent but by no means extinct. This juxtaposition of fire and water gives Martinique, the Island of Flowers, its distinctive and unmistakable character.

CLIMATE. – On Martinique, as on the neighboring islands, the climate is strongly influenced by the trade winds, which give rise to the climatic differences between the W and E coasts. On the E coast (the Côte au Vent), which is exposed to the trade winds, it rains much more frequently than on the W coast (Côte sous le Vent). In the hilly northern part of the island the difference between the windward and leeward sides is particularly striking. On the eastern flanks of the hills dense mists are a common occurrence, as are heavy rainfalls, increasing with altitude.

On the Côte au Vent the average annual rainfall at sea level is about 80 in./2000 mm, rising on the Mont Pelé to 400 in./10,000 mm. On the W side the air masses fall lower down and become warmer: here the average annual rainfall is about 60 in./1500 mm and in the extreme SW it is still lower.

From January to April is the dry season ("Carême", Lent); from July to December there is a kind of rainy season ("Hivernage"), during which some 75% of the annual rainfall occurs. The driest month is March, the wettest November. The rainy season, however, is not a period of constant rain: the rain falls in the form of brief but correspondingly violent showers, which usually die away during the afternoon at about the same time. The average humidity of the air is over 80%, but is made tolerable by the winds which blow all the time. From mid July to mid October there is the danger of tropical hurricanes, but statistics show that these are of devastating proportions only once every ten years. In 1979 Hurricane David caused considerable damage, particularly to the banana plantations in the N of the island. The Martinique meteorological service has developed an efficient early warning system, so that human casualties are rare.

The average annual temperature at sea level is 79 °F/25 °C, with only a small difference (some 5½ °F/3 °C) between the hottest and the coldest months. At the hottest time of day in summer the temperature can rise above 86 °F/30 °C, falling sharply at night – in winter to below 64 °F/18 °C. Temperature varies considerably with height: on Mont Pelé the average annual temperature is only 61 °F/16 °C.

For an island of such relatively small size (427 sq. miles/1106 sq. km) Martinique shows an extraordinary climatic diversity and a corresponding variety of vegetation. Above the cultivated land the slopes of the hills are covered with dense tropical forest to a height of some 3300 ft/1000 m, reaching farther down in the E than in the W. Above 3300 ft/1000 m, with increased humidity, the forest degenerates into thin tropical mountain forest, covered with moss (cloud forest). In the dry areas there are still patches of dry forest, but much of the land is covered with scrub or steppe, with a vegetation of cactuses and thorny bushes. On the coast there are large expanses of mangrove swamp.

HISTORY. – Like other islands in the Lesser Antilles, Martinique was probably occupied some 2000 years ago by Arawaks, a peaceable people who had already reached quite an advanced cultural level, as evidenced by archaeological finds to be seen in the Fort-de-France and elsewhere. The warlike Caribs who conquered the island, probably 1000 years later, are believed to have massacred all the Arawak men and spared only the women who submitted to them and became their slaves.

Columbus first appeared off Martinique in November 1493 but did not land on the island, since he was afraid of the natives – and also because he believed that the island was inhabited by the fierce Amazons of legend. He first set foot on Martinique in 1502, during his fourth voyage. Tradition has it that he and his men landed at Le Carbet on the W coast on June 15, 1502 and praised the island in these words: "It is the best, most fertile, most delightful and most charming land in the world. It is the fairest land I have ever seen, and I never tire of contemplating its magnificent verdure."

In spite of these fine words the island was forgotten for the next hundred years, and only the occasional European landed on Martinique – usually Spanish seamen who put in here to obtain food while on the way to other destinations.

In 1624 the French began to take an interest in Martinique, after shipwrecked mariners cast ashore on the island brought back glowing accounts of what they had seen.

The first settlement was established in 1635 by Belain d'Esnambuc, who landed at Le Carbet with a few hundred men and built Fort St-Pierre a few miles N. The Caribs put up fierce resistance but were unable to take the fort and drive out the French; in the end they were obliged to reach an accommodation with the invaders, and thereafter the island developed rapidly. Belain d'Esnambuc's nephew, Jacques du Parquet, from the Caux area in Normandy, who ruled the island from 1637 to 1658, is regarded as the real founder of Martinique. He brought in more settlers, made peace with the Caribs after a series of skirmishes and introduced new crops, including sugar-cane. At the end of the 17th c. the British and Dutch attempted to conquer the island from the French but were beaten off. In 1667 Martinique became the principal French possession in the Caribbean, and for many years was responsible for the administration of Guadeloupe. Fort-Royal, now Fort-de-France, was founded in 1669. At the end of the 17th c. sugar production enjoyed a considerable upswing, and the cultivation of coffee and cacao also developed. This required a considerably increased labor force, which was recruited mainly from black slaves and freed galley-slaves.

A further British attack on Martinique in 1759 was unsuccessful, but in 1762 British forces made good a landing on the island, withdrawing nine months later under the treaty of Paris, which confirmed the French loss of Canada. Thereafter Martinique was able to return to its former role.

In 1763 Joséphine Tascher de la Pagerie, who became Napoleon's wife in 1796 and empress of France in 1804, was born at Les Trois-Ilets, S of Fort-de-France. Divorced by Napoleon in 1809, she died at Malmaison, near Paris, in 1814.

The years of the French Revolution left their mark on Martinique. The population was split between royalists and those who supported the new ideas, and there was bitter and sometimes violent strife between the two parties. Finally the royalists gained the upper hand, with some help from the British, who occupied the island again in 1794 and remained there until 1802. Under the peace of Amiens Martinique reverted to France, and in 1814, under the treaty of Paris, it was finally recognized as a French possession, having in the meantime suffered a further brief British occupation in 1809.

The 19th c. saw the abolition of slave-owning (1848), the slave trade having already been banned in 1815. A French minister of Alsatian origin, Victor Schoelcher, is still honored by the black population for the decisive part he played in bringing about the abolition of slavery. More than 70,000 slaves were liberated and left the areas where they had been forced to work, often under inhuman conditions. The shortage of labor to which this gave rise was made good by bringing in indentured laborers from India and China, creating tensions between the different population groups on the island.

The beginning of the 20th c. was overshadowed by a natural catastrophe of massive proportions. An eruption of Mont Pelé razed to the ground the island's then capital St-Pierre, sometimes called the "Paris of the Antilles", and the 30,000 inhabitants (predominantly white) lost their lives with one single exception. Thereafter Fort-de-France became the administrative center of the island.

During the Second World War Martinique, like Guadeloupe, at first sided with the pro-Nazi Vichy regime and was blockaded by the Allies. In 1943, however, it joined the Committee of National Liberation, and the blockade was lifted. In 1946 it became a French overseas département (département d'outremer), and its inhabitants, whatever the color of their skin, are now French citizens with the same rights and duties as the people of mainland France.

ADMINISTRATION. – The overseas département of Martinique is administered in the same way as any other French département. The capital and seat of the Prefecture is Fort-de-France, which is also the administrative heart of the region of Martinique. There are sub-prefectures at Le Marin and La Trinité. The département sends three deputies and two senators to the French Parliament. The Conseil Général of the département consists of 36 representatives of communes and cantons.

POPULATION. – Martinique has a population of 330,000, predominantly of mixed blood, the descendants of French settlers, African slaves and Asian indentured laborers. Only a small percentage of the population – most of whom belong to the Roman Catholic Church – are of pure European descent. Six socio-ethnic groups can be distinguished in Martinique: (1) the "Békés" or "Blancs-Pays", in France

also called Creoles, who are whites born on the island; (2) persons of pure negro blood; (3) mulattoes, the largest group in the population, who in Martinique are usually lighter-skinned than in Guadeloupe; (4) Indians; (5) descendants of Arab immigrants, mainly from Syria and Lebanon; and (6) the "Blancs-France", whites from France, most of whom are only temporarily on the island and have little real connection with it.

All Martiniquais, whatever the color of their skin or ethnic origin, are equal in the eyes of the law, although complaints are sometimes heard from the colored population that whites are given preference in appointments to key positions, for example in the public service. There is no racism, and the various population groups get on well together. If there are occasional declarations in favor of self-government, or if radical parties sometimes seek to use skin color as a pretext for promoting their political purposes, this is inevitable in a democracy, and must be countered by the government with positive achievements and arguments. There has so far been no call for independence from France even among the main opposition groups, no doubt because all parties are well aware that the loss of the French social services, and of subsidies and imports from France, would bring the island to the verge of ruin.

With some 777 inhabitants to the sq. mile (300 to the sq. km), Martinique is a very densely populated territory; and if account is taken only of land suitable for human habitation the figure is as high as 1450 to the sq. mile (560 to the sq. km). The excess of births over deaths in the 1950s and 1960s was so high that in Martinique today, as in Guadeloupe, every other inhabitant is under 20. The annual rate of population increase is about 2.3%, with the mortality rate continuing to fall as a result of improved hygienic measures. At present, however, there are signs of a gradual slowing down of the rate of increase, since the government is promoting family planning and is also resettling many Martiniquais in more thinly populated territories such as French Guyana. Many have also voluntarily emigrated to France, where in Paris alone there are some 200,000 blacks from the Antilles.

The high density of population creates serious problems for the larger towns, in particular Fort-de-France. Roughly a third of the population live in the capital. There is a steady drift from the land into the towns. Unemployment, particularly among young people, is high, and this foments discontent. And even the island's social services and well-developed educational system – 98% of children go to school and illiteracy is down to under 10% – do little to help.

The French government is making great efforts to deal with these problems, but in the present state of the world economy no short-term solutions are in sight.

ECONOMY. – Until the end of the last war agriculture was the most important element in the economy and practically the only source of income for the population; and it still employs 50% of the working population. In the past a leading part was played by sugar-cane growing and the associated industry of rum distilling, but on Martinique as on other Caribbean islands the sugar industry is in a state of crisis. Cane-sugar production is becoming increasingly uneconomic and unable to compete with cheaper beet sugar. Sugar-cane is grown on some 20,000 acres, supplying only two factories which produce 15,000 tons of sugar. Sugar-cane products account for only 10% of the island's exports.

A corner of the harbor, Fort-de-France (Martinique)

Martinique rum, regarded as one of the best in the world, is still in great demand. Yearly production amounts to over 2 million gallons, most of it exported.

Banana plantations now take first place in Martinique's agriculture, with a crop of 300,000 tons in 1978, mostly exported to France and other EEC countries. Bananas account for half the island's exports. The crop is always vulnerable to weather conditions (e.g. hurricanes).

Since the last war increased attention has been given to the growing of pineapples (a fruit which was known to the Arawaks in pre-Columbian times). Recently there has been an increase in vegetable growing, and exports of egg plants and cucumbers have been rising. The island is still unable, however, to supply its own requirements of vegetables, which are flown in from Europe and sold at European prices.

Stock-farming is of relatively little importance, with some 50,000 head of cattle and 5000 sheep. Here too supplies must be imported to meet domestic needs.

Fishing is practiced only on a small scale, often with antiquated techniques and poor catches. Again imports are necessary, and much of the fish eaten in Martinique comes from Brittany or Normandy.

The development of **industry** has been promoted by the government on a considerable scale in recent years as a means of providing employment. Some 20 new projects have been carried through, including an oil refinery, canning plants, factories producing consumption goods and workshops making craft articles. The main industrial area is near Le Lamentin, SE of Fort-de-France.

Tourism has played an increasing role in the economy. Martinique now has accommodation for some 3000 visitors, compared with only 400 in 1965 – most of it in luxury hotels catering to Americans. – In the past hotel rates were often so high as to frighten off many visitors, but the situation has now changed and it is possible to find accommodation in the smaller hotels (often run by Creoles) at reasonable rates within the purse of the ordinary visitor. A new golf-course has been laid out and new moorings provided for sail boats. The Club Méditerranée has a luxurious establishment near Le Marin, and simpler accommodation can be found in the Latitude holiday village.

**Fort-de-France (0–590 ft/0–180 m; pop. 115,000), chief town and economic center of Martinique and the seat of the Prefecture of the département, lies in the western half of the island on the N side of the Baie de Fort-de-France. The town's central situation and its magnificent anchorage offered optimal conditions for the construction of a harbor; and the port of Fort-de-France is still a primary element in the town's life and an economic factor of major importance both to the town and to the island as a whole. This busy and lively town – a port of call for many cruise ships – reaches up into the foothills of the Pitons du Carbet in the N, so that some of the suburban districts command extensive views of the bay. During the last 30 years the population of Fort-de-France has been increasing at a feverish rate – indeed it has more than doubled over this period – and there is no sign of any pause in this development. Approximately 80% of the working population of Martinique live in and around the town, and a third of the island's total population is crowded into a relatively small area between Schoelcher in the W and Le Lamentin in the E. The problem is aggravated by the continuing drift of population from the land. Industry, administration, banking and agriculture are all concentrated around the capital, now almost threatened with suffocation.

HISTORY. – The town is named after Fort St-Louis, the fort commanding the harbor entrance, which was built during the governorship of Jacques du Parquet (1639). The first settlers were Dutch Protestants and Jews expelled from Brazil; but they were so beset by hostile Indians and disease that only a few survived. Soon afterwards the French, recognizing the strategic advantages of the situation, began the construction of the present town, then known as Fort Royal (1669). In

1676 Governor Baas moved his official residence to the new town, which in 1681 became capital of the island and of the French Antilles. In the course of the 18th c. Fort Royal, laid out on a geometric plan, expanded to fill the area between the fort and the Rivière Madame (i.e. the present town center). Particular attention was given to the draining of the swamps which had given the town a reputation for unhealthiness, and a drainage canal was cut for this purpose, broadly following the line of the present-day Boulevard du Général-de-Gaulle. The development of the town suffered repeated setbacks as a result of floods, hurricanes, earthquakes and an epidemic of yellow fever. During the periods of British occupation (1762, 1809) Fort Royal lost its role as capital of the island. Its name was changed during the French Revolution to Fort-République and later to République-Ville, and finally in 1802 it was renamed Fort-de-France by Napoleon. In 1839 400 inhabitants of the town lost their lives in an earthquake, and in 1890 it was almost completely destroyed by fire. After the catastrophic eruption of Mont Pelé in 1902 which wiped out St-Pierre, then the island's largest town, Fort-de-France developed rapidly, growing from a population of 10,000 at the turn of the century to 40,000 in 1936: a trend which continued after the Second World War and is still evident.

SIGHTS. – The central feature of the town is the tree-planted *Place de la Sayane, gay with flowers from all over the island, which is surrounded by hotels, restaurants and cafés and is bounded on the W by the business quarter of the town with its lively shopping streets. Here, immediately after sundown, the people of the town gather for the glass of punch which in Martinique

Statue of Belain d'Esnambuc, Fort-de-France

usually replaces the *pastis* of the home country. The girls who stroll past the cafés and shops are often claimed to be the prettiest in the Caribbean; there is much animated conversation and discussion, and the people give themselves up to the *douceur de vivre*. On special occasions and public holidays the square is the scene of processions, parades and events of all kinds. At the NW corner of the square stands a *statue in Carrara marble of Empress Joséphine, the Martinique-born wife of Napoleon I; a relief on the base depicts Joséphine's coronation in Notre-Dame in Paris. At the SW corner, near the landing-stage used by the launches which land passengers from the cruise ships, is a statue of *Belain d'Esnambuc*, leader of the French settlers who landed on Martinique in 1635. At the S end of the square, commanding the harbor, stands Fort St-Louis, surrounded by water on three sides.

Cathédrale St-Louis, Fort-de-France

From the statue of Joséphine, Rue de la Liberté runs SW past the Head Post Office to the *Musée Départemental de la Martinique, which gives an interesting picture of the early settlement, history and customs of the island. Particularly notable are the exhibits of Arawak and Carib material.

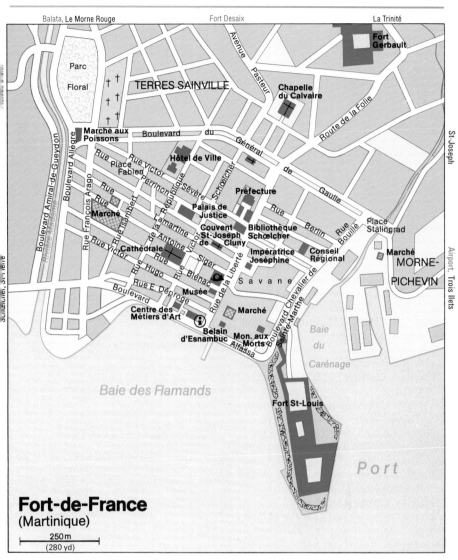

Balata, Le Morne Rouge · Fort Desaix · La Trinité

Fort Gerbault
Parc Floral
TERRES SAINVILLE
Chapelle du Calvaire
Marché aux Poissons
Boulevard du Général
Hôtel de Ville
Rue Place Fabien
Rue Victor
Parrinon
Rue François Arago
Boulevard Allègre
Boulevard Amiral-de-Gueydon
Rue
Marché
Rue Lamartine
Rue Antoine Victor
Rue Victor Hugo
Cathédrale
Palais de Justice
Préfecture
Couvent St-Joseph de Cluny
Bibliothèque Schœlcher
Impératrice Joséphine
Conseil Régional
Rue Berlin
Rue Boullé
Place Stalingrad
Marché
MORNE-PICHEVIN
Siger
Rue Blénac
Savane
Boulevard Rue E. Déproge
Musée
Centre des Métiers d'Art
Belain d'Esnambuc
Mon. aux Morts
Marché
Rue de la Liberté
Boulevard Alfassa
Rue Chevalier de Sainte-Marthe
Baie du Carénage
Baie des Flamands
Fort St-Louis
Port
St-Joseph
Airport, Trois Ilets

Fort-de-France
(Martinique)

├─── 250 m ───┤
(280 yd)

Rooms A and B are devoted to the early Arawak period, and contain the very fine pottery which demonstrates the artistic skill of these pre-Columbian Indians. Rooms D to G, continuing chronologically from the preceding rooms, display material of the later Arawak period and Carib sculpture and stone axes. Room H is concerned with the history of slave-owning. Rooms I and J are devoted to the people of Martinique, with costumes, implements, instruments and furniture, as well as displays illustrating the way of life and folk traditions of the island. Room K is concerned with the early Indian inhabitants of Martinique, and also depicts the present-day descendants of the original population, who came to the Antilles from Guyana and Venezuela, in their domestic setting.

At the far end of Rue de la Liberté, in the Boulevard d'Alfassa (on right, obliquely across from the landing-stage), is the **Office du Tourisme**. Farther along the Boulevard d'Alfassa, on the **Baie des Flamands** (named after the first Dutch settlers), the **Centre des Métiers d'Art**

displays and sells local handcrafts of fine quality. Just beyond this is Rue Victor-Schoelcher, one of the town's principal business and shopping streets, which leads to the **Cathédrale St-Louis**, re-built in 1978 to the design of the 19th c. architect Henri Pick. Previous churches on this site all fell victim to the ravages of war or natural catastrophes. The new church, built to be earthquake-proof, has fine stained glass (restored) and contains the tombs of leading Martinique figures.

Around the Cathedral is the **shopping center**, which offers a wide range of French luxury articles – perfume, spirits, culinary delicacies, jewelry, etc. – at very advantageous prices. Here too visitors will be tempted by a great variety of souvenirs and gift articles, including the popular headscarves and kerchiefs, dried fishes, shell necklaces, tortoiseshell articles, Creole jewelry, dolls and much else besides.

NW of the Cathedral the *Fruit and Vegetable Market (*Marché*), reached either by Rue Blénac or Rue Siger, is the scene of lively activity every morning – fragrant with exotic spices and overwhelming the European visitor with its profusion of tropical fruits. Adjoining the vegetable market is a smaller meat market. Some 220 yd/200 m farther W is the Rivière Madame, crowded, particularly in the early morning, with colorful fishing boats landing the catches made during the night. To the N, on the banks of the river, can be found the Fish Market (*Marché aux Poissons*), where an impressive selection of Caribbean fish and crustaceans are offered for sale. Immediately E of the Fish Market is Place Clémenceau, from which the Boulevard du Général-de-Gaulle runs E. Some 330 yd/300 m along this busy traffic artery, on the right, stands the modern Cultural and Administrative Centre. Turning right beyond this into Rue de la République and passing the Old Town Hall (*Hôtel de Ville*), a building of the colonial period, we come into Place Volny, to the left of which is the Law Court (Palais de Justice), and beyond this a small garden with a *statue of Victor Schoelcher*. Continuing towards Rue de la Liberté and turning left, we reach the *Schoelcher Library (*Bibliothèque Schoelcher*), a building in Romanesque-Byzantine style designed

by Henri Pick for the Paris Exhibition of 1880. To the N, facing the Library, is the Prefecture. – Above the town to the N are two old forts, *Fort Gerbault* and *Fort Desaix*.

> Warning. – Walkers venturing off the roads in the Fontaine-Didier area and the Case-Navire valley should keep a careful look-out for the highly venomous pit viper (French *trigonocéphale*), a relative of the rattlesnake which is relatively common in these areas. In an effort to combat these snakes mongooses were released all over Martinique; but these small predators, which are particularly fond of snake meat, are unwelcome visitors in populated areas, since they break into hen-runs and cause havoc there, as well as killing lizards and birds.

SURROUNDINGS of Fort-de-France. – From the surburban districts on the slopes of the hills and the immediate hinterland there are fine views of the town and the bay. Particularly to be recommended is a trip to the *Plateau Didier, a residential area which is reached by taking the Schoelcher road (N 2) and turning right into D 45. For some miles the road is lined with magnificent villas, many of them in luxurious colonial style with tropical gardens of breath-taking beauty, planted with exotic trees and gay with splendid colorful flowers. D 45 ends at the Fontaine Didier, a mineral spring, the water of which is much esteemed (bottled for use as table water).

Another sight in the immediate vicinity of Fort-de-France is the *church at *Balata* (by Wulfleff, 1928), which is modelled on the Sacré-Cœur in Paris. Situated amid a riot of tropical vegetation with the Pitons du Carbet as a backdrop, it seems quite out of place in this setting, but it is worth seeing as a curiosity – particularly since the road to it (N 3, signposted to Morne-Rouge) affords a succession of fine views of Fort-de-France.

3 miles/5 km W of Fort-de-France lies Schoelcher, a fishing village with a beach, the nearest to the capital. 1¼ miles/2 km beyond this is the beach of *Anse Collat*, at Fond-Lahaye. The beaches in this area, however, are not among the cleanest on the island, since the proximity of the capital is reflected in increasing pollution. The beaches on the peninsula S of Fort-de-France are to be preferred (accessible by motorboat from the town center).

Le Lamentin (65 ft/20 m; pop. 23,000), 4½ miles/ 7 km E of Fort-de-France on N 1 (expressway) is, like Schoelcher, now part of the Fort-de-France metropolitan area near which the largest industrial complex on the island can be found. At *La Californie*, half way between Fort-de-France and Le Lamentin, there is an oil refinery. Fort-de-France's international airport is situated S of Le Lamentin.

Fort-de-France to St-Pierre, returning via Morne-Rouge and the Route de la Trace (42 miles/68 km). – Leave Fort-de-France on N 2, going W.

3½ miles/5.5 km: Schoelcher, named after the Alsatian-born French minister who secured the abolition of slavery. In recent years this fishing village

Schoelcher Library, Fort-de-France

has developed into a residential suburb of the capital, thanks to a beautiful beach, excellent recreational facilities and a good anchorage in the *Case-Navire* bay.

The PARC NATUREL REGIONAL DE LA MARTINIQUE is not one continuous nature park but is a comprehensive term covering a number of separate areas under statutory protection and the bodies responsible for looking after them. The main features of interest in the Regional Park include the volcanic region in the NW of the island, with a Botanic Garden at Fonds-St-Denis and an Arboretum some 9 miles/15 km N of Fort-de-France on N 3; almost the whole of the southern highlands, with the Montravail forest N of Ste-Luce; and the Caravelle peninsula E of La Trinité, with the ruined Château Dubuc and a sport and recreation center in the Baie du Trésor.

Information: **Parc Naturel Régional de la Martinique,**
Caserne Bouillé,
Rue Redoute du Matouba,
F-97200 **Fort-de-France;**
tel. 72 19 30.
Office Départemental du Tourisme, Fort-de-France.

$4\frac{1}{2}$ miles/7.5 km: **Case-Pilote** (sea level; pop. 1800), one of the oldest settlements on the island, named after a Carib chief who was well disposed to the French and was called by them Pilote. It has an 18th c. Baroque church.

4 miles/6 km: **Bellefontaine** (sea level; pop. 1800), a village of fishermen and peasant farmers. Above the village (to right) is the *Panorame Verrier*, a fine lookout point.

$\frac{3}{4}$ mile/1 km: **Fond-Capot**, where the first Governor of the French Antilles, Baas, is buried.

An attractive detour can be made from here on D 20 to **Morne-Vert** (1300 ft/400 m), in the region known as **Petite Suisse** (Little Switzerland), notable for its lush green landscape and its magnificent view of the Pitons du Carbet.

4 miles/6.5 km: **Le Carbet** (sea level; pop. 3100), where Columbus and Belain d'Esnambuc are believed to have landed. The economy of this little town centers on its two rum distilleries. At the near end is the holiday village of *Latitude, a chalet settlement with an easy-going, almost family atmosphere.

The road continues along the coast, passing *Anse Turin*, where the painter Paul Gauguin lived in 1887.

2 miles/3.5 km: *St-Pierre (sea level; pop. 6200), the former capital of the island, which was totally destroyed by an eruption of Mont Pelé in 1902.

On the morning of May 8, 1902 a devastating explosion of Mont Pelé razed to the ground the oldest and finest town on the island, often called the "Paris of the Antilles". A cloud of burning gas with a temperature of over 3600 °F/2000 °C and a devastating rain of ash and stones blanketed the town and turned this flourishing little metropolis into a place of desolation and death. The population of over 30,000 died within minutes, leaving only one survivor, a prisoner named Siparis who was protected by the walls of his underground cell. Siparis later received a pardon and for some years was one of the sideshows in Barnum's Circus in the United States.

The catastrophe which destroyed St-Piere did not come as a complete surprise. For some years increased volcanic activity had been observed on Mont Pelé, and 14 days before the eruption earth tremors and unusually strong emission of steam gave further warning. On April 25 the first light rain of ash fell on the area around the town, and on April 30 there was a further fall of ash, accompanied by a dull rumbling within the volcano. Then at the beginning of May a shower of ash fell on the town itself for the first time; the rivers and streams in the area swelled to unprecedented size, and there was some loss of life. All wildlife, particularly the birds, had left the area some days before, but no one in the town heeded these warnings – least of all the municipal authorities, who were engaged in preparing for an election on the fateful May 8, which happened to be Ascension Day.

After the catastrophe the town never recovered its former importance, and all attempts to restore it to its earlier splendor failed. The present-day town has the air of an overgrown village, with mean little houses, huts and ruins in place of its former splendid colonial buildings.

Two parallel one-way streets form the town center. At the entrance to the town is a statue of the American vulcanologist *Frank A. Perret*, who founded the Vulcanological Museum here. In Rue Victor-Hugo, on right, stands the *Cathedral*, rebuilt after the catastrophe, with a small churchyard containing the graves of notable local families. 550 yd/500 m beyond this we find the *Musée Volcanologique*, with documents and pictures showing the old town and various items recovered by excavation. The violence of the eruption is demonstrated by such exhibits as molten glass, distorted flat-irons, twisted nails and metal parts, and a number of clocks which all stopped at the same time. – Beyond this are the **remains of the theater**, which was built at the end of the 19th c. on the model of the Grand Théâtre in Bordeaux; only a few walls and staircases and part of the stage remain to bear witness to its former splendor. N of the theater is *Siparis's prison*. A stone bridge of 1766 which survived the catastrophe leads into the Quartier du Fort. To the left, on the seafront stands a monument to *Belain d'Esnambuc*, founder of the French colony, on the site of the fort which he built after landing on Martinique in 1635. Farther N are the ruins of the *Eglise du Fort* (1640), the first church built on the island.

Excursion to Le Prêcheur and Anse Céron ($8\frac{1}{4}$ miles/13.5 km). – Continue NW from St-Pierre below the barren slopes of Mont Pelé, crossing the *Rivière Sèche* and the *Rivière Chaude*.

3 miles/5 km: the **Coffres-à-Morts**, a group of limestone hills from which the last Caribs are said to have thrown themselves to their deaths rather than surrender to the whites.

The road continues along a sunbathed but inhospitable stretch of coast.

$2\frac{1}{2}$ miles/4 km: **Le Prêcheur**, one of the oldest villages on the island, with an attractive church. Here François d'Aubigné, later Mme de Maintenon and wife of Louis XIV, spent part of her childhood.

Beyond this are some miles of steeply scarped coast.

3 miles/4.5 km: **Anse Céron**, with a beautiful beach. (NB: there is often dangerously heavy surf). Here and off the little island of La Perle there are good diving grounds.

From here a footpath (11 miles/18 km) leads to Grand'Rivière (see below).

Above St-Pierre N 2 climbs up the foothills of Mont Pelé.

4½ miles/7.5 km: *Le Morne-Rouge (1475 ft/450 m; pop. 5500), a little town and popular resort on the southern slopes of the volcano. It was destroyed by Mont Pelé in 1902, four months after the main eruption wiped out St-Pierre.

N 3 continues S over the plain of *Champ Flore*, with large pineapple plantations.

5 miles/8 km: **Deux-Choux**, amid luxuriant tropical forest, from which D 1 runs W to St-Pierre and E to Gros-Morne.

Alternative route from St-Pierre to Deux-Choux via Fond-St-Denis (8½ miles/14 km).

Soon after leaving St-Pierre there are magnificent views of the town, the sea and Mont Pelé. In 4 miles/6 km a road branches off on the right to the **Observatoire du Morne des Cadets**, where a constant watch is kept on the volcanic activity of Mont Pelé. From the observatory there are superb panoramic *views. The road continues through the deep gorges known as the *Porte d'Enfer* ("Gate of Hell") to Deux-Choux.

From Deux-Choux to Fort-de-France N 3 is a narrow asphalted road, which for most of the way follows a winding course through dense tropical forest. It is known to the local people as the* **Trace** or **Route de la Trace**.

1¼ miles/2 km: highest point on the Trace (2133 ft/650 m). From here there is a path to the *Pitons du Carbet.

The walk to the Pitons du Carbet takes about 8 hours. The route is steep and difficult, suitable only for experienced mountain walkers. Here too a watch must be kept for venomous snakes. The walk is best done in a group or with a guide. Route: via the *Piton Boucher* (3511 ft/1070 m), the *Piton Lacroix* (3924 ft/1196 m) to the *Piton de l'Alma* (3626 ft/1105 m) and then back to the Trace, or via the *Piton Daumaze* (3639 ft/1109 m) to the Colson Psychiatric Clinic.

The Trace continues to **Les Nuages**, with a plantation of the flamingo flower (*Anthurium*), and then passes the Psychiatric Clinic.

5 miles/8 km: **Maison de la Forêt**, on the edge of the *Arborétum de la Donis*. 1¼ miles/2 km beyond this is the spa of *Absalon*, with chalybeate mineral springs (86 °F/30 °C).

Then on via the **Camp de Balata** (1475 ft/450 m), from which there are magnificent views over the island, and past Balata church (see above, Surroundings of Fort-de-France) to –

7½ miles/12 km: **Fort-de-France**.

Fort-de-France to Le Morne-Rouge, Basse-Pointe and Grand'Rivière and back via La

Trinité and Gros-Morne (92 miles/148 km). – From Fort-de-France to Le Morne-Rouge on the Route de la Trace, described above, and on to –

20 miles/32 km: **Petite Savane**, where the road to the Aileron and Mont Pelé goes off.** Mont Pelé (4584 ft/1397 m) is the only active volcano on the island, though there are no outward signs of volcanic activity (no smoke, no fumes, no rumbling noises). Molten lava accumulates in the vent and the surface layer hardens; then when the pressure within the vent becomes too high the volcano explodes as it did in 1902.

Ascent of Mont Pelé. – 2 miles/3 km from Petite Savane there is a large car park, above the first mountain hut (2690 ft/820 m) and close to the television transmitter. From here there is a strenuous climb up a steep slope, now overgrown with vegetation, to the *Aileron* (3635 ft/1108 m), an outlier of Mont Pelé, with a fine view of the Caribbean and the Pitons du Carbet. The route continues along the rim of the crater to the *Calvaire* (4003 ft/1220 m) and on to the second hut; then downhill, bearing left, and up again to the volcanic cone of 1902 (4462 ft/1360 m). 440 yd/400 m W is a shelter which provides protection in bad weather. The main peak, also known as *Le Chinois* (4584 ft/1397 m), may then be climbed from the N. From the summit there are superb distant **views, extending in clear weather to the neighboring islands. Return to the car park by the same route.

From Petite Savane the road pursues a winding course to the NE, with fine views of the Atlantic coast.

5½ miles/9 km: **Ajoupa-Bouillon** (pop. 1900), a settlement founded in the 17th c., with a church of 1848. From here a rewarding trip can be made to the *Gorges de la Falaise*, amid lush tropical vegetation. At some points the track runs along the river bed. Waterproof footwear is essential.

1½ miles/2.4 km beyond this N 3 runs into N 1: turn left. The road passes the ruins of the *Habitation Capot*, an old sugar factory and plantation, and through a fertile area in which sugar-cane, bananas and pineapples are grown.

3 miles/5 km: **Basse-Pointe** (sea level; pop. 4400), the chief place on the northern Atlantic coast. Many Indians settled here in the mid 19th c., and this has left its mark in the form of a temple and some of the local customs.

3 miles/5 km: **Macouba** (sea level; pop. 1900), a banana-, coffee- and tobacco-growing center.

Beyond this is one of the most magnificently scenic stretches of road on the island, with views of the Atlantic and, in clear weather, of Dominica.

6 miles/10 km: *Grand'Rivière (sea level; pop. 1300), a pretty fishing village in a superb setting, with huge breakers rolling in from the Atlantic.

From Grand'Rivière there is a well-maintained path through luxuriant tropical forest to Anse Céron. At some points it is possible to find a way down to secluded beaches on the NW coast.

From Grand'Rivière return to the junction of N 3 and N 1 (13 miles/20.5 km) and continue SE on N 1.

4½ miles/7 km: **Le Lorrain** (sea level; pop. 8700), with a large beach (though bathing is dangerous on account of the heavy surf). Above the town is a residential school for 2000 children. Remains of buildings of the pre-Columbian period can be seen in the neighborhood.

Warning. – Bathing between Grand'Rivière and Marigot is dangerous because of the very heavy surf, and in many places it is prohibited.

3 miles/5 km: **Marigot** (sea level; pop. 3800), an old fishing village in which some new building is going on.

The road then runs along the *Anse Charpentier*, with a beautiful but not over clean sandy beach, and past the *Monastère de Fond St-Jacques*, a former Dominican monastery with a historic sugar factory which now houses a Center of Ancient Indian Studies. Visit recommended.

5 miles/8.5 km: **Sainte-Marie** (sea level; pop. 20,000), with a conspicuous white church of 1851. From the *Ilet*, an islet which can be reached at low tide on a narrow sandbank, there is an attractive view of the bay.

6 miles/9.5 km: **La Trinité** (sea level; pop. 11,000), in a sheltered bay, with a trim seafront promenade and 19th c. buildings.

Excursion to the *Caravelle peninsula (7 miles/ 11.5 km). – This narrow finger of land extending NE into the Atlantic is notable for the variety of its vegetation and the diversity of its coastal scenery. The E side is bleak and rocky, while the S side is gentle and attractive. The eastern part of the peninsula is a nature reserve. From the *Phare de la Caravelle* (489 ft/ 149 m), a lighthouse erected in 1861, there are magnificent distant *views. Ruins of *Château Dubuc*, an old plantation house. Facilities for swimming and other water sports at *Tartane*.

From La Trinité take N 4, which leads W through fertile country (pineapple plantations, etc.).

6 miles/9 km: **Gros-Morne** (pop. 10,000), situated on a hill. From here D 1 runs NW to the Montagne du Lorrain and Deux-Choux, at the beginning of the Route de la Trace (see above). N 4 continues to **St-Joseph** (pop. 11,000), on a winding road through lush tropical vegetation and in 14 miles/22 km reaches **Fort-de-France**.

Fort-de-France to Pointe du Bout, Le Diamant and Le Marin and back via Le Vauclin, Le François and Le Robert (95 miles/153 km). – From Fort-de-France the road runs E and then SE past the industrial area and airport of Le Lamentin.

12½ miles/20 km: **Rivière-Salée** (pop. 7200), named after the river which flows through the territory of the commune and reaches the sea a little way W of the town in the *Baie de Génipa*, an offshoot of the Baie de Fort-de-France. At the mouth of the river is an interesting bird sanctuary.

Turn right into D 7, which leads W to –

4½ miles/7.5 km: **Les Trois-Ilets** (sea level; pop. 3000), often claimed to be the prettiest village in Martinique. It takes its name from the little rocky islets off the *Pointe-aux-Pères*.

Birthplace of Empress Joséphine

Here in 1763 was born *Marie-Josèphe Tascher de la Pagerie*, better known as Napoleon's wife, the **Empress Joséphine** (d. 1814 at Malmaison). The little town still has many memories of Joséphine and her family, including the church in which her parents were married and she herself was baptized. The house in which she was born is now a museum, with various mementoes, and visitors are shown around some of the rooms.

3 miles/5 km: **Pointe du Bout**, now a regular little tourist center, with a marina, a number of luxury hotels and some beautiful beaches (sometimes artificially laid out). Nearby is a good 18-hole golf-course. From Pointe du Bout there are regular motorboat services to Fort-de-France.

Now return to D 7 and continue W to *Anse à l'Âne*, with a beautiful beach, a hotel and a shell museum; then S through hilly country to –

10½ miles/17 km: **Les Anses-d'Arlets** (sea level; pop. 3100), a popular resort, with beautiful beaches at *Grande Anse* and *Petite Anse*, crystal-clear water, magnificent vegetation and a very dry climate.

The road becomes narrower and climbs to 1300 ft/ 400 m, and then descends to the *Petite Anse du Diamant* and the *Pointe du Diamant*, from which there

View of Diamond Rock

is a good view of the* *Rocher du Diamant (590 ft/ 180 m), a steep-sided little rocky islet 1¼ miles/2 km off the coast.

In 1804 and 1805 the Rocher du Diamant (Diamond Rock) was the scene of a curious naval conflict between British and French forces.

During the fighting between British and French forces which went on intermittently at this period the British succeeded in landing on the rock a party of 200 sailors, with cannon and other arms, declared that the rock was now a warship (HMS "Diamond Rock") and bombarded any French vessel which came too close. For 17 months all French attacks were repelled, and finally the French had recourse to a stratagem. Learning through an indiscretion that the defenders of the rock were beginning to weary of their isolation, they caused a boat laden with rum to run aground on Diamond Rock. This had the expected effect: the British forces made short work of the rum, and thereafter the French had no difficulty in taking the rock.

7 miles/11.5 km:* Le Diamant (sea level; pop. 1700), one of the oldest villages on the island, in an incomparable setting, with a beautiful sandy beach and a view of Diamond Rock. From here a boat can be rented to go to the rock – though the crossing can sometimes be rough.

The road now continues E through an arid region of tropical scrub to a road intersection at *Les Coteaux*, from which one can turn N to Fort-de-France: turn right into the south-bound road.

9 miles/14.5 km: Trois-Rivières, with a beautiful beach and a noted rum distillery.

3½ miles/5.5 km: Sainte-Luce (sea level; pop. 4100), a fishing village with another beautiful beach. From here a short trip can be made to the *Forêt de Montravail*, with *Carib rock engravings* (signposted). From *Lépinay* there is a fine panoramic view.

Carib rock engravings, Martinique

4 miles/6 km: Rivière-Pilote (pop. 12,000). At the far end of the town are a number of huge erratic blocks (brought here in prehistoric times by glacial action). 2 miles/3 km NW, at the *Habitation Lescouet*, is a small private zoo.

Beyond Rivière-Pilote D 18a runs S to *Anse Figuiers*, which has excellent facilities for water sports.

6 miles/10 km: Le Marin (sea level; pop. 6000), in the Cul-de-Sac du Marin, an inlet with a beautiful sandy beach and a good anchorage for sailing craft.

Excursion to the Grande Anse des Salines (8½ miles/13.5 km) and the Savane des Pétrifications. – Take the road which runs S to Sainte-Anne. In 4½ miles/7 km a road goes off on the right to *Les Boucaniers*, with a fine public beach (charge) and a Club Méditerranée site. Sainte-Anne (sea level; pop. 3000) is the most southerly village on the island and a holiday resort popular with local people as well as visitors. It has an excellent beach, facilities for water sports and riding, a camp site, etc.

> **Warning.** – In this area, as in other Caribbean regions, the manchineel tree (French *mancenillier*) is fairly commonly found. This is a highly poisonous member of the spurge family, with fruits resembling small green apples. The French forestry authorities are attempting to eradicate these trees, and in many areas have marked them with red paint as a warning. The manchineel tree should not be touched.

Farther S is the *Grande Anse des Salines*, one of the best beaches on the island. From here the *Savane des Pétrifications*, a fascinating forest of petrified trees, can be reached on foot. To the E is the beautiful beach of *Anse Tràbaud*.

From Le Marin the road runs N through a region of scrub.

7 miles/11 km: Le Vauclin (sea level; pop. 8000), sometimes called the "capital of the South". It has a beach and facilities for water sports, as have the *Anses Macabou* to the S.

The road continues N. To the W rises the *Montagne du Vauclin* (1654 ft/504 m), the highest point in the southern part of the island.

9 miles/15 km: Le François (sea level; pop. 16,000), from which boat trips can be made to the small offshore islands.

6 miles/10 km: Le Robert (sea level; pop. 15,000), with one of the best bays on the island.

From Le Robert N 1 runs SW to Le Lamentin and –

12½ miles/20 km: Fort-de-France.

Mayaguana

Bahama Islands
Commonwealth of the Bahamas

Area: 110 sq. miles/285 sq. km.
Population: 800.
Administrative center: Nassau (on New Povidence).
Vehicles travel on the left.

ⓘ Ministry of Tourism,
Nassau Court,
P.O. Box N 3220,
Nassau,
Bahamas;
tel. (809) 322 7505.
See also Practical Information.

RECREATION and SPORT. – Sailing, deep-sea fishing, scuba diving, snorkeling, swimming, shooting, walking.

AIR SERVICES. – Scheduled services to Nassau (New Providence).

SHIPPING. – Mail boat and freighter services from Abraham's Bay to Nassau by way of Acklins, Crooked Island and Long Cay.

Some 300 miles/483 km SE of Nassau is *Mayaguana, the most easterly island in the Commonwealth of the Bahamas. It is one of the few islands to have preserved its original Indian name.

The island, well wooded and relatively well suited for agriculture, was uninhabited until 1812, after which it was only gradually settled by incomers from the neighboring Turks Islands. Still barely opened up to tourism, the island is a favorite of yacht-owners seeking a quiet and relaxing vacation, who can still find here unspoiled beaches and excellent fishing.

The chief town on the island is **Abraham's Bay**, on the S coast. – On the W coast are *Pirate's Well* and *Betsy Bay*, which offer good views of the **Mayaguana Passage** between Mayaguana and Acklins. – The island's airfield is part of a US Air Force Base.

See also **Bahamas.

Mayagüez
Puerto Rico
Estado Libre u Asociado de Puerto Rico
Commonwealth of Puerto Rico

District: Mayagüez.
Altitude: sea level.
Population: 96,200
(i) **Tourism Company of Puerto Rico,**
Edificio Banco de Ponce,
Muñoz Rivera Avenue,
San Juan/Hato Rey, PR 00708,
Puerto Rico;
tel. (809) 754 9292.
See also Practical Information.

HOTELS. – *Mayagüez Hilton*, Marina Sta., 150 r., T, golf; *El Sol*, El Sol Street, 40 r.; *La Palma*, Méndez Vigo Street, 90 r.

RESTAURANTS. – In *Hilton* and *El Sol* hotels; *El Pabellón*, Vista Verde Shopping Center (Italian); *Bolo's Place*, Guanajibo Playa; *Mesón Español*, Guanajibo Shopping Center (Spanish).

NIGHT CLUBS. – A number of private clubs, for which it is necessary to pay an annual subscription (usually quite moderate) to gain admittance.

SHOPPING. – Shops around the Alcaldía, and two large shopping centers, the Vista Verde Center and the Guanajibo Shoping Center, where the goods on offer include local handcrafts, embroidery, woodcarving and rum.

RECREATION and SPORT. – Swimming and sunbathing, sailing, various water sports, deep-sea fishing; tennis, riding, etc.

AIR SERVICES. – Regular flights to San Juan and Santo Domingo (Dominican Republic).

*Mayagüez, charmingly situated on the W coast of Puerto Rico and on the western fringes of the Cordillera Central, is primarily an industrial and university town. Alongside its modern quarters and its busy shopping centers it still preserves with its narrow side streets and elegant residential districts the charm of old Puerto Rico. It has a yachting and commercial harbor which is steadily increasing in importance.

HISTORY. – Columbus passed this way on his second voyage (1493), when he is said to have landed briefly near Mayagüez to take on water. At the beginning of the 16th c. the conquistador Juan Ponce de León conquered the island and decimated the Indian population, belonging to the Taino tribe, a branch of the Arawaks. The town was founded in 1760; its name means "place of the great waters" in the language of the Indians. Since then Mayagüez has shared the destinies of the rest of the island, with no particular incidents of note. During the past 20 years it has enjoyed an industrial boom, as a result of Puerto Rico's increasingly close association with the United States and the consequent efforts to decentralize industry.

SIGHTS. – The hub of the town's life is the beautiful ***Plaza Colón**, with a *statue of Columbus* and 16 other bronze statues which originally came from Barcelona. On the W side of the square stands the **Alcaldía** (Town Hall), on the E side a *Roman Catholic church*. Going E from the square and turning N into Calle Luna Ruta, we come in some 660 yd/600 m to the ***Estación Experimental Agrícola Federal** (Federal Agricultural Experimental Station), a large research center with an impressive collection of tropical plants from all over the Caribbean. To the NW, on Route 108, is the **Universidad de Puerto Rico de Agricultura y**

Plaza Colón, Mayagüez (Puerto Rico)

San Germán, once Puerto Rico's most important town after San Juan, is the main seat of the Inter-American University, which has more than 8000 students. SW of San Germán in the Bahía de Boquerón is the *Playa de Boquerón (Boquerón Beach), one of the finest beaches on the island.

Some 45 miles/72 km W of Boquerón, in the Mona Passage (Canal de la Mona) between Puerto Rico and Hispaniola, is the little Isla Mona.

S of Boquerón stands the *Faro de Punta Jagüey, a lighthouse erected to warn shipping of the dangerous rocks and currents off the double headland of Punta Jagüey/Cabo Rojo. In the vicinity are salt-pans which are worked to produce salt. 9 miles/15 km E of Punta Jagüey is the pretty fishing village of Parguera, and *Phosphorescent Bay, notable for the intensity of the marine phosphorescence to be seen here. At points where the sea is churned up by wave movement it appears to be illuminated by countless tiny dots of light.

Artes Mecánicas (University of Puerto Rico for Agriculture and Mechanical Arts), attached to which is an atomic research facility with a reactor. Farther out **Mayagüez Zoo**, run by the Puerto Rico Recreational Development Company, has a large collection of exotic birds and reptiles, a children's zoo, a museum and a park.

> **Marine phosphorescence** is a phenomenon caused by the accumulation of huge numbers of the minute transparent circular organisms known as flagellates, living just below the surface of the sea, which occur in this area in particular concentration. Waves or other disturbances of the water, caused for example by a boat or a swimmer, trigger off a metabolic process which leads to an emission of light. The phenomenon can be observed, in less striking form, on other Caribbean islands.

SURROUNDINGS. – 4¼ miles/7 km from the town on Route 2 a road leads W to the beautiful Anasco Beach. Farther NW is another fine beach, the Playa Tres Hermanos. From here a road runs via the little fishing town of Rincón to the *Punta Higuera, the most westerly point on the island, a favorite resort of surfers. Then via Aguada (pop. 26,000) to *Aguadilla (pop. 46,000), in Aguadilla Bay, where Columbus is said to have landed. Aguadilla has an excellent beach, good hotels and a lighthouse. N of the town, on the picturesque *Punta Borinquén, is an 18-hole golf-course. From the nearby airport there are regular flights to San Juan. The road continues via Isabela (pop. 30,000), with a beautiful beach near Punta Sardina, to Quebradillas (pop. 16,000), another beach resort with good sport and recreational facilities.

19 miles/30 km E of Mayagüez, at the beginning of the *Ruta Panorámica which runs through the interior of the island from W to E, we come to the little town of Maricao (fish hatcheries), surrounded by hills rising to 2600 ft/800 m. Farther E along the Ruta Panorámica is the *Monte del Estado, or Maricao State Forest, a statutorily protected area of tropical forest at an elevation of 2625 ft/900 m, with excellent facilities for visitors (footpaths, picnic areas, viewpoints).

An attractive trip from Mayagüez is to the Cabo Rojo lighthouse, to the S. The road runs via Poblado Sábalos and comes in 6 miles/10 km to Hormigueros, with the pilgrimage church of Nuestra Señora de Montserrat, which attracts large numbers of pilgrims on September 8. A few minutes' drive beyond this is Cabo Rojo (pop. 26,000), once the lair of the dreaded pirate Roberto Cofresí. To the E of Cabo Rojo, on the Río Guanajibo, San Germán (pop. 28,000) has attractive Spanish houses of the 16th and 17th c. and the little Porta Coeli church (early 17th c.), dedicated to the town's patron saint, St Germanus of Auxerre.

See also **Puerto Rico.

Montego Bay
Jamaica

Parish of St James.
Altitude: 0–330 ft/0–100 m.
Population: 60,000.
ⓘ **Jamaica Tourist Board,**
Cornwall Beach,
Montego Bay,
Jamaica;
tel. 952 4425
See also Practical Information.

HOTELS. – *Chatham Beach, 101 r., SP, T, beach, golf; *Half Moon, 190 r., SP, T, golf, beach; *Holiday Inn, 520 r., SP, T, golf, beach; *Montego Beach and Sunset Lodge, 125 r., SP, T, golf, beach; *Rose Hall Inter-Continental, 508 r., SP, T, golf, beach; *Round Hill, 111 r., SP, T, golf, beach; *Royal Caribbean, 165 r., SP, T, beach; *Tryall Golf Beach Club, 41 r., SP, T, golf, beach; Airport Hotel, 44 r., SP; Bay Roc, 120 r., SP, T, beach; Beach View, 36 r., SP; Blue Harbour, 24 r., SP; Buccaneer Inn, 45 r., SP; Carlisle Beach, 55 r., SP; Casa Montego, 125 r., SP; Chalet Caribe, 28 r., SP, beach; Coral Cliff, 32 r., SP; Doctor's Cave Beach, 75 r., SP; Harmony House, 23 r., SP; Holiday House, 14 r., SP, T, beach; Mahoe Bay Beach, 20 r., SP, T, beach; Malvern Gardens, 26 r., SP, T; Miranda Hill, 40 r., SP, T; Montego Bay Racquet Club, 60 r., SP, T; Montego Bay Club Resort, 97 r., SP, T; Montego

Gardens, 24 r., SP; *Ocean View*, 12 r.; *Richmond Hill Inn*, 23 r., SP; *Royal Court*, 25 r., SP; *Seawind Beach Resort*, 318 r., SP, T, beach; *Sign Great House*, 27 r., SP, T; *Spanish House*, 15 r., SP, beach; *Toby Inn*, 28 r., SP; *Trelawny Beach*, 350 r., SP, T, beach; *Upper Deck*, 109 r., SP; etc. – Numerous GUEST-HOUSES and HOLIDAY APARTMENTS.

RESTAURANTS in most hotels; also *Diplomat*, *Admiral's Inn*, *Calabash*, *Front Porch* and *Town House*.

NIGHT SPOTS. – There is a rich and varied night life. There are good floor shows in the night clubs of the *Holiday Inn* and *Rose Hall Inter-Continental Hotel* and in the *Banana Boat*.

SHOPPING. – A wide range of local handcrafts can be found in a number of galleries and specialized shops, in the *Crafts Market* at the corner of Strand and Creek Streets and in the *Crafts Boutique* at Cornwall Beach. – Luxury goods can be bought at advantageous prices in the *free port* (passport must be produced).

ART GALLERIES (a selection). – *Budhai's Gallery*, 9 Fort Street; *Gallery of West Indian Arts*, Orange Street; *Montego Gallery*, Half Moon Hotel; *Lester's Gallery*, Anchorage, Belmont; *Poulette's Gallery*, Market Street; *Stacy's Art Gallery*, 31 Union Street; *West Indian Gallery of Art*, Church Street.

RECREATION and SPORT. – Sailing, deep-sea fishing, water-skiing, parasailing, scuba diving, snorkeling; golf, riding, tennis, polo, cricket, walking.

AIR SERVICES. – INTERNATIONAL: scheduled services from Montego Bay to Atlanta, Chicago, Miami, New York and Philadelphia (USA), Montreal and Toronto (Canada) and London. – DOMESTIC: schedule services from Montego Bay to Kingston, Negril, Ocho Rios and Port Antonio.

SHIPPING. – Some cruise ships from Miami, Port Everglades (USA), San Juan (Puerto Rico) and other West Indian islands call at Montego Bay.

RAIL SERVICES. – Daily service of diesel trains from Montego Bay to Kingston (travel time 5 hours).

*Montego Bay, Jamaica's second largest town and the chief town of the parish of St James, lies near the western end of the N coast. Originally a sugar-exporting port, it has developed into the tourist capital of Jamaica, chiefly because of its excellent beaches. It is the regional center of western Jamaica.

The town lies on its beautiful bay, within a protective fringe of reefs, and is surrounded by wooded hills. The older part of the town, with areas of slums, extends around the relatively small Central Business District. To the N, along the coast and on the fringes of the Miranda Hills, is the hotel zone, bounded on the N by the International Airport. To the S, in an area of reclaimed swampland around the mouth of the Montego River, is the modern commercial and industrial district, with the free port. Near the town center are the middle-class and superior residential areas, some of them extending up the lower slopes of the hills. On the outskirts are a number of shanty towns which have grown up since the 1930s. As a result of the rapid growth of the town, through development of the hotel trade and of industry, a high percentage of the population are now incomers living in the slums.

SIGHTS. – The central feature of the town is *Sam Sharpe Square. On the SW side of the square stands the *Court House*, an early 19th c. colonial-style building. At the NE corner is the *Cage*, a small building of the same period which was used for the

Doctor's Cave Beach, Montego Bay (Jamaica)

detention of runaway or delinquent slaves. The *Strand Theatre* is situated at the corner of Church Street and Strand Street.

To the SE, at the corner of Church Street and St Claver Street, stands *St James's Parish Church* (18th c.), a Georgian building which was lovingly restored after suffering earthquake damage in 1957. Opposite it is the old *Town House*. In Church Street are a number of restored Georgian houses. Farther S, on the way to the *railway station* (diesel trains to Kingston; trips in the Governor's Coach, see below), we find the lively and colorful *Crafts Market, with a wide range of local handcraft items.

To the N of Sam Sharpe Square, in Fort Street, are the new *Court House*, the Post Office and the *City Centre Building*, with the town's largest shopping center. Nearby are the *Library* and the *Cord Theatre* and a little way N the *Roman Catholic church*.

At the near end of the hotel zone rises the imposing *Fort Montego*. Along the seafront and on the slopes of the Miranda Hills are many luxury hotels set in beautiful grounds, with a wide range of entertainment and sports facilities. The best beaches in this area are *Walter Fletcher Beach*, *Cornwall Beach*, *Sunset Lodge Beach* and above all **Doctor's Cave Beach, which in the early years of this century acquired a reputation for the curative properties of its water and attracted large numbers of distinguished visitors. – Farther N is the **Sir Donald Langster International Airport**, the island's largest airport, which handles some 700,000 passengers every year.

The area of swampland which formerly extended to the S of the mouth of the Montego River has been reclaimed in recent years and is now occupied by *Montego Bay Freeport, with a deep-water harbor, a duty-free area and an extensive industrial zone. The stretch of coast to the S and the Bogue Islands are still covered with mangrove swamps.

EXCURSIONS. – The Jamaica Tourist Board runs evening coach excursions to the Great River, SW of the town, with *canoe trips on the torch-lit river and open-air parties (barbecue, folk displays).

The Tourist Board also organizes weekly rail trips on the diesel-driven *Governor's Coach** to the *Appleton Sugar Factory*, in the center of the island. The train runs through magnificent tropical scenery and numbers of plantations, stopping at the most interesting spots.

Montego Bay to the Cockpit Country via Falmouth and Duncans (round trip 85 miles/ 137 km). – Leave Montego Bay on A1, which runs NE through the hotel zone and past the airport.

5½ miles/9 km: *Maho Bay*, with a fine reef-sheltered beach. Inland, occupying the site of old sugar plantations, is the golf-course of the *Ironshore Golf Club*. Farther E are beautiful beaches with large hotels and, inland, the *Half Moon Golf Club*.

Rose Hall Great House, Montego Bay

4½ miles/7 km: *Little River*, with a beautiful beach. To the S stands **Rose Hall Great House** (1760), one of the finest mansions in the West Indies; formerly the center of a huge sugar plantation, it has been converted into a luxury hotel with its own golf-course. A palatial three-story house approached by a flight of steps, it is set in carefully tended gardens and contains valuable 18th c. furniture. This was the home of the legendary Annie Palmer, the "white witch", of whom stories of murder and torture are told. – S of Rose Hall is *Palmyra Hill* (1368 ft/417 m).

6 miles/10 km: *Greenwood Plantation*, another handsome mansion in the old plantation style built by a relative of Elizabeth Barrett Browning. It contains fine furniture and a collection of old musical instruments.

The road continues E past *Flamingo Beach* and the *Salt Marsh*.

7 miles/11 km: *Falmouth* (sea level; pop. 5000), a pretty little fishing port, chief town of Trelawny parish, with handsome 18th c. buildings (restored). Particularly notable is the *Albert George Market*, with an interesting roof structure. The *Court House*, with a portico over the steps leading up to the entrance, is the reconstruction of an earlier building dating from the first half of the 19th c. Two fine churches are the late 18th c. *Parish Church* and the modern *Knibb Memorial Church*. The *Methodist Mansion*, at the end of Market Street, was once the home of Elizabeth Barrett Browning. To the N of the town is the picturesque *Half Moon Beach*; to the S a racecourse. Off the coast are interesting coral reefs.

2 miles/3 km S of Falmouth lies **Martha Brae**, from which there are attractive *bamboo raft trips on the *Martha Brae River*. The nearby Rafter's Village has a variety of recreational facilities.

9 miles/15 km S of Falmouth, in the upper part of the Martha River valley, is *Good Hope Plantation**, an

Bamboo raft on the Martha Brae River

old-established coconut and sugar plantation, with a cattle farm. Well-preserved relics of earlier days are the 18th c. *Great House* (valuable furniture), the huts once occupied by slaves and the old sugar-mill with its water-wheel.

Farther E, between Falmouth and Rock (*Fisherman's Inn restaurant), we find the *Luminous Lagoon*, so called after the marine phosphorescence to be seen here. (On marine phosphorescence, see under Mayagüez.)

5 miles/8 km: *White Bay Beach* (good swimming). Nearby is the village of *Coral Springs* (*Leeming's Steakhouse).

5 miles/8 km: **Duncans**, with the beautiful *Silver Sands Beach*. From here take B 10, which climbs S to –

7 miles/11 km: *Kinloss*. The road now runs W via *Duanvale* to –

6 miles/10 km: *Sherwood Content*. To the SW is the **Cockpit Country**, an area of very striking tropical terrain, sparsely wooded and difficult to reach.

This is a region of regularly alternating limestone cones and funnel-shaped depressions, with "pavements" of sharp ridges and furrows, inhospitable to human settlement and movement. During the Spanish colonial period the fringes of the area were the hiding-place of runaway slaves (Spanish *cimarrones*, English "maroons"), who maintained themselves by raiding the more densely populated parts of the island. The British authorities succeeded in putting an end to these activities only in the latter part of the 18th c.

The road continues SW to –

4 miles/6 km: the *Windsor Caves*, karstic caves with magnificent stalactitic formations. Only two of the caves are readily accessible.

The road now runs NW to two settlements founded after the liberation of the slaves in 1838, *Bunker's Hill* and –

15 miles/24 km: *Wakefield*.

2 miles/3 km: *Hampden Sugar Estate*. This huge sugar-cane plantation is open to visitors. – From here

the road runs W via *Adelphi* into the beautiful valley of the Montego River.

12 miles/19 km: *Sign Great House* (18th c.), an old plantation house, well restored and finely furnished (some furniture of the colonial period), which is now a hotel. There is a bird sanctuary on the site of the old plantation.

7 miles/11 km: **Montego Bay**.

Montego Bay to Black River via Negril (round trip 154 miles/248 km). – Leave Montego Bay by way of Barnett Street, taking a road which runs S and then W along the coast.

16 miles/26 km: **Sandy Bay**, with a fine beach and the famous *Tryall Golf Club* (luxury hotel). An interesting feature here is a huge water-wheel, almost 200 years old, which once irrigated the sugar-cane plantation. The road continues along the reef-fringed coast, past *Maggoty Cove* and *Mosquito Cove*.

9 miles/15 km: **Lucea** (sea level; pop. 4000), chief town of Hanover parish, with a sheltered harbor (export of bananas). To the N of the town stands the 18th c. *Fort Charlotte*. Farther W are two excellent beaches, *Watson Taylor Beach* and *Gull Bay*.

The road continues SW, rounds *North West Point* and passes *Lance's Bay, Cousin's Bay* and *Davis Cove*.

10½ miles/17 km: **Green Island Harbour**, a small sheltered harbor, with the ruins of an old fort.

The road continues S past *Orange Bay* with its protective reefs to the mangrove swamp known as the **Great Morass**, now in process of being drained, and further to the W coast, with the almost 7½ mile/12 km long *Negril Beach*, which takes in two bays, *Bloody Bay* and *Long Bay*. Since 1977 it has developed into one of Jamaica's largest resort complexes, drawing considerable numbers of visitors with its idyllic beach

Stalagmites in the Bamboo Cave

of white sand, its excellent hotels and its varied facilities for sport and recreation (sailing, deep-sea fishing, scuba diving, snorkeling, wind-surfing, water-skiing; golf, riding, tennis, walking).

11 miles/18 km: **Negril** (hotels: *Coconut Cove, 46 r., SP, T, golf, beach; *Negril Beach Village, 280 r., SP, T, beach; *Negril Beach Club, 95 r., SP, T, beach; Chorela Inn, 10 r., SP, T, beach; Sundowner, 25 r., beach; T-Water Cottages, 40 r., beach; Negril Villas, 60 r., SP, T. – Several holiday apartments. – Restaurants: Chicken Lawish, Rick's Café), an attractively situated little town, formerly a fishing village and in earlier days a notorious pirates' lair. Off the coast are a number of old wrecks bearing witness to past conflicts between European colonial powers in the Caribbean. Visitors can take interesting trips from Negril in a glass-bottomed boat.

The road continues SE up the valley of the Negril River through pastureland and large plantations of sugarcane. After passing through *Springfield, New Hope* and *Little London* it comes to –

18 miles/29 km: **Savanna-la-Mar** (sea level; pop. 15,000), situated near the mouth of the *Cabaritta River*. One of the oldest settlements in Jamaica, it is now the main town of Westmorland parish and an important sugar port. – 5 miles/8 km N is *Frome*, with one of the largest and most modern sugar factories on the island.

From Savanna-la-Mar A 2 runs SE via *Ferris Cross* to –

11 miles/18 km: *Bluefields*, an old pirate haunt, with a beautiful beach and an old fort. Then on past *Crab Pond Bay, Banister Bay* and *Parker's Bay* to –

8 miles/13 km: *White House*, which also has a beautiful beach.

12½ miles/20 km: **Black River** (sea level; pop. 5000), an attractive little colonial town, main settlement in the parish of St Elizabeth, situated at the mouth of the river from which it takes its name.

17 miles/28 km SE of Black River we come to the dyllic *Treasure Beach*. 8 miles/13 km farther SE is *Lover's Leap*, an overhanging cliff almost 650 ft/200 m high about which romantically sad tales are told.

From Black River take A 2, which runs N, roughly parallel to the *Black River* (formerly the home of large numbers of crocodiles), flowing in the opposite direction through an extensive area of swamp.

10 miles/16 km: **Middle Quarters**, still a center of the river fisheries. The road now turns E along the impressive *Bamboo Avenue*, with dense growths of bamboo forming a long green tunnel.

6 miles/10 km: *Lacovia Tombstone*, with two 18th c. tombs. From here a road runs N to –

7 miles/11 km: **Maggotty**. In the surrounding area are rich deposits of bauxite.

To the E is the fertile Interior Valley of **Appleton**. N and NE of Maggotty is the district of *Look Behind*, on the fringes of the Cockpit Country, once the hiding-place of runaway slaves, who were finally repressed by British troops after a bloody guerrilla war. – **Accompong**, 8 miles/13 km N of Maggotty, was originally founded by the runaway slaves ("maroons").

From Maggotty the route continues W to –

7 miles/11 km: **Ys**, on the river of the same name. From here B 6 leads NW into the wild and romantic valley of the *Great River* and continues to –

19 miles/31 km: **Anchovy**, with the well-known *Rocklands Feeding Station*, a bird sanctuary (with hummingbirds among many other species), where every evening visitors can feed the birds.

8 miles/13 km: **Montego Bay**.

See also **Jamaica.

Montserrat
Lesser Antilles
Windward Islands
British crown colony

Area: 39 sq. miles/101 sq. km.
Population: 13,000.
Administrative center: Plymouth.
Vehicles travel on the left.

ⓘ **Montserrat Tourist Board,**
P.O. Box 7,
Plymouth,
Montserrat, B.W.I.
See also Practical Information.

HOTELS. – PLYMOUTH: *Coconut Hill Hotel*, 10 r.; *Emerald Isle Hotel*, 10 r.; *Olveston House*, 6 r.; *Wade Inn*, 10 r. – ON OLD ROAD BAY: *Vue Pointe*, 68 r., SP, T, golf; *Caribelle*; *Hideaway*. – Many HOLIDAY APARTMENTS.

RESTAURANT. – *Rose and Compass*, Plymouth.

PUBLIC HOLIDAYS. – New Year's Day. – Good Friday. – Easter Monday. – Whit Monday. – Queen's

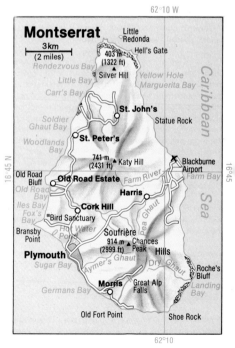

Montserrat

A farm on the E coast of Montserrat

Birthday (June). – *August Monday* (Commemoration of the Liberation of Slaves). – *Christmas Day*. – *Boxing Day* (December 26).

EVENTS. – Cricket matches (February to June); barbecues; sailing trips.

RECREATION and SPORT. – Swimming and sun-bathing, deep-sea fishing, scuba diving, snorkeling; golf, tennis, cricket, riding, walking.

AIR SERVICES. – Daily flights to and from Antigua (Coolidge International Airport); occasional flights to Nevis and St Kitts.

SHIPPING. – Irregular boat services to neighboring islands.

The hilly island of *Montserrat, in the inner arc of the Lesser Antilles, lies in latitude 16°45′ N and longitude 62°12′ W. Three volcanoes of different ages shape the topography of the island which is dissected by numerous rivers and streams.

The lower parts of the island, formerly occupied chiefly by sugar plantations, are now covered with scrub and grassland, while the steep slopes of the volcanic hills have a dense mantle of tropical rain forest. The larger settlements are all on the leeward side of the island, in the valleys between the volcanoes and on the fringes of the central coastal plain on the windward side.

HISTORY. – Columbus discovered the island in 1493 and named it after the similarly shaped mountain massif of Montserrat NW of Barcelona in Catalonia (Spain). In the first half of the 17th c. Irish Catholics driven out of Ireland by Cromwell settled on Montser-rat, leaving their mark on the island's place-names. For more than a hundred years France and Britain contended for possession of the island, but in 1783 it finally became British. From 1871 to 1956 it was administered as one of the British Leeward Islands, and from 1958 to 1962 it belonged to the short-lived Federation of the West Indies. In 1967 it became a crown colony with domestic self-government, under a Governor representing the Queen.

POPULATION and ECONOMY. – Over 90% of the population are blacks or mulattoes who, like the whites, belong chiefly to the Anglican, Methodist and Roman Catholic churches. – Between 1939 and 1970 there was a considerable fall in population as a result of emigration caused by the poor economic prospects on the island. Montserrat's economic difficulties have been somewhat relieved only in recent years, largely because of the establishment of small industrial concerns and a number of vocational and higher educational institutions. New jobs have also been created by the building boom resulting from the growth of tourism and the influx of retired people from the United States. At present there are some 150 hotel beds on the island. Each year about 15,000 visitors come to Montserrat.

On the sheltered W coast is the island's capital, **Plymouth** (pop. 4000), with a core of Georgian houses partly built with stone brought from Dorset in England in the form of ballast.

SIGHTS. – By the harbor is the colonial-style **Post Office and Treasury**, which produces the attractive stamps sought after by collectors. Nearby is the *War Memorial*, with a bell-turret. – Higher up, in Parliament Street, are the 18th c. *Court House* and the 19th c. *Methodist Church*. At the S end of the street a colorful market is held on Saturdays. The *Handicraft*

War Memorial and Post Office, Plymouth

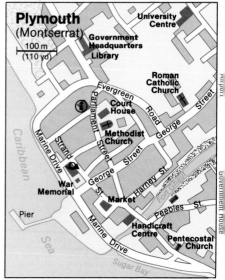
St. Anthony's Church, Pan Am Memorial

Centre close by displays and sells attractive local craft products. – On the E side of the town is the 18th c. *Roman Catholic Church*, with a school.

Outside the town, to the N, a *memorial stone* marks the spot of the first British settlement. – *St Anthony's Church* (Anglican; 17th, 18th and 19th c.), which during the fighting between Britain and France suffered several changes in its functions and architectural form, contains two silver communion chalices said to have been presented by freed slaves. In the adjoining churchyard stands the *Pan Am Memorial*, commemorating an aircraft crash on Chance's Peak in September 1965.

To the NE, on the lower slopes of Richmond Hill, an area of villas and vacation homes, is the **Montserrat**

Historical Society Museum, housed in the tower of an old sugar-mill, with exhibits illustrating the natural history and way of life of the island, including an interesting collection of postage stamps.

Farther NE is *St George's Hill* (1165 ft/ 355 m), with the ruins of an old fort and a large radio transmitter.

SURROUNDINGS of Plymouth. – To the S of the town, above *Sugar Bay* (beach of fine sand), stands **Government House**, which has an ornate gable. The house can be visited between 10 a.m. and noon. Farther S is *Fort Barrington* (18th c.), once a major element in the island's defences.

Hot Water Pond to the NW is of geological interest. Farther NW, on *Fox's Bay* (beautiful beach), is a bird sanctuary.

4 miles/6 km N of Plymouth is **Old Road Estate**, a vacation and retirement colony with a golf-course and other recreational facilities. Nearby are two excellent beaches, *Road Bay* and *Iles Bay*. 1¼ miles/2 km farther N we come to *Runaway Ghaut*, a defile which was the scene of a bloody battle between British and French forces. A little way N of this is a small beach in *Woodlands Bay*. The road continues through the village of **St Peter's** and comes in 3 miles/5 km to *Carr's Bay* and, just beyond this, *Little Bay*, two popular beaches.

3 miles/5 km S of Plymouth, on Old Fort Point, are the extensive installations of *Radio Antilles*, one of the leading transmitters in the Caribbean area.

The road from Plymouth to *Blackburne Airport*, the island's little airfield on the E coast, passes through **Harris**, with an Anglican church (19th and 20th c.), rebuilt after suffering severe destruction in a hurricane in 1928 and an earthquake in 1930.

WALKS and CLIMBS (strenuous; suitable clothing essential, local guide advisable in some cases). – **Plymouth to the Soufrière.** – SE of Plymouth is the *Soufrière*, the youngest and most southerly of the

Site of the first British settlement

island's volcanoes, with a number of separate peaks covered by dense tropical rain forest. On its highest point, *Chance's Peak* (2999 ft/914 m), a Pan Am aircraft crashed in September 1965. On the lower peaks of *Gage's Soufrière* to the W and *Galway's Soufrière* to the SE are impressive solfataras, pools of mud and hot springs.

Plymouth to the Great Alps Fall. – 2½ miles/4 km S of Plymouth lies the little settlement of Morris, from which a track runs up the deeply indented valley of the White River and climbs to the *Great Alps Fall*, a tropical waterfall which plunges over a 72 ft/22 m high rock into a picturesque pool.

Carr's Bay to Silver Hill. – From Carr's Bay the route runs up NE to the hamlet of **Rendezvous**, above Rendezvous Bay, and continues to the summit of *Silver Hill* (1322 ft/403 m), the highest point on the oldest and most northerly of Montserrat's volcanoes. On the coast to the NE of the hill is *Hell's Gate*, a bizarre rock formation.

Harris to the Centre Hills. – From Harris the route leads into the pleasant valley of the *Farm River* and then climbs through tropical rain forest to the summit of *Katy's Hill* (2431 ft/741 m), the highest point of the second oldest of the three volcanoes, centrally situated between the other two.

Mustique
See Grenadines

Nassau
Bahama Islands
New Providence
Commonwealth of the Bahamas

Altitude: 0–135 ft/0–41 m.
Population: 135,000.
(i) **Tourist Information Center,**
Bay Street,
Nassau,
Bahamas;
tel. 59171–2.
Branch offices on Prince George Wharf and at Nassau International Airport.
See also Practical Information.

HOTELS. – Out of the enormous range of hotels only a small selection can be given here.

CITY CENTER: *Sheraton British Colonial Hotel*, 225 r., SP, T; *Buena Vista*, 6 r.; *Graycliff*, 10 r., SP; *Parliament*, 20 r.; *Parthenon*, 20 r.; *Prince George*, 47 r.; *Towne Hotel*, 47 r., SP; etc. – WEST BAY STREET: *Atlantis*, 117 r., SP, T; *El Greco*, 26 r., SP; *International Club and Sports Hotel*, 15 r., SP, T; *Mayfair*, 94 r., SP; *New Olympia*, 53 r.; *Ocean Spray*, 30 r.; etc.

CABLE BEACH: *Ambassador Beach Hotel and Golf Club*, 400 r., SP, T, golf; *Bahamas Beach Hotel*, 114 r., SP, T; *Balmoral Beach Hotel*, 200 r., SP, T; *Cable Beach Hotel*, 700 r., SP, T, golf, casino, yacht harbor; *Nassau Beach Hotel*, 400 r., SP, T; *Cable Beach Manor Hotel*, 44 r., SP; *Casuarina*, 38 r., SP; etc.

PARADISE ISLAND: *Britannia Beach*, 252 r., SP, golf; *Club Méditerranée*, 300 r., SP, T; *Flagler Inn*, 250 r., SP, T; *Holiday Inn*, 532 r., SP, T; *Loew's Paradise Island Hotel*, 503 r., SP, T; *Ocean Club*, 70 r., SP, T; *Grosvenor Court Apartments*, 57 r., SP; *Paradise Beach Inn*, 10 r., SP; *Yoga Retreat*, 44 r.; etc.

EAST BAY STREET: *Montagu Beach and Racquet Club*, 30 r., SP, T; *Nassau Harbour Club*, 50 r., SP; *Pilot House*, 123 r., SP; etc.

OUT OF TOWN: *South Ocean Beach Hotel and Golf Club*, South West Road, 120 r., SP, T, golf; *Emerald Beach*, Emerald Beach, 367, r., SP; *Poincinia Inn*, Bernard Road, 27 r.; etc.

Many GUEST-HOUSES and HOLIDAY APARTMENTS.

RESTAURANTS in most hotels; also IN NASSAU CITY: *Androsia*, Cable Beach; *Blackbeard's*, on Harbour; *Boat House*, Paradise Island; *Bridge Inn*, East Bay Street; *Café de la Mer*. On W side of town; *Casuarinas*; *Cornucopia Health Food Bar*, East Bay Street; *Chinese Village Rice House*, Bay Street (Chinese); *East Hill Club*, East Hill; *Lofthouse Club*, corner of George and Marlborough Streets; *Da Vinci*, West Bay Street (Italian); etc. – PARADISE ISLAND: *Bahamian Club* (Bahamian); *Café Martinique* (French) and *Coyoba* (Polynesian), all in Britannia Beach Hotel; *Bräuhaus*, Bird Cage Walk (German); etc.

NIGHT SPOTS in some hotels; also *Banana Boat*, College Avenue; *Dirty Dick's*, Bay Street; *King and Knights Club*, West Bay Street; *Pink Pussycat*, Delancy and Augusta Streets; *Ports of Call*, East Bay Street.

Casinos at Cable Beach and on Paradise Island.

In the waterfront market, Nassau

SHOPPING. – Nassau city center is a very popular shopping area. In *Bay Street* and *Rawson Square* and in the excellently renovated area between Bay Street and *Woodes Rogers Walk* alongside the harbor, which has become famous as *Nassau International Bazaar*, the shops follow one another in almost endless succession. They offer South American craft products, cameras and photographic apparatus, watches, crystal, porcelain, jewelry, Mexican silver, electronic apparatus, linen, French lingerie and perfume, Scottish cashmeres, South American leather goods, spirits and other luxury imported goods at prices which, thanks to tax concessions, are very reasonable. Local handcrafts, in particular articles woven or plaited from palm leaves or straw, can be found in the Straw Market by the harbor and in Rawson Square.

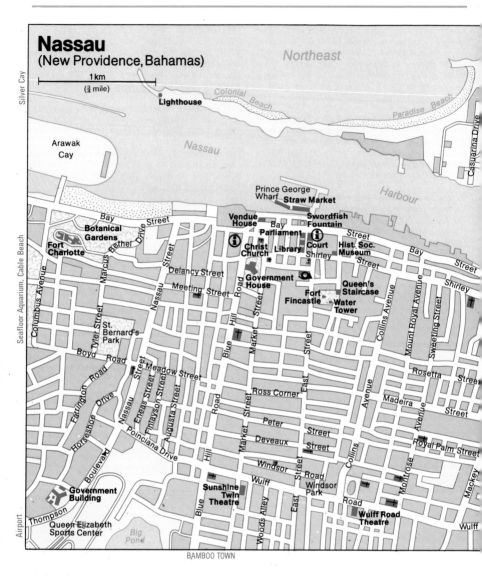

Nassau
(New Providence, Bahamas)

1 km
(¾ mile)

BAMBOO TOWN

EVENTS. – *Supreme Court Opening* (January, April, July, October). – *Red Cross Ball* (January). – *Miami–Nassau Yacht Race* (February). – *Heart Ball* (February). – *Red Cross Fair* (March). – *Miami–Nassau Sailing Race* (March). – *Independence Celebrations* (July). – *Commonwealth Fair* (July). – *Goombay Holiday* (July–August), with displays of goombay dancing, exhibitions, concerts, processions and music in the streets. – *Emancipation Day* (first Monday in August), commemorating the liberation of the slaves. – *Fox Hill Day* (second Tuesday in August), lively celebrations in memory of the freeing of the slaves in Fox Hill, one of the oldest slave settlements on the island. – *Discovery Day Regatta* (October), commemorating the discovery of the Bahamas by Columbus. – *Bahamas Humane Society Annual Dog Show* (November). – *Remembrance Day* (November). – *Miami–Nassau Power Boat Race* (December). – *Flying Treasure Hunt* (end November), followed by a great banquet. – *Junkanoo* (December 26 and January 1), colorful parades in costume.

AIR SERVICES. – INTERNATIONAL: from Nassau International Airport to Baltimore, Boston, Chicago, Fort Lauderdale, Miami, Newark, New York, Philadelphia, Washington D.C. and West Palm Beach (USA), Montreal and Toronto (Canada), Bermuda, London (UK), Frankfurt am Main (German Federal Republic), Luxembourg, Kingston (Jamaica), Port-au-Prince (Haiti), Turks Islands, Guayaquil and Quito (Ecuador) and Lima (Peru).

DOMESTIC: Marsh Harbour and Treasure Cay (Abaco); Andros Town, Mangrove Cay, San Andros and Congo Town (Andros); Chub Cay and Great Harbour Cay (Berry Islands); Alice Town Harbour (Bimini); The Bight (Cat Island); Crooked Island; Governor's Harbour, North Eleuthera and Rock Sound (Eleuthera); George Town (Exuma); Freeport International Airport (Grand Bahama); Inagua (Great Inagua); Deadman's Cay and Stella Maris (Long Island); San Salvador.

SHIPPING. – INTERNATIONAL SERVICES: Cruise ships sail regularly (often several times weekly) from Nassau to Miami (USA), St Thomas (US Virgin Islands), San Juan (Puerto Rico) and in summer also to New York and Bermuda. Occasional services to other Caribbean islands.

DOMESTIC SERVICES: Cruise ships several times weekly to Freeport (Grand Bahama) and weekly to Berry

Salt Cay

Providence   *Channel*

Paradise Island
(Hog Island)

Cabbage Beach

Cabbage Beach

Wenne

Gren
Road
Canal

French
Cloister

Versailles
Gardens

Paradise

Island

Drive

Golf   Course

Beach

Road

eaplane
ase

Hurricane
Hole

Potter's
Cay

Athol Island

Yacht Haven

The Narrows

Bay   Street

Fort
Montagu

Street

Shirley Street
Theatre

Street

Lake
Waterloo

Montagu Bay

Antiquities
Museum

Shirley

Street

Kemp Road

Yonder   Road

Dicks
Point

Eastern

Road

Kemp Road

Village
Road

Road

Richmond Road

Road

St. Andrew's Drive

Commonwealth Street

St. Augustine Monastery, SANDILANDS VILLAGE   Yamacraw Beach

Islands. Mail boats, often several times weekly, to the principal places on the Out Islands (i.e. all the Bahama Islands other than New Providence).

Junkanoo. – On New Year's Day and Boxing Day (December 26) Nassau is the scene of lively and colorful Junkanoo parades. From early morning the streets are taken over by crowds of splendidly costumed and masked figures, singing and dancing to the clamorous tones of *goombay* music – probably an import from West Africa – played by a band of whistles, small bells and rhythmically beaten drums.

The origins of Junkanoo, which is found in similar form in Jamaica and was formerly also known in the southern United States, are not certain, but it seems probable that elements from West African tribal dances brought in by slaves have fused with traditions inherited from the pre-Columbian inhabitants of the Caribbean. An alternative explanation is that the festival was originated by a legendary black slave named John Canoe.

**Nassau, capital of the Commonwealth of the Bahamas, is beautifully situated on the NE coast of the island of New Providence (see entry) amid carefully tended tropical vegetation. It takes its name from William of Orange-Nassau, who became king of the United Kingdom as William III in 1688. The town's long and narrow natural harbor, sheltered by Paradise Island, is one of the principal ports of call of the Caribbean cruise ships and a favorite rendezvous of yacht-owners, sailing enthusiasts, deep-sea fishermen and coral divers.

Nassau's colonial past is recalled by a number of forts and many charming old pastel-colored buildings, often lovingly restored. These are old-style grand hotels, luxurious modern establishments and

Sunset over Nassau Harbour

places of entertainment of all kinds, from modest rum-shops by way of calypso spots to the Casino with its glittering floor show. All bear witness to the long tradition and continuing vigor of the tourist trade in this cosmopolitan town.

SIGHTS. – In **Nassau Harbour** is **Prince George Wharf**, where the cruise ships moor. An old customs hall now houses the colorful * *Straw Market*, one of the largest of its kind in the Caribbean. The market extends into busy Rawson Square, just off the waterfront, in which can be seen the attractive *Swordfish Fountain*. Immediately S, around Parliament Square, are the much photographed colonial-style * **Parliament Buildings**.

Swordfish Fountain, Parliament Square, Nassau

The Parliament Buildings were erected about 1810 under the direction of American Loyalist architects. In the W wing is the *House of Assembly*, and adjoining this the *Senate*, in which Queen Elizabeth II read the speech from the throne on the occasion of her Silver Jubilee in 1977. To the E is the former Colonial Secretariat, now occupied by the Ministry of Tourism. – In front of the House of Assembly stands a fine marble statue of the young Queen Victoria.

Just beyond the Parliament Buildings are the *Supreme Court* and the *Garden of Remembrance*, with a Cenotaph. Close by, an octagonal building of the late 18th c. which was formerly a prison houses the well-stocked * **Public Library**, which contains much valuable material on the history of the town and the island as well as an elaborately carved chair used for ceremonial purposes by the pre-Columbian Arawak Indians. – Farther S are the *Royal Victoria Gardens*, the site of the historic old Royal Victoria Hotel, one of the first of the town's luxury hotels (1861), which flourished particularly in the time of the blockade-runners and liquor smugglers. Higher up is the modern *Post Office* (1971).

To the W, in East Hill Street, are some particularly attractive and well-preserved houses of the colonial period. Still farther W, beyond the bridge known as *Gregory's*

Government House, Nassau

a passage cut through the relatively soft calcareous sandstone at the end of the 18th c. by slave labor. – At the end of this passage is the modern *Princess Margaret Hospital* and farther N the *Historical Society Museum*, with an interesting collection of material on the history of the town and the island.

To the W of Rawson Square is the *Nassau International Bazaar, a shopping center consisting of numerous separate establishments, housed in excellently renovated old buildings, which extends between *Bay Street*, the town's principal business street, and *Woodes Rogers Walk*, on the harbor, where there is a fish, fruit and vegetable market.

Arch which gives access to the parts of the town beyond the hills, is *Government House, an imposing mansion crowning *Mount Fitzwilliam*.

This pink and white classical-style house, built in 1801, is the residence of the Governor-General, the Queen's representative in the Bahamas. – Half way up the long flight of steps leading to the entrance is a fine statue of Columbus. – Sentries stand guard in front of Government House, and there is a colorful Changing of the Guard ceremony on alternate Saturdays.

To the SE, above the Post Office, stands the commandingly situated *Fort Fincastle* (1793), in the shape of a ship's bow; it was built during the governorship of Lord Dunmore. Adjoining is the *Water Tower* (126 ft/38.4 m), from the platform of which there are magnificent panoramic *views.

Below the fort the long *Queen's Staircase*, a flight of 66 steps, leads down into

Queen's Staircase

On the W side of the town center the palatial pink *British Colonial Hotel, on a site once occupied by Fort Nassau (built 1697). Close by, in Bay Street, is *Vendue House*, where slaves were once auctioned, now occupied by the local electricity board. – Farther S, in King Street, stands *Christ Church Cathedral (Anglican), on the site of the first church in the Bahamas (1670).

This graceful church was completed by the Spaniards in 1753, after suffering destruction on a number of occasions, and served as the garrison church. It was enlarged in 1840–41. – The church has fine stained glass, several good pictures and a notable pulpit.

Fort Fincastle

Hurricane Hole yacht harbor, Paradise Island

At the W end of the town, above Arawak Cay, is *Fort Charlotte** (1787–89), another imposing fort built during the governorship of Lord Dunmore. This battlemented stronghold, complete with moat and dungeons, provides an effective backdrop for the *son et lumière* performances which are frequently given here. – Below the fort are the *Botanical Gardens*, with a colorful profusion of tropical plants. – To the W are the *Ardastra Gardens*, in which displays by trained flamingoes are presented. Immediately S is the *Seafloor Aquarium*, a showcase of underwater life where popular displays by trained dolphins are given.

the dolphins in the central lagoon is a daily tourist attraction. On the N coast of the island lies the excellently equipped *Cabbage Beach*. – In the eastern half of the island are the *Versailles Gardens*, laid out in French style with tropical plants and much sculpture and statuary. On higher ground the *French Cloister*, a ruined 14th c. Augustinian monastery, was brought from near Lourdes (France) and re-erected here. – Farther E is the fine *Paradise Golf Course*.

From Paradise Bridge, East Bay Street continues E, passing the busy Yacht Haven, to *Fort Montagu*, built in 1724 to protect the eastern entrance to the harbor. Below the fort is a fine beach. – $\frac{3}{4}$ mile/ 1 km SW, at the corner of Shirley Street and Kemp Road, the *Antiquities Museum*

Paradise Island

From Rawson Square *East Bay Street* runs E along **Nassau Harbour** which is crowded with craft of all kinds, to *Paradise Bridge*, then leads by way of *Potter's Cay* (fish market; huge mounds of shells) to **Paradise Island**, once a millionaires' retreat and now a vacationers' paradise.

The island (4 miles/6 km long and almost $\frac{3}{4}$ mile/1 km wide), formerly known as Hog Island, was acquired in the 1930s by a Swedish industrialist, Dr Axel Wenner-Gren, who began the development of the island – carried on still more vigorously by a later owner, the American financier Huntington Hartford, who gave it the more attractive name it now bears – into a luxury resort with top-class hotels and every facility for recreation. It provided the setting for the James Bond film "Thunderball".

At the far end of the bridge (toll point) is **Hurricane Hole**, a magnificent haven for luxury yachts. – In the center of the island is the *Casino*, one of the busiest gaming houses in the western hemisphere, with a large theater for shows (850 seats). – The feeding of

In the Casino, Paradise Island

contains much interesting material recovered from the seabed; the history of some exhibits is not always known. – Near the intersection of Deveaux Street and Bay Street is the *Pirates Museum, housed in a reproduction of the 18th c. frigate "Bonhomme Richard", with many objects recovered from the wrecks of Spanish galleons and other vessels.

SURROUNDINGS of Nassau. – 3 miles/5 km SE, on Monastery Heights, stands *St Augustine Monastery*, a Benedictine house with a church designed by the monk and architect Brother Jerome. Attached to the monastery are a natural history museum and a monastic school with a model farm. – To the E lies **Sandilands Village**, once the largest settlement of liberated slaves on the island. ¾ mile/1 km farther NE we come to *Blackbeard's Tower*, said to have been occupied by the notorious buccaneer Edward Teach.

1¼ miles/2 km S are the fine *Queen Elizabeth II Sports Centre* and the *Blue Hill Golf Club*. – Close by ***Jumbey Village** is an old Bahamian village reconstructed as an open-air museum. There is an interesting Art Gallery. – 2 miles/3 km farther W is *Bozine Hill* (118 ft/36 m; television tower), from which there are fine views. At the foot of the hill, in Harrold Road, is *Angelo's Art Centre* (local handcrafts).

To the S of the range of hills which slopes down to the S at *East End Point* are *Seabreeze Estate*, *Imperial Park* and *Yamacraw Beach Estate*, suburbs of Nassau.

BOAT TRIPS. – Trips in a glass-bottomed boat from Prince George Wharf to the world-famed ****Sea Gardens**, banks of coral off the eastern tip of Paradise Island with an extraordinary range of underwater life.

4 miles/6 km from Nassau is the idyllic palm-shaded islet of ***Sandy Cay**, often referred to as the "honeymoon island" or "treasure island".

See also ****Bahamas** and **New Providence.**

Navassa

See Jérémie

Netherlands Antilles/ Nederlandse Antillen

See Aruba, Bonaire, Curaçao, Saba, Sint Eustatius and Saint-Martin/Sint Maarten

Nevis

Lesser Antilles
Leeward Islands
St Kitts and Nevis

Area: 36 sq. miles/93 sq. km.
Population: 12,000.
Administrative center: Basseterre (on St Kitts).
Vehicles travel on the left.

ⓘ **Tourist Bureau,**
Main Street,
Charlestown,
Nevis, W.I.
See also Practical Information.

HOTELS. – CHARLESTOWN: *Cliff Dwellers*, 14 r.; *Pinney's Beach Hotel*, 36 r.; *Rest Haven Inn*, 31 r. – GINGERLAND: *Golden Rock*, 10 r.; *Old Manor*, 10 r.; *Zetlands Plantation*, 22 r. – MONTPELIER: *Montpelier Hotel*, 19 r. – NEWCASTLE: *Nisbett Plantation Inn*, 20 r. – Several GUEST-HOUSES and many HOLIDAY APARTMENTS.

RESTAURANTS in the hotels; also IN CHARLESTOWN: *Rookery Nook*, *Nevis Club*, *Cherry Tree*, *Docies*, *Tops Restaurant*, *Arcade* and *Harlem Shelter*.

PUBLIC HOLIDAYS and EVENTS. – *New Year's Day.* – *Statehood Day* (February 27). – *Good Friday.* – *Easter*; horse-races on Easter Monday. – *Labour Day* (first Monday in May). – *Whitsun.* – *Queen's Birthday* (second Saturday in June). – *August Monday* (first Monday in August), commemorating the liberation of the slaves; horse-races. – *Prince of Wales's Birthday* (November 14). – *Christmas Day.* – *Boxing Day* (December 26). – *Carnival* (December 26 to January 2), with parades through the streets.

RECREATION and SPORT. – Sailing, deep-sea fishing, wind-surfing, scuba diving, snorkeling, swimming and sunbathing; tennis, riding; walking, bird-watching expeditions; ball games.

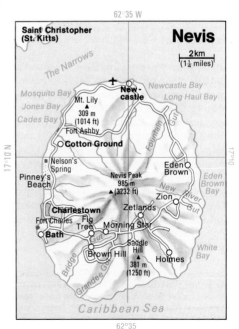

AIR SERVICES. – Regular flights from Newcastle Airport to St Kitts, Antigua and St Croix.

SHIPPING. – Ferry services daily (except Thursday and Sunday) from Charlestown to Basseterre (St Kitts). Occasional charters to some of the neighboring islands.

Nevis (pronounced Neevis), the smaller of the two islands which make up the self-governing state (independent since 1983) of St Kitts and Nevis, within the British Commonwealth, lies 2 miles/3 km SE of St Kitts, separated from it by the channel known as the Narrows, the bottom of which is covered with great expanses of coral reefs. Nevis consists of a single large volcano, Nevis Peak (3232 ft/985 m), which rises exactly in the center of the island and gives it its circular form. In contrast to St Kitts with its monoculture of sugar-cane Nevis produces mainly sea-island cotton and coconuts.

HISTORY. – Both Nevis, called "Ornalie" by the original Indian inhabitants, and St Kitts were discovered by Columbus on his second voyage (1493). In 1607 Captain John Smith landed on the island in order to hang some mutineers, erecting gallows on the beach for this purpose. The island was settled in 1628 from St Kitts. Alexander Hamilton, American statesman and aide to George Washington, was born on Nevis in 1757. The young Horatio Nelson spent some time on the island in the 1780s, when he met and married his wife. During the 18th c., too, John Huggins used the sulphurous water of the island's hot mineral springs to develop a spa establishment which in its day enjoyed a great reputation. During the last two centuries the history of Nevis has broadly been that of St Kitts. Following the decline in sugar-cane cultivation in recent times, some of the dilapidated 18th c. property has been restored and converted into accommodation for tourists.

Charlestown (pop. 2500) is the island's capital. Here on January 11, 1757 was born Alexander Hamilton, who became an aide to George Washington and later a member of the Continental Congress in Philadelphia. To the N of the town is the palm-fringed Pinney's Beach, one of the most beautiful in the Caribbean. Charlestown can also claim to have developed one of the earliest tourist trades in the West Indies, thanks to the hot mineral springs which in the 18th c. drew many visitors seeking a cure for rheumatism or gout.

Alexander Hamilton's birthplace, badly dilapidated, can be found in Low Street, at the N end of the town. In the center of Charlestown are the ferry port (services to Basseterre) and Main Street, the principal shopping street. At the intersection of Main Street

with Prince William Street is the Court House, with the **Public Library**, which contains a small collection of Carib stone engravings and old books on the history of the island. Opposite, in a small garden, is a *War Memorial* to the dead of both world wars. At the S end of the town the *Bath House* (spa establishment, 1778), has five hot baths (107 °F/42 °C) which are still in use. In Jews Street is the old *Jewish Cemetery*, with the graves of the first Jewish merchants to settle on Nevis. – The busy activity of a present-day Caribbean market can be observed on Saturday mornings in the *Public Market* near the harbor.

A TOUR OF THE ISLAND (*c.* 20 miles/32 km) is well worth making both for the sake of the magnificent scenery around Nevis Peak (3232 ft/985 m) and for the features of interest to be seen on the way. 2 miles/3.5 km N of Charlestown, to the S of Cotton Ground a track on the left leads to the *Nelson Spring*, where Nelson is said to have taken on water for his ships before sailing for North America where the War of American Independence was then raging. While the British fleet was at anchor here look-outs took up position in *Ashby Fort*, ¾ mile/1 km N of Cotton Ground, to watch for enemy shipping. – On the N coast is the picturesque village of *Newcastle*, with the island's airfield.

At *Eden Brown*, on the E side of the island, are the ruins of an 18th c. mansion, and 1 mile/1.5 km farther S a disused sugar-mill. – At Morning Star, 2½ miles/4 km E of Charlestown, is the privately owned **Nelson's Museum**, with pictures and mementoes of Nelson. In the neighboring *Fig Tree Village* stands St John's Church, in the registers of which are recorded the birth of Alexander Hamilton and Nelson's marriage to Frances (Fanny) Nesbitt (1787). The marriage took place in the nearby mansion of Montpelier, which belonged to his wife's uncle, then President of the island. Of the old manor house there remain only a few columns.

See also *St Kitts.

New Providence
Bahama Islands
Commonwealth of the Bahamas

Area: 80 sq. miles/207 sq. km.
Population: 135,000.
Administrative center: Nassau.
Vehicles travel on the left.

ⓘ **Ministry of Tourism,**
Nassau Court,
P.O. Box N 3220,
Nassau,
Bahamas;
tel. (809) 322 7505.
Tourist Information Centre,
Bay Street,
Nassau,
Bahamas;
tel. 59171–2.
See also Practical Information.

HOTELS. – See under Nassau.

RECREATION and SPORT. – Sailing, motorboat racing, deep-sea fishing, parasailing, wind-surfing, water-skiing, scuba diving, snorkeling, swimming and sunbathing; tennis, ball games.

Parasailing on Paradise Island, Nassau

Casinos (roulette, craps, blackjack, etc.): *Paradise Island Casino*, Paradise Island; *Playboy Casino*, Cable Beach.

ACCESS. – See under Nassau.

The island of * *New Providence lies in latitude 25° N and longitude 77°25′ W on the S side of the Northeast Providence Channel, which runs W from the Atlantic towards the Great Bahama Bank. It is the most important of the Bahama Islands from the economic point of view and the one which attracts most visitors. In the NE is the excellent natural harbor which favored the development of Nassau. The island is mostly flat, with a landscape patterned by lakes, areas of swamp and pine forests, with a range of low hills (135 ft/41 m)

traversing its northern part. Its excellent beaches, yacht harbors, golf-courses and other facilities for sports and recreation have made it one of the most popular and best equipped holiday areas in the Caribbean.

The island's capital, Nassau (see separate entry), which occupies almost a third of its area, is an important international financial center and conference site.

HISTORY. – Occupied in pre-Columbian times by Arawaks, the island became the second Bitish colony in the Caribbean in 1666. Its first settlement was Charles Town (after King Charles II), later renamed Nassau. During the the 17th and early 18th c. it became a pirates' lair. After the re-establishment of British authority Nassau developed into a central slave market. In 1776 the town was destroyed by United States warships, and six years later was attacked by Spaniards. At the end of the 18th c. many American Loyalists settled on the island. New villages were founded by blacks, particularly after the liberation of the slaves in 1834. During the American Civil War Nassau, and in particular the recently opened Royal Victoria Hotel, became the haunt of blockade-runners and spies, and during the Prohibition period in the United States a center of the illicit liquor trade. Since then the island has become the rendezvous of the world's financial aristocracy, and has been discovered and developed as a tourist resort. Its tourist trade has grown at a tremendous rate, particularly since the Second World War – a trend promoted by the planned development of its beaches and the transformation of Hog Island, off Nassau, into the Paradise Island resort. In 1973 Nassau became capital of the newly established independent Commonwealth of the Bahamas.

TOUR OF THE ISLAND. – Leave *Nassau (see separate entry) by way of West Bay Street. After passing *Highland Park* the road comes in 4 miles/6 km to the luxurious *Ambassador Beach Hotel and Golf Club*, in Goodman Bay (popular beach). Nearby are the *Playboy Casino* and the *Hobby Horse Race Track*, a well-known trotting course. – Just beyond this are the extensive resort facilities of *Cable Beach* which is bounded on the W by *Delaporte Point*. Inland lies little *Lake Cunningham*, its shores edged by mangrove swamps. – 1¼ miles/2 km farther W are *caves* which were once occupied by the pre-Columbian inhabitants of the island. At the turn-off of Blake Road, which runs around the mangrove-fringed *Lake Killarney* to the modern **Nassau International Airport**, we come to *Conference Corner*, with three trees planted by John F. Kennedy, Harold Macmillan and John Diefenbaker in 1962, to commemorate the Bahamas Conference.

The road continues W along *Love Beach* to Northwest Point, off which are fascinating coral gardens (seen from a glass-bottomed boat). – 1¼ miles/2 km S, in *Old Fort Bay, stands the ruined *Old Fort* (17th–18th c.); excellent beach. 2 miles/3 km SW the villa complex of **Lyford Cay** has magnificent amenities, including a golf-course and a marina. Offshore, to the W, is the little islet of *Goulding Cay*, with a lighthouse. – Farther S, on *Clifton Bluff*, can be found the **Clifton Power and Distillery Plant**, the largest power station and water distillation plant on the island.

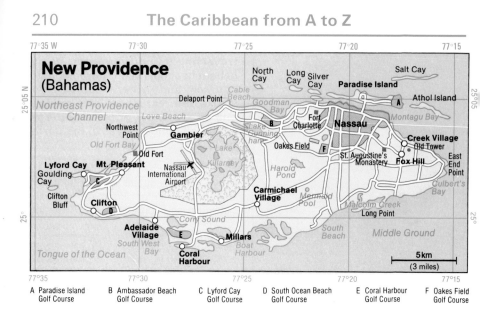

A Paradise Island   B Ambassador Beach   C Lyford Cay   D South Ocean Beach   E Coral Harbour   F Oakes Field
  Golf Course   Golf Course   Golf Course   Golf Course   Golf Course   Golf Course

1¼ miles/2 km E, above the ruins of an old fort, is the **South Ocean Beach** holiday park, with a golf-course. – From here the South West Road continues E through the *Pine Barrens*, a large area of natural forest (pines, casuarinas, palms), with many rare tropical orchids. This is now, however, increasingly being brought under cultivation, as the innumerable drainage channels show. – At the E end of the forested area lies **Adelaide Village**, an attractive little settlement with a beautiful beach originally founded by runaway slaves. Farther E *Coral Harbour*, a popular yacht harbor, is separated from the settlement of **Coral Heights**, a little way inland, by a golf-course. – 2½ miles/4 km E of Coral Harbour is the *Bacardi Rum Distillery*, one of the largest in the Bahamas.

3 miles/5 km E of Adelaide Village we reach the old settlement of *Carmichael Village*, on the S side of the *Government Experimental Farm*, which plays an important part in the development of agriculture in the Bahamas. 2½ miles/4 km beyond this a narrow road goes off on the left to *Hunt's Cave*, a cave with beautiful stalactites. ¾ mile/1 km S of the turn-off to the cave is the *Mermaid's Pool* in a secluded and very picturesque setting.

See also ****Bahamas**.

Ocho Rios

Jamaica

Altitude: 6–65 ft/0–20 m.
Population: 11,000
(i) **Jamaica Tourist Board,**
   Ocean Village Shopping Centre,
   P.O. Box 240,
   Ocho Rios,
   Jamaica;
   tel. 974 2570 and 974 2582.
   See also Practical Information.

HOTELS. – *Inter-Continental*, 357 r., SP, T, golf, beach; *Couples*, 139 r., SP, T, beach; *Jamaica Hilton*, 265 r., SP, T, golf, beach; *Jamaica Inn*, 49 r., SP, T, golf, beach; *Sheraton Ocho Rios*, 385 r., SP, T,

beach; *Sans Souci*, 73 r., SP, T, beach; *Shaw Park Beach*, 118 r., SP, T, golf, beach; *Carib Ocho Rios*, 27 r., SP, T, beach; *Hibiscus Lodge*, 20 r.; *Inn on the Beach*, 46 r.; *Plantation Inn*, 62 r., T; *Silver Seas*, 42 r., SP, T, golf; *Turtle Beach Towers*, 115 r., SP, T; etc. – Many HOLIDAY APARTMENTS and GUEST-HOUSES.

RESTAURANTS in most hotels; also *Moxon's*, Boscobel Lagoon.

RECREATION and SPORT. – Sailing, deep-sea fishing, scuba diving, snorkeling, wind-surfing, water-skiing, parasailing, swimming and sunbathing; golf, tennis, riding, cycling, walking.

AIR SERVICES. – Regular flights to Kingston and Montego Bay; occasional charters to Port Antonio.

SHIPPING. – Ocho Rios is a frequent port of call for cruise ships, mostly from Miami (USA) and San Juan (Puerto Rico).

*Ocho Rios, once a small fishing port, has developed into one of the most frequented tourist centers in Jamaica, particularly since the Cuban revolution diverted a large flow of vacationers from North America to other areas.

The town is attractively situated in a crescent-shaped bay on the N coast; but unfortunately it is now torn between the demands of tourism and an immediately adjacent bauxite terminal. The fallout of reddish bauxite dust and the heavy shipping traffic are having a deleterious effect on the attractions of Turtle Beach in the center of Ocho Rios Bay.

SIGHTS. – Interesting colonial-period buildings are the *Geddes Memorial Church* and the *Anglican Church* to the S of the town. The *Cove Theatre* is also

Beach scene, Ocho Rios

worth a visit. The town's business and shopping area is *Pineapple Place*. To the W of the town lies the *Ruin, an attractive recreation area laid out around the rock terraces of the *Eden Falls*, with buildings in neo-Spanish-colonial style

Ocho Rios to Port Maria (round trip 69 miles/ 111 km). – Leave Ocho Rios on A 4, which runs E along the reef-protected *Mallard's Bay* and *Sandy Beach Bay*, both with beautiful beaches, passing several luxury hotels.

2½ miles/4 km: *Shaw Park, a magnificent tropical park above Shaw Park Beach, a favorite site for the lively parties known as boonoonoonoos.

¾ mile/1 km: **White River Bay**, with *Glitter Beach*, the starting-point of attractive evening boat trips along the *White River*. – 4 miles/6 km S is *Upton Country Club* (golf-course), set in marvellous gardens.

2 miles/3 km: *Frankfort.* – In 1¼ miles/2 km S we reach *Prospect Estate, a large model plantation where interested visitors can see something of the island's agriculture (daily conducted tours in open mini-buses). – To the E is the little *Tower Isle*, with a well-preserved watch-tower of the colonial period.

3 miles/5 km: *Rio Nuevo*, at the mouth of the river of that name. In the 17th c. this was the scene of a battle between Spanish and British forces contending for possession of the island. – The road continues E, passing a number of luxury hotels.

6 miles/9 km: **Oracabessa** (presumably from Spanish, "golden head"; *Golden Head Beach Hotel, 65 r., SP, T, beach), an agricultural center (coconuts, bananas, citrus fruits). To the E of the village is *Firefly*, once the home of the actor and dramatist Noel Coward, who died in Jamaica in 1973.

8 miles/13 km: **Port Maria** (Casa Maria Hotel, 30 r., SP, T), chief town in the parish of St Mary, on the beautiful *Pagee Beach*. It has a number of well-preserved buildings of the colonial period. – The road now turns S, away from the coast.

2 miles/3 km: *Trinity.* – 2 miles/4 km W of Trinity, beyond *Bailey's Vale*, lies the model plantation of *Brimmer Hall (conducted tours daily; shopping center, restaurant), where the growing of bananas and coconuts in particular can be studied.

5 miles/8 km: *White Hall.* – From here take B 2, which climbs towards the S.

Tower Isle, off Jamaica's N coast

3 miles/5 km: *Highgate, a charming artists' colony, surrounded by banana and coconut groves. The road now turns W through hilly plantation country, passes through *Dean Pen*, enters the romantic valley of the *Rio Sambre* and ascends the valley to *Palmetto Grove*, then continues W via *Carron Hall*.

14 miles/23 km: Guy's Hill, in the center of the uplands N of the plain of St Thomas in the Vale.

From here continue N on B 13.

7 miles/11 km: *Lucky Hill*. The road now runs W over the White River and through the settlement of *Goshen*.

9 miles/15 km: the road joins A 3. Near here are large deposits of bauxite.

The road continues N through *Fern Gully, a former river valley 4 miles/6 km long which owes its particular charm to magnificent tree ferns.

7 miles/11 km: Ocho Rios.

Ocho Rios to Discovery Bay (round trip 88 miles/142 km). – From Ocho Rios the road runs W, passing the dusty bauxite-loading installations of the Reynolds concern. The bauxite is brought from the workings by cableway.

Dunn's River Falls

3 miles/5 km: *Dunn's River Falls (c. 605 ft/185 m), one of Jamaica's most popular tourist attractions.

Here Dunn's River surges down over a series of rock terraces and flows into the sea near a beautiful beach. It is possible to walk up and down the *cascades, with pools which offer a refreshing dip. On Thursday afternoons open-air parties ("Dunn's River feasts") are held here.

1¼ miles/2 km: *Roaring River Bridge, one of the few surviving bridges of the Spanish colonial period.

2 miles/3 km: *Drax Hall*, with a large polo ground.

2 miles/3 km: St Ann's Bay, an attractive little place with picturesque old lanes, the chief town of the parish of St Ann. The black nationalist leader Marcus Garvey was born here (statue). To the W of the town can be found the ruins of *Sevilla Nueva, the island's first capital, founded in 1509 by the Spanish Viceroy Diego Colón, whose residence was in Santo Domingo. There is a fine statue of Columbus, which was cast in his native Genoa.

The road continues along the beautiful N coast. The offshore coral reefs were severely battered by Hurricane Allen in the autumn of 1980.

10 miles/16 km: *Runaway Bay (hotels: *Club Caribbean, 116 r., SP, T, golf, beach; *Eaton Hall Great House, 36 r., SP, golf; *Runaway Bay Hotel and Golf Club, 152 r., SP, T, golf, beach; Berkley Beach, 76 r., SP, T, golf, beach; Silver Spray, 19 r., SP), a very modern vacation settlement with a magnificent *beach and a golf-course, which was originally established as an offshoot of Ocho Rios. *Cardiff Hall is a fine 18th c. mansion recalling the heyday of the plantation system on the N coast. Nearby are the *Runaway Caves, with impressive stalactites and stalagmites. Here runaway slaves are said to have taken refuge. In the *Green Grotto* is an underground lake (boat trips).

5 miles/8 km: Discovery Bay, where Columbus is believed to have made his first landing on Jamaica on May 4, 1494. The port established here by the Spaniards under the name of Puerto Seco now has large industrial installations belonging to the Kaiser Bauxite Company – which, as at Ocho Rios, have spoiled some of the neighboring beaches and reduced the teeming underwater life of the coral reefs. The attractive *Columbus Park (3 acres) contains ruined buildings of the Spanish colonial period. On land belonging to Kaiser Bauxite are *Mystery House*, with a small local museum, and the *Kaiser Lagoon* (spring).

6 miles/10 km: *Rio Bueno, a charming little fishing town, now also known for its artists' colony.

From here take B 5, which runs inland (S), with many bends.

8 miles/13 km: *Jackson Town* (road intersection). From here take B 11, which leads E via *Stewart Town* to –

10 miles/16 km: *Brown's Town* (road intersection). Take B 3, which runs S on to the limestone plateau of the *Dry Harbour Mountains, with large expanses of typical karstic landscape and areas of upland grazing.

9 miles/14 km: *Alexandria*. From here take a road which runs E through beautiful scenery, passing *Mount Albion* (2759 ft/841 m) and the village of *Bonneville*, to –

18 miles/29 km: Claremont, a small country town. Continue on A 1, going SE, to –

2 miles/3 km: *Golden Grove*, from which a road runs NE via *Lyford (large bauxite workings, open to visitors) and through Fern Gully to –

12½ miles/20 km: Ocho Rios.

See also **Jamaica.

Peter Island
See Tortola

Isla de Pinos
See Isla de la Juventud

Ponce
Puerto Rico
Estado Libre y Asociado de Puerto Rico
Commonwealth of Puerto Rico

District: Ponce.
Altitude: sea level.
Population: 189,000.

(i) **Tourism Company of Puerto Rico,**
Edificio Banco de Ponce,
Avenida Muñoz Rivera,
San Juan/Hato Rey, PR 00918,
Puerto Rico;
tel. (809) 754 9292.
See also Practical Information.

HOTELS. – *Holiday Inn de Ponce*, Highway 2, 120 r., SP, T, golf; *Meliá*, Plaza Central, 80 r., *San José*, Calle Cristina, 18 r.; *El Coche*, La Rambla, 20 r.

RESTAURANTS. – In *Holiday Inn* and *Hotels Meliá* and *El Coche*; also *El Ferrocarril*, Calle Ferrocarril.

RECREATION and SPORT. – Swimming and sunbathing at El Tuque; sailing, deep-sea fishing; tennis, golf, baseball.

EVENTS. – *Carnival*.

AIR SERVICES. – Daily flights to and from San Juan.

* Ponce, Puerto Rico's second largest town, known as the "Pearl of the South", has preserved its original Spanish character, with old colonial buildings, a Cathedral, a picturesque old fire station, an important museum and two plazas. In more recent times it has acquired a number of modern buildings, shopping centers, hotels and industrial plants which have given it a fresh lease on life. It is also becoming an increasingly popular tourist attraction – either as an excursion from San Juan, combined with very rewarding drives through the Cordillera Central, or because of its yacht harbor, the best on the Puerto Rican S coast.

HISTORY. – The town takes its name from the Spanish conquistador and first governor of Puerto Rico Juan Ponce de León, who landed on the island in 1506 and explored it in the hope of finding the legendary Fountain of Youth. He had no mercy on the Indian population, which was almost completely exterminated. The site of present-day Ponce was occupied in the mid 17th c. by Spanish settlers, who recognized the possibilities of the harbor. A chapel dedicated to the Virgin of Guadalupe was built in 1670, and the town was officially founded in 1692. In subsequent centuries Ponce shared the history of the rest of the island. During the last 25 years it has enjoyed rapid industrial, commercial and tourist development.

SIGHTS. – In the center of the town are two adjoining squares of the colonial period, *Plaza Degetau* and *Plaza Muñoz Rivera* – often known merely as the **Plaza Central** – dominated by the **Cathedral of Nuestra Señora de Guadalupe**. A short distance behind the Cathedral is the gaudily painted ***Parque de Bombas**, an old fire station (1883) which is a favorite

Plaza Central and Cathedral, Ponce

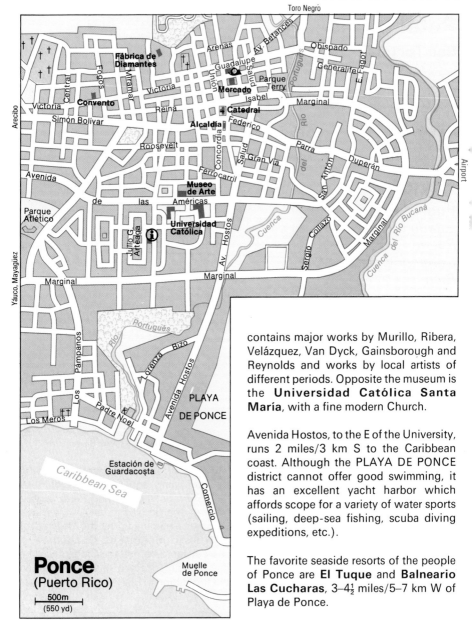

Ponce
(Puerto Rico)

|— 500m —|
(550 yd)

contains major works by Murillo, Ribera, Velázquez, Van Dyck, Gainsborough and Reynolds and works by local artists of different periods. Opposite the museum is the **Universidad Católica Santa María**, with a fine modern Church.

Avenida Hostos, to the E of the University, runs 2 miles/3 km S to the Caribbean coast. Although the PLAYA DE PONCE district cannot offer good swimming, it has an excellent yacht harbor which affords scope for a variety of water sports (sailing, deep-sea fishing, scuba diving expeditions, etc.).

The favorite seaside resorts of the people of Ponce are **El Tuque** and **Balneario Las Cucharas**, 3–4½ miles/5–7 km W of Playa de Ponce.

SURROUNDINGS. – 6 miles/10 km W along the Caribbean coast, beyond El Tuque, lies *Playa de Guayanilla*, on the bay of the same name. On the

target for tourist cameras. Nearby are old Spanish houses with their characteristic wrought-iron balconies and window grilles. To the S of Plaza Degetau stands the *Alcaldía* (Town Hall).

In the Avenida de las Américas we find the *Museo de Arte, a museum of much more than local importance built in 1965 by Edward Durell Stone, who was also responsible for the Museum of Modern Art in New York. Notable features of this fine two-story building are the hexagonal rooms and the patio with its fountain and its elegant curved staircase. The museum

Lago de Yáuco, Puerto Rico

stretch of coast to the SW American forces landed in 1898 during the Spanish-American War. The area is now occupied by the **Reserva Forestal Guánica**, a statutorily protected expanse of tropical scrub and cactus country. From **Yáuco**, W of Guayanilla, a road runs N to join the Ruta Panorámica. On this Panoramic Highway, half way between Yáuco and *Indiera Alta*, is the ***Lago de Yáuco**, a reservoir in a beautiful setting on the southern fringes of the Cordillera Central. It was created in the 1960s by the Autoridad de las Fuentes Fluviales de Puerto Rico under an irrigation scheme initiated in 1914, designed primarily to supply water for sugar growing in the arid southern coastal plain.

From Ponce there are opportunities for attractive trips, e.g. on Route 139 into the **Cordillera Central**, which reaches its highest point in the *Cerro de Punta* (4390 ft/1338 m). Around the highest peaks in the Cordillera extends the ***Toro Negro National Forest**, which is traversed by the magnificent *Ruta Panorámica*, affording a succession of superb views of the hills, valleys and lakes and the sea beyond. In the eastern part of the National Park is the *Area Recreo Doña Juana*, a well-equipped recreation area with footpaths, picnic sites, benches and a swimming pool. – Going N from here on Route 149, another fine panoramic road with magnificent views all the way, and then NW on Route 144, we come to *Jayuya* and Utuado, through typical cordillera scenery.

Utuado (pop. 39,000) is a coffee-growing center and also a popular resort, within easy reach of the ***Indian Ceremonial Ball Park**, an old Indian ball court constructed by the Taino Arawaks.

This ancient ritual complex, laid out some 700 years ago, comprises a number of paved roads and plazas and two parallel rows of standing stones. The megaliths differ in size and color, and some of them bear engravings. The ritual ball game played here seems to have been similar to that played in ancient Mexico. The rubber ball could be played only with the head, shoulder, hip or knee, never with the hand, and must never be allowed to touch the ground; otherwise a player was penalized. In contrast to the Mexican practice, however, a defeated player was not, so far as we know, beheaded. The ball court has been well restored, and there is a small museum.

The return to Ponce can be on Route 10, which follows a winding course through the Cordillera by way of the coffee-growing center of *Adjuntas*.

12¼ miles/20 km E of Ponce on Route 1 is the beach resort of *Santa Isabel*. 7½ miles/12 km beyond this, in the Bahía de Rincón, we reach *Salinas* and the beach of Playa Salinas. Farther E is **Guayama** (pop. 40,000), a town with the atmosphere of colonial Spain at the S end of the winding Route 15. The road leads to Cayey (pop. 41,000) on the Ruta Panorámica. Half way between Guayama and Cayey is a reproduction of the Grotto of Lourdes.

See also **Puerto Rico**.

Port Antonio
Jamaica

Parish of Portland.
Altitude: 0–490 ft/0–150 m.
Population: 18,000.

ⓘ **Jamaica Tourist Board**,
City Centre Plaza,
P.O. Box 151,
Port Antonio,
Jamaica;
tel. 993 3051.
See also Practical Information.

HOTELS. – *Frenchman's Cove*, 70 r., SP, T, golf, beach; *Dragon Bay*, 100 r., SP, T; *Goblin Hill*, 40 r., SP, T, golf; *Trident*, 50 r., SP, T, golf; *Bonnie View*, 27 r., SP, T; *De Montevin Lodge*, 15 r., SP; etc. – Many GUEST-HOUSES and HOLIDAY APARTMENTS.

RESTAURANT. – *Trident*.

EVENTS. – *Annual Marlin Tournament* (autumn).

RECREATION and SPORT. – Sailing, deep-sea fishing, water-skiing, scuba diving, snorkeling, swimming and sunbathing; riding, tennis, cycling, walking; *raft trips on the Rio Grande.

AIR SERVICES. – Regular flights to Kingston and Montego Bay; occasional charters to Ocho Rios and other places in the Caribbean.

SHIPPING. – Regular calls by Caribbean cruise ships, mostly from Miami (USA) and San Juan (Puerto Rico).

A raft on the Rio Grande, Jamaica

*Port Antonio, chief town of Portland parish, is charmingly situated on two natural harbors along the luxuriantly green NE coast of Jamaica. Formerly an important banana-shipping port, it has now developed into one of the most exclusive resorts in the West Indies.

The town, built on the slopes of the hills which rise above the East Harbour and West Harbour, was originally founded by the Spaniards. In 1793 Captain Bligh of the "Bounty" landed here, bringing the first breadfruits.

SIGHTS. – At the tip of the *Titch Hill* promontory between the two harbors looms *Fort George (18th c.), with a fine view of little *Navy Island* (boats; recreation facilities). The town contains some handsome old colonial buildings, including the 18th c. *Court House* and the 19th c. *Parish Church*.

On the S side of the East Harbour are two beautiful parks, *Oliver Park* and *Carder Park*. Around the West Harbour are warehouses, small craft workshops and a boatyard.

On the Folly promontory which bounds the East Harbour on the NE stands *Folly Great House* which was built in 1906 by an American millionaire named Alfred Mitchell. The house fell into ruin in the 1930s.

SURROUNDINGS. – To the E of the town are a number of luxury hotels on magnificent beaches, among them *Frenchman's Cove.

Frenchman's Cove, on the NE Jamaican coast

An impressive natural feature is the *Blue Hole, an immensely deep inlet linked with the sea by a narrow passage, with deep blue water which contrasts strikingly with the lush green vegetation on the enclosing rocks.

SE of Port Antonio in the *Seven Hills of Athenry* (plantations) are the *Nonsuch Caves, with fossils of marina fauna and flora and impressive stalactites and stalagmites. The caves are the home of numerous bats.

S of Port Antonio lies **Berrydale**, embarkation point for *raft trips on the Rio Grande, a diversion said to have been originated by the film actor Errol Flynn. These trips (2–3 hours), on long narrow bamboo rafts of the type formerly used for transporting bananas, follow the lower course of the Rio Grande, Jamaica's largest river, passing through impressive tropical rain forest, and end in *St Margaret's Bay*, W of Port Antonio.

Port Antonio to Hector's River (52 miles/84 km). – The A 4 runs E from Port Antonio, passing many beautiful *beaches and entering a region of luxuriant tropical vegetation and large plantations.

9 miles/15 km: **Boston Bay**, with the very popular *Boston Beach*.

5 miles/8 km: **Long Bay**, which also has an excellent beach.

7 miles/11 km: *Manchioneal, a prettily situated little fishing village, named after the poisonous manchineel tree which is common in this area.

The road runs past beautiful *Innis Bay* and comes to –

2 miles/3 km: **Hector's River**, surrounded by extensive coconut groves.

The return is by the same route to –

26 miles/42 km: **Port Antonio**.

Port Antonio to Bowden (34 miles/54 km). – A very attractive drive along the valley of the *Rio Grande* to the forbidding country of the *John Crow Mountains and the northern slopes of the Blue Mountains, which in earlier days was the retreat of runaway slaves and later of liberated slaves. Under the influence of the NE trade winds this area has a very heavy rainfall and is in consequence covered with dense tropical rain forest. Typical "maroon" settlements (established by runaway slaves, known as maroons) are *Moore Town* and *Cornwall Banks. – S of *Comfort Castle* is the *Macca Sucker* (4380 ft/ 1335 m), which is almost perpetually shrouded in mist. In the upper valley of the Rio Grande is the village of *Bowden*.

Port Antonio to Annotto Bay (60 miles/96 km). – From Port Antonio the road runs W along the N coast, through ever varying scenery.

6 miles/10 km: *St Margaret's Bay*, where the Rio Grande flows into the sea. The raft trips from Berrydale end here.

4½ miles/7 km: **Hope Bay**, near which are the *Somerset Falls, a picturesque and much visited series of cascades and pools on the *Daniels River*, amid dense tropical rain forest.

The road continues via *Black Hill* to –

5 miles/8 km: *Orange Bay*, with a magnificent beach.

4½ miles/7 km: **Buff Bay**, a little coastal town at the end of B 1, the most magnificently scenic road in Jamaica, which runs N from Kingston through the Blue Mountains and down the beautiful *valley of the *Buff Bay River* (see under Kingston, Surroundings).

Then on via *Windsor Castle* and *Golden Grove* to –

7½ miles/12 km: *Iter Boreale*, with a fine old mansion of the 17th–19th c. (small museum of local interest).

14 miles/23 km S of Annotto Bay on A 3, half way to Kingston, we reach **Castleton**, with one of the finest *botanical gardens on the island, laid out in the second half of the 19th c. above the valley of the *Way Water River*.

The return is by the same route to –

30 miles/48 km: **Port Antonio**.

See also **Jamaica.

Port-au-Prince

Haiti
République d'Haïti

Département de l'Ouest.
Altitude: 0–985 ft/0–300 m.
Population: 800,000.

ⓘ **Office National du Tourisme,**
Avenue Marie-Jeanne,
Port-au-Prince,
Haïti;
tel. 2 17 20.
See also Practical Information.

DIPLOMATIC MISSIONS. – *British Consulate*: 21 Avenue Marie-Jeanne, Cité de l'Exposition, P.O. Box 1302, tel. 2 12 27 and 2 22 25. – *United States Embassy*: Harry Truman Boulevard, tel. 2 02 00. – *Canadian Embassy*: Delmas Street, Home of Champions Building, tel. 2 23 58.

HOTELS. – PORT-AU-PRINCE: *Beau Rivage*, Boul. Harry Truman, 40 r., SP, T; *Habitation Leclerc*, Martissant, 130 r., SP, T; *Royal Haitian Hotel and Casino*, Bizoton, 80 r., SP, T, casino; *Castel Haïti*, St Gérard, 100 r., SP; *Christopher Hotel*, Bourdon, 65 r., SP, T; *Holiday Inn Plaza*, Champ de Mars, 80 r., SP, T; *Grand Hôtel Oloffson*, Avenue Christophe, 25 r.; *Montana*, 55 r.; *Park*, Champ de Mars, 40 r., SP; *Prince Hotel*, Rue 3, 32 r., SP; *Sans Souci*, Avenue C.-Summer, 24 r., SP; *Splendid*, Avenue N, 40 r., SP; etc. –DELMAS: *Coconut Villa*, 50 r., SP; *Cotubanama*, 40 r., SP; *Haiti Holiday Hotel*, 54 r., SP; etc. – PETIONVILLE: *El Rancho*, 124 r., SP, T; *Ibo Lélé Hotel*, 70 r., SP; *Choucoune*, 42 r., SP; *Le Régent*, 24 r., SP; *Marabou*, 14 r., SP; *Montana*, 43 r., SP, T; *Villa Créole*, 80 r., SP; *Village*, 40 r., SP; *Villa Quisqueya*, 16 r., SP; etc. – ON POINTE AUX SABLES (45 miles/75 km NW): *Club Méditerranée*. – Many GUEST-HOUSES.

RESTAURANTS. – PORT-AU-PRINCE: Le Bistrot, Lalue 146; *Le Récif*, Route de Delmas; *Le Rond-point*, Avenue Marie-Jeanne; *Place Vendôme*, Avenue Marie-Jeanne. – PÉTIONVILLE: *La Lanterne*; *Belle Epoque*; *Chez Gérard*; *Le Belvédère*; *Le Gourmet*.

Casinos (roulette, baccarat, blackjack). *Casino International*, Boul. Harry Truman; *Royal Haitian Hotel and Casino*, Bizoton.

EVENTS. – In some hotels and discotheques there are ballet and dance performances every evening, as well as folk displays, including voodoo shows (though these have very little in common with the real voodoo ceremonies which usually take place at night in private). – There are regular open-air folk performances in the *Théâtre de Verdure*. – Cockfights in the *Arène* on Saturdays and Sundays.

SHOPPING. – The Haitian capital is a shoppers' paradise. Visitors will be tempted by a whole range of goods at bargain prices – jewelry and perfume, fine woodcarving and furniture (much of it in mahogany), basketwork, embroidery, etc. Particularly attractive is the naive painting which can be purchased in the main squares and markets.

ART GALLERIES (a selection). – PORT-AU-PRINCE: *Ambiance*, 15 rue M; *George Nader Art Gallery*, Rue du Magasin de l'Etat; *Jerusalem Art*, Rue du Magasin de l'Etat; *Centre d'Art*, 56 rue Roy; *Varieties, Art and Painting Centre*, Rue de l'Enterrement; etc. – PÉTION-VILLE: *Galerie Marassa*, 10 rue Lamarre; *Galerie Panaméricaine*, 24 rue Panaméricaine; *Mahfoud Art Gallery*, Rue Clervaux; *National Art*, 20 rue Panaméricaine; *Red Carpet Art Gallery*, 48 rue Panaméricaine; *Shishi of Haiti*, 38 rue Panaméricaine; etc.

RECREATION and SPORT. – Boat trips, sailing, snorkeling, scuba diving; tennis, soccer.

AIR SERVICES. – INTERNATIONAL: Port-au-Prince (Aéroport International François Duvalier) to New York and Miami (USA), Montreal (Canada), Nassau (Bahamas), Kingston and Montego Bay (Jamaica), San Juan (Puerto Rico), Saint Maarten and Curaçao (Netherlands Antilles). – DOMESTIC: scheduled flights to Cap-Haïtien, Jacmel, Jérémie and Les Cayes.

SHIPPING. – INTERNATIONAL SERVICES: Occasional cruise ships from Port-au-Prince to Miami (USA) and San Juan (Puerto Rico); in winter services to other Caribbean islands. – DOMESTIC SERVICES: Frequent

Market scene in Port-au-Prince

motorboats and coastal sailing vessels to all the main ports in the country and on the offshore islands.

Public transport. – The most important form of public transport is the *tap-tap*, a pick-up truck with a gaudily painted wooden superstructure for carrying passengers and goods. Painted on the tailgates of the tap-taps are mottoes intended to promote divine favor and ensure protection for the passengers on their journey – a journey which goes at a pretty rapid pace. Larger tap-taps, or *camions-bus* – trucks with a fairly ramshackle superstructure – run between Port-au-Prince and other towns, usually much overloaded.

Another form of public transport in Port-au-Prince is the *voiture publique* or public car, a kind of communal taxi, identified by a red band on the outside mirrors, which plies within the city limits. There are also *camionnettes*, small station wagons which have regular routes between Port-au-Prince and Pétionville.

In all forms of public transport there are no fixed stops, except in certain busy central squares and at the end of the line: to stop a vehicle, hold out your hand or shout. The fare, which is extremely low – is paid at the end of the journey.

**Port-au-Prince, the political, economic and cultural capital of the Republic of Haiti, lies in the Baie de Port-au-Prince, the innermost part of the Golfe de la Gonâve, with the Massif de la Selle rearing above it on the S and the Plaine du Cul-de-Sac flanking it on the N. It is the see of an archbishop and has several higher educational establishments. With the only port in the country adapted to modern requirements, an international airport and the largest concentration of industry in Haiti, Port-au-Prince is a magnet attracting large numbers of people from the country areas in quest of employment.

Although this influx of people who cannot gain an adequate living in the country still continues, however, very few of the incomers do in fact obtain the jobs in the city which they hope for, and the unemployment rate in Port-au-Prince has reached alarming proportions. Numbers of people scratch a living with casual work. Thus unemployment and underemployment are crucial problems – reflected in the swarms of street dealers, shoeshine boys, sellers of lottery tickets, barrow-pushers and "guides" who inhabit the streets of the city. The activity of the inner town which appears so "picturesque" to the tourist, has its deeper roots in the often desperate economic plight of whole classes of the population. Visible expression of the social problems of Port-au-Prince is provided by the slums on the outskirts of the town which are constantly spreading. A stay in Haiti inevitably becomes a permanent confrontation with poverty. Again and again a beggar will be encountered holding out his hand and often underlining his plight by pointing to his empty stomach.

HISTORY. – The town takes its name from the "Prince", a warship which was the first vessel to anchor off the coast here (c. 1700). It was not actually founded, however, until 1749, by Governor La Caze, and was then known as L'Hôpital, a name still borne by the hill below which the city lies. Only a year after its foundation it replaced Cap-Français as the administrative capital of the colony. During the 19th c. Port-au-Prince was involved in constant revolts, coups d'état and civil wars, as each of the rival political groups sought to gain control of the capital. The disturbances and general insecurity which prevailed at this time earned the town the name of "Port-aux-Crimes". Like Cap-Haïtien, Port-au-Prince has lost many of its old buildings as a result of wars and civil wars, fires, hurricanes and earthquakes.

SIGHTS. – The most eye-catching building in the town is the monumental domed ***Palais National**, the residence of Jean-Claude Duvalier, who became President for life in 1971.

The palace, built in 1918, has a high pillared entrance portico and a long white façade which stands out sharply against the blue of the sky. The design was modelled on the Capitol in Washington. Some rooms in the palace are open to the public at certain times,

Palais National, Port-au-Prince

including a hall containing busts of all the Presidents of Haiti.

In front of the palace, to the N, lies the *Place du Marron Inconnu*, surrounded by public buildings. On the N side of the square is the ***Statue du Marron Inconnu**, one of the great symbols of the national struggle for liberation.

The term *marron* (English "maroon") is the name given to the runaway slaves who fled from the plantations of the colonial period to inaccessible parts

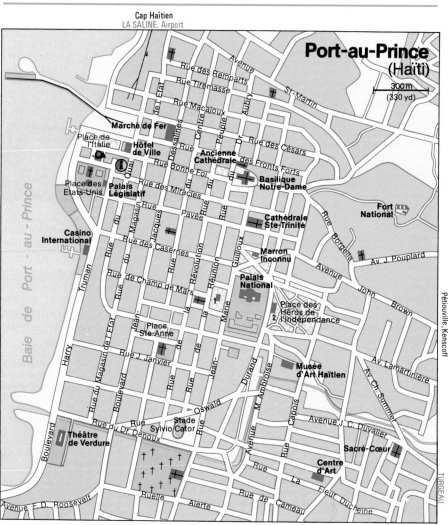

Cap Haïtien
LA SALINE, Airport

Port-au-Prince
(Haïti)

300m
(330 yd)

1 Mausolée de Dessalines et Pétion   2 Musée du Peuple Haïtien

of the country; these nameless men thus became the first to take up the fight against colonial rule. They are commemorated by this monument to the "Unknown Maroon". The bronze statue (1968) by the Haitian sculptor Albert Mangonès depicts a black slave, clad only in a loincloth, holding in his right hand a machete, the symbol of resistance, and in his left a conch, symbolizing the call to rise against the oppressors.

Only a few paces away is the *Monument de Toussaint L'ouverture* (by Normi Ulysse Charles), commemorating the man who with Dessalines ranks as the best known national hero. – To the E of the Palais National is the spacious *Place des Héros de l'Indépendance*, still generally know by its original name of *Champ de Mars*, on which Faustin I, second emperor of Haiti, was crowned in 1852.

The emperor, who had previously been President, reigned only for a few years. On January 15, 1859 he was overtaken by the same fate as many of his predecessors and successors and was overthrown by a coup d'état, withdrawing to exile in Jamaica. His reign was notable chiefly for two unsuccessful attempts to occupy the neighboring Dominican Republic.

In 1954, on the 150th anniversary of Haitian independence, statues of great figures in the fight for freedom, including Jean-Jacques Dessalines, Henry Christophe and Alexandre Pétion, were set up in the square. – On the W side of the square is the interesting *Musée du Peuple Haïtien, the most notable exhibits in which are the stone and pottery implements and utensils of the pre-Columbian Arawak Indians and the relics and mementos of the period of slavery. There is a map showing the places of origin of the slaves transported to Haiti. A small section of the museum is devoted to the origins and practices of the voodoo cult, with examples of objects used in the voodoo ceremonies. – To the S of the square, which is surrounded by public buildings, hotels and movie theaters we find the *Musée d'Art Haïtien, which presents an informative cross-section of the work of Haitian artists, in particular painters. – A large collection of Haitian art can also be seen in the *Centre d'Art, some distance SW in Rue du 22 Septembre 1957 (formerly Rue Roy).

To the W of the Presidential Palace is the *Mausolée de Dessalines et Pétion*, the mausoleum containing the remains of Dessalines, a black, and Pétion, a mulatto – their joint burial being conceived as a symbol of unity between these two different, and often rival, population groups.

Alexandre Pétion, noted for his support of Simón Bolívar during the South American struggle for liberation, was instrumental in founding Haiti's first higher educational establishment in Port-au-Prince.

The palatial buildings N and S of the mausoleum are the Ministries of Finance and Justice. To the E, in the grounds of the Presidential Palace, stand the Dessalines Barracks, housing the President's personal bodyguard.

To the S of the Presidential Palace are a number of academic institutes and a large sports stadium, the *Stade Sylvio Cator*. Beyond this is the *Cimetière Extérieur*, the city's principal cemetery, containing the monuments and mausoleums of influential Haitian families. Farther W, in the Boulevard Harry Truman, is the *Théâtre de Verdure*, an open-air theatre in which folk performances are given several times weekly. The city's largest cockfighting arena, nearby, caters for what is, after soccer, the most popular spectator sport in Haiti.

Colonial-style house, Port-au-Prince

SE of the Presidential Palace, in Avenue Jean-Claude Duvalier, is the attractive *Eglise du Sacré Cœur* (19th c.), adjoining which is a school associated with the church. – From the Place du Marron Inconnu *Rue Courte* runs N to the *Cathédrale de la Sainte-Trinité, with wall paintings which make it the most notable church in Port-au-Prince.

The ** wall paintings in the apse and the altarpiece are impressive examples of Haitian naive painting. The wall paintings set the Biblical stories against a Haitian background. Christ and the Apostles are depicted as blacks or mulattoes: only Judas is white. The scenery is that of Haiti, and the ordinary people are Haitian peasants with their characteristic yellow straw hats. Altogether the church contains 14 scenes from the life of Christ. The paintings were the work of Benoit, Bazile, Levêque, Obin and other artists.

A little way N stands the *Cathédrale Notre-Dame (R.C.), completed in 1915.

The Cathedral, attractively tinted in pink and white, is in neo-Romanesque style and is flanked by two towers. The structure of the towers and the nave is modelled on the Sacré-Cœur in Paris, though the large central dome is lacking. The five entrances on the façade are surmounted by small rose windows, and above these, separated from them by a balustrade, is a large rose made up of a series of smaller circles containing crosses.

In front of the Cathedral lies the *Parc Simone Duvalier*, a beautiful little garden named in honor of the present President's mother. – Immediately N stands the *Old Cathedral* (Ancienne Cathédrale), a wooden church dating from 1720 (restored 1970) which is one of the few surviving buildings of the French colonial period. – To the E are the *Archives Nationales* and, higher up, the 18th c. *Fort National*.

To the W, in Rue du Centre, is the *National Library* (Bibliothèque Nationale).

The *Boulevard Jean-Jacques Dessalines* (Grand'Rue) runs N to the **Iron Market (*Marché de Fer*), the scene of bustling

Cathédrale Notre-Dame, Port-au-Prince

activity, overflowing into the adjoining streets, which make it one of the great tourist attractions of the Caribbean.

The Market, erected in 1889, is an imposing iron structure painted bright red and green. In terms of construction it belongs to the same period as the Eiffel Tower and the Halles of Paris, demolished in the 70's. The Haitian President of the day immortalized himself with the inscription "Hyppolite Président d'Haïti 1889". On the roof of the building, which is in two sections, are four minarets. It is said that the Iron Market, with its Oriental features, came to Haiti only by mistake. At the same time as President Hyppolite ordered a market hall in France a similar building was commissioned from the same firm by a city in India, and through some misunderstanding the Haitian market hall went to India and the Indian one went to Haiti, where, after some initial surprise, it was accepted with enthusiasm.

Teeming with people, colorful, endlessly varied, the market beggars description. In the market hall itself, outside it and in the neighboring streets innumerable market women compete in offering their wares. Whatever you want, you will find it here. All the varied produce of Haiti is displayed on the stalls in a rich palette of color – rice, maize, beans, manioc, yams, all kinds of tropical fruits, mangoes, coconuts, pineapples and small livestock. On other stands are meat, fish and offal. Of particular interest to visitors are the many stalls in the market hall selling local handcrafts and naive paintings. Baskets, articles made of straw and sisal, woodcarving (particularly masks and statues) and naive pictures in endless variety make very popular souvenirs. But whatever you want to buy it is essential to bargain long and persistently over the price. Often the stranger – the "blanc", as the natives call the prosperous white man – will encounter in the busy market friendly and not aggressive Haitians who will offer their hand in an ingenuous way and explain that they would dearly love something to eat.

Characteristic Haitian souvenirs can also be found in the **Mahogany Market**, a few blocks farther N in the Grand'Rue. Here paintings and hand-made articles can be purchased at very reasonable prices, though here too this must be achieved by skilful bargaining.

Very different from the market quarter – where the truth of the saying "Haiti is Africa in the Caribbean" can be fully appreciated – is the *Cité de l'Exposition, only a few blocks away to the SW. This district, very modern in comparison with other parts of the town, is bounded by the Place de l'Italie, Avenue Marie-Jeanne and Boulevard Harry Truman. In the Place de l'Italie, on the N side of the district, with many art dealers' shops, are the *Town Hall* (Hôtel de Ville) and *Custom House* (Douane), adjoining which are the modern port installations and the quay used by cruise ships.

Most of the buildings in the Cité de l'Exposition date from 1949, when a great international exhibition was held here on the 200th anniversary of the foundation of Port-au-Prince. The exhibition pavilions, some of them decorated with attractive naive paintings, were later occupied by government departments and agencies.

On the S side of the Place de l'Italie is the *Head Post Office* (Administration Générale des Postes), with the *Tourist Office* (Office du Tourisme) opposite it.

Immediately to the S, in the Place des Nations-Unies, stand the *Chapelle Sixtine*, the *Palais Législatif* and a number of embassies, together with the beautiful *Fontaine Lumineuse*. – On the seafront is the *Casino International*, a popular rendezvous (gaming rooms).

In the northern district of LA SALINE is the **Port des Voiliers** (sailing ship harbor), the main base of Haitian coastal shipping.

Haiti which has no ocean-going fleet of its own possesses several hundred coastal ships with a total tonnage of about 400 BRT, which carry passengers and goods to parts of the country otherwise difficult to reach. Only a very small proportion of this fleet consists of modern motor-driven vessels: most of the boats are broad-beamed wooden sailing craft. In spite of competition from the developing road system these boats – still mostly built in northern Haiti – seem to be maintaining their position as a means of transport. There has even been a certain revival of the boat-building trade as a result of the illegal traffic that has developed in smuggling Haitians into the Bahamas and the United States. – Visitors should be wary of entrusting themselves to these boats. They are frequently unseaworthy as a result of inadequate maintenance, and the charcoal stoves they carry create a grave fire hazard.

Above the slum district of BOLOSSE, to the S, is *Fort Mercredi* (19th c.; 345 ft/ 105 m), from which there is a fine view over the city.

In the south-estern district of TURGEAU can be found the *Musée National, housed in the former residence of President Magloire.

In addition to many portraits of historical figures the museum contains a fine collection of material of the colonial period and the 19th c. The most notable item is the anchor, almost 13 ft/4 m long, of Columbus's flagship the "Santa Maria", which ran aground on the N coast of Haiti in 1492 and had to be abandoned. There are also ethnological and numismatic collections, contemporary furniture and utensils, and various items associated with great national leaders, including an elaborately decorated sword which belonged to Alexandre Pétion, Dessalines' sabre and the pistol with which Henry I shot himself. Another historic relic is the bell from the Ennery plantation with which Toussaint L'ouverture is said to have symbolically proclaimed the liberation of the slaves in 1793.

Port-au-Prince to Kenscoff (17 miles/28 km). The road climbs into the hills, past a long series of stalls where baskets, wooden and sisal articles and turtle shells are offered for sale. Purchasing turtle shells is very ill-advised, since many species are threatened with extinction and consequently a ban on the import was demanded by several countries. Here too will be seen many peasant women, as well as the "Madames Sarah", the women who buy up the peasants' agricultural produce. These women walk for many miles carrying baskets weighing up to a hundred pounds on their heads.

5 miles/8 km: **Pétionville** (985–1640 ft/300–500 m; pop. 40,000) has a pleasant climate which makes it a favorite residential area and tourist attraction (20% of all the hotel beds in the country). It has art galleries, souvenir shops and restaurants, a lively market and fine villas set in large gardens which form a stark contrast to the growing slum quarters of Port-au-Prince.

The road (D 101) continues uphill. At La Boule take a road to the right which leads to the *Distillerie Jane Barbancourt* (conducted tours and tasting of the local rum). A few miles farther on we reach *Boutillier* (3215 ft/980 m), from which there are superb *views of Port-au-Prince and the Golfe de la Gonâve. Nearby is the Old Heidelberg Restaurant.

12½ miles/20 km: **Kenscoff** (4920 ft/1500 m; pop. 3000), an attractively situated little hill town, famed for its colorful market (Tuesday and Friday mornings). In the neighborhood are several flower farms including *Le Châtelet des Fleurs* (open to visitors), which export flowers to the United States. *Fort Jacques* and *Fort Alexandre* in the *Fermathe Hills* both date from the 19th c.

On the road from Kenscoff into the hills of the *Montagne Noire* (7120 ft/2170 m) and the road to **Furcy** and the *Plateau de la Découverte* there are magnificent views of the **Massif de la Selle**. On market days travelers on these roads will encounter whole processions of women carrying fruit and vegetables to the distant markets of Kenscoff, Pétionville and Port-au-Prince.

Port-au-Prince to Arcahaie (c. 50 miles/80 km). – Along the stretch of coast between Port-au-Prince and **Saint-Marc** (see separate entry) are some of the finest beaches in Haiti – *Ibo Beach* on the **Ile des Caciques** (*Ibo Beach Club, 92 r., T), *Kyona Beach* (Kyona Beach Hotel), *Kaloa Beach* (*Kaloa Beach Club Resort, 300 b., SP, T, casino), *Ouanga Bay* N of **Arcahaie**, *Mai-Kai Beach*, *Xaragua Beach* (Le Xaragua, 48 r.), *Amai-y Beach* and *Pointe aux Sables* (*Club Méditerranée, SP, T), near **Montrouis**.

Port-au-Prince to Taino Beach. – At **Grand Goave**, 29 miles/47 km W of Port-au-Prince, is the splendid *Taino Beach* (Taino Beach Hotel, 50 r.), with good diving grounds. – Close by is the recently developed *Sun Beach*.

BOAT TRIPS (daily from the Casino Pier) to *Sand Cay Reef* (corals) and the scuba diver's paradise of *Grand Banc* in the Baie de Port-au-Prince.

See also **Haiti** and **Hispaniola**.

Port-de-Paix

Haiti
République d'Haïti

Département du Nord-Ouest.
Altitude: sea level.
Population: 16,000.

ⓘ **Office du Tourisme,**
Avenue Marie-Jeanne,
Port-au-Prince,
Haïti;
tel. 2 1720
See also Practical Information.

AIR SERVICES. – Occasional flights to Port-au-Prince.

RECREATION and SPORT. – Scuba diving, snorkeling.

*Port-de-Paix, main town of the Département du Nord-Ouest, one of the poorest in Haiti, is almost totally isolated, both geographically and economically.

HISTORY. – Columbus referred to the area around the present town of Port-de-Paix as "paradise valley". The town was founded in 1664 by buccaneers from the Ile de la Tortue, and during the French colonial period became one of the most prosperous settlements in the colony. Much of the town was destroyed by fire in 1902.

SIGHTS. – There are well-preserved remains of French fortifications. – Off the coast are magnificent *coral reefs, accessible only to scuba divers.

See also * *Haiti** and * *Hispaniola**.

Port of Spain

Trinidad
Republic of Trinidad and Tobago

Altitude: sea level.
Population: 100,000.

ⓘ **Trinidad and Tobago Tourist Board,**
56 Frederick Street,
Port of Spain,
Trinidad;
tel. 62 31932.
See also Practical Information.

DIPLOMATIC MISSIONS. – *British High Commission:* Furness House (4th floor), 90 Independence Square, P.O. Box 778, tel. 62 52861. – *United States Embassy:* 15 Queen's Park West, P.O. Box 752, tel. 62 26371. – *Canadian High Commission:* Colonial Building, 72–74 South Quay, P.O. Box 1246, tel. 62 34787 and 62 37254.

HOTELS. – *Trinidad Hilton, 442 b.; *Holiday Inn, 249 b.; Kapok, 72 b.; Bretton Hall, 90 b.; Normandie,

Port of Spain – a bird's-eye view

58 b.; *Chaconia Inn*, 46 b.; etc. – AT PIARCO AIRPORT: *Pan American*, 50 b.; *Bel Air*, 53 b.

EVENTS. –* **Carnival** (New Year to Shrove Tuesday: see under Trinidad).

TRANSPORT. – From Piarco Airport there are flights to London, New York, Miami, Toronto, Caracas, Georgetown and all the Caribbean islands. – Vehicles travel on the left.

* **Port of Spain, capital of the Republic of Trinidad and Tobago, lies in the NW of Trinidad on the wide sweep of the Gulf of Paria. The town, built on the flat coastal plain, is surrounded by hills, to the S of which is the swampy area around the mouth of the River Caroni. The population is a mixture of more than 40 races.**

SIGHTS. – The main sights of the town can easily be seen on foot. The center of commercial activity is *Woodford Square*, a little way E of the harbor area. On the E side of the square, Frederick Street running N–S, is lined with shops, handcraft boutiques and oriental bazaars.

On the W side of Woodford Square the Renaissance-style * **Red House**, rebuilt

after a fire in 1906, now houses the Parliament of Trinidad and Tobago. Behind it, to the W, are the police headquarters, originally built in 1877, destroyed by fire in 1881 and rebuilt in neo-Gothic style in 1884. – NW of the Red House are the Victorian *Law Courts*. – On the S side of Woodford Square stands the Anglican * **Holy Trinity Cathedral**, a new-Gothic building (1816–26) with a fine altar and beautiful woodcarving in the choir.

Beyond the Cathedral, at the E end of Queen Street is Trinidad's principal mosque, the *Jama Masjid*, with slender minarets. – From here Duncan Street runs S into *Independence Square*, actually a

Houses of Parliament, Port of Spain

Holy Trinity Cathedral, Port of Spain

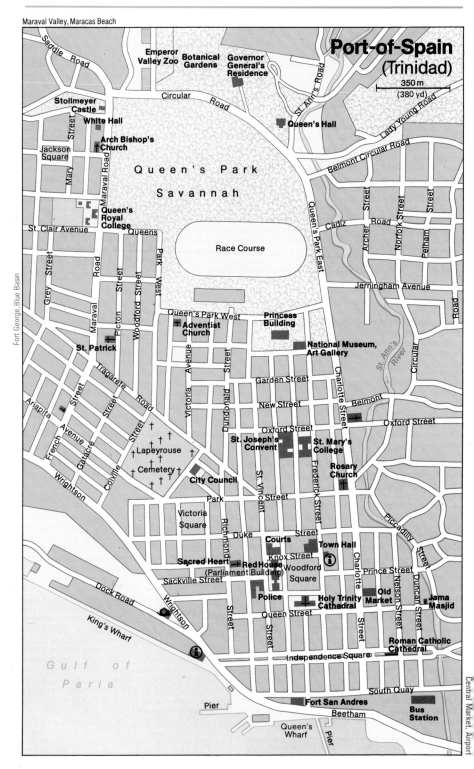

Maraval Valley, Maracas Beach

Port-of-Spain
(Trinidad)

350 m
(380 yd)

Emperor Valley Zoo
Botanical Gardens
Governor General's Residence
Saddle Road
Circular Road
St. Ann's Road
Stollmeyer Castle
White Hall
Arch Bishop's Church
Jackson Square
Mary Street
Queen's Hall
Belmont Circular Road
Lady Young Road

Queen's Park Savannah

Queen's Royal College
St. Clair Avenue
Queens Road
Maraval Road
Cadiz Road
Archer Street
Norfolk Street
Petham Street

Race Course

Grey Street
Maraval Road
Picton Street
Woodford Street
Park West
Park Street
Queen's Park East
Jerningham Avenue
Circular Road

Queen's Park West
Adventist Church
Princess Building
National Museum, Art Gallery
St. Ann's River

St. Patrick
Tragarete Road
Victoria Avenue
Dundonald Street
Garden Street
New Street
Charlotte Street
Belmont
Oxford Street

Ariapita Avenue
French Street
Galace Street
Colville Street
Oxford Street
St. Joseph's Convent
St. Mary's College
Wrightson Road
Lapeyrouse
Cemetery
City Council
Park Street
Frederick Street
Rosary Church
Piccadilly Street

Victoria Square
Richmond Street
Duke Street
Courts
Knox Street
Town Hall
St. Vincent Street
Charlotte Street

Sacred Heart
Red House
(Parliament Building)
Woodford Square
Sackville Street
Prince Street
Old Market
Nelson Street
Duncan Street
Jama Masjid

Dock Road
Police
Queen Street
Holy Trinity Cathedral
Roman Catholic Cathedral

King's Wharf
Wrightson Road
Independence Square
South Quay

Gulf of Paria

Pier
Fort San Andres
Beetham
Bus Station

Queen's Wharf
Pier

Fort George, Blue Basin

Central Market, Airport

wide boulevard running from E to W. Near the E end is the neo-Gothic **Cathedral of the Immaculate Conception** (R.C.; 1815–32), the main entrance flanked by curious three-story twin towers. – Farther S stands *Fort San Andrés*, built in 1785 to protect shipping in the harbor. Now lying a little inland, it is occupied by the traffic police. Here in 1792 the Spanish astronomer Don Cosma Damián de Chur-ruca established the first meridian of longitude in the New World.

At the N end of Frederick Street the **National Museum and Art Gallery** houses collections of material on the history of the island, works by Trinidadian artists and a dazzling display of Carnival costumes. At the entrance is an anchor said to have been lost by Columbus off Trinidad. – The street ends at the **Queen's Park Savannah**, with sports grounds

Cricket at Queen's Royal College, Port of Spain

and a racecourse. The park, a former sugar plantation which was presented to the town by its owner, Sir Ralph Woodford, is surrounded by buildings in a variety of styles. In Maraval Road can be seen **Stollmeyer Castle**, modelled on the medieval castles of the Rhine; immediately adjoining is the Moorish-style *White Hall*, residence of the Prime Minister; and farther S are the neo-Romanesque residence of the Roman Catholic archbishop and *Roudal House*, in French Empire style. – In Circular Road, which bounds the park on the N, stands the former Governor-General's Residence, in a mingling of Italian Renaissance and Victorian styles. Here too, on the slopes of the hill, are the *Botanical Gardens*, displaying the island's wealth of tropical plants. Adjoining the gardens is a small zoo.

From **Fort George** (1804), on a hill (1640 ft/500 m) to the NW of the town, there are panoramic *views, extending on clear days to the hills of Venezuela. Until the advent of radio communication the fort served also as a signal station.

SURROUNDINGS. – In **St Joseph**, 7½ miles/12 km E of Port of Spain on the Eastern Main Road, is the imposing *Jinnah Masjid* (mosque). – Near here, on a hill, stands the *Mount St Benedict Monastery*, from which there are far-ranging *views.

NW of Port of Spain on the Diego Martin Road lies the *Diego Martin Valley*, at the end of which is the **Blue Basin**, with a waterfall (swimming possible). It is advisable to wear stout footwear.

For a pleasant trip into beautiful hill scenery leave Port of Spain on Saddle Road, which runs N up the *Maraval Valley* into the picturesque and fertile *Santa Cruz Valley*. This leads back to the town, which is entered by way of the Eastern Main Road. – For a longer trip, also very rewarding, turn left N of Maraval into the North Coast Road, which runs through the *Northern Range* to *Maracas Beach*, the most beautiful in Trinidad. The winding coast road, at some points running high above the sea and offering a succession of beautiful views, leads to *Las Cuevas Bay* and beyond this to *Blanchisseuse*, on the bay of the same name (beach). From here take the Arima Blanchisseuse Road, which leads inland to the **Spring Hill Centre** (*Asa Wright Centre*), a former plantation in the Northern Range which is now a bird sanctuary. The special attraction here is a breeding colony, in a cave, of the nocturnal oilbird or guacharo. It is advisable, particularly during the rainy season, to have stout footwear, rainproof clothing and insect repellent. – The road continues to Arima, where it joins the Eastern Main Road: turn W along this. At *Arouca* is **Piarco Airport**. At *Tunapuna* the road enters the built-up area which extends to Port of Spain.

See also ****Trinidad** (Island) and ****Trinidad and Tobago**.

Puerto Plata

Dominican Republic
República Dominicana

Province: Puerto Plata.
Altitude: sea level.
Population: 80,000.
Dirección Nacional de Turismo e Información, César Nicolás Pensón Rosa Duarte,
ⓘ **Santo Domingo,**
República Dominicana;
tel. (809) 688 5537.
See also Practical Information.

HOTELS. – *Long Beach*, Av. Hermanas Mirabal, 100 r.; *Montemar* Av. Hermanas Mirabal, 60 r.; *Cabañas Cofresí*, Autopista Puerto Plata, 53 r.; *Caracol*, Av. Luperón, 18 r.; *Castilla*, Av. J.F. Kennedy, 17 r.; *Colimar*, Av. Luperón 9, 14 r.; *Costombar*, Jack Tar Village; *Dorado Naco*, Villas Caribe; **Playa Dorada*, 253 r.

RECREATION and SPORT. – Swimming, riding, tennis, golf.

Jinnah Mosque, St Joseph

AIR SERVICES. – Regular flights to Santo Domingo (Las Américas Airport), to Miami and New York, as well as to Puerto Rico (San Juan).

SHIPPING. – Occasional calls by cruise ships, usually from Miami (USA) and San Juan (Puerto Rico).

Puerto Plata, primary town of the province of the same name and the principal port on the N coast of the Dominican Republic, lies in a horseshoe-shaped inlet into which flows the Arroyo San Marcos. In addition to its freight traffic the port is now increasingly becoming a port of call for cruise ships. The luxuriant vegetation of the surrounding area, the agreeable climate, cooled by the Atlantic breezes, and the long beaches of white sand attract large numbers of visitors.

The development of the airfield at *La Unión* into an international airport capable of taking large-capacity aircraft and the creation of new infrastructures will, it is hoped, give a boost to the economy of this quiet provincial town.

HISTORY. – In pre-Columbian times the area was inhabited by the warlike Ciguayo-Macorixes, a branch of the Arawak Indians. After Columbus's discovery of Hispaniola on his first voyage (1492) his flagship the "Santa Maria" ran aground near Puerto Plata, and timber from the wreck was used to build a settlement which was given the name of Navidad. On Columbus's return he found the village destroyed and established a new settlement called *Isabela*, where on December 10, 1493, together with Juan Ponce de León, Alonso de Ojeda and the native chieftainess Anacaona, he attended the first mass celebrated on the island. The remains of Isabela can be seen to the W of Puerto Plata, which itself was founded in 1502.

SIGHTS. – The best view of the town and the harbor is from the summit of the *Pico de Isabel de Torres* (2602 ft/793 m), which is reached by cableway. On the summit is a monumental figure of Christ standing on a domed substructure.

On the promontory to the E of the harbor is *Fort San Felipe*, built between 1520 and 1585 to provide protection against Indian attacks and pirate raids. – In the center of the town there are still a few Victorian buildings. The Amber Museum, with a fine collection of specimens is well worth seeing.

SURROUNDINGS. – The N coast, also known as the *Costa Ámbar* on account of the amber found in the hinterland, has very beautiful sandy beaches. 2 miles/3 km E of Puerto Plata, near the airport, the new tourist center of *Playa Dorada* is being developed, with a good sandy beach 2 miles/3 km long, a golf-course and other sports facilities.

W of Puerta Plata (road inland to *Imbert*, then NW via *Luperón* to the coast) are the remains of *La Isabela*, founded by Columbus in 1493, with a later Spanish fort.

Farther E, along an unspoiled stretch of coast often called Long Beach, are *Monte Llano* and the little town of **Sosúa** (pop. 8000), with the beach of *Playa de Sosúa*. During the Second World War there was a refugee camp here for Jews from Germany and Austria, many of whom settled here, mostly taking up cattle-farming. Outside the town lie the health resorts of *Sosua Mar* and *Los Charamicos*.

37 miles/60 km farther E, beyond *Sabaneta de Yásica* and *Gaspar Hernández* and the long beaches of *Playa Magante*, is **Rio San Juan**, with the beautiful *Laguna Gri Gri*. Near here a luxury resort is being developed at * *Playa Grande*, with a magnificent beach 1 mile/1.5 km long, a golf-course, other sports facilities and first-class hotels. Farther E still is *Cabo Francés Viejo*, with the wreck of the "Conception", which came to grief here in 1641. SE of the cape the *Playa El Bretón* has a superb beach.

SE of Puerto Plata is the *Cordillera Septentrional*, the most northerly range in the Dominican Republic.

See also ****Dominican Republic** and ****Hispaniola**.

Puerto Rico
Greater Antilles
Estado Libre y Asociado de Puerto Rico
Commonwealth of Puerto Rico

Area: 3435 sq. miles/8897 sq. km
Capital: San Juan.
Population: 3,240,000.
Religion: Roman Catholic (over 90%); Protestant minorities.
Languages: Spanish, English.
Currency: US dollar of 100 cents.
Weights and measures: British/American system.
Time: Atlantic Time (AT), 4 hours behind GMT.
Vehicles travel on the right.
Travel documents: none required for US citizens

ⓘ **Government of Puerto Rico Tourism Company,**
Avenida Muñoz Rivera 268,
San Juan/Hato Rey, PR 00936,
Puerto Rico;
tel. (009) 754 9292.
See also Practical Information.

****Puerto Rico (formerly called Porto Rico), the smallest island in the Greater Antilles, lies between latitude 18° and 18°30′ N and between longitude 65°30′ and 67°30′ W. The Commonwealth of Puerto Rico also includes the island of Mona (21 sq. miles/54 sq. km) to the W and the islands of Vieques (51 sq. miles/132 sq. km) and Culebra (11 sq. miles/28 sq. km) to the E. – The principal** island extends from W to E for a distance of 110 miles/180 km, with a breadth which varies between 31 miles/50 km and 37 miles/60 km. It lies at the E end of the Greater Antilles, so that Puerto Rico is the half-way point of the chain of islands which extends in a wide arc from northern Central America by way of the Greater and Lesser Antilles to the N coast of South America.

Puerto Rico shows a harmonious mingling of Spanish and North American culture such as is found nowhere else in the world, and the island has successfully developed from an agricultural country primarily dependent on the growing of sugar-cane into a modern industrial state. The economic development of the Antilles, in the oldest zone of colonial settlement in the tropics, was conceived as a whole; Puerto Rico is a particularly interesting example of this trend, since its economic development was carried out by a single large industrial state, the USA. This close association with the United States has brought the island a considerable economic upswing during the last 30 years.

Puerto Rico owes its prosperity to its abandonment of an agrarian structure based on the monoculture of sugar-cane in favor of rapid industrial development. It is the exception among the Caribbean islands, formerly colonies and now developing third-world countries, whose principal concern over the last few decades has been to break free from their various mother countries. Even the smaller Caribbean islands – mere dots on the map of the world – felt this urge to achieve independence. Puerto Rico took the opposite course: this island with the relatively large population of over 3,200,000 has been moving towards ever closer association with its former colonial power, the United States. Its political development is headed not towards independence but towards the maintenance of the status quo, with a majority in favor of complete integration into the USA as a new state.

Puerto Rico has thus been swimming against the political current; but this has turned out to its advantage. While many of the neighboring Caribbean islands are still dogged by poverty and economic distress,

Puerto Rico has achieved the highest per capita income in Latin America after Venezuela – far ahead of its neighbors. Part of this is accounted for by transfer payments from the United States motivated by considerations of social policy; but in addition the island's economy shows an impressive growth rate. In spite of the social problems which still remain, Puerto Rico has developed from the "poorhouse of the Caribbean", as it was called 40 years ago, into the most prosperous island in the Greater Antilles.

This prosperity is clearly reflected in the present-day appearance of the island. The endless series of new tourist hotels along the Atlantic coast between the old town of San Juan and the airport, the high-rise office buildings in the Hato Rey banking district, the shopping centers on the American-style highways and the many new factories large and small around the capital are all symptoms of the transition from an agricultural to an industrial economy which has been achieved over the last few decades by this island, populous but poorly supplied with raw materials as it is.

TOPOGRAPHY. – Puerto Rico offers the visitor a varied landscape pattern, with the highland region in the center of the island as the dominant feature. Three main zones can be distinguished – the coastal plains, the uplands N and S of the Cordillera Central, and the Cordillera Central itself. The Cordillera, the island's backbone, reaches its highest point in the Cerro de Punta (4357 ft/1328 m), and the Sierra de Luquillo, beyond the Caraguas basin, rises to 3494 ft/1065 m. These two ranges are the eastern continuation of the Cordillera Central of Hispaniola and are thus part of the North American cordillera system extending southward into the Greater Antilles. The full scale of the relief in this part of the world is realized only when it is remembered that the Puerto Rico Trench immediately N of the island plunges down 30,185 ft/9200 m under the Atlantic. In spite of the rugged nature of much of the country the highland region is relatively well developed. The hilly topography, combined with the abundance of rain which falls particularly on the northern slopes, has been used to advantage for hydroelectric power.

The northern coastal plain is 9–12 miles/15–20 km wide; the one on the S no more than a few miles wide. In these plains many small streams flow down from the mountains, often passing through karstic formations. Between Arecibo-Manati and Aquadilla is a limestone region, belonging morphologically to the coastal plain and the foothills area, where the hot and humid climate has produced tower-like formations characteristic of tropical karstic country. These "haystacks" or *mogotes* form a backdrop to the extensive pineapple plantations around Manati.

CLIMATE. – Puerto Rico has a climate characteristic of the margins of the tropics, with an alternation between wet and dry seasons, rainfall in winter being relatively light compared with summer. Average temperatures in the coldest and hottest months are 74 °F/23 °C and 81 °F/27 °C, with temperatures in the mountains some 5½ °F/3 °C lower. There is no marked rainy season, but more rain falls between May and December than during the rest of the year. There is a difference of some 4% in relative humidity between January and September. An annual rainfall of 98 in./ 2500 mm is not unusual on the slopes exposed to the trade winds, and in the Sierra de Luquillo it may be three times as much. In contrast to this is the leeward side of the uplands, to the S, with under 39 in./ 1000 mm (Ponce 31 in./762 mm). Tropical hurricanes may sweep over Puerto Rico between August and October, but with modern early warning systems the danger can be recognized well in advance.

FLORA. – Puerto Rico has a rich plant life of some 3000 species. The original tropical rain forest on the humid northern slopes has largely fallen victim to human settlement and agriculture, but thanks to government protective measures it has survived, with a wide range of species, in the Sierra de Luquillo. In the El Yunque nature park there are 300 species of trees, 500 species of ferns and over 20 species of wild orchids. In this area are the trees which yield such valuable woods as teak, mahogany, ebony and the hard ansubo wood. Other species found in the forest include lianas, tree ferns, hibiscus, and here and there, orchids. Common all over Puerto Rico are flamboyants (flame-trees), tulip-trees, bougainvilleas (here called trinitarias) and the golden trumpet flower. Bamboos grow along the river valleys, while the beaches (such as the long Luquillo Beach) are fringed by coconut palms. At certain points on the coast there are mangrove swamps. In the arid SW of the island there are various species of cactus and other drought-loving plants.

Luquillo Beach, Puerto Rico

HISTORY. – Puerto Rico was discovered by Columbus on his second voyage (1493) and settled by the Spaniards, under the leadership of Ponce de León, from 1508 onwards. The island was originally inhabited by some 30,000 Arawak Indians, who called their country *Boriquén*: hence the Puerto Ricans call themselves Boriqueños, and their national anthem is "La Boriqueña". Columbus called the newly discovered island *San Juan Bautista*, and the arms of Puerto Rico, granted by Ferdinand and Isabella of Spain, still contain the lamb which is the symbol of John the Baptist.

The name Puerto Rico is due to the first Governor of the island, Ponce de León, who named the harbor in the Bay of San Juan *Puerto Rico*, the "rich harbor". Later the island and the town exchanged names.

Eighteen years after the discovery of the island the Spaniards began to work the gold which had been found, using Indian slave labor. In consequence the Indian population was rapidly decimated. After the gold became exhausted Puerto Rico remained a Spanish base and a place of refuge for their South American fleets. San Juan was strongly fortified, and the fort of San Felipe del Morro, with massive walls which withstood every attack, is still a major tourist attraction.

Increased number of settlers came to the island in the 17th c., and a plantation economy was developed for the production of sugar, followed in the 18th c. by tobacco and coffee. Cultivation was less intense, however, than on the neighboring islands, and fewer slaves were brought in from Africa. In 1873 slavery was abolished. In 1897 Luís Muñoz Rivera wrested a kind of dominion status from the Spanish crown, but this phase did not last long, for in 1898, during the Spanish-American War, United States forces occupied Puerto Rico, which then became an American colony. Again, however, Muñoz Rivera managed to secure an improvement in the country's status: in 1917 Puerto Rico ceased to be a colony, and the Puerto Ricans became American citizens. In 1948 they elected their first Governor, and in 1952 a new constitution came into force.

POLITICAL STATUS. – A major factor in promoting the economic development of Puerto Rico has been its political status. Since 1952, when the present constitution came into force, the island has been an autonomous political unit in voluntary association with the United States. It is represented in the US House of Representatives by a commissioner, elected by popular vote for a four-year term, who has all the rights of a Congressman except the right to vote. Every Puerto Rican is a citizen of the United States. The island has its own elected Senate, House of Representatives and Governor. Puerto Rico has its own flag, but in foreign affairs and defense the United States government is responsible.

Puerto Ricans do not pay US federal income taxes, but enjoy fiscal autonomy within a customs union with the United States. This allows Puerto Rico to offer entrepreneurs lower rates of tax than in the United States, while at the same time Puerto Rican firms can bring in raw materials from the United States and export their products to the large American market without payment of duty. This special status also simplifies movement between Puerto Rico and the United States (no restrictions on entry or exit, no waiting at customs, domestic air services for American businessmen, tourists and Puerto Ricans). Puerto Rico also receives some $2 billion of federal assistance annually.

In an election in 1976 the Partido Popular Democrático (PPD) led by Rafael Hernández Colón, which had been in power since 1940, lost control of both houses of the Puerto Rican Congress and of the appointment of Governor. The new Governor was Carlos Romero Barceló of the Partido Nuevo Progresista (PNP), mayor of San Juan. Under the PPD the island had achieved the status of commonwealth (Spanish *estado libre y asociado*): the PNP advocates full statehood for Puerto Rico, and the change of government, combined with a move in this direction by President Ford at the end of December 1976, has given a fresh stimulus to the discussions on the incorporation of Puerto Rico in the United States. The election of the governor in 1980 confirmed this trend but in 1981 there were acts of terrorism by a left-wing independence movement.

POPULATION. – In 1981 the population of Puerto Rico was 3.24 million, of whom more than 435,000 live in the capital San Juan (over 1.1 million in the San Juan metropolitan area). This gives a density of 927 to the sq. mile (358 to the sq. km), the highest in the Greater Antilles. Some 80% of the population are light-skinned. The small proportion of blacks reflects the fact that here, as in Cuba, the plantation system did not develop during the Spanish colonial period and slaves were not brought in on the same scale as in, for example, Haiti or Jamaica. Puerto Ricans with every shade of skin colour get on very happily together: the descendants of the original Indian inhabitants, Spanish settlers and black slaves have been mingling here for centuries, and no one thinks anything of it.

The density of population results from an extraordinarily high birth rate, which reached its highest point of 44 per 1000 in 1947. The annual rate of population increase over the period 1970–77 was still 2.8% – though this was accounted for partly by the return of large numbers of Puerto Ricans from the American mainland. Since 1930 the population has more than doubled. A safety valve for this population pressure was provided by emigration to the United States, and in the 1950s something like a million Puerto Ricans, 70% of them aged between 15 and 39, went there. More than a million Puerto Ricans now live in New York alone. As a result of this emigration the annual rate of population increase remained for many years below the Latin American average. One consequence of the development of industry on Puerto Rico has been an increased flow of returning emigrants, who already outnumber those leaving the island.

ECONOMY. – As a result of climatic conditions and the traditional productive structures Puerto Rican **agriculture** shows a very one-sided pattern. The main crop is sugar-cane, which is used to produce both sugar and rum and occupies an important place in the country's exports. Agriculture is therefore dependent on changes in world market prices for sugar, which has made it necessary to provide considerable subsidies in order to maintain the income of those employed in this sector. There are two main agricultural areas – the upland regions, in which the main crop during the Spanish period was coffee (now also some tobacco), and the coastal plains, which are drained in the N and irrigated in the S for the growing of sugar-cane. From the beginning of the 20th c. the Americans promoted the growing of sugar-cane and cut out coffee. Sugar-cane now occupies two-fifths

Pineapple plantation in the karstic region

of the cultivable land. There has also been a considerable development of pineapple growing in recent years.

Bananas, widely grown in Puerto Rico, together with citrus fruits, coconuts, mangoes, pawpaws, guavas and other tropical fruits and vegetables serve chiefly to meet local requirements. Rice – which, eaten with beans, is a staple item of diet – has to be imported from the continental United States. Pastureland and livestock have lost ground with the introduction of irrigated sugar-cane culture and the growth of mechanized agriculture. Under American influence the dairying industry has made great progress and is now established all over the island except in the Cordillera Central and the karstic regions. Most of the dairy farms lie within the catchment areas of the larger towns. The pasture available for the feeding of livestock is usefully supplemented by molasses, a by-product of the sugar industry. A Puerto Rican speciality is Creole cheese. Large numbers of pigs and poultry are reared and this meat is the principal element in Puerto Rican meals.

It is still necessary to import more than half the country's requirements of food, and increased efforts are therefore being made to achieve a higher agricultural output for domestic needs. Experiments in growing rice have given promising results and are to be extended.

The declining importance of agriculture within the economy as a whole is reflected in its reduced contribution to the gross domestic product. Although in 1960 agriculture and fishing still accounted for 9.8% of the GDP, by 1980 the percentage had fallen to barely 3. Over the same period the proportion of the working population employed in agriculture fell from 22.8% to 5.1%.

The unsatisfactory social structure in country areas has so far been only partly remedied. The land reform introduced in the 1940s by Luís Muñoz Marín, later Puerto Rico's first Governor, did not achieve all that was hoped. It is true that by 1959 58,000 jobs for agricultural workers had been created and the large estates had been carved up into 5000 small and medium-sized holdings and 83 state-run farms; but the rapid development of industry deprived the reform of much of its effect, and major problems were caused by the drift of thousands of workers away from the land and into industry.

The most serious decline in the economic situation of Puerto Rico took place between 1901 and 1920, against the background of an expansion of the monoculture of sugar-cane and the promotion of tobacco growing. During this period it became

The Areyto folk group (Puerto Rico)

necessary to import half the country's food require-ments. In 1920 94% of its needs came from the United States. This monoculture gave rise to grave difficulties during the world economic crisis, and between 1930 and 1935 per capita income fell from $122 to $86.

After the 1940 election and the victory of the Popular Democratic Party under Luís Muñoz Marín the development of **industry** was pushed ahead. The government began by promoting processing industries using locally available raw materials such as clay, sand and stone; and headway was also made with processing industries using sugar-cane – sugar factories, rum distilleries and molasses-processing plants – which in 1940 produced a third of total industrial output by value and employed a fifth of the industrial labor force.

The clothing industry, largely dependent on home workers, was then the major source of industrial employment, providing 61% of all industrial jobs and contributing 17% of the country's exports and 22% of total industrial output by value. The third place was taken by the tobacco industry, with 6% of industrial output. These three industries were the base from which the spectacular development of industry in Puerto Rico took off.

The Second World War and the consequent demand for industrial goods provided the initial impetus for Puerto Rico's industrial development. The establish-ment of the first state development company, PRIDCO, was accompanied by a law passed in 1947 which guaranteed foreign firms ten years' exemption from income tax and corporation tax. After these preliminary measures the newly established Economic Development Administration (EDA) set out in 1950 to carry through a complete restructuring of the Puerto Rican economy, in the program known as "Operation Bootstrap". This program of industrialization, initiated by Luís Muñoz Marín, has been carried on by his successors with little alteration, and over the last 30 years, in spite of some setbacks and disappointments, has given Puerto Rico one of the world's fastest growing economies.

The recipe was simple, and has since been copied by other countries, in particular Puerto Rico's Caribbean neighbors. Cheap labor (on wages which for many years were only half those of the United States), low taxes and duty-free access to the North American market are the principal attractions which Puerto Rico

holds out to foreign investors. The island is within the United States customs area but is not subject to United States taxes, and industrialists who invest in Puerto Rico are exempt from the high American income and corporation taxes. In addition Operation Bootstrap allows firms 10 to 25 years' exemption from local taxes. Finally in 1976 American firms gained a further concession under the Federal Tax Reform Act, which enables them, without limitation of time, to transfer profits to the United States without incurring any federal tax liability.

Industry established in Puerto Rico also has the advantage that raw materials and semi-finished products can be imported duty-free and industrial products made in Puerto Rico are admitted to the United States market without restriction. The govern-ment also promotes the establishment of industry with credits for the building of factories and the purchase of machinery. In many cases, too, it provides the factories (industrial estates), looks after the provision of the necessary infrastructure and meets the cost of training unskilled workers. In 1982, within the framework of the state promotion of industry, 1400 firms were established in 96 industrial areas.

Taking the economy as a whole, these measures for the promotion of industry have paid for themselves. The island's gross domestic product has been multiplied many times since 1950 and the net per capita income rose from $121 in 1940 to $3185 in 1980. According to United Nations statistics Puerto Rico is now one of the ten most highly industrialized countries in the world. The income per head is admittedly still lower than in the poorest American states, but it is the highest in Latin America after Venezuela.

Of the 500 largest American companies 111 have one or more plants in Puerto Rico. While the numbers employed in agriculture have fallen from 200,000 to below 60,000, some 130,000 new jobs have been created in industry and 300,000 in the commercial and services sector. If, in spite of this, the unemployment rate has not fallen below 12% and up to 1981 had again risen to 18%, it is mainly due to the drift from the land, the high birth rate and the higher average life expectancy, which has risen over the last three decades from 46 to 72 years. In terms of car ownership Puerto Rico ranks among the economically advanced countries, with one motor vehicle to 3.5 inhabitants.

Puerto Rico's exports consist primarily of industrial products including textiles, boots and shoes, pharmaceuticals, electrical apparatus and appliances. Sugar, which accounted for 62% of exports in 1940, has now fallen to under 1%. Imports consist chiefly of raw materials, consumption goods, motor vehicles and capital equipment, while 20% is accounted for by food from the USA. The level of imports reflects both the steep rise in income per head and the adoption of United States patterns of consumption. Only Canada, Japan, West Germany and Britain buy more from the United States than Puerto Rico. As a result of the high imports of food and consumption goods from the United States, however, Puerto Rico's external trade balance has gone into deficit – a deficit made good by income from tourism, remittances from Puerto Rican emigrants, payments from the American government and American capital investment. The balance of trade shows the close economic links between Puerto Rico and the United States: 92% of Puerto Rican exports go to the United States and 73% of imports come from there.

Over the last 20 years **tourism** has made great strides on Puerto Rico. The growth of tourism has been promoted by the Cuban revolution of 1959 and the policy of isolation to which it led, enabling San Juan to take the place of Havana, which had previously been the main Caribbean tourist attraction for Americans. Puerto Rico now has the largest number of visitors in the Caribbean – at present about 1.6 million annually (1966 – 0.7 million, 1970 – 1.1 million). With 6650 hotel rooms (1981) it has a high percentage of the total bed capacity of the Caribbean.

The full potential of tourism in Puerto Rico is still very far from being realized, and it contributes no more than 5% of the gross domestic product. One possible reason for this is that the hotel-building program has been tailored almost exclusively to the requirements of visitors from the United States and that there has been no broadly conceived strategy for the development of tourism. This defect will no doubt be corrected in future, particularly since the necessary infrastructures have now largely been provided.

See also *Culebra, *Mayagüez, *Ponce and **San Juan.

RECREATION and SPORT. – Sailing, deep-sea fishing, scuba diving, snorkeling, swimming and sunbathing.

AIR SERVICES. Occasional flights to Nassau and other neighboring islands.

SHIPPING. – Regular mail boats and freighters to Nassau.

The sickle-shaped *Ragged Island Range, a long string of islands extending W from Long Island for some 90 miles/145 km in the direction of Cuba, along the western side of Crooked Island Passage, is widely famed as a superb sailing area.

The largest of the islands, and one of the few that are inhabited, is **Great Ragged Island**, which like the neighboring islets is very dry on account of the almost constant wind. The chief place on the island is **Duncan Town**, named after the brother of Major Archibald Taylor, who together with Deveaux recovered New Providence in 1783. The people of the island formerly lived by extracting salt from the sea and trading with Haiti and Cuba; their main sources of income now are shipping, fishing and the production of souvenirs.

In recent years tourism has come to the Ragged Island Range, particularly in the form of yacht cruising. The ***Jumentos Cays** at the N end of the range and **Flamingo Cay** are particularly popular.

See also **Bahamas.

Ragged Island Range

Bahama Islands
Commonwealth of the Bahamas

Islands: Great Ragged Island, Hog Cay, Raccoon Cay, Narse Cay, Seal Cay, Flamingo Cay, Jumentos Cays, Lloyd Rock, Cay Verde, Cay Santo Domingo.
Area: 15 sq. miles/40 sq. km.
Population: 300.
Administrative center: Nassau (on New Providence).
ⓘ Ministry of Tourism,
  Nassau Court,
  P.O. Box N 3220,
  Nassau,
  Bahamas;
  tel. (809) 322 7505.
  See also Practical Information.

Redonda
See Antigua

La Romana
Dominican Republic
República Dominicana

Altitude: sea level.
Population: 60,000.
ⓘ Casa de Campo Hotel,
  Apartado Postal 140,
  La Romana,
  República Dominicana;
  tel. 682 9656.

HOTELS. – *Casa de Campo, in tourist center to E of town, 128 r., many bungalows; Roma, Ensanche la Oz, 14 r.; Romana, 77 r.

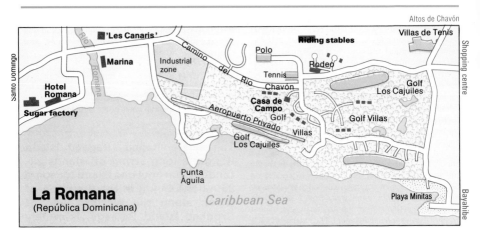

Altos de Chavón

La Romana
(República Dominicana)

Caribbean Sea

Shopping centre

Bayahibe

SPORT and RECREATION. – The tourist center has facilities for every variety of sport: *golf, tennis (many courts), clay pigeon shooting, riding, polo, canoeing, sailing, freshwater and sea fishing, water-skiing, snorkeling, scuba diving, etc.; instructors available. – Night club, discotheque.

TRANSPORT. – Air services to Las Américas International Airport, Santo Domingo. – Yacht harbor with marina and customs clearance facilities in La Romana. – Free bus services from Casa de Campo Hotel to yacht harbor, sports facilities, Altos de Chavón and Minitas Beach.

The provincial capital of La Romana lies on the SE coast of the island of Hispaniola some 75 miles/120 km E of Santo Domingo, capital of the Dominican Republic, at the mouth of the Río Romana. A major source of income is the sugar grown in the surrounding area (sugar factory). To the E of the town is a large **tourist center established in 1973, with several hotels, an airstrip, a golf-course, a polo ground, tennis courts and a wide range of other sports facilities.

The holiday complex, with an area of 7500 acres, is centered on the *Casa de Campo Hotel. Much of the coast here is rocky, but there are palm-fringed sandy beaches farther E at *Playa Minitas* and in *Bayahibe Bay*, which can be reached by minibus or boat.

Inland, to the NE, is *Altos de Chavón, a reproduction of a small Spanish colonial town of the 16th c. This is the home of an artists' colony, with workshops and studios, galleries and a museum.

SURROUNDINGS. – Off the coast lies the **Isla Catalina**, which can be reached on a schooner belonging to the hotel. The coastal waters offer ideal conditions for swimming, sailing and deep-sea fishing. Snorkelers and scuba divers can explore the magnificent coral gardens which abound with underwater life. There are instructors available for every kind of land and water sport.

E of La Romana are other beautiful bays. The road passes through extensive sugar-cane plantations to *La Laguna Beach*, with the Club Dominicus holiday village (60 bungalows). Still farther E is the *Bahía de Yuma*, a favorite with fishermen (see Higüey, Surroundings).

See also ****Dominican Republic** and ****Hispaniola**.

Islas de los Roques
See Isla de Margarita

Rum Cay
Bahama Islands
Commonwealth of the Bahamas

Area: 29 sq. miles/76 sq. km.
Population: 150.
Administrative center: Nassau (on New Providence).
Vehicles travel on the left.
ⓘ **Ministry of Tourism,**
Nassau Court,
P.O. Box N 3220,
Nassau,
Bahamas;
tel. (809) 322 7505.
See also Practical Information.

ACCOMMODATION. – Some rooms in private houses.

RECREATION and SPORT. – Scuba diving, snorkeling, deep-sea fishing, swimming and sunbathing; riding, shooting.

AIR SERVICES. – Occasional flights to Nassau and some of the neighboring islands.

SHIPPING. – Mail boat services from Port Nelson to San Salvador, Long Island, George Town (Great Exuma), Cat Island and Nassau (New Providence).

*Rum Cay, the second West Indian island visited by Columbus and named by him Santa María de la Concepción, lies in latitude 23°40′ N and longitude 74°50′ W. The land was brought into cultivation by American Loyalists who settled here during the Revolution. **This is a favorite port of call for sailing enthusiasts.**

This hilly island, originally a producer of cotton, switched to the production of salt after the collapse of the market for cotton in the first half of the 19th c. In 1853, however, the salt-working installations were devastated by a hurricane, and this, combined with American restrictions on the import of salt, led to a sharp fall in the island's population from its original 800 to the present figure of 150. The introduction of sisal and pineapple growing failed to halt the decline.

The chief settlement, **Port Nelson**, has a sheltered harbor on the S coast. To the E is the *Salt Pond*, which during the 19th c. was one of the most productive salt-pans in the Bahamas, with a peak annual output of 250,000 bushels of salt. – Around the island are a series of fine beaches, the best known of which are in *St George's Bay*, *Flamingo Bay* and **Hartford Cove*. In the NE of the island are *Lake George* and the little harbor of **Port Boyd**.

BOAT TRIP. – 12½ miles/20 km NW is **Conception Island**, a quiet little islet much frequented by deep-sea fishermen.

See also ****Bahamas**.

Saba

Lesser Antilles
Windward Islands
Netherlands Antilles

Area: 5 sq. miles/13.2 sq. km.
Population: 1100.
Administrative center: Willemstad (on Curaçao); regional centre Philipsburg (on St Maarten).
Vehicles travel on the right.
ⓘ **Saba Toeristenbureau,**
Windwardside,
Saba, N.A.
See also Practical Information.

HOTELS. – *Captain's Quarters*, 25 r., SP, terrace, bar, and *Scout's Place*, 5 r., both in Windwardside; *Caribe Guest House*, 5 r., and *The Bottom Guest House*, both in The Bottom.

EVENTS. – *Queen's Birthday* (April 30). – *Saba Day* (beginning of December), with folk displays. – *Kingdom Day* (December 15).

RECREATION and SPORT. – Hill walking and climbing, swimming, snorkeling, deep-sea fishing, sailing, boat trips.

AIR SERVICES. – Flights by light aircraft from the island of St-Martin/St Maarten.

SHIPPING. – Day trips from St-Martin/St Maarten. – Hydrofoil several times weekly from Philipsburg (St-Martin/St Maarten).

*Saba, one of the Windward Islands (Dutch Bovenvindse Eilanden) in the Netherlands Antilles, lies some 150 miles/24 km E of Puerto Rico and 30 miles/48 km S of St Maarten in latitude 17°37′ N and longitude 63°15′ W. This little island, almost circular in form and covered with lush green vegetation, is of volcanic origin. Its highest point is Mount Scenery (2900 ft/884 m), which is covered with tropical rain forest. The average temperature is about 77–79 °F/25–26 °C. The island has no beaches, being ringed with cliffs falling steeply down to the sea, and its appeal is primarily to individualists.

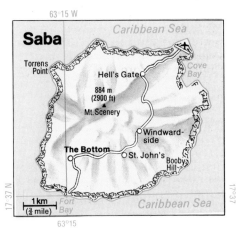

Saba was discovered by Columbus in 1493. The first Dutch settlers came here some 150 years later, and in 1690 the French tried unsuccessfully to establish a foothold. The island also became a pirates' lair. – The present-day population is almost equally divided between whites and blacks, and both are engaged in the growing of vegetables and in fishing.

Some of the men also work in the oil industry on Aruba (see p. 63), while the women produce beautiful embroidery (popular as souvenirs).

A road, completed in 1947 at the cost of much effort, runs across the island from NE to SW for 9 miles/14.5 km, linking the airfield with the harbor in Fort Bay. The little villages which cling to the hillside along this road are also accessible by stepped footpaths.

The chief town on the island is **The Bottom** (820 ft/250 m), in the SW. It is perched above the little *harbor* in Fort Bay, which has a breakwater 90 yd/80 m long and offers a safe haven for yachts. – The second largest settlement on the island is **Windwardside** (1805 ft/550 m), which has an island museum.

See also *Sint Eustatius (Statia)** and *Saint-Martin/Sint Maarten**.

Saint-Barthélemy (St Barts)

Lesser Antilles
Windward Islands

*French Antilles
Overseas Département of
Guadeloupe*

Area: 8½ sq. miles/22 sq. km.
Population: 3000.
Administrative center: Basse-Terre (on Guadeloupe).
Vehicles travel on the right.

(i) **Mairie de St-Barthélemy,**
F-97133 **Gustavia,**
St-Barthélemy, A.F.;
tel. 87 60 08.

HOTELS. – *PLM Jean-Bart*, St-Jean, 50 r., SP, private beach; *Autour du Rocher*, Lorient, 8 r.; *Baie des Flamands*; *Eden Rock*, St-Jean, 8 r.; *Emeraude Plage*, St-Jean, 14 r., private beach; *La Presqu'île*, Gustavia, 12 r.; *Le P'tit Morne*, Colombier, 10 r.; *Les Castelets*, Morne Lurin, 15 r., private beach; *Village St-Jean*, St-Jean, 26 r., private beach.

EVENTS. – *Fête Communale* (August 15), patronal festival.

RECREATION and SPORT. – Flying; sailing, deep-sea fishing, wind-surfing, water-skiing, scuba diving, snorkeling, swimming and sunbathing; walking.

AIR SERVICES. – Regular flights to Guadeloupe and St-Martin/St Maarten; occasional flights to other neighboring islands.

SHIPPING. – Occasional freighters to St-Martin/St Maarten.

*Saint-Barthélemy (also known in English as St Barts), lying in latitude 17°55' N and longitude 62°50' W, forms with St-Martin an arrondissement within the French overseas département of Gaudeloupe. With its beaches of fine sand fringed by fan palms and its turquoise and emerald-green water it is a holiday paradise, still largely undiscovered.**

Despite its small size the island has a varied topography, with much karstic terrain and a drought-loving vegetation reflecting the aridity of the soil. Trim little houses of northern European type give the villages a particular charm, and the island's past is reflected in a few Swedish street names which still survive and the starched white caps sometimes worn by the women, originally brought in by settlers from Normandy.

HISTORY. – Columbus discovered the island in 1493 and named it after his brother. A first attempt at colonization by French settlers from St-Christophe in 1648, when the island was still inhabited by Caribs, lasted only a few years, but a second settlement about 1660 by peasants from Brittany and Normandy was more successful. France was unable to hold on to the island, however, and in 1784 sold it to Sweden. The little coastal settlement of Le Carénage, now renamed Gustavia, became a free port. Thereafter the island, enjoying the benefits of neutrality in the conflicts between colonial powers, achieved a considerable degree of prosperity. This prosperity was destroyed by hurricanes and a great fire in Gustavia in 1852, and in 1877 the island, now impoverished, returned to France. – The population, over 90% of whom are white, live chiefly by trade and fishing.

*Gustavia, chief town on the island, is picturesquely situated on a sheltered natural harbor. The town was once defended by four forts, the ruins of which are still to be seen. Around the harbor are the *French Church* (R.C.) and the *Swedish Church* (Protestant). The town is still a free port, with many shops selling luxury goods at low prices. To the SE rises *Morne Lurin* (630 ft/192 m), below the S side of which is the *Anse du Gouverneur*, a romantic little cove accessible only on foot.

SURROUNDINGS of Gustavia. – 1 mile/1.5 km NW, beyond the *Anse du Public*, lies the picturesque little fishing village of *Corossol*, where the women still weave fabrics in the traditional way, using the leaf fibres of the fan palm. – To the NW, higher up, is the *Quartier du Colombier*, with a good view from the *Petit Morne* (528 ft/161 m) of the *Anse du Petit-Jean* and the vacation retreat of David Rockefeller. A footpath decends to the Anse du Colombier at the NW tip of the island, a secluded cove which offers good swimming and an anchorage for yachts. To the NW the *Ile Forchue*, rises out of the sea to a height of 341 ft/104 m and is a favorite port of call with yacht-owners.

2½ miles/4 km N of Gustavia, in the *Quartier des Flamands*, are the **Anse des Flamands* and the *Petite Anse*, two attractive little coves with good facilities for swimming. To the NE is a string of islets.

1½ miles/2.5 km N of Gustavia, also in the Quartier des Flamands, is the *Anse à Galets*, a beautiful little cove at the foot of the *Pointe à Etages* (469 ft/143 m).

1¼ miles/2 km NE of Gustavia, beyond the island's small airfield, is the charming **Baie de St-Jean*. – A narrow road continues E, coming in 1¼ miles/2 km to the *Anse de Lorient*, in the Quartier Lorient, with an interesting 19th c. church (R.C.). – The road then circles the island's highest peak, the *Montagne du Vitet* (922 ft/281 m; extensive views), and continues to the *Anse de Marigot* and the *Anse du Grand Cul-de-Sac*, two sheltered coves. Offshore lies the tiny *Ile de la Tortue* (115 ft/35 m). At the northeastern tip of the island, off the road, is the *Anse du Petit Cul-de-Sac* and 2½ miles/4 km farther on the *Anse du Grand Fond*, below the S side of the Montagne du Vitet. The road now runs NW to Lorient which has a beautiful beach. To the S, between the *Morne de Grand Fond* (899 ft/274 m) to the E and the Morne Lurin to the W, are to be seen the old salt-pans. Off the coast to the S are a number of islets and rocks.

See also **Guadeloupe*.

St Croix

Lesser Antilles
United States Virgin Islands
Territory administered by the United States

Area: 84 sq. miles/217 sq. km.
Population: 51,000.
Administrative center: Charlotte Amalie (on St Thomas).
Vehicles travel on the left.

ⓘ **United States Virgin Islands Division of Tourism,**
Christiansted, VI 00820,
tel. (809) 773 0495.
Custom House Building,
Frederiksted, VI 00840;
tel. (809) 772 0357.
See also Practical Information.

HOTELS. – CHRISTIANSTED: *Caravelle*, 46 r.; *Holger Danske*, 43 r.; *Club Comanche*, 40 r.; *King Christian*, 40 r.; *Anchor Inn*, 30 r.; *Charte House*, 26 r.; *King's Alley*, 22 r.; *Lodge*, 17 r.; *Pink Fancy*, 12 r. – **Buccaneer*, 1¼ miles/2 km E near Altona Lagoon, 152 r., T, golf, beaches, water sports; *Hotel on the Cay*, just outside the town to the E, 54 r. – *Doubles*, 64 r., NW of the town; *Queen's Quarter*, 50 r., SW of the town.

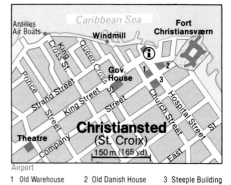

1 Old Warehouse   2 Old Danish House   3 Steeple Building

ON CANE BAY: *Cane Bay Plantation*, 20 r.

ON W COAST: *Sprat Hall*, 25 r., riding and sailing; *King Frederik*, 11 r.

FREDERIKSTED: *Frederiksted*, 38 r. – AT AIRPORT: *The Inn*, 25 r.

IN E OF ISLAND: **Grapetree Beach*, 153 r., SP, T, beach; *Coakley Bay Apartments*, 22 r.; *Reef Golf and Beach*, 34 r., golf.

RECREATION and SPORT. – Sailing, snorkeling, scuba diving, deep-sea fishing, swimming and sunbathing; golf, riding, tennis.

EVENTS. – *Crucian Christmas Fiesta*.

TRANSPORT. – Air services from the principal US airports and from other Caribbean islands. – Hydrofoil services to and from St John and St Thomas.

*St Croix is the largest and most southerly of the main islands in the US Virgin Islands group. It is mostly hilly, with expanses of pastureland and lush tropical vegetation – despite the fact that it suffers from a chronic shortage of water. In the NW the hills rise steeply up from the coast, with a gentler downward gradient towards the S.

Coastal scenery in the NE of St Croix

HISTORY. – Columbus discovered the island on November 14, 1493, on his second voyage, and named it *Santa Cruz*. The first settlers were Dutch and British; from 1650 to 1733 the island was French, and it then passed into the possession of the Danish West Indies Company which already owned the neighboring islands of St Thomas and St John. The growing of sugar-cane was introduced, and this brought the island great prosperity during the 18th and early 19th c. When the sugar industry collapsed in the latter part of the 19th c. Denmark sold the islands to the United States, of which they are now the most easterly outpost. A relic of the Danish occupation is that vehicles still travel on the left.

Other reminders of the island's Danish past are to be found all over St Croix, particularly in its two towns – Christiansted on the N coast and Frederiksted on the W coast.

Christiansted lies in a bay sheltered by a barrier reef and surrounded by hills.

SIGHTS. On the **harbor** is the well-preserved **Fort Christiansværn**, which was completed in 1774 and garrisoned until 1878. It was built of bricks brought from Denmark as ballast.

To the W of the fort is the **Old Danish Customs House**, now an art gallery, mostly dating from the early 19th c. Of only slightly later date is the *Scale House*, in which goods were weighed and checked. From here King Street leads to *Government House*, formed out of two older buildings about 1830. The central part dates from 1747, the W end from 1794 to 1797. Nearby can be found the colorful *Outdoor Market*.

To the S of the Scale House stands the old *Warehouse* of the Dutch West Indies Company, and opposite this the *Steeple Building*, the first Lutheran church on the island (1753). The neo-classical tower was added in 1794; small museum. Relics of pre-Columbian times.

An attractive BOAT TRIP from Christiansted (preferably in a glass-bottomed boat) is to ****Buck Island**, off the NE coast. The island and its coastal waters have been declared a national park, and are a paradise for divers. The *Buck Island Reef Nature Trail* is an underwater nature trail waymarked on the sea bottom ($\frac{1}{4}$ hour's swim). Since this is a nature reserve certain regulations must be observed: no fires may be lit on the island except on marked picnic sites, camping is not allowed and the collecting of marine organisms and underwater hunting are prohibited. – Other good diving grounds are to be found in *Sugar Bay*, half way along the N coast, and N of Frederiksted on the W coast. Sugar Bay (good view from Judith's Fancy) was where Columbus anchored in 1493.

Frederiksted (pop. 4000), the island's other town, has the advantage of a deep-water harbor. It is a sleepy little place which livens up when a cruise ship puts in. The buildings of the Danish period were largely destroyed in a fire in 1878, and the rebuilding was in Victorian style.

SIGHTS. – N of the pier is **Fort Frederik** (1755), where the abolition of slavery in the Danish possessions was proclaimed in 1848. It now houses a small art collection. – SE, in Market Street, stands the **Old Danish School** (1830). The market square dates from 1751.

To the S, in Princess Street, **St Patrick's Church** (R.C.) was built in 1843 on the site of an earlier 18th c. church. In Hospital Street, which runs parallel to Princess Street on the E, is an 18th c. building now occupied by the police.

From the pier Strand Street runs S along the coast. In this street are the old *Customs House* (late 18th c.) and the Victorian-style *Victoria House*. Parallel to Strand Street is King Street, a busy shopping area. A short distance S, at the corner of Queen Street and King Cross Street, we come to the striking **Apothecary Hall** (1839).

SURROUNDINGS of Frederiksted. – To the N of the town lies an extensive stretch of old plantation land; some of the plantation houses are now guest-houses. – Center Line Road leads NE from the town through a hilly region in which sugar-cane was grown until quite recently. In this area are a number of distilleries. The road passes *Whim Great House*, a restored plantation house with a sugar-mill; the house is now used for concerts, exhibitions, etc. To the left of the road is a *Botanical Garden*, and beyond this the *Fountain Valley golf-course*; to the right are the airport, the port installations of the aluminum-oxide plant and an oil refinery.

See also ***British Virgin Islands** and ***United States Virgin Islands**.

Street in Christiansted

Iles des Saintes

Lesser Antilles
Windward Islands
French Antilles
Overseas Département of
Guadeloupe

Area: 5½ sq. miles/14 sq. km.
Population: 4000.
Administrative center: Basse-Terre (on
Guadeloupe).
Vehicles travel on the right.

ⓘ **Office Départemental du Tourisme,**
Place de la Victoire,
B.P. 1099,
F-97110 Pointe-à-Pitre,
Guadeloupe, A.F.;
tel. 82 09 30.

HOTELS. – *Bois Joli*, 21 r.; *Jeanne d'Arc*, 10 r.;
Kanaoa, 10 r.; *La Colline*, 7 r.; *La Saintoise*, 10 r. – all
on Terre-de-Haut.

RECREATION and SPORT. – Sailing, deep-sea
fishing, scuba diving, snorkeling, swimming and
sunbathing; walking.

EVENTS. – ON TERRE-DE-BAS: *Fête Communale* (December 6, St Nicholas's Day). – ON TERRE-DE-HAUT:
Fête Communale (August 15), a colorful celebra-
tion of Assumption.

AIR SERVICES. – Regular flights from Terre-de-Haut
and Terre-de-Bas to Basse-Terre (Aérodrome de
Baillif) and Pointe-à-Pitre (Aéroport du Raizet) on
Guadeloupe.

SHIPPING. – Regular ferry services from Gros-Cap on
Terre-de-Bas and from Terre-de-Haut to Trois-
Rivières on Guadeloupe; occasional boats to Basse-
Terre.

The *Iles des Saintes (Les Saintes for
short) are one of the most beautiful
of the smaller groups of islands in
the Caribbean. Often described as a
"mini-Rio", with a series of attractive beaches, they lie 6 miles SE of
Basse-Terre, the volcanic western
part of Guadeloupe. They are the tips
of a submarine massif of volcanic
origin.**

Despite the proximity of the mountains of
Basse-Terre the rainfall is low, and the
islanders – who live mainly by fishing –
have had to construct cisterns to store
water. Within the last few years these
charming islets have been discovered by
the tourist trade.

HISTORY. – The islands, then apparently uninhabited,
were discovered by Columbus in November 1493 and
named by him *Los Santos*. French settlers established
themselves on the islands in 1648 and since then they
have shared the destinies of the mother island of
Guadeloupe. Soon their strategic importance was
recognized and they were strongly fortified. On April
12, 1782 the decisive naval battle of the Saints was
fought between Les Saintes and the neighboring
island of Dominica to the S, then under British rule. In
this encounter Admiral Rodney's British fleet defeated
a French fleet commanded by the Comte de Grasse: a
setback to the growing French influence in the
Caribbean which greatly strengthened the British
position in this area.

VEGETATION and ANIMAL LIFE. – The aridity of the
islands is reflected in the vegetation pattern, with its
many drought-loving plants and its wide range of
cactuses. – Visitors will encounter numerous little
lizards of varying size and species. Some of the caves
in less frequented parts of the islands are inhabited by
formidable-looking but harmless iguanas.

*Terre-de-Haut (0–1014 ft/0–309 m;
pop. 3000), the main island, has a varied
topography. It is made up of a number of
hills separated from one another by a
series of bays and inlets with beautiful
beaches.

The chief town on the island is **Terre-de-
Haut**, a picturesque little settlement of
small red-roofed houses, centrally located
on a curving bay between the hills. The
northern part of the town, *Mouillage*, is a
district of handsome villas, while the
southern part, *Fond de Curé*, has the
appearance of a fishing village. On the E
side of the town, near the airfield, is the
*Grande Anse, with a beautiful beach.

WALKS. – From Terre-de-Haut a track (⅓ hour's walk)
runs N through the *Quartier Maison-Blanche*, a
settlement once occupied by officers of the garrison,
to the well-restored *Fort Napoléon**, built at the
beginning of the 19th c. in Vaubanesque style to
replace an earlier 17th c. fort; it contains a small
museum.

In the NE of the island (⅓ hour's walk) is the pretty *Baie
de St-Pierre*, sheltered by the *Roches Percées*, which
lie offshore. A short distance S in the wild *Trou du
Grand Souffleur* the waves surge up against an
amphitheater-like inlet which has been gouged out of
the cliffs.

In the SW (1½ hours' walk) the *Morne du Chameau*
(1014 ft/309 m), the highest point on the island is
reached. From the top there are splendid panoramic
*views of Basse-Terre and Grande-Terre to the N and
NE, Marie-Galante to the E and Dominica to the S.

On the little *Ilet à Cabrit*, which rises out of the sea
to a height of 279 ft/85 m, stands *Fort Joséphine*
(19th c.), on the site of the earlier *Fort La Reine*.

*Terre-de-Bas (0–961 ft/0–293 m; pop.
1500), larger in area but more compact in
form, is separated from Terre-de-Haut by
the ¾ mile/1 km wide *Passe du Sud*. Its
highest points are the *Morne Abymes*
(961 ft/293 m) to the N and the *Morne
Paquette* (686 ft/209 m) to the S. On the

Pointe Sud is the recently constructed airfield. – The chief town on the island is *Gros-Cap*, with a small harbor from which boats ply to the reefs lying off the coast to the E and to the *Grand Ilet* (541 ft/165 m). On the NE coast, facing Terre-de-Haut, is the *Grande Anse*, with a sandy beach and a small 17th c. church.

See also *La Désirade, **Guadeloupe and *Marie-Galante.

St John
Lesser Antilles
United States Virgin Islands
Territory administered by the United States

Area: 20 sq. miles/52 sq. km.
Population: 3000.
Administrative center: Charlotte Amalie (on St Thomas).
Vehicles travel on the left.
(i) United States Virgin Islands Division of Tourism,
P.O. Box 200,
Cruz Bay, VI 00830;
tel. (809) 776 6450.
See also Practical Information.

HOTELS. –*Caneel Bay Plantation*, 168 r.; *Huldah Sewer's*, 20 r.; Cinnamon Bay; Maho Bay. – Several bungalows.

RESTAURANTS. – *Bamboo Inn*; *Fish Fry*; *Meada's*.

TRANSPORT. – Ferry services (*c.* 30 minutes) from Redhook Bay, St Thomas.

*St John is the smallest of the three major United States Virgin Islands. Some two-thirds of its area and large stretches of its coastal waters are now included in the *Virgin Islands National Park, established in 1956 on the initiative of Laurence S. Rockefeller, who bought this former sugar island and made it over to a foundation. It is now a great attraction for nature lovers and diving enthusiasts.

HISTORY. – The island was colonized by Denmark later than its sister islands, in 1717. The Danes cleared the whole island and laid out sugar-cane plantations; and the present tropical vegetation is a secondary growth, which developed after the working of the plantations had been first gravely hampered and then made impossible by a slave revolt in 1733 and the liberation of the slaves in 1848. The small population of the island now lives chiefly from tourism.

The ferry from St Thomas across the Pillsbury Sound puts in at **Cruz Bay**, the island's business center. In the little town is the Cruz Bay Visitors Center, where introductory talks about the National Park are given daily. This is also the starting point of conducted walks as well as excursions around the island in cross-country vehicles. There are boats from here to the Caneel Bay resort complex.

The standard TOUR OF THE ISLAND (15 miles/ 25 km) takes in the most beautiful of the bays on the N coast, the ruins of Annaberg sugar plantation and the look-out points in the interior of the island.

In *Caneel Bay*, to the N of Cruz Bay, is the exclusive *Caneel Bay Plantation* resort complex. From here the road continues past *Hawks Nest Bay* to *Trunk Bay*, one of the finest beaches in the Caribbean. In heavy surf swimming can be dangerous here, but there are life guards. For snorkelers there is a fascinating way-marked *Underwater Trail* through the coral gardens. – A camp site is situated in *Cinnamon Bay*, and another in *Maho Bay*. Above *Leinster Bay* are the ruins of *Annaberg Plantation* (18th c.).

At the E end of the island are two large inlets, *Hurricane Hole*, an excellent natural harbor, and *Coral Harbor*, – Above *Reef Bay*, half way along the S coast, are rock engravings attributed to the Arawaks, the pre-Columbian inhabitants of the island.

The interior of the island is traversed by waymarked footpaths. The best plan is to join a guided walk – essential requirements for which are stout footwear, insect repellent, food and drinking water. – Information about diving expeditions can be obtained in Cruz Bay.

See also *British Virgin Islands and *United States Virgin Islands

St Kitts (St Christopher)
Lesser Antilles
Leeward Islands
St Kitts and Nevis

Area: 101 sq. miles/262 sq. km (St Kitts 65 sq. miles/169 sq. km, Nevis 36 sq. miles/93 sq. km).
Capital: Basseterre (on St Kitts).
Population: 50,000, including 12,000 on Nevis.
Religion: predominantly Protestant (Anglicans and Methodists); some Roman Catholics.
Language: English; also some French patois.
Currency: Eastern Caribbean dollar (EC$) of 100 cents.
Weights and measures: British/American system.
Time: Atlantic Time, 4 hours behind GMT.
Vehicles travel on the left.
Travel documents: passport, onward or return ticket.

ⓘ **Tourist Board,**
Treasury Pier,
Basseterre,
St Kitts, W.I.;
tel. 2620.
See also Practical Information.

HOTELS. – BASSETERRE: *Fort Thomas Hotel*, 64 r., SP, T; *Ocean Terrace Inn*, 30 r., SP, T; *Banana Bay Beach Hotel*, 12 r., beach; *Blakeney Hotel*, 11 r.; *Canne-à-Sucre*, 10 r.; *Cockleshell*, 10 r., T, beach; *Fairview Inn*, 33 r., SP, T; etc. – FRIGATE BAY: *Royal St Kitts Hotel*, 138 r., SP, T, casino, golf, beach. – MOUNT PLEASANT: *Rawlins Plantation Inn*, 6 r., SP. – DIEPPE BAY: *Golden Lemon*, 10 r., SP. – CONAREEF BEACH: *Conareef Beach*, 7 r., T, beach; etc. – Several GUEST-HOUSES and many HOLIDAY APARTMENTS.

RESTAURANTS in most hotels; also IN BASSETERRE: *Avondale*, George Street; *City Gate*, Fort Street; *Hylyte*, Old Road; *Uncle T's*, Cayon Street; *Lennies*, Fort Street. – AT GOLDEN ROCK AIRPORT: *Wings*. – IN FRIGATE BAY: *The Anchorage*.

Casino in *Royal St Kitts Hotel*, Frigate Bay.

PUBLIC HOLIDAYS and EVENTS. – *New Year's Day*. – *Statehood Day* (February 27). – *Good Friday* and *Easter Monday*. – *Labour Day* (first Monday in May). – *Queen's Birthday* (second Saturday in June), with parade. – *August Monday* (first Monday in August). – *Prince of Wales's Birthday* (November 14). – *Christmas Day*. – *Boxing Day* (December 26). – *Carnival* (December 26 to January 2).

RECREATION and SPORT. – Golf, tennis, water sports, riding, cricket, softball, netball.

AIR SERVICES. – Regular flights to Nevis, Anguilla, Antigua, St Maarten, Tortola, St Thomas, St Croix, Puerto Rico and Guadeloupe; occasional charters to other places in the Caribbean.

SHIPPING. – Occasional calls by cruise ships, usually from San Juan (Puerto Rico) or Miami (USA) and visiting other Caribbean islands.

*St Kitts (less commonly called St Christopher), 19 miles/31 km long and up to 6 miles/10 km wide, lies in the inner arc of the Leeward Islands, at the northern end of the Lesser Antilles. Together with the neighboring island of Nevis – only half its size – and the coral islet of Sombrero it forms the state of St Kitts and Nevis. With their magnificent sandy beaches and idyllic bays and coves, framed by hills, the two main islands are among the most popular tourist destinations in the eastern Caribbean.

St Kitts and its neighbor Nevis (see separate entry) are geographically as well as politically linked. Both lie on a submarine rock base which was overlaid during the Tertiary era by a mighty range of volcanic mountains. The range traverses the oval island of St Kitts from NW to SE, continues along a narrow tongue of land with several salt lagoons, runs under the sea at a depth of only 26 ft/ 8 m below the surface and re-emerges on Nevis. The two islands are separated by the Narrows, a channel 2 miles/3 km wide the floor of which is covered with great expanses of coral reefs. While Nevis

The W coast of St Kitts, with Brimstone Hill; in the background the island of Saba

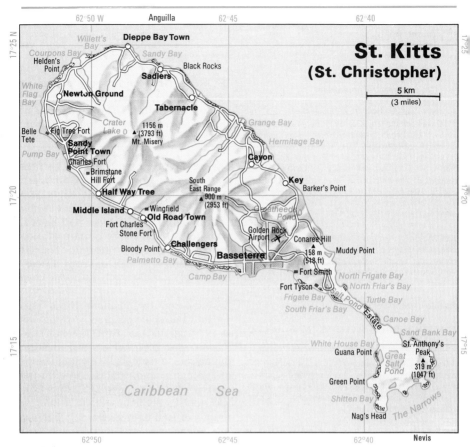

St. Kitts
(St. Christopher)

consists of a single volcano in the exact center of the island (Nevis Peak, 3232 ft/ 985 m), St Kitts has two volcanic massifs – in the SE are the steep-sided peaks of the South East Range, rising to 2950 ft/ 900 m, in the NW the crater walls of Mount Misery rearing up to 3793 ft/ 1156 m.

The dimensions of the crater of Nevis Peak are impressive. It has a diameter of some 1100 yd/1000 m and is about 790 ft/ 240 m deep. It was last active in 1692, when the small lake within the crater was formed. At several points sulphurous fumes at a temperature of between 212 and 392 °F (100 and 200 °C) emerge from crevices in the rock (solfataras). These indicate that volcanic activity is dying down, so that Mount Misery is unlikely to erupt again.

CLIMATE and VEGETATION. – Like the other Caribbean islands, St Kitts and Nevis lie within the tropical zone exposed to the trade winds. As a result of their mountainous structure, however, their climate has some distinctive characteristics, since the high central mountain regions produce a very uneven distribution of rainfall. The moisture-bearing trade winds blow throughout the year from the E and NE, releasing the moisture in the form of rain when they encounter the hills. Most of the rain falls in the summit regions, with an average of 148 in./3750 mm a year.

This can be observed from the coast, the hills being shrouded in dense cloud by noon.

Around the hills the rainfall lessens with decreasing height to an average of 47 in./1200 mm. In the wind

Coconut harvest, St Kitts

shadow of the South East Range, at Basseterre and on the S coast of Nevis, the figure falls to 30 in./750 mm, and 4–6 months in winter are arid: i.e. the evaporation is higher than the rainfall. This is true also of the narrow tongue of land at the SE end of St Kitts, extending towards Nevis. This area owes its low rainfall to the fact that there is no high ground to cause the moist trade winds to rise.

The climate of St Kitts and Nevis is healthy, particularly in the dry coastal areas, since the air lacks the high humidity usually found on tropical islands. Moreover, air temperatures throughout the year are equable and mild. The mean January temperature at Basseterre is 76.5 °F/24.7 °C, the mean for August 81.3 °F/27.4 °C. Extremes are 90 °F/32 °C in summer and 64 °F/18 °C in winter; but these figures are reached on only a few days in the year.

The natural vegetation varies with altitude. The highest summits are covered only with grass and are used as pasture. Immediately below this, at altitudes of 2625 ft/800 m and upwards, is cloud forest, and below this again is tropical rain forest, extending down to about 1000 ft/300 m. Below this level, reaching to the coast, is cultivated land, with the natural vegetation surviving only in patches here and there, except on the southeastern peninsula of St Kitts, where it has largely been preserved. Thus on the E coast opposite Basseterre there are still large mangrove swamps, and farther inland and towards the S there are narrow strips of thorn and succulent vegetation in the coastal hinterland, giving place to evergreen dry forest with increasing distance from the coast. It is planned to establish a nature park in this relatively unspoiled southern part of the island.

HISTORY. – St Kitts and Nevis were discovered by Columbus on his second voyage (1493), but for the next 150 years both islands remained in the possession of the indigenous Carib inhabitants. St Kitts was then known as *Liamuiga* ("fertile land"), for its volcanic soils provided subsistence for an unusually large Indian population. As the discoverer of the islands and the dominant power in the Caribbean, Spain laid claim to their ownership but made no attempt to settle them, being chiefly concerned at this time to secure the treasures of gold and silver of South and Central America. Towards the end of the 16th c., however, other European powers – England, France and the Netherlands – moved into the Caribbean. At first both the English and the French drew salt and timber from St Kitts, but in 1605 England took possession of the whole island. In 1623 the first 16 settlers, led by Sir Thomas Warner, established themselves on St Kitts, which became known as the mother colony of the British West Indies. A few years later, in 1628, Nevis was colonized from St Kitts. In 1625 a damaged French ship was given permission to put in at what is now Basseterre to carry out urgent repairs, and the French, led by Belain d'Esnambuc, then succeeded in gaining a foothold on the island. In 1626 St Kitts was divided between Britain and France, the N and S (Capesterre and Basseterre) going to France and the central part to Britain – a division still reflected in the place-names. The salt lakes in the extreme S of the island were worked by both British and French settlers. Over the next 157 years there were frequent conflicts between French and British, and it was only in 1783, under the treaty of Versailles, that France and Spain finally recognized St Kitts as a British possession. In 1871 it was incorporated,

together with Nevis, in the colony of the Leeward Islands. On September 19, 1983 the little island state became fully independent.

POPULATION. – St Kitts and Nevis has a population of some 50,000, the great majority of whom live in the coastal areas on both islands. The main concentrations of population are in the Capital, Basseterre (pop. 16 000) and Sandy Point Town on St Kitts and Charlestown (pop. 2500) on Nevis. The interiors of both islands are largely uninhabited, since the steep and densely wooded slopes of the volcanic hills can be cultivated only up to a height of about 1000 ft/300 m. The peninsula at the SE end of St Kitts, with its salt lakes, is also empty of population, since the poor soils and greater aridity make the land unsuitable for cultivation. The island of Sombrero which is also included within the state of St Kitts and Nevis is completely uninhabited.

The population of St Kitts and Nevis consists mainly of blacks (86%) and mulattoes (11%), the descendants of the slaves brought in from Africa; only some 2% of the population are Europeans, while 1% come from India.

Fishermen mending their nets, St Kitts

As on the neighboring islands, the considerable excess of births over deaths has given rise to serious problems. Since the local labor market, which is predominantly agricultural, cannot absorb the explosive increase in population, several hundred people leave the islands every year, most of them going to the US Virgin Islands.

ECONOMY. – Despite the government's efforts to promote the development of industry and the very considerable growth of tourism in recent years, St Kitts and Nevis remain a predominantly agricultural country. There are, however, major structural differences between the two islands.

St Kitts is an island of large agricultural holdings. Some 90% of the cultivable land belongs to 30 or so estates devoted to the monoculture of sugar-cane, extending up the slopes of the volcanic hills to about 1000 ft/300 m. Small mixed farming units, mostly producing high-quality sea-island cotton, are found in only three areas, at heights of between 650 ft/ 200 m and 1000 ft/300 m.

Sugar growing was introduced on St Kitts some 300 years ago, replacing the tobacco which had been grown by the early settlers when the tobacco surplus in Europe created by the large imports from colonies in the New World led to a sharp fall in price. The large sugar plantations were worked by many African black slaves brought in for the purpose. In spite of three centuries of this monoculture the yield per acre was more than doubled at the beginning of the 20th c. by the application of modern methods of cultivation, for the volcanic soils were fertile enough to show no signs of exhaustion after this long period under the same crop. Since 1964, however, yields have been falling, no doubt because the regenerative capacity of the soil has been overestimated and the extensive method of cultivation practiced on the large plantations affords no scope for the intensive use of fertilizers and the introduction of a system of crop rotation.

Although the total output of sugar-cane has thus fallen over the past 20 years from 43,000 to 27,000 tons a year (1983) it is still by far the most important element in the economy, accounting for 30% of the gross domestic product and 90% of the value of exports. Much of the foreign currency which it earns, however, must be spent on the import of food.

The entire St Kitts and Nevis sugar-cane crop is processed in a sugar factory in Basseterre. St Kitts also has a number of other industrial establishments, all in Basseterre – two cotton-ginning mills, a brewery, a textile factory, a cigarette factory and two factories producing television and radio sets and electronic switchgear for the American market.

The economic structure of the neighboring island of Nevis is quite different. Small peasant holdings predominate – Nevis has more than half the number of such holdings in the two islands – and there is little industry.

TRANSPORT. – Both islands have a good road system, enabling agricultural produce to be transported easily to the port of Basseterre, the capacity of which has been considerably increased by a new

deep-water harbor opened in 1981. The sugar-cane plantations are served by 36 miles/58 km of industrial railroad and 60 miles/96 km of road. The much smaller island of Nevis is even better served, with 62 miles/ 100 km of roads. The number of motor vehicles licensed in St Kitts and Nevis in 1975 was 3333. The recently improved airport at Golden Rock on St Kitts is used by three airlines which link the island with the larger international airports on Antigua, St Maarten, the Virgin Islands, Guadeloupe and Puerto Rico. With an eye to the further development of tourism the runway has been extended to take large-capacity aircraft.

Tourism has developed over the last two decades into an important element in the economy, second only to agriculture as an earner of foreign currency. The largest resort area, with the most modern infrastructure, is in Frigate Bay at the SE end of St Kitts.

Basseterre (pop. 16,000), capital of St Kitts and Nevis since 1727, lies in a wide, flat bay on the SW coast of St Kitts, against the backdrop of the *South East Range*, wooded volcanic mountains rising to 2950 ft/900 m. This is a typical little British colonial town with its streets laid out on a rectangular plan. It dates in its present form from the rebuilding following a fire in 1867 which destroyed four-fifths of the town. Founded by the French in the 17th c, it was developed by the British from 1706 onwards. Many buildings had already been destroyed by an earthquake in 1843. More recently, in August 1928, much of the town was

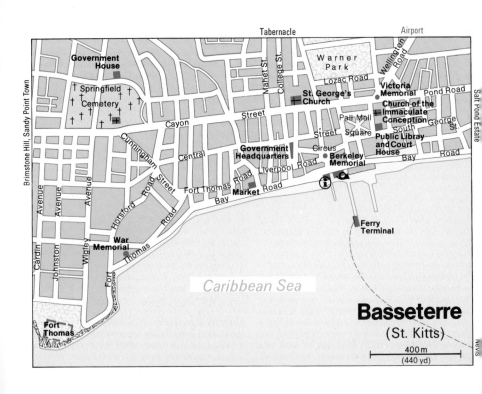

The Circus, Basseterre, with the Thomas Berkeley Memorial

devastated by a hurricane. An earthquake on October 8, 1874 caused only minor damage to buildings. Finally in 1979 the harbor front suffered severely from the effects of Hurricane David and Hurricane Frederick.

SIGHTS. – The life of the town revolves around the **Harbor**, with the old *Treasury Pier*, and the octagonal *Circus*, the heart of the business quarter, a few yards from the seafront. In the middle of the square stands the *Thomas Berkeley Memorial*, commemorating a former president of the Legislative Assembly. From here Bank Street runs E to *Pall Mall Square* which is surrounded by Georgian buildings; the gardens in the square occupy the site of the old slave market. At the SE corner of the square is the *Court House*, the first floor of which is occupied by the **Public Library**, with valuable old books and maps on the West Indies and stone engravings and implements of the Caribs who were the indigenous inhabitants of St Kitts. A few yards N is the *Church of the Immaculate Conception* (R.C.), with a façade flanked by twin towers. Going past the church and turning left along Cayon Street, we come to **St George's Church** (on right), which was originally built by the French in 1670, burned down by the British in 1706, rebuilt four years later and thereafter three times destroyed and rebuilt. The present church dates from 1868. – Also worth a visit is the *Public Market* in Bay Road, W of the harbor.

A worthwhile excursion from Basseterre is a TOUR OF THE ISLAND by hired car (37 miles/60 km). – At the W end of Basseterre Bay are the ruins of *Fort Thomas*,

St George's Church, Basseterre

Brimstone Hill, St Kitts

built by the French. 3 miles/5 km W of the town on the coast road we reach the *Fairview Inn*, built about 1720 as the headquarters of the French commandant and converted into a modern hotel in 1968–70. Beyond this is *Bloody Point*, where British and French forces inflicted an annihilating defeat on the Caribs in 1626. A few miles farther on comes **Old Road Town**, capital of the British sector of the island until 1727, and the oldest town in the British West Indies; from here Nevis, Antigua and Montserrat were colonized. At the entrance to the town are the ruins of *Fort Charles*, scene of a bloody encounter between British and French forces in 1666. Old Road Town was founded on January 28, 1623 by Sir Thomas Warner, leader of the first settlers on St Kitts and later Governor-General of the British West Indies. Near the town are some *Carib rock engravings. To the N is *Wingfield Manor Estate*, on a site once occupied by the principal Carib settlement.

The next place on the coast road is *Middle Island*, with the **grave of Sir Thomas Warner** (d. 1648), founder of the colony. Then comes Half-Way Tree, immediately beyond which, on the right, rises *Brimstone Hill**, crowned by the ruins of Brimstone Hill Fort (partly restored; visitors' center). This formidable stronghold, begun in 1690, has been called the Gibraltar of the West Indies. It was the scene in 1782 of one of the fiercest engagements in the Caribbean, when British forces captured the fort from the French and gained control of the whole of the island. Within the fort is a munitions depot and a hospital, beside which lies a cemetery for victims of yellow fever.

The road continues through *Sandy Point Town*, the second largest settlement on St Kitts, and round the NW end of the island to the **Black Rocks**, on the E coast, where the lava flows from Mount Misery reached the sea. The ascent of the volcano is a rewarding experience (an 8-hour trip, starting from Harris Estate; local guide advisable). – From the Black Rocks the road returns via Frigate Bay to Basseterre.

See also **Nevis**.

Carib rock engravings, St. Kitts

St Lucia

Lesser Antilles
Windward Islands
Commonwealth of St Lucia

Nationality letters: STL.
Area: 238 sq. miles./616 sq. km
Capital: Castries.
Population: 125,000.
Religion: 90% Roman Catholics; 10% Protestants
(Anglicans, Methodists).
Local administration: 11 quarters.
Language: English; Creole patois of French.
Currency: Eastern Caribbean dollar (EC$) of 100
cents.
Weights and measures: British/American system.
Time: Atlantic Time, 4 hours behind GMT.
Vehicles travel on the left.
Travel documents: passport, onward or return ticket.

St Lucia Tourist Board,
Port Entrance,
Jeremy Street,
P.O. Box 221,
Castries,
St Lucia;
tel. 2479.
See also Practical Information.

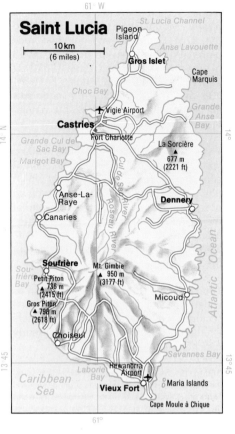

HOTELS. – CASTRIES: *Halcyon Beach Club*, Choc
Beach, 88 r., SP, T; *Hotel La Toc*, 164 r., SP, T, golf,
beach; *Halcyon Sands*, Vigie Beach , 47 r.; *Malabar
Beach Hotel*, Vigie Beach, 80 r., beach; *Villa Hotel*,
The Morne, 28 r.; etc. – SOUFRIÈRE: *Anse Chastanet
Beach Hotel*, 25 r.; *Dasheene Live Inn Resort*, 22 r.;
Home Hotel, 4 r. – VIEUX-FORT: *Halcyon Days Hotel*,
256 r., SP; *Cloud's Nest Hotel*, 14 r.; *Kimatrai Hotel*,
14 r. – CAPE ESTATE: *Steigenberger Cariblue Hotel*,
102 r., SP, T, golf, beach; *Smugglers Village*, 75 r. –
REDUIT BEACH: *St Lucian* (formerly Holiday Inn), 190
r., SP, T, beach. – LABORIE: *Hewanorra Hotel*, 14 r. –
Many GUEST-HOUSES and HOLIDAY APART-
MENTS.

RESTAURANTS in most hotels; also IN CASTRIES:
Nick's Place; Coalpot; Calabash, Mongiraud Street;
Rain Restaurant, Columbus Square; *Dolittle's*, Mari-
got des Roseaux; *Marigot Inn*, Marigot Bay; *Green
Parrot*, The Morne. – SOUFRIÈRE: *Hook's Hideaway*;
The Still. – REDUIT BEACH: *Pelican Restaurant*, near St
Lucian Hotel, Gros Islet Highway.

PUBLIC HOLIDAYS and EVENTS. – *New Year's Day*.
New Year's Holiday (January 2), celebrations in
Columbus Square, Castries. – *Carnival* (first week in
February). – *National Day* (February 22). – *Indepen-
dence Day; St Peter's Day* (June 29), festival of the
inshore fishermen. – *Feast of St Rose of Lima* (August
30), flower festival. – *Feast of St Margaret Mary
Alacoque* (October 17), flower festival. – *Christmas
Day*.

RECREATION and SPORT. – Golf (Cap Estate Golf
Club, La Toc Hotel, Halcyon Days Hotel, Halcyon
Beach Hotel), tennis (courts at all the large hotels);
water sports; riding (Cap Estate Stables).

AIR SERVICES. – From Hewanorra International
Airport, 40 miles/64 km from Castries at the S end of
the island, there are direct connections with Miami,
New York, Toronto, London, Paris (via Martinique),
Düsseldorf and Frankfurt am Main. Domestic services
(within the Caribbean) use Vigie Airport, 2 miles/3 km
N of Castries.

SHIPPING. – Regular calls by Caribbean cruise ships
at Castries.

****St Lucia has some of the most
beautiful scenery in the eastern
Caribbean, with magnificent
beaches, modern hotels, beautiful
secluded coves, good communications and a climate characteristic of
the Windward Islands, under the
influence of the trade winds, which
is pleasantly tolerable for visitors
from more northern climes.**

Like the neighbouring islands of Martinique, 20 miles/32 km N, and St Vincent,
30 miles/48 km S, St Lucia (27 miles/
44 km long, 14 miles/22 km wide)
consists almost wholly of volcanic
rock, with a geologically older volcanic
massif in the N and a younger one in the
central part of the island. The two areas
are sharply distinguished by the very
different superficial topography. The
northern part of the island has been worn
down by erosion during the Tertiary era to
a height of about 1640 ft/500 m, while the
central part, geologically much younger,
is a region of markedly mountainous
character slashed by innumerable mountain streams. In this region are the island's

highest sugarloaf-shaped peaks known as *pitons* – Mount Gimie (3117 ft/950 m), to the E of Soufrière, and the two rock pinnacles which rear up on the coast S of the town, the Grand Piton (2618 ft/ 798 m) and the Petit Piton (2415 ft/ 736 m). These two striking landmarks are among the most remarkable natural features in the Caribbean.

The southern part of the island is in sharp contrast to the rest; a flat coastal plain of alluvial soil deposited by the rivers which flow into the sea here, varied only by an occasional hill. At the southernmost tip of the island is the Moule-à-Chique peninsula, a narrow promontory rising to 728 ft/ 222 m which separates the Atlantic from the Caribbean.

The coasts of St Lucia show a pattern as variable as the interior, in which small secluded coves at the mouths of rivers alternate with sheer cliffs and long sandy beaches.

CLIMATE. – The climatic pattern of St Lucia is set by the NE trade winds which blow throughout the year. There are, therefore, only minor differences between the seasons, both average monthly temperatures (about 75–81 °F/24–27 °C) and rainfall showing relatively little variation over the year. A more important differentiating factor is altitude: temperatures in the hills are markedly lower than on the coast, while rainfall is considerably higher. In the hills, which cause the moisture-carrying trade winds to move upwards, there may be up to 150 in./3800 mm of rain in the year, while in the northern and southern coastal areas the rainfall is about 46 in./1160 mm. Between these two extremes the figures vary widely according to altitude and exposure to wind. The tourist areas are in the regions with the lowest rainfall. The best time to visit St Lucia is between December and June, when the relative humidity of the air is lower and the chances of being caught in a tropical hurricane are at a minimum.

VEGETATION. – Not much is left of the island's natural vegetation, varying according to altitude and exposure to the wind. The primeval forests were ruthlessly felled for their timber and were replaced by the secondary forest which now covers half the island. Some remnants of the natural tropical rain forest have survived only in the higher and more inaccessible highland regions.

HISTORY. – Unusually for the Caribbean, it is not known when St Lucia was discovered, or by whom. It has been supposed that Columbus sighted it – but did not land here – on St Lucia's Day (June 18) in 1502, during his fourth voyage, and this would explain the name of Santa Lucia which was given to the island by the Spaniards and later became the French Sainte-Lucie and the English St Lucia. Lack of any European interest in the island and the hostile attitude of the indigenous Caribs long prevented any attempt at settlement, though European vessels frequently anchored off the island. Spanish expeditions came here in quest of slaves to work in their mines; French

freebooters used the island as a lair; and English ships put in to take on water. The first settlement was established in 1605 by 67 Englishmen making for Guiana on the South American mainland. They took the wrong course and when their provisions began to run low resolved to settle on St Lucia, probably in the Vieux Fort area. As a result of internal dissension and Carib attacks, however, the settlement was a failure.

Later St Lucia was claimed by France, and in 1635 the French king made grants of land to various Frenchmen. However, the next attempt to establish a settlement was again made by Englishmen, a small party of whom came to St Lucia in 1638 but were driven out by the Caribs two years later. In 1642 Louis XIII granted the island to the French West Indies Company; but several governors appointed by the Company were murdered by the Caribs, and peace was not established until 1660, when a treaty was concluded between the British, the French and the Caribs. It was not long, however, before France and Britain were again at odds, with the result that St Lucia changed hands no fewer than 14 times, until it was finally taken by Britain in 1803 and became a British crown colony under the Peace of Paris in 1814. In 1871 it was incorporated in the larger administrative unit of the Windward Islands.

Remote though it was from the actual battle areas, St Lucia was inevitably affected by the First and, even more strongly, the Second World War. A shortage of essential supplies as a result of the interruption of normal shipping services was not the islanders' only problem. As a British colony, St Lucia sent troops to Europe and allowed the Americans to establish an air base at Beane Airfield near Vieux Fort (now Hewanorra Airport) as well as a naval base. On March 9, 1942 a German submarine torpedoed two vessels in Castries harbor.

In February 1967 the island was granted the status of a state associated with the United Kingdom but with full internal self-government, Britain remaining responsible only for external affairs and defense; and on February 22, 1979 it became a wholly independent state within the British Commonwealth. The head of government is the Queen, who is represented by a Governor-General.

POPULATION. – St Lucia has a population of 125,000 some four-fifths of whom are concentrated in the capital (pop. 45,000) and the surrounding area in the valley of the Castries River and around Vieux Fort in the southern coastal plain. The rest are mostly in the town of Soufrière and some other coastal settlements. The lower areas in the interior of the island, particularly the fertile valleys, also support a significant population, but the highland regions in the center of the island are practically uninhabited.

Some 66% of the population consists of blacks and 30% of mulattoes, the descendants of the island's 13,000 slaves, who were liberated between 1834 and 1840. A further 4% are Indians, descended from contract workers recruited in India. Only some 0.5% of the population is of European extraction.

Like most of the Caribbean islands, St Lucia has a very high annual rate of population increase – almost 2.7%, a not unusual figure in developing countries. The visible expression of the problems to which this gives rise can be seen in the corrugated iron shacks and primitive wooden houses in the poorer districts of the capital. The poverty which is rife in this overpopulated island state has been a major factor in the social unrest of recent years.

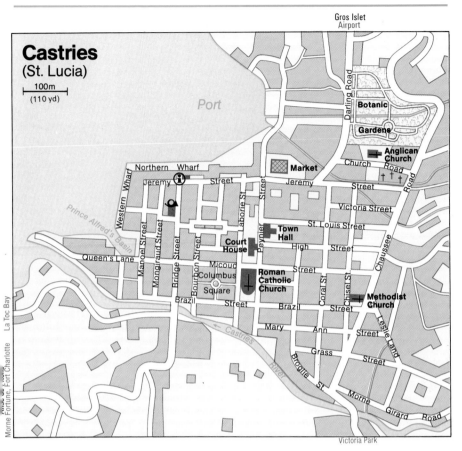

Castries
(St. Lucia)

100m
(110 yd)

ECONOMY. – Despite the government's efforts to promote the development of industry, St Lucia's economy is still based on **agriculture**, which accounts for almost four-fifths of the value of exports and employs two-fifths of the working population. In addition there are some 10,000 small agricultural holdings growing subsistence crops.

For more than 200 years St Lucia was a major producer of sugar, but since the 1950s the growing of sugar-cane has steadily declined, giving way to the less labor-intensive growing of bananas. The old sugar-growing areas in the larger valleys (Roseau, Cul de Sac, Dennery) are now covered by large banana plantations, using modern methods of cultivation including the use of light aircraft for pest control. The last sugar factory on the island closed down in 1963. In addition to bananas, which now make up over 80% of exports, coconuts and cacao are also grown on a considerable scale. Soufrière has a plant for extracting copra oil and making soap. Cattle-farming and dairying are being promoted by government assistance, with the object of making the island self-sufficient in meat and dairy products and thus obviating the need for expensive imports.

Although only about a third of the island's total area is under cultivation, agriculture makes its very large contribution to exports ·as a result of the high productivity achieved by intensive methods of cultivation on small and medium-sized holdings. Some 46% of agricultural land is on holdings of under 50 acres; large estates account for about 40%.

The only significant amount of non-agricultural employment is in the capital, Castries, and (on a very small scale indeed) in Soufrière, Vieux Fort and Gros Islet. There is practically no **industry**. Of much more importance are craft production, commerce and banking, together with **tourism**, which has developed into a valuable source of foreign currency, and employment. In 1974 St Lucia had more than 2400 beds available for visitors, 51,800 of whom spent almost 10 million Eastern Caribbean dollars, or more than 10% of the gross domestic product. In 1979 153,000 overseas visitors came to St Lucia, of whom 64,000 were on cruises and 13,000 on yachts. In 1980 the island's tourist infrastructure suffered severe damage from Hurricane Allen.

***Castries** (pop. 45,000), capital of St Lucia, is attractively located in a sheltered bay on the W coast, surrounded by hills. There is a magnificent view of the town and the harbor from the Morne Fortune (853 ft/260 m), 1 mile/1.5 km S of the town center, crowned by Fort Charlotte (1794). Castries is a town of modern appearance, since numerous earthquakes, hurricanes and fires have destroyed all its older buildings. The town lost the last remnants of its former colonial charm in a great fire in 1948 which, in spite of the efforts of American fire-fighting aircraft, destroyed four-fifths of the· old wooden houses.

The strategic importance of St Lucia, with its excellent natural harbor, was recog-

Castries (St Lucia)

nized from the earliest days of European settlement in the New World, and Britain and France fought bitterly for possession of the island. Its strategic situation brought economic advantages, leading at the turn of the 19th c. to a considerable boom as a result of the heavy shipping traffic using the port. At the end of the century Castries occupied 14th place among the world's ports in terms of freight handled. Between 1880 and 1930 coal bunkering accounted for over half St Lucia's gross domestic product, the ships being loaded by women carrying hundred pound sacks on their heads.

The only building of major consequence in Castries is the *Cathedral of the Immaculate Conception* (1894–97), on the E side of the gardens in Columbus Square. The Market in the N of the town is a lively scene on Saturday mornings.

The most celebrated tourist attraction on St Lucia is on the W coast, S of Castries. The road crosses the Cul-de-Sac valley, and reaches *Marigot Bay*, one of the most

beautiful natural yacht harbors in the Caribbean, with hotels, restaurants and facilities for water-sports. It then follows a winding course to the fishing village of *Soufrière*. From the last ridge of hills before Soufrière there is the finest view of the best known landmarks in the Caribbean – the two ****Pitons**, volcanic cones respectively 2618 ft/798 m and 2415 ft/ 736 m in height, formed of the lava from volcanoes which were originally much larger. A short distance inland are the impressive **Sulphur Springs*, in a volcanic

A sulphur spring on St Lucia

The Pitons (St Lucia)

crater which can be easily reached by car: hence St Lucia's claim to possess the only drive-in volcano in the world. Nearby are the island's well-known sulphur baths, said to have been in use as early as 1785. The plans which had been in existence for many years to use the geo-thermal energy of these volcanic phenomena for the production of electric power were revived in September 1979, when the St Lucia government applied to the Organization of American States for financial support.

From Soufrière the road continues S to **Vieux Fort**, formerly capital of St Lucia but now outshadowed by Castries. It is to be developed over the next few years into a tourist resort, a role favored by the proximity of *Hewanorra Airport* (from the Indian name for St Lucia), which was enlarged in 1969. From here a modern road follows the Atlantic coast and across to Castries.

A shorter EXCURSION from Castries is to **Pigeon Island**, off the N end of St Lucia. On the island are remains of Arawak occupation and a fort of 1778. Pigeon Island is now connected to the main island by a causeway, and has become *Pigeon Point*. A long sandy beach has been created, and the adjoining swampland converted into a resort complex (vacation apartments, marina, yacht anchorage) called *Rodney Bay*, after the 18th c. admiral, who had his headquarters here for a time. The unexpected consequence of this development has been a major change in the direction of the coastal currents which has destroyed other beaches and killed the lobster fisheries of a nearby fishing village.

Saint-Marc

Haiti
République d'Haïti

Département de l'Artibonite.
Altitude: sea level.
Population: 26,000.

(i) **Office National du Tourisme,**
Avenue Marie-Jeanne,
Port-au-Prince,
Haïti;
tel. 2 1720.
See also Practical Information.

*Saint-Marc, a port founded in the 18th c., lies in a beautiful setting on the bay of the same name, bounded on the S by the foothills of the Chaîne des Matheux. It is still an important center of the charcoal trade.**

Saint-Marc was the port of embarkation for an expeditionary corps of 800 men which the then French colony of Saint-Domingue sent to help the Americans in their War of Independence. Among the volunteers in this force was Henry Christophe, later king of northern Haiti. – There are imposing remains of fortifications, and beautiful beaches in the immediate vicinity of the town.

Saint-Marc to Verrettes. – It is advisable before undertaking this excursion to inquire about the state of the road. – 19 miles/30 km E of Saint-Marc, at the village of **Petite Rivière de l'Artibonite**, is the *Fort de la Crête à Pierrot*, the heroic defense of which

against French forces commanded by General Leclerc in March 1802 is one of the memorable episodes in Haitian history. Nearby are the ruins of Henry Christophe's grandiose *Palais des 365 Portes*. 5 miles/8 km farther S, at **Verrettes**, is the *Hôpital Albert Schweitzer*, established in the early fifties by the American Dr W. L. Mellon: one of the few effective health care facilities available to the rural population in Haiti.

See also **Haiti** and **Hispaniola**.

Saint-Martin/Sint Maarten

Lesser Antilles
Leeward Islands
French Antilles (Overseas Département of Guadeloupe)/Netherlands Antilles

Northern part: *French territory*
Area: 21 sq. mile/54 sq. km.
Population: 7000.
Administrative center: Basse-Terre (on Guadeloupe).

(i) **Mairie de Saint-Martin,**
F-97150 **Marigot,**
Saint-Martin, A.F.;
tel. 87 50 04.

Southern part: *Dutch territory*
Area: 13 sq. mile/34 sq. km.
Population: 19,000.
Administrative center: Willemstad (on Curaçao); regional center Philipsburg.

(i) **St Maarten Toeristenbureau,**
De Ruyterplein,
Philipsburg,
St Maarten, N.A.;
tel. 2327.

HOTELS. – ST MAARTEN: *Great Bay Beach Hotel*, 225 r., SP, T, casino; *Little Bay Beach Hotel*, 120 r., SP, T, casino; *St Maarten Sheraton*, 622 r.; *Holland House*, 42 r.; *Dawn Beach*; *Maho Reef and Beach Resort*, 140 r., SP, T, casino; *Sint Maarten Beach Club Hotel and Casino*, 78 r., SP, T, casino; *Belair Beach Hotel*; *Concord Hotel*, 160 r., SP, T, casino; *Caribbean Hotel*, 54 r.; *Castle Cove Inn*, 10 r., SP; *Central Hotel*, 70 r.; *Mary's Boon*, 10 r.; *Oyster Pond Yacht Club*, 20 r., T; *Pasanggrahan*, 20 r.; *Seaview*, 50 r.; *Summit Hotel*, 70 r., SP, T; *Caravanserai*, 60 r., SP, T; etc. – Many GUEST-HOUSES. – HOLIDAY APARTMENTS.

ST-MARTIN: *La Samanna*, Baie Longue, 85 r., SP, T; *PLM St-Tropez*, Marigot, 134 r., SP, T; *Beauséjour*, Marigot, 12 r.; *Coralita Beach Hotel*, Quartier d'Orléans, 40 r., SP; *Le Galion*, Quartier d'Orléans, 48 r.; *Le Grand Saint-Martin Beach Hotel*, Marigot, 60 r., SP; etc. – Several PENSIONS. – HOLIDAY APART-MENTS.

RESTAURANTS. – PHILIPSBURG: *West Indian Tavern*; *Antoine's*; *L'Escargot*. – MARIGOT: *Mini-Club*. – GRAND-CASE: *Fish Pot*.

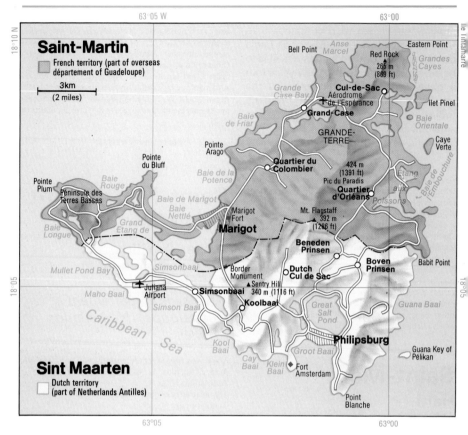

63°05 W   63°00

Saint-Martin

▢ French territory (part of overseas
   département of Guadeloupe)

3km
(2 miles)

Eastern Point
Bell Point   Anse Marcel
Red Rock   Grandes Cayes
265 m (869 ft)
Grande Case Bay   Cul-de-Sac
Aérodrome de l'Espérance   Îlet Pinel
Grand-Case   Baie Orientale
GRANDE-TERRE   Caye Verte
Baie de Friar
Pointe Arago
Pointe du Bluff   Quartier du Colombier   424 m (1391 ft)
Pointe Plum   Baie de la Potence   Pic du Paradis   Étang aux Poissons
Baie Rouge   Quartier d'Orléans   Baie de l'Embouchure
Péninsule des Terres Basses   Baie de Marigot
Baie Nettlé   Mt. Flagstaff 392 m (1286 ft)
Baie Longue   Grand Étang de   Marigot Fort   **Marigot**
Mullet Pond Bay   Beneden Prinsen
Simsonbaai   Boven Prinsen   Babit Point
Border Monument   Dutch Cul de Sac
Maho Baai   Juliana Airport   ▲Sentry Hill   340 m (1116 ft)
Simson Baai   ○Simsonbaai
Koolbaai
Caribbean Sea
Kool Baai   Great Salt Pond   Guana Baai
Sint Maarten
Cay Baai   **Philipsburg**
▢ Dutch territory
   (part of Netherlands Antilles)
Klein Baai   ♦Fort Amsterdam   Groot Baai   Guana Key of Pélikan
Point Blanche

Île Tintamarre

63°05   63°00

Casinos in St Maarten Sheraton, Maho Reef and Beach Resort, Sint Maarten Beach Club Hotel and Casino, Great Bay Beach Hotel, Little Bay Beach Hotel and Concord Hotel, all in St Maarten.

SHOPPING. – Thanks to their status as free ports Philipsburg (St Maarten) and Marigot (St-Martin) are shoppers' paradises, where high-quality imported goods can be bought at prices up to 50% cheaper than in Europe or the United States. Optical, electronic and precision instruments and appliances, perfume and clothing from many different countries are on sale here at very reasonable prices.

PUBLIC HOLIDAYS and EVENTS. – *New Year's Day.* – *Carnival* (St-Martin: from first Sunday after Epiphany to Ash Wednesday). – *Good Friday.* – *Easter Carnival* (St Maarten: mid-April). – *Queen's Birthday* and *St Maarten Trade Winds Race* (St Maarten: April 30). – *Labour Day* (May 1). – *Ascension.* – *Whitsun.* – *Fête Nationale* (St-Martin: July 14), French National Day. – *Schoelcher Day* (St-Martin: July 21), commemorating the liberation of the slaves. – *All Saints* (St-Martin: November 1). – *St Martin's Day* (November 11). – *Kingdom Day* (St Maarten: December 15). – *Christmas.*

RECREATION and SPORT. – Sailing, deep-sea fishing, water-skiing, wind-surfing, scuba diving, snorkeling, swimming and sunbathing; golf, tennis; cycling, walking.

AIR SERVICES. – From Juliana Airport (St Maarten) regular flights to St-Barthélemy, Saba, Sint Eustatius, Anguilla, St Kitts, Antigua, Guadeloupe, St Thomas and St Croix (US Virgin Islands), Tortola (British Virgin Islands), San Juan (Puerto Rico), Curaçao, Port-au-Prince (Haiti), Miami and New York (USA),

Montreal and Toronto (Canada) and Caracas (Venezuela). – From Grand'Case airfield (St-Martin) flights to St-Barthélemy and Guadeloupe.

SHIPPING. – Many cruise ships call in at Philipsburg (St Maarten), mostly from Miami (USA), San Juan (Puerto Rico) and Curaçao. – Regular boat services from Philipsburg (St Maarten) to Saba, Sint Eustatius and Anguilla and from Marigot (St-Martin) to St-Barthélemy and Anguilla.

BOAT TRIPS. – From both Philipsburg and Marigot there are trips around the island, evening cruises and excursions to Anguilla, St-Barthélemy, Saba and Sint Eustatius.

The island of *Saint-Martin/Sint Maarten, the northern part of which belongs to France and the southern part to the Netherlands, lies in the outer arc of the Lesser Antilles in latitude 18°5′ N and longitude 63°10′ W. It is an arid limestone island eroded by karstic action which is divided into two parts geographically as well as politically.

While the lower southern part of the island, belonging to the Netherlands, is characterized by sand-spits, coastal lagoons and salt-pans the French half, known as Grande-Terre, is a region of forest-covered hills, with the island's highest point, the Pic du Paradis (1391 ft/ 424 m). Around the island are a series of beautiful beaches, many of which in recent years have been opened up to tourism.

HISTORY. – Columbus is believed to have discovered the island, then inhabited by Caribs, on St Martin's Day in 1493, and named it in honor of the Saint. At first little attention was paid to it by Europeans; then in the 17th c. a few French filibusters established themselves on the island, which was declared a French possession in the reign of Louis XIII. A few years later the Dutch built a fort on the S coast. In 1640 the Spaniards, for strategic reasons, occupied the island, but abandoned it eight years later. Both the Dutch, led by Peter Stuyvesant, and the French now sought to gain control of the island, and in 1648 a treaty was signed dividing the island between France and the Netherlands on a basis of peaceful coexistence. In 1794 the island was captured by British forces, but was recovered two years later by Victor Hugues, who then made it over to the Dutch. It was again occupied by British forces in 1799 and 1808. The present line of division between France and Holland was finally established in 1816. The main pillars of the island's economy were then sugar production and pastoral farming, together with the salt extraction and fishing. Since then the Dutch part of the island has shared the destinies of the other islands in the Netherlands Antilles, which in 1954 were granted full self-government within the Kingdom of the Netherlands. The French part of the island, along with the island of St-Barthélemy, has been an arrondissement of the overseas département of Guadeloupe since 1963.

POPULATION and ECONOMY. – The population of the island consists predominantly of the descendants of Dutch or French settlers and black slaves from Africa. Half of them are Roman Catholics and half Protestants. Over the past 20 years the population has been increased by immigrants from the poorer neighboring islands – a consequence of the rapid growth of tourism, first in the Dutch part of the island and later in the French part, both of which can offer the attractions of their beautiful beaches. Thanks to the North American and European capital which has been attracted to the island and the advantages offered by its free port status St-Martin/St Maarten has enjoyed a great tourist boom, which is now spreading to the small neighboring islands of Saba, Sint Eustatius, St-Barthélemy and Anguilla.

*__Philipsburg__, capital of the Dutch part of the island, lies on a 1650 yd/1500 m long strip of land which separates the Great Salt Pond (salt-working) from the *Groot Baai*. The town was founded in 1763 by John Philips, a Scotsman in the Dutch service. For two centuries the inhabitants lived mainly by salt extraction and fishing; but within the last 20 years, thanks to its status as a free port, the town has enjoyed a great economic upswing as a result of the rapidly growing tourist trade. Work is now in progress to reclaim land from the Great Salt Pond in order to provide room for expansion.

The town's busy main square is the rectangular *De Ruyterplein*, around which are the principal public buildings. At its S end is the *Little Pier*, from which the excursion boats start. The De Ruyterplein links the two principal streets, the *Voorstraat*, with shops, restaurants and bistros, and the quieter *Achterstraat*. At the NE corner of the De Ruyterplein and Voorstraat is the *__Courthouse__, built in 1793 and destroyed by a hurricane a few years later, which now houses the *Town Hall* and the *Post Office*. To the E of the De Ruyterplein are several old Dutch-style burghers' houses. Between Nisbetsteeg and Kerksteeg, two charming little lanes leading to the beach, stands the __Roman Catholic Church__. Farther E are the *Government Buildings* (offices of the government of the Dutch Leeward Islands). – To the W of De Ruyterplein is the colorful *Market*.

SURROUNDINGS of Philipsburg. – To the SW of the town, on a promontory between the Groot Baai and the Klein Baai (beautiful beach), are the ruins of *__Fort Amsterdam__ (17th c.), the first Dutch fort on the island.

__Marigot__, capital of the French part of the island and seat of the sub-prefecture of St-Martin and St-Barthélemy, lies at the NE corner of the *Grand Etang de Simsonbaai*. Its two principal streets, Rue de la Republique and Rue de la Liberté, run parallel to the coast. The little fishing harbor is very attractive. Behind the Sous-Préfecture a footpath goes up to the old Fort du Marigot, from which there is a fine *view of the western part of the island.

TOUR OF THE ISLAND (24 miles/39 km). – The road runs NW from Philipsburg.

1¼ miles/2 km: side road to __Dutch Cul de Sac__, a tobacco-, sugar- and indigo-growing center in the 18th and 19th c. Near here is the oldest graveyard on the island. – The main road continues, with extensive views, along the southeastern slopes of *Sentry Hill* (1116 ft/340 m) and *Cole Bay Hill.*

1¼ miles/2 km: *view of Cay Bay, where in 1644 Peter Stuyvesant was severely wounded by a cannonball during an attempted landing on the island, then held by Spain.

¾ mile/1 km: *Koolbaai,* where the main road to Marigot goes off.

Half way between Koolbaai and Marigot, on the boundary between the Dutch and French parts of the island, is a small monument commemorating the peaceful coexistence of the two territories for more than 300 years.

In *Kool Baai*, S of the village, is a beautiful beach. Notable remains of the pre-Columbian period have been discovered here.

2 miles/3 km: *Simsonbaai, a picturesque little Dutch-style fishing village on the narrow strip of land along the S side of the Grand Etang de Simsonbaai, much patronized by sailing, wind-surfing and water-skiing enthusiasts.

¾ mile/1 km: Juliana Airport. – The road runs NW past *Maho Bay* and *Mullet Pond Bay*, two beautiful beaches of fine sand with excellent facilities for swimmers.

2 miles/3 km: The road crosses the Dutch-French boundary on to the Péninsule des Terres-Basses, the most westerly part of the island, with beautiful beaches; then along the *Baie Nettlé* to –

5 miles/8 km: Marigot.

1½ miles/2.5 km: *Quartier du Colombier*. From here a narrow road climbs to the *Pic du Paradis (1391 ft/424 m; extensive views), the highest point on the island.

1¼ miles/2.5 km: *Grand'Case, on a strip of land between an old salt-pan (airfield) and a superb beach.

From here there is an attractive WALK to the charming *Anse Marcel*, 2 miles/3 km NE, with a beautiful beach.

1½ miles/2.5 km: road on left to Cul-de-Sac, 1 mile/1.5 km NE, a little port much favored by yacht-owners. Offshore are the little *Ilet Pinel*, with a fine sandy beach, and the larger *Ile Tintamarre*, which also has beautiful beaches.

The road now turns S along the E side of the *Montagne de France* (1319 ft/402 m), with a view of the *Baie Orientale* (magnificent beach).

2½ miles/4 km: Quartier d'Orléans, a little settlement on the *Etang aux Poissons*, to the E of which is the *Baie de l'Embouchure*. There are several holiday complexes in the surrounding area.

To the W of the village, on the slopes of *Mount Flagstaff* (1286 ft/392 m; extensive views), is a site where pre-Columbian remains were found.

1 mile/1.5 km: French-Dutch boundary. Just beyond this is the little hamlet of *Beneden Prinsen*.

1¼ miles/2 km: *Boven Prinsen*, where a narrow road goes off to the E coast, on which are a number of hotel complexes.

1¼ miles/2 km: side road running E from the *Great Salt Pond* to *Guana Bay Point* (beach).

1¼ miles/2 km: Philipsburg.

See also *Anguilla, **Guadeloupe and *St-Barthélemy.

St Thomas

Lesser Antilles
United States Virgin Islands
Territory administered by the United States

Area: 32 sq. miles/83 sq. km.
Population: 48,000.
Administrative center: Charlotte Amalie.
Vehicles travel on the left.

(i) United States Virgin Islands Department of Tourism,
P.O. Box 6400,
Charlotte Amalie, VI 00801,
St Thomas;
tel. (809) 774 8784.
Government Tourist Information Center,
Waterfront Highway.

HOTELS. – CHARLOTTE AMALIE: *Bluebeard's Castle, 100 r.; Windward Passage, 144 r.; Mafolie, 23 r.; Harbor View, 8 r. – SE OF TOWN: *Frenchman's Reef, 350 r., SP, T, beach; *Yacht Haven, 218 r.; *Limetree Beach, 84 r., T, diving, night club; *Bolongo Bay Beach, 37 r., T, diving sailing; Scott Hotel, 31 r.; Morning Star, 24 r.; Watergate Vacations (apartments), 100 r.

ON WATER ISLAND: Sugar Bird Beach, 99 r., T; West Indies Terrace (apartments), 4 r. – AT AIRPORT: Carib Beach, 92 r.; Island Beachcomber, 49 r.; Michele Motel, 42 r.

AT W END OF ISLAND (not on coast): *Virgin Isle Hotel, 200 r.; Shibui Resort, 25 bungalows; Villa Olga Hotel, 18 r.; Crown Colony, 17 r.

ON N COAST: *Mahogany Run, 200 r., T, golf; Magens Point, 32 r.; The Inn at Mandahl, 8 r. – ON E COAST: *Pineapple Beach, 154 r., night club; *Point Pleasant, 130 r., T, sailing; Sapphire Beach Resort, 110 r.; Secret Harbour, 46 r.; Pavilions and Pools, 25 r.; Cowpet Bay Apartments, 90 r.; Sapphire Bay Beach Apartments, 82 r.

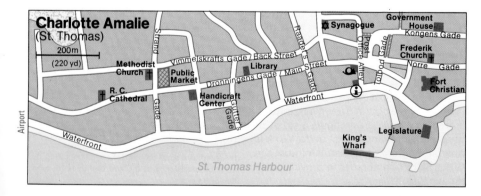

ART GALLERIES. – *A. H. Rijse's*; *Craft Co-op*; *Harbor Arts*; *Virgin Islands*; *Yorkshire House*; *Jim Tillett's*.

RECREATION and SPORT. – Sailing, scuba diving, deep-sea fishing, golf, tennis.

TRANSPORT. – Air connections with New York, Washington, Miami (USA) and San Juan (Puerto Rico). – Hydrofoils to St Croix and St John. – Boat services to offshore islands.

*St Thomas, second largest of the US Virgin Islands (12¼ miles/20 km long, 3 miles/5 km wide), lies between the Atlantic Ocean to the N and the Caribbean Sea to the S. Like St Croix and St John, it is of volcanic origin. The island is traversed by a ridge of hills rising to 1510 ft/460 m; at the N end Magens Bay cuts deep inland, and at the S end is the bay containing the harbor of Charlotte Amalie, capital of the US Virgin Islands.

Charlotte Amalie lies in a bay on the S coast which is sheltered by *Hassel Isle* (private property) and *Water Island* and forms an excellent deep-water harbor (St Thomas Harbor). The town is perched on the slopes above the bay, with *Signal Hill* (1401 ft/427 m) rearing up to the NW.

The town was already a busy port and cosmopolitan trading center in the 18th c., a place noted for its tolerance – and also one of the world's largest slave markets. It rose to prosperity through the growing of sugar, but a predominant part is now played in the island's economy by tourism. Many cruise ships make St Thomas a port of call, and large numbers of visitors, particularly from the United States, take advantage of the wide range of duty-free wares in its shops.

SIGHTS. – At the E end of the town, near *King's Wharf*, is **Fort Christian**, built in 1672 by the first Danish settlers and named after King Christian V. It contains a small museum with Arawak and Carib material and mementoes of the Danish period. – NW of the fort is the little *Emancipation Park*, commemorating the liberation of the slaves in 1848.

From Emancipation Park Tolbod Gade leads into the town's principal traffic artery, Main Street and its continuation to the W, Dronningens Gade. Immediately on the left is the *Post Office*, with murals by Stephen Dohanos.

On the N side of Norre Gade is *St Frederick's Church* (18th c.), one of the oldest buildings in the town. – Reached by way of Kongens Gade or a stepped lane is *Government Hill*, on which is the *Hotel 1829* (Lavalette House), built in the early 18th c. for a French sea-captain; it has a beautiful courtyard. Farther E is **Government House**, built in 1867 as the seat of the Danish Colonial Council, now the residence of the Governor of the US Virgin Islands. The house, part of which is open to the public, has wall paintings of episodes in the island's history and

A street in Charlotte Amalie (St Thomas)

contains a collection of pictures, including works by the French Impressionist Camille Pissarro, born on St Thomas in 1830.

Between Hotel 1829 and Government House are the "Ninety-Nine Steps", which lead up to the top of the hill, with **Crown House** (18th c.), once the residence of high Danish officials; still containing some of the original furnishings. – Near here are the remains of the 17th c. **Fort Skytsborg** (Blackbeard's Tower) and the impressive Bluebeard's Tower, now part of a hotel.

On Synagogue Hill, to the W of the town, stands the **Synagogue** (Crystal Gade), the oldest synagogue on United States soil. In accordance with tradition the floor is strewn with sand – symbolizing the Jews' 40 years of wandering in the wilderness (or, according to another interpretation, a symbol of the Diaspora – the dispersion of the Jews). – From here Back Street (Vimmelskrafts Gade) leads to the busy *Market Square*, with covered stalls. In earlier days the slave market was held here.

Outside the town to the W is **French Town** (known as "Cha Cha Town" from the straw hats which are made here), the inhabitants of which still speak a northern French dialect. – Farther out, the road comes to the **Orchidarium**, and beyond this road goes off on the right to *Crown Mountain* (1509 ft/460 m), from which there are magnificent *views. From here the N coast of St Thomas can be reached. – The road continues W past the *Harry S. Truman Airport*. To the S is *Lindbergh Bay*, to the N a golf-course. – Off the W end of St Thomas are good *diving grounds, with coral reefs and abundant marine life.

The N coast, beyond the range of hills which runs across the island, is wetter and quieter than the S. In **Magens Bay** the Atlantic drives a deep wedge into the land. From *Drake's Seat* there are very fine views. To the NW of the bay lie the islets of *Outer Brass* and *Inner Brass*, to the NE *Little Hans Lollick* and *Big Hans Lollick* (diving grounds). To the E of the bay is Mahogany Run golf-course, and beyond this, on *Coki Beach*, is the **Coral World** underwater observatory, in which visitors can watch the teeming marine life of the coral reefs, with sharks, rays, barracudas and moray eels (restaurant, duty-free shop). Offshore is the islet of *Thatch Cay* (good diving grounds). From *Redhook*

Bay there is a ferry to **St John** (see separate entry).

Along the bay SE of Charlotte Amalie is a long stretch of beach with numerous hotels. In a large underwater cavern to the SE of *Bolongo Bay* scuba divers can observe nurse sharks (depth *c.* 35–65 ft/ 10–20 m).

See also ***British Virgin Islands** and ***United States Virgin Islands**.

St Vincent

Lesser Antilles
Windward Islands
St Vincent/Grenadines

Nationality letters: WV.
Area: 150 sq. miles/389 sq. km (including the islands of Bequia, Mustique, Canouan, Mayero, Union, Petit Martinique, etc.).
Capital: Kingstown.
Population: 125,000.
Religion: predominantly Protestant (Anglicans, Methodists) and Roman Catholic.
Language: English; Creole patois of English in everyday use.
Currency: Eastern Caribbean dollar (EC$) of 100 cents.
Weights and measures: British/American system.
Time: Atlantic Time, 4 hours behind GMT.
Vehicles travel on the left.
Travel documents: passport, onward or return ticket.

ⓘ **St Vincent Tourist Board,**
P.O. Box 834,
Halifax Street,
Kingstown,
St Vincent/Grenadines.
See also Practical Information.

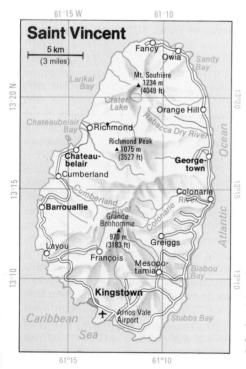

HOTELS. – KINGSTOWN: *Cobblestone Inn,* 20 r.; *Haddon,* 16 r., T; *Heron Hotel; Waterloo House;* etc. – IN INDIAN BAY: *Coconut Beach,* 10 r.; *Grand View Beach,* 12 r.; *Indian Bay Beach Hotel,* 40 r., beach; *Villa Lodge,* 10 r.; *Yvonette Beach,* 18 r.; etc. – ON BLUE LAGOON: *CSY Yacht Club.* – ON S COAST: *Sunset Shore Beach Hotel,* 20 r., beach. – MOUNT PLEASANT: *RaWaCou,* 60 r., SP. – ON YOUNG ISLAND: **Young Island Resorts,* 50 r., SP, T, beach. – Some APARTMENTS and GUEST-HOUSES.

RESTAURANTS. – KINGSTOWN: *Bounty* and *Chubby's Eat Out,* both in Halifax Street; *Ikaya,* Middle Street; *Fish Net,* Grenville Street. – VILLA: *Harbour Light; Umbrella.*

Casino in the Valley Inn, at the Aqueduct Golf Club (on the road from Kingstown to Layou).

PUBLIC HOLIDAYS and EVENTS. – *New Year's Day.* – *Discovery Day* (January 22), commemorating the discovery of the island by Columbus. – *Good Friday.* – *Easter.* – *Labour Day* (May 1). – *Whitsun Regatta,* yacht race from Kingstown to Bequia and back. – *Whitsun.* – **Carnival* (last week in June to first Tuesday in July), a colorful occasion, with lively celebrations and parades, reaching a climax on *Carnival Tuesday* (second Tuesday in July). – *August*

A beach on the E coast of St Vincent

Monday (first Monday in August), commemorating the liberation of the slaves. – *Independence Day* (October 27). – *Christmas Novena* (December 15–24), morning Advent fairs. – *Christmas* (December 24–25). – *Boxing Day* (December 26).

RECREATION and SPORT. – Sailing, deep-sea fishing, scuba diving, swimming and sunbathing; golf, tennis, cricket; walking, botanical excursions.

AIR SERVICES. – Regular flights to Union, Canouan, Mustique and Carriacou (Grenadines), Grenada and Barbados from Arnos Vale Airport; occasional charter flights to other Caribbean destinations.

SHIPPING. – Mail boats several times weekly to the inhabited Grenadines and Grenada; boat to Bequia daily (except Sundays). – Calls by cruise ships on their way to Miami (USA), San Juan (Puerto Rico), Barbados or Curaçao.

St Vincent, the "Emerald Isle" or the "Pearl of the Antilles", is the principal island (18 miles/29 km long, 10½ miles/17 km wide) of the independent state of St Vincent in the eastern Caribbean, lying just over 70 miles/113 km W of Barbados and about the same distance S of Martinique. Together with the Grenadines to the S it belongs to the southern Windward Islands group. In spite of its magnificent beaches and sailing waters the island has only quite recently begun to attract large numbers of visitors. One of the reasons for this may have been the

dark coloring of the sand on its beaches.

St Vincent is wholly made up of volcanic rocks. It is a hilly island, reaching its highest point in its youngest hill, the still active volcano of Soufrière (4049 ft/ 1234 m), in the N. This is the most active volcano in the eastern Caribbean after Mont Pelé on Martinique. The earliest recorded eruption, which was observed from passing ships, was in 1718. This was followed by a further eruption in 1812 which claimed 56 lives. An eruption in 1902 created the present crater (depth 1640 ft/500 m, diameter 1 mile/1.5 km), which soon afterwards filled with water. This eruption, in which 2000 people lost their lives, was accompanied by a cloud of gas rising to 6¼ miles/10,000 m and heavy showers of ash, some of which came down as far away as Barbados. After almost 70 years of quiescence a small island was formed in the crater lake in 1971; in 1978 there was a further eruption; and only a year later, on April 17, 1979, another huge cloud of gas and ash towered up into the sky over St Vincent. More than 20,000 people had to be evacuated, and large areas of the banana plantations were destroyed by the rain of ash.

CLIMATE. – Like the other Caribbean islands, St Vincent lies in the tropical trade wind zone. The winds which blow from the NE throughout the year take up moisture from the Atlantic and, coming up against the steep slopes of the volcanic hills, deposit it in the form of rain. The heaviest rain (98 in./2500 mm) falls on the sides exposed to the wind, particularly on the main island. Not surprisingly, therefore, the beaches are on the much drier SW side of St Vincent, with an annual rainfall of 51 in./1300 mm. As a result of the island's proximity to the Equator air temperatures vary little betweeen summer and winter (January average 77.2 °F/25.1 °C, September 81.2 °F/27.3 °C). The best time to visit St Vincent is in March or April, with a rainfall of only 3½ in./90 mm, compared with the November maximum of 12 in./305 mm.

HISTORY. – St Vincent was discovered by Columbus in 1498, on his third voyage. In 1672 the island, then still occupied by Caribs, was claimed by Britain; but the fierce resistance of the Caribs prevented the establishment of any European settlements until 1763, when British troops occupied St Vincent – in breach of an agreement with France that it should be neutral.

In 1675 a ship laden with a cargo of slaves from Africa was wrecked off the Grenadine island of Bequia, and the blacks who survived found their way from Bequia to St Vincent, mingled with the Caribs and adopted their way of life, becoming known as the "black Caribs". From 1763, apart from a brief period of French occupation in 1779–83, St Vincent remained in British hands, and under the treaty of Versailles (1783) became a crown colony. In 1795 there was a

Carib rising, with French support, but this was quickly repressed. Most of the Caribs were then deported to the island of Roatán (now in Honduras). In 1871 St Vincent was incorporated in the colony of the Windward Islands.

Almost a hundred years later, in 1969, St Vincent became a British Associated State with full internal self-government, Britain remaining responsible only for external affairs and defense. On October 27, 1979 this status was ended by agreement and St Vincent became a completely independent state within the British Commonwealth, with Milton Cato as Prime Minister. In a general election on December 5, 1979 Cato's moderate Labour Party took 11 out of the 13 seats in Parliament. The head of state is still the Queen, who is represented by the Governor-General. Britain gave the new state initial development assistance of £10,000,000, and is continuing to give technical assistance. St Vincent has also received assistance from Cuba, which is seeking to extend its influence in the eastern Caribbean.

POPULATION. – St Vincent has a population of 125,000, 95% of whom live in the coastal regions of the main island. The main concentration of population is in the capital, Kingstown, which has some 30,000 inhabitants. The interior of the island is largely uninhabited, as the steep and densely wooded slopes of the volcanic hills do not lend themselves to cultivation. Some 65% of the population are blacks, descended from African slaves, and a further 30% are mulattoes. The descendants of indentured laborers brought in from India from 1861 onwards account for 4% of the population. Only an insignificant proportion of the population are of European extraction, most of them being the descendants of Portuguese indentured laborers who came to the island from 1846 onwards.

St Vincent has the high rate of population increase (over 3%) characteristic of a developing country. Considerably more than half the population are under 20. Since only the most limited progress has been made in developing industry, many thousands of people emigrate every year, mainly to Trinidad, Curaçao and Aruba.

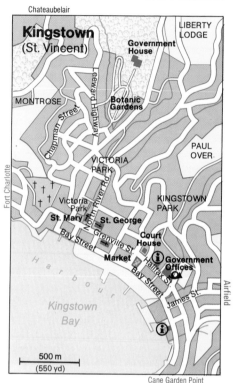

ECONOMY. – St Vincent is still a predominantly agricultural country. The only significant non-agricultural employment is in the capital, Kingstown (tourism, banking, craft production, industry). Some 90% of the gross domestic product is accounted for by agriculture. Although half the island's area has an angle of slope greater than 30° and only a twentieth has a gradient of less than 5°, cultivation is intensive. One factor which contributes to this is the fertile volcanic soil, which is regularly revitalized by the

Washing day in a mountain stream on St Vincent

Kingstown, capital of St Vincent

showers of ash deposited during eruptions of Sou-frière; but equally important is the pattern of landholding, which – in contrast to the pattern on most of the other islands in the Lesser Antilles – shows a reasonable balance between large estates and small peasant holdings.

Large estates account for only a third of the total area under cultivation. The peasant holdings, supported by the government, are no longer limited to the subsistence farming which was formerly the rule: they still grow yams, cassava and sweet potatoes for their own consumption, but most of their effort is devoted to producing cash crops for export. The main crop is bananas, which since the 1950s have steadily displaced arrowroot (used in the manufacture of starch), previously predominant. The once dominant sugar-cane began to give place to arrowroot around 1900, and sugar and rum production is now confined to meeting domestic requirements. Other exports are sea-island cotton (among the best in the world), cocoa, sweet potatoes and spices.

Tourism is now becoming important. In 1980 50,000 visitors arrived on the island by air and a further 20,000 came on cruise liners.

*__Kingstown__ (0–597 ft/0–182 m; pop. 35,000), capital of St Vincent, was founded at the beginning of the 18th c. Beautifully situated in Kingstown Bay, at the SW corner of the island, it has the country's only deep-water harbor, which handles all the agricultural exports of St Vincent and the Grenadines. Since its completion in 1964 a number of factories have been established here, including plants for making starch (mostly exported to the USA) and for ginning the island's high-quality sea-island cotton. As the only sizeable town on St Vincent, Kingstown has a public library and a teachers' training college. A road around the coast links the capital with all the main settlements on the island. There are regular boat services to the Grenadines, and there are

daily flights from Arnos Vale airfield (inaugurated 1962) to Barbados, Trinidad, St Lucia and Martinique.

SIGHTS. – Prominent landmarks in Kings-*Cathedral* (Anglican; 1820, fine windows) in Greenville Street and the neighboring *St Mary's .Church* (R.C.), built about 1890, restored 1940, in an extraordinary mixture of styles – Romanesque, Gothic, Renaissance and Baroque. Of notable interest are the *__Botanic Gardens__, the oldest in the whole of America, founded in 1765. They contain a breadfruit tree, said to be descended from one brought to the Caribbean from Tahiti by Captain Bligh of the "Bounty" in 1793. – There is a fine view of the town from *Fort Charlotte* (1803), which is named after George III's queen and was occupied by British troops until 1873. – The __Market__ in the center of Kingstown is a colourful scene on Saturday mornings. The St Vincent Museum in the Chief Agricultural Officer's House is to be recommended.

It is unfortunately not possible to do a complete tour of St Vincent, since there is no road around the NW corner of the island. – A rewarding day trip is to the volcano of *__Soufrière__ (4049 ft/1234 m), from the summit of which there are superb views of St Vincent and the Grenadines. The climb is best tackled from *Georgetown*, on the E coast. 2½ miles/4 km N of the town, just beyond the Rabacca landing-stage, a road leading to the foot of the volcano goes off on the left. The topography of the mountain was altered by the volcanic activity of 1979–80 – for a time the crater lake disappeared – and it is therefore advisable to get a local guide. An attractive detour can be made into the wild and romantic valley of the *Rabacca Dry River* (dry because the water usually seeps away into the porous volcanic ash which forms the subsoil). Instead of returning by the same route it is possible to walk down to *Châteaubelair* on the W coast, taking a bus from

A village on the E coast of St Vincent

there to Kingstown. – The road continues N from Georgetown up the E coast. The first part of the road, which passes a copra-processing plant N of Orange Hill, is perfectly adequate but the final stretch leading to the village of *Fancy*, at the northernmost tip of the island, is narrow and difficult.

The most attractive place on the W coast is the fishing village of **Barrouallie**, at the entrance to which is an Indian stone altar. Whaling is still carried on here, following methods inherited from the 18th c. The whaling season is in spring. – On a side road 1¼ miles/ 2 km N of *Layou* is a *rock engraving of a human face dating from about A.D. 600, one of the finest in the Caribbean. There are other rock engravings at *Escape* (near Argyle), at Colonaire and on the S coast opposite the Aquatic Club. – The W coast road ends a few miles N of Châteaubelair. From there it is a 6 mile/ 10 km walk to the N coast – well worth it for the sake of the grand *Falls of Baleine**. Half way there are the remains of a Carib settlement, the occupants of which had withdrawn for safety to this remote spot.

A short trip (6 miles/10 km) offering a good *view of Kingstown and the Grenadines is on *Queen Elizabeth Drive*, which branches off at Dorsetshire Hill–Sion Hill, E of Kingstown, and runs inland, ending at Arnos Vale airfield. – One excursion which should not be missed is into *Marriaqua Valley**, one of the most intensively cultivated valleys in the eastern Caribbean; it is enclosed between high ridges, with huge banana plantations and other tropical crops. There is a marvellous view from the Montreal Gardens. The valley also contains mineral springs whose water has long been esteemed for its curative properties.

Excursions can be made by boat or light aircraft to the **Grenadines (see separate entry), S of St Vincent. Most of these islands are practically uninhabited; their waters are a paradise for sailing enthusiasts.

Bahía de Samaná

Dominican Republic
República Dominicana

Provinces: Samaná and El Seibo.
(i) **Dirección Nacional de Turismo e Información,**
César Nicolás Pensón/Rosa Duarte,
Apartado 497,
Santo Domingo,
República Dominicana;
tel. (809) 688 5537.
See also Practical Information.

HOTELS. – SABANA DE LA MAR: *Brisa de la Bahía*, Duarte 1, 21 r. – SAMANÁ: *Cayacoa*, 62 r.

RECREATION and SPORT. – Sailing, deep-sea fishing, scuba diving, snorkeling, swimming and sunbathing; shooting, walking.

AIR SERVICES. – Occasional flights from Samaná airfield to the Las Américas International Airport.

The beautiful **Bahía de Samaná, traversed by many reefs, lies at the northeastern end of the island of Hispaniola. The eastward continuation of the Cibao rift valley, it separates the Samaná peninsula to the N – geologically a more recent feature belonging to the Cordillera Septentrional – from the Cordillera Oriental to the S. The Río Yuna forms an extensive delta in the bay. Samaná Bay ranks among the finest fishing waters in the world, and it also has many attractive beaches (some of them accessible only by boat).

The hills on the **Península de Samaná** (40 miles/64 km long, 5–11 miles/8–18 km wide, area 297 sq. miles/768 sq. km) rise to over 2000 ft/600 m). Until recently it could be reached only by boat, but it is now linked to the rest of the country by a new road.

The area was occupied in the 18th c. by settlers from the Canary Islands; then in the 1820s several hundred liberated black slaves from the United States founded a number of the Protestant settlements which are still a characteristic feature of the peninsula. – On the N side of the bay is *Samaná** (sea level; pop. 10,000), a well-preserved old fishing village which is now the chief town of the province of Samaná. Americans settled here in the 19th c. Thanks to its convenience as a base for fishing and diving expeditions, particularly to the *Cayos Levantados*, SE of the town, and to the excellent beaches in the area it has now developed into a modest tourist area.

8 miles/13 km E of Samaná is the *Playa Playuela, a beautiful beach. – 6 miles/10 km N is the charming *Bahía del Rincón, near which remains of pre-Columbian settlement have been found.

21 miles/34 km W of Samaná in the NW corner of the bay lies the port of Sánchez (pop. 9000: difficult access for boats). 25 miles/40 km from Sanchez lies the first-class beach of Playa Las Terrenas (vacation center).

From the little port of Sabana de la Mar (pop. 10,000), opposite Samaná on the S side of the bay, there are ferries to various places in the bay. There are beautiful beaches around the town.

19 miles/30 km E of Sabana de la Mar is the *Bahía de la Jina, on the N coast, with a magnificent beach.

8 miles/13 km W of Sabana are the *Cuevas de Caño Honde, interesting caves which are unfortunately difficult to reach.

SW of the town is the very interesting karstic region – rugged and with a dense growth of vegetation over much of its area – of **Los Haitises, part of which has been declared a National Park.

The W end of the bay, formed by the delta of the Río Yuna, is a swampy area which provides good sport for wildfowlers.

See also **Dominican Republic and **Hispaniola.

San Juan

Puerto Rico
Estado Libre y Asociado de Puerto Rico
Commonwealth of Puerto Rico

Altitude: 0–138 ft/0–42 m
Population: 435,000; Metropolitan Area 1.1 million.

(i) Puerto Rico Tourism Company,
Calle San Justo,
Esq. Recinto Sur,
San Juan,
Puerto Rico 00903;
tel. (809) 721 2400.
Tourism Information Center,
Old San Juan, near Pier 1.
See also Practical Information.

HOTELS. – VIEJO SAN JUAN (Old San Juan): El Convento, 100 Cristo, 95 r., SP; La Fortaleza, 252 Fortaleza, 45 r. – PUERTA DE TIERRA: *Caribe Hilton, 707 r., SP, T, beach; Ocean Side, 54 Muñoz Rivera, 34 r. – MIRAMAR: Capitol, 800 Ponce de León, 126 r.; Excelsior, 801 Ponce de León, 140 r., SP; Olimpo Court, 603 Miramar, 100 r.; Toro, 605 Miramar, 44 r. – 603 Miramar, 100 r.; Toro, 605 Miramar, 44 r. – CONDADO: *Condado Beach, Ashford Avenue, 251 r., SP, beach; *Condado Holiday Inn, 999 Ashford, 580 r., SP, beach; *Dupont Plaza San Juan, 1309 Ashford, 450 r., SP, beach; *Howard Johnson's Nabori Lodge, 1369 Ashford, 150 r., SP; *La Concha, Ashford Avenue, 224 r., SP, T, beach; Aquarena Beach, 1123 Seaview Avenue, 18 r.; Condado Lagoon, corner of Clemenceau and Joffre, 44 r., SP; Diplomat, 1126 Ashford, 60 r., SP; Dutch Inn and Towers, corner of Condado and Ashford, 144 r., SP; El Canario, 1317 Ashford, 20 r., SP; El Prado, 1350 Luchetti, 15 r.; Lindomar, 4 Condado, 27 r.; Ramada 96 r.; Regency, 1005 Ashford, 129 r., SP; Rose Marie's by the Sea, 1125 Seaview, 9 r.; Tanamá, Joffre, 95 r.; etc. – SANTURCE: Bolívar, 609 Bolívar, 38 r.; Pierre, De Diego, 180 r., SP; Simar, 166 Villamil, 11 r. – OCEAN PARK: Arcade Inn, 8 Taft, 19 r.; La Condesa, 2071 Cacique, 8 r.; Lily's, 2064 España/Rampla del Almirante, 7 r.; Lutece on the Beach, 1 Atlantic Place, 20 r.; San Antonio, 1 Tapia, 7 r. – PUNTA LAS MARIAS: Almendro by the Sea, 2 Almendro, 7 r.; Buena Vista, 2218 General Del Valle, 14 r.; Sea and Sun, 2210 Park Boulevard, 10 r.; Villa Mare, 4 Caoba, 14 r., beach. – ISLA VERDE: *Carib Inn, Route 187, 225 r., SP, T; *Continental de Puerto Rico, Loíza/Jupiter, 238 r., SP, beach; *Isla Verde Holiday Inn, Route 187, 410 r., SP, T. beach; *Palace, Route 187, 450 r., SP, beach; Don Pedro, 4 Rosa, 22 r., SP; Duffy's, 9 Route 187, 16 r.; El Patio, 87 Tres Oeste, Bloque D 8, 14 r., SP; Green Isle, 36 Uno Este, Villamar, 14 r., SP; Interline, 20 Uno Este, Villamar, 12 r., SP; International Airport, Airport Terminal Building, 82 r.; La Casa Mathiesen, 14 Uno Este, Villamar, 12 r., SP; etc.

RESTAURANTS in most hotels; also *La Fonda del Callejón, Old San Juan, 317 Fortaleza; *La Zarago-zana, Old San Juan, 356 San Francisco (Spanish/ Cuban); Beeflover, Hato Rey, 238 F. D. Roosevelt; El Cid, Condado, Joffre/Marseille (Spanish); El Mesón Vasco, Old San Juan, 47 Cristo (Basque); El Zipperle, Hato Rey, 352 F. D. Roosevelt (Spanish and German); Hostal Castilla, Condado, 1408 Magdalena; La Gallega, Old San Juan, 309 Fortaleza (Spanish); La Góndola, Old San Juan, 305 Recinto Sur (Italian); Scotch and Sirloin, Condado, La Rada Building; Swiss Chalet, Santurce, De Diego (Swiss); etc.

NIGHT SPOTS. – San Juan offers a wide range of late-night entertainment. There are good floor shows in the night clubs in the leading hotels; also *Ocho Puertas, Old San Juan, Cristo/Fortaleza; El Barril de Vino, Santurce, Ashford/De Diego. – DISCOTHEQUES in some of the large hotels, among them *Julianna's (in Caribe Hilton) and Isadora (in Condado Holiday Inn); also Discoteca Otelo, Old San Juan, 203 Tanca; Warehouse Discotheque, Old San Juan, 151 San Justo; Rod's Discotheque, Old San Juan, 206 O'Donnel.

Casinos. – Casino El Centro, government-run; also casinos in Caribe Hilton Hotel, Carib Inn, Condado Holiday Inn, El San Juan Hotel and Isla Verde Holiday Inn.

EVENTS. – San Juan and the surrounding area offer an endless range of cultural events, lively festivals and religious ceremonies throughout the year. Details are given in the brochure issued monthly, free of charge, by the Puerto Rico Tourism Company, "Que Pasa", and in the newspapers. The principal events in the annual program are the *Fiesta de San Juan Bautista (June), a ten-day festival in honor of St John the Baptist, with carnival parades and mass swimming events; the *Casals Festival (June); the Summer Art Festival; the State Fair (autumn), a large amusements park at the Hiram Bithorn Stadium in Hato Rey; and the Orchestra Season (autumn and winter). All year round there is the *LeLoLai Festival run by the Tourism Company, a weekly series of folk events based on the traditional Jibaro festivals, with dancing on the beach. Other events include drama, ballet, concerts and art exhibitions organized by the Institute of Puerto Rican Art and the University of Puerto Rico and performances by the *Areyto Folkloric Ballet and the Puerto Rico Symphony Orchestra.

SHOPPING. – Stimulated by the rapid growth of tourism, particularly via cruise ships, the old town of San Juan has developed into a major shopping area with many shops and department stores offering a tempting range of luxury goods from all over the world – often organizing shopping "events" to the accompaniment of music. Items particularly worth looking for include local craft products – carved figures of saints, hand-woven fabrics, pottery, jewelry and Indian-style straw work (hanging mats) – as well as fashion clothing, cigars and rum.

ART GALLERIES (a selection). – *Institute of Puerto Rican Culture*, Convento Dominicano; *Ateneo Puertorriqueño*, Ponce de León, by the Capitol; *José E. Alegria*, 152–154 Cristo; *Amparo Porcelain Inn*, 53 Cristo; *Butterfly People*, 152 Fortaleza; *Galeria Botello*, 208 Cristo; *Galeria de Caleta*, 74 Caleta de San Juan; *Galeria Colibri*, 156 Cristo.

AIR SERVICES. – INTERNATIONAL: scheduled flights from San Juan International Airport to Atlanta, Baltimore, Boston, Chicago, Cleveland, Dallas, Detroit, Miami, Newark, New Orleans, New York, Philadelphia and Washington (USA), Mexico City (Mexico), Caracas (Venezuela), Madrid (Spain), Frankfurt am Main (German Federal Republic), Zurich (Switzerland) and all the main islands in the Caribbean (except Cuba). – DOMESTIC: scheduled

flights from San Juan to Mayagüez, Ponce, Vieques and Culebra.

SHIPPING. – Many Caribbean cruise ships are based in San Juan, and most of the others call in there on their way to other West Indian destinations.

San Juan – gateway to the Caribbean. – Centrally located and with a well-developed infrastructure, San Juan has become *the* great traffic junction of both airborne and seaborne tourism in the Caribbean. It is linked with the airline networks of North, Central and South America, and many services from Europe to Central and South America also put in here. In addition almost all the Caribbean islands, with the exception of Cuba, are linked with San Juan by cruise lines or can be reached by chartered boat or aircraft.

**San Juan, capital of the Commonwealth of Puerto Rico, lies on a sheltered natural harbor at the E end of the island's northern coastal plain. With almost a third of Puerto Rico's total population concentrated in its metropolitan area, it is the country's cultural and economic hub, the see of a Roman Catholic archbishop, a university town and a considerable industrial city, as well

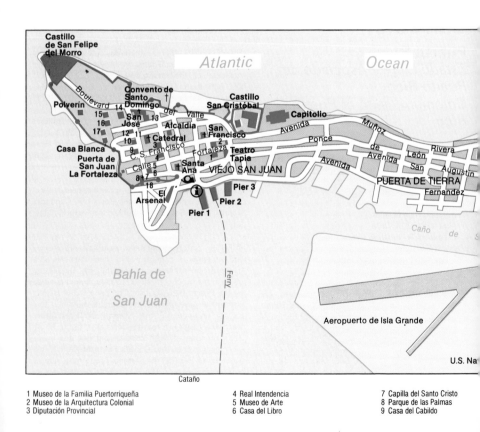

1 Museo de la Familia Puertorriqueña	4 Real Intendencia	7 Capilla del Santo Cristo
2 Museo de la Arquitectura Colonial	5 Museo de Arte	8 Parque de las Palmas
3 Diputación Provincial	6 Casa del Libro	9 Casa del Cabildo

as being one of the focal points of tourism in the Caribbean.

The townscape of San Juan is characterized by a not unattractive contrast between modern American high-rise buildings and Spanish and Moorish architecture. Old San Juan (Viejo San Juan) is a world of its own, with wrought-iron balconies, old-world Spanish street lamps and streets paved with stone brought to Puerto Rico in the 17th and 18th c. as ballast in Spanish merchant vessels; and the old town is still dominated by the fortress of El Morro. Old San Juan is connected with the newer part of the town by three bridges. The big luxury hotels are in the districts of Condado and Isla Verde, the modern business center in Santurce, the banking quarter in Hato Rey.

The problems of planning and land use in Puerto Rico have been complicated by the concentration of most of the country's economic activity in and around San Juan. The decision to industrialize Puerto Rico led to increased development in San Juan Metropolitan Area, since this was the only place with the port installations and infrastructure required for handling imports and exports. Accordingly industry began to concentrate there; and during the early years of the industrialization program (1942–55) some 60% of all new jobs were created in the San Juan area, in which at that time fewer than 20% of the population of Puerto Rico lived.

The result of this uncontrolled growth of industry was, not unexpectedly, an increasing concentration of other economic activities in San Juan, together with a large-scale movement of population into the capital from other parts of the country. In consequence the population of San Juan increased by more than 50% within ten years (1960–70), with effects similar to those observable on other Caribbean islands which have experienced this drift from the country areas to the towns.

This increasing concentration of industry and population in San Juan was the consequence of the primacy given to the capital over the rural areas, and despite some successful projects by the government planning authorities aimed at halting the movement the trend still continues. The only prospect of preventing the continuance of this unhealthy growth of the metropolis lies in a determined and

San Juan
(Puerto Rico)

500 m
(550 yd)

Atlantic

Ocean

10	Convento de las Carmelitas	13	Casa Suazo	16	Casa de Beneficencia
11	Seminario Conciliar	14	Cuartel de Ballaja	17	Casa Rosa
12	Palacio Episcopal	15	Antiguo Maniconio	18	Presidio de la Princesa

effective policy of decentralization. The government of Puerto Rico recognized the problem at an early stage and put in hand a program of industrial decentralization as early as 1953. As a result of these efforts the rate of migration to the capital was reduced, offering the hope of a more balanced relationship between San Juan and the rest of the country.

HISTORY. – The first settlement in this area was founded by Ponce de León in 1508 at *Caparra*, on the S side of the Bahía de San Juan. Some years later a settlement was established on the little island on the N side of the bay which is separated from the main island by the Caño de San Antonio and the Laguna del Condado – a site whose strategic importance was recognized at an early stage. In 1533 work began on the construction of extensive fortifications, which withstood a series of attacks from the sea. The town, at first known as Puerto Rico ("rich harbor") and later renamed San Juan, developed into an important bridgehead between Spain and its colonial territories. During the 19th c. the town was embroiled in confused domestic political strife.

The American occupation of Puerto Rico in 1898 and the later grant of limited rights of American citizenship to the inhabitants at first brought little benefit to San Juan. It was only after Puerto Rico was granted a limited form of self-government in 1952 and "Operation Bootstrap", a program of economic development based on self-help, was launched that the town began to expand and to attract an influx of population from the rural areas. In the 1960s and early 1970s the tourist trade boomed, partly as a result of the Cuban revolution which put Havana out of bounds for American visitors. Around 1975 the tourist trade went through a crisis period, with many firms going out of business; but the situation has since improved, contributory factors being the restoration program in the old town, the construction of a huge Convention Center and the improvement of the port facilities to accommodate the largest cruise liners.

Columbus Monument, Old San Juan

Sightseeing in San Juan

The Old Town

VIEJO SAN JUAN (OLD SAN JUAN), the whole of which has been under statutory protection as a national monument since 1949, lies picturesquely on a long narrow islet at the NE entrance of the Bahía de San Juan which is separated from the main island by the *Caño de San Antonio* and the *Laguna del Condado*. Almost all the cruise ships which call here moor on the waterfront in the neighborhood of Calle Marina. At Pier No. 1 is the *Museo del Mar* (Museum of the Sea), with a collection of old nautical instruments, ship models and well-preserved documents (including charts) of the Spanish colonial period. From here Calle

Commercio runs NE to the little *Museo de la Fundación Arqueológica*, housed in the former municipal baths, which has a rich collection of pre-Columbian material and also puts on periodic special exhibitions. To the N is the busy *Plaza de Colón* (Columbus Square), which was originally larger and known as Plaza de Santiago. The **statue of Columbus** was erected in 1893 on the 400th anniversary of the discovery of Puerto Rico. On the S side of the square is the *Teatro Tapia* (1832), named after Alejandro Tapia y Rivera, the first great Puerto Rican actor. The theater was completely renovated in 1976.

NE of the Plaza de Colón is ***Fort San Cristóbal** (1766–72; *son et lumière* shows). Standing 150 ft/45 m above sea level and covering an area of almost 27 acres, this consists of five separate structures linked by underground passages and was designed to protect not only the seaward side but also the E flank of the town.

To the W of the Plaza de Colón in Calle Fortaleza is the *Casa de Callejón, an attractively restored 18th c. burgher's house which is now occupied by the *Museo de la Arquitectura Colonial* (Museum of Colonial Architecture), with models of fortifications and old plans and documents, and the *Museo de la Familia Puertorriqueña* (Museum of the Puerto Rican Family), a folk museum. A short distance NW, in Calle San Francisco, is an attractive church, the *Iglesia de San Francisco* (1645).

Farther W we come to the *Plaza de Armas*, originally the town's main square, with four 19th c. statues of the Seasons. On the N side of the square stands the *Alcaldía (Town Hall), begun in 1604 and enlarged in later periods. The façade with its double arcade flanked by towers is modelled on the Madrid Town Hall. The *Real Intendencia*, a neo-classical building of 1851 on the W side of the square, once housed the royal Treasury and is now occupied by the law courts. An earlier 17th c. building on the site was used as a prison and barracks. To the N is the 18th c. *Diputación Provincial*, formerly the Bishop's Palace. – Farther W, in Calle Cristo, stands the *Casa del Cabildo* (16th c.), the original Town Hall. Obliquely opposite it is the *Cathedral, which dates in its present form from the early 19th c.

The first Cathedral, begun after 1521, was destroyed soon afterwards by a hurricane. The present church, begun around 1540, has an interior in Gothic style and a handsome spiral staircase. This too was damaged by a hurricane, and also by British troops under the command of the Earl of Cumberland, but was later radically rebuilt. In 1862 the relics of the Roman martyr San Pio were deposited in the Cathedral. In 1908 the remains of Juan Ponce de León were brought here from the Iglesia de San José and housed in a marble sarcophagus.

Facing the Cathedral, in Caleta de las Monjas (to W), we find the 17th c. *Convento de las Carmelitas*, a house of Carmelite nuns.

Farther N, at the corner of Calle Cristo and Calle Sol, is a former Jesuit college, the *Seminario Conciliar* (1832). Close by, at the corner of Calle Cristo and Calle San Sebastián, stands the 16th c. *Palacio Episcopal* (Bishop's Palace), which was burned down by the Dutch in 1625 and thoroughly restored in 1733.

NE of the Cathedral, at the corner of Calle Luna and Calle San José, the old *Casa de los Dos Zaguanes* now houses the very interesting *Museo del Indio (Museum of the Indian), with a wide range of Indian artifacts and other material (stone objects, pottery, carved wood, shells and bones, cult objects, etc.).

Farther NW is the attractive *Plaza de San José*, planted with lignum vitae trees; here stands a statue of Juan Ponce de León (1797), made from British cannonballs. Dominating the square is the *Iglesia de San José* (1532), one of the earliest and finest Gothic churches in the western hemisphere.

The church was originally the chapel of a Dominican convent, dedicated to St Thomas Aquinas, but later became the family church of Ponce de León's descendants. The remains of Juan Ponce de León himself were deposited in the church in 1559 and remained there until their transfer to the Cathedral in 1908. The church contains a fine 16th c. *Crucifixion presented by the Ponce de León family.

Adjoining the church is the *Convento de Santo Domingo, begun in 1523, which houses the first university in America with a *studium generale*. The large patio surrounded by a double-columned gallery is now used for various cultural events. The convent, like all other religious houses in Puerto Rico, was closed in 1838. In 1898 it became the headquarters of the United States Army, and since 1966 it has been occupied by the Instituto de Cultura Puertorriqueña.

Beside the Iglesia de San José is the *Museo Pablo Casals, with mementoes of the great cellist. Close by is the *Casa

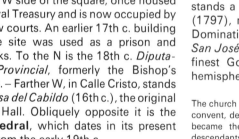
Cathedral, Old San Juan

Castillo de San Felipe del Morro

de los Contrafuertes (17th c.), with massive buttresses, which is probably the oldest private house in the town. It now houses a pharmacy museum, a collection of Puerto Rican *santos* (carved figures of saints) and a gallery of graphic art.

To the W of the Dominican convent stands the *Cuartel de Ballaja* (1864), with a spacious patio and an imposing staircase leading up to the entrance.

To the NW, in the fine *Cementerio de San Juan* below the town walls (1865), are the graves of many noted Puerto Ricans. The domed circular cemetery chapel is dedicated to Santa María de la Magdalena de Pazzis.

W of the Convento de Santo Domingo, beyond the *Campo San Felipe del Morro* (the old parade ground), can be seen the ***Castillo de San Felipe del Morro**, the town's oldest fort and once one of the principal strongholds of Spanish colonial power.

The building of the fort began in 1539, and it was strengthened in 1591 to provide protection on the landward as well as the seaward side. An attack by Sir Francis Drake was repelled in 1595. In 1598 the Earl of Cumberland managed to capture the town when the garrison was weakened by a severe epidemic of dysentery, but was soon compelled to withdraw, as was a Dutch attacking force in 1625. The fort was given its present form at the end of the 18th c. It is built on six levels, rising to a height of 130 ft/40 m above sea level, with a complex system of underground passages.

From El Morro a massive wall of sandstone blocks, up to 50 ft/15 m in height, extends round Old San Juan. Begun around 1630, it had six gates and a series of look-outs which were manned day and night.

The *Polvorín de Santa Elena* (1782), an old powder magazine, now houses the *Museo del Niño* (Museum of Childhood). To the E is the *Antiguo Manicomio* (Old Hospital, 1683), and beyond this the *Casa de Beneficencia* (1844), a former hospice. Adjoining this is the *Casa Rosa*, a fine example of 19th c. Spanish colonial architecture. Finally at the S end of the castle precincts is the ***Casa Blanca** (1521), one of the oldest houses in the town, formerly occupied by the family of Ponce de León, first Governor of the island. In the 18th c. it became the headquarters of the Spanish military commandant, and at the end of the 19th c. was taken over by the commander of the American occupation forces. It is now occupied by a museum illustrating life in Puerto Rico in the 16th and 17th c.

Two picturesque little stepped lanes parallel to Calle Cristo, the *Callejón de las Monjas* and the *Caleta del Hospital*, run down from the castle precincts to the Plaza de la Catedral. At the end of the Caleta de las Monjas is the *Plazuela de la Rogativa*, with an attractive monument, erected in 1971 on the 450th anniversary of the town's foundation, commemorating a procession of women led by the Bishop during the British occupation in 1797. Lower down, at the end of Caleta San Juan, is the *Puerta de San Juan* (1635), the oldest of the town gates, which leads to a small bay which in those days was much used as an anchorage.

Farther S stands the *Fortaleza* (16th c.), San Juan's oldest fort. Originally consisting only of a tower designed to give the inhabitants of the young settlement protection against Indian attack, it was later enlarged to serve as the Governor's residence, and is now one of the oldest continuously occupied seats of government in the western hemisphere. It was given its present form during the reign of Isabella II (19th c.).

Farther E is the *Parque de las Palomas*, from which there is a fine *view of the harbor. On its E side we find the *Capilla del Cristo* (1753), said to have been founded by a horseman badly injured in a fall in gratitude for his miraculous preservation; it contains a splendid *silver altar. Obliquely opposite is the *Casa del Libro* (18th c.), a museum of old books and printing and adjoining this, in a handsome colonial mansion, the *Museo de Arte Puertorriqueña* (Museum of Puerto Rican Art), with a good collec-

Capilla del Santo Cristo

tion of painting and sculpture of the 18th, 19th and 20th c.

Outside the town gate, to the S, is the *Presídio de la Princesa* (1837), a former prison which is due to be restored. Farther W, in Calle Tetuán, is the *Bastión de las Palmas*, on the town walls, another excellent look-out point. To the E is the *Iglesia Santa Ana* (18th c.).

To the S of the town walls lies the little district of **La Puntilla**, with the *Arsenal* (c. 1800), which once housed more than 30 coastal guard-boats. Beyond this are the local headquarters of the *US Coast Guard*.

Capitol, San Juan

Puerta de Tierra

Immediately E of Old San Juan is the PUERTA DE TIERRA district, still on the island N of the Caño de San Antonio. The dominant feature here is the *Capitol (Capitolio)*, in Avenida Muñoz Rivera, seat of the Puerto Rican Parliament. It is an imposing domed building (begun 1925) designed by the Puerto Rican architect Rafael Carmoega on the model of the Capitol in Washington, D.C. An urn, centrally situated in the interior, contains a copy of the Puerto Rican constitution of 1952. There are various other government buildings, higher educational establishments and schools in the neighborhood.

Both the Avenida Muñoz Rivera and the parallel Avenida Ponce de León lead to the **Parque Moñoz Rivera**, ¾ mile/1 km E. The park was originally laid out in the 1920s but was completely renovated in 1976 and equipped with a variety of recreational facilities. Near the *Polverín*, an old powder magazine, is a statue of Luís Muñoz Rivera. Round the park are

US military and naval establishments. To the E stands the handsome building occupied by the *Supreme Court* (Corte Suprema).

At the E end of the island lies the *Playa Escambrón*, with large luxury hotels. On its eastern tip is *Fortín Sa Jerónimo, a small fort built in 1788 which was severely damaged by a British attack in 1788 but rebuilt in 1799. It now contains a Military Museum, with ship models, old charts and other documents and uniforms of different periods.

The island is linked with the mainland of Puerto Rico by two heavily used bridges, at the ends of which are yacht clubs.

Condado

The CONDADO district lies on the spit of land between the **Laguna de Condado** (part of which is used as a yacht anchorage) and the Atlantic and on the coastal area to the E. The massive development of high-rise building in this district began after the last war and was accelerated after the Cuban revolution to cater for the steadily increasing flow of vacationing visitors from North America. There is now a huge concentration of hotels and recreational facilities in all price categories, tending to reduce the appeal of what was originally a very beautiful beach. Since the hotel crisis of the mid seventies the further development of this area has been pursued with the greatest restraint. The main traffic artery is the *Avenida Ashford*, along which are many luxury hotels. An attractive new feature is the *Condado Convention Center*, the largest and most modern establishment of

its kind in the Caribbean, which can seat more than 4000 people at the same time. The Center is used also for events in the *LeLoLai Festival* and for art exhibitions.

Santurce

To the S of Condado is the densely built-up SANTURCE district, extending to the *Caño de Martín Peña* and the *Laguna San José*. Since the last war this has developed into a modern business district. Its principal street is the Avenida Ponce de León, a wide avenue designed on the North American model, as are two modern expressways, the Baldorioty de Castro Expreso to the N and Luís Muñoz Rivera to the W and S.

On a peninsula to the W of the MIRAMAR district is the *Aeropuerto de Isla Grande*, with a United States naval base. – On the SE side of the **Bahïa de San Juan** is the *Puerto Nuevo*, a new port and industrial area still in course of development, surrounded by large estates of detached family houses.

The modern district of Hato Rey

Hato Rey

S of the Caño de Martín Peña we come to HATO REY, a district of ultra-modern high-rise buildings housing banks and offices. Its principal traffic arteries are the Avenida Luís Muñoz Rivera and Avenida Ponce de León, both running N and S.

Farther W, on the *Río Piedras*, is the extensive **Parque de las Américas**, with the large *Hiram Bithorn Stadium*. To the N is *Las Américas Shopping Center*, one of the largest in the West Indies.

Río Piedras

Immediately S of Hato Rey is the RIO PIEDRAS district, with the campus of the

Laguna de Condado, San Juan

University of Puerto Rico, founded in 1903 (22,000 students). There is an interesting *University Museum*, with archaeological and historical collections and art exhibitions which change every month. The *University Theatre* has a full program of dramatic performances, and the annual Casals Festival is held here. In the vestibule of the Library is a huge painting by Rufino Tamayo, "Prometheus".

To the S is the **Agricultural Experimental Station**, with a large *Botanic Garden*. There is a magnificent display of orchids, and other notable features are the Lotus Lagoon, the Bamboo Avenue and the Liana Jungle.

High-rise apartment buildings in the Isla Verde district

Isla Verde

The hotel and apartment zone extends from Condado by way of *Ocean Park* to the *Punta las Marías*, and is continued in the ISLA VERDE district. Here a further group of luxury hotels has grown up in convenient proximity to the busy **Aeropuerto Internacional de Isla Verde**, which lies between the *Laguna de San José* and the *Laguna La Torrecilla* with its mangrove swamps. In the *Boca de Cangrejos* are the interesting *Jardines Submarinos* (Underwater Gardens), a marine aquarium with many rare species of fish and other sea creatures. On the E side of the entrance to the lagoon is the *Bosque Estatal de Piñones*, a nature reserve (woodland; birds).

BOAT TRIPS. – **Around the harbor** (1½ hours): from the Tourist Pier in Old San Juan to the Puerto Nuevo with its large industrial installations; then via Catano to the Isla de Cabras and Punta del Morro, and back from there.

Bacardi tour: from the Tourist Pier to **Catano** (pop. 26,000), on the opposite side of the harbor; from there

a conducted tour of the world-famous* **Bacardi rum factory** (facilities for tasting).

Laguna La Torrecilla (1 hour): from the Boca de Cangrejos in the Isla Verde district to the mangrove swamps in the lagoon, then on to the *Bosque Estatal de Piñones* nature reserves.

San Juan to Arecibo (round trip 173 miles/ 278 km). – Leave San Juan on A 2, going SW.

6 miles/9 km: *ruins of Caparra, in the commune of **Guaynabo** (pop. 80,700) and immediately S of the *large Fort Buchanan Military Reservation*.

Caparra, the first Spanish settlement on Puerto Rico, was founded on Ponce de León in 1508. The *Museo Ponce de León* contains interesting excavation finds and documents on the history of Caparra. – To the N is the industrial suburb of **Catano**, with the *Bacardi rum factory*.

The road continues W, crossing the *Río Bayamón*, to –

3 miles/5 km: **Bayamón**, (pop. 196,000), once a separate villa suburb but now swallowed up by San Juan. It has beautiful parks and gardens and several higher educational establishments.

7 miles/11 km: turn right into route 165, which runs N via **Toa Baja** to –

4 miles/6 km: **Dorado**, a popular holiday resort (golf-course). N of the town is the *Playa de Dorado*, a beautiful beach.

Continue W on Route 693, which runs parallel to the coast, passing the excellently equipped beaches of *Playa Dorado-Sardinera*, *Playa los Tocores* and *Playa Cerro Gordo*, with exclusive hotels (*Dorado Beach Hotel, 308 r., T, SP, golf, casino; *Cerromar Beach Hotel, 508 r., T, SP, golf, beach, casino).

10 miles/16 km: **Vega Baja**, in a fertile region of pineapple, citrus fruit and sugar-cane plantations. – From here N on Route 686 through a swampy area.

4 miles/6 km: *Playa de Vega Baja*, and beyond this *Playa Puerto Nuevo*, two fine beaches.

Farther W, on the spit of land between the Atlantic and the *Laguna Tortuguero* (military training area), is *Playa Tortuguera*, and beyond this *Playa Mar Chiquita* – two more attractive beaches, the latter enclosed by rugged cliffs. – Now S on Route 685.

9 miles/15 km: **Manatí**, in the center of an intensively cultivated area (pineapples, sugar-cane, pastureland).

From here W on A 2, over the *Río Grande de Manatí* and past the *Reserva Forestal de Cambalache*.

17 miles/27 km: *Arecibo (0–50 ft/0–15 m; pop. 86,800), a port at the mouth of the *Río Grande de Arecibo*; the second largest town on the N coast. The town, founded by the Spaniards in the early 16th c., is apparently named after an Indian chief. Under the government's industrialization program Arecibo has developed into an active industrial town. The *Ronrico rum distillery* can be visited (tasting). In the harbor is a handsome lighthouse. 4 miles/6 km NE of the town is the *Cueva del Indio*, a cave occupied in pre-Columbian times, probably a cult site, with interesting rock engravings.

To the S and E of Arecibo is the *Karst Country, along the northern edge of which are swarms of the conical hills known as "haystacks", formed by karstic action and erosion. The wooded karstic region to the S is extremely striking with its steep-sided karstic cones and towers and numerous funnel-shaped cavities.

12½ miles/20 km S of Arecibo (Routes 129, 635 and 625) is the **Observatorio de Arecibo (open to visitors only on Sunday afternoons, 2–4.30), with the largest radio-telescope in the world, belonging to Cornell University and the National Science Foundation. The reflector, which has an area of over 20 acres, spans a huge saucer almost 440 yd/400 m across and over 295 ft/90 m deep which is surrounded by karstic cones. Some 590 ft/180 m above the reflector hangs a lattice suspended from three masts. With this apparatus it is possible to record the radio impulses of cosmic background radiation and other sources of radiation in space.

From Arecibo A 10 leads up the valley of the Río Grande de Arecibo and through the Karst Country (see above) to –

12½ miles/20 km: *Embalse Dos Bocas, a man-made lake consisting of one main and several subsidiary basins, the water in which is used chiefly for the production of electric power. Boat trips on the lake.

To the W of the lake is the *Reserva Forestal Río Abajo (5800 acres), a beautiful nature park with facilities for recreation. There are a number of look-out points offering a prospect of the Karst Country. There is a sawmill, still in operation. The predominant tree here is teak, the foliage of which reaches astonishing dimensions. The best time to visit the forest is between August and December, when the teak trees are in blossom.

Continue on A 10, which climbs towards the S.

7¼ miles/12 km: Utuado (Hotel Hacienda Roses, 7 r.), from which the Indian Ceremonial Park (see under Ponce) can be visited. – From here take Route 111, which runs SW and in 4½ miles/7 km joins Route 140.

Route 140 goes N through beautiful scenery, passing the Embalse Coanillas (reservoir), and then winds its way down through the Karst country to the northern coastal plain, where it joins A 2.

Continue SW on a winding section of road.

9 miles/14 km: Collores. – From here continue on Route 144, which runs E along the northern slopes of the Cordillera Central to –

3 miles/5 km: *Jayuya (Parador Hacienda Gripiñas, 9 r., SP), once a coffee-growing center, now a holiday resort in the hills.

7½ miles/12 km: junction with Route 157. Continue up the valley of the Río Toro Negro.

2½ miles/4 km: Route 157 joins the Ruta Panorámica (see under Ponce). This beautiful road (here No. 143) runs E through the hills of the Cordillera Central, with plantations of coffee, tobacco, bananas and oranges and the attractive Area Recreo Doña Juana (see under Ponce).

23 miles/37 km: junction with Route 162. – 2 miles/3 km N is the picturesque resort of *Barranquitas,

birthplace of the writer and statesman Luis Munoz Rivera. The house in which he was born is now a museum. There is a picturesque market (craft goods). – The road now runs S.

5 miles/8 km: junction with A 14. Continue on A 14, which runs NE via Aibonito.

6 miles/10 km: junction with Route 173. Take this road, which runs N to –

7½ miles/12 km: Cidra (Treasure Island Resort). To the E is a beautiful man-made lake, the Embalse de Cidra.

Route 173 continues NE via Sumidera to –

6 miles/9 km: the *Cuevas de Aguas Buenas, a group of caves which are among the most interesting on the island. – Then back via the little town of Aguas Buenas to –

20 miles/33 km: San Juan.

San Juan to Fajardo and Humacao (round trip 141 miles/227 km). – Leave San Juan on Autopista 26, which runs SE past the Laguna San José.

12½ miles/20 km: junction with A 3. Continue E via Carolina to –

6 miles/9 km: Loíza. 6 miles/10 km N, at the mouth of the Río Loíza, is the fishing village of Loíza Aldea, scene of the *Fiesta de Santiago Apóstol (July), which draws many visitors every year. The special charm of this festival of St James lies in its mingling of Spanish, Indian and African traditions.

5 miles/8 km: Río Grande. 3 miles/5 km N is a well-equipped beach with a luxury holiday complex (*Río Mar Hotel, 111 r., SP, T, golf, beach).

From Río Grande a detour can be made on Route 186 up the beautiful valley of the Río Espíritu into the *Sierra de Luquillo, a range of steep wooded hills – the continuation of the Cordillera Central – which rises out of the northern coastal plain. Most of this region, now conveniently accessible by road, is a nature reserve, with palms, tree ferns, pineapples and a lichen-like growth known as old man's hair.

4 miles/6 km: Palmer, from which a road leads through the hills to El Yunque.

From Palmer the road runs S through magnificent scenery, climbing into the dense rain forest of El Yunque (3494 ft/1065 m), long scheduled as the *Caribbean National Forest, Luquillo Division. The only tropical forest under the control of the US National Parks Administration, this has an area of 28,000 acres and is notable for the extraordinary variety of its vegetation (over 240 different species of trees). Situated in an area exposed to the trade winds, it has a very high rainfall. The forest is the home of a number of rare species of parrot. In addition to El Yunque it contains two other peaks, El Toro (3524 ft/1074 m) to the SW and the Pico de Este (3448 ft/1051 m) to the SE. At the N entrance to the National Park is the Vivero Forestal La Catalina, an interesting tropical tree nursery. In the center of the forest is the Area Recreativa La Mina, with excellent recreational facilities, from which footpaths run through magnificent scenery to the surrounding peaks.

3 miles/5 km: *Playa de Luquillo*, a palm-fringed beach of fine sand, one of the finest on the island. – The road continues via **Luquillo** (Parador Martorell, 7 r.) to –

6 miles/10 km: **Fajardo** (*El Conquistador Hotel, 381 r., SP, T, golf, beach, casino; etc. – Flamboyán Restaurant), a pretty little fishing port which was once the haunt of pirates and smugglers. – 1¼ miles/2 km E is *Playa de Fajardo*, from which there are ferry services to Vieques and Culebra. Boat trips to the little coral islets of *Isla Palominos*, *Isla de Aves*, *Cayo Lobos* and *Cayo Icacos* to the NE. 2 miles/3 km NE of Fajardo is the beautiful beach of *Playa Sardinera*, and another 2 miles/3 km beyond this, at the rugged northeastern tip of the island, are two other beaches, *Playa Las Croabas* and *Playa Soroco*.

A 3 continues S through large sugar-cane plantations, passing through the little town of *Ceiba* and along the excellently equipped beach of *Playa de Humacao* (*Palmas del Mar Hotel, 400 r., SP, T, golf).

22 miles/35 km: **Humacao** (246 ft/75 m; pop. 46,000), formerly an agricultural center and now a growing industrial town (petrochemicals, textiles, sugar). It has an offshoot on the coast with a small harbor which has developed in recent years into a popular sailing and fishing center. – On the little offshore coral island of *Cayo Santiago* lives a colony of monkeys.

From here A 3 continues S.

2½ miles/4 km: junction with Route 906. – 4½ miles/7 km S is *Playa de Guayanés*, with a small harbor, formerly used for the shipment of sugar.

7 miles/11 km: **Yabucoa**, in the intensively cultivated Yabucoa plain.

The road continues through the *Cuchilla de Pandura*, a range of low hills, passing the second highest point in the range, the *Cerro La Pandura* (515 ft/157 m), and comes to **Maunabo**, near which are a beautiful beach and the *Punta Tuna* lighthouse (extensive views).

15 miles/24 km: *Puerto Patillas*. – 2 miles/3 km NW is *Patillas*, above which is the *Embalse de Patillas*, a man-made lake created under the program, initiated in 1914, for irrigating the southern coastal plain. – To the SW, near *Punta Guilarte*, is the well-equipped beach of *Playa las Palmas*.

9 miles/14 km: **Guyama**, a developing industrial town, with attractive Spanish colonial houses in the old town center.

1¼ miles/2 km: junction with Route 179.

This beautiful hill road runs S, passing the *Embalse Carite* (reservoir), into the *Sierra de Cayey*, a southeastern offshoot of the Cordillera Central. The central part of the range is a forest reserve, the *Reserva Forestal Carite*.

22 miles/35 km: junction with A 1, which runs N into the *Caguas basin* between the eastern Cordillera Central, the Sierra de Luquillo and the northern uplands. This is a region of sugar-cane, vegetable and tobacco plantations and dairy farms.

9 miles/15 km: **Caguas** (pop. 118,000), Puerto Rico's largest inland town, an industrial center which developed at a tremendous rate during the 1960s and 1970s.

From here A 1, now of highway standard, continues through the *Altos de San Luís* and past the *Embalse Río Grande de Loíza*, the island's largest man-made lake, to –

22 miles/35 km: **San Juan**.

Excursion to Vieques. – Vieques (area 51 sq. miles/132 sq. km; pop. 7000; Casa del Francés, 19 r.; etc.), reached either by air from San Juan or by ferry from Playa de Fajardo, is an island on the coastal shelf 7½ miles/12 km E of Puerto Rico which in terms of structure and topography belongs to the Virgin Islands. Much of the island is occupied by the US Navy as a training ground. The chief place is **Isabel Segunda** (pop. 3500), to the N of which is the *Punta Mula lighthouse* (extensive views). On the S coast of the island is the charming beach of *Playa Sombe*.

See also ****Puerto Rico.**

San Salvador (Watling's Island/ Guanahani)

Bahama Islands
Commonwealth of the Bahamas

Area: 68 sq. miles/175 sq. km
Population: 1000.
Administrative center: Nassau (on New Providence).
Vehicles travel on the left.

ⓘ **Ministry of Tourism,**
Nassau Court,
P. O. Box N 3220,
Nassau,
Bahamas;
tel. (809) 322 7505.
See also Practical Information.

HOTELS. – *Riding Rock Inn*, Cockburn Town, 45 r., SP, tennis; *Pat's Place*, Cockburn Town, 4 r.; *Sea View Villa*, Cockburn Town, 6 r.

RECREATION and SPORT. – Scuba diving, snorkeling, sailing, deep-sea fishing, swimming and sunbathing; tennis.

AIR SERVICES. – Scheduled flights to Nassau.

SHIPPING. – Mail boat services from Cockburn Town via Cat Island or Rum Cay and George Town (Great Exuma) to Nassau.

The island of *San Salvador, an eastern outpost of the Bahamas, lies in latitude 24° N and longitude 74°30′ W. Tradition has it that Columbus made his first landing in the New World here on October 12, 1492.

San Salvador, a flat island with an extensive system of inland lakes and a few hills rising to about 165 ft/50 m, lies on a

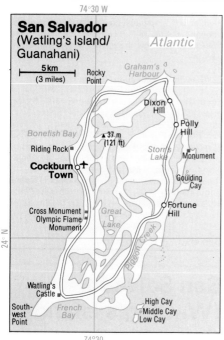

San Salvador
(Watling's Island/
Guanahani)

northern offshoot of the eastern Bahama Bank, surrounded by magnificent *underwater canyons. The island is highly regarded by fishermen.

HISTORY. – The island, known to the pre-Columbian inhabitants as **Guanahani**, was only briefly occupied by the Spaniards. In the 17th c. it became the haunt of freebooters and pirates of many nations. About 1680 a pirate captain named John Watling sought refuge here: hence the name of **Watling's Island** which was in use until 1926. In the late 18th c. it was settled by American Loyalists, who established cotton plantations, some of which still exist. Further economic change came to the island with the establishment of a US rocket base in 1951.

The chief settlement on the island is **Cockburn Town**, on the sheltered W coast. The town, dominated by its imposing Roman Catholic church, has an interesting New World Museum with a large collection of pre-Columbian material.

To the S of the town is *Fernandez Bay*, with a fringe of palms and bay grapes. Farther S is *Long Bay*, Columbus's probable landing-place, with the *Cross Monument* to commemorate the event. Nearby is the *Olympic Flame Monument*, commemorating the passage of the Olympic flame on its way to Mexico City for the 1968 Olympic Games.

On **Southwest Point** are the ruins of *Watling's Castle*, a mansion on an old cotton plantation which is said to have

been built by the pirate, Captain Watling. In the neighborhood are some impressive caves and bizarre rock formations.

Off *French Bay*, on the S coast, are good diving grounds offering a great variety of underwater life. – Off the SE tip of the island are a group of islets rising prominently out of the sea – *High Cay*, *Middle Cay*, *Low Cay* and *Boat Rock*.

On the E coast with its two large inlets, *Pigeon Creek* and *Storr's Lake*, lie a number of small settlements, some of which have grown out of former plantations. To the S of *Polly Hill* is another monument to Columbus. – On a low hill at the NE corner of the island stands the *Dixon lighthouse* (1855–56).

N of Cockburn Town is *Riding Rock Point*, with a large resort complex which attracts many visitors. – Farther N is *Bonefish Bay*, a sheltered fishing area.

SCUBA DIVING. – The precipitous *submarine canyons off *French Bay* and *Southwest Point* are rated the best diving grounds in the Bahamas, with extensive and varied coral formations and an equally varied underwater life. – There is also good diving to be had on the reef off the W coast, between Southwest Point and Cockburn Town.

See also **Bahamas.

Santiago de los Caballeros

Dominican Republic
República Dominicana

Province: Santiago
Altitude: 1017 ft/310 m.
Population: 285,000.

ⓘ **Dirección Nacional de Turismo e Información,**
César Nicolás Pensón/Rosa Duarte,
Santo Domingo,
República Dominicana;
tel. (809) 688 5537.
See also Practical Information.

HOTELS. – *Matum*, Las Carreras, 50 r.; *Mercedes*, 30 de Marzo, 36 r.; *Don Diego*, Estrella Sahdalá, 35 r.; *Corona*, Estrella Sahdalá, 28 r.; *Carmino Real*.

RESTAURANTS. – *El Dragón*; *El Pez Dorado*.

AIR SERVICES. – Occasional flights to Santo Domingo (Las Américas).

Santiago de los Caballeros, capital of Santiago province and the second

largest town in the Dominican Republic, lies on the banks of the Río Yaque del Norte in the fertile Cibao valley. The economic and cultural center of the country's northern region and a university town, it still preserves the *atmosphere of a country town of the colonial period.

SIGHTS. – The hub of the town's life is the **Parque Duarte**, near which are the *Cathedral* (Iglesia Mayor de Santiago Apóstol), the *Gobernación Provincial* (headquarters of the provincial government) and the *Palacio Consistorial* (Town Hall). Farther E, on the Rio Yaque del Norte, is *Fort San Luís*.

In Calle del Sol, the town's principal street, is the *Parque Colón*, with an interesting church, the *Iglesia de la Altagracia*. Farther E the street opens into a large roundabout, with the impressive *Monumento a los Héroes de la Restauración* (fine *views). – Also of interest is the *Tomás Morel Museum of Folk Art*.

SURROUNDINGS. – To the N of the town is the *Cordillera Septentrional*, extending from Montecristi in the NW to the swampy low-lying Samaná peninsula in the SE. In this region there are rich deposits of *amber (fossil resin of the Miocene era), particularly around Tamboril. The highest peaks in the range are the *Pico Diego de Ocampo* (4131 ft/1259 m) and the *Pico Jicomé* or *Murazo* (3553 ft/1083 m).

SE of Santiago is the *Vega Real*, a fertile and intensively cultivated region which in addition to cacao and coffee for export also produces bananas, maize, sweet potatoes, manioc and rice. It has a population of about a million – a third of the total population of the Dominican Republic. The towns of *La Vega* (pop. 43,000), *Moca* (pop. 34,000) and **San Francisco de Macoris** (pop. 64,000) are busy market centers. – To the S of the Vega Real is the **Cordillera Central**, the eastern part of the island's main range, which in Haiti is formed by the northwestern highlands and the Massif du Nord. Within the Dominican Republic the range splits into two chains, the lower of which, taking in the highlands of Castellanos and Seibo, extends eastward as the Cordillera Oriental, while the higher and more southerly runs down to the Caribbean coast as the *Sierra de Ocoa*.

Most of the Cordillera Central, which is rich in raw materials, is now a nature park. It contains the two highest peaks in the whole of the Antilles, the **Pico Duarte** 10,417 ft/3175 m) and *Yaque* (9991 ft/3045 m).

The mountain region has been opened up to traffic by the Carretera Duarte and the new road from Constanza into the Cibao valley. The high valley of Constanza (c. 3950 ft/1200 m), an area of European appearance, produces crops normally grown in the world's temperate zones. The idyllic side valleys are already

drawing many visitors, whose needs are catered for by a fine hotel at Constanza and another at Jaracaboa (1970 ft/600 m), to the N.

See also **Dominican Republic** and **Hispaniola**.

Santo Domingo
Dominican Republic
República Dominicana

Distrito Nacional.
Altitude: sea level.
Population: 1,300,000; metropolitan area 1,600,000.

ⓘ **Dirección Nacional de Turismo,**
Calle César Nicolás Pensón 59,
Santo Domingo,
República Dominicana;
tel. 688 5537.
Centro Dominicano de Información Turistica,
Calle Arzobispo Meriño 156;
tel. 685 3282.
See also Practical Information.

DIPLOMATIC MISSIONS. – *British Embassy:* Avenida Independencia 506, Apartado 1352, tel. 682 3128. – *United States Embassy:* César Nicolás Pensón/Leopoldo Navarro, tel. 682 2171. – *Canadian Honorary Consul:* Mahatma Gandhi 200, tel. 689 0002.

HOTELS. – *Embajador, Av. Sarasota, 310 r., SP, T, casino; *Hostal Nicolás de Ovando, Las Damas, 60 r., SP; *Jaragua, Av. Independencia, 250 r., SP, T, casino; *Melia, 316 r., SP. T; *Naco, Av. Tiradentes 22, 105 r., SP, T, casino; *Plaza Dominicana, Av. Anacoana, 316 r., SP, T; Dominican Concorde, Av. Anacoana, 300 r., SP. T, golf; *Santo Domingo, Av. Independencia, 220 r., SP, T; *Sheraton, Av. George Washington, 271 r., SP, T, casino; Anacoana, Palo Hincado 303, 15 r.; Cervantes, Cervantes 202, 96 r.; Comercial, El Conde 201, 75 r.; Comodoro Av. Bolivar 193, 87 r.; Continental, Av. Máximo Gómez, 100 r.; Hispaniola, Av. Independencia, 165 r., SP; San Gerónimo, Av. Independencia 205, 72 r.; Nupolitano 78 r., Av. George Washington; etc. – Several PENSIONS and HOLIDAY APARTMENTS.

RESTAURANTS in most hotels; also D'Agostino, Av. Máximo Gómez; Da Ciro, Av. Independencia 38; Vesuvio, Av. George Washington; El Bodegón, Calle Arzobispo Merino 19; Mesón de la Cava, Av. Mirador del Sur; Plaza Criolla, Av. 27 de Febrero; Mesón 1503, Calle Hostos; La Fromagerie, Av. Pasteur 18; El Caserío, Av. George Washington; Lago Enriquillo, Paseo de los Indios; La Gran Muralla, Av. 27 de Febrero; Viejo Roma, Calle Mercedes 605; Rincón Argentino, Av. George Washington; etc.

NIGHT SPOTS in the leading hotels; also Le Petit Château, Autopista 30 de Mayo; Maunaloa, Centro de los Héroes.

Casinos in Embajador, Jaragua, Naco and Sheraton Hotels and in Maunaloa Club.

THEATERS. – Teatro Nacional, Plaza de la Cultura; Palacio de Bellas Artes, Av. Independencia/Av. Máximo Gómez; Casa de Teatro, Calle Arzobispo Meriño.

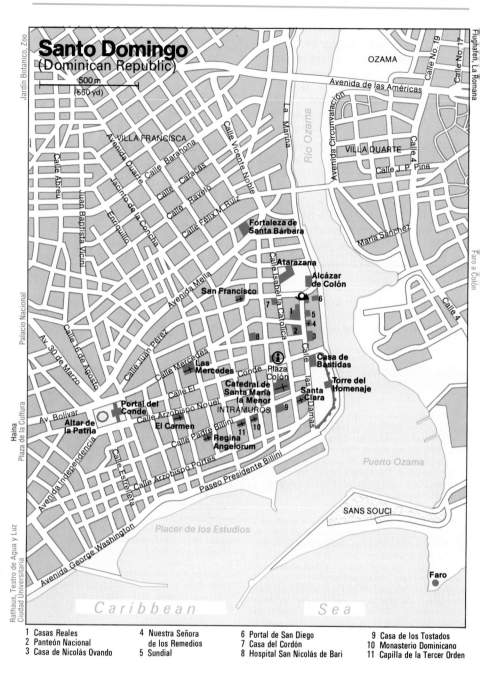

Santo Domingo
(Dominican Republic)

500 m
(550 yd)

Jardín Botánico, Zoo

Flughafen, La Romana

OZAMA

Avenida de las Américas

Calle No. 19
Calle No. 17

Faro a Colón

Calle 4

VILLA DUARTE

Calle J. P. Pina

Z. VILLA FRANCISCA

Calle Abreu

Avenida Duarte

Calle Barahona

Calle Caracas

Calle Ravelo

Calle Félix M. Ruiz

Calle Vicente Noble

La Marina

María Sánchez

Río Ozama

Avenida Circunvalación

Juan Baptista Vicini

Enriquillo

Jacinto de la Concha

Fortaleza de
Santa Bárbara

Avenida Mella

Atarazana

Alcázar
de Colón

San Francisco

7

Calle Isabela la Católica

6

1

5
4

2

3

8

Palacio Nacional

Calle 16 de Agosto

Calle Juan Pérez

Las
Mercedes

Calle Mercedes

Conde

Plaza
Colón

Casa de
Bastidas

Calle El

Catedral de
Santa María
la Menor

Santa
Clara

Torre del
Homenaje

Calle las Damas

Av. 30 de Marzo

Av. Bolívar

Portal del
Conde

Altar de
la Patria

Calle Arzobispo Nouel

INTRAMUROS

9

Casa de los Tostados

El Carmen

Calle Padre Billini

11 10

Regina
Angelorum

Haina
Plaza de la Cultura

Avenida Independencia

Calle Estrelleta

Calle Arzobispo Portes

Paseo Presidente Billini

Puerto Ozama

SANS SOUCI

Rathaus, Teatro de Agua y Luz
Ciudad Universitaria

Avenida George Washington

Placer de los Estudios

Faro

C a r i b b e a n   *S e a*

1 Casas Reales	4 Nuestra Señora	6 Portal de San Diego	9 Casa de los Tostados
2 Panteón Nacional	de los Remedios	7 Casa del Cordón	10 Monasterio Dominicano
3 Casa de Nicolás Ovando	5 Sundial	8 Hospital San Nicolás de Bari	11 Capilla de la Tercer Orden

SHOPPING. – The range of goods in Santo Domingo is broadly the same as in other Caribbean tourist areas. Particular bargains are the famous Dominican amber and various craft products (straw work, articles made from mahogany, pottery). – The principal shopping street is the Avenida Mella, with the well-stocked *Mercado Modelo, in which hundreds of sellers offer a wide range of craft objects, sometimes of excellent quality. Another shopping area which has recently come to the fore is the *Plaza Criolla*, in Avenida 27 de Febrero.

ART GALLERIES (a selection). – *Auffant*, Av. El Conde 513; *Carías*, Av. México/Alma Mater; *Candido Bido*, Av. Mella 9B; *Casa de Teatro*, Arzobispo Merino 110; *El Greco*, Av. Tiradentes; *Nader*, La Atarazana 7; *Taller Giotto*, Calle Arzobispo Merino 31.

RECREATION and SPORT. – Sailing, deep-sea fishing, swimming and sunbathing; golf, riding, tennis.

AIR SERVICES. – Scheduled flights from Las Américas International Airport (19 miles/30 km E) to Aruba and Curaçao (Netherlands Antilles), Mayagüez and San Juan (Puerto Rico), Port-au-Prince (Haiti), Miami, Detroit and New York (USA), Caracas (Venezuela), Barranquilla and Bogota (Colombia) and Madrid (Spain).

SHIPPING. – Regular calls by Caribbean cruise ships, usually from Miami and Fort Lauderdale (USA), San Juan (Puerto Rico) and Willemstad (Curaçao). Occasional passenger-carrying cargo ships to North America and Western Europe.

Santo Domingo, capital of the Dominican Republic, lies in a bay on the SE coast of the island of Hispaniola at the mouth of the Río Ozama. For a long time the principal center of Spanish power in the New World, it has preserved many fine colonial buildings, which in recent years have been carefully restored.

HISTORY. – The settlement of *Nueva Isabela*, which later became Santo Domingo, was founded by Columbus's brother Bartholomew in 1496, and thereafter it became a base for expeditions to the neighboring islands and the American mainland. The first university in the New World was founded here in 1538. During the 16th and 17th c. Santo Domingo became the target of raids by buccaneers and freebooters of all kinds, and in 1586 it was plundered by Sir Francis Drake. Hispaniola's political troubles also hampered the town's development until 1844, but it flourished after the Dominican Republic was established as an independent state – although Spanish colonial influence continued to make itself felt.

Cathedral, Santo Domingo

Subsequently the development of the town was again held back by political instability. After disturbances which almost amounted to civil war the country, and with it the capital, was under United States control from 1916 to 1924. In 1930 a coup d'état brought Rafael Leónidas Trujillo to power, and during his Presidency Santo Domingo was renamed *Ciudad Trujillo*. – After Trujillo's murder in 1961 and the brief Presidency of Juan Bosch the country was involved in further disturbances and finally (1965) in civil war, which caused severe damage in the town and led to the intervention of US troops.

It was not until 1966 that the newly elected President was able to take steps for the preservation of Santo Domingo's historic old buildings, and these measures have since produced some notable results. The town has also benefited in recent years from the development – still continuing – of the Plaza de la Cultura, the modern buildings in which contrast effectively with the old colonial town, now restored.

Columbus died in 1506 in the Spanish town of Valladolid and was buried there; but in accordance with his last wishes his remains were later taken to Santo Domingo and deposited in the Cathedral. In 1795, however, his remains – or what were believed to be his remains – were exhumed and taken first to Havana and later to Seville, where they were housed in a tomb erected in the Cathedral. Dominican historians believe that these were actually the remains of Columbus's grandson Luis and that the true coffin of the Discoverer was not found in Santo Domingo Cathedral until 1877 and is still there.

SIGHTS. – The central feature of the old town of Santo Domingo, known as INTRAMUROS, is the *Parque Colón* (Columbus Park), with a monumental bronze statue of Columbus by the French sculptor Gilbert (1897). On the E side of the square is the *Palacio de Borgellá*, residence of the Governor during the Haitian occupation (1822–44); on the W side is the old Town Hall; and on the S side is the Renaissance façade of the **Catedral de Santa María la Menor.** As the first Cathedral in America (built 1521–40) it enjoys the title of *Catedral Primada de América*. Near the main entrance is the magnificent tomb of marble and bronze created by the Spanish sculptor Carbonell to house the remains of Columbus, who Dominican historians believe is buried here.

The INTERIOR of the Cathedral is in Gothic style. It has a *high altar* of beaten silver and a silver *carillon* by Benvenuto Cellini. The rich Cathedral *treasury* contains, among much else, the crown of Queen Isabella of Castile, which was pawned to meet the cost of Columbus's first voyage of discovery.

One block S of the Cathedral, at the corner of Calle Arzobispo Merino and Calle Padre Billini, is the **Casa Tostado** which was built at the beginning of the 16th c. for Francisco de Tostado and which later became the Archbishop's Palace; it now houses the *Museo de la Familia Dominicana del Siglo XIX* (Museum of the Dominican Family in the 19th c.).

From here Calle Padre Billini runs E, passing the Hospice and *Church of Santa Clara* (1522) on the right, into Calle de las Damas. On the far side of this street,

Torre del Homenaje

within the precincts of the fort of **Ozama** commanding the harbor, is the **Torre del Homenaje** (Tower of Homage, 1502). – A little way N is the handsome *Casa Bastidas*, built (probably by Rodrigo de Bastidas) at the beginning of the 16th c.

and rebuilt in the 18th c., with an inner courtyard resembling a cloister. It now houses the ceramic department of the Museo de las Casas Reales. – One block N, on right, is the *Casa de Nicolás Ovando*, home of the man who played a prominent part in the planning of the town. Opposite it, in a former Jesuit house (1714–45), is the *Panteón Nacional* (National Pantheon), which commemorates great national figures.

N of Nicolás de Ovando's house we come to the *Capilla de Nuestra Señora de los Remedios*, which was used as a church before the building of the Cathedral. – Farther N is an old *sundial*.

Opposite, in two early 16th c. buildings (much altered in later periods), the place occupied by the Real Audiencia y Cancilleria de las Indias and the residence of the Governor and Captain-General, is the *Museo de las Casas Reales. The museum's collections, superbly displayed, illustrate the social, economic,

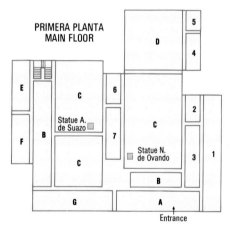

Museo de las Casas Reales
Santo Domingo
(República Dominicana)

Palacio de la Real Audiencia y Cancillería de Índias
Palacio de los Gobernadores y Capitanes Generales de la Isla Española

PRIMERA PLANTA (Main Floor)
A Vestibulo (Entrance Hall)
B Galeria (Gallery)
C Patio (Inner Courtyard)
D Traspatio (Rear Courtyard)
E Sanitario (Toilets)
F Cafeteria
G Sala de Exposiciones Temporales (Room for Temporary Exhibitions)

1 Cartografia (Maps)
2 Sanidad y Farmacologia (Health and Medicines)
3 Mineria (Mining)
   Economia Agropecuaria (Agriculture and Stock-Farming)
   Presencia y Uso del Tabaco en la Colonia (Tobacco in the Colony)
4 Caballerizas (Stables)
5 Polverín Santa Bárbara (Powder Magazine)
6 Despensa (Store)
7 Trasporte (Transport)
   Cocheras (Coach-houses)

SEGUNDA PLANTA (Upper Floor)
A Galeria de la Audiencia (Court Room)
B Galeria (Gallery)
C Sala de Paso (Lobby)

8 Numismática y Contaduria (Coins and Bookkeeping)
9 Legislación (Legislation and Justice)
10 Secretarios de la Audiencia (Clerks of Court)
11 Despacho del Oidor Principal (Office of Chief Judge)
12 Sala de Espera (Waiting Room)
13 Salón del Real Acuerdo (Court Room)
14 Sala de Ayudantes (Ushers' Room)
15 Despacho del Capitán General (Office of Captain General)
16 Urbanismo y Arquitectura (Town Planning and Architecture
17 Naval (Seafaring) I:
    Comercio y Navegación (Trade and Navigation)
    Exploración y Conquistadores (Exploration and the Conquistadors)
    Construcción Naval (Shipbuilding)
18 Naval (Seafaring) II:
    Corsarios (Pirates)
19 Militar (Military Matters)
20 Gran Salón de Gobernadores (Governors' Hall)

Alcázar de Colón, Santo Domingo

political and military history of the island from its discovery down to the so-called "period of temporary independence" (Independencia Efímera, 1821).

N of the junction of Calle de las Damas and Calle Emiliano Tejera is the *Alcázar de Colón (Fortress-Palace of Columbus, 1510–14), in which Columbus's son Diego lived. The interior, with its galleries, reception rooms and other state apartments furnished in the style of the colonial period, gives some impression of the splendor of life at the court of a Spanish Viceroy.

In the Alcázar de Colón

A flight of steps leads down to the group of buildings known as the *Atarazana* in which naval supplies were once stored; it dates from before 1507. Skilfully restored, these eight buildings now house a restaurant, exhibition rooms, art galleries and shops selling craft goods.

To the NW, at the W end of Calle G. Puello, is the *Fortaleza de Santa Bárbara*, a fort built in 1574, with the gate of the same name.

SW of the Atarazana, at the corner of Calle Tejera and Calle Isabel la Católica, is Santo Domingo's oldest surviving house, the *Casa del Cordón* (c. 1500), which was the residence of Viceroy Diego Colón before the completion of the Alcázar.

Two blocks W are the ruins of the Church and *Convent of San Francisco* (1512–44). – From here Calle Hostos leads S to the ruins of the *Hospital of San Nicolás de Bari*, the first hospital in the New World, founded by Nicolás de Ovando in 1508.

Four blocks W along Calle General Luperón is the *Convent of Las Mercedes*

Convent of San Francisco

(1555–76), which lost most of its treasures when it was plundered by Sir Francis Drake in 1586.

Calle de las Mercedes runs SW to the *Parque de la Independencia*, in which, on a site once occupied by Fort Concepción, is the *Portal del Conde*, an old town gate. Beyond it are the **Altar de la Patria**, where the Dominican Republic was proclaimed in 1844, and the **National Mausoleum**, of marble and concrete, in which the founders of the Republic are buried.

To the NW, in the elegant SAN CARLOS district, is the massive domed *Palacio Nacional*, faced with pink marble. – Farther W in the GASCUE district, on the E side of the Avenida Máximo Gómez, is the grandly conceived ****Plaza de la Cultura**. Grouped around this huge square, its spacious lawns decorated with modern sculpture, are the *Teatro Nacional*, the *Biblioteca Nacional* (National Library), the ***Museo del Hombre Dominicano** (Museum of Dominican Man), with anthropological and ethnological collections, and the ***Museo de Arte Moderna** (art of the 20th c.). To the S, in Calle Nicolás Pensón, is the *Museo de Historia Natural* (Natural History Museum).

In the National Pantheon

There are two new museums worthy of a visit: *Museo Duarte* (Avenue Isabal la Católica 138) has souvenirs of Juan Pablo Duarte, the champion of Dominican independence; the *Pre-Spanish Art Hall* (Avenue San Martín) houses one of the best collections of pre-Columbian art.

Modern sculpture, Santo Domingo

From the *Placer de los Estudios*, the bay on the S side of the old town, the Avenida George Washington runs SW along the seafront, with several good hotels and restaurants. In 1¼ miles/2 km it comes to the *Ciudad Universitaria* (University City), successor to the university founded in 1538, the first in the New World.

Farther SW is the *Centro de los Héroes de Constanza, Maimón y Estero Hondo*, commemorating the heroes of the war of independence. In the vicinity are various government buildings, including the *Palacio del Congreso*, together with the *Town Hall* and an open-air theater, the *Teatro de Agua y Luz*. – To the W, on Avenida Anacoana, is the *Paseo de los Indios*, an amusement park.

In the new district of ARROYO HONDO on the NW side of the town is the *Jardin Botánico* (Botanical Garden; area 445 acres), with a Japanese Garden and a remarkable display of orchids. – A short distance N is the *Jardin Zoológico* (Zoo; area 320 acres), in which the animals are shown in their natural surroundings; there is a large aviary.

On the E side of the Río Ozama, in the VILLA DUARTE district, is the *Faro a Colón*, a huge memorial to Columbus with a ground-plan in the form of a cross ½ mile/

800 m long. – 1¼ miles/2 km farther E, to the right of the Autopista de las Américas, is the karstic cave known as *Los Tres Ojos (the "Three Eyes"), with three turquoise-blue lakes on different levels and magnificent stalactites and stalagmites.

SURROUNDINGS of Santo Domingo. – The coastal highway, the Autopista de las Américas, runs E to Santo Domingo's international airport, the Aeropuerto de las Américas. At the entrance is the *Parque La Caleta* (Indian cemetery, museum).

E of the airport, in the Boca Chica, is a beautiful beach (water sports). Other good beaches are *Guayacanes* and *Juan Dolio*. – 50 miles/80 km from Santo Domingo lies the port of **San Pedro de Macoris**, with an excellent tourist infrastructure.

The Autopista Sánchez runs W from Santo Domingo to the little resort of *Haina* and on to **San Cristóbal**, with a mahogany house which belonged to Trujillo. The road continues via *Bani* to the marvelously beautiful *Bahía de Ocoa*, at the NW corner of which is the town of **Azua**, with the much frequented *Playa Monte Rio*. 12½ miles/20 km W of Azua a road branches off on the right and goes NW to the town of **San Juan**, around which are the well-preserved remains of Indian settlements. – 50 miles/80 km W of Azua, on the E side of the *Sierra de Baoruco*, a favorite game-shooting area, is the port of **Barahona**, a center of the sugar industry. From here a road leads NW, passing the *Lago del Rincón*, to the *Lago Enriquillo* (area 116 sq. miles/300 sq. km), which lies 144 ft/ 44 m below sea level in a rift valley of extreme aridity between the Sierra de Baoruco and the *Sierra de Neiba* (nature park taking in most of the range; shooting). The *Isla de Cabritos* has recently been declared a National Park. Around the lake are a number of Indian sites.

See also **Dominican Republic** and **Hispaniola**.

Sint Eustatius (Statia)

Lesser Antilles
Leeward Islands
Netherlands Antilles

Area: 8 sq. miles/20.8 sq. km.
Population: 1500.
Administrative center: Willemstad (on Curaçao); regional center: Philipsburg (on St Maarten).
Vehicles travel on the right.

ⓘ St Eustatius Toeristenbureau,
by Fort Oranje,
Orangestraat,
Oranjestad,
St Eustatius, N.A.
See also Practical Information.

HOTELS. – *Antillian*, 40 r.; *Statia Strandhotel*, 20 r.; *Old Gin House*, 22 r.; *Golden Rock Resort*, on Atlantic coast, 10 r. in individual houses, SP, terrace; *Ocean View Guesthouse*, 12 r.

EVENTS. – *Queen's Birthday* (April 30). – *Kingdom Day* (December 15).

RECREATION and SPORT. – Hill walking and climbing, walks along beach; swimming, snorkeling, scuba diving, surfing, sailing, deep-sea fishing.

AIR SERVICES. – By light aircraft from St Maarten.

SHIPPING. – Twice-weekly ferry from St Maarten.

The little island of *St Eustatius (commonly called Statia), in the Leeward Islands group, lies 35 miles/ 56 km S of the Dutch island of St Maarten and 6 miles/10 km NW of St Kitts in latitude 17°29′ N and longitude 62°59′ W (Oranjestad). Extinct volcanoes covered with green rain forest rear up at the N end of the island and in the SE (Quill, 1949 ft/ 594 m). The average temperature is about 77–79 °F/25–26 °C. St Eustatius differs from its sister island of Saba in having some beautiful stretches of beach.

The population, almost exclusively black, live by farming, rearing small livestock and fishing. Half way along the island, in the plain between the two ranges of volcanic hills, is a small airfield. The port of Oranjestad on the SW coast has a deep-water quay 1100 yd/1000 m long.

HISTORY. – The island has had an eventful history. It was discovered by Columbus, together with Saba, in 1493, on his voyage to the Virgin Islands. Thereafter attempts were made by French and English settlers to colonize it. The first Dutchmen arrived in 1636, and during the next 150 years the island changed hands more than 20 times. It was finally assigned to the Netherlands in the Peace of Utrecht (1713).

During the second half of the 18th c. the island enjoyed a period of considerable prosperity. As the base of the Netherlands West Indies Company it developed into one of the principal trading centers in the Caribbean, and it would often have well over a hundred ships in the harbor loading and discharging slaves, as well as rum, sugar, tobacco and other goods. The population grew to several thousands, and the island became known as the "Golden Rock". During the War of American Independence, in 1775–76, St Eustatius became a depot for supplies from Europe. – In 1776 Fort Oranje fired the first salute in honor of the new Stars and Stripes. In 1781 a British force under Admiral Rodney captured the island and destroyed many installations. The end of the Dutch West Indian trade relegated St Eustatius to relative insignificance. Great hopes are now attached to tourism as a means of reviving the island's economy.

The chief settlement on the island is **Oranjestad**, its upper town and fort rising magnificently above the deep blue sea on the SW coast.

SIGHTS. – The principal attraction of Oranjestad is the 17th c. * **Fort Oranje** with its imposing bastions (restored 1976). Here on November 16, 1776 a salute was fired for the first time in honor of the new American flag, the Stars and Stripes, flying on an American vessel (commemorative tablet). From the fort there is a fine view of the sea and the ruined buildings around the old harbor.

In the 17th and 18th c. the town and port installations were directly on the waterfront, filled with life by seamen of many nations. Some remains of this LOWER TOWN, with its warehouses and other commercial buildings, can still be seen; others have sunk into the sea and can be explored only scuba divers and snorkelers, who can also investigate the wreck of an old Spanish galleon.

The present UPPER TOWN contains a number of notable buildings. At Oranjestraat 4 is a *half-timbered house* of traditional type, though actually built in the 20th c., and in Kerweg *Three Widows' Corner*, a restored 18th c. house. The **Stadhuis** (Town Hall) in Fort Oranjestraat is a typical colonial-style building. At Tonningenweg 2 stands the *Graaf House*, Admiral Rodney's headquarters in 1781. – Also of interest are the *Gertrude Judson Memorial Library* and the *Honen Dalim Synagogue* (begun 1740), with an old Jewish cemetery.

The road to *Fort de Windt* runs past the ruins of the *Dutch Reformed Church*, with an old graveyard. In the vicinity are the remains of an old sisal factory and sugar-mill.

Further EXCURSIONS can be made on donkey-back or by taxi. – A popular occupation on moonlit nights is catching large land crabs in the crater of the extinct volcano at the S end of the island, **Quill** (1949 ft/594 m).

See also * **Saba** and * **Saint-Martin/Sint Maarten.**

Sint Maarten
See Saint-Martin/Sint Maarten

Sombrero
See Anguilla and St Kitts

Statia
See Sint Eustatius

Tobago
Lesser Antilles
Windward Islands
Republic of Trinidad and Tobago

Area: 116 sq. miles/301 sq. km.
Population: 40,000.
Administrative center: Port of Spain (on Trinidad).
Vehicles travel on the left.
ⓘ **Trinidad and Tobago Tourist Board, Scarborough,**
    Tobago;
    tel. 639 2195.
    See also Practical Information.

HOTELS. – IN AND AROUND SCARBOROUGH: *Mount Irvine Bay Hotel*, 110 b., golf-course, * *Arnos Vale,*

Mount Irvine Golf Course, Tobago

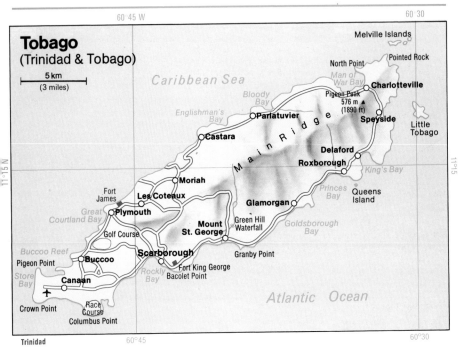

Tobago
(Trinidad & Tobago)

5 km
(3 miles)

Caribbean Sea

Melville Islands
Pointed Rock
North Point
Man of
War Bay
Charlotteville
Bloody
Bay
Pigeon Peak
576 m
(1890 ft)
Englishman's
Bay
Parlatuvier
Speyside
Castara
Little
Tobago
Delaford
Roxborough
King's Bay
Moriah
Princes
Bay
Queens
Island
Fort
James
Les Coteaux
Glamorgan
Great
Courtland Bay
Plymouth
Golf Course
Mount
St. George
Green Hill
Waterfall
Goldsborough
Bay
Buccoo Reef
Scarborough
Granby Point
Pigeon Point
Buccoo
Store
Bay
Canaan
Rockly
Bay
Fort King George
Bacolet Point
Atlantic Ocean
Crown Point
Race
Course
Columbus Point

Trinidad

28 b., and *Turtle Beach*, 52 b., all on the coast to the NW; *Tabc*, 30 b., *Della Mira*, 20 b., *Castle Cove*, 30 b., and *Robinson Crusoe*, 25 b., all near Rockly Bay. – TO THE W: *Crown Point*, 100 b.; *Crown Reef*, 150 b.

TRANSPORT. – Air services to and from Trinidad (Piarco Airport).

*Tobago, the smaller of the two islands which make up the state of Trinidad and Tobago, lies 22 miles/ 35 km NE of Trinidad. The backbone of the island is the range of hills known as Main Ridge, consisting mainly of metamorphic and volcanic rock, which traverses it from SW to NE. The highest point in the range rises to 1890 ft/576 m.

Topographically Tobago is very different from its sister island. This results from the fact that Tobago drifted away from Trinidad long before that island became detached from the South American land mass.

While Trinidad pulses with life, the smaller island of Tobago (25 miles/40 km long, up to $7\frac{1}{2}$ miles/12 km wide) is the place for a restful vacation.

Almost the whole of the island's area is covered with tropical vegetation and is intensively cultivated. The inhabitants, predominantly of African origin, gain their subsistence from a plantation economy (coconuts, cacao) and from fishing. The tourist trade is important to Tobago,

which attracts both excursionists from Port of Spain (Trinidad) and visitors from farther afield.

Tobago claims to be the island on which Robinson Crusoe was cast away, though the honor properly belongs to the Chilean island of Juan Fernández in the Pacific. Defoe based his story on the real-life adventures of a Scottish seaman named Alexander Selkirk but moved the setting to Tobago, which suited his purpose better. The so-called Robinson Crusoe's Cave on the NW coast of the island has no connection with Alexander Selkirk.

HISTORY. – In pre-Columbian times Tobago had a considerable population of Arawak Indians, as is shown by the remains of many settlements. When Columbus sailed S from Grenada to Trinidad in 1498 he must have sighted the smaller island, but there is no reference to it in his log. Later settlers gave it the name of *Tobago*, after the local form of tobacco pipe (*tabaco*). In the 17th c. Dutch settlers introduced the growing of sugar-cane, which became the island's

Scarborough from Fort King George

Buccoo Bay, Tobago

principal crop during the 18th c. and brought great wealth to the planters. – After changing hands several times and suffering pirate raids and invasions Tobago finally became a British possession in 1803 (although in the previous year, under the Peace of Amiens, it had been assigned to France). Sugar production suffered severe setbacks and increasingly gave way to fruit trees. – In 1889 Tobago was joined with Trinidad in the colony of Trinidad and Tobago, which in 1962 became an independent republic within the British Commonwealth.

The island's capital and principal port is **Scarborough** (pop. 17,000). The commandingly situated *Fort King George* (18th c.) affords a fine *view of Rockly Beach and the S coast, extending as far as Trinidad. – NW of the town is *Fort William*, residence of the President of Trinidad and Tobago. Farther NW is the conspicuously sited Courland Monument, commemorating the settlers who came from the Baltic province of Courland in the 17th c.

An attractive EXCURSION is to the western tip of the island. The best beaches are on *Pigeon Point* and in *Store Bay*. 1 mile/1½ km off Pigeon Point lies the *Buccoo Reef*, a happy hunting ground for scuba divers and snorkelers. There are daily trips to the reef

from Pigeon Point, Buccoo Point and Store Bay in glass-bottomed boats which enable visitors to observe the beautiful coral gardens and the brilliantly colored fish which inhabit them. NE of Buccoo is the widely famed *Mount Irvine Golf Course*, designed by John Harris.

Buccoo Reef

Equally rewarding is a drive up the SE coast to the northern tip of the island. A few miles from Scarborough is *Mount St George*, from which a road runs inland to the *Green Hill Waterfall*. The main road continues NE, with beautiful views of the bays along the coast and the offshore islets. After passing through *Roxborough* and *Delaford*, in King's Bay, it comes to the charming little fishing town of **Speyside**, from which a boat can be taken to the island of **Little Tobago**, the only place in the world outside New Guinea where birds of paradise – introduced by Sir William Ingram in 1909 – live in the wild state. This bird sanctuary also contains other tropical species. The best times for seeing the birds are the early morning and late afternoon.

Beyond Speyside the road turns inland and cuts across the island to *Charlotteville* on the N coast. Above this little fishing settlement, situated above *Man o' War Bay*, one of the finest natural harbors in the Caribbean, rears *Pigeon Peak* (1890 ft/576 m).

See also **Trinidad** (Island) and **Trinidad and Tobago**.

Rockly Beach from Fort King George

Tortola
Lesser Antilles
British Virgin Islands
British crown colony

Area: 25 sq. miles/64 sq. km.
Population: 9000.
Vehicles travel on the left.

ⓘ **British Virgin Islands Tourist Board,**
P.O. Box 134,
Road Town,
British Virgin Islands;
tel. (809) 494 3134.
See also Practical Information.

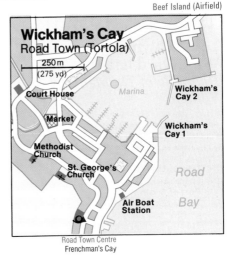

Beef Island (Airfield)

Road Town Centre
Frenchman's Cay

HOTELS. – ROAD TOWN: *Prospect Reef Resort*, 172 b.,
SP, sailing, snorkeling, scuba diving, water-skiing,
deep-sea fishing, tennis; *Treasure Isle Hotel*, 70 b., SP,
sailing, snorkeling, tennis; *Long Bay Hotel*, 68 b., SP,
beach; *Moorings-Mariner Inn*, 48 b., SP, yacht
charters, tennis; *Sugar Mill Estate*, 50 b., SP, beach;
Village Cay Marina, 26 b.; *Sebastians on the Beach*,
62 b., beach, sailing, snorkeling, surfing. – WEST END:
Smuggler's Cove, 30 b., beach, fishing, sailing,
rowing, diving.

RECREATION and SPORT. – Sailing, deep-sea
fishing, scuba diving, snorkeling.

EVENTS. – *Election of the Island Queen* (July–
August), with processions, musical contests, horse-
races, etc. – *Regatta* (spring).

TRANSPORT. – Air taxis to Virgin Gorda, Anegada
and St Thomas, linking up with international air
services via San Juan (Puerto Rico). – Boat services to
neighboring islands.

*Tortola is the largest of the British
Virgin Islands, and its capital, Road
Town, is the administrative center of
the group. It is separated from the
US Virgin Islands, to the SW, by the
Narrows and from the islands of
Norman, Peter, Salt, Cooper and
Ginger Island to the SE by the Sir
Francis Drake Channel. The south-
ern part of the island has a
vegetation consisting mainly of
scrub and low trees, while the N is a
region of bananas, mango trees and
palms.

Road Town, capital of the island and of
the whole group, lies in Road Bay, on the
S coast. It has both a pleasure harbor
(yacht charters) and a deep-water commercial harbor. The little town has
excellent shopping facilities and has
preserved a number of old buildings. On a
hill to the S are the ruins of a fort. – At the
N end of the town is the *Wickham's
Cay holiday center, with a marina, hotels,
holiday apartments and restaurants.

5 miles/8 km off Road Bays is **Peter
Island,** with a yacht harbor.

In the SW of the island, around *Mount
Sage* (1782 ft/543 m), is a *National Park*
which contains a remnant of the original
tropical rain forest. It is most easily
reached from the road which runs SW
down the coast from Road Town. Footpaths lead into the hills; there is a superb
panoramic *view from the summit of
Mount Sage. – Near the western tip of
Tortola is *West End*, from which there is a
ferry to St Thomas (US Virgin Islands).
Offshore lies the little island of *Frenchman's Cay*. – To the NW is the island of
Jost van Dyke, originally settled by
Quakers, with beautiful beaches.

The road E from Road Town skirts the
wide arc of *Road Bay* and follows the
much indented coast, fringed by coral
reefs which offer good diving grounds.
Beyond *East End* the *Queen Elizabeth
Bridge* (1966) crosses *Beef Island Channel* to the neighboring **Beef Island,** with
Tortola's airfield and tourist accommodation. On the N coast is *Long Bay*, with a
very fine *beach.

See also *British Virgin Islands.

Trinidad (Island)

Lesser Antilles
Windward Islands
Republic of Trinidad and Tobago

Area: 1864 sq. miles/4827 sq. km.
Population: 1,200,000.
Administrative center: Port of Spain.
Vehicles travel on the left
(i) **Trinidad and Tobago Tourist Board,**
56 Frederick Street,
Port of Spain,
Trinidad;
tel. 623 1933 and 623 1142.
See also Practical Information.

HOTELS. – PORT OF SPAIN: see separate entry. – AT
PIARCO AIRPORT: *Pan American Guesthouse*, 50 b.; *Bel Air Hotel*, 53 b. – SAN FERNANDO: *Farrell House*, 18 r. –
POINT FORTIN: *Gulf Coast Hotel*, 15 b. – IN MAYARO
BAY: *Atlantis Beach*, 25 b.

SPORT. – Golf-course (18 holes) at Moka (Maraval).

EVENTS. – *Carnival (New Year to Shrove Tuesday).
– *Divali*, the Hindu Festival of Lights (October–
November). – *Hosein*, a Moslem festival (winter).

TRANSPORT.– Flights from Piarco Airport, 9 miles/
15 km SE of Port of Spain, to London, New York,
Miami, Toronto, Caracas, Georgetown and all Caribbean islands.

****Trinidad, the most southerly of the
Caribbean islands, lies barely
15 miles/24 km from the South
American coast, off the delta of the
Orinoco. Forty-five different races
have gone to the making of the
Trinidadian people, whose lively
temperament and joie de vivre find
their fullest expression in the
spectacular Carnival. Trinidad is the
home of the calypso and the
steelband.**

Geologically Trinidad is a continuation of
the Venezuelan coastal cordillera, as is
shown by the three parallel ranges running from W to E which are the most
striking features of its superficial topography. The **Northern Range** is a chain
of sharply contoured mountains built up
of metamorphic rocks which falls steeply
down to the N coast and is covered with
dense rain forest and montane forest; its
highest peaks are the *Cerro del Aripo*
(3087 ft/941 m) and *El Tucuche* (3074 ft/
937 m). The **Central Range**, formed
from Oligocene and Miocene limestones,
have a gentler pattern of relief, barely
rising above 1000 ft/300 m. The **Southern Range**, consisting of Tertiary

sediments, rises to over 1000 ft/300 m in
the *Trinity Hills* at the southeastern tip of
the island, which suggested the name of
Trinidad to Columbus. This thinly populated upland region is also covered with
dense rain forest and has remained hostile
to human penetration. – The areas between the hills have been filled up by
alluvial sediments and now form what is
known as the **Naparima Peneplain**. The
larger rivers, including the *Caroni, Navet,
Orupuche* and *Ortoire*, from extensive
lagoons and mangrove swamps around
their mouths.

PLANT and ANIMAL LIFE. – In view of the fact that
Trinidad was once connected with the South American mainland it is not surprising that it has the widest
range of plant and animal species in the Caribbean
islands.

The frangipani (*Plumeria acuminata*) is renowned for
its perfume, as are the pink poui (*Tabebuia penta-
phylla*) with its lavender-pink trumpet-shaped
flowers and the yellow poui (*Tabebuia serratifolia*). A
particularly attractive flower is *Cassia fistula*, well
named "golden shower". At its best in June is the
magnificent "pride of India" (*Lagerstroemia spe-
ciosa*) with its rose-like flowers. One of the most
striking of the flowering trees, with flame-colored
crimson blossoms, is the immortelle (*Erythrina* spp.),
also known as "madre de cacao" because it is used to
shade the cacao plants. Another common species is
the jacaranda (*Jacaranda acutifolia*) with its
lavender-blue flowers. The national flower of Trinidad
and Tobago is the wild poinsettia or chaconia, with
vivid red leaves, which grows in wooded areas,
especially along the N coast. There are over 700
species of orchids and numerous lilies, the best known
of which are the sweet-smelling ginger lily (*Hedy-
chium coronarium*) and the river lily (*Spathiphyllum
cannafolium*).

HISTORY. – Originally part of the South American
sub-continent, Trinidad became an island after the last
Ice Age, when the sea level rose. This explains the
variety of its vegetation and animals, reflected in
the Indian name of the island, *Iere* ("land of the
hummingbirds"). – The earliest traces of settlement
were left by the Arawaks, who crossed the Gulf of
Paria on to the island more than 2000 years ago,
probably coming from the territory of present-day
Venezuela or Guyana. They remained on the island for
many centuries and moved on from there to the smaller
Antilles islands to the N. Some time later they were
followed by the warlike Caribs, also coming from the
NE of the South American sub-continent, but the
newcomers were unable to do more than establish a
bridgehead on the island from which they advanced
northward to other islands, hitherto thinly populated,
such as the Grenadines, Barbados and St Lucia.

Columbus discovered the island on his third voyage
and – probably struck by the three peaks at the SE tip
– named it *Trinidad*. Later the Spaniards founded a
settlement which they called San José de Oruña (now
St Joseph), using it as a base from which to explore
the N coast of South America and to search for the
fabled land of El Dorado. The island's development
was hampered by inadequate financial support from
Spain, and it was frequently exposed to raids by
Caribbean adventurers looking for plunder. In 1595

Sir Walter Raleigh discovered the Pitch Lake and used its asphalt to caulk his ships. During the 17th c. the colony, now with large numbers of African slaves, was repeatedly plundered by Dutch and French free-booters.

In the second half of the 18th c. Philippe de St-Laurent, a French settler from the island of Grenada, was given authority by the Spanish king to develop the island. The growing of sugar-cane was introduced, and the island prospered. During this period many French settlers came to Trinidad from Haiti, then in turmoil as a result of slave rebellions and the influence of the French Revolution. During the war between France and Britain, in 1797, a British force captured the island, and under the Peace of Amiens (1802) it was finally assigned to Britain. After 1834, when the slaves were liberated and became peasant farmers, the large landowners brought in indentured laborers from India to replace them – a practice which continued until 1914. The result was that even before the First World War almost 50% of the population of Trinidad consisted of Hindus, Moslems and Parsees. – At the beginning of the 20th c. Arthur Cipriani, a popular hero of Corsican origin, fought for justice and unity in the island's medley of races and gained a great reputation as mayor of Port of Spain over a long period of years.

During the Second World War a number of American bases were established on the island in order to protect Allied shipping. – From 1947 onwards, during the Governorship of Sir John Shaw, the development of industry began – a process which has continued down to the present day, with government assistance. – Trinidad was granted independence in 1962, and on August 1, 1976, together with Tobago, it became a presidential republic within the British Commonwealth.

CULTURE. – The ethnic diversity of the population of Trinidad is reflected in a rich cultural life. The country's multinational heritage finds expression not only in place-names but also in the architecture of the island's towns and villages, in which Roman Catholic and Anglican churches rub shoulders with mosques and Hindu temples and British colonial buildings in Victorian style alternate with houses and shops showing Spanish and French influence, the simple huts occupied by ordinary people, many of them the descendants of black slaves, and the houses occupied by indentured laborers with their Indian or Far Eastern characteristics.

This ethnic variety is reflected in the island's place-names. Port of Spain and St Mary are English, Puerto de España, San Fernando, Manzanilla, Sangre Grande, Monos and Diego Martin are Spanish, Blanchisseuse, Matelot, Biche, Basse Terre and Pointe-à-Pierre are French, Barrackpore and Sad-hoowa stem from India, Chaguaramas, Chacachacare, Chaguanas, Arima, Naparima and Paria are Carib, and so on.

Although there are sometimes tensions between members of different racial groups the government is trying to develop a Trinidadian national conscious-ness. A number of indigenous cultural phenomena help towards this end.

Xango. – The Xango or Shango cult is a combination of African and American elements which appeals particularly to the descendants of black slaves. It is a mingling of ceremonies inherited from the Yoruba, Ewe, Fon, Ashanti and other West African tribes with rites of Roman Catholic or Protestant origin, native Indian traditions and features taken over from Islam, Hinduism, Buddhism and spiritualism.

The supreme god of this cult is Shango, one of the principal divinities of black Africa, who also incor-porates characteristics of the rice gods of India as well as some attributes of John the Baptist. He is attended by 12 obas, who resemble the 12 Apostles, and he is frequently represented as the master of thunder and lightning. His favorite sacrificial animal is the ram, and his symbol is the battle-axe of the pre-Columbian inhabitants of the Caribbean. As in Africa, his worshippers wear colored chains, usually red and white.

New rites and new divinities come to the fore almost daily in this cult, reflecting the dynamism of this emerging new religion, which, like the voodoo cult of Haiti or the *santería* of Cuba, is part of a vigorous Afro-American religious movement.

Calypso. – The infectious rhythms and melodies (in $\frac{2}{4}$ or $\frac{4}{4}$ time) of the calypso were originally created by the black inhabitants of Trinidad, but it has since become widely popular throughout the whole of the Carib-bean area and has also spread to the United States and the cities of Western Europe.

The word calypso is probably an anglicized form of the West African word *kai-so*, a term of encouragement or approval. The words and tune of a calypso are usually composed by the same person, and frequently improvised on the spur of the moment. The com-monest themes are love and sex, but calypsos often deal with topical subjects taken from politics, sport or

Folk dancers, Trinidad

Carnival, Trinidad

social life. The words, full of satirical allusions and double entendres, are accompanied by catchy rhythms.

Musically the calypso took on characteristics borrowed from the music of the different races represented in Trinidad – Spanish colonial influences from Venezuela, features from French, English and Irish music – but African rhythms have remained strongly predominant. In recent years elements have also been assimilated from Indian and Chinese music.

Calypso singers often adopt high-sounding names like King Pharaoh, Lord Nelson, the Mighty Sparrow or Lord Kitchener. Rose McCartha Lewis, known as Calypso Rose, was the first woman to win the national calypso competition, gaining the "road-march title" in the 1978 Carnival.

The steelband. – Like the calypso and limbo, this has become one of the most characteristic features of Caribbean life. Music-making with the typical hollow-topped cylindrical metal drums first came to the fore in Trinidad in 1945, and from there rapidly spread over the whole Caribbean.

Present-day steelbands may have anything up to 20 or more of these steel drums, known as **pans**, ranging from the *bass pan* with 3 or 4 notes by way of the *cello pan* (5–6 notes) and the *guitar pan* (14 notes) to the *ping-pong pan* with 26 to 32 notes. The repertoire of a steelband may range from Mozart or Rossini to the latest calypso tunes.

The pans are made by cutting off the bottom end of an old oil drum, beating the top into a concave shape and marking out the notes with a hammer and cold chisel. They are beaten with a rubber hammer to produce the desired bell-like notes.

Pan music, said to have originated on the little island of Antigua, had its big breakthrough when pans were used by members of a Trinidadian bamboo band during the VE Day celebrations in 1945. It is clearly derived from the music of the shango drums, brought

from West Africa by black slaves but banned by their colonial masters. – A legendary figure in the world of steelbands, founder of a band whose fame extended far beyond the bounds of Trinidad, was *Ellie Manette*, who played a major part in bringing about the renaissance of drum music now to be observed particularly in the black quarters of New York and other cities.

The Carnival. – The great annual event in the life of Trinidad is the *Carnival*, an unforgettable spectacle of color and gaiety, an endless succession of costume parades, calypso singing, dancing in the streets and music by steelbands. Preparations begin several months before the actual Carnival, which lasts from the New Year to Ash Wednesday, as masqueraders design their costumes, steelbands practice new tunes and calypso singers polish their lyrics.

Originally brought in by French settlers, the Carnival has developed into a characteristically Trinidadian event which incorporates pre-Christian traditions from the Mediterranean region as well as customs taken over from the many different races represented on the island.

Around the turn of the year the program for the forthcoming Carnival, the "road march", is determined in a series of competitions to select the best steelbands, calypso singers and so on – a process which attracts wide public interest. To be chosen as the composer or singer of the winning calypso is a particular distinction, and the Calypso King, with his Queen, graces the principal events in the Carnival with his presence. The celebrations reach their climax on *Joo Vay* (from "jour ouvert": the Monday before Ash Wednesday) and *Vaval* (Shrove Tuesday), when the streets are filled with brilliantly costumed figures dancing, skipping and singing to the accompaniment of throbbing rhythms and tunes. In the early hours of Ash Wednesday the excitement abruptly subsides; and it is not very long before everyone begins thinking about next year's Carnival.

Divali. – This Hindu Festival of Lights, celebrated in October or November, is one of the most beautiful and moving events of the year. Devout Hindus place thousands of little earthenware lamps around their homes and temples, providing a spectacle which is particularly impressive at night. During this period a ceremony of purification known as *Katik Nannan* is celebrated at Manzanilla on the Atlantic coast, when hundreds of Hindus bathe in the sea.

Hosein. – This Moslem winter festival is held ten days after new moon in the month of Mohurran in the Islamic calendar. It is celebrated by processions in splendid costumes, with music, singing and dancing, and with beautifully made and painted models of mosques ("tadgeahs").

Street scene near Port of Spain

TOUR OF THE ISLAND (*c.* 174 miles/ 280 km). – A tour of the island will introduce the visitor to Trinidad's beautiful tropical scenery and the racial diversity of its people, taking in the agricultural areas with their large sugar-cane and coconut plantations, the industrial centers with their refineries and factories, the inhospitable swamps, the extensive lagoons and beautiful sandy beaches, the forests of teak and the lush tropical vegetation of the island.

Leave the capital, * **Port of Spain** (see separate entry), on the Beetham Highway, going E, and in 6 miles/10 km turn S into the Princess Margaret Highway. This soon comes to the entrance to the **Caroni Bird Sanctuary**, a large area of swamp into which visitors are taken in motor-boats. Here they will see a variety of species, including herons, flamingoes and the scarlet ibis which is Trinidad's national bird. The birds' return to their nesting-places in the late afternoon is an impressive sight. The boats follow a winding course through canals, lagoons and mangrove swamps, in which alligators are occasionally to be seen.

The Princess Margaret Highway continues to **Chaguanas**, a village mainly inhabited by Indians in which Indian filigree work can be bought. – From here it is possible to take either the direct road to San Fernando on the Solomon Hochoy Highway, running inland, or the Southern Main Road via *Couva* and **Pointe-à-Pierre** (large oil refinery).

San Fernando (pop. 40,000), Trinidad's second largest town, also has a large Indian population. Thanks to the nearby refineries it is now developing into the island's principal industrial area. From *Naparima Hill* there is a fine view of the town and the *Gulf of Paria* at the E end of the island.

From San Fernando the Southern Main Road runs SW and later W along the coast to *La Brea*, just beyond which is the ** **Pitch Lake**, the largest deposit of asphalt in the world (89 acres/36 ha). It was discovered in 1595 by Sir Walter Raleigh, who used the bitumen to caulk his ships. Since the beginning of this century more than 15 million tons of asphalt have been extracted, most of it being exported. The Pitch Lake is some 300 ft/90 m deep and has a constant inflow of asphalt; it is estimated that the deposit will last at least another half-century.

Returning 7 miles/11 km from the Pitch Lake, turn S into the road to *Fyzabad*, with the largest oilfield on the island. – 4 miles/ 6.5 km SE is **Siparia**, with the pilgrimage church of the Divina Pastora (1758),

Hosein festival

Pitch Lake, Trinidad

which contains a leather-clad Black Virgin, surrounded by votive offerings (festival and procession in May).

NE of Siparia and E of San Fernando is *Princes Town*, from which the route continues on the Mayaro Road. Just beyond Princes Town can be seen the *mud volcanoes* of the *Devil's Woodyard*. The road continues via *Rio Claro* to reach the Atlantic at *Pierreville*, near the S end of the E coast.

To the S of Pierreville lies *Mayaro Bay*, to the N *Cocos Bay* and *Manzanilla Bay*. Along this stretch of coast there are beautiful beaches, but the heavy surf tends to make swimming dangerous. Moreover, the water is sometimes polluted by the oil drilling which is taking place off the E coast of Trinidad.

The road N from Pierreville runs through extensive plantations of coconut palms between the sea, lagoons and *Nariva Swamp*, and in 17 miles/27 km turns NW and runs inland, leading back to Port of Spain by way of *Sangre Grande* and the Churchill-Roosevelt Highway. – From Sangre Grande an attractive detour can be made to the N coast (see under Port of Spain, Surroundings).

*Port of Spain: see separate entry.

Trinidad and Tobago

Lesser Antilles
Windward Islands
Republic of Trinidad and Tobago

Nationality letters: TT.
Area: 1980 sq. miles/5128 sq. km.
Capital: Port of Spain.
Population: 1,240,000.
Local administration: 9 counties.
Religion: Roman Catholic (*c.* 35%); Protestant (*c.* 30%); Hindu (25%); Jewish minority.
Language: English.
Currency: Trinidad and Tobago dollar (TT$) of 100 cents.
Weights and measures: British system.
Travel documents: passport, immigration card, onward or return ticket.

ⓘ **Trinidad and Tobago Tourist Board,**
  56 Frederick Street,
  Port of Spain,
  Trinidad; tel. 623 1933 and 623 1142.
  See also Practical Information.

Trinidad and Tobago, the most southerly of the Caribbean island states, lies off the N coast of Venezuela. The islands, generally regarded as the most exotic of the West Indian islands, have also one of the strongest economies in the Caribbean, thanks largely to their large reserves of oil. In spite of this a considerable proportion of the population, which is of very mixed racial origin, live in relatively poor conditions. The state became independent in 1962, and is now a republic within the British Commonwealth.

CLIMATE. – As a result of their nearness to the Equator the islands have average monthly temperatures in the range 75–81 °F/24–27 °C. Rainfall is over 118 in./3000 mm a year in the hills near the E coast, but falls to below 55 in./1400 mm on the NW and S coasts. The rainy season is from July to December. Trinidad and Tobago are almost immune from the dreaded hurricanes which ravage the more northerly Caribbean islands. The least agreeable time of year for Europeans and North Americans is from early summer to late autumn, the period of heavy rain and high humidity of the air.

Oil Pump, Trinidad

Fire-eater, Trinidad

GOVERNMENT and ADMINISTRATION. – Trinidad and Tobago were amalgamated in 1889 as a British colony, became independent in 1962 and a presidential republic within the British Commonwealth in 1976. The head of state is the President, the head of the government the Prime Minister. The legislature consists of a House of Representatives, with 36 members elected for a 5-year term, and a Senate of 31 appointed members. The state is divided into 9 counties and 48 lower local government units.

The Republic of Trinidad and Tobago is a member of the United Nations, the Organization of American States (OAS), the Caribbean Common Market (CCM) and the Sistema Económica Latino-Americano (SELA) and an associate of the European Community.

POPULATION. – The population of some 1,240,000 is of great ethnic variety. Nearly three-fifths are blacks and mulattoes, while some two-fifths are (Asian) Indians. In addition to sizeable minorities from the Middle and Far East there are some 2% of whites, the descendants of Spanish, Portuguese, Dutch, French and British settlers. The official language is English, but in many areas dialects of Hindi are still spoken, and a Creole patois is also widely used. The largest religious community is the Roman Catholics, followed by various Protestant denominations. Hindus, Moslems and Jews. In addition large numbers of people of African origin are influenced by the syncretist creed of the Spiritual Baptists and the Shango cult.

Some 16% of the working population are employed in agriculture, over 30% in industry (half of these in building and civil engineering), more than 50% in the service trades. Major problems are presented by the high rate of unemployment, now about 14% – mainly affecting young people, women and blacks. In the past the islands' poor economic situation led to a high rate of emigration: between 1962 and 1972 alone more than 18,000 people, mostly skilled workers, left the country.

The main concentration of population is in the Port of Spain and Arima metropolitan area, where almost half the inhabitants of Trinidad and Tobago live on a tenth of its area. The second largest town is San Fernando (pop. 40,000), near the S end of the W coast.

Copra-working, Trinidad

Hindu temple, Port of Spain

In recent years considerable sums have been spent on developing the health and educational services, with a view particularly to reducing the rate of increase of the population. The slum quarters on the outskirts of Port of Spain are also being steadily improved and rebuilt. – The old Imperial College of Tropical Agriculture in St Augustin has become the Faculty of Agriculture of the University of the West Indies.

ECONOMY. – Agriculture is still an element of major importance in the economy of Trinidad and Tobago. Almost a third of the area of Trinidad – particularly in the fertile alluvial plains – is intensively cultivated. Some 7% of the area is occupied by the monoculture of sugar-cane, more than 10% of cacao, coffee and citrus fruits. In recent years many farms devoted to the growing of vegetables, mostly belonging to Indians, have been established around Port of Spain.

The dominant element in the economy is the *oil industry*, which accounts for some 80% of the total volume of exports and produces 40% of the state's revenue. Oil is worked in southern Trinidad, which also has the Pitch Lake (area 100 acres), the largest deposit of asphalt in the world. In the last few years oil has also been discovered in the shelf off the E and W coasts. The annual production of oil is at present about 60 million barrels, but in order to use the full capacity of the three refineries at Pointe-à-Pierre, Brighton and Point Fontin more than 100 million barrels a year are imported from Venezuela and the Middle East. The output of the refineries is mostly exported to neighboring Caribbean states and to North America.

More than half the working population, particularly those employed in the processing industries and the service trades, live in the Port of Spain/Arima area, a prominent place being taken by the food and clothing industries. The development of industry in the secondary sector, however, has been inadequate. The processing industries other than those connected with oil have suffered severely from foreign competition, particularly that of the low-wage countries of SE Asia.

One rapidly growing branch of the economy is tourism, which developed in the first place on Tobago, thanks to its magnificent beaches and coral reefs. In more recent years Trinidad has begun to draw increasing numbers of visitors, its particular attractions being the beautiful scenery of its N coast and the newly established nature reserves with their rich plant and animal life. In 1976 more than 100,000 holiday visitors came to Trinidad and Tobago.

See also *Port of Spain, *Tobago and **Trinidad (Island).

Turks and Caicos Islands

Bahamas Group
British crown colony

Islands: Grand Turk, Salt Cay, South Caicos, Middle Caicos, North Caicos, East Caicos, Pine Cay, Providenciales, Five Cays.
Area: 166 sq. miles/430 sq. km.
Population: 7500.
Administrative center: Cockburn Town (on Grand Turk).
Currency: US dollar.
Vehicles travel on the left.
(i) Turks and Caicos Tourist Board,
Cockburn Town, Grand Turk,
Turks and Caicos Islands, B.W.I.;
tel. 2321.
See also Practical Information.

HOTELS. – GRAND TURK: *Kittina*, 23 r.; *Turks Head Inn*, 10 r.; *Salt Raker Inn*, 11 r. – SALT CAY: *Mount Pleasant Guest-House*, 5 r.; *Brown House*, 7 r. – SOUTH CAICOS: *Admiral's Arms*, 15 r. – NORTH CAICOS: *Prospect of Whitby*, 25 r., SP, T, beach. – PINE CAY: *Meridian Club*, 75 r., SP, T, beach. – PROVIDENCIALES: *Third Turtle Inn*, 20 r.

RESTAURANT. – GRAND TURK: *Red Devil*.

PUBLIC HOLIDAYS and EVENTS. – *New Year's Day*. – *Good Friday*. – *Easter*. – *Commonwealth Day* (May); start of the *South Caicos Regatta. – Queen's Birthday* (June). – *Constitution Day* (June 12). – *Emancipation Day* (August 7), commemorating the liberation of the slaves. – *Carnival* (end of August). – *Peacemaker's Day* (November 9). – *Christmas Day. – Boxing Day* (December 26).

RECREATION and SPORT. – Sailing, deep-sea fishing, *scuba diving, snorkeling, wind-surfing, swimming and sunbathing; tennis, *archaeological exploration, walking.

AIR SERVICES. – From **Grand Turk** there are regular flights to Salt Cay, South Caicos, Middle Caicos, Pine Cay, Providenciales, Miami (USA) and Port-au-Prince (Haiti). From **South Caicos** there are regular flights to Grand Turk, Middle Caicos, Pine Cay, Providenciales, Nassau (Bahamas), Miami (USA) and Port-au-Prince and Cap-Haïtien (Haiti).

SHIPPING. – Charter services between Turks and Caicos Islands and neighboring Caribbean islands.

BOAT TRIPS. – Fascinating expeditions to the *submarine gardens and *national parks in the Turks and Caicos Islands are run from Cockburn Town (Grand Turk), Salt Cay, Cockburn Harbour (South Caicos), Whitby (Middle Caicos), Pine Cay and Providenciales.

The *Turks and Caicos Islands lie at the southeastern tip of the Bahamas group between latitude 21° and 22° N and between longitude 71° and 72°30′ W. Only six of the 30 or so islands are inhabited. Tourism has come to the islands only in quite recent years, but it has already developed into their main source of revenue.

The little archipelago of the Turks Islands, with its innumerable coral reefs and submarine rocks, lies in the SE of the group and includes the principal island and seat of the colony's government, Grand Turk. It is separated by the 20 mile/32 km wide Turks Islands Passage, plunging precipitously down to a great depth, from the Caicos Islands, the highest points on the submarine Caicos Bank. The largest settlement in the Caicos group is Cockburn Harbour on South Caicos. The almost uninhabited central Caicos Islands straggle from E to W, separated by channels. The narrow northern coastal zone, rising to over 130 ft/40 m and falling steeply down to the Atlantic, is formed of old coral reefs; to the S is an area with a sparse vegetation of cactuses and a number of salt lakes; and this in turn merges almost imperceptibly into a flat coastal zone.

These almost virginal islands attract not only well-to-do vacationers seeking seclusion and tranquillity but also visitors in quest of untouched sandy beaches and snorkeling and scuba diving enthusiasts, for whom they are a happy hunting ground teeming with underwater life.

CLIMATE. – The climate of the Turks and Caicos Islands is characterized by very high average temperatures, 6 to 8 months of great aridity and an annual rainfall of 20–31 in./500–800 mm – low figures, given the high evaporation. The vegetation accordingly consists mainly of cactuses and thorny scrub, with areas of salt meadowland. The islands have relatively frequent hurricanes.

HISTORY. – Ponce de León is believed to have discovered both groups of islands in 1515. Already inhabited in pre-Columbian times, they were settled from Bermuda during the 17th c. and onwards. They supplied salt, obtained from specially constructed salt-pans, to the people of Bermuda. In the 18th c. American Loyalists established themselves on the islands, which were administered from Nassau until 1848. Thereafter, following disputes between the population and the colonial government, they were governed from Jamaica, an arrangement which lasted until 1962. Then – despite their close proximity to the Bahamas – they became a separate crown colony.

Since 1976 the colony has had internal self-government, subject to some restrictions. The Queen is represented by a Governor, who presides over an Executive Council of three ex-officio members and four members appointed by the Legislative Assembly (which has three ex-officio members, three appointed members and eleven elected members).

POPULATION and ECONOMY. – The Turks and Caicos Islands have a population of 7500, a third of whom live in the capital, Cockburn Town. They are predominantly the descendants of African slaves and belong for the most part to various Protestant denominations. – Only a small proportion of the land is suitable for cultivation, and only subsistence farming is possible. A major contribution to the economy is made by the catching of crustacea and shellfish, mostly exported. In recent years there has been a carefully planned development of **tourism**, and this is now the inhabitants' principal source of income. It has so far been possible to pursue this development without unduly disturbing the delicate ecological balance of the islands.

Grand Turk. – The principal island of the Turks and Caicos group, a favorite resort of anglers and scuba divers, lies in latitude 21°28′ N and longitude 71°10′ W. On the W coast of the island, which extends from N to S for a distance of 6 miles/10 km and is up to 2 miles/3 km wide, is ***Cockburn Town**, the picturesque little capital of the colony, built in a style reflecting the influence of Bermuda.

The town's handsomest buildings are to be seen in its two principal streets, Duke Street and Front Street. Horse-drawn and donkey-drawn vehicles are still a common form of transport and are now used also for excursions by tourists. In the *Old Library* is a well-preserved seat of the Lucayan period.

SURROUNDINGS of Cockburn Town. – A road runs along *North Creek* to the N end of the island (alt.

102 ft/31 m), where there are a lighthouse and a US base. – At the S end of the island is *Governor's Beach, the finest on the island. Nearby is another military base.

BOAT TRIPS. – For anglers, scuba divers, bird-watchers and those interested in insect life there are rewarding trips to the cays E and S of Grand Turk. *Gibb's Cay* and *Round Cay* (both 1¼ miles/2 km E of Grand Turk) and *Penniston Cay* (3 miles/5 km S of Grand Turk) are designated nature reserves. *Long Cay*, *Pear Cay*, *East Cay* and *Cotton Cay* (all S and SE of Grand Turk) have charming anchorages and beaches.

Salt Cay. – The second largest of the Turks Islands, Salt Cay, lies 6 miles/10 km S of Grand Turk. It was formerly a center of salt production. – On the W coast are the chief settlement on the island, **Balfour Town**, and old *salt-pans, with sluices and windmills. On the N coast is an excellent *beach; 7 miles/11 km S is *Big Sand Cay*, also with a good beach.

South Caicos. – This island rises to a height of 151 ft/46 m above one of the most impressive coral reefs in the West Indies, on the E side of the Caicos Bank. On the SW coast is **Cockburn Harbour**, an excellent *natural harbor where the annual South Caicos Regatta is held. The little town, the second largest in the colony, has long been an important export-oriented fishing center. The island, some 7 miles/11 km long and only a few hundred yards wide at the N end, has beautiful beaches of fine white sand, made more easily accessible by the recent construction of a new road.

BOAT TRIPS. – SW of Cockburn Harbour is **Long Cay**, and beyond this are the **Six Hill Cays**, all now designated nature reserves, with teeming *underwater life.

14 miles/23 km SW, beyond the little *Fish Cays*, is **Big Ambergris Cay**, with a magnificent beach in *Long Bay*. Both this island and its neighbor to the W, **Little Ambergris Cay**, are favorite haunts of anglers and scuba divers.

*****Middle Caicos.** – This attractive island, with magnificent beaches and beautiful scenery, is also the most interesting island in the colony from the archaeological point of view. It is the central element in the main Caicos chain, which extends for 42 miles/67 km from SE to NW, with a breadth of up to 10 miles/16 km.

From the little airstrip in the NW of the island it is a short distance to the****Conch Bar Caves**, limestone caves – still barely explored, with impressive pure white stalactites and stalagmites and eerie

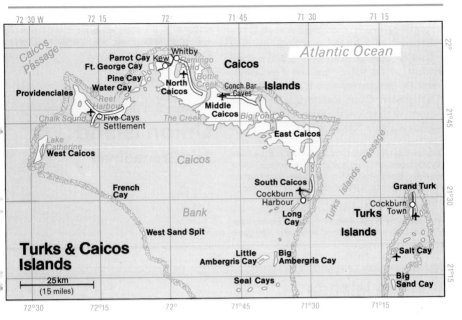

underground salt lakes. – 6 miles/10 km W, between the villages of **Bambarra** and **Lorimer**, are the very interesting remains of a **settlement of the Arawak and Lucayan Indians. The site with its cave-dwellings has recently attracted the interest of American archaeologists, and there are thought to be other sites in the neighbourhood. – 2 miles/3 km S of Lorimer is the *Big Pond*, now a nature reserve, with rich and varied plant and animal life.

East Caicos. – This almost untouched island is separated from Middle Caicos by the **Windward Going Through**. With its brackish meadows and ponds and its narrow coral reefs it forms a transition to South Caicos.

At the NW corner of the island are the small *Iguana Cay* and the larger *Joe Grant's Cay*, now designated as nature reserves for the protection of their many varieties of coral and their rare plant and animal life. They are rated one of the finest nature reserves in the area.

North Caicos. – This is the most northerly island in the group, separated from Middle Caicos by a narrow channel. With its beautiful beaches and excellent fishing it has recently become popular with vacationers in the upper income brackets. The first development was the exclusive holiday complex of **Whitby** at the N end of the island, from which a road runs W to the pretty little village of **Sandy Point**, 3 miles/5 km S of which is the

charming hamlet of **Kew**. To the S of Whitby lies the *Flamingo Pond*, a nesting-place of this species, now rare in the wild state.

6 miles/9 km SE of Whitby are the secluded **Bottle Creek Settlements**, on the E coast of the island (fine beaches), whose inhabitants live mainly from catching fish, shellfish and crayfish. – To the E, on the far side of Bottle Creek, is *Bay Cay*, a low-lying and almost untouched little island.

BOAT TRIP. – 4 miles W of Whitby are the *Three Mary Cays* (nature reserve), which will appeal to lovers of unspoiled natural beauty.

*Pine Cay.** – On this little coral island (private property), with a **beach on the SW coast which is rated one of the most beautiful in the world, is one of the most exclusive holiday developments in the western hemisphere, the *Meridian Club*. – Off the N coast of Pine Cay is *Fort George Cay** (National Park), with the ruins of a British fort. On both islands traces of pre-Columbian settlement can be found with the help of a local guide. – *Water Cay* and *Little Water Cay*, off the S coast, are happy hunting grounds for shell collectors.

*Providenciales.** – The development of this charming island is now in full swing. British and American firms are building hotels and second homes, which are to be supplied with the produce of small farm holdings. A lobster and shellfish farm has also been established, producing for the North American as well as the local market.

The chief place on the island is **Five Cays Settlement**, situated in a beautiful bay on the S coast, with an airstrip and a small harbor. – To the S are the *Five Cays*, recently designated as a National Park. – To the W is * *Chalk Sound*, a land-locked lagoon with recent deposits of limestone, which is also a National Park.

3 miles/5 km N of Five Cays Settlement is **Blue Hills Settlement**, on * *Reef Harbour*, a marvelous marine garden. – 5 miles/8 km NE of Five Cays Settlement are the little fishing villages known as the *Bights Settlements*.

The island of **West Caicos** (7 miles/11 km long, 2 miles/3 km wide), separated from the central chain of islands by a shallow channel 5 miles/8 km wide studded with sharp rocks, offers excellent fishing and diving.

See also** **Bahamas**.

Union Island
See Grenadines

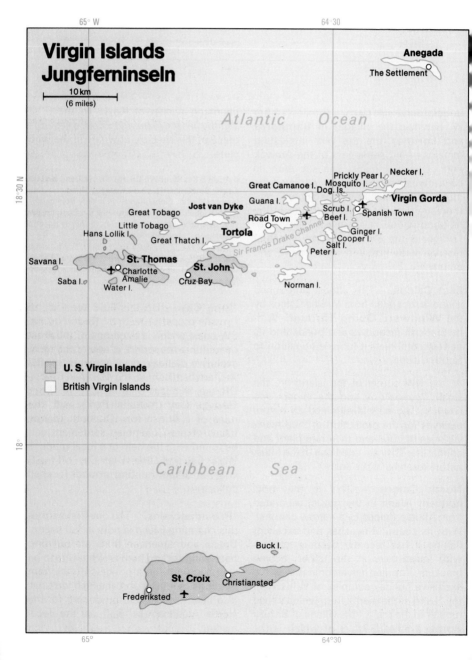

United States Virgin Islands

Lesser Antilles
United States Unincorporated Territory

Area: 133 sq. miles/344 sq. km.
Population: 96,000.
Administrative center: Charlotte Amalie (on St Thomas).
Vehicles travel on the left.
ⓘ **US Virgin Islands Division of Tourism,**
P.O. Box 1692,
Charlotte Amalie, VI 00801,
St Thomas, U.S.V.I.;
tel. (809) 774 1331.
P.O. Box 200,
Cruz Bay, VI 00830,
St John, U.S.V.I.;
tel. (809) 776 6450.
P.O. Box,
Christiansted, VI 00820,
St Croix, U.S.V.I.;
tel. (809) 773 0495.
Custom House Building,
Frederiksted, VI 00840,
St Croix, U.S.V.I.;
tel. (809) 772 0357.
See also Practical Information

The * United States Virgin Islands are the south-western part of the group of Virgin Islands lying to the E of Puerto Rico; the north-eastern part is the British colony of the Virgin Islands. In addition to the three main islands – St Croix, St Thomas and St John – the archipelago is made up of some 50 smaller islets and reefs.

Originally occupied by British and Danish settlers, the islands were acquired by the United States in 1917. The inhabitants are United States citizens but are not entitled to vote in federal elections.

The climate is tropical, but is pleasantly cooled by the trade winds which blow all year round. The islands' main sources of revenue are tourism, sugar-cane and stock farming; there is little industry. The only industrial complex is situated on St Croix, where there is an oil refinery as well as an aluminum-oxide works. The duty-free shops offer a tempting array of imported goods at bargain prices.

See also * St Croix, * St John, * St Thomas and * British Virgin Islands.

Venezuelan Islands

See Isla de Margarita

Isla de Vieques

See San Juan

Virgin Gorda

Lesser Antilles
British Virgin Islands
British crown colony

Area: 8 sq. miles/21.5 sq. km.
Population: 1000.
Administrative center: Road Town (on Tortola).
Vehicles travel on the left.
ⓘ **British Virgin Islands Tourist Board,**
P.O. Box 134,
Road Town,
Tortola, B.V.I.;
tel. (809) 494 3134.
See also Practical Information.

HOTELS. – *Little Dix Bay Hotel*, 140 b., T, beach, sailing, scuba diving, water-skiing, fishing, riding; *Biras Creek Hotel*, 60 b., beach, SP, T; *Bitter End Yacht Club*, 28 b., beach; *Ocean View*, 24 b.; *Olde Yard Inn*, 20 b.; holiday apartments in *Fischers Cove Beach Hotel*, 30 b., and *Guavaberry Spring Bay*, 20 b., beach.

RECREATION and SPORT. – Sailing, deep-sea fishing, snorkeling, scuba diving; walking.

EVENTS. – *Easter Festival*, with procession, musical contests and dancing.

TRANSPORT. – Air taxis to Anegada, Tortola and St Thomas, linking up with international services via San Juan (Puerto Rico). – Boat services to neighboring islands.

Virgin Gorda lies NE of Tortola, the principal island of the British Virgin Islands group. The relatively flat and more populous southern part of the island is joined by a narrow isthmus to the hillier northern part, which rises to 1362 ft/415 m in Virgin Gorda Peak. The part of the island lying above 1000 ft/300 m, now a National Park, is fine walking country.

The ferry from Tortola puts in at **Spanish Town**, which is sheltered by a barrier reef. The airstrip used by the air taxis is a short distance E. – On the beautiful rocky coast SW of the town are the *Baths*, a complex of eerie sea caves, rock basins and channels. Near *Copper Mine Point* on the SE coast is an abandoned copper-mine, worked in the 16th c. by the Spaniards and in the 19th c. by settlers from Cornwall. – Off the S tip of Virgin Gorda are the curiously shaped rocky islets known as *Fallen Jerusalem* and *Broken Jerusalem*.

There are beautiful beaches on *North Sound*, in the NE of the island, which is sheltered by a string of little islets and has good moorings for sailing boats. The much indented coast has some of the finest scenery in the whole group.

See also *British Virgin Islands.

Virgin Islands

The **Virgin Islands lie E of Puerto Rico in the Lesser Antilles. The group consists of six major islands and a number of smaller ones. The eastern part is British; the western part belongs to the United States.

The climate is tropical, pleasantly cooled by the constant winds off the sea (average winter temperature 79 °F/26 °C, summer 82 °F/28 °C). There is no real rainy season – merely occasional showers. The islands' main sources of revenue, apart from tourism, are sugar-cane and cotton, together with a certain amount of stock farming.

See also *British Virgin Islands, *Anegada, *Tortola and Virgin Gorda; United States Virgin Islands, *St Croix, *St John and *St Thomas.

Watling's Island
See San Salvador

Practical Information

Warning

Visitors to the Caribbean should keep a watchful eye on their belongings at all times. Political, economic and social tensions have led in many areas to a serious increase in crime and to increasingly frequent acts of aggression, sometimes directed against visitors. (It should be remembered that most islanders regard all foreigners as wealthy, since they spend about as much in one day as many local inhabitants earn in a month.) Particularly in the neighborhood of slum areas visitors should be on their guard against verbal or physical aggression, theft or robbery with violence; and in certain areas and towns it is better not to go out after dark without a knowledgeable local escort.

When cruising about in the islands in a small boat visitors should be wary of unpleasant encounters in lonely and apparently deserted coves. In some ports visitors' boats are besieged by a swarm of locals, mostly youths, offering every conceivable service; and in these circumstances the best way of avoiding trouble is to hire one or more reliable persons to act as guides and attendants for the duration of your stay and to err on the side of generosity in paying them. **Boats should never be left unattended**, since they are a magnet for thieves and are in demand for smuggling.

The police are anxious to help, but are often powerless in the face of criminal activities by organized gangs. In cases of attack or robbery they can usually do no more than prepare a report on the occurrence (which will of course be required for the purposes of a claim for insurance).

The loss of traveler's checks or credit cards should be reported at once by cable to the bank or other agency concerned so that payment can be stopped.

Recommended precautions

- Never let your baggage out of your sight.

- Deposit anything of value (particularly personal documents, money, traveler's checks, keys, etc.) in the hotel safe or carry it with you.

- Carry only enough money for your immediate requirements.

- Change money only at a bank. Money offered in the street is often counterfeit or no longer current. Moreover, there are heavy penalties on some islands for the illegal changing of currency.

- Do not buy from street hawkers, since they frequently deal in stolen goods.

- To avoid any risk of getting involved in the smuggling of narcotics, do not allow yourself to be persuaded to carry any package or parcel on behalf of a person unknown to you.

Regatta in the Bahamas

When to Go; Weather

The Caribbean climate does not show the marked differentiation between the seasons found in the temperate latitudes of Europe and North America. Between latitude 10° N and the Tropic of Cancer summer and winter vary only slightly in the length of the day, the position of the sun at noon, the average duration of sunshine and the average temperature. There is, however, a considerable difference between summer and winter in the amount of rainfall: the winter is dry, making it the best time of year for a visit to the Caribbean, while in summer there are sometimes heavy showers of rain and hurricanes are almost a matter of course.

Although the Caribbean islands, with the exception of the northern Bahamas, lie within the tropics the *trade winds* which blow throughout the year bring most of them cooling sea breezes which make the climate readily tolerable by visitors from more northern climes. It should not be forgotten, however, that even when these winds are blowing the sun's rays remain powerful and some form of protection is essential. – For a fuller account of climatic conditions in the Caribbean, see pp. 18–23.

When planning a trip to the Caribbean it is worth remembering that during the main tourist season prices are often higher and some resorts may be overcrowded.

Travel Documents

A valid **passport** is required by British visitors to some of the former British colonies (Bahamas, Barbados, Bermuda, Caymans, Jamaica, Trinidad and Tobago, Turks and Caicos), the French and Dutch territories, the US territories (visa required), the Dominican Republic, Haiti and Venezuela. For other ex-British colonies only proof of identity is required, but it is advisable in any event to have a passport which is the best form of identity document.

United States citizens require only proof of citizenship for entering most of the Caribbean states. Passports are required for Trinidad and Tobago and Venezuela.

Canadian nationals require only proof of citizenship for entry to most of the Caribbean states. Passports are required for Cuba, Trinidad and Tobago and Venezuela.

Almost all the Caribbean states also require visitors to produce an onward or return ticket, and in some states visitors must show that they have enough money to maintain themselves for the period of their stay.

National **driving licenses** are usually recognized, but it will sometimes help to have an *international driving license*.

It is advisable to check the current regulations on passports, etc., with the national tourist office or diplomatic or consular office before departure.

Health

Visitors to the Caribbean should take precautions against certain possible health hazards. Protection against the strong light and the fierce heat of the sun is advisable. The high humidity of the tropics can give rise to circulatory problems, and the climate is favorable to the development of certain diseases (e.g. malaria). Food goes off quickly in the warm, moist climate, so that there is always a risk of stomach and intestinal disorders. At higher altitudes the climate may call for a period of acclimatization.

Moreover, hygienic conditions in many places fall short of European and North American standards, and particular care is required in this respect. Visitors should consult their doctor before departure and make sure that they have any injections required. Injections are advisable against tetanus, cholera, typhus, poliomyelitis, hepatitis and yellow fever, and precautions should also be taken against malaria. It is advisable to take your international vaccination certificate with you.

It is important to take clothing suitable for the tropics (no synthetic fibres!), particularly if it is intended to do much walking. Stout footwear, knee-length stockings, trousers and long-sleeved shirts give protection against scratches or grazes which may take some time to heal and against mosquito and snake bites. –

Swimmers should make a point of leaving the beach before it begins to get dark if they want to avoid being attacked by swarms of sand-fleas.

Avoid drinking water, raw meat, fruit, salads, ices and ice cubes in your drink unless you are sure they are clean, since otherwise there is always a risk of salmonella infection or intestinal troubles.

Do not swim in rivers or ponds where there may be a danger of bilharzia. If in doubt, inquire locally.

Before leaving home it is advisable to take out suitable short-term *health insurance.* – It should be remembered that in the remoter parts of some of the Caribbean islands medical attention may not always be readily available.

Islands or states	Currency	Import of local currency	Export of local currency
Anguilla	E. Caribbean dollar (EC$)	unrestricted[1]	as declared
Antigua/Barbuda	E. Caribbean dollar (EC$)	unrestricted[1]	as declared
Bahamas	Bahamian dollar (B$)	prohibited	70 B$
Barbados	Barbados dollar (BDS$)	unrestricted	100 BDS$
Bermuda	Bermuda dollar (BD$)	unrestricted	250 BD$
Caymans	Cayman dollar (CI$)	unrestricted	unrestricted
Dominica	E. Caribbean dollar (EC$)	unrestricted[1]	as declared
Dominican Republic	Dominican peso (RD$)	prohibited	prohibited
Grenada	E. Caribbean dollar (EC$)	unrestricted[1]	as declared
Guadeloupe	French franc (F)	unrestricted	5000 F
Haiti	gourde (gde)	unrestricted	unrestricted
Jamaica	Jamaican dollar (J$)	prohibited	prohibited
Margarita	Venezuelan bolívar (Bs)	unrestricted	unrestricted
Martinique	French franc (F)	unrestricted	5000 F
Montserrat	E. Caribbean dollar (EC$)	unrestricted[1]	as declared
Netherlands Antilles	Netherlands Antilles gulden (NAfl)	100 NAfl	100 NAfl
Puerto Rico	US dollar (US$)	unrestricted	unrestricted
St Kitts and Nevis	E. Caribbean dollar (EC$)	unrestricted[1]	as declared
St Lucia	E. Caribbean dollar (EC$)	unrestricted[1]	as declared
St Vincent/Grenadines	E. Caribbean dollar (EC$)	unrestricted[1]	as declared
Trinidad and Tobago	Trinidad and Tobago dollar (TT$)	prohibited	prohibited
Turks and Caicos	US dollar (US$)	unrestricted	unrestricted
Virgin Islands (British and US)	US dollar (US$)	unrestricted	unrestricted

[1] must be declared

Customs Regulations

In general visitors to the Caribbean islands are allowed to take in duty-free their personal effects and equipment. In some cases items of particular value (cameras and movie cameras, radios, tape-recorders, fishing tackle, sports gear, etc.) must be specially declared. The regulations on taking in sporting guns and spear-guns (which in some places are banned) vary from island to island. – Small quantities of tobacco goods and alcohol for personal consumption may also be taken in duty-free. There are heavy penalties for the possession of narcotics, even in the smallest quantities. Visitors who bring pills, etc., with them should keep the original pack to show what they are.

Full information about the regulations for the various countries can be obtained from travel agents and national tourist offices.

Currency

In general there are no restrictions on the import of foreign currency into the Caribbean states. It is advisable, however, to declare the amount of foreign currency carried when entering a country in order to avoid possible difficulty when leaving it.

In order to change back any unused local currency it is frequently necessary to produce the receipt for the original purchase of local currency: any such receipts should therefore be carefully preserved.

It is practically impossible to cash Eurocheques or traveler's checks in currencies other than American dollars. Money should therefore be taken in *dollar traveler's checks*, and any cash taken should also be dollars.

Credit cards (American Express, Diners' Club, etc.) are widely accepted.

Weights and Measures[1]

Weight

1 ounce (oz)	=	28.35 g	100 g	=	3.527 oz
1 pound (lb)	=	453.59 g	1 kg	=	2.205 lb
1 stone	=	6.35 kg	10 kg	=	1.57 stone

Length

1 inch (in)	=	2.54 cm	1 cm	=	0.39 in
1 foot (ft)	=	30.48 cm	10 cm	=	0.33 ft
1 yard (yd)	=	91.44 cm	1 m	=	1.196 yd
1 mile (mi)	=	1.61 km	1 km	=	0.62 mi

Area

1 sq. inch (in²)	=	6.45 cm²	1 cm²	=	0.155 in²
1 sq. foot (ft²)	=	9.290 dm²	1 dm²	=	0.108 ft²
1 sq. yard (yd²)	=	0.836 m²	1 m²	=	1.196 yd²
1 sq. mile (mi²)	=	2.590 km²	1 km²	=	0.386 mi²
1 acre	=	0.405 ha	1 ha	=	2.471 acres

Liquid measure

British

1 pint (pt)	=	0.568 l	1 l	=	1.76 pt
1 quart (qt)	=	1.136 l	1 l	=	0.88 qt
1 gallon (gal)	=	4.546 l	10 l	=	2.20 gal

United States

1 pint (pt)	=	0.473 l	1 l	=	2.114 pt
1 quart (qt)	=	0.946 l	1 l	=	1.057 qt
1 gallon (gal)	=	3.785 l	10 l	=	2.642 gal

Pressure

1 lb/in²	= 0.7 kg/cm²		1 kg/cm²	= 14.2 lb/in²
20 lb/in²	= 1.41 kg/cm²		1.5 kg/cm²	= 21.3 lb/in²

Temperatures

K(elvin)	$°C$(elsius)	$°F$(ahrenheit)	
373	100	212	*boiling*
323	50	122	*point*
318	45	113	
313	40	104	
310	37	98.6	*body*
308	35	95	*heat*
303	30	86	
298	25	77	
293	20	68	
288	15	59	
283	10	50	
278	5	41	
273	0	32	*freezing*
268	− 5	23	*point*
263	−10	14	
258	−15	5	
255.3	−17.7	0	
253	−20	− 4	
248	−25	−13	
243	−30	−22	

Conversion

$$°C = \frac{5\,(°F - 32)}{9}$$

$$°F = 1.8 \times °C + 32$$

Relationship °C/F

$$°C : °F = 5 : 9 \qquad °F : °C = 9 : 5$$

[1]British and American weights and measures are still in use in the English-speaking islands, though metrication is under way in some areas.

Time

The Caribbean islands fall within two time zones. The eastern Caribbean as far as the Dominican Republic observes *Atlantic Standard Time* (4 hours behind Greenwich Mean Time), while the western half is on *Eastern Standard Time* (5 hours behind GMT). – Some islands have *Summer Time* (Standard Time + 1 hour) from May or June to October.

Electricity

Electric voltages vary from island to island, with voltages of 110, 130, 220 and 240 and frequencies of 50 or 60 cycles. Types of power socket also vary: it is advisable, therefore, to take a set of adaptors.

Light Conditions in the Caribbean
(Hints for Photographers)

Visitors from more northern latitudes should bear in mind that in the Caribbean, lying closer to the Equator, the length of the day varies relatively little over the year. The longest day in summer lasts about 12¾ hours, the shortest day in winter 11¼ hours, and the difference between summer and winter becomes steadily less towards the S. The period of twilight, averaging some 20 minutes, is markedly shorter than in Europe or North America. Thus in the morning it quickly becomes light enough to take photographs, while in the evening it equally quickly becomes too dark. The period around midday is even less suitable for taking color photographs than it is farther N, since the sun is very high in the sky: light and shadow are hard and sharply contrasted, and there is no chance of getting the soft side lighting which is best for many subjects.

Most people in the Caribbean dislike being photographed, feeling it, on religious or other grounds, to be an intrusion. Before taking a photograph of anyone, therefore, it is essential to ask for permission to do so; and it may sometimes help to offer some small financial reward.

Getting There

Most visitors to the Caribbean islands go by air, since this is by far the quickest way.

There are direct flights from London and other European airports to the principal islands, and numerous flights from United States airports. Travelers from Europe can also reach the Caribbean by linking up with an American service, e.g. from New York or Miami. The dense network of inter-island flights provides connections to the smaller islands. – Package holidays using chartered aircraft make it possible to visit the Caribbean at very reasonable rates, but some airlines have introduced special tariffs for flights to the West Indies which compare very favorably with the rates for charter flights.

Going by sea takes considerably longer, particularly for visitors from Europe – and in any event there are now very few transatlantic passenger liners. One possibility is to sail one way and fly the other.

One good way of seeing the islands is on a Caribbean cruise ship. The cruises usually begin and end either in Miami (USA) or San Juan (Puerto Rico).

Air Services

Within the Caribbean area a considerable number of airlines provide services between the various islands and connections with the nearer airports on the mainland of North, Central and South America. Many of these services are flown by quite small aircraft, and occasionally by seaplanes or flying boats. This extensive network makes it easy to get about from island to island ("island hopping"). The international airport of San Juan (Puerto Rico) is an important junction for air traffic in the Caribbean. Among leading regional airlines flying scheduled services are *Bahamasair* (Nassau to the main islands in the Bahamas and to Florida), *Prinair* (San Juan to other places in Puerto Rico, the Virgin Islands and some of the Lesser Antilles) and *Liat* (Antigua, Barbados and San Juan to all the larger islands in the eastern Caribbean).

Cruising

A good way of seeing the Caribbean islands is offered by the wide range of cruises operated by various shipping lines

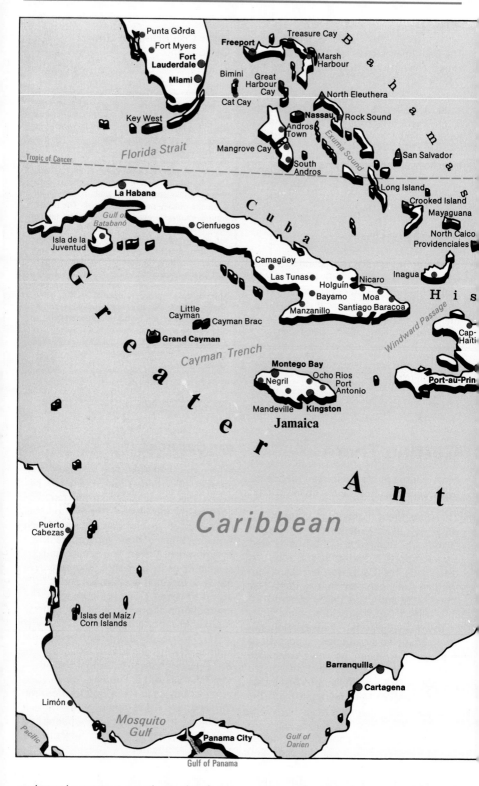

and travel operators, mostly starting from Miami (USA), San Juan (Puerto Rico), Bridgetown (Barbados) or Curaçao. Some cruises also call in at ports on the South American mainland. The cruise ships offer every amenity and a full program of entertainments, with land excursions from the ports of call (usually at additional cost).

A number of operators run cruises from USA.

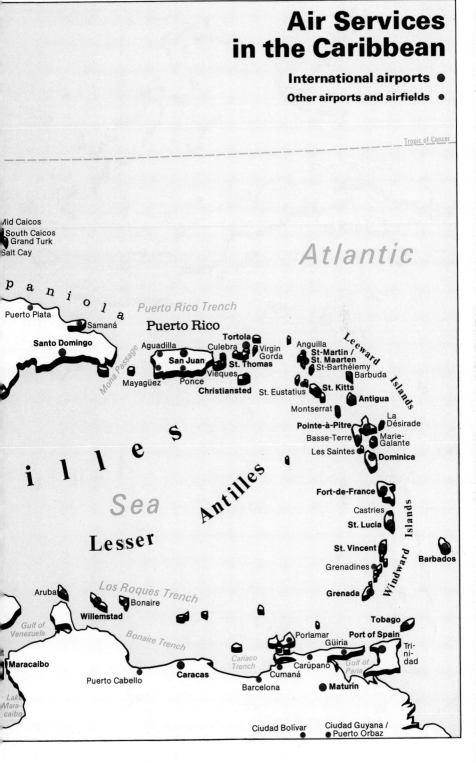

Air Services in the Caribbean

International airports ●
Other airports and airfields ●

Tropic of Cancer

Atlantic

Mid Caicos
South Caicos
Grand Turk
Salt Cay

panio la
Puerto Plata
Samaná
Santo Domingo

Puerto Rico Trench
Puerto Rico
Tortola
Aguadilla   Culebra   Virgin Gorda
Mona Passage   San Juan   St. Thomas
Mayagüez   Ponce   Vieques
Christiansted   St. Eustatius

Anguilla
St-Martin /
St. Maarten
St-Barthélemy
Barbuda
St. Kitts
Antigua
Montserrat

Leeward Islands

illes

Pointe-à-Pitre
Basse-Terre
Les Saintes

La Désirade
Marie-Galante
Dominica

Sea   *Antilles*

Fort-de-France
Castries
St. Lucia
St. Vincent
Grenadines
Grenada

Windward Islands

Lesser

Aruba
Bonaire
Willemstad

Los Roques Trench

Barbados

Gulf of Venezuela

Bonaire Trench

Tobago
Porlamar   **Port of Spain**
Güiria   Tri-ni-dad
Cariaco Trench
Maracaibo   Carúpano
Puerto Cabello   **Caracas**   Cumaná   *Gulf of Paria*
Barcelona   ● **Maturin**
Lake Mara-caibo

Ciudad Bolívar   Ciudad Guyana / ● Puerto Orbaz

Shipping lines offering cruises from USA (a selection)

Chandris Cruise Inc.,
666 Fifth Avenue,
New York, NY 10019;
tel. (212) 586 8370.

Costa Line Inc.,
733 Third Avenue,
New York, NY 10017;
tel. (212) 682 3505.
Cunard Line Ltd,
555 Fifth Avenue,
New York, NY 10017;
tel. (212) 880 7500.

Holland America Cruises,
2 Pennsylvania Plaza,
New York, NY 10001;
tel. (212) 290 0100.

Norwegian American Cruises,
29 Broadway,
New York, NY 10006;
tel. (212) 422 3900.

Norwegian Caribbean Lines,
1 Biscayne Tower,
Miami, Florida 33131;
tel. (305) 358 6670.

Princess Cruises,
2029 Century Park East,
Los Angeles, Cal. 90067;
tel. (213) 553 1770.

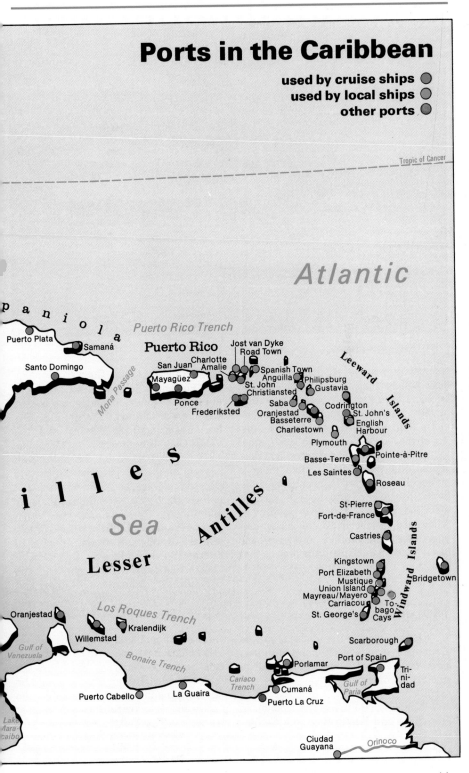

Ports in the Caribbean

used by cruise ships ⊙
used by local ships ⊙
other ports ⊙

Tropic of Cancer

Atlantic

Puerto Rico Trench

Puerto Plata
Samaná
Puerto Rico Jost van Dyke
Road Town
Santo Domingo San Juan Charlotte
Amalie Anguilla Philipsburg
Mayagüez Spanish Town Gustavia
St. John
Ponce Christiansted
Frederiksted Saba Codrington
Oranjestad St. John's
Basseterre English
Charlestown Harbour
Plymouth
Basse-Terre Pointe-à-Pitre
Les Saintes
Roseau

Mona Passage

Leeward Islands

St-Pierre
Fort-de-France
Castries

S

illes

Sea

Lesser *Antilles*

Windward Islands

Kingstown
Port Elizabeth Bridgetown
Mustique
Union Island
Mayreau/Mayero To-
Carriacou bago
St. George's Cays

Los Roques Trench

Oranjestad
Kralendijk
Willemstad Scarborough

Gulf of Venezuela *Bonaire Trench* Port of Spain
Tri-
Porlamar ni-
dad
Cariaco Trench Cumaná *Gulf of Paria*
Puerto Cabello La Guaira Puerto La Cruz

Lake Mara-caibo

Ciudad
Guayana *Orinoco*

Royal Caribbean Cruise Line,
903 South America Way,
Dodge Island,
Miami, Florida 33132;
tel. (305) 379 2601.

An attractive alternative for those who like a more individual holiday and can afford the time is a trip on a cargo-passenger ship sailing to Caribbean ports. This is more unpredictable than an organised cruise, since the vessels have no exact timetables and may have their itinerary altered at short notice. Moreover cargo vessels are not usually fitted with stabilisers,

Cruise ships in the Caribbean

so that in a heavy sea they tend to be less steady than passenger ships. No medical service is available on cargo ships unless they have accommodation for more than 12 passengers. On the other hand they go to ports and anchorages which are normally not reached by cruise ships, and they have a more intimate atmosphere than the large cruising liners, with closer relationships between passengers (usually few in number) and crew. They also usually allow the passengers more time ashore at their ports of call and leave them free to spend the time as they please.

Motoring

In general driving regulations in the Caribbean islands are in line with international standards, but it is as well to check the position on arrival.

In Hispaniola (Haiti and the Dominican Republic) and Puerto Rico, the Nether-lands Antilles (Aruba, Curaçao, Bonaire, Sint Eustatius, Saba and Sint Maarten), the French Antilles (Guadeloupe and its associated islands, Martinique, St-Barthélemy and St-Martin) and the Venezuelan islands (Isla de Margarita, etc.) vehicles travel on the right, with passing on the left. In former British and Danish colonies and in territories still under British rule – the Bahamas, Turks and Caicos, Caymans, Jamaica, Virgin Islands (including both the US and British islands), Anguilla, Barbuda, Antigua, St Kitts and Nevis, Montserrat, Dominica, St Lucia, Barbados, St Vincent and the Grenadines, Grenada, Trinidad and Tobago, Bermuda – traffic keeps to the left, with passing on the right.

On all the larger Caribbean islands, but not in Bermuda, it is possible to rent self-drive cars: for the names of car-rental firms see under Practical Information. It should be noted that neither road conditions nor the cars available for rent are likely to be up to European or North American standards.

Language

The languages spoken on the Caribbean islands are as varied as their histories, often showing characteristic local divergences from the standard language. – The most widely spoken language is **Spanish**, the language of the Dominican Republic, Puerto Rico and the Venezuelan islands. English is spoken in Bermuda, the Bahamas, the Turks and Caicos Islands, the Caymans, Jamaica, the Virgin Islands,

Antigua and Barbuda, St Kitts and Nevis, Montserrat, Dominica, St Lucia, Barbados, Grenada, St Vincent and the Grenadines and Trinidad and Tobago. **French** is the official language of Haiti, St-Martin, St-Barthélemy, Guadeloupe and Martinique, **Dutch** of Sint Maarten, Sint Eustatius, Saba, Curaçao, Bonaire and Aruba.

A number of mixed (Creole) languages have developed out of the languages of the original European settlers and other tongues spoken in the Caribbean – languages of simple structure which arose out of the need for a lingua franca enabling people of mixed racial origin to understand one another but which have never attained the status of a written language. Regional forms of this kind are the *Papiamento* (in which Portuguese, Spanish and Dutch influences are predominant) still spoken in the Dutch Leeward Islands, the *Patois* (French and English influences predominant) spoken on some former British colonies and the *Créole* (mainly French influences) of Haiti and the islands still belonging to France.

Visitors should use the standard language, since the islanders tend to resent being addressed by a foreigner in a dialect which carries with it the implication of lower social status.

Accommodation

Hotels, Guest-Houses and Pensions

As one of the world's most popular, and until quite recently most exclusive vacation areas, the Caribbean region is well equipped with hotels and other accommodation for visitors.

The **hotels** of the higher categories in towns and resorts are fully up to international standards, but although the service is efficient they tend to have little atmosphere. Hotels under local management have more individuality, and there are also hotels under European management which are likewise usually more pleasant. Outside the main tourist centers the same standard of comfort cannot be expected.

On many islands most of the accommodation is in luxury hotels, often built with North American or European capital. These expensive but very comfortable establishments are equipped with every amenity, including private beaches, swimming pools, tennis courts and facilities for water sports; many of them

Gosier hotel complex, Guadeloupe

	Rates per day
AP (American plan): accommodation + three meals	$36–$93 (£25–£65)
MAP (modified American plan): accommodation + breakfast and dinner	$32–$83 (£22–£58)
CP (continental plan): accommodation + breakfast	$19–$46 (£13–£32)
EP (European plan): accommodation only	$16–$36 (£11–£25)

even have their own yacht harbors and golf-courses. Most of them have restaurants – often of high quality – and night clubs, and some of them have their own casinos.

Most of the middle-category hotels are in line with European standards, but tend to be more expensive than their equivalents in Europe. Hotels in the lower price category are often relatively cheap, but standards of amenity frequently leave much to be desired.

The above table gives an indication of the approximate range of prices for accommodation and meals in Caribbean hotels.

Rates are highest during the main winter season, between December 15 and April 30, and during this period it is advisable to book well in advance. Around Christmas and Easter and during the Carnival accommodation is likely to be at a premium. With the increased flow of visitors from Europe hotels on some of the Caribbean islands now also charge higher rates during the main summer season, the European school holiday period.

Tariffs may be reduced by up to 40% during the early summer and autumn, and prices are at their lowest between September and mid December – though many of the better hotels are closed during this period.

In **Bermuda**, lying much farther N, the season lasts almost for the whole year, and only during the winter are small reductions offered by some hotels. The Bermudian hotels, almost all offering a very high standard of comfort and amenity, are expensive.

Accommodation of more modest standard is provided by **guest-houses** and **pensions**, with tariffs of the order of $9–$20 (£6–£14) per night (accommodation only).

Holiday Apartments

In recent years many islands have offered accommodation for visitors in holiday apartments. The starting-point of this development was the conversion of old plantation houses, often luxuriously appointed, into separate apartments, but more recently holiday villages and apartment houses have been specially built for the purpose. Standards of comfort in these apartments are very variable. In most cases domestic help is available at very modest charges.

Camping

On most Caribbean islands camping is prohibited. Where it is permitted it can be recommended only for the hardy and adventurous traveler, for the amenities provided on organized camp sites are of the most spartan character.

Food and Drink

Caribbean cuisine incorporates elements from all the various cultures represented in the population, including influences from the native Indian population, Africa and the Far East as well as from the countries of the various European settlers. Much use is made of spices and herbs, particularly peppers and curry powder.

The various kinds of tropical vegetables also feature largely in the diet of the Caribbean – plantains (cooking bananas), breadfruit, cassava, taro, yams, okra, pumpkin, etc. There are many different ways of serving them, found in similar form on all the islands.

There are greater differences in the meat dishes, evidently related to the cuisines of

Crayfish – a Guadeloupe delicacy

the different colonial powers. Stock farming was relatively little practiced in the Caribbean area, except in the former Spanish colonies, and in consequence beef rarely appears on the menu: much use is made, however, of wild goat meat, lamb, pork and also poultry. On Dominica, in particular, "mountain chicken" – the meat of giant frogs – ranks as a particular delicacy.

The waters of the Caribbean are well stocked with fish and shellfish. One particular local specialty is turtle meat, but since turtles living in the wild state are threatened with extinction they are strictly protected and the demand is met by large turtle farms. Other favorite dishes are crayfish, various kinds of shellfish, sea-urchins and flying fish.

There is a wide range of fruit – citrus fruits, bananas, pineapples, coconuts, mangoes, pawpaws (known in Cuba as *fruta bomba*), etc.

> **Warning.** – There is always a risk of stomach or intestinal infection from drinking water of doubtful purity (sometimes even tap-water) or eating salads, unskinned fruit and vegetables or ices. Remember to take appropriate medicines with you!

The Caribbean Menu

Many dishes are found all over the Caribbean but, depending on the local language, may be known by different names.

HORS D'ŒUVRES. – Fritters with prawn meat or stockfish (stamp and go, *accras, cala, bacaleitos*); prawns with rice (*matété de crabes, matoutou*); fried and marinated fish (*escovitch, escabeche*); plantain chips; black sausage and knuckle of pork (pudding and souse); avocados (avocats); prawn croquettes (*bombas de camarones*).

SOUPS. – Vegetable soup (*soupe z'habitant*); turtle soup (*soupe de tortue*); black bean soup (*sopa de frijol negro*); prawn soup (*callaloo, calalou*); bread-fruit soup (*soupe au fruit de pain*); soups made with avocados, pawpaws, coconuts, etc.; cold soups.

MAIN DISHES. – Stuffed plantains (*piononos*); rice with beans and meat (*moros y cristianos*); rice with mushrooms (*riz au djon djon*); pepper pot (a highly seasoned stew of meat and peppers); and a wide range of dishes based on local vegetables such as breadfruit, okra (*gombo*), paprika, pumpkin (*calabaza, calebasse*), pawpaws, plantains, taro, yams and cassava. – MEAT DISHES. – Beef is almost always imported and often of poor quality. The kinds of meat more generally found are pork (*porc, cerdo*; sucking pig, *cochon de lait, lechón*), lamb (*agneau, cordero*), turtle meat (*tortue, tortuga*) and poultry.

FISH. – The commonest type of fish and seafood are stockfish, flying fish and other species of seafish, crayfish, prawns and various kinds of shellfish.

DESSERT. – Most commonly various tropical fruits including pineapples, bananas, coconuts, guavas, citrus fruits, mangoes, etc.

SPICES AND SEASONINGS. – Caribbean dishes tend to be highly seasoned, much use being made of the various species of pepper and of curry. Where spices and sauces are served separately it is a good idea to begin by taking only very small quantities.

Drinks

Fruit juices (pineapple, guava, lime, maracuja, grapefruit, etc.), freshly pressed sugar-cane juice and coconut milk and the various local *mineral waters* make good thirst-quenchers. Excellent *beer*, both imported and locally brewed, is available everywhere. *Wine* is generally found only in the better-class restaurants.

Rum, one of the best known products of the West Indies, is the basis of many drinks. Among the most popular are *daiquiri* (3 parts of white rum, 1 part of sugar syrup, 1 part of lime juice, 2 ice cubes), *piña colada* (2 parts white rum, 1

part coconut syrup, 3 parts pineapple juice, 1 part lime juice, 2 ice cubes) and *rum punch* or *planter's punch* (French *planteur*: 2 parts brown rum, 1 part sugar syrup, 4 parts fruit juice).

> **Rum** (Spanish *ron*, French *rhum*) is distilled from fermented sugar-cane juice. Depending on the quality of the raw material and the method of production and processing, it is available in a wide range of color and aroma. White rum is described as "young", while brown rum, like cognac, is aged in oak casks.
>
> Brown rum of lower quality – usually sold as industrial rum – is produced from fermented molasses (a by-product of the process of sugar production).

West Indian *coffee* enjoys world renown. A major producer is the island of Hispaniola.

Manners and Customs

The pattern of life on the West Indian islands shows a variety of ethnic, religious, social and economic contrasts – largely, but not exclusively, resulting from the past history of the region. European visitors in particular should remember that many of the tensions in the Caribbean stem from the behavior of the islands' former colonial rulers. In consequence the present rapid development of tourism, mostly financed by North American and European capital, is regarded by many islanders as a continuation of the colonial system in another form, and the encounter between the local inhabitants with their relatively low standard of living and the visitors, who are generally regarded as enjoying great wealth, can sometimes give rise to conflicts. In some particularly backward areas the first stirrings of xenophobia can be detected, and there are occasional assaults on tourists which cannot be put down solely to a hereditary tradition of piracy. Visitors to the Caribbean should accordingly always bear the special circumstances of the area in mind and not judge it by the standards of the highly developed industrial countries of the western world.

The proverbial friendliness of the Caribbean people makes visitors feel welcome; but it should not allow them to forget that even the simplest people have a well-developed sense of their own dignity and may also sometimes feel a shade of resentment against the visitors who seem to them so relatively wealthy. Visitors should, therefore, avoid any criticism of the local way of life and customs and should show tact in the discussion of political matters. The people of the Caribbean cannot understand the impatience sometimes shown by visitors, and punctuality is not one of their virtues, so that at least half an hour's grace must be allowed for appointments, opening times, etc.

Many of the local people are notably helpful to visitors, but sometimes their helpfulness may go no farther than a polite gesture. A degree of generosity on the visitor's part will usually promote good relations and a display of zeal, and it is, therefore, a good idea to have a supply of small change always available. The tactful offer of an appropriate sum will sometimes help to overcome particular difficulties – when a hotel is full, an office is closed, tickets for some event are sold out, and so on. It may help to avoid possible unpleasantness to reward some service rendered even if it is unwanted.

Tipping is a general practice throughout the Caribbean. Many hotels and restaurants add a service charge to the bill, but it is still usual to tip waiters, chambermaids, porters, lift attendants, bellhops, etc. Custodians at tourist sights and usherettes in movie-theaters and theaters also expect a tip. Taxi-drivers should be given something on top of the fare. On some islands officials, often poorly paid, expect some pecuniary recognition for services (e.g. customs examination) which are part of their official duties – a payment which is not in any sense regarded as a bribe.

Tipping on cruise ships takes on considerable proportions. Shipping lines and travel agents recommend allowing at least 5% of the fare for tips. On a week's cruise the chief steward will expect at least $8 (£5), the cabin steward at least $9 (£6), the deck steward at least $4 (£2.50). Special services call for an additional payment.

Guides lie in wait for tourists at airports and landing-stages as well as at the main sights and outside the large hotels. European and North American visitors will be surrounded by a swarm of potential guides, mostly youthful, offering their services. The best way of avoiding difficulty is to select a suitable person, after checking on his local knowledge and linguistic ability, and make a bargain with him. Have nothing to do with the touts – often posing as official guides or tourist police – whose only object is to entice their customers into particular shops or restaurants.

A good deal of importance is attached, particularly in the former British colonies, to proper **dress**, especially on festive occasions, in the better restaurants and hotels and on cruise ships. Tourists are granted a certain indulgence, but should not abuse this freedom.

On many cruise ships there are recommended standards of dress, information about which can be obtained from the shipping line or travel agent. On board ship during the day and on shore excursions informal dress is appropriate (not forgetting the need for stout footwear and protection against rain and sun); in the evening women wear a cocktail dress, men a jacket and tie. On special occasions, such as the captain's reception or gala buffet, most passengers put on formal evening wear. There may also be a fancy dress party.

In areas with a considerable white element in the population and a European or American oriented elite, social standards are similar to those prevailing in Europe and North America and attitudes are more liberal. Among the colored population, however, the *position of women* is often very different, particularly in relation to the institution of marriage.

The wife is the pillar of the family. Brought up from early childhood to work hard, she runs the house and looks after the children. The husband, on the other hand – who is often attracted to two or more women – frequently makes only a relatively small contribution to the maintenance of the family.

The question of **prostitution**, which visitors may sometimes encounter, must be considered with this in mind. Some of the women are highly emancipated and may be prepared to enter into temporary liaisons which are not to be judged by European or North American standards. Often, too, women and girls are driven to prostitution on economic grounds.

Tolerance and tact are essential in religious matters, given the great variety of religions and sects. Visitors should enter churches only if suitably dressed, and if they are allowed into a mosque, temple or Afro-American cult center or to be present at religious ceremonies of any kind, they should avoid giving offence by excessive curiosity, inappropriate behavior, photography or missionary zeal.

Sport and Recreation

Sailing

The Caribbean is famed as one of the finest sailing regions in the world, but it differs in a number of respects from the sailing waters of the temperate zones. On the one hand it is exposed throughout the year to the northeastern trade winds, which drive the long swell of the Atlantic into the Caribbean area; on the other there is the danger of hurricanes, the course of which can be charted in advance but which build up dangerous seas. The islands have plenty of good natural harbors but few lights, so that it is necessary to reach an anchorage before nightfall (which occurs very suddenly, with only a brief twilight).

Boats can be rented, with or without a

crew. Visitors who want to "go it alone" rather than hire an experienced local skipper will be required to demonstrate their competence. – There are also organized flotilla cruises.

Information about firms running sailing holidays can be obtained from travel agents.

Yacht Harbors and Anchorages   (Map, pp. 314–315)

1 **Green Turtle Cay**
   (Abaco; Bahamas)

2 **Treasure Cay**
   (Abaco; Bahamas)

3 **Walker's Cay**
   (Abaco; Bahamas)

4 **Man-o'-War Cay**
   (Abaco; Bahamas)

5 **Marsh Harbour**
   (Abaco; Bahamas)

6 **Sandy Point**
   (Abaco; Bahamas)

7 **West End**
   (Grand Bahama; Bahamas)

8 **Freeport**
   (Grand Bahama; Bahamas)

9 **Lucaya**
   (Grand Bahama; Bahamas)

10 **Alice Town**
   (Bimini; Bahamas)

11 **Cat Cay**
   (Cat Cays; Bahamas)

12 **Chub Cay**
   (Berry Islands; Bahamas)

13 **Great Harbour Cay**
   (Berry Islands; Bahamas)

14 **Nicholl's Town**
   (Andros; Bahamas)

15 **Fresh Creek**
   (Andros; Bahamas)

16 **Mangrove Cay**
   (Andros; Bahamas)

17 **Nassau**
   (New Providence; Bahamas)

18 **Paradise Island**
   (New Providence; Bahamas)

19 **Harbour Island**
   (Eleuthera; Bahamas)

20 **Spanish Wells**
   (Eleuthera; Bahamas)

21 **Hatchet Bay**
   (Eleuthera; Bahamas)

22 **Governor's Harbour**
   (Eleuthera; Bahamas)

23 **Cape Eleuthera**
   (Eleuthera; Bahamas)

24 **Rock Sound**
   (Eleuthera; Bahamas)

25 **George Town**
   (Great Exuma; Bahamas)

26 **Cockburn Town**
   (San Salvador; Bahamas)

27 **Clarence Town**
   (Long Island; Bahamas)

28 **Duncan Town**
   (Ragged Island; Bahamas)

29 **Matthew Town**
   (Great Inagua; Bahamas)

30 **Abraham's Bay**
   (Mayaguana; Bahamas)

31 **Providenciales**
   (Turks & Caicos)

32 **Caicos Bank**
   (Turks & Caicos)

33 **Cockburn Harbour**
   (South Caicos; Turks & Caicos)

34 **Cap Haïtien**
   (Hispaniola; Haiti)

35 **Fort Liberté**
   (Hispaniola; Haiti)

36 **Baie de l'Acul**
   (Hispaniola; Haiti)

37 **Môle St-Nicolas**
   (Hispaniola; Haiti)

38 **Gonaïves**
   (Hispaniola; Haiti)

39 **Port-au-Prince**
   (Hispaniola; Haiti)

40 **Santo Domingo**
   (Hispaniola; Dominican Republic)

41 **La Romana**
   (Hispaniola; Dominican Republic)

42 **Boca de Yuma**
   (Hispaniola; Dominican Republic)

43 **Samaná**
   (Hispaniola; Dominican Republic)

44 **Puerto Plata**
   (Hispaniola; Dominican Republic)

45 **Mayagüez**
   (Puerto Rico)

46 **Arecibo**
   (Puerto Rico)

47 **Ponce**
   (Puerto Rico)

47a **Puerto de Calas**
   (Humacao, Puerto Rico)

48 **San Juan**
   (Puerto Rico)

49 **Fajardo**
   (Puerto Rico)

50 **Culebra**
   (Puerto Rico)

51 **Buck Island**
   (US Virgin Islands)

52 **Christiansted Harbor**
   (St Croix; US Virgin Islands)

53 **Frederiksted**
   (St Croix; US Virgin Islands)

54 **Port Alucroix**
   (St Croix; US Virgin Islands)

55 **Port Harvey**
   (St Croix; US Virgin Islands)

56 **Benner Bay**
(St Thomas; US Virgin Islands)

57 **Charlotte Amalie/St Thomas Harbor**
(St Thomas; US Virgin Islands)

58 **Cowpet Bay**
(St Thomas Bay; US Virgin Islands)

59 **Redhook Bay**
(St Thomas; US Virgin Islands)

60 **Canegarden Bay**
(Tortola; British Virgin Islands)

61 **Marina Cay**
(Tortola; British Virgin Islands)

62 **Maya Cove**
(Tortola; British Virgin Islands)

63 **Roadtown**
(Tortola; British Virgin Islands)

64 **Soper's Hole**
(Tortola; British Virgin Islands)

65 **The Baths**
(Virgin Gorda; British Virgin Islands)

66 **Gorda Sound**
(Virgin Gorda; British Virgin Islands)

67 **Yacht Harbour Virgin Gorda**
(Virgin Gorda; British Virgin Islands)

68 **Caneel Bay**
(St John, US Virgin Islands)

69 **Cooper Island**
(British Virgin Islands)

70 **Coral Harbor and Bay**
(St John; US Virgin Islands)

71 **Cruz Bay**
(St John; US Virgin Islands)

72 **Francis Bay**
(St John; US Virgin Islands)

73 **Hawknest Bay**
(St John; US Virgin Islands)

74 **Peter Island**
(British Virgin Islands)

75 **Norman Island**
(British Virgin Islands)

76 **Rendezvous and Fish Bay**
(St John; US Virgin Islands)

77 **Salt Island**
(British Virgin Islands)

78 **Trunk Bay**
(St John; US Virgin Islands)

79 **Great Harbour**
(Jost van Dyke; British Virgin Islands)

80 **Anegada Reef Hotel**
(Anegada; British Virgin Islands)

81 **Road Bay**
(Anguilla)

82 **Marigot**
(St-Martin)

83 **Oyster Bay**
(St Maarten)

84 **Philipsburg**
(St Maarten)

85 **Simson Lagoon**
(St Maarten)

86 **Fort Baai**
(Saba)

87 **Oranjestad**
(St Eustatius)

88 **Anse du Colombier**
(St-Barthélemy)

89 **Baie de St-Jean**
(St-Barthélemy)

90 **Gustavia**
(St-Barthélemy)

91 **Ile de la Fourche**
(St-Barthélemy)

92 **Cocoa Point**
(Barbuda)

93 **Spanish Point**
(Barbuda)

94 **Basseterre**
(St Kitts)

95 **Pointe de Sable**
(St Kitts)

96 **Charlestown**
(Nevis)

97 **Plymouth**
(Montserrat)

98 **Carlisle Bay**
(Antigua)

99 **English Harbour**
(Antigua)

100 **Five Islands Harbour**
(Antigua)

101 **Falmouth**
(Antigua)

102 **Indian Creek**
(Antigua)

103 **Mamora Bay**
(Antigua)

104 **Mosquito Cove**
(Antigua)

105 **Parham Harbour**
(Antigua)

106 **St John's Harbour**
(Antigua)

107 **Willoughby Bay**
(Antigua)

108 **Anse-à-la-Barque**
(Basse-Terre; Guadeloupe)

109 **Basse-Terre**
(Basse-Terre; Guadeloupe)

110 **Baie Deshaies**
(Basse-Terre; Guadeloupe)

111 **Ste-Marie**
(Basse-Terre; Guadeloupe)

112 **Grand Cul-de-Sac Marin**
(Grande-Terre; Guadeloupe)

113 **Pointe-à-Pitre**
(Grande-Terre; Guadeloupe)

114 **Le Petit Havre**
(Grande-Terre; Guadeloupe)

115 **Ste-Anne**
(Grande-Terre; Guadeloupe)

116 **St-François**
(Grande-Terre; Guadeloupe)

117 **Bourg des Saintes**
(Les Saintes)

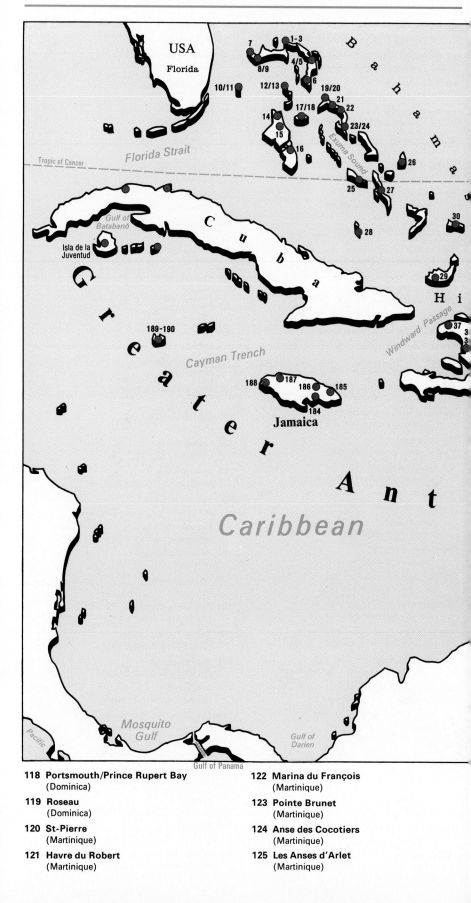

Yacht Harbors and Anchorages in the Caribbean

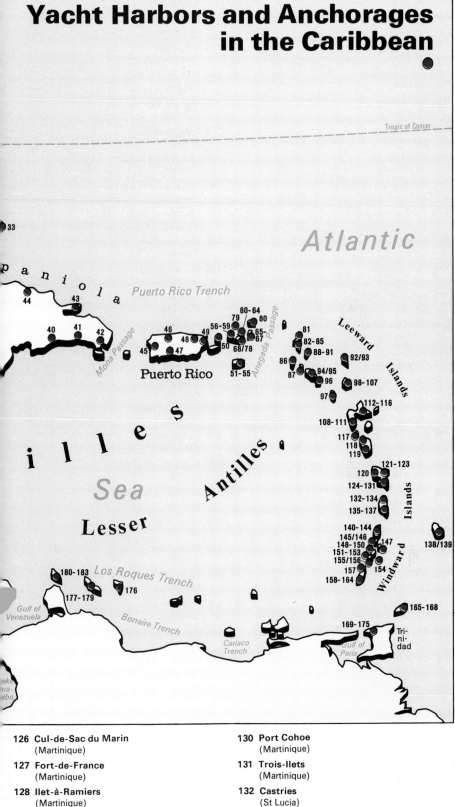

Tropic of Cancer

Atlantic

Puerto Rico Trench

Puerto Rico

Mona Passage

Anegada Passage

Leeward Islands

Sea

Lesser

Antilles

Los Roques Trench

Bonaire Trench

Cariaco Trench

Gulf of Venezuela

Gulf of Paria

Windward Islands

Trinidad

126 Cul-de-Sac du Marin (Martinique)	**130 Port Cohoe** (Martinique)
127 Fort-de-France (Martinique)	**131 Trois-Ilets** (Martinique)
128 Ilet-à-Ramiers (Martinique)	**132 Castries** (St Lucia)
129 Pointe-du-Bout (Martinique)	**133 Cul de Sac Bay** (St Lucia)

Beach on the S coast of Bermuda

The best areas for wind-surfers are Maracas Bay on *Trinidad*, the W coast of *Barbados*, the S coast of *Grande-Terre* (Guadeloupe), Frigate Bay on *St Kitts*, parts of the W coast of *Puerto Rico*, parts of the N and W coasts of Jamaica and the coastal waters of *Eleuthera* (Bahamas).

Water-skiing

Motorboats and equipment can be rented at many resorts, large hotels and tourist centers on the coasts.

Snorkeling

The shallow coastal lagoons inside the barrier reefs offer ideal conditions for snorkeling, which opens up a varied and colorful microcosm of marine life – corals, fishes, molluscs and crustaceans. Since the Caribbean coastal fisheries are relatively underdeveloped the inshore waters have not been fished out as they have in many other countries, and the crystal-clear water is ideal for observing, photographing or filming the underwater fauna and flora. In some areas there are very interesting underwater nature trails.

Snorkelers may sometimes forget that salt water and the hot tropical sun can bring on severe sunburn: it is a good idea, therefore, to wear a cotton shirt or T-shirt. Caution is advisable in touching unknown marine creatures, which may have poisonous spines: stout rubber gloves will give protection. On no account should you feel inside cavities in the banks of coral. – The collecting of marine organisms is prohibited in many areas, and even where it is not snorkelers should not do it, in order to avoid disturbing the delicate ecological balance in the coastal waters.

Bathing and Swimming

The Caribbean is renowned for its crystal-clear water and its beaches of fine sand. Near towns and hotel complexes the beaches may tend to be crowded, but there are plenty of secluded spots easily reached by boat. Many hotels have their own swimming pool. – On the Atlantic coasts there are often heavy seas.

The only **naturist beaches** are on Jamaica and in the French Antilles, usually attached to large hotels; but nude bathing is tolerated on many secluded beaches.

Surfing

From December to April the northeastern trade winds build up a powerful swell on the open sea which is driven W to break on the coasts facing the Atlantic. During this period the Atlantic coasts of the Caribbean islands (particularly Puerto Rico, Barbados and Trinidad) offer excellent conditions for surfing.

Wind-surfing

Thanks to the trade winds which blow almost constantly throughout the year and to the many reef-sheltered bays, wind-surfing has developed into one of the most popular water sports in the Caribbean. Competitions are held in many places, on some islands world championship contests. At most tourist resorts surfboards can be hired and instructors are available.

Scuba Diving

Since the coasts of the Caribbean islands are sheltered by coral reefs for much of their length and the marine fauna in their crystal-clear waters has not been decimated by over-fishing they are a happy hunting ground for scuba divers.

It should be borne in mind that the waters of the tropical zone contain more poisonous sea creatures than are found in more temperate waters. Fire corals, sea anemones and jellyfishes (particularly the Portuguese man-of-war, *Physalia physalis*) can give a sharp sting; hatpin sea-urchins have poisonous spines which break off easily; the red firefish, scorpion-fish and stonefish have poisonous spines

Scuba diver in the Bahamas

adaptor for connecting cylinders of a different type. – Visitors renting scuba diving equipment are usually required to produce evidence of competence.

Fishing

Deep-sea fishing for big fish (big game fishing: swordfish, sailfish, shark, barracuda, tunny, etc.) is a very popular sport in the Caribbean. In most ports it is possible to charter boats complete with crew, fishing tackle and bait.

Strong tackle is also required for *shore fishing* (surf fishing). A sufficient length of cast can be achieved only with heavy weights ($3\frac{1}{2}$–$5\frac{1}{2}$ oz/100–150 g upwards) and correspondingly stout rods. Moreover, you may hook into some pretty powerful fish. The line should be at least 500 ft/150 m long and $\frac{1}{5}$ in./0.5 mm thick.

on their fins; and moray eels, rays, barracudas and sharks can also be dangerous. It is only sensible, therefore, to inquire locally about possible hazards before diving in unknown waters. Regard should also be had to the local regulations on underwater hunting; spear-guns are frequently prohibited.

The scope for *freshwater fishing* varies from island to island. Inquiry should be made locally about the possibilities and the local regulations.

If you are traveling by air, considerations of weight are likely to rule out any idea of taking your own equipment. The best plan is to rent from a local diving school or organizer or to join a specially organized diving trip. If you are able to take your own breathing apparatus you may need an

Tennis

Almost all the islands have tennis courts, either attached to hotels or belonging to clubs. Many of them have floodlighting, and there are often coaches available. Grass courts are becoming increasingly rare, and most courts are now hard-surfaced. After rain they need some time to dry out before becoming playable.

Golf

This is a very popular game in the Caribbean. There are many golf-courses, frequently associated with hotels or resort complexes and often set in very beautiful scenery.

Feather stars, Grand Cayman

There are first-rate courses on *Grand Bahama* (Lucayan), *Eleuthera* (Cotton Bay) and *New Providence* (South Ocean) in the Bahamas, on the N cost of *Jamaica* (Half Moon, Runaway, Rosehall, Iron Shore, Tryall), in the *Dominican Republic* at La Romana (Cajuiles), in *Puerto Rico* (Dorado Beach, Cerromar), on *St Croix* (Fountain Valley), on *Barbados* (Sandy

Lane), on *Tobago* (Mount Irvine) and in *Bermuda* (Mid Ocean, Port Royal, Castle Harbour, Riddell's Bay, Belmont, Princess).

Riding

Riding horses can be rented in most of the regions developed for tourism, and on the smaller islands a horse has advantages over the automobile as a means of seeing the country.

Public Holidays

Anguilla, St Kitts and Nevis

New Year's Day
Statehood Day (February 27)
Good Friday
Easter Monday
Labour Day (first Monday in May)
Whit Monday
Queen's Birthday (second Saturday in June)
August Monday
Prince of Wales's Birthday (November 14)
December 25
Boxing Day (December 26)

Antigua and Barbuda

New Year's Day
Good Friday
Easter Monday
Labour Day (first Monday in May)
Whit Monday
Queen's Birthday (second Saturday in June)
August Monday and Tuesday (Summer Carnival)
State Day (November 1)
December 25
Boxing Day (December 26)

Bahamas

New Year's Day
Good Friday
Easter Monday
Whit Monday
Labour Day (first Friday in June)
Queen's Birthday (first Monday in June)
Independence Day (July 10)
Emancipation Day (first Monday in August)
Discovery Day (October 12)
December 25
Boxing Day (December 26)

Barbados

New Year's Day
Good Friday
Easter Monday
May 1
Whit Monday

Emancipation Day (first Monday in August)
United Nations Day (first Monday in October)
Independence Day (November 30)
December 25
Boxing Day (December 26)

Bermuda

New Year's Day
Good Friday
Empire Day (Monday nearest May 24)
Queen's Birthday (Monday nearest second Saturday in June)
Cup Match Days (Thursday and Friday before first Monday in August)
Remembrance Day (November 11)
December 25
Boxing Day (December 26)

British Virgin Islands

New Year's Day
Good Friday
Easter Monday
Commonwealth Day (May 24)
Whit Monday
Queen's Birthday (June)
Territory Day (July 1)
August Monday and Tuesday
St Ursula's Day (October 21)
Prince of Wales's Birthday (November 14)
December 25
Boxing Day (December 26)

Cayman Islands

New Year's Day
Ash Wednesday
Good Friday
Easter Monday
Commonwealth Day (third Monday in May)
Queen's Birthday (second week in June)
Constitution Day (first Monday in July)
Remembrance Day (Monday after Remembrance Sunday)
December 25
Boxing Day (December 26)

Dominica

New Year's Day
Carnival Monday and Tuesday
Good Friday
Easter Monday
Labour Day (May 1)
Whit Monday
Emancipation Day (first Monday in August)
Dominica National Days (November 3 and 4)
December 25
Boxing Day (December 26)

Dominican Republic

New Year's Day
Día de la Virgen de Altagracia (January 21)
Día de Juan Pablo Duarte (January 26)
Día de la Independencia (February 27)
Día del Trabajo (May 1)
Corpus Christi
Día de la Restauración (August 16)
Día de la Virgen de las Mercedes (September 24)
December 25

Grenada

New Year's Day
January 2
Independence Day (February 7)
Good Friday
Easter Monday
Tuesday after Easter
Labour Day (May 1)
Whit Monday
Queen's Birthday
Corpus Christi
August Bank Holidays
National Day of Prayer (November 25)
December 25
Boxing Day (December 26)

Guadeloupe and Martinique

New Year's Day
Mardi Gras (Shrove Tuesday)
Good Friday
Easter Monday
Fête du Travail (May 1)
Ascension
Whit Monday
National Day (July 14)
Victor Schoelcher Day (July 21)
Assumption
All Saints
Jour de l'Armistice (November 11)
December 25

Haiti

New Year's Day
Jour des Héros de l'Indépendance (January 2)
Carnival Tuesday
Maundy Thursday
Good Friday
Jour Mondial de la Santé (April 7)
Pan-American Day (April 14)
Jour du Travail (May 1)
Jour de la Souveraineté Nationale (May 22)
Ascension
Corpus Christi
Assumption
Jour de J.-J. Dessalines (October 17)
Jour des Nations Unies (October 24)

All Saints
All Souls
Jour de l'Armée (November 18)
December 25

Jamaica

New Year's Day
Ash Wednesday
Good Friday
Easter Monday
National Labour Day (May 23)
Independence Day (first Monday in August)
National Heroes' Day (third Monday in October)
December 25
Boxing Day (December 26)

Isla de Margarita

New Year's Day
Maundy Thursday
Good Friday
Día del Levantamiento (April 19)
Día del Trabajo (May 1)
Día de la Batalla de Carabobo (June 24)
Día de la Independencia (July 5)
Anniversario de Simón Bolívar (July 24)
Día de Colón (October 12)
December 25

Montserrat

New Year's Day
Good Friday
Easter Monday
Labour Day (first Monday in May)
Whit Monday
Queen's Birthday (June)
Bank Holiday (first Monday in August)
December 25
Boxing Day (December 26)

Netherlands Antilles

New Year's Day
Good Friday
Easter Monday
Queen's Birthday (April 30)
Labour Day (May 1)
Ascension
Whit Monday
National Day (December 15)
December 25 and 26

Puerto Rico

New Year's Day
January 6
Anniversario de De Hostos (January 11)
Anniversario de Washington (third Monday in February)
Día de la Emancipación (March 22)
Good Friday
Anniversario de José de Diego (April 16)
Día de la Independencia (July 4)
Anniversario de Muñoz Rivera (July 17)
Día de la Constitución (July 25)
Anniversario del Dr José Celco Barbosa (July 27)
Día del Trabajo (September 1)
Día de Colón (second Monday in October)
Día de los Veteranos (fourth Monday in October)
Descubrimiento de Puerto Rico (November 19)
Thanksgiving Day (November)
December 25

St Lucia

January 1 and 2
Good Friday
Easter Monday
Labour Day (May 1)
Whit Monday
Corpus Christi
Queen's Birthday (June)
Bank Holiday (August)
Thanksgiving Day (October)
St Lucia Day (December 13)
December 25
Boxing Day (December 26)

St Vincent and Grenadines

New Year's Day
Discovery Day (January 2)
Carnival Tuesday
Good Friday
Easter Monday
Labour Day (May 1)
Whit Monday
Caricom Day (first Monday in July)

The * *Carnival (French and Spanish Carnaval), an event rooted in Roman Catholic tradition which is celebrated in most of the Spanish and French islands, is a splendidly colorful traditional occasion – with magnificent costumes, parades through the streets and musical and folk competitions – which reaches its climax on Shrove Tuesday (Mardi Gras).

No less renowned, however, is the Carnival on the island of Trinidad, with the traditional "road march" through Port of Spain, when the steelbands, mounted on open trolleys, are pushed through the town by their fans and thousands of gaily costumed people dance in the streets. – The Carnival is preceded by months of work on the making of the costumes, which are new every year. The variety of figures and masks and the elaboration of the costumes are of overwhelming effect. The figures, mounted on wheels and propelled by the unseen person within, represent flowers, plants and animals (particularly marine animals) with the liveliest imagination and gayest of colors. The celebrations end with the award of prizes for the most original figures and the most popular calypsos and calypso singers.

August Monday (first Monday in August)
Thanksgiving and Statehood Day (last Monday in October)
December 25
Boxing Day (December 26)

Trinidad and Tobago

New Year's Day
Good Friday
Easter Monday
Labour Day (June 19)
Whit Monday
Corpus Christi
Caribbean Day (first Monday in August)
Independence Day (August 31)
December 25
Boxing Day (December 26)

Turks and Caicos

New Year's Day
Good Friday
Easter Monday
Commonwealth Day (third Monday in May)
Queen's Birthday (June 10)
Constitution Day (June 12)
Emancipation Day (first Monday in August)
Peacemaker's Day (November 9)
December 25
Boxing Day (December 26)

United States Virgin Islands

New Year's Day
January 6
Roosevelt's Birthday (January 30)
Washington's Birthday (February 22)
Transfer Day (March 31)
Carnival Week (end of April)
Maundy Thursday
Good Friday
Easter Monday
Memorial Day (May 30)
Organic Act Day (June 22)
Independence Day (July 4)
Supplication Day (July 25)
Labour Day (first Monday in September)
Columbus Day (October 12)
Local Thanksgiving Day (October 25)
Liberty Day (November 1)
Veterans' Day (November 11)
Thanksgiving Day (last Thursday in November)
December 25 and 26

Shopping and Souvenirs

Many of the Caribbean islands have free ports or levy only low rates of duty on imported goods, and in consequence they are a shoppers' Mecca, particularly for visitors from North America, since such things as cameras, electronic apparatus, watches, porcelain and perfume may be up to 60% cheaper than in the United States. It is well worth while, however, to compare prices carefully before deciding that you have found a bargain; and visitors from Europe must consider the restrictions imposed by their air baggage allowance and their own customs regulations, and must also make sure that service facilities will be available at home for any appliance or apparatus they may buy.

In addition to the imported goods which are the staple of the displays in the tourist shops it is worth looking for examples of **folk art** and **local handcrafts**, of which there is a wide choice (mainly textiles, printed fabrics, basketwork, leather articles, hammocks and pottery.

Good **pictures** and *drawings* can be found in Haiti (naive painting), Jamaica and Puerto Rico – though careful consideration is required before ·making a purchase. **Jewelry** made of *tortoiseshell* and black *coral* (beware of imitations!) is sold in Barbados, the British Virgin Islands, the Caymans and the Dominican Republic, which is also noted for its *amber* and the blue semi-precious stone called *larimar*. Items made from larimar should be bought only in reputable shops. – Since Caribbean turtles are an endangered species any articles made of tortoiseshell are liable to be impounded by the United States customs.

Other popular souvenirs of the Caribbean are **rum** and liqueurs, *cigars* (Puerto Rico) and *spices* (Grenada).

Opening Times

On most of the West Indian islands there are official closing times (usually 6 p.m.) for *stores*, but in practice many small shops (including foodshops) stay open from early morning until late evening. *Banks* are normally open from 9 to 12 Mondays to Fridays, but on some islands they ·are also open in the afternoon, closing not later than 5.

Museums, churches and other major sights are usually open from 9 to 5; often they are closed on one day in the week.

Information

Anguilla

Anguilla Department of Tourism,
The Valley, Anguilla;
tel. 451 and 479.

Anguilla Tourist Information Office,
25 West 39th Street,
New York, NY 10018;
tel. (212) 840 6655.

Airline
WIA
(*Windward Island Airways*),
The Valley, Anguilla

Antigua and Barbuda

Antigua Tourist Board,
P.O. Box 363,
High Street,
St John's, Antigua;
tel. 2 00 29.

Antigua Tourist Board,
Suite 311,
610 Fifth Avenue,
New York, NY 10020;
tel. (212) 541 4117.

Antigua Tourist Board,
Suite 205,
60 St Clair Avenue East,
Toronto, Ontario M4T 1L9.
tel. (416) 961 3085

Airline
LIAT
(*Leeward Islands Air Transport*),
Coolidge Airfield,
St John's, Antigua.

Car rental
Avis,
Fort Road,
St John's, Antigua;
tel. 2 18 15.

Hertz,
c/o Ramco Car Rentals,
Upper Nevis Street,
St John's, Antigua;
tel. 2 33 97.

Europcar,
All Saints Road,
P.O. Box 405,
St John's, Antigua;
tel. 2 21 13.

Bahamas

Ministry of Tourism,
Nassau Court,
P.O. Box N 3220,
Nassau, Bahamas;
tel. (809) 3 22 75 05.

Bahamas Tourist Office,
30 Rockefeller Plaza,
New York, NY 10112;
tel. (212) 757 1611.

Also in Atlanta, Boston, Chicago, Dallas, Houston, Los Angeles, Miami, Philadelphia, San Francisco and Washington D.C.

Bahamas Tourist Office,
1255 Phillips Square,
Montreal, Quebec H3B 3G1.

Also in Toronto and Vancouver.

Airlines

Air Bahama,
3 Beaumont House Arcade,
Bay Street,
P.O. Box N 4887,
Nassau, Bahamas.

Bahamasair,
British Colonial Arcades,
Nassau, Bahamas;
tel. 7 85 11.

Car rental

Avis,
P.O. Box N 8300,
Nassau, Bahamas;
tel. 3 27 71 21.

P.O. Box F 2414,
Freeport, Bahamas;
tel. 3 52 76 66.

Hertz,
Windsor Field,
P.O. Box N 3948,
Nassau, Bahamas;
Tel. 3 27 72 31 and 3 27 83 00.

P.O. Box F 2055,
Freeport, Bahamas;
tel. 3 52 93 08.

Barbados

Barbados Board of Tourism,
P.O. Box 242,
Harbour Road,
Bridgetown, Barbados;
tel. 7 26 23 and 6 46 56.

Barbados Board of Tourism,
800 Second Avenue,
New York, NY 10017;
tel. (212) 986 6516.

Barbados Board of Tourism,
11 King Street West,
Toronto, Ontario M5H IA3;
tel. (416) 869 0600.

Also in Montreal.

Airline

Caribbean Airways,
Lower Bay Street,
Bridgetown, Barbados;
tel. 6 01 10.

Car rental

Avis,
P.O. Box 605C,
Bridgetown, Barbados;
tel. 0 31 41.

Hertz,
Tweedside,
Bridgetown, Barbados;
tel. 7 50 94.

Bermuda

Bermuda Department of Tourism,
Old Town Hall,
Hamilton 5–23, Bermuda;
tel. (809) 2 92 00 23.

Bermuda Department of Tourism,
630 Fifth Avenue,
New York, NY 10111.

Also in Atlanta, Boston and Chicago.

Bermuda Department of Tourism,
Suite 510,
1075 Bay Street,
Toronto, Ontario M5S 2B1.

British Virgin Islands

British Virgin Islands Tourist Board,
P.O. Box 134,
Road Town, Tortola, B.V.I.;
tel. (809) 4 94 31 34.

British Virgin Islands Information Service,
370 Lexington Avenue,
New York, NY 10017;
tel. (212) 696 0400.

British Virgin Islands Information Service,
801 York Mills Road, Suite 201,
Don Mills, Ontario M3B 1X7;
tel. (416) 441 1981.

Airline

Air BVI,
Airport,
Beef Island, Tortola, B.V.I.

Cayman Islands

Cayman Islands Department of Tourism,
Government Building,
P.O. Box 67,
George Town, Grand Cayman;
tel. 9 48 44.

Cayman Islands Department of Tourism,
Suite 2312, 420 Lexington Avenue,
New York, NY 10170;
tel. (212) 682 5582.

Also in Chicago, Houston, Los Angeles and Miami.

Cayman Islands Department of Tourism,
Earl B. Smith,
Suite 406, 11 Adelaide Street West,
Toronto, Ontario M5H 1L9;
tel. (416) 362 1550.

Airline

Cayman Airways,
West Wind Building,
George Town, Grand Cayman;
tel. 9 53 11.

Car rental

Avis,
P.O. Box 400,
George Town, Grand Cayman;
tel. 24 58.

Hertz,
P.O. Box 53,
George Town, Grand Cayman;
tel. 9 22 80 and 9 29 32.

Europcar,
P.O. Box 1105,
George Town, Grand Cayman;
tel. 9 47 90.

Dominica

Dominica Tourist Board,
Cork Street,
P.O. Box 73,
Roseau, Dominica;
tel. 23 51 and 21 86.

Dominica Tourist Board,
P.O. Box 1061,
Elmhurst, New York,
NY 11373;
tel. (212) 271 9285.

Dominican Republic

Dirección Nacional de Turismo e Información,
César Nicolás Pensón/Rosa Duarte,
P.O. Box 497,
Santo Domingo, República
Dominicana;
tel. (809) 6 88 55 37.

Dominican Tourist Information Center,
485 Madison Avenue,
New York, NY 10022;
tel. (212) 826 0750.

Also in Miami.

Airline

Dominicana Airlines
(*Compañia Dominicana de Aviación*),
Calle El Conde 407,
Santo Domingo;
tel. (809) 6 85 91 71.

Car rental

Avis,
Calle Sarasota,
Santo Domingo;
tel. (809) 5 65 39 27.

Hertz,
Avenida de la Independencia,
Santo Domingo;
tel. (809) 6 88 22 77.

Europcar,
Avenida Lincoln 210,
Santo Domingo;
tel. (809) 5 66 27 47 and 5 65 55 61.

Grenada

Grenada Tourist Bureau,
P.O. Box 293,
St George's, Grenada;
tel. 20 01 and 22 79.

Grenada Mission and Information Office,
Suite 905, 141 East 44th Street,
New York, NY 10017;
tel. (212) 599 0301.

Consulate of Trade and Tourism,
Suite 101, 143 Yonge Street,
Toronto, Ontario M5C 1W7;
tel. (416) 368 1332.

Car rental

Hertz,
Young Street,
P.O. Box 46,
St George's, Grenada;
tel. 25 14 and 20 31.

Guadeloupe

Office Départemental du Tourisme,
Place de la Victoire,
B.P. 1099,
F-97159 **Pointe-à-Pitre,** Guadeloupe;
tel. 82 09 30.

Office du Tourisme de Guadeloupe,
5 Square de la Banque,
B.P. 1099,
F-97181 **Pointe-à-Pitre,** Cédex,
Guadeloupe Antilles Françaises;
tel. 82 09 30.

French Government Tourist Office,
610 Fifth Avenue,
New York, NY 10020;
tel. (212) 757 1125.

Services Officiels Français du Tourisme,
1840 Ouest rue Sherbrooke,
Montréal, Quebec;
tel. (514) 931 3855.

Airlines

Air France,
Boulevard Legitimus Assainissement,
B.P. 372,
F-97110 **Pointe-à-Pitre**, Guadeloupe;
tel. 82 50 00.

Air Guadeloupe,
Aéroport du Raizet,
F-97110 **Pointe-à-Pitre**, Guadeloupe;
tel. 82 28 35.

Car rental

Avis,
Aéroport du Raizet,
F-97110 **Pointe-à-Pitre**, Guadeloupe;
tel. 82 33 47.

Hertz,
Route de la Gabarre,
F-97110 **Pointe-à-Pitre**, Guadeloupe;
tel. 82 38 20 and 82 07 18.

Europcar,
Quai Gatine 1,
B.P. 89,
F-97110 **Pointe-à-Pitre**, Guadeloupe;
tel. 82 30 40.

Haiti

Office National du Tourisme,
Avenue Marie-Jeanne,
Port-au-Prince, Haiti;
tel. 2 17 20.

Haitian Government Tourist Office,
1270 Avenue of the Americas,
New York, NY 10020;
tel. (212) 757 3517.

Also in Chicago and Miami.

Haitian Government Tourist Office,
920 Yonge Street,
Toronto, Ontario M4W 3C7;
tel. (416) 923 7833.

Also in Montreal.

Airline

Haïti Air Inter,
Aéroport Dr François Duvalier,
Port-au-Prince, Haiti.

Car rental

Avis,
Rue Panaméricaine,
Pétionville, Haiti;
tel. 7 13 25.

Hertz,
Rue Delmas,
Port-au-Prince, Haiti;
tel. 6 14 45, 6 19 35 and 6 11 32.

Europcar,
105 rue Pavée,
Port-au-Prince, Haiti;
tel. 2 38 56 and 6 01 81.

Jamaica

Jamaica Tourist Board,
New Kingston Office Complex,
P.O. Box 284,
Kingston, Jamaica;
tel. 92 9 80 70.

Jamaica Tourist Board,
866 Second Avenue,
New York, NY 10017;
tel. (212) 688 7650.

Jamaica Tourist Board,
2221 Yonge Street,
Toronto, Ontario M4S 2B4;
tel. (416) 482 7850.

Airline

Air Jamaica,
72–76 Harbour Street,
Kingston, Jamaica.

Car rental

Avis,
2 Haining Road,
Kingston, Jamaica;
tel. 92 6 15 60.

Sangster Airport,
Montego Bay, Jamaica;
tel. 95 2 14 81.

Main Street,
Ocho Rios, Jamaica;
tel. 97 4 20 57.

7 Harbour Street,
Port Antonio, Jamaica;
tel. 99 3 26 26.

Europcar,
Knutsford Boulevard,
Skyline Plaza,
Kingston, Jamaica;
tel. 92 9 72 07.

54 Half Way Tree Road,
Kingston, Jamaica;
tel. 92 6 16 21.

International Airport,
Montego Bay, Jamaica;
tel. 95 3 28 24.

Isla de Margarita

Corporacion de Turismo,
EDO. Nueva Esparta,
Edif. Santiago Mariño,
Av. Santiago Mariño,
Av. Velasquez;
Porlamar, Venezuela;
tel. (095) 2 46 51.

Airline

Viasa
(*Venezuelan International Airways*),
Aeropuerto Internacional,
Santiago Marino,
Porlamar, Venezuela;
tel. 2 30 78.

Car rental

Avis,
Santiago Marino International Airport,
Porlamar, Venezuela;
tel. (095) 2 24 38.

Hertz,
Santiago Marino International Airport,
Porlamar, Venezuela;
tel. (095) 2 24 06 and 2 23 27.

Prefecture, Fort-de-France (Martinique)

Martinique

Office Départemental du Tourisme,
Boulevard Alfassa,
B.P. 520,
F-97206 **Fort-de-France,** Martinique;
tel. 71 79 60.

See under **Guadeloupe,** above, for
addresses of French Government Tourist
Office in the United States and Canada.

Montserrat

Montserrat Tourist Board,
P.O. Box 7,
Plymouth, Montserrat, B.W.I.

Netherlands Antilles

Aruba Toeristenbureau,
A. Schuttestraat 2,
Oranjestad, Aruba;
tel. 2 37 77.

Bonaire Toeristenbureau,
Breedestraat 1,
Kralendijk, Bonaire;
tel. 83 22 and 86 49.

Curaçao Toeristenbureau,
Plaza Piar,
Willemstad, Curaçao;
tel. 61 33 97.

Sint Eustatius Toeristenbureau,
Oranjestraat,
Oranjestad, Sint Eustatius.

Sint Maarten Toeristenbureau,
De Ruyterplein,
Philipsburg, Sint Maarten;
tel. 23 27.

Saba Toeristenbureau,
Windwardside, Saba.

Cabinet of the Minister
Plenipotentiary of the Netherlands
Antilles,
Badhuisweg 175,
NL-2597 JP **The Hague;**
tel. (070) 51 28 11.

Aruba Tourist Bureau,
1270 Avenue of the Americas,
New York, NY 10020;
tel. (212) 246 3030.

Also in Miami.

Bonaire Tourist Bureau,
685 Fifth Avenue,
New York, NY 10022;
tel. (212) 838 1797.

Curaçao Tourist Board,
400 Madison Avenue, Suite 311,
New York, NY 10017;
tel. (212) 751 8266.

St Maarten, Saba and St Eustatius
Tourist Information Office,
445 Park Avenue,
New York, NY 10022;
tel. (212) 688 8350.

St Maarten, Saba and St Eustatius Tourist Information Office,
243 Ellerslie Avenue,
Willowdale,
Toronto, Ontario M2N 1Y5;
tel. (416) 223 3501.

Airlines

KLM,
Prinses Beatrix Airport,
Orangestad, Aruba;
tel. 24 67.

c/o Bonaire Trading Co. Ltd,
Kerkweg 9,
Kralendijk, Bonaire;
tel. 83 00.

Kerkstraat 1,
Willemstad, Curaçao;
tel. 1 19 44.

Juliana Airport,
Sint Maarten;
tel. 42 30.

ALM
(*Antillanse Luchtvaart Maatschappij*),
Nassaustraat 74,
Oranjestad, Aruba;
tel. 18 52.

c/o Bonaire Trading Co. Ltd,
Kerkweg 9,
Kralendijk, Bonaire;
tel. 83 00.

c/o Mr M. F. da Costa,
Gomezplein 5,
Willemstad, Curaçao;
tel. 1 27 00.

Emmaplein,
Philipsburg, Sint Maarten;
tel. 22 02.

WIA
(*Windward Islands Airways*),
Philipsburg, Sint Maarten.

Car rental

Avis,
Kolibristraat 14,
Oranjestad, Aruba;
tel. 2 87 87.

Gouverneur N. Debrotweg 42B,
Kralendijk, Bonaire;
tel. 83 10.

Fokkerweg 6A,
P.O. Box 677,
Willemstad, Curaçao;
tel. 61 47 00.

Cul de Sac,
Philipsburg, Sint Maarten;
tel. 23 16.

Hertz,
Prinses Beatrix Airport,
Oranjestad, Aruba;
tel. 48 00.

Perseusweg 22,
P.O. Box 402,
Willemstad, Curaçao;
tel. 3 57 99 and 3 60 41.

Juliana Airport,
Sint Maarten;
tel. 42 31.

Europcar,
Tanki Leendert 170,
P.O. Box 150,
Oranjestad, Aruba;
tel. 2 19 67.

Curaçao Airport,
P.O. Box 476,
Willemstad, Curaçao;
tel. 3 58 44 and 3 62 85.

Backstreet 61,
P.O. Box 249,
Philipsburg, Sint Maarten;
tel. 24 68.

InterRent,
Sabana Blanco 35,
Oranjestad, Aruba;
tel. 18 45/30 55.

Puerto Rico

Puerto Rico Tourism Company,
Calle San Justo,
Esq. Recinto Sur,
San Juan,
Puerto Rico 00903;
tel. (809) 7 21 24 00.

Tourism Information Center,
Isla Verde International Airport,
San Juan, Puerto Rico 00913;
tel. (809) 7 91 10 14.

Puerto Rico Tourism Company,
1290 Avenue of the Americas,
New York, NY 10019;
tel. (212) 541 66 30.

Puerto Rico Tourism Information Center,
10 King Street East,
Toronto, Ontario;
tel. (416) 367 01 90.

Airlines

PRINAIR,
Isla Verde International Airport,
San Juan, Puerto Rico 00913;
tel.(809) 7 24 42 29.

SUN International Airways
Isla Verde International Airport,
San Juan, Puerto Rico 00913;
tel. (809) 7 91 24 29.

Car rental

Avis,
Calle Begonia,
P.O. Box 3746,
San Juan, Puerto Rico 00918;
Tel. (809) 7 91 52 12.

Hertz,
Isla Verde International Airport,
San Juan, Puerto Rico 00913;
tel. (809) 7 91 08 40.

P.O. Box 3687,
Carolina, Puerto Rico 00630;
tel. (809) 7 91 18 05.

St Kitts and Nevis

St Kitts and Nevis Tourist Board,
Treasury Pier,
P.O. Box 132,
Basseterre, St Kitts;
tel. (809) 465 2620.

Eastern Caribbean Tourist Association,
220 East 42nd Street,
New York, NY 10017,
tel. (212) 986 9370.

Car rental

Avis,
Liverpool Row,
Basseterre, St Kitts;
tel. 26 31.

St Lucia

St Lucia Tourist Board,
Jeremy Street,
P.O. Box 221,
Castries, St Lucia;
tel. (809) 455 4094
      (809) 455 2479.

St Lucia Tourist Office,
Suite 315, 41 East 42nd Street,
New York, NY 10017;
tel. (212) 867 2950.

St Lucia Tourist Office,
151 Bloor Street West,
Toronto, M5S 1P7;
tel. (416) 961 5606.

Car rental

Avis,
26 Brazil Street,
Castries, St Lucia;
tel. 27 00.

Hertz,
36 St Louis Street,
Castries, St Lucia;
tel. 32 95.

Europcar,
Gros Islet Highway,
P.O. Box 542,
Castries, St Lucia;
tel. 87 21.

St Vincent and Grenadines

St Vincent Tourist Board,
Halifax Street,
P.O. Box 834,
Kingstown, St Vincent;
tel. 6 12 24.

Car rental

Hertz,
P.O. Box 144,
Kingstown, St Vincent;
tel. 6 18 23 and 6 17 43.

Trinidad and Tobago

Trinidad and Tobago Tourist Board,
56 Frederick Street,
Port of Spain, Trinidad;
tel. 623 19 32.

Tourist Bureau, **Piarco Airport;**
tel. 644 51 96.
Tobago Tourist Bureau,
Scarborough;
tel. 639 21 95.

Trinidad and Tobago Tourist Board,
400 Madison Avenue,
New York, NY 10017;
tel. (212) 838 7750.

Trinidad and Tobago Tourist Board,
York Centre,
145 King Street West and
University Avenue,
Toronto, Ontario M5H 1J8;
tel. (416) 367 0390.

Airline

BWIA International,
Long Circular Road,
Kent House, Maraval,
Port of Spain, Trinidad;
tel. 6 22 12 41.

Car rental

Hertz,
44 New Street,
Port of Spain, Trinidad;
tel. 6 25 30 11 and 6 25 30 21.

Turks and Caicos Islands

Turks and Caicos Tourist Board,
Cockburn Town, Grand Turk,
Turks and Caicos Islands, B.W.I.;
tel. 23 21.

Turks and Caicos Tourist Board,
P.O. Box 592617,
Miami FL 33159;
tel. (305) 592 6183.

Airline

TCNA,
Cockburn Town, Grand Turk,
Turks and Caicos Islands.

United States Virgin Islands

US Virgin Islands Division of Tourism,
P.O. Box 1692,
Charlotte Amalie, VI 00801,
St Thomas, U.S.V.I.;
tel. (809) 7 74 13 31.

US Virgin Islands Division of Tourism,
1270 Avenue of the Americas,
New York, NY 10020;
tel. (212) 582 4520.

United States Virgin Islands Division of Tourism,
234 Eglington Avenue East,
Toronto, Ontario,
M4P 1K5;
tel. (416) 488 4374.

Also in Chicago, Los Angeles, Miami, San Francisco, Seattle and Washington D.C.

Airline

Aero Virgin Islands,
Christiansted, St Croix,
VI 00820, U.S.V.I.;
tel. (809) 7 78 00 05.

Charlotte Amalie, St Thomas,
VI 00801, U.S.V.I.;
tel. (809) 7 74 50 00.

Car rental

Avis,
Harry S. Truman Airport,
P.O. Box 1172,
Charlotte Amalie, St Thomas;
tel. (809) 7 74 14 68.

Alexander Hamilton Airport,
Christiansted, St Croix;
tel. (809) 7 72 13 65.

58 King Street,
Christiansted, St Croix;
tel. (809) 7 33 43 77.

Hertz,
Harry S. Truman Airport,
Charlotte Amalie, St Thomas;
tel. (809) 7 74 18 79.

Alexander Hamilton Airport,
Airport Road,
Christiansted, St Croix;
tel. (809) 7 78 14 02.

Buccaneer Hotel,
Christiansted, St Croix;
tel. (809) 7 73 21 00.

Europcar,
Harry S. Truman Airport,
Charlotte Amalie, St Thomas;
tel. (809) 7 74'62 20.

Alexander Hamilton Airport,
P.O. Box 7012,
Christiansted, St Croix;
tel. (809) 7 78 04 30.

Dollar Rent-a-Car,
9B Contant Street,
Charlotte Amalie, St Thomas;
tel. (809) 7 74 20 95.

Radio

Radio stations in British, former British and United States territories broadcast in English. The Dutch and French territories have regular news programs in English.

Telephoning

All the islands covered by this Guide have telephone services, and there are no difficulties about telephoning to or from Europe or North America. Many islands can be dialed direct (area code 809).

TELEPHONE COMPANIES. – *ITT, RCA*: Dominican Republic, Haiti, Puerto Rico. – *Jamintel*: Jamaica. – *Textel*: Trinidad and Tobago. – *P. & T.*: French Antilles. – *Landsradio & Telegraafdienst*: Netherlands Antilles. – **Cable and Wireless**: Anguilla, Antigua, Barbados, Bermuda, British Virgin Islands, Cayman Islands, Dominica, Grenada, Montserrat, St Kitts and Nevis, St Lucia, St Vincent and Grenadines, Turks and Caicos Islands. – State-run services in the Bahamas, the Dominican Republic and Haiti.

Source of illustrations

Barbados Board of Tourism, Frankfurt am Main (pp. 22, 44, 72) Ph. Bastin, Fort-de-France, Martinique (pp. 16, 33, 180, 181; 191, top; 192)

Bermuda Department of Tourism, Hamilton (pp. 15, 79, 80; 81, top; 85, right; 86, three; 87, two; 89, below; 90, left; 91, 317, 319)

Charles, Grand Cayman (p. 32, lower left)

Dexter, West Nyack, New York (pp. 31; 204, top; 228, 263; 265, two; 266, left)

Divald, Basseterre, St Kitts (p. 244, top)

Secretaria de Estado de Turismo de la República Dominicana, Santo Domingo (p. 158)

French Government Tourist Office, Frankfurt am Main (pp. 148, below; 191, below)

Gaf/Pana-Vue, Newark, N.J. (pp. 9; 32, lower right; 85, left; 89, upper left and right; 104, upper and lower right; 120, left; 194, 274; 275, three; 276, left; 318, below)

Office du Tourisme de la Guadeloupe, Pointe-à-Pitre (pp. 149; 152, left; 307, 309)

Parc Naturel de Guadeloupe (pp. 25, right; 29, right; 139, 142, 146, 147)

Prof. Dr Hans-Dieter Haas, Munich (pp. 12, 23, 27; 28, top left and lower right; 29, left; 46, lower right; 61, 66, 69, 74, 76, 109, 110, 111, 115; 130, left; 136, 143, 162, 164, 165, 170, 172, 174, 175; 197, right; 211, two; 213, 214, 216; 225, below; 229, 235, 236, 240; 243, top; 248, top and lower left; 253, 255, 256, 262; 266, right; 285, right; 287; 288, lower left)

Haitian Government Tourist Office, Munich (pp. 96, 218)

Jamaica Tourist Board, Frankfurt am Main (pp. 195, 215)

Helmut Linde, Reutlingen (pp. 18; 24, left; 28, upper right; 30, right; 53; 81, below; 101, right; 102; 104, upper right; 105, upper left and right; 106, 118, 141; 148, upper left; 185; 186, two; 188, 199; 200, two; 205, three; 206, top; 220, left; 243, below; 276, right; 326)

Tom McCarthy, Grand Cayman (p. 105, below)

Rolf Nonnenmann, Pforzheim (pp. 13, 17; 28, lower left; 35, 36, 45; 46, lower right; 98, 99, 100; 101, left; 120, right; 125; 152, right; 153, 155, 156, 157, 217; 220, top; 273; 288, right)

Norwegian Caribbean Line, Miami (p. 306)

Puerto Rico Tourism Company, San Juan/Hato Rey (pp. 230, 264, 267)

Robinsons, Orlando, Florida (pp. 7, 55, 67, 68; 70, two; 92; 122, two; 123; 126, two; 201, 204, below; 206, below; 209, 297; 318, top)

Georg Scherm, Munich (pp. 37, 49, 75, 116, 117, 129; 130, right; 131, 132; 133, two; 239, 241; 244, below; 248, lower right; 257, 258)

Bildagentur Schuster GmbH, Oberursel (pp. 166, 196; 197, left; 212)

Nancy Sefton, Kalt, Grand Cayman (p. 32, middle left)

Hartmut Stelter, Eningen (pp. 24, right; 30, left; 223, top; 279; 280, top and lower left; 286)

Trinidad and Tobago International Marketing Organization, Geneva (pp. 25, left; 32, top; 223, lower left and right; 225, top; 278; 280, lower right; 283, 284; 285, left; 288, upper left)

Zentrale Farbbild Agentur GmbH (ZEFA), Düsseldorf (cover picture; p. 47, left)